Second Edition

VAX®
Assembly Language

Sara Baase

San Diego State University

PRENTICE HALL
Englewood Cliffs, New Jersey 07632

Library of Congress Cataloging-in-Publication Data

BAASE, SARA.
   VAX assembly language / Sara Baase. -- 2nd ed.

      p.   cm.
   Rev. ed. of: VAX-11 assembly language programming.
   Includes index.
   ISBN 0-13-942152-1
   1. VAX-11 (Computer)--Programming.   2. Assembler language
(Computer program language)   I. Baase, Sara. VAX-11 assembly
language programming.   II. Title.
QA76.8.V32B33 1992
005.2'45--dc20   91-29207
                                               CIP

Editorial/Production Supervision and Interior
   Design: *Kris Ann E. Cappelluti*
Editor-in-Chief: *Marcia Horton*
Prepress Buyer: *Linda Behrens*
Manufacturing Buyer: *David Dickey*

Cover Design: *Bruce Kenselaar*
Supplements Editor: *Alice Dworkin*
Copy Editor: *Zeiders & Associates*
Editorial Assistant: *Diana Penha*

 © 1992, 1983 by Prentice-Hall, Inc.
A Simon & Schuster Company
Englewood Cliffs, New Jersey 07632

The author and publisher of this book have used their best efforts in preparing this book. These efforts include the development, research, and testing of the theories and programs to determine their effectiveness. The author and publisher make no warranty of any kind, expressed or implied, with regard to these programs or the documentation contained in this book. The author and publisher shall not be liable in any event for incidental or consequential damages in connection with, or arising out of, the furnishing, performance, or use of these programs.

Trademark Information
DIGITAL, MicroVAX, PDP-11, RMS, VAX, VAX-11, VAXstation and VMS are registered trademarks of
   Digital Equipment Corporation.
Intel, 80186, 80286, and 80386 are registered trademarks of Intel Corporation.
68000, 68010, 68020, and 68030 are registered trademarks of Motorola Corporation.
IBM is a registered trademark of International Business Machines Corporation.

Printed in the United States of America
10   9   8   7

ISBN 0-13-942152-1

Prentice-Hall International (UK) Limited, *London*
Prentice-Hall of Australia Pty. Limited, *Sydney*
Prentice-Hall Canada Inc., *Toronto*
Prentice-Hall Hispanoamericana, S.A., *Mexico*
Prentice-Hall of India Private Limited, *New Delhi*
Prentice-Hall of Japan, Inc., *Tokyo*
Simon & Schuster Asia Pte. Ltd., *Singapore*
Editora Prentice-Hall do Brasil, Ltda., *Rio de Janeiro*

Contents

Figures

Tables

Preface

This book is intended as a text for an assembly language course such as CS 3: Introduction to Computer Systems in the ACM's Curriculum '78. It is also for anyone who wants to learn about the instruction set and assembly language for the VAX family of computers. The book is written primarily for readers who do not already know any assembly language; the VAX is used partly as a vehicle for teaching about features and principles common to many modern computers and assembly languages. The book is suitable for readers who are already familiar with assembly language if some sections are skimmed. The summary sections at the ends of the chapters include reference tables that should be helpful to both the novice and those experienced in assembly language who want to learn about the VAX. It is assumed that the reader is familiar with high-level language programming.

The book has been organized to make the chapters easy to cover in sequence in a class where students begin programming early and write programs regularly on the material as it is encountered. With this aim in mind, I introduce some topics and instructions informally as needed before they are covered in complete detail, and I intersperse chapters on topics that would be the subject of programming assignments (e.g., branching, procedures) with chapters on topics that would not be (e.g., machine code, assembler expressions). Topics are not divided up in precise, logically distinct chunks as they are in manuals. For example, although loop control instructions "belong" in Chapter 7,

"Branching and Looping," one loop instruction is introduced in Chapter 6 so that students can use it in programs.

In our one-semester course we cover almost all of the text. A few addressing modes (in Chapter 8), Section 9.10, bit field instructions (in Chapter 12), packed decimal instructions (in Chapter 13), Chapter 14, and some of the long examples are skipped. (Sometimes Chapter 16 is omitted.)

Chapters 1 and 2 are very short introductory chapters and may be covered quickly. Chapter 3 on hexadecimal numbers and two's complement representation may be skimmed if that material has been covered in an earlier course.

Chapter 4 begins the presentation of machine instructions and assembly language. The VAX has a very large set of operand addressing modes. Some of the simpler ones are described in Chapter 4, while some more complex and less commonly available ones are left for Chapters 7 and 8.

While Chapters 1–4 are being covered in class, my students do assignments to familiarize them with the basic VAX/VMS commands, the editor they will be using, and electronic mail on the VAX.

Chapter 5 contains a diverse group of topics intended to get students started on their first program. The only section that pertains specifically to VAX assembly language is Section 5.2 on the MOV instructions, including MOVA (MOVe Address). Two new concepts that are difficult for students who have programmed only in high-level languages like Pascal and Fortran are the distinction between address and contents, and the need to calculate addresses. This chapter contains several exercises, including two suitable for programming assignments, to provide practice with these ideas. Since students have not yet learned how to convert integers from character code to two's complement representation and vice versa, the programming exercises use character string input and output.

To allow students to do simple I/O at a terminal, I have defined some I/O macros that can be used quite easily. The VAX Run-Time Library contains procedures that do terminal I/O, but the macros are simpler for students to use. The macros are READLINE, READRCRD, PRINTCHRS, and DUMPLONG. Their functional characteristics and argument formats are described in Section 5.1. The macro definitions and related procedures are given in Appendix D. They are available on diskette from the publisher.

Section 5.3 contains the VAX/VMS commands for assembling, linking, and running a program. Section 5.4 is a completely new section introducing the VAX Debugger.

After Chapter 6 students can write programs with loops and can convert between character code and two's complement. Chapter 7 covers conditional branching and looping. The displacement modes for operand addressing are included here.

I suggest that Chapters 1–7 be covered first, in order. (Some sections may be omitted.) Although the remaining chapters have occasional references to each other, the order in which they are covered is not critical.

In some ways Chapter 8, "Machine Code Formats, Translation, and Execution," is the most important chapter, even though it has little to do with programming. Here, probably for the first time, students will begin to see how a computer executes instructions and how assembly language statements are translated. One very instructive, but long, programming assignment for this chapter is writing an emulator (in a high-level language) for a small subset of the VAX instructions and addressing modes. My students found the project difficult, but said they understood the instruction execution process much better after doing it.

Chapter 8 follows the chapter on branching and looping because by now students should be writing a program with conditional branching. However, since they will see machine code on their program listings and will need to understand a little about instruction formats and execution to interpret and correct errors, it is a good idea for the instructor to present some material form Chapter 8 (particularly Section 8.8, which explains some of the execution-time error messages) before completing Chapter 7. This is what we do in class, but it seemed awkward to break these chapters up into smaller, intermingled pieces.

Chapter 9 considers the problems involved in communicating between procedures and the programs that call them. It describes several techniques used for solving those problems but focuses mainly on the VAX procedure calling standard. A short section is included on the VAX conventions for linking assembly language with other languages. The information in this section should suffice for many straightforward situations, but it does not cover all argument types. A new section briefly considers the treatment of local variables, recursion, and reentrant code.

Chapter 10 presents more about the assembler (and linker): mainly the treatment of expressions and the distinction between absolute and relocatable expressions.

The VAX macro facility is not a particularly powerful or elegant one, but it does include many of the standard features, such as argument concatenation, assembler-generated labels, and a variety of conditional assembly directives. These features and some general points about writing macros are presented in Chapter 11.

Chapter 12 presents the bit and logical instructions and includes a section on the VAX variable-length bit field data type and instructions.

The floating-point and packed-decimal data types and instructions are presented in Chapter 13. The accuracy problems in floating-point computations are illustrated.

Chapter 14 describes the high-powered character string manipulation instructions, including search, translate, and edit instructions. Although the instructions and examples in this chapter are interesting, such instructions are not typically available on many computers. If one's purpose in using this book is to learn about basic concepts and commonly available features, this chapter can be skipped.

Chapter 15 is a new chapter introducing interrupts. This chapter is less specific to the VAX than the other chapters in the book. The goal of the chapter is for students to understand what interrupts are and the basic issues and techniques involved in servicing them. Interrupt servicing on the VAX is used as the main example, but the description of what is done on the VAX is substantially simplified to emphasize the main techniques rather than VAX details.

Chapter 16 is a brief introduction to the VAX Record Management Services. It will enable the reader to do some I/O without using the macros presented in Chapter 5.

Chapters 15 and 16 give the reader some idea of the complexity of input and output. I have chosen not to include a more detailed discussion of I/O devices and operations in this book.

The book does not describe all the instructions in the VAX instruction set or all the assembler directives. Some instructions (e.g., for quadword arithmetic) are introduced only in exercises. The VAX instruction set includes some powerful and unusual machine instructions that are designed specifically to efficiently implement high-level language constructs (e.g., CASE) and to implement some common operating systems functions (e.g., queuing). These are not covered. (All machine instructions are included in the instruction table in Appendix A.) It is expected that students will be able to intelligently consult the *VAX MACRO and Instruction Set Reference Manual* to look up additional instructions and directives.

CHANGES FROM THE FIRST EDITION

Two major additions are the introduction to the VAX Debugger (in Chapters 5, 6, and 9) and the new Chapter 15 on interrupts. A new section was added to Chapter 9 to briefly cover treatment of local variables, recursion, and reentrant routines. In Chapter 11 the section on the macro string functions has been expanded. New examples were added in some chapters; for example, Section 7.2 is a new example on processing free-format input.

Based on my experience teaching our assembly language course, I have moved some topics to different places so that the book corresponds more closely to how I cover material in class. I have also added and clarified explanations of concepts that students find confusing.

I have added more than 125 new exercises. In some of the old exercises, I have changed details while exercising the same ideas. As in the first edition, the book contains exercises ranging from short-answer questions to problems that are suitable for programming assignments. Appendix E now contains solutions to most of the odd-numbered exercises.

DISKETTE

Instructors who are teaching a course using this book may request a diskette from the publisher. It contains the files with the I/O macro definitions and procedures described in Appendix D and some of the programs used as examples in the book (including the linked list manipulation program from Chapter 9).

REFERENCES

The following references have been helpful in the preparation of this book and/or in preparing material for our course. All but the last are VAX manuals published by Digital

Equipment Corporation. The first manual listed is the primary reference for VAX assembly language.

VAX MACRO and Instruction Set Reference Manual

VMS Debugger Manual

VMS DCL Concepts Manual

VMS DCL Dictionary

VMS Linker Utility Manual

Introduction to the VMS Run-Time Library

Introduction to VMS System Routines

VMS Record Management Services Manual

VMS I/O User's Reference Manual

Guide to VAX C

VAX FORTRAN User Manual

VAX Pascal User Manual

VAX COBOL User Manual

VAX Architecture Reference Manual, edited by Timothy E. Leonard, DEC Books, 1987.

ACKNOWLEDGMENTS

I would again like to express my appreciation to the people acknowledged in the first edition of this book: Richard Hager, Tom Teegarden, John van Zandt, and Jack Revelle.

For the second edition, I am grateful to Robin Fishbaugh for converting the first edition from hardcopy to electronic copy, to Ron Sukel for proofreading the manuscript, to Eric Vaitl for writing solutions for many of the exercises and for suggestions for improving the text, to Vernor Vinge, Jack Revelle, and Kasi Anantha for reading and helping to improve the new Chapter 15, to Clark Thomborson for giving me material from his course, and to many of my colleagues in the Computer Science Division at San Diego State, and Mike McCurdy, our VAX system manager, for answering miscellaneous questions. I thank Marcia Horton, Kris Ann Cappelluti, and the others at Prentice Hall who worked on this book, especially the following Prentice Hall reviewers: Keith B. Olson, Montana Tech and Ida M. Flynn, University of Pittsburgh. I also thank my birding friends for time spent watching red-tailed hawks, wood ducks, and nesting hummingbirds, instead of characters on a computer screen.

> *TO ALL THE STUDENTS
> I'VE ENJOYED HAVING IN MY CLASSES*

1

Introduction

1.1 WHAT IS ASSEMBLY LANGUAGE AND WHY STUDY IT?

An assembly language is a programming language in which instructions correspond closely to the individual primitive operations that are carried out by a particular computer. These primitive operations, encoded in a form the computer can act on directly, comprise the machine language of the computer.[1] By studying assembly language we get an introduction to the components of a computer and what they do. We also learn how data and data structures are actually represented and manipulated in a computer, better understand what a pointer is, learn more about how procedures communicate with each other (including how recursion works), and see how the control structures of high-level languages (conditional branches and loops) are implemented at the machine level.

This introductory section and the two examples on the next page are intended to give you a general idea of what assembly language "looks like," what kinds of instructions it has, and how it differs from high-level languages and machine languages. In this book we will be studying the assembly language of the VAX family of computers made by Digital Equipment Corporation (DEC for short). Each of the examples shows a state-

---

[1] The design of modern computers has many levels of complexity. We will sometimes make simplifications in our general discussions to focus on the main ideas. For example, here we are not mentioning microcode.

ment in a high-level language and a possible translation of it into the VAX assembly language (called VAX MACRO) and VAX machine language.

Perhaps the most glaring difference among the three types of languages is that as we move from high-level languages to lower levels, the code gets harder to read (with understanding). The major advantages of high-level languages are that they are easy to read and are machine independent. The instructions are written in a combination of English and ordinary mathematical notation, and programs can be run with minor, if any, changes on different computers. Each computer has compilers to translate high-level language programs into its machine language.

Some parts of the assembly language instructions are decipherable: In Example 1.1 the variable names appear, and one may guess from their names what some of the instructions do. MULF2 does multiplication and ADDF3 does addition. The machine code is totally unintelligible without further explanation, and one can see that even knowing all the translation rules would not make reading or writing in machine language an easy or enjoyable task.

Example 1.1: Fortran, Assembly Language, and Machine Code

Fortran

COST = BASE + NUM*VAR

Assembly Language   **Machine Code**

```
COST:   .BLKF   1
BASE:   .BLKF   1
VAR:    .BLKF   1
NUM:    .BLKL   1

        . . .
        CVTLF   NUM,R3                                      53DBAF4E
        MULF2   VAR,R3                                      53D3AF44
        ADDF3   BASE,R3,COST                            C4AF53CBAF41
```

Example 1.2: Pascal, Assembly Language, and Machine Code

Pascal

if *tag* < 0 **then** *sum* := *sum* + *amount* [*i*]

Assembly Language   **Machine Code**

```
        TSTB    (R2)                                            6295
        BGEQ    NEXT                                            0418
        ADDL2   (R4)[R5],R6                                  566445C0
NEXT:   [next instruction]
```

The second most visible difference among the different types of languages is that several lines of assembly language instructions are needed to encode one line of a high-level language program. One line of a high-level language may include several operations; in assembly language (roughly speaking) each instruction performs one operation. Early computers had a small number of primitive instructions to perform such operations as integer addition, integer subtraction, sign tests, branching, certain logical operations, input and output, and movement of data. Integer multiplication and division and floating-point arithmetic had to be programmed using the primitive operations. Now many computers have more sophisticated instructions: instructions that do integer multiplication and division, floating-point arithmetic, and many more complex logical and data-manipulation operations. Still, as the examples illustrate, one line in a high-level language can do more than a single instruction in assembly language.

Let us look at the examples in more detail. Execution of the Fortran statement in Example 1.1 requires several operations: conversion of the integer datum NUM to floating point, a multiplication, an addition, and an assignment of the result to COST. In many modern computers the conversion would require a long sequence of instructions, and each of the other operations would be performed by a separate instruction. The VAX has a very powerful set of instructions, though; the conversion is done in one instruction (CVTLF), and the add instruction adds and stores the result. In the second example, the Pascal **if** statement is translated to a sign test (TSTB), a conditional branch (BGEQ, branch if greater than or equal zero), and an addition. On other computers more instructions might be required to specify the desired element of the array *amount*, but the VAX has very powerful and flexible ways to specify the location of data.

Machine code, along with data, is stored in the computer's memory. The machine code for an entire program segment would be one continuous sequence; it is broken up into separate lines in each example to show the correspondence between sections of the machine code and the assembly language instructions. Actually, machine code is slightly worse than shown here; it consists of a long string of bits (i.e., 0's and 1's). What we see in the examples is a shorthand notation; each digit and letter represents a group of four bits. The notation used is the hexadecimal number system. Hexadecimal numbers are used extensively for machine code, memory addresses, and data, and will be discussed in Chapter 3.

The assembly and machine language sequences in the examples are not the only possible translations of the Fortran and Pascal statements shown. They depend on some assumptions about the context of the statements. In Example 1.1, for instance, the first four lines allocate memory space for the variables, but similar lines do not appear in Example 1.2. In assembly language, all variable names must be defined (i.e., roughly speaking, a position in memory must be assigned to them). In many cases it is possible to refer to variables by name, as in Example 1.1 and in high-level languages. For Example 1.2, we assumed that the statement is in a subroutine or procedure, and *tag*, *sum*, and *amount* are arguments. Space must be allocated elsewhere for the data the routine acts on, but the variable names (if any) are not available for use here. We may not even use formal argument (i.e., dummy argument) names as we do in high-level language procedures or subroutines.

The machine code contains no declarations, variable names, or statement labels (e.g., NEXT in Example 1.2). It contains only executable instructions; references to data and instructions are encoded in ways to be described in Chapter 8.

In situations where programming in a high-level language is not appropriate, it is clear that assembly language is to be preferred to machine language. Assembly language has a number of advantages over machine code aside from the obvious increase in readability. One is that the use of symbolic names for data and instruction labels frees the programmer from computing and recomputing the memory locations whenever a change is made in a program. Another is that assembly languages generally have a feature, called macros, that frees the user from having to repeat similar sections of code used in several places in a program. Assemblers do bookkeeping and other tasks for the user. Often compilers translate into assembly language rather than machine code.

If one has a choice between assembly language and a high-level language, why choose assembly language? The fact that the amount of programming done in assembly language is quite small compared to the amount done in high-level languages indicates that one generally does not choose assembly language. However, there are situations where it may not be convenient, efficient, or possible to write programs in high-level languages. The first compiler, for example, could not be written in the high-level language it translates because there would be no way to run the compiler. (Actually, nowadays, compilers are usually written in high-level languages.) Programs to control and communicate with peripheral devices (input and output devices) are usually written in assembly language because they use special instructions that are not available in high-level languages, and they must be very efficient. Some systems programs are written in assembly language for similar reasons. In general, since high-level languages are designed without the features of a particular machine in mind and a compiler must do its job in a standardized way to accommodate all valid programs, there are situations where to take advantage of special features of a machine, to program some details that are inaccessible from a high-level language, or perhaps to increase the efficiency of a program,[2] one may reasonably choose to write in assembly language.

Although assembly language programs must be translated into machine code, the translation task is simpler than for a high-level language because of the close correspondence between the assembly and machine language for a particular computer. A program that translates assembly language into machine language is called an *assembler*.

Some of the major reasons for studying assembly language have little to do with its practical use as a programming language. We already mentioned that it contributes to our understanding of how data and control structures of high-level languages are implemented. This understanding requires some knowledge of the internal structure of a computer. Consider that Fortran was developed in the 1950s when computers were made of vacuum tubes. The same Fortran program that ran on such a machine could also run on a computer in the 1960s made of transistors, on a computer today with integrated circuits, and on a future computer that uses some new technology. Clearly, learning Fortran (and other high-level languages) teaches one virtually nothing about what a computer is and how it actually works. We will not be studying computer hardware here, but the point— that there have been dramatic changes over the years, all virtually invisible to high-level language programmers—is equally true about *computer architecture*, that is, the conceptual structure and functional characteristics of a computer. One purpose of studying assembly language is to learn something about computer architecture; in fact, part of

---

[2] Optimizing compilers may eliminate this last reason, as some very good ones produce code whose efficiency rivals that of code written by experienced assembly language programmers.

Digital Equipment Corporation's definition of architecture is "the attributes of a system as seen by the assembly language programmer." Thus, along with learning how to write programs in assembly language, we will study the structure of the computer, its instruction set, how it decodes and executes instructions, and the schemes used to specify memory locations. All these topics and others covered in assembly language texts help us understand more about how the computer works and more about the task performed by the compilers that must translate high-level language programs.

Computer architecture and assembly languages differ very much from what they were thirty or forty years ago. There are also significant differences among computers available today from different manufacturers, but of course they also have many features and characteristics in common. Why study the VAX assembly language rather than some other? To be honest, the choice of which assembly language to learn is usually determined by what computer is available at one's university or place of work, and the decision to acquire that particular machine probably depended on many factors having little to do with the merits of its assembly language. If a programmer must use a VAX and intends to write in assembly language, he or she will probably write in VAX MACRO.[3] On the other hand, if one's purpose is to learn about the architecture of a modern computer, there are several to choose from that would serve the purpose. The VAX is not the only choice, but it is a very good one. As we indicated in the examples, the VAX has some instructions and ways of accessing data that are more powerful and flexible than those of other computers. The VAX and its assembly language also have many features that are typical of modern machines. It has, as computer people would put it, a nice architecture. Throughout this book we will often mention similarities and differences between the VAX and other computers.

1.2 WHAT IS "THE" VAX?

We have been speaking of "the VAX" as though it were one specific computer. It is not. The VAX is a family of computers, covering a wide range of cost and performance, from desktop systems (e.g., VAXstations and MicroVAXes) to high-performance, multiprocessor, multiuser systems. What ties them together, what makes them a "family" that we can describe in one book, is that they have the same architecture. Recall that architecture is the conceptual structure and functional characteristics of a computer at the machine language level. It used to be that machine (and assembly) languages corresponded closely to the physical design of a computer. When a computer manufacturer updated the design to take advantage of new ideas and technology, or simply designed another machine to achieve different performance goals, the machine language changed (requiring rewriting of compilers for high-level languages and rewriting assembly language programs and routines). In the 1960s some computer manufacturers began to separate the conceptual design of a computer system from the specific hardware implementation, so that as technology and hardware designs change, the machine language does not. The

---

[3] PDP-11 assembly language programs may be run on the VAX in what is called compatibility mode, but we will not consider that in this book.

first VAX, the VAX-11/780, introduced in 1978, was a fast, modern computer at the time. It is no longer sold, in part because improvements in circuit technology allow increased speed, circuit density, and reliability. Comparable performance can be obtained today in a newer member of the VAX family that is smaller and cheaper than the 780. However, although the physical size, chip technology, and so forth, are different on the newer machines, the machine language is the same. Programs written for one member of the VAX family, even one that is no longer sold, can be used on others.

Earlier we said that one reason to learn assembly language is to learn how a computer works—high-level languages, more or less unchanged over many years and running on computers of greatly varying designs, do not reflect what is actually happening in the computer. But now we have just said that the machine language does not change to reflect changes in hardware. In fact, computer architectures do change as new and better ideas are developed, and at any one time, there will be a variety of architectures available for different purposes and from different manufacturers. They do not change as fast as the hardware or as slowly as high-level languages. Studying assembly language will give us a good understanding of the internal logical structure of a computer.

1.3 SOME TERMINOLOGY

In this section we give definitions and brief explanations of some commonly used terms, many of which should be somewhat familiar to the reader. This is not intended as a complete glossary, but rather as a review of some general terminology.

Data are pieces of information of some kind, often numbers or character strings. The singular form of data is *datum*.

A *bit* is often defined as a binary digit (i.e., a 0 or a 1). It also may mean a place (in a computer memory, for example) where a 0 or a 1 may be stored. In many computers, including the VAX, bits are organized in groups of eight called *bytes*. In such machines the byte is considered the basic unit of memory. Half a byte is defined by some computer makers, including DEC, as a *nibble*. (Yes, computer scientists have a sense of humor.) To *complement* a bit does not mean to say something nice about it (that is a "compliment"). It means to reverse its value, that is, to change a 0 to a 1 and a 1 to a 0. To complement a bit string means to complement each bit in the string.

A *compiler* is a program that translates a high-level language into assembly language. Compilers usually provide a program listing and error messages for syntax errors in the program being translated.

An *assembler* is also a translation program; its purpose is to translate assembly language into machine language. The input to a compiler or assembler is a program written by a programmer; it is called a *source program* (or *source file* or *source module*). The primary output from the compiler or assembler is called an *object module* (or *object file*). Like a compiler, an assembler also provides error messages and a program listing. The listing shows the machine code produced by the assembler.

Because a program may consist of several modules or procedures assembled separately, and because the assembler does not know where in memory a program will be when it runs, the object file is not the final machine-code translation. Another program, called a *linker*, combines the various object modules and puts them in executable form. The output of the linker is called an *executable image* or *execution file*.

An *executable instruction*, in assembly language or a high-level language, is an instruction that gets translated into one or more machine language instructions. Other instructions appearing in a program, such as declarations and header statements, provide information or instructions to the assembler or compiler.

As suggested above, a program goes through three stages: assembly, linkage, and execution. When learning and programming assembly language, it is often important to understand which operations take place in which of these stages. Thus we will talk about an operation, or perhaps an error, occurring at *assembly time* or at *execution time*. *Assembly time* does not mean the amount of time used to translate the program, but the time span, or stage, when assembly takes place. The same is true for *execution time*.

A *procedure* is a program section that performs a particular task on (zero or more) arguments that are given to it when it is called by another routine. A procedure can be assembled (or compiled) as an independent unit. (In Fortran, procedures are called subroutines.)

We have used the term *module* several times. Since it is used in many contexts, its definition is fairly vague. A *module* is a section of a program, as an abstract entity or in some representation such as source or object code, treated as a unit for some purpose. When we use the term, we will most often mean a section of assembly language source code assembled as a unit. A module would generally be either a main program or a procedure.

Multiprogramming means concurrent execution of several programs. The computer's CPU (central processing unit) executes only one instruction at a time, but it is so fast that, to avoid wasting this valuable resource, several programs are kept available in memory at once so that while one is waiting for a relatively slow operation (maybe one that takes a few dozen milliseconds) to finish, another program may be executing. The slow operation may involve reading data from a disk, or something really slow: a person sitting at a terminal deciding what to do next.

An *operating system* is a collection of programs that controls and allocates the resources of the computer system. It handles the scheduling of all the jobs in the system, the communications necessary for doing input and output, and record and file management. The standard VAX operating system is called VAX/VMS. The letters stand for Virtual Address eXtensions/Virtual Memory System.

2

Machine Organization

A computer system generally consists of three subsystems (as illustrated in Figure 2.1): the memory, the central processing unit, and the I/O subsystem. In this chapter we present a brief overview of their logical structure.

2.1 MEMORY AND DATA ORGANIZATION

Physical Memory

The *physical memory*, also called *main memory* or *main storage*, of a computer is where instructions and data that the processor can directly fetch and execute or manipulate are stored. The VAX uses MOS (metal oxide on silicon) memory, which consists of chips containing thousands of tiny electric circuits each of which may be open or closed at any time. One state is taken to represent 0 and the other to represent 1. In the past, computer memories have been made of other materials, including, for example, magnetic rings, called cores, that could be magnetized in one of two directions, and thus also could represent one bit. In the VAX (and many other computers) the bits are logically grouped in units of eight called *bytes*.

The amount of main memory on a VAX may be from 2 to 32 megabytes (MB) for smaller systems and up to several hundred MB for large systems. (A megabyte is roughly one million bytes.)

8

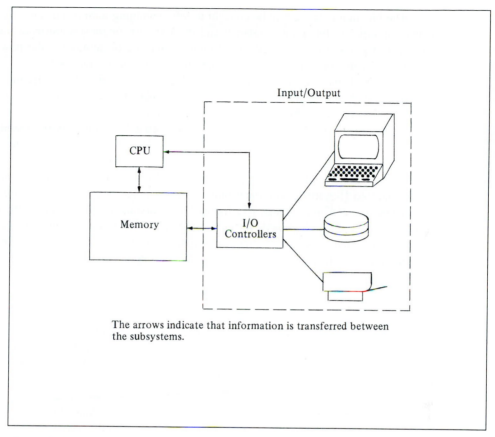

Input/Output

CPU

Memory

I/O
Controllers

The arrows indicate that information is transferred between
the subsystems.

Figure 2.1   The subsystems of a computer

The Logical Structure of Memory

Conceptually, memory consists of a sequence of bytes numbered from 0 to the maximum
available in the given installation. The number of a byte is called its *address*. When
programming in a high-level language, we do not think about memory addresses at all.
We use names for variables, and we leave it to the compiler to find some space in
memory for each variable and keep track of where it is. Variable names are a convenience for the programmer; they do not exist in machine code. Thus copying a character,
for example, in a high-level language is done with an assignment statement. The corresponding machine instruction might tell the machine to "Copy the byte in address 491 to
the byte at address 387." As we saw in the examples in Chapter 1, in assembly language
we can sometimes use names for variables, but an assembly language programmer will
have to understand some new concepts related to the use of memory addresses for specifying the locations of operands. These ideas are introduced and used throughout several
chapters, beginning in Chapter 4.

The bits in a byte are numbered right to left, beginning with 0. Thus the rightmost, or least significant, bit is bit number 0 and the leftmost, or most significant, bit is bit number 7. The bits are numbered right to left so that the bit number is the power of 2 represented by that bit when the datum is interpreted as a binary number.

Since each bit may have one of two values, 0 or 1, 256 (2^8) configurations are possible in one byte. A byte may be used to store a character or a small integer. (Characters are encoded in seven bits; the eighth, or leftmost, is always zero.)

Bytes are too small a unit of memory for storing large integers or floating-point numbers. They are grouped in various ways to provide larger units of storage for data that require more space.

A *word* consists of two contiguous bytes, or 16 bits. The bits of a word are numbered from 0 to 15 starting with the rightmost, or least significant, bit. Words are used to store signed integers in the range –32,768 to 32,767 and unsigned integers in the range 0 to 65,535. There are two choices for how to arrange the bytes of a word (or one of the larger memory units described below) in memory: with the least significant byte first or with the most significant byte first. Suppose, for example, that the integer 558 is represented in binary in a word as

00000010	00101110

and this word is to be stored in memory beginning at the byte whose address is 74. Figure 2.2 illustrates the two possible arrangements. Both arrangements are used by different machines. On the VAX, for all multibyte integers, the least significant byte is stored first in memory. (The Intel 80x86 series microprocessors follow this scheme too. The Motorola M68000 Family and IBM mainframes store the most significant byte first.) For machines like the VAX that store the least significant byte first, when the bytes are shown together on one line in the natural way, with the most significant byte at the left, the bytes of memory are actually in right-to-left order, as illustrated in Figure 2.2. This may cause some confusion, so be forewarned! (Alas, to compensate for this backwardness, machine code on program listings and dumps is printed out showing memory contents from right to left on a line, so while integers may be read easily, data that are stored in the natural way appear backward. This takes some getting used to.)

A *longword* consists of four contiguous bytes, or 32 bits. The bits are numbered from 0 to 31, right to left. Longwords may be used to store very large signed or unsigned integers. They may also be used to store single-precision floating-point numbers.

A *quadword* consists of eight contiguous bytes, or 64 bits, numbered 0 to 63, right to left. Quadwords may be used to store extremely large integers or double-precision floating-point numbers. An *octaword* consists of 16 contiguous bytes, with bits numbered 0 to 127. The VAX provides a complete set of integer arithmetic instructions for byte, word, and longword integers, but not for quadwords or octawords.

Each of the larger units just described has an address in memory: the address of its first, or lowest-numbered, byte. For example, if an instruction is to perform an operation on the longword in memory at address 780, it will use bytes 780, 781, 782, and 783.

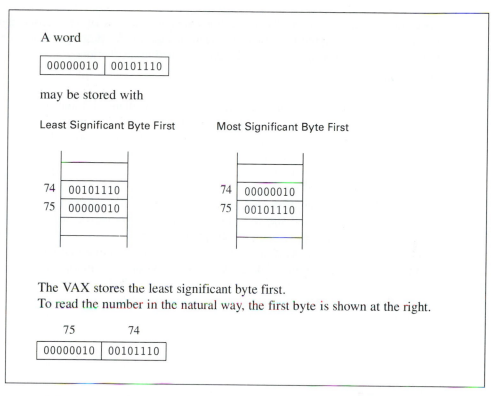

Figure 2.2   An integer in a multibyte memory unit

Bytes may be grouped in other ways for other types of data. For example, one byte can hold the character code for one character, so a contiguous sequence of bytes may be grouped together to store a character string. The number of bytes used will depend on the length of the character string.

Different computer systems have different word sizes, generally in the range of 16 to 60 bits; 16 and 32 are very common sizes. Supercomputers, intended for scientific computations on real numbers with a high degree of accuracy, tend to have large words (e.g., 64 bits). In some computers the basic unit of memory is the word, not the byte, and only words have addresses.

For storing very small numbers or a lot of numbers that do not require an integral number of bytes, it may be an inefficient use of space to think of bytes as the basic unit of memory. On the VAX, arbitrary strings of (at most 32) contiguous bits anywhere in memory (ignoring byte boundaries) may be treated as a unit, called a *variable-length bit field*.

The notation for specifying a range of bits within a byte, word, longword, or quadword specifies the numbers of the first and last bit in the range, separated by a colon. Since the lower-numbered bits are to the right of the high-numbered ones, the lower number is written on the right. For example, the bits of the second byte of a longword may be referred to as bits 15:8. (This notation is for descriptive or documentation purposes; it is not the way bit fields are specified in instructions.)

Virtual Memory

In a multiprogramming system like the VAX, parts of many different users' programs and their data are in main memory at the same time. However, a programmer may write a program that requires more space than there is in main memory. The VAX uses a *virtual memory* system. One definition of *virtual* is "being functionally or effectively, but not formally, of its kind." With virtual memory the user may imagine that (and program as if) the computer has a much larger amount of main memory than it really has. Since only a small part of a program and its data is being used at any time, that part can be kept in main memory and the rest stored on a mass storage device, usually a disk. Programs are divided into segments, called pages, of 512 bytes each. When a page that is not in main memory is needed, the hardware and the operating system detect this and load the required page from the disk. On the VAX the virtual memory can contain up to approximately 4.3 billion bytes, or four gigabytes. (A gigabyte is roughly one billion bytes.) The limit on the size of virtual memory comes from the fact that addresses are 32-bit integers, and the largest integer that can be represented in binary in 32 bits is 4,294,967,295. The actual amount available depends on the mass storage devices at a particular installation.

The memory locations we use when writing assembly language programs are virtual locations; however, throughout the rest of this book we will think of them as actual locations. The hardware and the operating system translate virtual addresses into physical memory addresses. The beginning assembly language programmer does not have to be concerned about the distinction.

Representation of Data in Memory

It should be clear that since memory contains only 0's and 1's, all the data types that we wish to use—integers, floating-point numbers, character strings, and so on, as well as machine instructions—must be encoded as strings of 0's and 1's. For some data types, integers for example, there are fairly standard encodings used by many different computers. For other types there is more variation. As we consider each of the data types, we will describe its representation, or encoding. We will also describe the encoding of instructions.

Since many different types of data may be stored in the same place in memory at different times, how can we, or the computer, tell if a particular location contains a signed integer, a floating-point number, an instruction, or something else? The answer is that we cannot tell just by looking at the string of bits; we, and the computer, must know what type of datum is supposed to be there before we can interpret it properly. The type is generally determined from the context in which the datum is used. To emphasize the necessity of knowing the context or the data type in order to decode data, we show next six different valid interpretations of the same longword.

Contents of the longword in hex:	63654440

Longword integer:	1,667,580,992
Two word integers:	17472 and 25445
Four byte integers:	64, 68, 101, and 99
Instruction:	ADDF2 (R5)[R4],(R3)
Characters:	@Dec
Floating-point number:	192.38826

This is not an exhaustive list of the valid interpretations of the longword. The datum could be an address, part of a packed-decimal number or a double-precision floating-point number, or various other things.

In many places throughout this book we will diagram or list the contents of memory locations to illustrate the effects of instruction. We will show the data in memory units of a size appropriate to the topic being considered. (If the size of the units used is not explicitly stated, the reader should be able to figure it out from the amount of data shown.) It is important to remember that to the computer, memory is one long sequence of consecutively numbered bytes. The amount of data it will use for a computation, or store as a result, depends on the instruction used, not the diagrams drawn as a conceptual aid for people.

2.2   THE CENTRAL PROCESSING UNIT

The central processing unit (CPU) is responsible for decoding and executing machine instructions. Decoding instructions includes determining what operation is to be performed and determining the locations of the operands. After the operands are fetched, the CPU performs the operation using its arithmetic and logical units. The CPU also keeps track of its place in the program it is executing and keeps other status information about the program.

The machine instruction set on the VAX has more than 300 instructions, including some that do arithmetic and logical operations on integer and floating-point data of various sizes, arithmetic and logical operations on packed-decimal data (another format for numbers), manipulation of character and bit data, program flow control (i.e., testing and branching), manipulation of special data structures called stacks and queues, other special operations (e.g., editing data to be printed), and various others.

A *general register* is a special storage location in the CPU rather than main memory. It takes much less time to access and modify data in registers than it takes for data in memory, so computation is often done on data in registers rather than memory. Some computers have separate registers for data and for addresses (e.g., some CDC machines and some microprocessors like the M68000 series), but the VAX does not. The VAX has 16 general registers, each of which has 32 bits, numbered 0 to 31, right to left. The first 12 registers, named R0, R1, . . . , R11, are used by assembly language programs for intermediate results of computations (involving data and/or addresses), temporary storage of data and/or addresses, and the like. The remaining four registers play special roles.[1] Their names are AP (argument pointer),[2] FP (frame pointer), SP (stack pointer), and PC (program counter). AP, FP, and SP are used for procedure and subroutine linkage. The details of how they are used will be discussed in Chapter 9. The stack pointer has other uses that will be described later.

In many computers the program counter is a special register that is used to keep track of the address of the next instruction to be executed; as each instruction is fetched, its length is quickly determined by the CPU and the program counter is automatically incremented by that amount, so that when the execution of the current instruction is completed, the program counter already points to the next one. The principle is the same for the VAX's PC, but because the VAX has an extremely flexible instruction format, making it difficult to determine the length of an instruction, the PC is usually incremented several times while processing one instruction. It first points to the beginning of the instruction, where the operation code is, then is incremented to point to the parts of each operand specifier in turn, and finally will point to the beginning of the next instruction. The instruction decoding process is described in detail in Chapter 8.

In machine instructions on the VAX, register references are encoded by the numbers 0 through 15; AP, FP, SP, and PC are encoded as 12 through 15.

Although general registers R0 through R11 are available to the assembly language programmer, some instructions have side effects that change the contents of these registers. Some I/O instructions use R0, and several other instructions use R0 through R5. Thus it is good practice for the programmer to use R6 through R11 most of the time. The lower-numbered registers may be used, carefully, for temporary data.

A general register contains as many bits as a longword. When instructions that act on bytes or words use data in general registers, they use the rightmost byte or word in the register.

Table 2.1 in the chapter summary (Section 2.4) summarizes the uses of the general registers.

The VAX has many special-purpose registers that are used by the CPU and the operating system to execute instructions, manage the resources and programs in the system, and do input and output. Most of these registers are not accessible by the user and their uses are so far "behind the scenes" that they will not be discussed in this book. Parts of one of the special registers, however, can be affected and accessed by assembly language instructions, so it is of importance to the assembly language programmer. This special register is the processor status longword (PSL). The PSL contains a variety of status flags. Those that are available to the user are in the low-order half of the PSL, called the processor status word (PSW); the other half is reserved for the system. An example of the first kind of flag is the *overflow condition code*, which is set when the

---

[1] It may seem strange to have special-purpose "general" registers. They are general in the sense that they can all be used in similar ways in machine code.

[2] R12 is an alternative name for the AP register. However, because it is too easy to forget that R12 and AP are the same register, we will not use the name R12 in this book.

> General registers
>
> PSL
>
> Other registers (for use by CPU)
>
> Instruction decoder
>
> Arithmetic and logic units

Figure 2.3   The central processing unit (CPU)

result of an arithmetic operation is too large to fit in the space designated in an instruc-tion. This condition code may be tested by a program and appropriate action taken. An example of the second kind of flag is one that specifies the level of privilege of the program. The operating system has a higher privilege level than an ordinary user and can execute some instructions that the user cannot, including instructions that change the privilege level. The PSL contains some of the critical information that must be saved when a program is interrupted to give another program a chance to use the CPU. The PSL is automatically stored in memory and reloaded when execution of the program continues. We will add more detail about the PSL as we cover instructions that affect and access it.

Figure 2.3 shows some of the important components of the CPU.

2.3   INPUT AND OUTPUT

Input and output are very complex operations, much more so than the arithmetic and logical operations that are carried out by the CPU. I/O is complex because it involves communicating with devices external to the computer, such as disks, terminals, tape drives, and printers. Since a variety of devices may be attached to a computer at any installation and each type has its own rules for formatting and transmitting data, numer-ous parameters must be specified to describe how and where I/O will be done. For several reasons, the user has neither the privilege nor the responsibility to program I/O directly. Most of the necessary work is done by systems programs that the user can access. Details about physical characteristics of I/O devices and the physical location or format of data files are handled by the systems programs and are invisible to the user, who may think of data as being organized in whatever way is most appropriate to the application. The user is responsible for specifying this logical structure.

Aside from eliminating the need to know and program many I/O details, there is another reason for not allowing the user to directly control I/O devices in a multipro-gramming system: to prevent interference among different users. Imagine, for example, two programs running concurrently that are both writing data out on the same printer; the data from the two programs would be intermingled—and not particularly useful to either user. Thus the operating system manages and schedules the I/O operations requested by a program.

The VAX has a utility called Record Management Services (RMS) that handles file organization and input and output operations for the user. Even though RMS allows the user to do I/O without considering all the many details inherent in such operations, it still requires a fair amount of background. We will describe some of the capabilities of RMS in Chapter 16. In Chapter 5 we will provide some very easy-to-use instructions that do simple I/O.

2.4 SUMMARY

A computer has three subsystems: memory, the central processing unit, and the I/O subsystem. The bits in the main memory of many computers are grouped in units of eight, called bytes. The bytes may be further grouped for storing large data. Some of the units that instructions can act on as a whole on the VAX are words (two bytes), longwords (four bytes), quadwords (eight bytes), and octawords (16 bytes). These memory units may begin at any byte in storage (except of course at the very end, where there is not enough room), but processing is more efficient if they begin at a byte whose address is divisible by the size of the unit. The bits within a byte, word, longword, or quadword are numbered consecutively from zero beginning at the right, or least significant, end. Bytes may be grouped in other ways for character strings and packed-decimal data. Up to 32 bits may be grouped without regard to byte boundaries to form a unit called a variable-length bit field.

Bytes are numbered consecutively from zero to one less than the number of bytes in memory. The number assigned to a byte is called its address. When bytes are grouped to form larger memory units, the address of the unit is the address of its lowest-numbered byte.

The VAX uses a virtual memory system; that is, the programmer may program as if the memory were much larger than it really is. The system stores part of the program on a disk and fetches segments, called pages, as they are needed. The system handles the translation of virtual addresses used by the program into the physical addresses where the data and instructions have actually been stored in main memory.

Since all data are encoded in 0's and 1's, we and the computer must know the context in which data are used to interpret them.

The CPU decodes and executes machine instructions.

A *register* is a special storage location in the CPU that can be accessed faster than main memory. The CPU has 16 general registers, 12 of which, R0 through R11, may be used by the assembly language programmer for "scratch work," that is, temporary storage of addresses and intermediate results of computation. The other four general registers, AP, FP, SP, and PC, have special roles. The first three are used primarily for procedure and subroutine linkage. PC is the program counter; it contains the address of the next instruction to be executed or the address of the next segment of the current instruction. The roles of the registers are summarized in Table 2.1.

The CPU has a special register called the Processor Status Longword. It contains various flags and condition codes that provide information about the status of the program.

TABLE 2.1   GENERAL REGISTERS

Registers	Uses
R0–R5	General use; affected by side effects of some instructions
R6–R11	General use
AP	Argument pointer (for procedures)
FP	Frame pointer (for procedures)
SP	Stack pointer (for procedures and other uses)
PC	Program counter (not used directly by the programmer)

Input and output are very complex operations because they involve communicating between the computer and the outside world. Many of the details of I/O programming are handled by the operating system.

2.5   EXERCISES

1. How many bits are in a byte? A word? A longword?

2. How many bytes are in a word? A longword? A quadword?

3. How does the computer determine whether a longword in memory contains an integer or a string of four characters?

4. An integer is represented in a longword of memory consisting of bytes with addresses 488, 489, 48A, and 48B. Which byte contains the most significant bits of the integer?

5. Are the general registers in main memory or in the CPU?

3

Binary and Hexadecimal Numbers and Integer Representation

3.1 THE BINARY AND HEXADECIMAL NUMBER SYSTEMS

Since all data are stored in memory encoded in 0's and 1's, it seems natural to store positive integers in their binary representation. To examine and interpret data and instructions in memory, we could read long binary strings or frequently convert back and forth between binary and decimal. Both of these choices would lead to many errors and wasted time. The hexadecimal (base 16) number system is very convenient to use as an intermediate notation between binary and decimal. Conversion between binary and hexadecimal (called hex for short) is simple, but hex is much more compact than binary; only about one-quarter as many digits are needed to represent a number. We will find that in many cases where we would usually use the decimal system, we can use hex almost as easily, so we will not have to convert between hex and decimal very often. In this section we review the principle underlying all these positional representation number systems, and we present algorithms for converting between them and algorithms for doing arithmetic in hex.

To say that a number system uses *positional representation* means that the value represented by a digit depends on its position in the representation of a number. For example, the 3 in 437 represents the value thirty, while the 3 in 3692 represents three thousand. An example of a different kind of number system is the Roman numeral system where, for example, X always represents ten (or negative ten). The value repre-

18

sented by a digit in a positional representation system is the digit's own value multiplied by a power of the base, or radix, of the particular system being used. Thus if a number is written as

$$d_n \, d_{n-1} \cdots d_2 d_1 d_0$$

where the d's are digits, then, for each i between 0 and n, d_i represents the value of the digit d_i multiplied by the radix raised to the ith power. Thus, in decimal, we call the rightmost position the ones (10^0) place, the next (from the right) position the tens (10^1) place, the next the hundreds (10^2) place, and so on. For an arbitrary radix r, the rightmost place is the ones (r^0) place, the next is the r's place, the next the r^2's place, and so on. Using the radix r, the number written above would have the decimal value

$$\left(\overline{d}_n \times r^n \right) + \left(\overline{d}_{n-1} \times r^{n-1} \right) + \cdots + \left(\overline{d}_2 \times r^2 \right) + \left(\overline{d}_1 \times r^1 \right) + \overline{d}_0 \tag{3.1}$$

where $\overline{d}_i$ is the decimal value of the radix r digit d_i, for i between 0 and n. We will return to this formula and do some examples later.

The hexadecimal number system is the positional representation number system with radix 16. The first few positions (from the right) in a hexadecimal number are the ones place, the 16's place, the 256's place, and the 4096's place. (It is often useful to know these first few powers of 16.)

If r is the radix being used, we need digits, or distinct symbols, to explicitly represent the numbers 0 through $r-1$; we can represent r by putting a 1 in the r's place and a 0 in the ones place, and we can represent higher numbers similarly by putting digits in the various positions. For radices no larger than ten, we can use the usual digits 0 through $r-1$, but for larger radices (e.g., 16) we have to invent new digits. By convention, the digits for the hexadecimal system are 0, 1, 2, . . . , 8, 9, A, B, C, D, E, and F, where A through F represent ten through fifteen, respectively.

Converting between Hex and Binary

In binary, using four bits, we can represent the numbers zero through fifteen. The correspondence between the bit patterns and the decimal and hexadecimal representations is shown in Table 3.1. Each four-bit binary number corresponds to one hexadecimal digit, and vice versa. Thus we may think of hexadecimal as a shorthand for binary. To convert a hex number to binary we simply replace each hex digit in the number by its binary equivalent. For example, we convert 2B70F3 as follows:

2	B	7	0	F	3
0010	1011	0111	0000	1111	0011

We can omit the first two zeros without changing the value of the number, but the hex zero must be encoded as four binary zeros, and in general leading zeros in the encoding of each hex digit, except the leftmost, must be included. They are needed as place savers. To convert from binary to hex, we reverse the process we just used: i.e., replace each group of four bits by the hex digit with the same value. Since the number of bits may not be divisible by four, we must start grouping the bits from the right end of the string. If

TABLE 3.1   BINARY AND DECIMAL VALUES OF HEXADECIMAL DIGITS

Binary	Decimal	Hexadecimal
0000	0	0
0001	1	1
0010	2	2
0011	3	3
0100	4	4
0101	5	5
0110	6	6
0111	7	7
1000	8	8
1001	9	9
1010	10	A
1011	11	B
1100	12	C
1101	13	D
1110	14	E
1111	15	F

the last, or leftmost, group has fewer than four bits, we pad with extra zeros on the left. Thus 1101001000111010100110010 is converted as follows:

$$\underbrace{0001}_{1} \quad \underbrace{1010}_{A} \quad \underbrace{0100}_{4} \quad \underbrace{0111}_{7} \quad \underbrace{0101}_{5} \quad \underbrace{0011}_{3} \quad \underbrace{0010}_{2}$$

We have not justified the validity of the conversion methods, but rather than do a formal proof (which we leave to the mathematically inclined reader), we will use the example to indicate how the argument would go. Consider the digit 5 in $1A47532_{16}$. Since it is in the third place from the right, it represents 5×16^2. The corresponding bits in the binary string, 0101, are in the 2^8 through 2^{11} places, so we can compute the value they represent as follows:

$$(0 \times 2^{11}) + (1 \times 2^{10}) + (0 \times 2^9) + (1 \times 2^8)$$
$$= [(0 \times 2^3) + (1 \times 2^2) + (0 \times 2^1) + (1 \times 2^0)] \times 2^8$$
$$= (5) \times (2^4)^2$$
$$= 5 \times 16^2$$

the same value represented by the 5 in $1A47532_{16}$.

Converting from Hex or Binary to Decimal

The evaluation formula (3.1) is used to convert numbers from a radix other than ten into decimal. It is fairly easy to use if you have a table of powers of the radix (or are willing to compute them) and can do addition and multiplication.

Example 3.1: Converting from Hex and Binary to Decimal

$$E2407_{16} = (14 \times 16^4) + (2 \times 16^3) + (4 \times 16^2) + (0 \times 16^1) + (7 \times 16^0)$$
$$= 917,504 + 8192 + 1024 + 7$$
$$= 926,727$$

$$10011101_2 = (1 \times 2^7) + (0 \times 2^6) + (0 \times 2^5) + (1 \times 2^4) + (1 \times 2^3)$$
$$+ (1 \times 2^2) + (0 \times 2^1) + (1 \times 2^0)$$
$$= 128 + 16 + 8 + 4 + 1$$
$$= 157$$

The multiplications can be eliminated, simplifying the conversion, by keeping larger tables that contain the values of $d \times r^p$ for each nonzero digit d and each power p up to some reasonable limit. Such a table for radix 16 appears in Appendix B. It contains columns for powers between 0 and 7; that is sufficient to convert the contents of a longword to decimal. The entries in the table are all decimal numbers. (A similar table appears in the *VAX-11 Programming Card*.) Suppose that a longword contains $00014A2E_{16}$ and we want to convert it to decimal. (To emphasize that bits are never "empty"—they always have value 0 or 1—when specifying the contents of a register or a memory location, we will show leading zeros.) We use the hex conversion table in Appendix B as follows to do the conversion.

Begin at the right end of the number. Look in the rightmost column, the 16^0 column, and the row for the digit E. We find the value 14; write it down. Then, moving left one place in the longword and left one column in the table to the 16^1 column, we look in the row for the digit 2 and find 32. Write that down. Moving left in the longword and in the table again, we look in the row for the digit A and find 2560. For the digits 4 and 1 we find the values 16,384 and 65,536, respectively. Since zeros in any position have the value 0, we are finished looking up table entries, and we now add up the values found. The result is 84,526. The computation is summarized in Fig. 3.1.

We did not really have to look up all five nonzero digits in the table. After a bit of familiarization with hexadecimal numbers, the first three could be done directly. E is 14,

---

The caret (^) points to the digit being evaluated in each line.

00014A2E	14
^	
	+
00014A2E	32
^	
	+
00014A2E	2560
^	
	+
00014A2E	16384
^	
	+
00014A2E	65536
^	
	84526

Figure 3.1   Converting from hexadecimal to decimal

a 2 in the 16's place is obviously 32, and multiplying by ten (A) is always easy; in this case one must only remember that 16^2 is 256. There are many times when it is more efficient to use one's head, with care, than to use tables or follow an algorithm slavishly.

Note that the first row in the table gives the powers of 16 and may be useful for purposes other than conversion. For example, if we want to determine how many numbers can be represented using four hexadecimal digits (a word of memory) we can just look up 16^4, since each of the four digits may have any one of 16 values. This explains why the range of unsigned integers that can be represented in a word is 0 through 65,535.

Converting from binary to decimal can be done by the same method, using the evaluation formula 3.1, but with binary there is no need for multiplications, since the only digits are 0 and 1. Thus the 1's simply tell us which powers of 2 to add up. A conversion table comparable to the hexadecimal conversion table in Appendix B would be much shorter but much wider; we need 2^0 through 2^{31} to evaluate a longword. A list of these powers of 2 is included in Appendix B.

Another way to convert binary to decimal is first to convert to hexadecimal by the straightforward substitutions described earlier, then convert from hex to decimal. When the hex conversion table is available, this method probably will require less work because there will be fewer values to add up (at most eight rather than 32 for a longword). Fig. 3.2 illustrates both methods.

Converting from Decimal to Hex

Converting from decimal to another radix involves division instead of multiplication. We will present two methods for decimal-to-hex conversion. The first is a general method for converting numbers from decimal to a different radix. The second method makes use of the hexadecimal conversion table (and could be generalized to other radices if we had the appropriate tables).

The first method uses the evaluation formula for an $(n + 1)$-digit number in radix r. Notice that in the formula

$$value = (\overline{d_n} \times r^n) + (\overline{d_{n-1}} \times r^{n-1}) + \cdots + (\overline{d_1} \times r^1) + \overline{d_0}$$

all the terms are clearly divisible by the radix except the last, d_0, the rightmost digit of the hex number. Since d_0 is in the range 0 to $r - 1$, it is the remainder when the number is divided by the radix. Thus, starting with a decimal number, we can find the rightmost digit of its hex representation by dividing the number by 16 and finding the remainder. The arithmetic is all done in decimal. The quotient from the division is

$$(\overline{d_n} \times r^{n-1}) + (\overline{d_{n-1}} \times r^{n-2}) + \cdots + (\overline{d_2} \times r^1) + \overline{d_1}$$

Now every term is divisible by r except d_1, so d_1 is the remainder if we divide this new number by r. (If $d_1 = 0$, it is divisible by r, but then the remainder is 0 too.) The new quotient will be

$$(\overline{d_n} \times r^{n-2}) + (\overline{d_{n-1}} \times r^{n-3}) + \cdots + (\overline{d_3} \times r^1) + \overline{d_2}$$

Problem: Convert 110100010000001110 (binary) to decimal.

Method 1: Add up the powers of 2 corresponding to the 1's in the number.

11010001000000111̬0	2^1	2
		+
1101000100000011̬10	2^2	4
		+
110100010000001̬110	2^3	8
		+
11010001̬0000001110	2^{10}	1024
		+
110̬100010000001110	2^{14}	16384
		+
1̬10100010000001110	2^{16}	65536
		+
1̬10100010000001110	2^{17}	131072

The result is: 214030

Method 2: Convert to hex, then use the hex conversion table.
  Convert to hex:

11	0100	0100	0000	1110
3	4	4	0	E

  Then, using the table:

3440E̬	14
	+
3440E̬	1024
	+
3440E̬	16384
	+
3̬440E	196608

214030 is the result again

Figure 3.2   Converting from binary to decimal

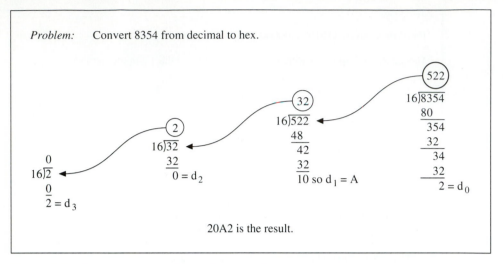

Figure 3.3   Converting from decimal to hexadecimal

and clearly we can continue the procedure of dividing by the radix and finding the remainder to get all the digits of the radix-r representation of the original decimal number. We quit when we get a zero quotient. The method is illustrated in Fig. 3.3.

The second method for converting from decimal to hexadecimal uses the hex conversion table in Appendix B. The first step determines how many hex digits there will be in the result and also determines the leftmost digit. Let k be the decimal number to be converted. Look in the table and find the largest entry that is not larger than k. The column in which this number is found indicates the number of digits in the hex representation of k: one more than the power of 16 at the top of the column. The hex digit in whose row we are looking is the leftmost digit of the result. At this point it is a good idea to mark a space for each digit and write down the leftmost. Subtract the number found in the table from k, and let k now be the difference. (All the arithmetic is done in decimal.) Move one column to the right in the table and again look for the largest value that is not larger than k. If all the values in this column are too large, the next digit is 0, and we move right another column. Otherwise, the next digit is the digit in whose row we found the largest number not larger than k. Once again, subtract this number from k, and let k now be the difference. Repeat this digit-finding procedure until all the digits are filled in. This method is illustrated in Figure 3.4.

Converting from Decimal to Binary

A decimal number can be converted to binary by using either of the two methods just described for decimal-to-hex conversions. For the second method, the powers-of-2 table would be used. A third method is first to convert the decimal number to hexadecimal, then substitute the four-bit binary representations of each hex digit.

Problem: Convert 584,972 from decimal to hex.

Let $k = 584,972$.
The largest entry in the table no larger than k is 524,288. It appears in row 8 of the 16^4 column, so the hex result will have 5 digits and the first is 8. Thus we write down

8 _ _ _ _

$$\begin{aligned} \text{Subtract:} \quad k = \ & 584,972 \\ & -524,288 \\ \hline \text{New } k = \ & 60,684 \end{aligned}$$

In the 16^3 column we find 57,344 is the largest number that doesn't exceed k. It is in the E row, so we write E as the next digit.

8 E _ _ _

$$\begin{aligned} \text{Subtract:} \quad k = \ & 60,684 \\ & -57,344 \\ \hline \text{New } k = \ & 3,340 \end{aligned}$$

In the 16^2 column we find 3,328 in row D, so we now have

8 E D _ _

$$\begin{aligned} \text{Subtract:} \quad k = \ & 3,340 \\ & -3,328 \\ \hline \text{New } k = \ & 12 \end{aligned}$$

All the numbers in the 16's column are larger than 12, so the next digit is 0.

8 E D 0 _

Finally, in the 16^0 column (or from memory) we find that 12 is C, so the resulting hex number is

8 E D 0 C

Figure 3.4 Converting from decimal to hex using a conversion table

Arithmetic in Hex

Sometimes we have to add or subtract (and occasionally, multiply) hex numbers. Of course, it is possible to convert the numbers to decimal, do ordinary decimal arithmetic, and convert the results back to hex, but this involves extra work and increased opportunity for making mistakes. Doing arithmetic in hex is not much different from doing arithmetic in decimal; the principle is the same; we just have to remember that we carry

Problem: Add 30E4 and 29A7.	30E4 +29A7
Working right to left: 4 + 7 = 11, which is B in hex.	30E4 +29A7 ――― B
E + A is 14 + 10 = 24. 24 = 16 + 8, so write 8 and carry 1.	¹ 30E4 +29A7 ――― 8B
1 + 9 = 10, which is A in hex	¹ 30E4 +29A7 ――― A8B
3 + 2 = 5.	¹ 30E4 +29A7 ――― 5A8B

Figure 3.5   Addition in hex

only when the sum of a column of digits exceeds 15, not 9, and when we "borrow" for a subtraction, we borrow 16, not 10. When adding or subtracting a column of digits, it may be easiest to translate the digits indicated by letters (A through F) to decimal in your head and do the digit sums and differences in decimal. Figures 3.5 and 3.6 show examples of addition and subtraction in hex.

Generally, when we have to multiply hex numbers, one of the numbers has only one digit, often 2, 4, or 8. Again, you may find it easiest to do the digitwise multiplications in decimal, switching back and forth between hex and decimal in your head. See Fig. 3.7 for an example.

Why Hex?

We said at the beginning of this section that hex is a good shorthand notation for binary. We have since seen that each hex digit corresponds exactly to a group of four bits, making the conversion between hex and binary very easy. But it would be just as easy to convert between binary and octal (base 8) or between binary and base 32; if the radix is a power of 2, one digit for the radix corresponds exactly to a group of bits. Some computer systems, in fact, use octal instead of hexadecimal. The choice depends on the architecture of the system. In the VAX there are 16 general registers, numbered 0 through 15. Thus a reference to a register in a machine instruction is encoded in four bits, or one hex digit. The instruction set for the VAX (excluding instructions for certain

Problem: Subtract 19B8 from 30E4.

$$\begin{array}{r} 30E4 \\ -19B8 \\ \hline \end{array}$$

4 is less than 8, so we must borrow 16 from the next place, leaving D there and giving us $16 + 4 = 20$ in the ones place.

$$\begin{array}{r} {\scriptstyle D20} \\ 30E4 \\ -19B8 \\ \hline \end{array}$$

$20 - 8 = 12$, which is C.

$$\begin{array}{r} {\scriptstyle D20} \\ 30E4 \\ -19B8 \\ \hline C \end{array}$$

$D - B = 2$.

$$\begin{array}{r} {\scriptstyle D} \\ 30E4 \\ -19B8 \\ \hline 2C \end{array}$$

0 is less than 9, so borrow to get 16. $16 - 9 = 7$

$$\begin{array}{r} {\scriptstyle 216} \\ 30E4 \\ -19B8 \\ \hline 72C \end{array}$$

Finally, $2 - 1 = 1$.

$$\begin{array}{r} {\scriptstyle 2} \\ 30E4 \\ -19B8 \\ \hline 172C \end{array}$$

Figure 3.6 Subtraction in hex

extra data types) has slightly fewer than 256 machine instructions; thus most operation codes use eight bits, or two hex digits. The VAX uses eight bits to encode a character; thus character codes are given as two hex digits. The VAX has 14 different addressing modes (ways to specify where the operands of an instruction are to be found); thus it is convenient to use a hex digit to specify the mode. Once we know the formats of the machine instructions (which will be covered in detail in Chapter 8), if we look at the encoding of an instruction in hex we can easily pick out the component parts. 5B53A0 is the encoding of a simple instruction. The operation code is at the right end, hence is A0, the code for an add instruction. The other two pairs of digits each include an addressing mode specifier and a register number. Thus both operands are addressed in mode 5, which means that the operands are in registers, and the registers used are R11 and R3.

Computers that have eight registers and 64 or fewer instructions, or perhaps close to 512 (8^3) instructions, and use six bits to encode characters, are more likely to use octal instead of hexadecimal, since the encoding of three bits by one octal digit would make the encodings easy to interpret. In some such computers, the number of bits in a word is a multiple of three.

Problem: Multiply 4CA9 by 8.

$$\begin{array}{r} 4CA9 \\ \times 8 \\ \hline \end{array}$$

$8 \times 9 = 72$, but this result must be converted back to hex. $72 = 64 + 8$, and $64 = 4 \times 16$, so we write 8 and carry 4.

$$\begin{array}{r} \overset{4}{4}CA9 \\ \times 8 \\ \hline 8 \end{array}$$

Now $8 \times 10 + 4 = 84$ and $84 = 5 \times 16 + 4$, so we write 4 and carry 5.

$$\begin{array}{r} \overset{54}{4}CA9 \\ \times 8 \\ \hline 48 \end{array}$$

$8 \times 12 + 5 = 101$ and $101 = 6 \times 16 + 5$, so we write 5 and carry 6.

$$\begin{array}{r} \overset{654}{4}CA9 \\ \times 8 \\ \hline 548 \end{array}$$

$8 \times 4 + 6 = 38$, which is 26 in hex, so finally:

$$\begin{array}{r} \overset{654}{4}CA9 \\ \times 8 \\ \hline 26548 \end{array}$$

Figure 3.7 Multiplication in hex

3.2 INTEGER REPRESENTATION

Signed integers are used in computers in several ways. They may be data themselves or they may be a part of another type of data (e.g., the exponent in a floating-point number). They are also used as parts of instructions, to specify the location of operands. An obvious representation for nonnegative integers is the binary number system, and it is the representation used for most of these purposes.

The interesting problem is how to represent negative integers. We will consider three possible solutions, including the two's complement representation used on the VAX and many other computers (including the Motorola 68000 Family and the Intel 80x86 microprocessors). All three methods have one common feature: one bit in the integer is reserved to represent its sign. By a convention standard throughout the computer industry, the leftmost bit is the sign bit, 0 indicates a positive (or nonnegative) number, and 1 indicates a negative number. The choice between the different representations depends partly on how quickly a computer can do commonly performed operations on data. For each representation scheme, we will consider how to negate a (positive or negative) integer and how to add two integers.

For all our examples we will use 16 bits (i.e., a word). The largest integer we can accommodate is 0111111111111111, or 32,767. The representation schemes described can easily be generalized to any number of bits (greater than one).

Sign-Magnitude

The simplest way to handle negative integers is to represent the absolute value of the integer in binary and just use the leftmost bit to indicate the sign. This method is called *sign-magnitude* representation, because the sign and the magnitude (absolute value) are represented separately.

Example 3.2: Sign-Magnitude Representation of 92 and –92

92	0000000001011100
–92	1000000001011100

Negating a sign-magnitude integer is very easy; we simply complement (i.e., reverse) the sign bit. Addition is done in the usual way, but in binary. If both integers have the same sign, we add their magnitudes and put the same sign in the result. If the signs are different, we determine which integer has the larger magnitude and subtract the other from it. The sign of the result is the sign of the operand with the larger magnitude. This does not seem very complicated, but it involves tests, decisions, and different potential courses of action. Sign-magnitude is a poor choice for an integer representation when we would like a computer to do millions of additions per second.

One's Complement

The next representation scheme is called *one's complement*. To represent a negative integer, we write out its absolute value in binary, then complement all the bits. Note that this will make the sign bit be 1, as it should be. In the examples for one's complement and two's complement, we will show the hex equivalent of the bit strings. The operations that we (humans) will sometimes have to do on integers (interpretation and addition, for example) can be done just as easily, if not more so, using the hex shorthand. Note that complementing a bit is the same as subtracting the bit from 1, so complementing the bits, given their hex representation, can be done by subtracting the hex digits from F (or 15_{10}), because $F_{16} = 1111_2$.

Example 3.3: One's Complement Representation of 92 and –92

92	0000000001011100	005C
-92	1111111110100011	FFA3

To negate a positive or negative integer, complement all the bits.

Addition can be done without regard to the signs of the operands. We add the two integers as if they were unsigned binary numbers: that is, treat the sign bits just like the others. If we carry a 1 out of the leftmost bit position, it is added in at the right, or least significant, bit.

Example 3.4: Adding 45 and –92 in One's Complement Notation

```
      45     0000000000101101      002D
   +(-92)   +1111111110100011     +FFA3
   ------    ----------------     -----
     -47     1111111111010000      FFD0
```

(0 carry)

Example 3.5: Adding 1637 and –101 in One's Complement Notation

```
    1637     0000011001100101      0665
  +(-101)   +1111111110011010     +FF9A
  -------    ----------------     -----
            10000010111111111     105FF

                           +1        +1
             ---------------     -----
    1536     0000011000000000      0600
```

We leave it as an exercise for the reader to add two negative integers and verify that the same method works. Also, the theoretically inclined reader may wish to consider how to prove that this method always works.

Since there are no decisions to make and the steps followed are always the same (the carry bit is always added back in at the right, but is sometimes 0, as in the first example), addition of one's complement integers is relatively easy and fast on a computer. Unfortunately, though, adding in the carry bit may involve almost as much work as adding the two operands; in the second example the addition of the carried 1 caused ten bits of the result to change. One's complement notation has a peculiarity that, along with the extra work required for adding the carry bit, has made it an unpopular choice for integer representation. The number zero is represented by 0000000000000000. What happens if we negate it? We complement all the bits and get 1111111111111111. Thus –0 has a different representation from +0, but algebraically, –0 = +0. The different representations of zero cause problems when doing tests on results of arithmetic operations. Suppose that we add two integers and test the result for zero. For example:

```
    -8     1111111111110111      FFF7
    +8    +0000000000001000     +0008
    --     ----------------     -----
     0     1111111111111111      FFFF
```

= – 0, not = 0

Some computers do use one's complement representation and regularly check the results of arithmetic, converting –0, when it occurs, to +0. Most computers now use a variation of one's complement, called two's complement, that eliminates the problem of the two zeros.

Two's Complement

To represent a negative integer in *two's complement*, we start with its absolute value in binary, then complement all the bits and add 1 to the result.

Example 3.6: Two's Complement Representation of 92 and −92

92	0000000001011100	005C
Complement the bits	1111111110100011	FFA3
Add 1	+1	+1
−92	1111111110100100	FFA4

To negate a negative integer we must reverse this process. It is not obvious, but is nonetheless true, that we use the same steps. That is, given a negative integer in two's complement representation, to find its absolute value we complement all the bits and add 1.

Example 3.7: Negating −92

−92	1111111110100100	FFA4
Complement the bits	0000000001011011	005B
Add 1	+1	+1
92	0000000001011100	005C

Thus, negating an integer (either positive or negative) is easy and does not depend on the sign of the integer being negated. But does this method always work? We will present a formal justification of it at the end of this section.

How do we add two's complement integers? We simply add the two bit strings as unsigned binary integers and ignore the carry from the leftmost bit position if there is one.

Example 3.8: Adding 92 and −45 in Two's Complement Notation

92	0000000001011100	005C
+(−45)	1111111111010011	FFD3
	10000000000101111	1002F
Drop the carry	0000000000101111	002F

The result is 47.

Example 3.9: Adding −102 and −58 in Two's Complement Notation

−102	1111111110011010	FF9A
+(−58)	+1111111111000110	+FFC6
−160	1111111101100000	1FF60
Drop the carry	1111111101100000	FF60

To check the result, we observe that it is negative because bit 15 is 1, and we determine its absolute value by complementing the bits and adding 1.

Result	1111111101100000	FF60
Complement	0000000010011111	009F
Add 1	+1	+1
	0000000010100000	00A0
| Result |	$2^7 + 2^5 = 160$	$10 \times 16 = 160$

It is just about as easy to negate and add two's complement integers as it is to do these operations on one's complement integers. What about the problem of the two representations of zero? Suppose that we start with 0 and find its two's complement negation.

0	0000000000000000
Complement	1111111111111111
Add 1	+1
	10000000000000000
Drop the carry	0000000000000000

So −0 = +0, as it should.

On the VAX, two's complement representation is used for integer data, which may be stored in bytes, words, longwords, or quadwords, or in the rightmost byte or word of a general register, or in a full register. As we will see in Chapter 8, it is often necessary to store integers (negative or positive) in instructions to indicate the location of an operand of the instruction. Two's complement is used there too.

In our discussion of addition we assumed that the result of the addition would fit in a word. Of course, that is not always the case. For example, if we add 29,676 and 3204, both of which are less than the maximum 16-bit integer, 32,767, we get 32,880, which is too big. What happens when we carry out the two's complement addition?

29,676	0111001111101100	73EC
+3,204	+0000110010000100	+0C84
32,880	1000000001110000	8070

Because the leftmost bit of the sum is a 1, the result would be incorrectly interpreted as a negative integer. Integer arithmetic instructions set a bit in the Processor Status Word (PSW), called the overflow condition code, when the result of an arithmetic operation will not fit in the designated space. It is the programmer's responsibility to check this bit if the data being used might cause an overflow. For the data in our example, there would have been no problem if we had been using longwords; then bit 31, not bit 15, would have been the sign bit.

Table 3.2 shows the interpretation of each three-bit pattern using each of the representation schemes we have discussed; bit 2 is the sign bit. Notice that −0 has a distinct representation from +0 in sign-magnitude as well as in one's complement. Since there is only one representation of 0 in two's complement, there is an extra bit pattern; using only three bits, as in the table, we find that we can represent −4 in two's complement but not in one's complement or sign-magnitude.

Why Two's Complement Works

To show that complementing the bits and adding 1 always negates a two's complement integer, and to show that the rules for addition of two's complement integers are correct, it is useful to use another characterization of negative two's complement integers. Let s be the number of bits in the representation ($s = 16$ in all the examples in this section). Let n be a negative integer and let $|n|$ be its absolute value. Then the two's complement

TABLE 3.2 INTEGER REPRESENTATION

Bit pattern	Sign-magnitude	One's complement	Two's complement
000	0	0	0
001	1	1	1
010	2	2	2
011	3	3	3
100	-0	-3	-4
101	-1	-2	-3
110	-2	-1	-2
111	-3	-0	-1

representation of n is the binary encoding of $2^s - |n|$. This is true because complementing the bits of $|n|$ is the same as subtracting $|n|$ from s 1's, and s 1's represents $2^s - 1$, so

$$|n| \text{ with bits complemented:} \quad 2^s - 1 - |n|$$

$$\text{Add 1 to get } n \text{ in two's complement:} \quad 2^s - 1 - |n| + 1 = 2^s - |n|$$

Now, what happens when we start with a negative integer in two's complement and reverse the procedure? Again, suppose that the number is n. Thus we start with $2^s - |n|$:

$$n \text{ (negative) in two's complement:} \quad 2^s - |n|$$

$$\text{Complement the bits:} \quad (2^s - 1) - (2^s - |n|) = -1 + |n|$$

$$\text{Add 1. The result is } -n \text{ (i.e., } |n|): \quad -1 + |n| + 1 = |n|$$

When s is a multiple of 4, as it is for the standard memory units, we can write the hex representation of a negative integer n in two's complement as $16^{s/4} - |n|$. An argument similar to the one above shows that the steps we described for negating and adding two's complement numbers written in hex are also correct.

Using the characterization of the two's complement representation of a negative integer n as $2^s - |n|$, it is not hard to prove that adding the bit strings and ignoring the carry always correctly adds two's complement integers (if the result fits in s bits). We leave the details as an exercise.

3.3 SUMMARY

The hexadecimal number system is used as a shorthand for bit strings. Hexadecimal is the positional number system with radix 16. Conversion between binary and hex is very easy: Each four-bit pattern corresponds to one hex digit, and vice versa. Conversion between hex or binary and decimal can be done by several methods, some of which use the tables in Appendix B.

Arithmetic in hex is similar to arithmetic in decimal, but one must take care to handle carries and borrows correctly.

Hex is particularly well suited to the VAX because the various components of machine instructions take up four, eight, 16, or 32 bits and can therefore be encoded separately by one, two, four, or eight hex digits. Also, character codes use eight bits, or two hex digits.

There are several schemes for representing signed integers in a computer. Three of these are sign-magnitude, one's complement, and two's complement. For all three, positive integers are represented in binary, and the leftmost bit is used to represent the integer's sign, with 0 indicating "plus" and 1 indicating "minus."

The two's complement notation is used in the VAX. To represent a negative integer in two's complement, we first write out its absolute value in binary, then complement all the bits, then add 1. Alternatively we can write its absolute value in hex, then subtract each digit from F (15, decimal), and then add 1.

Two's complement is used because it does not have two distinct representations for +0 and −0, as one's complement and sign-magnitude do, and because addition and subtraction of two's complement integers are very straightforward and independent of the signs of the operands. Two signed two's complement integers are added as if they were unsigned binary numbers. If there is a carry from the leftmost bit, it is ignored. Arithmetic can be done on the hex representations instead of long bit strings.

Another way to look at the two's complement representation of a negative integer n is that it is $2^s - |n|$ in binary, or $16^{s/4} - |n|$ in hex, where s is the number of bits used in the representation.

If the result of an arithmetic operation does not fit in the designated space, the overflow condition code bit in the PSW is set.

3.4   EXERCISES

1. Convert the following numbers from hexadecimal to binary.
    (a) 2409
    (b) E0625
    (c) CAB
    (d) 3B70

2. Convert the following numbers from binary to hex.
    (a) 11011011111001011
    (b) 11110011100010
    (c) 1000000000
    (d) 11110000

3. Convert the following numbers from hex to decimal.
    (a) 45C
    (b) 2095FA
    (c) D0
    (d) 10000

4. Convert the following numbers from decimal to hex.
    (a) 75
    (b) 250
    (c) 4293 (Use both methods described in Section 3.1.)
    (d) 12,782,439

5. Convert the following numbers from binary to decimal.
    (a) 1110011010
    (b) 1111101111
    [None of the methods given in the text is the quickest way to do part (b). Use some ingenuity.]

6. Convert the following numbers from decimal to binary.
    (a) 135
    (b) 452

7. Do the following addition problems. All numbers shown are in hex.

   (a) 62E8   **(b)** 84B2
       +CD2A   +2FA

8. Do the following subtraction problems. All numbers are in hex.

   (a) 5A047   **(b)** 23A5
       -6B2C   -1C96

9. Do the following multiplication problems. All numbers are in hex.

   (a) 3CA4   **(b)** 73
       × 4   × 8

10. Prove that the hex-to-binary conversion method given in the text is correct: that is, if each hex digit is replaced by its four-bit binary equivalent, the resulting binary number has the same value as the original hex number.

11. Write the 16-bit representation of −182 in sign-magnitude, one's complement, and two's complement. Show the answers as four hex digits (rather than in bits).

12. Show the bit pattern for the negative integer with the largest magnitude using s bits in one's complement. Do the same for two's complement.

13. What decimal number is represented by FF38 in two's complement notation? What data type is this number—byte, word, longword, or quadword?

14. Find the decimal equivalent of each of the following two's complement integers.

   (a) FFFF   **(c)** 907B
   (b) FC00   **(d)** FFFFFD87

15. Represent each of the following decimal integers in two's complement form, using the smallest unit of memory among bytes, words, and longwords that is large enough for each datum. Do the conversion and show your results in hex.

   (a) −632   **(c)** 128
   (b) −38   **(d)** −20,480

16. There is an integer that can be represented in two's complement form using eight bits but whose negative cannot. What is this integer?

17. What are the largest and smallest two's complement integers that can be represented in a byte? In a word? In a longword?

18. Prove that adding two's complement integers as if they were unsigned binary numbers and dropping the carry, if any, from the leftmost place always gives the correct two's complement sum (if the sum does not overflow).

19. Suppose that the decimal integers 37,412 and −548 are represented as longword two's complement integers. Show their representations (use hex) and add them. Show the two's complement result in hex.

20. Describe an efficient method the computer could use to subtract one two's complement integer from another. Your method should be independent of the signs of the operands.

21. Figure out a rule or rules that the computer might use to determine if overflow occurred when it added two two's complement integers.

4

Introduction to Assembly Language

Most assembly language source statements contain some or all of the following four fields: a label field, an operator field, an operand field, and a comment field. In this chapter we begin to examine the components of the fields, describe some frequently used assembler directives, and show how to put together a complete program. Since one of our aims is to provide enough information so that the reader can begin to write complete simple programs relatively soon, we do not give a thorough presentation of all the details and options for the topics covered in this chapter. More information may be found in later chapters and in DEC manuals. Also, we will use some machine instructions in examples without formal explanations. Their general functions should be clear; they will be explained in more detail in later chapters.

Note that unless the programmer indicates otherwise, the assembler will interpret as decimal numbers all numbers that appear in instructions.

4.1 SYMBOLS AND LABELS

Symbols are names of things. They name variables, arrays, and other data areas, and they label instructions. The names of general registers (R0, ..., R11, AP, FP, SP, and PC) and instructions are permanent symbols.[1] Symbols used to label instructions and data, and other symbols given values by the programmer, are called *user-defined symbols*.

---

[1] Although PC is a permanent symbol, it is not used directly by a programmer.

A symbol may consist of up to 31 characters from among letters, digits, and the underline (_). The first character may not be a digit. (Dollar signs and periods are acceptable too, but should be avoided; they are used in system-defined symbols.)

Assemblers have a counter, called the *location counter*, for keeping track of the number of bytes used in the translation of a program section. The assembler sets the location counter to zero at the beginning of the assembly of each program section and increments it by the number of bytes required for each machine instruction translated and each data area reserved. Thus, the value of the location counter is always the address of the next available byte (relative to the beginning of the program section).

User-defined symbols are most often defined (i.e., given a value) by being used in the label field of an instruction. The value assigned to the symbol is the value of the location counter at that point; hence it is the location of the instruction or datum the symbol names. The assembler stores the symbol and its value in a symbol table so that when other instructions use the symbol the assembler can look it up, find its value, and properly encode the address in the translation of the other instructions. It is important to understand that to the assembler, the value of a variable name is the location of the variable, not the contents of the location—what we usually think of as the value of the variable in a high-level language. To emphasize the distinction, we will work through an example.

Suppose that a program contains the following statements, which direct the assembler to initialize longwords in memory with the specified values. (Note that a symbol used as a label must be followed by a colon.) Suppose that the value of the location counter is 108_{16} (addresses are always given in hex) when the assembler encounters these statements.

```
ALPHA:   .LONG   1186
BETA:    .LONG   -28
GAMMA:   .LONG   35
```

The assembler sees the symbol ALPHA in the label field, so it assigns to ALPHA the current value of the location counter, that is, the address of the next available byte. The assembler converts 1186_{10} to a two's complement longword integer, 000004A2, to be stored in memory at the current location. Recall that for longwords, the byte with the least significant bits is stored first, so this longword will appear in memory as follows:

Address	Memory Contents
ALPHA = 00000108	A2
00000109	04
0000010A	00
0000010B	00

The assembler increments the location counter to $10C_{16}$, the address of the next available byte. In the diagram below we group the bytes of each longword on one line, and show the addresses and labels on the right (since the rightmost byte of a longword is the one that is first in memory). Also, since the assembler always uses 32 bits to keep track of addresses, we show addresses with leading zeros.

Memory Contents	Address	Symbol
000004A2	00000108	ALPHA
FFFFFFE4	0000010C	BETA
00000023	00000110	GAMMA

The values of the symbols ALPHA, BETA, and GAMMA are 108_{16}, $10C_{16}$, and 110_{16}, respectively. We may write, simply, ALPHA = 108, BETA = 10C, and GAMMA = 110. It is *not* correct, as it would be in a high-level language, to say ALPHA = $4A2_{16}$ or ALPHA = 1186_{10}. A commonly used notation for the contents of a memory location or a register consists of the name (or address) of the location or register enclosed in parentheses. So (ALPHA) means "the contents of ALPHA." In this example, (ALPHA) = 000004A2, (BETA) = FFFFFFE4, and (GAMMA) = 00000023. Note that (ALPHA) may change often during execution of the program, whereas ALPHA never changes (unless the program is changed).

Now, suppose that the program contains the following instruction, which copies a longword of data from the location specified by the first operand to the location specified by the second one.

```
MOVL    ALPHA+4,GAMMA
```

What gets moved into the longword at GAMMA? Not 000004A6, for that would be (ALPHA)+4. ALPHA+4 = $10C_{16}$, the address of the second longword shown. Thus the instruction moves FFFFFFE4 into GAMMA. (In fact, ALPHA+4 = BETA.)

Aside from emphasizing that the value of a symbol is an address, this example illustrates that a symbol may be combined with other terms to make up an expression that designates the location of an operand. We will cover the rules for forming expressions later; for now, if you remember that a symbol represents an address, not the contents of an address, it is safe to assume that any reasonably simple expression is valid.

User-defined symbols may be defined by explicitly equating them to the desired value in what is called a *direct assignment statement*. The format for such a statement is

$$symbol = expression$$

If any symbols appear in the expression, they must have been defined previously in the program. Direct assignment statements have many uses, one of which is to make it easier to read and modify a program by naming constants. In many instances they are used like the **const** declaration in Pascal. The assembler does not allocate any memory space for a symbol defined in a direct assignment statement; it just records the value of the symbol in its symbol table.[2] We will see examples of the use of direct assignment statements in subsequent sections.

---

[2] Unlike Pascal, a symbol that is defined in a direct assignment statement may be redefined (i.e., assigned another value later in the program) any number of times. These changes are recorded by the assembler in its symbol table at assembly time, not at execution time. Such changes are useful in macros. Until we discuss macros, it is reasonable to think of symbols defined in direct assignment statements as constants.

4.2 OPERATORS

The operator field specifies the operation or action to be performed by the statement. There are three categories of operators: machine instructions, assembler directives, and macros. *Machine instructions* are those that are translated by the assembler to machine code and perform execution-time operations such as arithmetic, data movement, and branching. *Assembler directives* are instructions to the assembler to perform various bookkeeping tasks, storage reservation, and other control functions. (To be consistent with DEC's terminology, we will use the term "argument" for an operand of an assembler directive.) A *macro instruction* is a pseudoinstruction invented by a programmer (or provided in a system library) to denote a certain sequence of machine instructions, assembler directives, and/or other macros.

To perform a machine instruction, the computer needs several pieces of information: the operation to be performed, the number, locations, and types of the operands, and the type and location for the result. Some of this information is provided in the instruction name (some implicitly), the rest in the operand specifiers. In almost all machine instruction names, the first three or four letters indicate the operation to be performed. For many instructions the next letter (or in a few cases, the next two letters) specify the data type(s) of the operands and the result. (Usually, the operands and the result are the same type.) The letters used for the types are

Letter	Data Type
B	Byte
W	Word
L	Longword
Q	Quadword
P	Packed decimal
F	Floating point (single precision)
D	Double-precision floating point
G	G_floating
H	H_floating
C	Character
V	Variable-length bit field

The number of operands is implicit for some instructions; for others it is specified by a digit at the end of the instruction name. Thus it is easy to figure out what many of the instructions do. Consider these examples:

MULW3	MULtiply Word integers, three operands.
CVTLF	ConVerT Longword to Floating point.
SUBB2	SUBtract Byte integers, two operands.
	(The first operand is subtracted from the second.)
CMPF	CoMPare Floating-point numbers.

CLRL	CLeaR Longword (i.e., set it to zero).
INCW	INCrement a Word integer by 1.
MOVC3	MOVe (actually, copy) Characters, three operands.
BEQL	Branch if EQuaL (used after a comparison).

For ease of distinguishing them from machine instructions, assembler directive names begin with a period. A directive name is usually a word or an abbreviation for a word that indicates what the directive does. Some frequently used directives are presented in Section 4.4.

Macros can be very complex; we will present and use some in Chapter 5, but we defer most of our discussion of them to Chapter 11.

4.3 OPERAND ADDRESSING

The VAX has an unusually large variety of operand addressing modes, that is, ways of specifying the locations of operands. With some exceptions, any addressing mode may be used with any machine instruction. This is different from some computers where each instruction requires specific operand formats.

In instructions that have more than one operand, the order in which they are written determines which operands play which roles. For example, we indicated that in a subtract instruction, the first operand is subtracted from the second. Usually, the *destination* operand (i.e., the place where the result of an operation goes) is the last operand. Almost all of the addressing modes may be used to specify both the locations of data to be operated on and locations for results. The exceptions are fairly obvious; for example, an addressing mode that specifies a constant would not be used for the result of an operation.

An operand may be in a general register, in memory, or in the instruction itself. We will describe some simple addressing modes for specifying operands in each of these categories. All of the additional, more complex, addressing modes are for specifying operands in memory. We will describe a few in this section and leave some for later.

Remember that these addressing modes are for machine instructions; they specify locations of operands at execution time. The formats for assembly directive arguments are different (and will be described later).

Register Mode: R*n*

Register mode is used to indicate that the operand is in a general register. The operand specifier is simply the name of the register. It may be any of R0, ..., R11, or AP, FP, or SP.

For data types such as B and W that use fewer than 32 bits, the rightmost byte or word of the register is used. The leftmost portion of the register is ignored; it is not changed by a B or W instruction. For data types such as quadwords and double-precision floating-point numbers that take up 64 bits, or two general registers, the operand is in Rn and Rn+1. (For data types that have more than 64 bits, the appropriate number of registers is used beginning with Rn.)

General registers should be used for intermediate results and data that are used often because it takes less time to access registers than memory.

Example 4.1: Register Mode

Suppose that R6 contains `00280E45` and R9 contains `FFFFF3A6`. After the MOVe, or copy, instruction

```
        MOVL    R6,R9
```

is executed, both R6 and R9 will contain `00280E45`. However, if the instruction had been

```
        MOVW    R6,R9
```

then R9 would contain `FFFFF0E45`.

Relative Mode: *address*

Relative mode may be used for operands in memory. The operand specifier is an expression, usually just a symbol, whose value is the address of the datum to be used (or the address of the location where the result of the operation is to be stored). The reason why this is called relative mode will be explained when we consider its machine language encoding.

Example 4.2: Relative Mode

```
        MOVC3   #32,TITLE,LINE+12        ; Move title to output line
```

This instruction moves (i.e., copies) a string of characters from TITLE to LINE+12. The second and third operands are in relative mode. The first operand is a literal, the addressing mode that is explained next.

Literal and Immediate Modes: *#number* or *#expression*

Normally, an operand specifier specifies the *location* of the datum to be used in the instruction. In a literal or immediate mode operand the actual datum to be used is specified in the instruction. Literal and immediate mode operands may be integer, floating point, or character constants. (Negative numbers are permitted.) The constant may be described by a number or an expression (usually, just a symbol). The restrictions on the kinds of expressions that may be used will be described later. The constant is preceded by a # to indicate that it is a literal rather than an address.

In assembly language literal and immediate mode operand specifiers look the same, but in machine code they are different. (The assembler chooses between them depending on how much space is needed to assemble the constant. A literal is six bits long; an immediate datum may be longer. The machine code will be examined in detail in Chapter 8.)

Example 4.3: Literal Mode

The instruction

```
MOVW     #25,R11                        ; Put max size in R11
```

puts the (decimal) integer 25 in the rightmost word of R11. For example:

R11

Before execution   EFFE0972

After execution   EFFE0019

An alternative way of doing the same thing is

```
MAX_SIZE = 25
            .
            .
            .
       MOVW     #MAX_SIZE,R11            ; Put max size in R11
```

The use of the symbol MAX_SIZE makes the program clearer, and if the max size is ever changed, only the direct assignment statement need be modified; the programmer would not have to search through the program for all relevant instances of the number 25.

It is a common mistake for beginners to forget the # in a literal or immediate operand. If we had written

```
       MOVW     25,R11                   ; Put max size in R11
```

the assembler would encode the 25 as an address and the CPU would try to copy the memory word whose address is 25 into R11. Most likely this would cause an execution-time error called an *access violation*, because memory location 25 is not in the section of memory available to the program. The error would also occur if MAX_SIZE were used without the #, because MAX_SIZE is not a label; it is equal to the constant 25.

Another common mistake for beginners is to use # in the arguments of assembler directives, for example, to write

```
    MAX_SIZE = #25                       ; This is wrong
```

The # is used only in machine instruction operands, where it distinguishes literal data from addresses.

We sometimes want to specify a character constant; the value of the constant is the ASCII code(s) for the character(s). The format for such constants is

$$^\wedge A/char/$$

For example:

```
    STAR = ^A/*/
```

This has the advantage of being clearer than writing STAR = 42, and saves the programmer the trouble of looking up the ASCII code for '*'. If a character constant is used as a literal, the # is needed. Thus we may write

```
MOVB    #^A/*/,LINE
```

or

```
MOVB    #STAR,LINE
```

to put the ASCII code for the asterisk into the byte labeled LINE. The assembler translates ^A/*/ into binary or machine code exactly as it translates 42, so the instructions above are equivalent to MOVB   #42,LINE. Use of ^A is a convenience for the programmer and makes a program easier to understand.

Branch Mode: *destination*

The branch destination may be specified by an expression; usually, it is a symbol used as a label on an instruction. Branch mode is used to specify a location to which the program should branch if certain conditions are met. If the operator is an unconditional branch or if it is a conditional branch and the condition is satisfied, the destination address is loaded into the PC (program counter) register, so the next instruction executed is the one at that address. There are limits on how far from the current instruction the branch address may be. These will be discussed when we describe branch instructions in Chapter 7.

Branch mode may look just like relative mode in assembly language, but they are encoded differently in machine language.

Example 4.4: Branch Mode

The unconditional branch instruction

```
BRB     NEXT
```

causes a branch to the instruction labeled NEXT.

The next three addressing modes specify operands in memory. The reader who wishes to begin writing some short programs as soon as possible may skim or skip these for now and return to them after reading Chapter 5.

The notation Rn used for describing the addressing modes denotes any of the registers R0 through R11 or AP, FP, or SP.

Register Deferred Mode: (Rn)

In register deferred mode the address of the operand, not the operand itself, is in a general register. Recall the notational convention that an address or register name enclosed in parentheses means the contents of the address or register. Thus in register deferred mode, the *location* of the operand is (Rn), the contents of Rn.

Example 4.5: Register Deferred Mode

The instruction

```
        ADDW2    R5,(R8)                    ; Add food cost to budget
```

adds the word in (the right end of) R5 to the word in memory whose address is in R8.

Suppose that before the instruction in the preceding example is executed, the data are as follows:

	Memory	Address
R5	F543	00000840
EFFE002E	FFFF	00000842
	FFB9	00000844
R8	001C	00000846
00000846	074D	00000848
	12C0	0000084A

The only locations changed by the instruction are bytes 846_{16} and 847_{16}. Since $002E+001C = 004A$, the result is

Memory	Address
.	.
.	.
.	.
004A	00000846
.	.
.	.
.	.

Note that the left half of R5 is ignored, but since addresses are always 32 bits long, all of R8 is used. We have diagrammed memory as a list of words because the instruction in Example 4.5 acts on words. In general, in diagrams, we break up memory into units of a size appropriate to the example being considered. It is important not to be misled by the pictures. We could have drawn memory as a list of longwords like this (before execution of the instruction):

Memory	Address
FFFFF543	00000840
001CFFB9	00000844
12C0074D	00000848

The instruction would have the same effect; the affected area would be shown as

Memory	Address
004AFFB9	00000844

Autoincrement Mode: (R*n*)+

Autoincrement is one of several addressing modes that are especially useful for processing data in arrays. The address of the operand is in a general register. After the operand is determined, the register is automatically incremented so that it contains the address of the next array entry. The amount by which R*n* is incremented is the amount appropriate for the data type of the operand: 1 for a byte, 2 for a word, 4 for a longword or floating-point number, 8 for a quadword or eight-byte floating-point number, and 16 for octawords and 16-byte floating-point numbers. (For other data types, such as character strings, R*n* is incremented by 1, so autoincrement mode is not useful for them.)

Example 4.6: Adding Array Entries with Autoincrement Mode

A loop that adds up all entries in an array needs only two instructions, one that does the addition and one that handles the loop control. Suppose that the address of the beginning of a longword array AMOUNTS has been put in R10, and R7 has been cleared for the sum.

```
ADD:    ADDL2   (R10)+,R7              ; Add next entry
;               [loop control instruction]
```

The loop control instruction would cause a branch to ADD if there are more entries to be added.

Assume that the ADDL2 instruction has been executed several times and the contents of registers and memory before the next execution of it are as follows:

	Memory	Address
R7	000102E7	000009A4 = AMOUNTS
00034CD6	.	.
	.	.
	.	.
	FFFF8A30	000009D8
R10	00000671	000009DC
000009D8	.	.
	.	.
	.	.
	FFFFFA09	00000B30 (end of array)

After the next execution of the ADDL2 instruction we have

R7

00020706

(No changes in memory)

R10

000009DC

Note that when the loop finishes, R10 will contain 00000B34, the address of the first byte following the end of the array.

Since Rn is incremented after the operand is determined, rather than after the operation is performed, if Rn is used in autoincrement mode to specify two operands in the same instruction, the operands are in different locations and Rn is incremented twice. For example, suppose that R8 contains 000102C7. The instruction

```
MOVB     (R8)+,(R8)+                ; Copy flag byte
```

will determine that the first operand is the byte at address $102C7_{16}$, increment R8 by 1 (since the operand is a byte), determine that the destination (second operand) address is $102C8_{16}$, increment R8 by 1, and finally, copy the byte at $102C7_{16}$ into $102C8_{16}$. R8 will contain 000102C9.

Autodecrement Mode: –(Rn)

The operand size (1, 2, 4, 8, or 16, as for autoincrement) is subtracted from Rn; then the new contents of Rn is used as the operand address.

Autodecrement mode may be used to process an array backward: that is, starting with the higher-addressed entries and moving toward the lower ones. It is particularly useful for adding items to a data structure called a stack (described in Chapter 9) and, in conjunction with autoincrement, for searching arrays or strings.

Example 4.7: Autodecrement Mode

The instruction

```
CLRW     -(R5)
```

affects R5 and a word in memory as follows:

		Memory	**Address**

Before execution:

R5	95B5	000008D2
000008D4	7051	000008D4

After execution:

R5	0000	000008D2
000008D2	7051	000008D4

Note that there are two differences between autoincrement mode and autodecrement mode. Autoincrement mode *increments* the register *after* using the address it contained to locate the operand, while autodecrement mode *decrements* the register *before* using its contents to locate the operand.

4.4 RESERVING AND INITIALIZING DATA AREAS

In this section we cover two types of assembler directives: those that reserve blocks of storage (initializing the contents to zero) and those that reserve storage and initialize the contents to values specified by the programmer. Recall that the assembler assumes any numbers used in source statements to be decimal numbers, unless the programmer indicates otherwise.

Reserving Space

The .BLKx directives tell the assembler to reserve storage for various types of data; the x indicates the type. The .BLKx directives are

.BLKB	for bytes
.BLKW	for words
.BLKL	for longwords
.BLKQ	for quadwords
.BLKO	for octawords
.BLKA	for addresses (longwords)
.BLKF	for floating-point numbers (longwords)
.BLKD	for double-precision floating-point numbers (quadwords)
.BLKG	for G_floating type (quadwords)
.BLKH	for H_floating type (octawords)

The format for these directives is

$$.\text{BLK}x \quad expression$$

The expression specifies the number of units of storage to allocate. It is usually just a constant or a simple expression. Any symbols used must be defined before the .BLKx statement appears. (There are other restrictions on expressions used in this and other assembler directives, but they need not concern us yet.) The assembler fills all the reserved space with zeros.

Example 4.8: Storage Reservation Directives

```
MAX = 100                          ; Number of entries in amounts array
REC_SIZE = 52                      ; Account record size
NUM = 70                           ; Number of accounts
AMOUNTS:  .BLKL   MAX
ACCOUNTS: .BLKB   NUM*REC_SIZE
MPG:      .BLKF   40
```

The .BLKL directive reserves 100 longwords, or 400 bytes. The .BLKB directive reserves $70 * 52 = 3640$ bytes for the ACCOUNTS array. The .BLKF directive reserves space for a floating-point array called MPG with 40 elements. Using named constants for array and record sizes is a good habit.

What do we actually mean when we say that the assembler reserves space? Recall that the assembler updates its location counter as it processes source statements. Reserving space means increasing the location counter by the appropriate amount. The location counter is denoted by a period, and its value is always shown in hex. Thus if the current value of the location counter is 104 (denoted $. = 104$) and the assembler is to reserve two bytes, it assigns $. = .+2 = 106$.

Example 4.9: How the Assembler Processes a Storage Directive

Suppose that $. = 000009A4$ (hex, as usual) when the assembler begins processing the statements in Example 4.8. No space in the program is reserved for the three direct assignment statements; the assembler simply puts the symbols and their assigned values in its symbol table. When the assembler encounters the .BLKL directive with the label AMOUNTS, it puts the symbol AMOUNTS in the symbol table and gives it the value 000009A4. Then it determines that 400 bytes are to be allocated. Since $400_{10} = 190_{16}$, it updates . by setting $. = .+190 = 00000B34$. Then when it processes the next statement, ACCOUNTS will be assigned the value 00000B34.

There is no .BLK*x* statement for explicitly reserving space for character strings or packed decimal data. The programmer decides how many bytes will be needed for such data and may use the .BLKB directive.

Example 4.10: Reserving Space for a Character String

```
LINE:   .BLKB   80              ; Output line
```

This statement reserves 80 bytes for a character string with up to 80 characters.

Initializing Integer Data

Directives for initializing data cause the assembler to store data in specified areas in memory. The directive name specifies the type of data to be stored and the argument(s) specify the values. (If a value specified is too large for the data type, an error message will be issued.) The argument formats differ slightly, depending on the type. The first group of data storage directives we consider are

.BYTE	*argument_list*
.WORD	*argument_list*
.LONG	*argument_list*

For each of these directives, the argument list may contain one or more arguments, separated by commas. Each argument has the form

$$datum[repetition\_factor]$$

Both the datum and the repetition factor may be expressions. The assembler will store in the next available locations the number of copies of the datum specified by the repetition factor. The data are stored in two's complement form. The repetition factor is optional. If it is not used, a value of 1 is assumed. If it is used, it must be enclosed in square brackets as shown, and any symbols in the expression must already be defined.

Example 4.11: Initializing Storage

Suppose . = 0000058A when the assembler encounters the following statements:

```
COORDS:   .WORD    2,27,-180,492
ALPHA:    .BYTE    5[3]
```

After these statements are processed, the affected area of memory will look like this:

Memory	Address
0002	0000058A
001B	0000058C
FF4C	0000058E
01EC	00000590
0505	00000592
05	00000594

Two symbols have been defined:

$$COORDS = 0000058A$$

$$ALPHA = 00000592$$

The final value of the location counter is 00000595.

Example 4.12: Initializing Storage

Suppose that instead of just reserving space for the ACCOUNTS array used in Example 4.8, we want to initialize all the bytes in the array to −1. Instead of using the .BLKB directive, we could use

```
ACCOUNTS:  .BYTE   -1[NUM*REC_SIZE]                    ; Unopened accounts
```

For storing eight bytes of data, the .QUAD directive may be used. Its format is

.QUAD *constant*

or

.QUAD *symbol*

The .QUAD directive can have only one argument, which cannot be a general expression, and it cannot have a repetition factor. (The VAX does not support the quadword data type as fully as the other integer types; that is, there are fewer instructions and less flexible assembler directives for quadwords than there are for the other types.)

Initializing Character Data

The VAX uses ASCII character codes to represent characters (letters, numerals, punctuation, special characters, and control characters). Each ASCII code has seven bits, so they are stored one per byte, with the eighth, or leftmost, bit always 0. Appendix C contains a list of the codes. (They appear in the *VAX-11 Programming Card* too.) ASCII stands for American Standard Code for Information Interchange.

A character string—a sequence of characters—is represented in memory in a contiguous sequence of bytes, one ASCII character code to a byte. The .ASCII directive (and a few variations of it) tell the assembler to store a character string. Headings and other messages to be printed by a program are set up using these directives. We will use the .ASCII and .ASCIZ directives. Their formats are

.ASCII   *character_string_specification*

.ASCIZ   *character_string_specification*

The .ASCII directive stores the string in the next available bytes; the first character in the string in the first (lowest-numbered) byte, and so on. .ASCIZ stores the string in the same way, but it also adds an extra byte at the end of the string containing 0's. For some uses of character strings, it is handy to have the end of the string marked in this way. In Chapter 5 we will see some criteria for choosing between .ASCII and .ASCIZ.

The simplest way to specify a character string is to write it out preceded and followed by a delimiter character. The slash is most commonly used as a delimiter.

Example 4.13: Initializing a Character String

```
TITLE:   .ASCII   /Daily Sales/
```

This directive stores the following data:

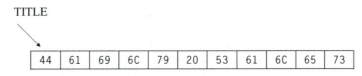

TITLE

| 44 | 61 | 69 | 6C | 79 | 20 | 53 | 61 | 6C | 65 | 73 |

The assembler assigns as the value of the symbol TITLE the address of the first byte of the character string.

If a slash appears in the string, it cannot be used as the delimiter. Any other printable character (except space, tab, equal sign, semicolon, or left angle bracket) that does not appear within the string may be used.

Control characters are ASCII codes that do not correspond to a printable symbol but rather indicate that some action, such as a carriage return, is to occur. If we want to include such a character in a string to be stored in memory, we cannot simply type it; in the case of a carriage return, it would terminate the statement we were typing. In the .ASCII and .ASCIZ directives, control characters must be represented by their ASCII code. The code must be enclosed in angle brackets *outside* the delimiters that delimit the rest of the string. (Noncontrol characters also may be specified this way, but it is clearer just to type them.)

Example 4.14: A Character String Containing Control Characters

The statements

```
LINEFEED = 10                       ; ASCII code for linefeed
. . .
HEADER:   .ASCIZ   <LINEFEED><LINEFEED>/THIRD LINE/
```

would cause the assembler to fill the next 13 bytes of memory as follows:

HEADER

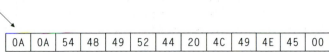

| 0A | 0A | 54 | 48 | 49 | 52 | 44 | 20 | 4C | 49 | 4E | 45 | 00 |

The value of the symbol HEADER will be the address of the first byte of the character string. If this string were printed or displayed at the terminal, two lines would be skipped because of the line feed characters, and the string "Third line" would appear on the third line. Note that a blank, or space, is a character and has an ASCII code. Note also that the symbol LINEFEED is used for clarity.

Example 4.15: More Character Strings

```
CR = 13                                    ; ASCII carriage return
LF = 10                                    ; ASCII linefeed
. . .
TITLE:   .ASCIZ  /DAILY TRANSACTIONS/
DEP:     .ASCII  /Page 1/<CR><LF>/DEPOSITS/
DATE:    .ASCII  '9/14/92'
```

The .ASCIZ directive defines a simple character string of length 18; it reserves 19 bytes altogether because of the extra byte of zeros added at the end. In the first .ASCII directive, the character string is broken up into several segments, each enclosed in delimiters. The complete string has length 16. If it were printed on a terminal or printer, "Page 1" would appear on one line and "DEPOSITS" at the beginning of the next line. In the last .ASCII statement, because slashes appear in the character string, apostrophes are used as the delimiters.

Example 4.16: Initializing a String of Blanks in Memory

```
BLANK = ^A/ /
LINE:    .BYTE   BLANK[80]         ; 80 blanks
```

The .BYTE directive initializes each of the next 80 bytes of memory to contain the ASCII code for a blank. We used the ^A notation, introduced in Section 4.3, to specify the code for blank. Note that even though we may think of the data in memory as character codes, we did not use an .ASCII directive here to fill the bytes.

4.5 BEGINNING AND ENDING A PROGRAM

Suppose that we want to write a program to compute (BETA) = 3*(ALPHA)–20, where ALPHA and BETA are the addresses of longword integers. (If we were describing the computation for a high-level language, say Pascal, we would write *beta := 3*alpha − 20*. We use the parenthesized notation here to reinforce the idea that in assembly language, ALPHA and BETA are addresses, not variable values.) From the examples we have seen so far we know how to write the instructions to do the arithmetic and the directives to initialize ALPHA and reserve space for BETA. We may do as follows:

```
; DATA
;
ALPHA:  .LONG   224
BETA:   .BLKL   1
;
;
; Program to compute (BETA) = 3*(ALPHA)-20
;
; Register use:  R6      intermediate results
;
        MULL3   #3,ALPHA,R6             ; 3*(ALPHA) in R6
        SUBL3   #20,R6,BETA             ; 3*(ALPHA)-20 in BETA
```

How does the computer know that the instructions begin at the third longword and that it should not try to execute the data? It does not, unless we tell it. How will the computer know that it is supposed to stop executing instructions after the SUBL3 instruction? Again, it does not. (One might argue that it should stop after the last instruction, but there is always *something* in the next memory location; the computer does not know what we intend to be the last instruction unless we tell it.) Several instructions and directives are needed to control assembly and execution of a program.

The statements described below are the standard statements for VAX assembly language programs. In Chapter 5 we will describe some macros that must be used in place of some of these if the I/O macros defined in this book are used. Readers who plan to use our I/O macros should not skip the discussion here, however.

The .ENTRY Directive

Part of the task of specifying where execution of a program section begins is accomplished by the .ENTRY directive, which establishes an *entry point*. An entry point is a place in a routine (a main program or a procedure) at which it can be entered, that is, at which execution of that routine may begin. The format of the .ENTRY directive is

.ENTRY   symbol,entry_mask

The symbol is the name of the entry point. The assembler assigns to the symbol the current value of the location counter. We will consider the role of the entry mask when we study procedures. Until then, it is a good idea for beginning assembly language programmers to use ^M<IV>. This entry mask sets the IV (Integer oVerflow) trap bit in the PSW so that an error message will be given (and the program terminated) if the result of an integer arithmetic operation overflows the space allotted. (If the entry mask is 0, the IV trap bit will not be set, and overflow will be ignored.) The .ENTRY directive should be placed just before the first instruction to be executed.

The .END Directive

The .END directive is placed at the very end of the source file; it tells the assembler that it has reached the physical end of the module that it is translating. The format of the .END directive is

.END *transfer_address*

The transfer address is a symbol that specifies where execution of the program is to begin. There is a distinction between the transfer address and an entry point. A main program and each procedure would have an entry point, the point where execution of that routine is to begin. The transfer address is where execution of the entire program begins, the entry point of the main program. It must be specified on the .END directive of a main program; it must be omitted from the .END directive in a procedure because execution of the program does not begin in a procedure.

The $EXIT_S Macro

$EXIT_S may be used to terminate execution of a program. $EXIT_S is a macro; that is, the assembler replaces it with a sequence of instructions that do the necessary work and transfer control back to the operating system.

A Complete Program

Here we have rewritten our sample program segment as a complete program. The asterisks along the left margin indicate the statements that have been added; they (the asterisks) are not part of the program.

Example 4.17: A Complete Program

```
        ; DATA
        ;
        ALPHA:   .LONG   224
        BETA:    .BLKL   1
        ;
        ;
        ; Program to compute (BETA) = 3*(ALPHA)-20
        ;
        ; Register use:   R6     intermediate results
        ;
*                .ENTRY  COMPUTE,^M<IV>
                 MULL3   #3,ALPHA,R6              ; 3*(ALPHA) in R6
                 SUBL3   #20,R6,BETA             ; 3*(ALPHA)-20 in BETA
*                $EXIT_S
*                .END    COMPUTE
```

We now have a correct program that can be assembled, linked, and executed.

Note that we placed the data ahead of the machine instructions. If data and instructions are properly separated, the data may be placed before or after the executable portion of the program. However, for reasons that will be explained in Chapter 8, it is good practice to put the data first as we did here.

Every program should contain comments at the beginning explaining what it does and what the general registers are used for. Most instructions should have a brief comment that explains what the instruction does in terms of the problem. For example:

```
        MULL3   R7,R9,R10        ; bytes = blocks * size
```

Comments like "put product of R7 and R9 in R10" provide no more information than the instruction itself and just clutter up a program. (We will sometimes use such comments in this book when explaining new instructions.) Note the use of blank comment lines to visually separate parts of the program.

Although the sample program in Example 4.17 is complete and will execute properly, it does not print any output. In the next chapter we describe instructions for doing input and output.

4.6 STATEMENT FORMATS

To increase the clarity of an assembly language program, the fields of each statement should be aligned in columns. (Tabs may be used for convenience.) Only comments, labels, and direct assignments should begin in the first column. The operator field and operand field must be separated by at least one space or tab. The individual operands are separated by commas. The label field is terminated by a colon (:), and the comment field must begin with a semicolon (;).

A statement may be continued on more that one line by the use of a hyphen as the last nonblank character (before the comment, if any) on each line being continued. If the only field on the first line is the label field (and perhaps a comment), the hyphen may be omitted. If a statement is continued over more than one line, it should be broken up at logical points, such as between fields or operands.

The VAX assembler is not case-sensitive. We show all assembly language statements (except comments) in uppercase letters, but lower case works also. The .ASCII and .ASCIZ directives, however, do generate the ASCII codes for the exact characters typed in their string arguments; that is, they do distinguish between upper and lower case.

4.7 SUMMARY

Most assembly language statements may have four fields: a label field (beginning in column 1), an operator field, an operand field, and a comment field. A consistent indenting style, aligning the fields in columns, should be used to make a program easier to read.

Symbols are used to name data, instructions, and constants. User-defined symbols may be given a value by being used in the label field of a statement or by being explicitly assigned a value in a direct assignment statement. In the first case, the more common one, the value assigned to the symbol is the current value of the location counter. Thus the value of a symbol defined this way is an address, not the datum stored at the address.

There are three kinds of operators: machine instructions, assembler directives, and macros. The name of a machine instruction is a mnemonic for the operation it performs, the data type(s) it operates on, and (in some cases) the number of operands.

TABLE 4.1 SOME ADDRESSING MODES

Mode name	Notation	Location of operand	Other features
Register	R*n*	In register	Uses rightmost byte or word for B or W instruction; R*n* and R*n*+1 for Q, D, or G; R*n*, ..., R*n*+3 for H
Relative	*address expression*	In memory	
Literal	*#expression*	In instruction	
Branch	*destination*	In memory	
Register deferred	(R*n*)	In memory, address in R*n*	
Autoincrement	(R*n*)+	In memory, address in R*n*	R*n* incremented by data type size
Autodecrement	–(R*n*)	In memory, address in R*n* after decrementing	R*n* decremented by data type size

TABLE 4.2 STORAGE RESERVATION AND INITIALIZATION DIRECTIVES

Directive		Remarks
.BLK*x*	*expression*	The expression indicates the number of units to reserve; *x* indicates the type. (*x* = B, W, L, O, A, F, D, G, or H.)
.BYTE	*list*	Store the listed values in successive bytes, words,
.WORD	*list*	or longwords, respectively. Repetition
.LONG	*list*	factors (enclosed in square brackets) may be used.
.QUAD	*value*	Store the value in the next quadword.
.ASCII	*string*	Store the character string. .ASCIZ adds a byte
.ASCIZ	*string*	of zeros at the end of the string.

Machine instruction operands use a positional protocol; that is, the order in which the operands appear determines what role each one plays. The operands may be in registers, in memory, or in the instruction itself. The result of an operation, if any, usually goes in the last operand.

The VAX has an unusually large variety of operand addressing modes. Some of the more commonly used modes are summarized in Table 4.1.

The storage reservation and initialization directives described in this chapter are summarized in Table 4.2. The assembler reserves storage by incrementing the location counter by the required number of bytes. The assembler stores integer data in two's complement.

Character strings are represented in memory in ASCII code in a sequence of contiguous bytes, one character per byte. In the .ASCII and .ASCIZ directives, the string to be stored is written between matching delimiters. Control characters are specified by their ASCII code enclosed in angle brackets.

The assembler interprets numbers that appear in machine instruction operands or assembler directive arguments as decimal numbers unless the programmer instructs otherwise.

The .ENTRY directive defines an entry point for a program module; it indicates where execution of that module is to begin. The .END directive tells the assembler where the end of the source module is. The argument on the .END directive in a main program specifies the main program's entry point, to indicate where execution of the whole program begins. The $EXIT_S macro may be used to terminate execution of a program.

Data must be separated from executable instructions in a program. Generally, storage reservation and initialization directives are placed at the beginning of a module, ahead of the .ENTRY directive.

4.8 EXERCISES

1. Write an instruction that assigns the symbol BUFFER_SIZE the value 80.

2. What are some of the differences between the location counter and the program counter (PC)?

3. Suppose that . = $00000C74_{16}$ when the assembler encounters the following statements:

```
LENGTH: .WORD   21                      ; Length of rectangle
WIDTH:  .WORD   7                       ; Width of rectangle
```

What is the value of LENGTH? What is the value of WIDTH?

4. Suppose that along with the statements shown in Exercise 3, the program has

```
AREA:     .BLKW   1                     ; Area of rectangle
```

Write an instruction that computes the area of a rectangle whose length and width are stored in LENGTH and WIDTH; the area should be stored in AREA.

5. Try to figure out what each of the following instructions does, and write a brief explanation for each.
   (a) SUBD3
   (b) CMPC3
   (c) DIVW3
   (d) BLSS
   (e) MOVO
   (f) CVTBL
   (g) CLRB
   (h) DECL
   (i) ADDP

6. Write an instruction to add the word contents of R3 and R9 and put the sum in R7.

7. Explain the differences between the following assembler directives.

```
ALPHA: .LONG   2     and     ALPHA: .BLKL   2
```

8. Explain the differences between the following statements.

```
ALPHA: .LONG   2     and     ALPHA = 2
```

9. Suppose that R6 contains the address of an array of longwords. What is the address of the third entry in the array?

10. R5 contains the address of a byte integer. Write an instruction to put the integer in R9 and an instruction to put the address of the integer in R10.

11. The CVTLW instruction converts its first operand, a longword integer, to a word, its second operand. If 00183490 is in R5 and 001A38E4 is in R8 before the execution of the following instruction, what will be in R5 and R8 afterward?

    ```
    CVTLW    (R5)+,(R8)                    ; Truncate datum to word
    ```

12. Write an instruction to put the number 21 in the rightmost byte of R3 and an instruction to put 21 in the byte of memory whose address is in R4.

13. Write an instruction to put the number 1,000,000 in registers R8 and R9 as a quadword integer.

14. Suppose that each character of a character string called TEXT with length 22 is to be examined, starting from the end of the string, and that R7 will be used with the autodecrement addressing mode to address the characters. What number should be put in R7 to start?

15. What is the value of MPG in Example 4.8, assuming that . = 000009A4 when the statements in Example 4.8 are encountered by the assembler? (See Example 4.9 for some help.)

16. Write instructions to allocate a block of 35 longwords called IDS, a byte array called CODES with 35 entries, and an array NAMES with 35 character strings, each of length 16.

17. Write assembly language statements to reserve 80 contiguous bytes of memory and define symbols with the following values:

Symbol	Value
LINE	The location of the first byte
COL1	The location of the ninth byte
COL2	The location of the seventeenth byte
COL3	The location of the forty-first byte

18. Suppose that a program starts with the following directives.

    ```
    ONE:     .LONG    12
    TWO:     .BYTE    15
    TEXT:    .ASCIZ   /Mark Twain/
    ```

    (a) Give the values of ONE, TWO, and TEXT.
    (b) How many bytes of memory will be used by these directives?

19. Suppose that the following statements appear at the beginning of an assembly language program (so . = 0 when the assembler begins processing them). For each statement, state the value of the symbol defined in that statement, and how many bytes of memory are reserved by that statement.

```
LF = 10
MAX = 12
LIST:    .BLKL   MAX
PQR:     .BLKW   8
XYZ:     .BYTE   5,-2
LINE:    .ASCIZ  <LF>/Thomas Jefferson/
```

20. Suppose that $. = 00000628_{16}$ when the assembler encounters the following state-ments. Show the contents of all affected areas of memory, list the values of all the symbols defined, and give the final value of the location counter.

```
ALPHA:   .LONG   1024,5000
BETA:    .BLKW   3
TAG:     .BYTE   1
LABEL:   .ASCII  /VAX/
GAMMA:   .BLKW   6
```

21. Write a directive to store each of the following character strings. Give each one an appropriate label.
  (a) Pi is approximately 22/7   **(b)** **** SYMBOL TABLE ****

22. Why is it preferable to initialize 80 bytes with the ASCII code for a blank by using

```
BLANK = ^A/ /                          ; ASCII code for blank
         .BYTE    BLANK[80]
```

rather than an .ASCII directive? (How would you do it with an .ASCII directive?)

23. Write a complete program to do the following task: There are three consecutive longwords of memory beginning at the location NUMBERS. The first number is initialized by an assembler directive to contain some value. When the program terminates the second longword should contain twice the number in the first longword, and the third should contain twice the number in the second.

24. Write instructions to compute $2y^2 + 5y - 12$ where y is a longword integer in R6. Put the result in R8.

5

I/O, MOVe Instructions, System Commands, and the Debugger

This chapter covers several topics. Only Section 5.2 directly concerns VAX assembly language. It covers the MOVe instructions and introduces examples where we do computation on addresses. It should be read by all users of this book.

Section 5.1 describes a set of I/O macros written for this book. They allow us to write programs with input and output before learning the complexities of I/O. The I/O macros presented here are *not* a VAX utility. A macro library containing the macro definitions in Appendix D must be created before these macros can be used, and the I/O module (also described in Appendix D) must be linked with the program (as described in Section 5.3).

Section 5.3 presents the VAX/VMS system commands to assemble, link, and run assembly language programs. It also gives a brief description of the information provided in assembler listing files. Section 5.4 introduces the VAX VMS Debugger.

5.1 I/O MACROS

Input and output on a computer are complex processes. Many of the details are handled by the operating system, but even the use of operating system procedures and macros requires more background than the reader may have at this point. In this chapter we present some fairly easy-to-use macro instructions that free the user from having to learn the intricacies of system I/O functions until later. Macros are pseudoinstructions; wherever they appear in a program, they will be replaced by the assembler by a sequence of other instructions that do the desired operations.

There are four macros that do specific I/O operations: input a line from a terminal, input a record from a disk file, output a line (or several) to a terminal, and output (dump) hex data to the terminal. There are also two macros that do necessary initialization and termination chores related to I/O.

The macros presented here use registers R0 and R1 for their own work. Thus the user should not leave any important data in those registers. Some of the macros return useful information to the program in R0. (The conventions that we use here—that I/O macros may destroy the old contents of R0 and R1, and may use them to pass information back to the program—are conventions used by system I/O macros also.) The SP (stack pointer) register should not be used to specify arguments for the macros; the contents of this register are changed immediately by the macros before they carry out their task.

I/O Processing Macros

READLINE.   The purpose of the READLINE macro is to input a line from the terminal. It displays two question marks (followed by a blank) as a prompt, then reads the line of text typed at the terminal. The format of the instruction is

READLINE destination

The input string will be stored, one character to a byte, in memory beginning at the byte addressed by the argument *destination*.

The length of the input line is the number of characters typed (including spaces and tabs) before the carriage return. READLINE will read up to 80 characters. It will place the length of the line read in R0 for use by the program.

Example 5.1: Reading Input from the Terminal

Suppose that a program contains the directive

```
LINE:    .BLKB    80
```

and the instruction

```
READLINE   LINE
```

Before the program is executed, the 80 bytes at LINE contain zeros. Suppose that when READLINE is executed and the prompt appears, the person at the terminal types the line shown below and then hits the return key. (The input begins with the character 2; the blank after the question marks is part of the prompt.)

```
?? 25     -18
```

The line will be read and stored in memory beginning at LINE. The result is

LINE	LINE +1	LINE +2						LINE +8	LINE +9			LINE +79
32	35	20	20	20	20	2D	31	38	00		· · ·	00

R0 will contain 00000009. Since the input line has only nine characters, the remaining 71 bytes reserved still contain zeros.

Note that the bytes in memory in Example 5.1 contain the ASCII codes for the characters in the input line; they do not contain the two's complement representation of the integers. Conversion of integers to two's complement is not automatic in assembly language as it is in high-level languages. In Chapter 6 we will see how to convert between character code and two's complement.

In Example 5.1 we reserved 80 bytes for the line of input even though we expected the user to type only two integers. Should we have saved space by reserving only, say, 10 or 15 bytes? Suppose that we had reserved only 15 bytes and the user happened to type a line with 17 characters. What happens to the "extra" two characters? When READLINE is executed, the CPU does not know how many bytes were reserved for the input; it just reads all the characters typed by the user (up to READLINE's built-in limit of 80) and puts them in memory beginning at the address specified, in this case LINE. Thus the sixteenth and seventeenth characters will be put in the next two bytes of memory following the 15 that were reserved for the line. Those next two bytes may contain data important to the program; that data would be overwritten and lost. To protect a program against both innocent errors on the part of the user and against malicious users, when input is to be read from a terminal, a programmer should reserve space for the maximum input size, even when a short line is expected.

READRCRD.   The purpose of the READRCRD (READ ReCoRD) macro is to read a record from a sequential disk file called DATA.DAT. For now, records may be thought of simply as lines of text. A *sequential file* is a collection of records arranged in sequential order (i.e., there is a first record, a second record, etc.). When a program begins executing, a pointer is set to the first record in the file. Each time the macro READRCRD is executed, the record pointed to will be read and the pointer will be moved ahead to the next record. This is done automatically by the VAX Record Management Services. The file on the disk is unchanged; a copy of the record read is stored in memory. If READRCRD is used, the data file to be read must be named DATA.DAT.

The format of READRCRD is

READRCRD destination

As with READLINE, *destination* is the address where the record is to be put in memory, READRCRD reads records of length up to 80, and it puts the length of the record in R0. (If a record in the file is longer than 80 characters, only the first 80 are read.)

If READRCRD is executed after all the records in the file have been read and the record pointer is at the end of the file, a branch is taken to the instruction labeled EOF. Any program module that uses READRCRD must have an instruction labeled EOF, even if the programmer does not expect to read past the end of the file.

Example 5.2: Reading from a Disk File

If the first record in DATA.DAT is "25   -18," then READRCRD will affect memory and R0 the same way that READLINE did in Example 5.1.

PRINTCHRS.   PRINTCHRS displays (prints) a string of characters at the terminal. The address of the first byte of the string must be given as the first argument. The end of the string is indicated by a byte of zeros in memory following the last character, or by specification of the string length as a second argument. If a length is specified, it should be a word integer. Each control character, if any, counts as one character. If the string contains any bytes of all zeros, no further bytes will be printed even if a larger length was specified.

The formats for PRINTCHRS are

PRINTCHRS string

and

PRINTCHRS string,length

The first version is most convenient for printing a message or heading initialized in memory using an .ASCIZ directive. It frees the user from the chore of counting the characters. If the length operand is omitted, PRINTCHRS has a default maximum length of 85 (thus allowing for one full line and several control characters, such as line feeds).

PRINTCHRS always begins on a new line at the left margin. Any appropriate addressing modes may be used for the arguments.

Note that PRINTCHRS expects the memory locations specified for the string to contain ASCII code. It will not print two's complement data; such data must be converted to character code by the program before printing.

Example 5.3: Printing a Heading

Headings may be set up and printed as follows:

```
HDG:    .ASCIZ  /Output from Assignment 1/
        .
        .
        .
        PRINTCHRS HDG
```

Example 5.4: Printing Several Lines at Once

The ASCII codes for control characters "carriage return" and "line feed" may be included in a string to accomplish the indicated control operations. Consider the following statements.

```
CR = 13                     ; ASCII carriage return
LF = 10                     ; ASCII line feed
PAGE:   .ASCIZ  /Page 1/<CR><LF>/June 12/<LF><LF>
        .
        .
        .
        PRINTCHRS PAGE
```

PRINTCHRS will print June 12 on the line after Page 1, both beginning at the left margin, then skip down two lines.

Example 5.5: Variations

To emphasize the independence between the initialization of the character string in memory and the printing of it, we show three variations on Example 5.4. It does not matter if one or several .ASCII and .ASCIZ directives are used to set up a string to be printed with one PRINTCHRS statement, or if several PRINTCHRSs are used, as long as the correct ASCII codes are in memory, the string is terminated by a byte of zeros or is of the correct length, and the PRINTCHRS statements specify correct starting addresses.

(a) Using the .ASCIZ directive in Example 5.4, we could have obtained the same result with

```
         PRINTCHRS PAGE,#6
         PRINTCHRS PAGE+8
```

because the first character of "June 12" is in the byte whose address is PAGE+8. PRINTCHRS always starts printing at the left end of a new line, so the first two control characters were not included in the strings to be printed. A length is needed on the first PRINTCHRS because there is no zero byte immediately after the bytes containing "Page 1."

(b)
```
PAGE:    .ASCIZ  /Page 1/
DATE:    .ASCIZ  /June 12/<LF><LF>
           .

           .

           .

         PRINTCHRS PAGE
         PRINTCHRS DATE
```

(c)
```
PAGE:    .ASCII  /Page 1/<CR><LF>
DATE:    .ASCIZ  /June 12/<LF><LF>
           .

           .

           .

         PRINTCHRS PAGE
```

Note that in (c) .ASCII is used in the first directive instead of .ASCIZ.

Example 5.6: Printing a Record Read from the Disk File DATA.DAT

We must reserve space for a record to be read; if we do not know its size, we can reserve 80 bytes, the maximum READRCRD will read. Since a record in general will not be terminated by a byte of zeros, we must know the actual length of the record to print it. READRCRD puts the length in R0, so we may use R0 as the length argument in PRINTCHRS.

```
RECORD: .BLKB    80
           .

           .

         READRCRD  RECORD
         PRINTCHRS RECORD,R0
```

Remember that PRINTCHRS may change the contents of R0, so we can no longer expect it to contain the length of the record.

DUMPLONG.   DUMPLONG prints the contents of longwords (in memory or registers) in hex. It can be used to examine the results of computation before one learns how to convert data from two's complement to character code. It can be used to examine the internal representation of the various data types and machine instructions. It can be used as a simple debugging tool, since it can easily be inserted at various points in a program to display intermediate results, addresses, and so on. If the VAX Debugger is available, it may be used instead of DUMPLONG; it can accomplish all that DUMP-LONG does and much more.

The format of the DUMPLONG macro is

DUMPLONG arglist

where the arglist may contain up to 12 arguments separated by commas and using any addressing modes. (Since DUMPLONG may change the contents of R0 and R1, if these registers are specified as arguments, the output shown for them may not be the original contents. To dump R0 and R1, their contents should be copied to other registers.)

DUMPLONG always prints a header and trailer line to mark its output, and it prints the operand specifier for each longword it dumps.

Example 5.7: The DUMPLONG Format

The output generated by

```
DUMPLONG  LINE,LINE+4,R10,ALPHA,R7,(R7)
```

has the following form. (The data at LINE and LINE+4 are from Example 5.1.)

```
** DUMPLONG OUTPUT **
LINE       20203532
LINE+4     312D2020
R10        FFFFFFE7
ALPHA      00000019
R7         0074020B
(R7)       FFFFFFFC
**  END  DUMPLONG  **
```

Initialization and Termination Macros

The initialization and termination macros are BEGIN and EXIT. If any of the I/O macros are used in a program, BEGIN and EXIT must be used instead of .ENTRY and $EXIT_S (described in Chapter 4), respectively, in the main program (even if the I/O is done in procedures).

The format of the BEGIN macro is

BEGIN entry_point_name

This statement will be replaced by an .ENTRY directive that specifies the entry point name and sets the integer overflow trap. Also, instructions to initialize the I/O files will be inserted in the program. The entry point name should appear as the argument of the program's .END directive.

The termination macro is

EXIT

It has no arguments and is used wherever $EXIT_S would be.

Storage reservation and initialization directives must be separated from executable instructions. Generally, they are placed before the BEGIN statement as in the next example.

Example 5.8: A Complete Program Using DUMPLONG for Output

```
; ALPHA and BETA contain longword integers. This program
; computes 6*(ALPHA)+(BETA) and stores the result in RESULT.
;
LF = 10                                 ; ASCII line feed
;
TITLE:  .ASCIZ   /Computation of 6*(ALPHA)+(BETA)/<LF>
ALPHA:  .LONG    3
BETA:   .LONG    450
RESULT: .BLKL    1
;
; Register use: R5   scratch
;
        BEGIN       EXAMPLE
        PRINTCHRS   TITLE            ; Print heading
        DUMPLONG    ALPHA,BETA       ; Show data
        MULL3       #6,ALPHA,R5      ; 6*(ALPHA)
        ADDL3       R5,BETA,RESULT   ; 6*(ALPHA)+(BETA) in RESULT
        DUMPLONG    RESULT           ; Show result
        EXIT
        .END        EXAMPLE
```

The output from the program is

```
Computation of 6*(ALPHA)+(BETA)

** DUMPLONG OUTPUT **
ALPHA      00000003
BETA       000001C2
**  END  DUMPLONG  **
** DUMPLONG OUTPUT **
RESULT     000001D4
**  END  DUMPLONG  **
```

In Section 5.4 we will show how to examine the data in this program using the VAX Debugger instead of DUMPLONG.

5.2 MOV INSTRUCTIONS

Move Instructions

The MOV*x* (move) instructions copy the first operand into the second. The general format is

MOV*x*   *source,destination*

where x = B, W, L, Q, or O. For types B and W, only the rightmost byte or word of a register is copied if register mode is used for the source, and only the rightmost byte or word is modified if register mode is used for the destination. If R*n* is specified as an operand of MOVQ or MOVO, the actual operand occupies two or four consecutive registers, respectively. The MOV instructions set condition code bits in the PSW to indicate the sign of the datum copied; they can be tested for conditional branching.

Copying Character Strings—The MOVC3 Instruction

Formatting data for output often requires moving (actually, copying) character strings from one place in memory to another. The MOVC3 (MOVe Characters, three operands) instruction does this task. Its format is

MOVC3   *length,source,destination*

The length, a word integer, is the number of characters to be copied from the source to the destination. The last two operands specify the addresses of the first byte of the source and the destination, respectively. The source and destination must be in memory; MOVC3 does not copy characters to or from a register. The source string will be unchanged (unless it overlaps the destination).

Warning: MOVC3 uses registers R0–R5, destroying the original contents of these registers.

Example 5.9: Formatting Characters for Output (A Complete Program)

Suppose that the DATA.DAT file contains data for a telephone directory in which each record consists of a name and a phone number. This program displays the directory on the screen.

Recall that READRCRD causes a branch to the instruction labeled EOF if an attempt is made to read past the end of the file.

Note the use of named constants and expressions in directive arguments and instruction operands.

```
; PROBLEM STATEMENT
;
; This program reads a telephone directory from the file
; DATA.DAT and prints it at the terminal in an easy-to-
; read format.
;
; DATA FORMATS
;
```

```
; Each record in the file contains a 20-character name
; (which may be padded with blanks) followed by an 8-
; character telephone number. The entries will be printed
; with 10 blanks separating the name and phone number.
;
; CONSTANTS
;
TAB = 9                                             ; ASCII tab
LF = 10                                             ; ASCII line feed
BLANK = ^A/ /                                       ; ASCII blank
NAME_SIZE = 20                                      ; Name field length
;
; STORAGE RESERVATION AND INITIALIZATION
;
HDG:    .ASCIZ   <TAB>/TELEPHONE DIRECTORY/<LF><LF>
LINEIN: .BLKB    NAME_SIZE+8                        ; Input buffer
NAME:   .BLKB    NAME_SIZE
        .BYTE    BLANK[10]                          ; Blanks
PHONE:  .BLKB    8
;
        BEGIN    PRINT_PHONES
        PRINTCHRS HDG                               ; Print heading
READ:   READRCRD LINEIN                             ; Read entry from file
        MOVC3    #NAME_SIZE,LINEIN,NAME             ; Copy name
        MOVC3    #8,LINEIN+NAME_SIZE,PHONE          ; Copy phone number
        PRINTCHRS NAME,#NAME_SIZE+18                ; Print entry
        BRB      READ                               ; Branch to READ
EOF:    EXIT                                        ; Done
        .END     PRINT_PHONES
```

Moving Addresses

In many examples where we have character strings in memory, we have a label for the byte containing the first character in the string. For example, LINE is the address of the first character in the line in Example 5.1. There are no labels on the bytes containing the other characters. Suppose that we want to write instructions that perform some operation on each of the characters in turn (e.g., search for a particular character) or need to know the address of the next available byte after the end of the string. In either case we can solve our problem by putting the address of the first character into a register and then incrementing the register by the appropriate amount. How do we put an address into a register? The MOVAx instructions do it. They have the following format:

$$\text{MOVA}x \quad \textit{source,destination}$$

where x = B, W, L, Q, or O. The first operand *address* is put into the destination operand. The datum addressed by the first operand is not accessed or affected at all. Addresses are always 32 bits, so the destination must be a longword or register.

Example 5.10: Putting an Address in a Register

The instruction

```
MOVAB    LINE,R7
```

puts the address LINE into R7. The instruction name would be read as "MOVe the Address of a Byte."

It is important to understand how the MOVAB instruction in Example 5.10 differs from

```
MOVB     LINE,R7
```

Normally, an instruction operand tells the location of the datum to be operated on. MOVB means "MOVe Byte." The first operand, LINE, is interpreted as the location, or address, of the byte to be copied, so this instruction goes to memory location LINE, reads the byte in that location, and puts a copy of it into R7. The MOVe Address instructions do not fetch the operand from memory; they just determine the operand address and put the address in the destination.

Example 5.11: Address Computation

Now suppose that we have read a line of characters and stored them in memory beginning at LINE. We want to store a byte of zeros in the next available byte.

```
MOVAB    LINE,R7       ; Address of first character
ADDL2    R0,R7         ; Add line length
MOVB     #0,(R7)       ; Store 0 in next byte
```

It is tempting to try the following shortcut for the first two instructions:

```
MOVAB    LINE+R0,R7    ; This is wrong
```

The assembler will reject this; expressions may combine user-defined symbols and constants, but not registers.[1] The ADDL2 instruction performs the addition on the address at execution time.

Why is there a different MOVA instruction for each data type when they all move a 32-bit address? The reason has to do with side effects of the instructions. Recall that the autoincrement and autodecrement addressing modes increment or decrement the register used to address the operand by the number of bytes in the operand data type. An instruction of the form

$$\text{MOVA}x \quad (Rn)+,Rm$$

---

[1] There are addressing modes, called displacement modes, that can be used to add LINE and the contents of R0 to compute an address; we will discuss them in Chapters 7 and 8.

will copy the contents of R*n* to R*m*, then increment R*n* by 1, 2, 4, 8, or 16 if *x* is B, W, L, Q, or O, respectively.

5.3 SYSTEM COMMANDS AND PROGRAM LISTINGS

The reader now has enough information to begin to write and run small programs. The commands described in this section are the VAX/VMS commands to assemble, link, and run a program. They are to be typed following the system prompt ($).

To assemble a program using the I/O macros presented in this chapter:

MACRO name+[directory]IOMAC/LIB

where *name* is the name of the file containing the program and *directory* is the name of the directory that contains the macro library file IOMAC.MLB described in Appendix D. The program file type should be MAR; the .MAR extension does not have to be specified in the command.

The MACRO command produces an object file, that is, a file containing the translation of the program. The file name is *name*.OBJ (where *name* is the same name as the source program, or .MAR file).

The /LIST option on the MACRO command will cause the assembler to create a listing file. The form of the command is

MACRO/LIST name+[directory]IOMAC/LIB

The listing file will be given the name *name*.LIS.

The linker combines object files to create an executable program. It must be used even if the entire program is in one object file. (Later we will see that the linker performs other important tasks.) To link:

LINK name,[directory]IOMOD

where *directory* is the name of the directory that contains the IOMOD.OBJ file described in Appendix D. Note that the .OBJ extension on the program file and the IOMOD file does not have to be included in the LINK command. The linker creates an executable file, *name*.EXE.

To run the program:

RUN name

Figure 5.1 illustrates the action of these commands. Note that program errors can show up at any of the three stages: assembly, linkage, or execution.

In Chapter 9 we will show how the steps described here must be modified to assemble, link, and run programs that use procedures.

Program Listings

We will give a brief description of the format of the program listings produced by the VAX MACRO assembler. Figure 5.2 shows the listing for the program in Example 5.9. The right-hand half of the listing is a copy of the source program with line numbers just

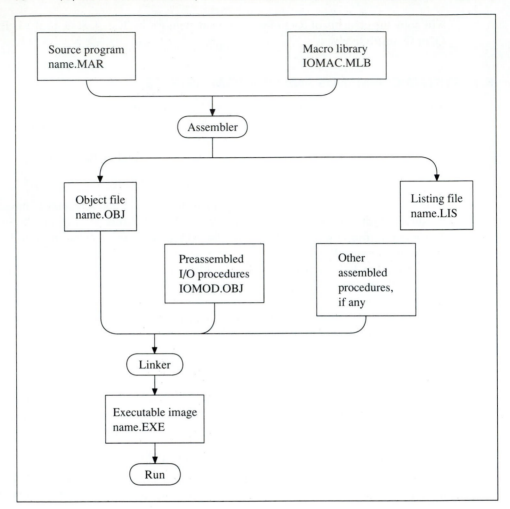

Figure 5.1   Assembling, linking, and running a program

to the left of the statements. The column of four-digit numbers to the left of the line numbers shows the value of the assembler's location counter at each line. The leftmost section shows (in most cases) the machine code or data stored for the statement on the same line. Note that the first (lowest-addressed) byte of each instruction is the one shown closest to the location counter value, so the machine code must be read right to left. The instructions that are substituted by the assembler for the I/O macros are not shown in the listing, but we can determine how many bytes they take up by observing the increase in the location counter value between a line containing a macro and the next line. See the notes on Fig. 5.2 for more detail about the listing.

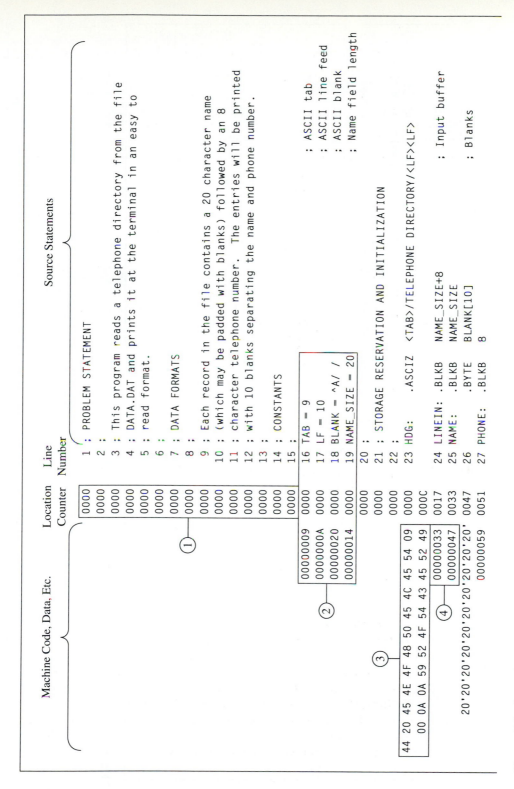

Machine Code, Data, Etc.	Location Counter	Line Number	Source Statements
	0000	1	; PROBLEM STATEMENT
	0000	2	;
	0000	3	; This program reads a telephone directory from the file
	0000	4	; DATA.DAT and prints it at the terminal in an easy to
	0000	5	; read format.
	0000	6	;
	0000	7	; DATA FORMATS
	0000	8	;
	0000	9	; Each record in the file contains a 20 character name
	0000	10	; (which may be padded with blanks) followed by an 8
	0000	11	; character telephone number. The entries will be printed
	0000	12	; with 10 blanks separating the name and phone number.
	0000	13	;
	0000	14	; CONSTANTS
	0000	15	;
00000009	0000	16	TAB = 9 ; ASCII tab
0000000A	0000	17	LF = 10 ; ASCII line feed
00000020	0000	18	BLANK = ^A/ / ; ASCII blank
00000014	0000	19	NAME_SIZE = 20 ; Name field length
	0000	20	;
	0000	21	; STORAGE RESERVATION AND INITIALIZATION
	0000	22	;
44 20 45 4E 4F 48 50 45 4C 45 54 09 / 00 0A 0A 59 52 4F 54 43 45 52 49 49	0000	23	HDG: .ASCIZ <TAB>/TELEPHONE DIRECTORY/<LF><LF> ; Input buffer
00000033	0017	24	LINEIN: .BLKB NAME_SIZE+8
00000047	0033	25	NAME: .BLKB NAME_SIZE
20 20 20 20 20 20 20 20 20 20	0047	26	.BYTE BLANK[10]
00000059	0051	27	PHONE: .BLKB 8 ; Blanks

Figure 5.2 Part of a program listing (continued next page).

```
                                28  ;
          0059        5   0059  29        BEGIN     PRINT_PHONES
                          00A9  30        PRINTCHRS HDG                        ; Print heading
                      6   00B9  31 READ:  READRCRD  LINEIN                     ; Read entry from file
                          00C9  32        MOVC3     #NAME_SIZE,LINEIN,NAME     ; Copy name
                          00D1  33        MOVC3     #8,LINEIN+NAME_SIZE,PHONE  ; Copy phone number
                          00D9  34        PRINTCHRS NAME,#NAME_SIZE+18         ; Print entry
                      6   00E7  35        BRB       READ                       ; Branch to READ
                          00E9  36 EOF:   EXIT                                 ; Done
                          0119  37        .END      PRINT_PHONES
7  FF62 CF  FF49 CF  14  28
   FF78 CF  FF55 CF  08  28
                  D0  11
```

1. The location counter is not incremented for comments.
2. The values of symbols defined in direct assignment statements are entered in the symbol table and shown on the listing, but they are not stored in memory; the location counter has not changed.
3. ASCII code stored in memory.
4. On storage reservation directives, the listing shows the location of the next available byte following the bytes reserved.
5. The BEGIN macro takes up 80 bytes.
6. The number of bytes used by the PRINTCHRS macro depends on its arguments. The first instance of PRINTCHRS here uses 16 bytes; the second only 14.
7. Machine code.

Figure 5.2 (concluded)

72

5.4 INTRODUCTION TO THE VAX/VMS DEBUGGER

A debugger is a utility that a programmer can use to help debug a program by monitoring and controlling its execution. Debuggers allow the programmer to run a program one line at a time and examine the values of variables. They have a variety of other features and capabilities. In this section we will describe some of the simpler features of the VMS Debugger.

A debugger is used to track down and correct *run-time* errors (errors that show up after the RUN command). Typical evidence of run-time errors includes incorrect output, infinite loops, and program crashes (providing system error messages). Errors that generate error messages from the assembler or linker must be corrected before using the debugger.

The VAX debugger can be used in different ways depending on the power of the workstation or terminal the programmer is using. We will describe the command interface, the most general way to use the debugger. This introduction will be brief. Some of the commands we present have many more capabilities than we describe here. There is on-line help available, and readers may consult the *VMS Debugger Manual* to learn more about the capabilities of the debugger and its extra features for use with workstations and special terminals.

Here are some of the things we can do with the debugger. Throughout this discussion, we will use the term *variable* to mean the contents of a memory location or a register.

- Control execution of a program. For example, we can tell the debugger to pause after executing each instruction and wait for a command from the programmer.
- Display the current values of selected variables.
- Instruct the debugger to report whenever selected variables are changed, and then wait for a command from the programmer. The selected variables are called *watched* variables, and the process of specifying them is called *setting watchpoints*.
- Instruct the debugger to report whenever selected instructions are executed, and then wait for a command from the programmer. Such points where the debugger pauses are called *breakpoints*, and the process of specifying them is called *setting breakpoints*.
- Modify data and continue execution.

The debugger is called a *symbolic* debugger because we specify the variables we want to examine by using their symbolic names. Symbols are a convenience for programmers. Normally, when an assembler translates an assembly language program to machine code, it replaces the symbols by memory addresses (or information the CPU can use to compute the addresses). After assembly, the symbols are irrelevant and they need not be kept. If a symbolic debugger is to be used, we must tell the assembler not to throw away its symbol table. The linker also generates a symbol table that normally can be discarded. We must tell the linker to include the symbol tables with the executable image it creates so that they will be available to the debugger. This is done by specifying the /DEBUG option on both the MACRO and LINK system commands. Depending on whether or not one wants a listing file, and depending on whether or not a program uses the I/O macros described in Section 5.1, the following commands may be used to assemble a program.

MACRO/DEBUG   name

or

MACRO/LIST/DEBUG   name+[directory]IOMAC/LIB

where name.MAR is the source program file and directory is the directory containing the I/O macro library. The LINK command (if using the I/O macros) would be

LINK/DEBUG   name,[directory]IOMOD

If a program is assembled and linked with the /DEBUG option, then when the RUN command is used to run the program, the debugger will be in control. Instead of just executing the program from start to finish, as the RUN command normally does, the debugger will prompt the programmer for commands to be entered from the terminal.

We will use a simple program to illustrate some of the debugger commands. More complex examples will be presented in later chapters. The program used here is the short, complete program from Example 5.8. The DUMPLONG instructions have been removed. Here is the revised program.

```
; ALPHA and BETA contain longword integers. This program
; computes 6*(ALPHA)+(BETA) and stores the result in RESULT.
;
LF = 10                                 ; ASCII line feed
;
TITLE:  .ASCIZ  /Computation of 6*(ALPHA)+(BETA)/<LF>
ALPHA:  .LONG   3
BETA:   .LONG   450
RESULT: .BLKL   1
;
; Register use: R5   scratch
;
        BEGIN       EXAMPLE
        PRINTCHRS   TITLE               ; Print heading
        MULL3       #6,ALPHA,R5         ; 6*(ALPHA)
        ADDL3       R5,BETA,RESULT      ; 6*(ALPHA)+(BETA) in RESULT
        EXIT
        .END        EXAMPLE
```

It is always a good idea to know what you expect a program to do before you try to determine if its results are correct. So, by doing a quick computation, we find that the value computed by the program and stored in RESULT should be 468_{10}.

Here are the assembly, link, and run commands and then the response from the debugger. The program is in a file called PROGRAM.MAR, and the I/O files are in the same directory. The commands typed by the programmer are tinted.

```
$ macro/debug program+iomac/lib
$ link/debug program,iomod
$ run program


        VAX DEBUG Version V5.2-015

%DEBUG-I-INITIAL, language is MACRO, module set to .MAIN

DBG>
```

The debugger is now awaiting a command. DBG> is the debugger prompt.

The GO command. The GO command tells the debugger to execute the program. If there are no errors in the program, and no watchpoints or breakpoints have been set, the program will run to completion and the debugger will issue the message in the following example.

```
DBG> go
Computation of 6*(ALPHA)+(BETA)

%DEBUG-I-EXITSTATUS, is '%SYSTEM-S-NORMAL, normal successful completion'
DBG>
```

There are several things to note about this example. First, the output from the program appears on the screen as usual when the program runs.

Second, normally when a program finishes execution, the system prompt ($) appears on the screen. When running a program under the control of the debugger, we do not automatically return to the system at the end of the program; we have the debugger prompt. At this point we can exit the debugger (using the EXIT command) or examine final values of variables. If we choose to exit, the screen shows

```
DBG> go
Computation of 6*(ALPHA)+(BETA)

%DEBUG-I-EXITSTATUS, is '%SYSTEM-S-NORMAL, normal successful completion'
DBG> exit
$
```

Third, since the GO command was the first command given, the debugger began execution at the beginning of the program (i.e., at the user transfer address specified on the program's .END directive). The GO command is also used after the debugger pauses at watchpoints, breakpoints, and other points where the program has been partially executed. In such cases, the GO command causes execution to continue from the point at which it was suspended.

The EXAMINE command.   The EXAMINE command is used to examine the values of variables. In the following example, we examine the contents of ALPHA, BETA, and RESULT before and after execution of the program.

```
$ run program

        VAX DEBUG Version V5.2-015

%DEBUG-I-INITIAL, language is MACRO, module set to .MAIN.

DBG> examine alpha,beta,result
.MAIN.\ALPHA:    00000003
.MAIN.\BETA:     000001C2
.MAIN.\RESULT:   00000000
DBG> go
Computation of 6*(ALPHA)+(BETA)

%DEBUG-I-EXITSTATUS, is '%SYSTEM-S-NORMAL, normal successful completion'
DBG> examine alpha,beta,result
.MAIN.\ALPHA:    00000003
.MAIN.\BETA:     000001C2
.MAIN.\RESULT:   000001D4
DBG>
```

The EXAMINE command shows the contents of ALPHA, BETA, and RESULT as hex longwords. It shows longwords because space for the variables is reserved with .LONG and .BLKL directives. If the variables examined were reserved as bytes or words, EXAMINE would display the appropriate number of digits. The EXAMINE command shows the data in hex unless the programmer requests a different option. We can convert 000001D4 to decimal to check that the result is what we expect, but it is easier to let the debugger do the conversion. In the following example, we use the DECIMAL qualifier on the EXAMINE command to request that the values be shown as decimal numbers. We examine TITLE to see that the debugger recognizes the .ASCIZ directive and displays the character string rather than the hex codes. This example also illustrates that we may abbreviate command and qualifier names, and that we may examine the contents of registers.

```
$ run program

        VAX DEBUG Version V5.2-015

%DEBUG-I-INITIAL, language is MACRO, module set to .MAIN.

DBG> examine/decimal alpha,beta,result,r5
.MAIN.\ALPHA:    3
.MAIN.\BETA:     450
.MAIN.\RESULT:   0
```

```
.MAIN.\EXAMPLE\%R5:       0
DBG> ex title
.MAIN.\TITLE:     'Computation of 6*(ALPHA)+(BETA).'
DBG> go
Computation of 6*(ALPHA)+(BETA)

%DEBUG-I-EXITSTATUS, is '%SYSTEM-S-NORMAL, normal successful completion'
DBG> ex/dec alpha,beta,result,r5
.MAIN.\ALPHA:     3
.MAIN.\BETA:      450
.MAIN.\RESULT:    468
0\%R5:   18
DBG>
```

(After the EXIT macro is executed, the contents of some registers may be changed. If the programmer wants to examine the final contents of registers, it may be necessary to set a breakpoint at the EXIT macro.)

The EXAMINE command has many other qualifiers that control the format used to display the requested data. Most are not of much interest to us now because we have not learned enough assembly language to appreciate their use.

In the examples we have given so far, the variables listed on the EXAMINE commands are symbols and a register. We may also specify expressions and array elements. Here is an example with an expression. Remember that the value of a symbol defined as a label is an address, and since BETA follows ALPHA in memory, ALPHA+4 = BETA.

```
DBG> ex/dec alpha,alpha+4,beta
.MAIN.\ALPHA:     3
.MAIN.\BETA:      450
.MAIN.\BETA:      450
DBG>
```

If a symbol is defined on a .BLKx directive specifying more than one memory location of type x, the debugger will treat the symbol as the name of an array. For example, suppose that a program contains the declaration

```
LIST:    .BLKW    10
```

and has stored data in these words. If we specify the symbol LIST in an EXAMINE command, it will display the entire array. Here is an example. Notice that the debugger indexes arrays beginning at 0. If we want to display the contents of the eighth element of the array, we examine LIST[7], as in the example.

```
DBG> ex/dec list
.MAIN.\LIST
    [0]:        3
    [1]:        7
    [2]:        11
    [3]:        25
```

```
        [4]:          19
        [5]:          23
        [6]:          57
        [7]:          31
        [8]:          35
        [9]:          30
DBG> ex/dec list[7]
.MAIN.\LIST[7]: 31
```

The HELP command. The HELP command provides information about debugger commands, qualifiers, and other features. To get information about a particular command, type HELP followed by the command name.

The STEP command. The STEP command causes the debugger to execute one instruction, then pause for another command. Here is an example. Notice that the debugger displays the *next* instruction to be executed, not the one it just completed. (Observe where the output appears and where the contents of R5 and RESULT change.)

```
$ run program

        VAX DEBUG Version V5.2-015

%DEBUG-I-INITIAL, language is MACRO, module set to .MAIN.

DBG> step
stepped to .MAIN.\EXAMPLE\%LINE 14
    14:         PRINTCHRS   TITLE                ; Print heading
DBG> step
Computation of 6*(ALPHA)+(BETA)

stepped to .MAIN.\EXAMPLE\%LINE 15
    15:         MULL3       #6,ALPHA,R5          ; 6*(ALPHA)
DBG> ex/dec r5
.MAIN.\EXAMPLE\%R5:     0
DBG> step
stepped to .MAIN.\EXAMPLE\%LINE 16
    16:         ADDL3       R5,BETA,RESULT       ; 6*(ALPHA)+(BETA) in RESULT
DBG> ex/dec r5,result
.MAIN.\EXAMPLE\%R5:     18
.MAIN.\RESULT: 0
DBG> step
stepped to .MAIN.\EXAMPLE\%LINE 17
    17:         EXIT
DBG> ex/dec r5,result
.MAIN.\EXAMPLE\%R5:     18
.MAIN.\RESULT: 468
DBG> step
%DEBUG-I-EXITSTATUS, is '%SYSTEM-S-NORMAL, normal successful completion'
DBG>
```

Note that even though the assembler replaces the BEGIN, PRINTCHRS, and EXIT macros with several instructions, the debugger treats each macro as one "step."

The SET WATCH command. If we are interested in a particular variable, we do not have to step through the entire program one instruction at a time. We can tell the debugger to watch for changes in that variable. When the debugger pauses, it displays the instruction that changed the watched variable, the old and new values of the variable, and the next instruction to be executed. In this example we watch RESULT.

```
$ run program

        VAX DEBUG Version V5.2-015

%DEBUG-I-INITIAL, language is MACRO, module set to .MAIN.

DBG> set watch result
DBG> go
Computation of 6*(ALPHA)+(BETA)

watch of .MAIN.\RESULT at .MAIN.\EXAMPLE\%LINE 16
    16:          ADDL3      R5,BETA,RESULT        ; 6*(ALPHA)+(BETA) in RESULT
    old value: 00000000
    new value: 000001D4
break at .MAIN.\EXAMPLE\%LINE 17
    17:          EXIT
DBG> go
%DEBUG-I-EXITSTATUS, is '%SYSTEM-S-NORMAL, normal successful completion'
DBG>
```

The SET BREAK command. We can use the SET BREAK command to tell the debugger to pause at particular instructions (specified by a label on the instruction or its line number) or at the beginning of each procedure called. The debugger will display the next instruction to be executed.

There are no labeled instructions in the program we are using for our example. If we wanted to suspend execution at an instruction labeled, say, NEXT, we would give the following command.

```
DBG> set break next
```

We can use a listing file to find line numbers (or just count lines). The following example shows how to set a breakpoint at the ADDL3 instruction.

```
$ run program
        VAX DEBUG Version V5.2-015
%DEBUG-I-INITIAL, language is MACRO, module set to .MAIN.

DBG> set break %line 16
DBG> go
Computation of 6*(ALPHA)+(BETA)
```

```
break at .MAIN.\EXAMPLE\%LINE 16
    16:         ADDL3       R5,BETA,RESULT          ; 6*(ALPHA)+(BETA) in RESULT
DBG>
```

Note that the format for specifying a breakpoint by a line number is "%LINE" followed by the number. If we just wrote the line number by itself, the debugger would assume that it is an address. Consider the following example.

```
DBG> set break 16
%DEBUG-E-NOACCESSR, no read access to virtual address 00000016
DBG>
```

This is an error message saying that the memory location with address 16 is outside the memory area allocated to the program. This may seem surprising. We will illustrate the EVALUATE command next and find out where our program is in memory.

The EVALUATE command.   The EVALUATE command displays the value of an expression. In the following example we use it to determine the values of some of the symbols in the program. Remember, again, that the values of the symbols are addresses. We use the /ADDRESS qualifier on the command. The symbol EXAMPLE is defined on the BEGIN macro, not as a label; it is the entry point of the program, and we determine its address. As usual, the command and qualifier may be abbreviated.

```
DBG> evaluate/address title,alpha,beta
0000061B
0000063C
00000640
DBG> eval/addr example
00000648
DBG>
```

Why are the values of the symbols so high? TITLE is the label on the first byte of the program. (The comments and direct assignment statement do not cause any space to be allocated in memory.) We have explained that the assembler starts its location counter at zero when it translates a source program file, so to the assembler TITLE = 0. But a program is not usually loaded into memory at location 0. The values the assembler assigns to the symbols are relative to the beginning of the program. The address of the actual location labeled by the symbol will depend on where the program is loaded. This depends in part on where the linker puts the program when it links with other files (e.g., procedures or the IOMOD file used for our I/O macros). We can see from the debugger's output that the program in our example begins in memory at location $61B_{16}$. Note that the values of ALPHA and BETA differ by 4, as they should; each value is 61B larger than we would have expected. The reader may be wondering how the assembler translates instruction operands into machine code when it does not know where the operands will really be in memory. We will see the solution to this problem when we study machine code in Chapter 8.

Table 5.1 summarizes the debugger commands described in this section.

TABLE 5.1 SOME DEBUGGER COMMANDS

Command	Qualifiers	Arguments	Action
EVALUATE	ADDRESS	Expression	Display value
EXAMINE	DECIMAL	Memory locations, registers	Display contents
	ASCII		
EXIT			Terminate debugging
GO			Continue execution
HELP		Command name	Display information
SET WATCH		Memory locations, registers	Display changes
SET BREAK		Label, line number, address	Pause at breakpoint
STEP			Execute one step

Using Tools

The debugger can be of great help in finding program errors. However, like any tool, it must be used sensibly. The VAX debugger is very powerful, but it cannot think. Before beginning a debugger session, you should have a plan of action. Based on the symptoms (e.g., incorrect output or system error message) you should think of possible causes and decide what evidence the debugger can provide to help you determine which one is actually responsible for the error.

For the small programs you write while learning VAX assembly language, careful thinking about the possible causes of the error, followed by careful examination of your program, is often sufficient to find the bug without using the debugger.

5.5 SUMMARY

The I/O macros described in this chapter are not VAX system macros. To use them the macro library described in Appendix D must be created and the I/O module described in Appendix D must be linked with the program.

These macros may change the data in R0 and R1. The SP register should not be used to address arguments of the macros.

READLINE *destination*.   READLINE reads a line from the terminal and stores it in memory, beginning at the address specified by the argument *destination*. READLINE prompts with "?? ". The maximum number of characters read is 80; the actual length is placed in R0.

READRCRD *destination*.   READRCRD reads the next record from the sequential disk file called DATA.DAT. It stores the record in memory beginning at *destination*. It reads at most 80 characters and puts the number of characters in R0. If an attempt is made to read past the end of the file, a branch will be taken to the statement labeled EOF; there must be such a statement in the program.

PRINTCHRS *string,length*.   PRINTCHRS prints at the terminal the ASCII string whose address is specified by the first argument. The length, a word, is optional and specifies the maximum number of characters to be printed. Fewer characters may be printed if the string is terminated with a byte of zeros.

DUMPLONG *arglist*.   DUMPLONG dumps its arguments at the terminal in hex. It may have up to 12 arguments.

BEGIN *entry_point_name*.   BEGIN must be used in place of .ENTRY to indicate the entry point of the main program in a program that uses any of the I/O macros described above. It does initialization needed by these macros.

EXIT.   EXIT does termination operations for the I/O files and should be used instead of $EXIT_S to terminate a program that uses any of the I/O macros described above.

Move instructions.   MOV instructions copy the datum specified by the first operand into the location specified by the second operand. MOVA instructions put the address of the first operand into the location specified by the second operand. The MOVC3 instruction copies a character string from one place in memory to another.

5.6 EXERCISES

1. Write a complete program to print out your name at the terminal.
2. Run your program for Exercise 1.
3. Write a complete program to print at the terminal the message "What is today's date?," read in the response, and print it out.
4. Run your program for Exercise 3.
5. Write instructions (including storage initialization) to print the words in the pattern shown below. "FIRST" should begin at the left margin.

```
FIRST
     SECOND
              THIRD
```

6. How many bytes of memory are used by each .ASCIZ and .ASCII directive in Example 5.4 and parts (b) and (c) of Example 5.5?
7. In Example 5.6 we reserved space for an input line by using a .BLKB directive that initialized the reserved bytes to zeros, but we specified a length argument on the PRINTCHRS macro that printed out the line. Why? That is, why is it not a good idea to rely on the zeros stored by the .BLKB directive to terminate the character string to be printed?
8. Create a file called DATA.DAT that contains a list of names, each at most 24 letters long. Write and run a program to read the list and print it out at the terminal. The printed list should have an appropriate heading, separated from the names by a blank line.

9. Create a file called DATA.DAT containing people's names in the following format: The family name appears first and is 12 characters long, and the given name appears next and is 10 characters long. (If the actual names are shorter, they are padded with blanks.) Then write and run a program that reads the names from the file and prints them out at the terminal with the given name first.

10. Suppose that the DATA.DAT file contains data for a mailing list where each record has the following format:

Name	20 characters
Street address	20 characters
City	13 characters
State	2 characters
Zip code	5 characters

    Write instructions to read a record and print out the name and address on three lines with at least one space between the city and state and between the state and zip code.

11. Write and run a program that uses DUMPLONG to dump the contents of registers R2 through R11. (The output may show that you cannot assume that the registers are cleared when a program begins execution.)

12. Write and run a program that initializes longwords ALPHA, BETA, and GAMMA to contain 25, −13, and 58 respectively, then computes the product of the three numbers and prints it using DUMPLONG.

13. Suppose that R3 contains 00502A3C, R4 contains FFDE7582, and the two longwords in memory beginning at address 502A3C contain 000000A2 and 0063C715 before *each* of the following instructions is executed. Show what will be in R3 and R4 after each instruction.

    (a) MOVL   R3,R4   (c) MOVB   R3,R4

    (b) MOVL   (R3),R4   (d) MOVB   (R3)+,R4

14. Assuming the same register and memory contents as in Exercise 13, show what will be in R3 and R4 after each of the following instructions is executed. Are the contents of any memory locations changed by any of these instructions? If so, give the address of each byte changed.

    (a) MOVAL   (R3)+,R4

    (b) MOVAB   (R3)+,R4

    (c) MOVAW   -(R3),R4

15. A character string of length 12 begins at the byte labeled STRING in memory. Write an instruction to put the address of the last byte of the string into R10.

16. R6 contains the address of the first character in a character string. Write an instruction to put the address of the second character in R6.

17. Suppose that a sequence of character strings of varying lengths is to be stored in memory beginning at TEXT, with the length of each string stored in one byte at the beginning of the string. For example:

TEXT

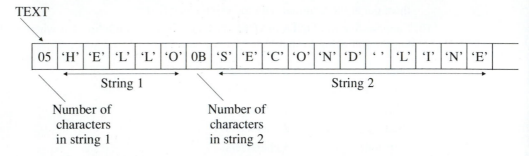

Suppose that some strings have already been read and stored, and R10 contains the address of the next available byte. Write instructions to read a character string from a terminal, store the length of the string in the memory byte whose address is in R10, store the character string in memory beginning at the next byte, then change R10 to contain the address of the next byte after the end of the string.

18. Suppose that several character strings have been stored in memory as described in Exercise 17, and suppose that R8 contains the address of the length byte for one of the strings. Write instructions to print that string and change R8 to contain the address of the length byte for the next string.

19. Write and run a program that does the following operations in the order given:

Prompt the user for his or her last name. Read it.

Prompt the user for his or her first name. Read it.

Print on the screen a message like the one below, but using the names the user typed. There should be one space between the first and last names.

```
Hello, Benjamin Tucker
```

20. Write and run a program that prompts the user for the name of his or her favorite writer, reads the name, then prints it on the screen in the following format:

```
*************************

*****  Oscar Wilde  *****

*************************
```

There are two spaces before and after the name, and a blank line before and after the line with the name. The first and last lines should have the same length as the middle line.

21. Redo Exercise 12 using the debugger instead of DUMPLONG to examine the result.

6

Integer Instructions

6.1 AN OVERVIEW

In this chapter we discuss instructions to do arithmetic on signed integers, integer conversion, and a few other operations. Almost all these operations can be performed by a single instruction for each of the three main integer data types: byte, word, and longword. Arithmetic on quadword integers cannot be done directly, but it can be programmed using other instructions.

All integer arithmetic instructions described in this chapter assume that the data are represented in two's complement form. There are other instructions that treat data as unsigned (i.e., nonnegative) binary integers. Table 6.1, in Section 6.7, shows the ranges of the integer data types.

All the instructions described in this chapter set condition code bits in the PSW to indicate the sign of the result of the operation and to indicate whether or not the result overflows the space allotted for it. We will consider how to use these bits in Chapter 7. (If IV is included in the program module's entry mask, an overflow will cause a program interrupt, normally resulting in termination of the program.)

When a general register is specified as the location of a byte or word source operand (i.e., an operand to be used in the operation) the CPU always takes the operand from the rightmost byte (bits 7:0) or word (bits 15:0) of the register. The rest of the register is ignored. When a register is specified for a byte or word destination operand, the result of the operation is placed by the CPU in the rightmost byte or word. The remaining portion of the register is unchanged. (This differs from the practice on some other machines, where the sign bit of the result is extended through the high-order part of the register, so that the result always appears as a 32-bit two's complement integer.) All operands other than the destination operand remain unchanged by the instructions (unless the destination operand specifies the same location as a source operand).

6.2 ARITHMETIC

There is an instruction for each of the four arithmetic operations (addition, subtraction, multiplication, and division) for each of the integer data types (byte, word, and longword), with either two or three operands. Thus 24 instructions are formed by choosing from the options shown below.

Operation	Type	Number of Operands
ADD	B	2
SUB	W	3
MUL	L	
DIV		

For all these instructions, the result goes in the last operand. If there are only two operands, the second is overwritten by the result. If the number of operands is omitted from the instruction name, the assembler will assume that "2" was intended. In the 3-operand instructions, only the first two operands participate in the arithmetic operation. For example, ADDL3 adds two integers, not three. (Exercise 20 considers addition of quadwords.)

ADD and MUL

Since addition and multiplication are commutative, there is no confusion about the roles of the operands. The action of the instructions is

$$\text{ADD}x2 \quad op1,op2 \qquad\qquad op1 + op2 \rightarrow op2$$
$$\text{ADD}x3 \quad op1,op2,sum \qquad op1 + op2 \rightarrow sum$$
$$\text{MUL}x2 \quad op1,op2 \qquad\qquad op1 * op2 \rightarrow op2$$
$$\text{MUL}x3 \quad op1,op2,prod \qquad op1 * op2 \rightarrow prod$$

where x = B, W, or L. The number of significant bits in the product of two integers may be twice as many as in the operands, so the programmer should take care to use a large enough data size.

SUB

The first operand of a subtract instruction is subtracted from the second. This is probably easiest to remember by reading the instruction from left to right as: SUBtract $op1$ from $op2$. Schematically,

$$\text{SUB}x2 \quad op1,op2 \qquad op2 - op1 \to op2$$
$$\text{SUB}x3 \quad op1,op2,dif \qquad op2 - op1 \to dif$$

where x = B, W, or L.

DIV

The first operand of a division instruction is the divisor; the second is the dividend. Thus

$$\text{DIV}x2 \quad op1,op2 \qquad op2/op1 \to op2$$
$$\text{DIV}x3 \quad op1,op2,quo \qquad op2/op1 \to quo$$

where x = B, W, or L. The quotient is truncated if necessary so that the result is an integer. Negative quotients are truncated toward zero. For example, the result of dividing -5 by 2 is -2. If the divisor is zero, an execution-time error occurs.

How Arithmetic Is Done

In Chapter 3 we explained how addition of two's complement integers is done and gave some examples. The operands are added as if they were unsigned binary numbers, ignoring the carry, if any, from the most significant bit position. Since $a - b = a + (-b)$, subtraction is done by negating (two's complementing) the subtrahend (in this case, b) and then adding the result to the minuend (a). Thus the hardware for addition and negating is used for subtraction. For computations on paper, there is a simpler method for subtracting two's complement integers: One number is subtracted from the other as if the operands were unsigned binary integers. If a borrow is needed in the leftmost place, we borrow as if there were another bit to the left.

Example 6.1: Subtracting Two's Complement Integers

Subtract the word integer 0107 from 005E.

Method 1: Negate and add.
The negation (two's complement) of 0107 is FEF9.

Binary	Hex	Decimal
0000000001011110	005E	94
1111111011111001	FEF9	-263
1111111101010111	FF57	-169

Method 2: Subtract as unsigned integers.

Binary	Hex	Decimal
Assumed extra 1		
10000000001011110	1005E	94
-0000000100000111	-0107	-263
1111111101010111	FF57	-169

Suppose the multiplier is 00001110 and the multiplicand is 00001011 (both shown in binary). We show the results of each step. (Note that the operands are sign-extended.)

Multiplier	Multiplicand	Product
0000000000001110	0000000000001011	0000000000000000
	No add	
0000000000000111	0000000000010110	0000000000010110
	Add multiplicand:	
0000000000000011	0000000000101100	0000000001000010
	Add multiplicand:	
0000000000000001	0000000001011000	0000000010011010
	Add multiplicand:	
0000000000000000	0000000010110000	
	No add	

There are more bits to be considered in the multiplier, but since they are all zeros, there will be no further change in the result. Note that bit 7 of the product is a 1, but bits 15:8 are zeros. The product has overflowed the allotted space, and the byte stored in the destination operand will not be the arithmetically correct product. The overflow bit in the PSW will be set. We can check our result by redoing the example in decimal. The multiplier is 14 and the multiplicand is 11. Their product, 154, is outside the range for signed byte integers.

Figure 6.1   Multiplying two's complement integers

Multiplication and division are more complicated, of course, but the principles behind the operations are the same as for decimal integers. Let us consider multiplication. We describe here a basic, straightforward method. Actual implementations in the CPUs of different computers use various tricks to save time and space.

The two operands of a multiplication are called the *multiplier* and the *multiplicand*. A place for the product, twice as long as the operands, is cleared (i.e., set to zero). If the rightmost bit of the multiplier is a 1, the multiplicand is added to the product. The multiplicand is shifted one bit to the left (a 0 fills the vacated bit at the right), and the multiplier is shifted one bit to the right (with the old rightmost bit disappearing). Then, again, the (new) rightmost bit of the multiplier determines if the (shifted) multiplicand is added to the product. The process continues until each bit of the multiplier has been examined. Overflow occurs if any of the bits in the high-order half of the product are different from the sign bit in the low-order half. Figure 6.1 shows an example of multiplication.

Example 6.2: Instruction Action

Suppose that before *each* of the instructions below, registers and memory contain the data shown. Examine carefully the results in the "Effect" column to be sure that each example is understood.

Registers	Memory	Address
R4		
FFED01A2	401A0010	00021044 = ALPHA
R6	FFFFF104	00021048 = BETA
123400D7	27480A3B	0002104C = GAMMA
R10		
00021044		

Instruction		Effect	
ADDB2	#25,ALPHA	ALPHA:	401A0029
ADDW2	R4,R10	R10:	000211E6
ADDL2	R4,R10	R10:	FFEF11E6
ADDL2	R4,(R10)	ALPHA:	400701B2
MULW2	ALPHA,R6	R6:	12340D70
DIVB3	BETA,R4,GAMMA	GAMMA:	27480AE9
SUBL3	BETA,ALPHA,R6	R6:	401A0F0C
SUBB	BETA+1,R10	R10:	00021053

Example 6.3: Computation

```
; This program segment computes 3x^2+12x-17, where x is the
; longword in X. The result is stored in Y.
;
; Register use:         R0, R1   scratch
;
        MULL3   X,X,R0        ; x^2 in R0
        MULL2   #3,R0         ; 3x^2 in R0
        MULL3   #12,X,R1      ; 12x in R1
        ADDL2   R1,R0         ; 3x^2+12x in R0
        SUBL3   #17,R0,Y      ; 3x^2+12x-17 in Y
```

We have several remarks on Example 6.3. Note that R0 and R1 are used for intermediate results. These registers are used for data that are needed only briefly because some instructions have side effects that destroy their contents. (The arithmetic instructions do not.)

Instead of using R0, one might have written

```
        MULL2   X,X
        MULL2   #3,X
```

to compute $3x^2$ in X. The major reason why this is not good is that it destroys the original value of *x*. As a general rule, the input data used in a problem should not be modified by the program (unless modifying the data is inherent in the nature of the task to be performed—for example, rearranging a list to put the entries in order). Most programs that a programmer writes are only parts of much larger programs written by many people, and the data may be needed by other parts of the program.

It is faster to put intermediate results in registers than in memory. The location Y could have been used in place of R0 or R1, but that would have required more memory references. Also, as we shall see in Chapter 8, the instruction itself takes up less space if the operands are in registers.

The program segment in Example 6.3 is not the most efficient way to solve the problem. See Exercise 3.

Example 6.4: Computation

Compute R7←R4^4+R3∗R6, where the registers contain word integers. [Note that to be technically correct, we should write (R4)^4+(R3)∗(R6) to denote the contents of the registers, but for brevity we omit the parentheses. We also omit them in the comments in the program.]

```
MULW3    R4,R4,R7              ; R4^2 in R7
MULW2    R7,R7                 ; R4^4 in R7
MULW3    R3,R6,R0              ; R3*R6 in R0
ADDW2    R0,R7                 ; R4^4+R3*R6 in R7
```

Example 6.5: Computation

In this example, as in many others from now on, we assume that the data operated on have been appropriately initialized.

```
; PROBLEM STATEMENT
;
; TOTAL is a longword containing the total cost of an order
; that qualifies for a 20% discount. The amount to be
; billed is computed and stored in the longword AMOUNT.
;
; Money is represented by integers by storing the amount in cents.
;
; Register use:          R7       amount of discount
;
        DIVL3    #5,TOTAL,R7              ; Compute discount
        SUBL3    R7,TOTAL,AMOUNT         ; Subtract discount
```

Some Special-Purpose Instructions

Some special cases of arithmetic operations are performed so often that some computers have specialized instructions that perform them faster and take up less space than the usual arithmetic instructions. The VAX has special instructions to set a register or memory location to zero, increment (add 1), decrement (subtract 1), and negate. These operations can be accomplished with the MOV, ADD, SUB, and MUL instructions, respectively, using appropriate operands, but the special-purpose instructions, CLeaR, INCrement, DECrement, and Move NEGated, are more efficient and should be used instead. The MNEG instructions have two operands; the negation of the first, or source, operand is put in the second, or destination, operand. The formats of the instructions are

CLR*x*	*operand*	*x*= B, W, L, Q, or O
INC*x*	*operand*	*x*= B, W, or L
DEC*x*	*operand*	*x*= B, W, or L
MNEG	*source,destination*	*x*= B, W, or L

(Recall that CLRQ and CLRO with operand R*n* will clear R*n* and R*n*+1, or R*n*, R*n*+1, R*n*+2, and R*n*+3, respectively.)

Example 6.6: Instruction Action

Suppose that before *each* of the instructions below is executed, R8 contains 00009AFF.

Instruction		R8 After Execution
CLRL	R8	00000000
CLRB	R8	00009A00
INCB	R8	00009A00
INCW	R8	00009B00
DECB	R8	00009AFE
DECL	R8	00009AFE
MNEGL	R8,R8	FFFF6501
MNEGW	R8,R8	00006501
MNEGB	R8,R8	00009A01

Example 6.7: Computation

```
; Compute the average of SCORE1, SCORE2, and SCORE3 (longwords),
; and store the rounded result in AVERAGE.
;
        ADDL3   SCORE1,SCORE2,R0    ; Add first two scores
        ADDL2   SCORE3,R0           ; Add third score
        INCL    R0                  ; Add 1 to force rounding
        DIVL3   #3,R0,AVERAGE       ; Divide; store average
```

6.3   A SIMPLE LOOP INSTRUCTION (SOBGTR) AND ARRAY ADDRESSING

The VAX has several specialized loop control instructions. We will cover these and other conditional branch instructions in Chapter 7, but we are introducing one simple loop instruction here so that the reader can write and run nontrivial programs. The instruction is SOBGTR, which stands for Subtract One and Branch if GreaTeR than zero. It is particularly useful for loops that must be executed a specific number of times. Its format is

SOBGTR   *index,destination*

The index may be in a general register or in memory; it must be a longword. The destination operand uses branch mode. The instruction operates as follows:

$$index \leftarrow index{-}1$$

if $index > 0$, then branch to *destination*

　　　　　　　　　else continue with the next instruction

The following scheme describes the usual way SOBGTR is used.

$$index \leftarrow \text{number of times loop is to be executed}$$

LOOP:　　　first instruction in loop

　　　　　　　.

　　　　　　　.

　　　　　　　.

　　　　　　SOBGTR　　　*index*,LOOP

If the instruction is used this way, the index is always the number of times the loop is still to be executed; when *index* becomes 0, control passes to the instruction following the loop.

The SOBGTR instruction is convenient for implementing some common kinds of loops in high-level languages like the following Pascal, C, and Fortran statements.

for *index* := *initial_value* **downto** 1 **do**

```
for (index = initial_value; index > 0; index--)
```

DO *s* INDEX = INITIALVALUE,1,−1

The initial value of the loop counter does not appear in the SOBGTR instruction itself; as illustrated in many of the following examples, the index must be initialized before the loop begins. Also, to properly implement the high-level language loop statements, we must prevent the loop from being executed at all if the initial value of the index is 0 (or negative). The SOBGTR instruction itself cannot take care of this because it occurs at the end of the loop. We will return to this point in Chapter 7 when we introduce conditional branching instructions.

Example 6.8: Programming with an Array

Problem: Write a program segment to double each entry in a word array DATA. The number of array entries is stored in the longword NUM.

Discussion of solution: The solution is straightforward. We use a register, R6, to address each array entry in turn. A variable (or register) that contains an address is usually called a pointer, so we will call R6 our array pointer. To initialize R6, that is, to get the address of the first array entry into R6, we use the MOVAW (MOVe Address of a Word) instruction.

The autoincrement addressing mode is appropriate here; after doubling an entry, R6 will automatically be incremented to contain the address of the next entry.

Solution:

```
; PROBLEM STATEMENT
;
; This program segment doubles each entry in the word array DATA.
; The number of array entries is in the longword NUM.
;
; REGISTER USE
```

```
;
;          R6          array pointer
;          R9          loop counter
;
; INITIALIZATION
;
           MOVAW    DATA,R6        ; Array pointer
           MOVL     NUM,R9         ; Number of entries
;
; THE LOOP
;
DOUBLE: ADDW2    (R6),(R6)+        ; Double entry, increment ptr
        SOBGTR   R9,DOUBLE         ; Loop control
```

Remark: Note that the second operand address in the ADDW2 instruction is computed before R6 is incremented, and that this address is used for both the second summand and the location for the sum.

The program segment in the example above contains more lines of comments than of instructions. This is not unusual. Documentation is extremely important, even more so in assembly language programs than in high-level language programs because assembly language is harder to read. The documentation block at the beginning of a program segment should contain a statement of the problem and of the data types used, a description of the method that points out any special or unusual things done, and a list of registers used and their roles. The program above does not describe the method used to solve the problem because it is straightforward.

Example 6.9: Programming with an Array

Problem: Write a program segment to store in each entry of a longword array LIST the entry's index number (starting with 1). The array size is stored in NUM, a longword.

Discussion of solution: The index used to control the loop in the SOBGTR instruction may also be used as the value to be stored in the array entries, but since SOBGTR counts down from the maximum index value to zero, we will fill the array backward. Therefore, the autodecrement addressing mode is the appropriate mode to use for addressing the array entries. Since this mode decrements an address before using it, we should initialize our array pointer just beyond the end of the array. Each entry takes up four bytes, so the address after the last entry is LIST+4*(NUM). See Figure 6.2 for an illustration.

Solution:

```
; PROBLEM STATEMENT
;
; This program stores in each entry of the longword array LIST
; the entry's index number. The array size is in NUM, a longword.
;
; METHOD
;
; The array is filled from the end to the beginning so that
; the loop counter may be used as the array index value also.
```

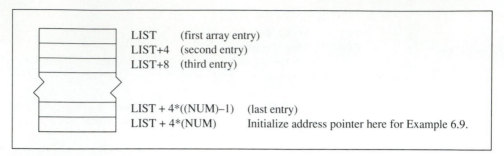

LIST   (first array entry)
LIST+4   (second entry)
LIST+8   (third entry)

LIST + 4*((NUM)–1)   (last entry)
LIST + 4*(NUM)   Initialize address pointer here for Example 6.9.

Figure 6.2   Addresses of array entries

```
;
; REGISTER USE
;
;       R0       scratch
;       R6       loop counter
;       R10      array pointer
;
; INITIALIZATION
;
        MOVL     NUM,R6           ; Number of entries
        MOVAL    LIST,R10         ; Initialize array pointer
        MULL3    #4,R6,R0         ;    4*(NUM) in R0
        ADDL2    R0,R10           ;    LIST+4*(NUM)
;
; THE LOOP
;
STORE:  MOVL     R6,-(R10)        ; Decrement ptr, store index
        SOBGTR   R6,STORE         ; Loop control
```

This example illustrates or suggests several important points about loops, arrays, and some of the particular instructions used.

The index, or counter, used to control the loop may be used in other instructions in the loop. One must be careful, though, to ensure that the loop counter is not modified by any but the loop control instruction so that the instructions are executed the proper number of times.

What if (NUM) = 0? That is, what if the array were empty? The loop would be executed one time because the SOBGTR instruction occurs at the end of the loop, and the loop counter is not tested earlier. A longword 0 would be stored at LIST–4 (i.e., the longword just before the beginning of the array), overwriting whatever was there. To avoid such errors, we will use instructions in Chapter 7 to test the loop index before the loop begins.

The computation of the initial value for the array pointer required several instructions. Expressions are permitted for operands, so a novice might have thought of trying

```
MOVAL    LIST+4*NUM,R10              ; This is wrong.
```

This will not work because the value of NUM to the assembler is the *address* where the array size is stored. The assembler will multiply the *address* by 4. The contents of NUM is unknown at assembly time; it may be read in as input or computed by another part of the program. (Even if initialized in a storage directive, it can change at execution time.) So we used MULL3 and ADDL2 to compute the desired address at execution time.

If we wanted the program to compute the address of the last array entry, it could do so as follows:

```
MOVAL    LIST-4,R10
MULL3    #4,NUM,R0
ADDL2    R0,R10
```

The (address) expression LIST–4 can be computed by the assembler; a SUB instruction is not needed at execution time to subtract the 4.

Because of the variety of loop control instructions and addressing modes available on the VAX, this programming problem could have been solved several other ways.

Example 6.10: Two-Dimensional Arrays

Problem: Compute the trace of a square *n*-by-*n* array of longwords. (The trace is the sum of the entries on the main diagonal.)

Discussion: Two-dimensional arrays are usually stored row by row. That is, the first entry of the second row is stored in memory immediately following the last entry of the first row, and so on, as illustrated in Fig. 6.3. (Fortran compilers store two-dimensional array entries column by column, but that is not the usual scheme.) Thus the diagonal entries are $n + 1$ entries, or $4 * (n + 1)$ bytes, apart.

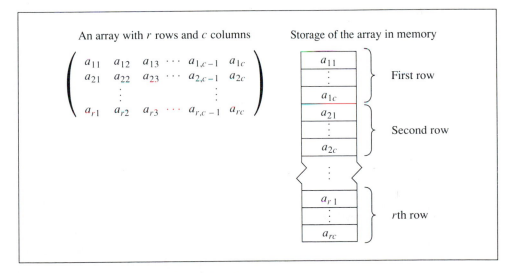

Figure 6.3 Storage of two-dimensional arrays

Solution:

```
; PROBLEM STATEMENT
;
; The trace of a square array is the sum of the entries on the
; main diagonal. This program segment computes the trace of
; MATRIX, an n by n array of longwords, where n is a longword
; stored in N.
;
; METHOD
;
; For an n by n array, the main diagonal entries are n+1 entries
; apart, so the diagonal entries will be accessed by starting at
; the first entry and adding 4*(n+1) to the pointer to get each
; succeeding one.
;
; REGISTER USE
;
;       R6        address of a diagonal entry
;       R7        loop counter
;       R8        trace
;       R9        4*(n+1), the address increment
;
        MOVAL    MATRIX,R6          ; Set pointer to first entry
        MOVL     N,R7               ; Initialize loop counter
        CLRL     R8                 ; Clear for trace
        ADDL3    #1,R7,R9           ; n+1 in R9
        MULL2    #4,R9              ; 4*(n+1)
;
ADD:    ADDL2    (R6),R8            ; Add diagonal entry
        ADDL2    R9,R6              ; Increment pointer
        SOBGTR   R7,ADD             ; Loop control
        MOVL     R8,TRACE           ; Store trace
```

Example 6.11: Reading and Storing an Entire File

Problem: The disk file DATA.DAT contains a list of names, each with 20 characters (some of which may be blanks). Reserve space in memory for 50 names at NAMES. Read the list into memory, keeping a count of the names actually read from the file, and print the list out at the terminal. Store the number of names in the longword COUNT.

Discussion of solution: When the end of the file is reached, the READRCRD macro automatically causes a branch to the instruction labeled EOF. Thus there will be an exit from the loop when the end of the file is encountered. However, since the file may contain more than 50 records, we must explicitly ensure that no more than 50 records are read in; otherwise, instructions and/or other data could be overwritten.

Solution:

```
MAX = 50                           ; Maximum number of records to store
REC_SIZE = 20                      ; Length of each record
NAMES:  .BLKB    MAX*REC_SIZE      ; Space for the list of names
COUNT:  .BLKL    1                 ; The number of names actually read
```

```
;
; REGISTER USE
;
;        R6        array pointer
;        R7        loop counter
;
; INITIALIZATION
;
         MOVAB    NAMES,R6                 ; Initialize array pointer
         MOVL     #MAX,R7                  ; Read at most MAX records
;
READ:    READRCRD (R6)                     ; Read next name
         PRINTCHRS (R6),#REC_SIZE          ; Print name
         ADDL2    #REC_SIZE,R6             ; Increment pointer
         SOBGTR   R7,READ                  ; Loop control
EOF:     SUBL3    R7,#MAX,COUNT            ; Compute and store COUNT
```

6.4   CONVERTING AMONG INTEGER TYPES

The VAX has CVT (ConVerT) instructions to convert between the various signed integer types. Conversion of a signed integer to one with more bits is done by sign extension— that is, by copying the sign bit into all the new bit positions at the high-order end of the destination operand. Converting from a longer representation to a shorter one is done by dropping the leftmost bits. Of course, it is possible that the source operand may not fit in the smaller destination; in this case the overflow condition code is set (and a program interrupt will occur if IV was specified in the entry mask). Conversion from a long representation to a shorter one is successful if all the bits dropped are identical to the sign bit of the result.

The instructions are as follows:

$$\text{CVT}xy \quad source, destination \qquad x = \text{B, W, or L}$$
$$y = \text{B, W, or L}$$
$$x \text{ not equal } y$$

Example 6.12: Integer Conversions

Suppose that R5 contains FFE729A0 before *each* of the following instructions.

Instruction		Effect on R5
CVTBW	R5,R5	FFE7FFA0
CVTWL	R5,R5	000029A0
CVTBL	R5,R5	FFFFFFA0

Example 6.13: Integer Conversions

Suppose that R6 contains 000000B4. The instruction

```
         CVTLW    R6,(R8)
```

will put 00B4 in the word whose address is in R8. The instruction

```
CVTWB    R6,(R8)
```

will put B4 in the byte whose address is in R8, but this is not a proper conversion because the word integer 00B4 is positive, but the (two's complement) byte integer B4 is negative. This instruction will set the overflow condidion code.

Example 6.14: Integer Conversion

We wish to compute

$$number \leftarrow 10 * number + digit$$

where *number* is a longword in R9 and *digit* is a byte in memory whose address is in R10. We want to replace the current value of *number* by the result and increment R10 so that it will contain the address of the next byte in memory. The following program segment does this.

```
MULL2    #10,R9             ; 10*number
CVTBL    (R10)+,R0          ; Convert digit to longword
ADDL2    R0,R9              ; Add digit
```

Why is the conversion in this example necessary? Suppose that the four bytes beginning at the address originally in R10 contain 04, 02, 01, and 07 (all in hex). We want to add 04 to R9, but if we had used an ADDL instruction to add the digit, the longword 07010204 would have been added. If we had used an ADDB instruction, only the 04 would have been added, but using ADDB to add a byte to a longword can sometimes produce an incorrect result, as the next example shows.

Example 6.15: Adding a Byte and a Longword

Suppose that R9 contains 000000E6 (230_{10}), the byte in BYTE contains 23 (35_{10}), and we want to add these integers. After

```
ADDB2    BYTE,R9            ; This is wrong
```

we would want R9 to contain 265_{10} (00000109), but instead, R9 will contain 00000009. Recall that a byte instruction will affect only the rightmost byte of the register.

Example 6.16: Integer Conversion

Problem: Add up the entries in the byte array BLOCKS, assuming that the sum will be too large for a byte. The number of entries is in the byte NUM, and the sum should be stored in the word TOTAL.

Discussion of solution: Each entry in the array will be converted to a word before being added; the addition will be done with an ADDW instruction. The loop control instruction SOBGTR requires a longword index, so the array size must be converted to a longword. The sum will be accumulated in a register rather than in TOTAL because the addition instruction may be executed many times in the loop, and register references are faster than memory references.

Solution:

```
; PROBLEM STATEMENT
;
; This program segment adds the entries of the byte array
; BLOCKS. The number of entries is in the byte NUM, and
; the sum will be stored in the word TOTAL.
```

```
        ;
        ; REGISTER USE
        ;
        ;       R6       array pointer
        ;       R7       converted entry
        ;       R8       loop counter
        ;       R9       sum
        ;
        ; INITIALIZATION
        ;
                MOVAB    BLOCKS,R6        ; Array pointer
                CVTBL    NUM,R8           ; Loop counter
                CLRW     R9               ; Clear for sum
        ;
        ; COMPUTE SUM
        ;
        NEXT:   CVTBW    (R6)+,R7         ; Fetch and convert entry
                ADDW2    R7,R9            ; Add
                SOBGTR   R8,NEXT          ; Loop control
                MOVW     R9,TOTAL         ; Store sum
```

Conversion instructions for unsigned integers are introduced in Exercise 36.

6.5   CONVERSION BETWEEN CHARACTER CODE AND TWO'S COMPLEMENT

The Problem

When input is read by an assembly language program, it is read as a sequence of characters and stored in memory in character code, one to a byte. If the data are integers and we want to do a lot of computation with them, or if we wish to store a large number of integer data, we convert the character code to two's complement representation. Two's complement is used because arithmetic is faster on numbers in this form, and because it takes less space to store an integer in two's complement than in character code. Many computers, including the VAX, have an intermediate data type called packed decimal. Packed-decimal data are more compact than character code, but not as compact as two's complement. There are instructions that do arithmetic on packed-decimal integers, but they are slower than two's complement arithmetic instructions. Packed-decimal instructions will be covered in Chapter 13; in this section we will be interested in this format only as an intermediate step in the conversions between character code and two's complement.

Conversion between two data representations is not a trivial task. It requires a lot of work—and a lot of thought about how to accomplish the task. The VAX has powerful conversion instructions. Many microprocessors (and other large computers) do not have such instructions. In this section we will describe the VAX instructions for converting between character code and two's complement. In Chapter 7, after we have more tech-

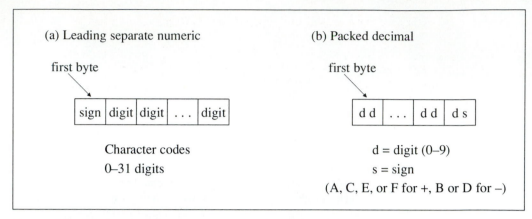

Figure 6.4   Leading separate numeric and packed-decimal data formats

niques available, we will consider the problem in more depth to see how it might be solved on a computer without special conversion instructions.

Leading Separate Numeric and Packed-Decimal Data

The VAX has a data format called *leading separate numeric*, which is simply a signed integer in character code (with at most 31 digits). The sign may be a plus, minus, or blank. The character codes occupy consecutive bytes of memory, with the sign in the first, or lowest-addressed, byte. (Thus here we draw diagrams of memory in the natural way with the lowest-addressed byte at the left.) Figure 6.4(a) shows the format of a leading separate numeric string. The address of the string is the address of its sign byte (i.e., its lowest-addressed byte).

Example 6.17: Leading Separate Numeric String

For any character c, 'c' denotes its character code in hex. Note that the character codes for digits are in the range 30_{16}–39_{16}.

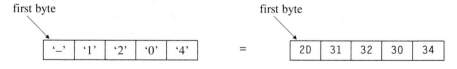

In *packed-decimal* format, digits are "packed" two to a byte. This can be done because the value of each decimal digit can be represented in four bits in binary (0000–1001). The sign of the integer is in the rightmost half of the last byte; that is, the sign shares a byte with the integer's least significant digit. Since the bit patterns 0000–1001 are used for digits, the patterns 1010–1111 (the hex digits A–F) are available to represent signs. They are used as follows:

$$A, C, E, \text{ and } F \qquad \text{represent } +.$$
$$B \text{ and } D \qquad \text{represent } -.$$

C and D are the representations used by instructions that convert data to packed decimal form.

A packed decimal number may have at most 31 digits. Its address is the address of its lowest-numbered byte. As with leading separate numeric, the diagrams show the lowest-addressed byte at the left so that the datum can be read naturally, left to right. Figure 6.4(b) shows the format for packed decimal.

Example 6.18: A Packed-Decimal Number

first byte

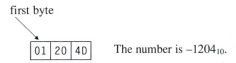

01 20 4D   The number is -1204_{10}.

Converting from Character Code to Two's Complement

The VAX has an instruction that converts from leading separate numeric to packed decimal, an instruction that converts from packed decimal to a two's complement longword, and two instructions that reverse these conversions. We will consider first the conversions that would be done on input—conversion from character code to two's complement.

The CVTSP instruction converts leading separate numeric to packed decimal. Its format is

CVTSP   *s_num_digits,lsn,p_num_digits,packed*

The first operand is the number of digits (*not* counting the sign) in the leading separate numeric string, and the second operand is the string (specified by the address of the byte containing the sign). The third operand is the number of digits (*not* the number of bytes) to be put in the packed-decimal result, and the last operand is the result (specified by the address of the first byte). If the number of digits specified for the packed-decimal result exceeds the number specified for the source, the leftmost digits will be filled with zeros. (If too few digits are specified, the result will be truncated, perhaps producing an incorrect value.) The leading separate numeric and packed operands must be in memory; they cannot be in registers.

> *Warning: CVTSP, and the other conversion instructions described in this section, use registers R0–R3 for scratch work, destroying the original contents of these registers.*

The CVT instructions must be used with care; there are many ways in which errors can occur. The source operand must be a leading separate numeric string; that is, the first byte must contain the character code for a plus, minus, or blank, and each of the other bytes must contain the character code for a digit. If the source contains a bad byte, or if the number of digits specified for either operand is outside the range 0–31, then a program exception, called a *reserved-operand fault* (an error condition usually causing program termination), will occur. If the source and destination operands overlap, the results of the instruction are unpredictable; in other words, a leading separate numeric string cannot be converted to packed decimal "in place."

Example 6.19: Converting from Leading Separate Numeric to Packed Decimal

Suppose that the bytes beginning at DATUM are as follows:

DATUM

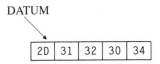

The instruction

```
CVTSP    #4,DATUM,#5,PKD
```

will cause the bytes beginning at PKD to be filled as follows:

PKD

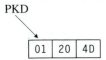

Note that a packed-decimal number always has an odd number of digits. If the programmer had specified #4 as the third operand of the CVTSP instruction in Example 6.19, three full bytes would have been filled (with five digits) anyway.

The CVTPL instruction converts from packed-decimal format to a two's complement longword integer. Its format is

$$CVTPL \quad p\_num\_digits, packed, long$$

The first operand is the number of digits (not the number of bytes) in the packed-decimal datum. The third operand is the longword result.

Many of the warnings mentioned above for the CVTSP instruction apply to CVTPL also: R0–R3 are used for scratch work (but they can be used as the destination operand because the result is stored last), the number of digits must be between 0 and 31, and the source operand must be in packed-decimal format. Overflow can occur with CVTPL, since the largest two's complement longword integer has only ten digits. CVTPL will work properly if the operands overlap.

Example 6.20: Converting Packed Decimal to Two's Complement

Continuing Example 6.19, the instruction

```
CVTPL    #5,PKD,R7
```

puts the two's complement representation of -1204_{10} in R7.

Example 6.21: A Program to Read and Convert Data

```
; PROBLEM STATEMENT
;
; This program reads a line (from the terminal) that contains
; six 4-digit signed integers. The integers are converted to
; two's complement and are stored in the word array NUMBERS.
; The format of the integers in the line is assumed to be
;
;       sddddbbbsddddbbbsddddbbbsddddbbbsddddbbbsdddd
;
; where     s = sign (+, -, or blank)
;           d = digit (There may be leading zeros.)
;           b = blank
;
NUMBERS:.BLKW   6
LINE:   .BLKB   80
PKD:    .BLKB   3
;
; REGISTER USE
;
;       R6      array pointer
;       R7      pointer to leading separate
;               numeric string to be converted
;       R8      loop counter
;       R9      scratch
;
        BEGIN   CONVERT
        MOVAW   NUMBERS,R6              ; Initialize array pointer
        MOVAB   LINE,R7                 ; Initialize string pointer
        MOVL    #6,R8                   ; Initialize loop counter
        READLINE LINE                   ; Read the line
;
CVT:    CVTSP   #4,(R7),#4,PKD          ; Convert to packed
        CVTPL   #4,PKD,R9               ; Convert to longword
        CVTLW   R9,(R6)+                ; Convert to word and store
        ADDL2   #8,R7                   ; Increment string pointer
        SOBGTR  R8,CVT                  ; Loop control
;
;       [instructions to do some work on the data]
;
        EXIT
        .END    CONVERT
```

Remarks: The rigid format of the input makes the programmer's task of finding and convert-ing the input data quite simple. However, it would be more convenient for the user of the program if the input could be typed in a less rigid format (e.g., not requiring leading zeros on numbers with fewer than four digits). The test, comparison, and branching instructions presented in Chapter 7 are used there to process free-format input.

Converting from Two's Complement to Character Code

To print out integer data that are represented internally in two's complement, the process described above is reversed; that is, we convert first from two's complement to packed decimal, then to leading separate numeric. The instructions used are CVTLP and CVTPS.

$$\text{CVTLP} \quad long, p\_num\_digits, packed$$

converts a longword (the first operand) from two's complement to packed decimal.

$$\text{CVTPS} \quad p\_num\_digits, packed, s\_num\_digits, lsn$$

converts from packed decimal to leading separate numeric. (The source and destination operands must not overlap.) CVTPS always puts a + or − character in the leading separate numeric result (i.e., it does not leave the sign blank for a positive number).

For both instructions, if the number of significant digits in the source operand is smaller than the number specified for the destination, leading zeros will be filled in. If the actual number of digits is larger than what is specified for the destination, overflow occurs and the result stored is not the correct value.

Example 6.22: Converting and Printing a Result

Suppose that R4 contains a longword integer known to be no larger than 50,000, and we want to print the integer with an appropriate message. The following assembler directives set up the message and reserve storage space used in the conversions.

```
LINE:   .ASCII  /The answer is /
LSN:    .BLKB   7                       ; 6 for lsn, one zero byte
                                        ;   to terminate the string
PKD:    .BLKB   3
```

Suppose that R4 contains 000001E3. The conversion instructions and their effects are

```
        CVTLP   R4,#5,PKD               ; Convert answer to packed
```

which produces

PKD

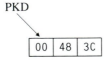

```
        00 | 48 | 3C
```

and

```
        CVTPS   #5,PKD,#5,LSN           ; Convert answer to lsn
```

which produces

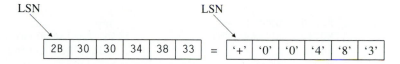

The message and the number may be printed using

```
        PRINTCHRS LINE                        ; Print answer
```

which prints the line

```
The answer is +00483
```

Usually, we do not want the plus sign and the leading zeros to be printed. They can be eliminated, but not, in the general case, with instructions we have covered so far. (If the result is known to be positive, we could use a MOVB instruction to blank out the plus sign.)

6.6 A DEBUGGER EXAMPLE

In this section we illustrate the use of the VAX Debugger to debug an incorrect version of the program in Example 6.21. We go through the example in detail, as much to illustrate debugging strategy as to show the use of the debugger itself. Here is the program.

```
; PROBLEM STATEMENT
;
; This program reads a line (from the terminal) that contains
; six 4-digit signed integers. The integers are converted to
; two's complement and are stored in the word array NUMBERS.
; The format of the integers in the line is assumed to be
;
;     sddddbbbsddddbbbsddddbbbsddddbbbsddddbbbsdddd
;
; where      s = sign (+, -, or blank)
;            d = digit (There may be leading zeros.)
;            b = blank
;
NUMBERS:.BLKW    6
LINE:    .BLKB    80
PKD:     .BLKB    3
;
; REGISTER USE
;
;          R6       array pointer
;          R7       pointer to leading separate
;                   numeric string to be converted
;          R8       loop counter
;          R9       scratch
```

```
        ;
                BEGIN    CONVERT
                MOVAW    NUMBERS,R6          ; Initialize array pointer
                MOVAB    LINE,R7             ; Initialize string pointer
                MOVL     #6,R8               ; Initialize loop counter
                READLINE LINE                ; Read the line
        ;
        CVT:    CVTSP    #4,(R7),#4,PKD      ; Convert to packed
                CVTPL    #4,PKD,R9           ; Convert to longword
                CVTLW    R9,(R6)+            ; Convert to word and store
                ADDL2    #7,R7               ; Increment string pointer
                SOBGTR   R8,CVT              ; Loop control
        ;
        ;       [instructions to do some work on the data]
        ;
                EXIT
                .END     CONVERT
```

Suppose that we assemble, link, and run without using the debugger. The program prompts for input, and we type the following line:

```
    0001     0002     0003     0004     0005     0006
```

The following error message will appear on the screen:

```
%SYSTEM-F-ROPRAND, reserved operand fault at PC=000006E2, PSL=03C00020
%TRACE-F-TRACEBACK, symbolic stack dump follows
module name     routine name                    line      rel PC      abs PC

.MAIN.          CONVERT                                   00000068    000006E2
```

What might have caused this error? In Section 6.5 we mentioned that the CVTSP instruction is a common cause of reserved operand faults. There are two ways we can find out if the CVTSP instruction is the culprit here.

If we have a listing file for the program, we can use the "rel PC" (relative PC) value in the message to locate the error. The "rel PC" is the contents of the program counter when the error occurred, relative to the entry point of the program. So add the "rel PC" value to the location of the BEGIN statement. The result will indeed be the location of the CVTSP instruction.[1]

The second, and usually simpler, way to find the offending instruction is to let the debugger tell us which it is. After assembling and linking the program with the /DEBUG option, and then running it, we get the following message from the debugger.

---

[1] As we will see in Chapter 8, sometimes this method gives the address of the next instruction following the one that caused the error.

```
$ run program

        VAX DEBUG Version V5.2-015

%DEBUG-I-INITIAL, language is MACRO, module set to .MAIN.

DBG> go
??  0001    0002    0003    0004    0005    0006
%SYSTEM-F-ROPRAND, reserved operand fault at PC=000006E2, PSL=03C00020
break on unhandled exception at .MAIN.\CONVERT\CVT
    32: CVT:    CVTSP   #4,(R7),#4,PKD              ; Convert to packed
DBG>
```

The debugger displays the error message and the instruction that caused it.

What can go wrong with the CVTSP instruction? A reserved operand fault occurs if any of the bytes in the leading separate numeric operand are not of the correct type (sign or digit), or if the number of digits specified is outside the legal range. A quick glance at the instruction lets us rule out the second possibility; the numbers of digits are stated as literals, and they are clearly within range (0–31). Something is wrong with the leading separate numeric string in memory beginning at the address in R7. It may be that the data are bad, or it may be that the pointer itself (the address in R7) is wrong. At this point we should check that we typed the input in the correct format—there may be nothing wrong with the program itself. Read the description of the input format in the program, and check the input line shown above. The input line is typed correctly,[2] so we conclude that the program probably does have a bug.

R7 should contain an address somewhere in the input line. We do not know exactly where it will be, because we do not know if some of the numbers in the input have already been correctly converted. That is, we do not know how many times the statements in the loop were executed before the error occurred. What information should we request from the debugger? Any of the following may be helpful.

- The value of LINE and the contents of R7: to see where in the line R7 is pointing.

- The contents of memory locations pointed to by R7.

- The contents of R8, the loop counter: to see how many of the input integers have already been converted.

Here is the transcript of our requests and the debugger's response.

```
DBG> eval/addr/dec line
1575
DBG> ex/dec r7,r8
.MAIN.\CONVERT\%R7:     1582
.MAIN.\CONVERT\%R8:    5
DBG>
```

---

[2] The READLINE prompt includes one blank. The input line itself begins with one blank.

We requested the value of LINE and the contents of R7 in decimal to make the subtraction easy. We see that R7 contains the address of the eighth byte of the line. (Are you convinced that it is the eighth byte, not the seventh?) R8 contains 5, and since it was initialized to 6, the loop was executed once already, and the program is now trying to convert the second integer in the input line.

To examine the byte pointed to by R7, we specify its address in hex. Rather than do the conversion ourselves, we ask the debugger for the pointer value in hex (the default for the EXAMINE command).

```
DBG> ex r7
.MAIN.\CONVERT\%R7:        0000062E
DBG> ex/ascii 62e
.MAIN.\LINE[7]: ' '
```

The byte contains a blank, which is okay because the first byte of a leading separate numeric operand must be a sign or blank. Have you found the problem yet?

Suppose that we have not yet figured out what is wrong. We examine all the bytes in the CVTSP operand. We expect them to contain '0002'. Here are the results of our examination.

```
DBG> ex/ascii line[7],line[8],line[9],line[10],line[11]
.MAIN.\LINE[7]: ' '
.MAIN.\LINE[8]: ' '
.MAIN.\LINE[9]: '0'
.MAIN.\LINE[10]:          '0'
.MAIN.\LINE[11]:          '0'
DBG>
```

The second byte contains a blank, not a digit. That caused the reserved operand fault. A CVTSP operand must be a sign (or blank) followed by digits. Where is the '2'?

```
DBG> ex/ascii line[12]
.MAIN.\LINE[12]:          '2'
```

So R7 is not pointing to the sign byte for the second input number, '0002' (i.e., the byte that precedes its first digit). At this point we may want to check the input line again to make sure that we did not type an extra blank before the second integer in the line. We did not. So R7 points to the wrong byte; the address in R7 should be larger by 1 than it is. Since the first input was converted without error, we may assume that R7 was properly initialized. (We can check by looking at the MOVAB instruction; it is fine.) Was R7 incremented correctly? The ADDL2 instruction near the end of the loop adds 7 to R7. There is the program error! The integers in the input are eight spaces apart, not seven. If we change the operand #7 to #8 in the ADDL2 instruction, the program will run correctly.

Notice that the most important part of the work done in this example was the thinking. The debugger helps provide clues and helps confirm (or eliminate) guesses. To debug efficiently, the programmer must generate theories, determine what evidence will be useful, collect the evidence, interpret it, and perhaps modify the theories a few times, and repeat the process.

TABLE 6.1 INTEGER RANGES

Type	Bits	Range (signed)	Range (unsigned)
—	n	-2^{n-1} to $2^{n-1} - 1$	0 to $2^n - 1$
Byte	8	-128 to 127	0 to 255
Word	16	$-32{,}768$ to $32{,}767$	0 to 65,535
Longword	32	$-2{,}147{,}483{,}648$ to $2{,}147{,}483{,}647$	0 to 4,294,967,295
Quadword	64	-2^{63} to $2^{63} - 1$	0 to $2^{64} - 1$

6.7 SUMMARY

There are signed integer arithmetic instructions to add, subtract, multiply, and divide bytes, words, and longwords. There are two-operand and three-operand versions of each kind of instruction. Integer division instructions truncate the quotient toward zero. Table 6.1 shows the ranges of integers that may be stored in the various memory units.

Byte and word instructions with register operands use only the rightmost byte or word, respectively, of the register. There are special instructions to increment, decrement, clear (set to zero), and negate.

Integer arithmetic instructions and virtually all other instructions described in this chapter set condition code bits in the PSW to indicate the sign of the result and to indicate if the result overflowed. The SOBGTR instruction is a loop control instruction that may be used to execute instructions in a loop a specified number of times.

The CVT (ConVerT) instructions convert data from one data type to another. Conversion between integer types is straightforward: conversion to a longer integer is done by sign extension (i.e., by copying the sign bit into the left end of the result) and conversion to a shorter type is done by dropping bits at the left. (Overflow may occur in the latter case.)

Conversion between character code and two's complement is a more complex process and uses the data types *leading separate numeric* and *packed decimal* as intermediate data formats. The CVTSP, CVTPL, CVTLP, and CVTPS instructions do the conversions.

Table 6.2 lists all the instructions introduced in this chapter.

Some general guidelines for good programming are

- Document programs well. Include a statement of the problem, a description of the data used, an explanation of the method used to solve the problem, a list of the registers used and their roles, brief comments on the instructions, and blank comment lines to separate sections of a program.

- Use registers rather than memory locations for intermediate results of a computation; fetching and storing data in memory takes more time than using data in registers.

- Do not destroy or modify input data if you do not need to. The data may be needed by another part of the program.

TABLE 6.2 INSTRUCTIONS

		Arithmetic	
ADDx2	$op1,op2$	x = B, W, or L	$op1 + op2 \rightarrow op2$
ADDx3	$op1,op2,sum$	"	$op1 + op2 \rightarrow sum$
SUBx2	$op1,op2$	"	$op2 - op1 \rightarrow op2$
SUBx3	$op1,op2,dif$	"	$op2 - op1 \rightarrow dif$
MULx2	$op1,op2$	"	$op1*op2 \rightarrow op2$
MULx3	$op1,op2,prod$	"	$op1*op2 \rightarrow prod$
DIVx2	$op1,op2$	"	$op2/op1 \rightarrow op2$
DIVx3	$op1,op2,quo$	"	$op2/op1 \rightarrow quo$
INCx	op	"	$op + 1 \rightarrow op$
DECx	op	"	$op - 1 \rightarrow op$
MNEGx	$source,dest$	"	$-source \rightarrow dest$
CLRx	$dest$	x = B, W, L, Q, or O	$0 \rightarrow dest$

	Loop instruction	
SOBGTR $index,dest$	$index$ is longword	$index - 1 \rightarrow index$; if $index > 0$, branch to $dest$

	Data conversion	
CVTxy $source,dest$	x and y = B, W, or L $x \neq y$	$source$ (of type x) converted to type $y \rightarrow dest$
† CVTxy $n1,src,n2,dest$	x = S and y = P, or x = P and y = S; $n1$ and $n2$ are words (0–31)	src (with $n1$ digits), converted from type x to type y (with $n2$ digits) $\rightarrow dest$
† CVTPL $n,pkd,long$	n is a word	pkd (with n digits) converted from packed to 2's comp. $\rightarrow long$
† CVTLP $long,n,pkd$	"	long converted from 2's comp. to packed (with n digits) $\rightarrow pkd$

† Uses R0–R3.

6.8 EXERCISES

1. Write an instruction to multiply the word at GALLONS by 8 and store the product in the word PINTS.

2. Write an instruction to subtract the byte at USED from the byte at ONHAND, leaving the result in ONHAND.

3. Redo Example 6.3 using only four instructions and one register for scratch work.

4. Write instructions to compute $15x^2 - 3x^4 + 17$ and store the result in the word VALUE. Assume that x is in the word DATUM and the numbers are small enough that overflow will not occur.

5. Subtract the two's complement byte integer B7 from the two's complement byte integer 0A using both methods described in the text. Is there a carry from the leftmost bit when you use the negate-and-add method? Is there a borrow in the leftmost place when you directly subtract?

6. Using the characterization of negative two's complement numbers described in Chapter 3 (i.e., that a negative number n is represented by $2^s - |n|$, where s is the number of bits in the representation), show that the second method described in Section 6.2 for doing subtraction (i.e., subtracting as unsigned binary integers, with a borrow at the leftmost position, if needed) will always work no matter what the signs of the operands (assuming no overflow).

7. In Fig. 6.1 two positive integers are multiplied. Use the method shown there to multiply two negative byte integers. Does it work correctly?

8. For integer division, what is the relationship between the sign of the dividend and the sign of the remainder (when the remainder is not zero)? Are they always the same? Always opposite? Sometimes the same and sometimes opposite? Justify your answer with an argument or examples.

9. Write four different instructions each of which has the effect of setting all bits in R5 to zero.

10. Suppose that the following statement appears in a high-level language program where all the variables are longword integers. (Assume that *SQR* is a function that squares its argument.) Write assembly language instructions to carry out the computation.

```
K := SQR(7*I+J/LL)
```

11. Write instructions to determine the profits made by an organization's fund-raising dinner using the following data. Advertising, speaker fees, and other fixed costs were $528, and the dinners cost $19 each (tax and tip included). The ticket price was $30 each, or $225 for a group of eight. Seventy-six individual tickets and three group-of-eight tickets were sold. Use a data size you consider reasonable and include data-initialization directives for the variables in the problem. (The program segment should be written so that only the data initialization, not the machine instructions, need be changed to use the program for another fund-raising dinner.)

12. For *each* of parts a, b, and c below, start with the following data in R7, R8, and R9. (All data in registers are shown in hex.)

R7   00012CA2

R8   00000002

R9   00000023

(a) After the instruction

```
MULW3    R8,R9,(R7)+
```

is executed, what will be in R7, R8, and R9? Are the contents of any memory locations changed by this instruction? If so, give the address of each byte changed.

(b) What will be in R7 and R8 after executing the following instruction?

```
CVTWL    R7,R8
```

(c) What will be in R7 and R9 after executing the following instruction?

```
SUBL2    R9,R7
```

13. Assume that the contents of registers and memory are as shown below before *each* of the instructions below is executed. For each instruction, show the new contents of all registers and memory locations that are changed by the instruction and indicate which, if any, will cause overflow.

Registers	Memory	Address
R4		
00013B64	003520C1	00013B60
R7	FFFFFE75	00013B64
FFFAFF1C	.	.
R8	.	.
0000258A	.	.
R9	000009B4	00C27DE8
00C27DE8	00175B3D	00C27DEC

(a) ADDL2 (R9)+,(R4)   (e) CVTLW R7,R7
(b) DIVB2 #4,R9   (f) MNEGW R4,R4
(c) DIVB3 R7,R4,(R9)   (g) DECW   (R4)+
(d) CVTBL R7,R8   (h) CLRW   (R4)

14. In Example 6.5 the following instructions were used to compute an amount to be billed, assuming a 20% discount:

```
DIVL3    #5,TOTAL,R7           ; Compute discount
SUBL3    R7,TOTAL,AMOUNT       ; Subtract discount
```

Suppose that these instructions were used instead:

```
MULL3    #4,TOTAL,R7           ; 4*total
DIVL3    #5,R7,AMOUNT          ; 80% of total
```

Will the result in AMOUNT be the same in both cases? Comment on any other differences you think there might be in speed, accuracy, or clarity between the two sequences of instructions.

15. Write instructions to compute the average of five integers stored in the word array SCORES, and put the result in the word AVERAGE. Do not use a loop.

16. Suppose that 80 bytes of memory beginning at the byte labeled LINE have been initialized so that each byte contains the character code for a blank. There is a name in memory (in ASCII code) beginning at a byte labeled NAME; the length of the name is in R6. Write instructions to copy the name to the *center* of the 80-byte line. (In other words, when you are done, there should be an equal number of blanks before and after the name. If the length of the name is odd, it does not matter whether the one "extra" blank is before or after the name.)

17. Suppose that you want to divide the positive longword in ALPHA by the positive longword in BETA and put the result in the longword GAMMA, but you want a rounded, rather than truncated, result. Write instructions to do this. (Three instructions suffice.) Will your method work if the divisor and/or dividend may be negative? If so, explain why. If not, show an example where it gives the wrong answer.

18. The formula for converting a temperature from Fahrenheit to centigrade is

$$centigrade = \frac{5}{9}\,(Fahrenheit - 32).$$

Write instructions to convert the word integer at FAREN to centigrade and store the result in the word integer at CENT.

19. Suppose that the VAX did not have the special-purpose instructions INCx, DECx, and MNEGx. For each of the following instructions, write one other instruction that would accomplish the same thing.

    (a) INCW   R3   **(c)** MNEGL   (R5)+,(R10)
    (b) DECL   (R7)+

20. Quadword addition can be done using the ADDL2 and the ADWC (AdD With Carry) instructions. Like ADDL2, ADWC adds its first operand (a longword) to its second operand (a longword), but it also adds the value of the C (Carry) condition code bit. The ADD instructions set the C bit to 1 if there is a carry out of the most significant bit. Write instructions to add the quadword at QUAD to the quadword in R8 and R9 (with the least significant part in R8).

21. **(a)** Suppose that ALPHA and BETA contain unsigned byte integers. That is, if bit 7 is on, it represents 2^7; it is not a sign bit. The product of the two integers could be as large as a word. Write instructions to compute the unsigned product and store it in the word at GAMMA.

    (b) Suppose that ALPHA and BETA contain two's complement (signed) byte integers. Write instructions to compute the full word-length two's complement product and store it in the word at GAMMA. (Recall that the MULB instructions produce only a byte result. If the product is too large for a byte, only the least significant half is stored in the result and overflow occurs.)

22. What will be in R6 and R9 at the end of the program segment in Example 6.8?

23. Write instructions to add up all the entries in the longword array LIST and put the sum in the longword SUM. Assume that the longword COUNT contains the number of array entries.

24. Write instructions to subtract 1 from every fourth entry in the word array COUNT-ERS, beginning with the fourth entry. The number of entries is in the word NUM. You may assume there are at least four entries, but the number of entries may not be divisible by four.

25. Suppose that we want to copy the entire word array A1 into the word array A2, and the longword NUM contains the number of entries. This could be done with a simple loop similar to those in examples in Section 6.3. However, it can also be done using only two instructions. Show how.

26. What is the maximum number of times the body of a loop controlled by an SOBGTR instruction can execute?

27. What number will be in R10 after the following statements are executed?

```
          CLRL     R10
          MOVL     #10,R8
LOOP:     INCL     R10
          DECL     R8
          SOBGTR   R8,LOOP
```

28. Suppose that you are given a word array DATA and a longword N containing the number of array entries. Suppose that we denote the entries $a_1, a_2, \ldots, a_n$, where $n = (N)$. For each i between 1 and n, we define the ith partial sum to be $a_1 + a_2 + \cdots + a_i$. That is, the ith partial sum is the sum of the first i entries. Write a program segment to replace the entries by the partial sums; when your program segment finishes executing, the ith partial sum should be in DATA[i]. (*Hint:* This can be done with a surprisingly short loop, only two instructions, using autoincrement mode appropriately. Look at Example 6.8.)

29. What will be in R6 at the end of the program segment in Example 6.9 if (NUM) = 0?

30. What happens if the file read in Example 6.11 is empty? Will the program crash? If not, what will be in COUNT when it terminates?

31. Suppose that MATRIX is a two-dimensional longword array whose dimensions are stored in the longwords ROWS and COLMS. The row and column numbering begins at 1. Assume that I and J are longwords containing a row number and a column number, respectively. Write a formula for the address of the entry that would be denoted in a high-level language by MATRIX[I,J]. Do the same problem for an array where the row and column numbers start at 0.

32. Suppose that A is a $p \times q$ longword matrix and B is a $q \times r$ longword matrix. The formula for entries in the product matrix, $C = A \times B$, is

$$c_{ij} = \sum_{k=1}^{q} a_{ik}b_{kj} \quad \text{for } 1 \leq i \leq p \text{ and } 1 \leq j \leq r.$$

Write instructions to compute the product matrix.

33. Suppose that PRICE is an array with 250 entries containing the price of a stock on 250 consecutive trading days. In another array, called MOV_AVG, compute the average price of the most recent five days. (This is called the 5-day moving average.) In other words (using Pascal notation) MOV_AVG[I] = the average of PRICE[J] for J = I–4, I–3, I–2, I–1, and I. You may simply store zeros in the first four entries of MOV_AVG. Compute rounded averages instead of truncated averages. (You may assume that all the data are positive.) There are several solutions for this problem; try to find an efficient one.

34. Will the overflow condition code be set as a result of executing the instruction in Example 6.15? Why or why not?

35. Could the problem in Example 6.16 be solved by adding the elements in the array BLOCKS using an ADDB instruction, then converting the total to a longword with a CVTBL instruction? Why or why not?

36. The MOVZxy (MOVe Zero-extended) instructions (for xy = BW, BL, and WL) extend the first operand by adding zeros at the left end, and put the result in the second operand. How do these instructions differ from the CVT instructions? Could a MOVZ instruction have been used in place of either of the CVT instructions in Example 6.16?

37. The entries in the byte array DELTA are to be subtracted from the corresponding entries in the longword array VALUES; the new values should replace the old ones in the VALUES array. The number of entries in each array is in the longword POINTS. Write instructions to do this.

38. Using the record format described in Exercise 10 of Chapter 5, write a program to read all the records in the file and store them in memory in a character array called MAILING_LIST, then go through the array and format and print the entries as described in that exercise with a blank line after each one. The program should reserve space for 20 entries and should make sure that no more than 20 are read and stored.

39. Show the representation of the number -4927_{10} in
    (a) Leading separate numeric format.
    (b) Packed decimal format.

40. Given the data shown, for each instruction below tell if it will cause a reserved-operand fault, and if not, show what it puts in the bytes beginning at PKD.

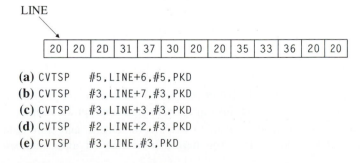

LINE

20	20	2D	31	37	30	20	20	35	33	36	20	20

(a) CVTSP   #5,LINE+6,#5,PKD
(b) CVTSP   #3,LINE+7,#3,PKD
(c) CVTSP   #3,LINE+3,#3,PKD
(d) CVTSP   #2,LINE+2,#3,PKD
(e) CVTSP   #3,LINE,#3,PKD

41. Show the contents of R7 (in hex) after the CVTPL instruction in Example 6.20 is executed.

42. Write instructions to convert the word at ALPHA from two's complement to character code and print it preceded by a message saying ALPHA = .

43. Suppose that a program contains the following statements:

```
BLANK = ^A/ /
TEMP:    .BLKB    2                    ; Space for packed
MSG:     .ASCII   /My car is/
AGE:     .BLKB    3
         .ASCIZ   / years old./
         .
         .
         .
         CVTLP    R6,#2,TEMP
         CVTPS    #2,TEMP,#2,AGE
         MOVB     #BLANK,AGE
         PRINTCHRS MSG
```

Suppose that R6 contains 0000000B when the instructions are executed. Show what will be in the two bytes beginning at TEMP and in the three bytes beginning at AGE after they are executed. Show exactly what will be printed by the PRINTCHRS statement. (Show clearly where there are blanks.)

44. Write instructions to convert and print out all the longword integers in the array NUMBERS, assuming that the longword NUM contains the number of entries and each entry has at most six digits. The numbers should be printed in a column with an appropriate heading.

45. Write a complete program that reads I, J, and LL from the terminal, computes the expression in Exercise 10, and prints out K. The program documentation should describe the format in which the input data are expected.

46. Suppose that the file DATA.DAT contains the list of courses a student is taking this semester. The first line tells the number of courses (one digit). The remaining lines each contain a course name (using eight spaces), a blank, and the number of units for that course (one digit, always in column 10). Here is an example:

```
5
CS 237    3
PE 100    2
CHEM 200 5
CS 310    3
ENG 101   3
```

Write a program to print the list of courses on the screen and print the total number of units the student is taking this semester. Include appropriate headings.

47. Write a program to read, convert to two's complement, and store data for a two-dimensional longword array. You may assume that all input numbers have five digits (including leading zeros) and are arranged in the input line in a standard format. The first line of input is to contain the array dimensions, number of rows first. You may assume that the number of rows and the number of columns are at most 10. After the line containing the dimensions, there is one line for each row of the array.

48. Write instructions to print a two-dimensional longword array. The entries have at most five significant digits, and ROWS and COLMS are longwords containing the number of rows and columns, respectively. You may assume that the number of columns (i.e., the number of entries in each row) is at most 10. If you have done Exercise 47, combine it with this one, and run the program to read, store, and then print the array.

49. Write instructions to print a longword array in two-column format. Assume that the longword N contains the number of entries. You may assume that (N) is even. The first half of the array should appear in the first column, and the second half in the second column.

7

Branching and Looping

7.1 CONDITION CODES AND BRANCHING

Condition Codes and Branch Instructions

A branch instruction is an instruction that can load a new address into the program counter, so that the instruction executed next will be the one at that new address instead of the one that is physically next in memory. Most branch instructions are *conditional branches*; that is, they may or may not change the PC, depending on the condition of data just operated on. The VAX, and many other computers, use one-bit flags called *condition codes* to record properties of the operands of instructions. The conditional branch instructions test these flags to determine whether or not to change the PC.

On the VAX, the condition codes are the first (rightmost) four bits of the PSW. Their names are N, Z, V, and C, and they are located in the PSW as follows:

The most frequent uses of the codes are as follows:

N—Negative   N = 1 if the result of an operation is negative.

                       After a comparison, N = 1 if the first operand is less than the second.

Z—Zero   Z = 1 if the result of an operation is zero.
                After a comparison, Z = 1 if the operands are equal.
V—oVerflow   V = 1 if the result of an operation overflowed the space allotted
                for it.
C—Carry   C = 1 if an operation had a carry or borrow in the leftmost bit.
                After an integer comparison, C = 1 if the first operand is
                less than the second as unsigned integers.

Thus, conditional branching involves two steps. First the condition codes are set, either explicitly by a test or comparison instruction, or implicitly as a side effect of another instruction. Almost all instructions affect the codes. All integer arithmetic, move, and convert instructions set N, Z, and V to indicate whether the result of the operation is negative, zero, or overflowed. (If a result overflows, N and Z indicate the condition of the true result, not the truncated part stored in the destination operand.) Arithmetic instructions for other data types (floating point and packed decimal) affect the N and Z bits similarly. Integer addition instructions set the C bit if there was a carry from the leftmost bit (and clear it otherwise). Integer subtraction instructions set the C bit if there was *not* a carry from the leftmost bit during the addition of the negated sutrahend and the minuend. Another way to interpret the C bit for subtraction is that it is set if there is a borrow for the leftmost bit when subtracting the operands as unsigned binary integers. The treatment of V and C for other data types depends on the particular instruction. From now on, whenever we introduce new instructions, we will indicate how they affect the condition codes. In general, the reader who wants more detail than we present in this book can consult the *VAX-11 Programming Card* or the *VAX MACRO and Instruction Set Reference Manual*.

The second step in conditional branching includes testing the condition codes to determine whether the branch should be taken, and if so, loading the branch address into the PC. Usually, the second step is performed by a conditional branch instruction, though some instructions perform both steps. SOBGTR, for example, does a subtraction on the loop index, setting the condition codes, then tests the codes and branches if the appropriate condition holds.

The VAX has a large set of conditional branch instructions. They include instructions to be used after operations on signed data (two's complement integers, floating-point numbers, and packed decimal numbers), some to be used after operations on unsigned data (e.g., unsigned binary integers and addresses), instructions that test for carry and overflow, and a few others. The interpretation (by the programmer) of the branch instruction depends on the context in which the condition codes were set. After a test or an arithmetic operation, for example, they reflect the condition of one datum; after a comparison, they describe the relation between the two data compared. The CPU interprets the conditional branch instructions as indicating specific tests to be done on the condition codes. For example, BEQL will cause a branch if and only if the Z bit is 1; BGTR will cause a branch if and only if both Z = 0 and N = 0. The conditional branch instructions themselves do not change the current settings of the condition codes. Table 7.1 lists the branch instructions and their interpretations. The two unconditional branch instructions, BRB and BRW, which cause a branch no matter what values the condition codes have, are included in the table.

The format of the branch instructions is

$$B\textit{xyz} \quad \textit{destination}$$

where xyz = one of the many branch conditions. The destination is specified by an address expression. For all the branch instructions in Table 7.1 there is a limit on how far away the branch destination may be. For all but BRW, the machine code for the instruction allows one byte to encode the distance to the branch destination, so it must be within approximately 127 bytes from the branch instruction. As we will see in Chapter 8, the number of bytes needed to encode an instruction can vary quite a bit depending on the addressing modes used, but we can make a rough estimate of 4–5 bytes per instruction on the average. Thus the branch instructions can branch over roughly 25–30 instructions. For BRW, a word is used to encode the distance to the destination, so BRW can be used to branch to instructions that are quite far away.

Example 7.1: Conditional Branching

Problem: A person's bank balance is in the longword whose address is in R8, and R6 contains the amount of a check written on the account. There is a 20-cent check charge. All money amounts are stored as integers representing the number of cents. Compute and store the new balance if the check clears; branch to OVRDRN otherwise.

Discussion: The SUB instructions set the condition codes to indicate the sign of the result of the subtraction; thus a conditional branch may be used immediately after subtracting the amount of the check and check charge. The subtractions will be done in a register so that the old balance is not changed in the case where the account is overdrawn.

Solution:

```
; REGISTER USE
;
;       R6        amount of check
;       R8        address of balance
;       R10       computation
;
        SUBL3     R6,(R8),R10              ; Subtract check
        SUBL2     #20,R10                  ; Subtract check charge
        BLSS      OVRDRN                   ; Branch if overdrawn
        MOVL      R10,(R8)                 ; Store new balance
```

Suppose that the balance was $150.00 and the check is written for $149.95. The result of the first subtraction is positive, but the result after subtracting the check charge is negative. The following table shows the values of the condition codes after each instruction.

INSTRUCTION		N	Z	V	C
SUBL3	R6,(R8),R10	0	0	0	0
SUBL2	#20,R10	1	0	0	1
BLSS	OVRDRN		unchanged		

There is a branch to OVRDRN because N = 1.

The C bit is set by SUBL2 because subtraction of 20 from 5 requires a borrow in the leftmost place. Specifically:

$$
\begin{array}{rr}
100000005 & 5 \\
-\ 00000014 & -20 \\
\hline
\text{FFFFFFF1} & -15
\end{array}
$$

TABLE 7.1   BRANCH INSTRUCTIONS

Instruction	Interpretation by Programmer		
	After a Test Branch if	*After a Comparison Branch if*	*Branch If and Only If*
For signed data			
BEQL	operand = 0	operands are equal	Z = 1
BNEQ	operand ≠ 0	operands not equal	Z = 0
BGTR	operand > 0	op1 > op2	N = 0 and Z = 0
BLEQ	operand ≤ 0	op1 ≤ op2	N = 1 or Z = 1
BGEQ	operand ≥ 0	op1 ≥ op2	N = 0
BLSS	operand < 0	op1 < op2	N = 1
For unsigned data			
B*xyz*U where *xyz* may be any of the six conditions above		Same as above	As above, but with C in place of N
For overflow and carry			
BVS		Branch if overflow	V = 1
BVC		Branch if no overflow	V = 0
BCS		Branch if carry	C = 1
BCC		Branch if no carry	C = 0
Unconditional branches			
BRB		Always branch	
BRW		Always branch	
Bit 0 tests			
BLBS *op,dest*		Branch if bit 0 is set	These do not use condi-
BLBC *op,dest*		Branch if bit 0 is clear	tion codes.

Note that there are some pairs of conditional branches where both instructions branch on exactly the same condition code settings (for example, BEQL and BEQLU). They are really one machine instruction that has two names for the convenience of the programmer.

Test and Compare Instructions

Sometimes we want a conditional branch depending on the status of data that were not just used in an instruction. We can set the the condition codes explicitly with a test (TST) or compare (CMP) instruction. The formats of these instructions (for integer data) are

TSTx operand x = B, W, or L
CMPx op1,op2 x = B, W, or L

The main effect of these instructions is to set the condition codes; their operands are not modified at all. (Just like other instructions, they may alter the contents of registers used to address the operands if, for example, autoincrement mode is used.)

The TST instructions test two's complement integers. The N and Z bits indicate whether the operand is negative or zero; the C and V bits are cleared (set to 0).

The CMP instructions compare two operands as two's complement integers and also as unsigned integers. Z indicates whether or not the operands are equal, N indicates whether the first is less than the second as signed integers, and C indicates whether the first is less than the second as unsigned integers. V is cleared.

The CMP instructions actually work by subtracting the second operand from the first (the reverse of what the SUB instructions do). The N and Z condition codes are set to indicate the sign of the result of the subtraction. Thus, for example, N is set if *first op – second op* is negative, or in other words, if the first operand is less than the second. The subtraction is done in a CPU scratch area and the result is discarded; the operands are not changed.

Example 7.2: How a CMP Instruction Affects the Condition Codes

With the data

ALPHA   BETA

| 6A | | 94 |

the instruction

```
        CMPB      ALPHA,BETA
```

sets the condition codes as follows:

N = 0   because, as two's complement integers, (ALPHA) is positive and (BETA) is negative, so (ALPHA) is not less than (BETA).

Z = 0   because the operands are not equal.

V = 0   always after a CMP instruction.

C = 1   because, as unsigned binary integers, $6A_{16} < 94_{16}$.

Programming Considerations

Careful thought should be given to the organization of a program segment using conditional branches. The programmer should try to arrange instructions to satisfy the following two goals:

Use as few branches as possible.

Except for loops, branches should always go forward, not backward, in a program.

There are two reasons for these guidelines. One is clarity. It is difficult to understand (and write correct) programs in which the branching resembles tangled spaghetti. Also, branching is expensive (in terms of time) in many computers. Normally, the next instruction, or several instructions, are fetched from memory to a CPU scratch area, called an instruction buffer, before they are needed, so that when the CPU finishes executing one instruction, the next one will be available immediately. When a branch is taken, the prefetched instructions may all have to be discarded, and the CPU must wait briefly while the instruction at the branch destination is fetched.

It is helpful to write out conditional statements in a high-level language, then follow some straightforward guidelines to translate them into assembly language. Often a branch is used to distinguish between two cases where in one case some extra steps must be performed, while in the other case nothing special must be done. This situation is described by the high-level language **if** statement and flowchart segment in Fig 7.1. As Fig. 7.1(c) indicates, the programmer should choose the conditional branch instruction to branch on the condition for which the extra instructions are *not* performed. Then the two guidelines above are likely to be met. Compilers translate **if** statements this way.

Example 7.3: An if-then Statement

Problem: NAMES is an array of names, each 22 characters long. The array SCORES contains word integers; each entry is associated with the name at the corresponding position in the NAMES array. The longword COUNT contains the number of entries in each array. The problem is to print the names associated with scores between 75 and 85, inclusive, or, in other words:

$$\text{if } 75 \leq \text{score} \leq 85 \text{ then print name}$$

Solution:

```
; PROBLEM STATEMENT
;
; This program segment searches the array SCORES and prints
; names from the array NAMES in positions that correspond
; to scores between LOW and HIGH, inclusive.
;
; DATA
;
```

```
;       SCORES      word array
;       NAMES       character array, N_LENGTH characters per entry
;       COUNT       the number of entries in each array (longword)
;       N_LENGTH    the name length
;
; CONSTANTS
;
LOW = 75
HIGH = 85
N_LENGTH = 22
;
; REGISTER USE
;
;       R6          SCORES pointer
;       R7          NAMES pointer
;       R8          loop counter
;
        MOVL    COUNT,R8            ; Initialize loop counter
        BEQL    DONE                ; Branch if arrays are empty
        MOVAW   SCORES,R6           ; Initialize SCORES pointer
        MOVAB   NAMES,R7            ; Initialize NAMES pointer
;
COMPR:  CMPW    (R6),#LOW           ; Compare score to LOW
        BLSS    NEXT                ; If score < LOW, don't print
        CMPW    (R6),#HIGH          ; Compare score to HIGH
        BGTR    NEXT                ; If score high, don't print
        PRINTCHRS (R7),#N_LENGTH    ; Print name
NEXT:   ADDL2   #2,R6               ; Increment SCORES pointer
        ADDL2   #N_LENGTH,R7        ; Increment NAMES pointer
        SOBGTR  R8,COMPR            ; Loop control
;
DONE:   ; [next instruction]
```

Remarks: Note that the conditional branch instructions were chosen to branch on the negative of the condition in the **if** statement.

We have added a new feature to the documentation in this example: a list in tabular form of the data used and their types and roles. Putting it in tabular instead of paragraph form makes it easy to refer to. Such a table is useful, even for moderate-sized programs, both to the programmer, to avoid getting confused and making errors, and to anyone else who has to read or modify the program.

Why was autoincrement mode not used for the SCORES pointer? If it were used in the first CMPW instruction, then R6 would not be pointing to the same score when the second CMPW was executed, thus potentially causing incorrect results. If autoincrement mode were used on the second CMPW, then after the branch back to COMPR we would not know if R6 were pointing to the next score or still pointing to the previous

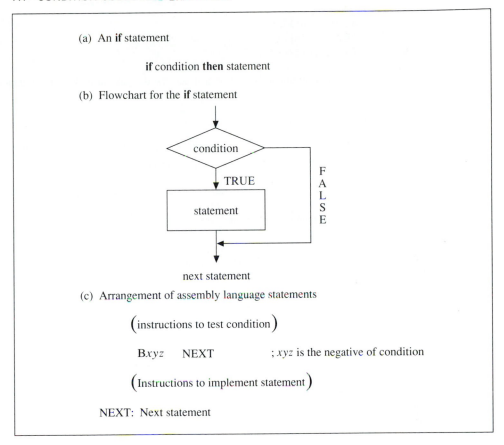

(a) An **if** statement

    if condition **then** statement

(b) Flowchart for the **if** statement

    condition

    TRUE   FALSE

    statement

    next statement

(c) Arrangement of assembly language statements

    $($ instructions to test condition $)$

    Bxyz NEXT   ; xyz is the negative of condition

    $($ Instructions to implement statement $)$

    NEXT: Next statement

Figure 7.1   Translating an **if** statement to assembly language

one, because the second CMPW instruction is not executed every time through the loop. So R6 is incremented explicitly at NEXT every time.

The **if-then-else** statement describes the situation where there are always two alternative sequences of operations to be performed, depending on some condition. Figure 7.2 shows a flowchart and pattern of assembly language statements for this situation.

Example 7.4: Branching to Far Destinations

Recall that the branch destination for conditional branches must be within roughly 127 bytes from the branch instruction. What should a programmer do if the branch destination is farther away? Suppose, for example, that we had the sequence

```
BGTR    THERE
[next instruction]
```

but that when assembling the program, the assembler gave an error message saying that the branch destination is out of range. Here is a solution:

```
        BLEQ    NEXT
        BRW     THERE
NEXT:   [next instruction]
```

Recall that BRW is an unconditional branch and the destination may be thousands of bytes away.

Comparing Character Strings

There are two instructions intended for comparing character strings. The simpler one is

$$\text{CMPC3} \quad length, string1, string2$$

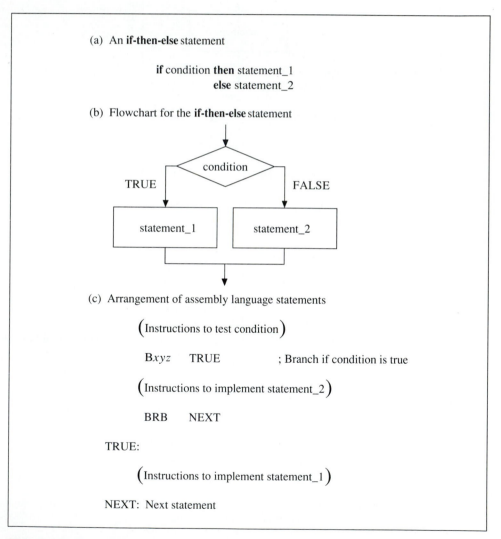

(a) An **if-then-else** statement

if condition **then** statement_1
                else statement_2

(b) Flowchart for the **if-then-else** statement

condition

TRUE   FALSE

statement_1   statement_2

(c) Arrangement of assembly language statements

$\left(\text{Instructions to test condition}\right)$

B*xyz*   TRUE   ; Branch if condition is true

$\left(\text{Instructions to implement statement\_2}\right)$

BRB   NEXT

TRUE:

$\left(\text{Instructions to implement statement\_1}\right)$

NEXT: Next statement

Figure 7.2 Translating an **if-then-else** statement

CMPC3 can compare long strings of bytes; the bytes may contain data other than character codes, though comparing character strings is what it is most commonly used for. Like the TST and integer CMP instructions, it does not modify its operands; its main effect is to set the condition codes.

The first operand gives the length of, or number of bytes in, each string. It must be a word integer and may be specified by a literal or any other addressing mode. The second and third operands specify the addresses of the first byte of each string. The strings must be in memory, not in registers or literals.

CMPC3 compares corresponding bytes in the two strings until it finds unequal bytes or reaches the ends of the strings (determined by the length operand). It sets the condition codes in the same ways as the integer CMP instructions (i.e., it does both signed and unsigned comparisons of the bytes).

The ASCII character codes for the letters of the alphabet are in numerical order; that is, the character code for "A" is less than the code for "B", and so on. Thus the condition code settings after a CMPC3 instruction can be used to sort (alphabetize) character data. The reader should look over the ASCII codes in Appendix C to see where various groups of characters are in the sequence of codes. For example, capital letters precede lowercase letters, and digits precede letters. The code for the blank character is less than the codes for letters and digits, so, for example, the strings "Mill   " and "Miller" could be put in the proper order without being treated as a special case.

If the strings compared do contain character codes, the N and C bits will have the same values, because all ASCII character codes are 0 in the leftmost bit and are interpreted as positive integers. Thus the signed or unsigned conditional branch instructions can be used with CMPC3 for searching and sorting character data.

Warning: The CMPC3 instruction uses R0–R3, destroying the original contents of these registers.

Example 7.5: Comparing Character Strings

R7 contains the address of an eight-character name. Another eight-character name is stored in memory immediately after the first. If the names are not in correct alphabetical order, they must be interchanged. In other words, the problem is to program the statement

if first name > second name **then** interchange names

We assume that an eight-byte area called TEMP is available for temporary use.

```
        ADDL3   #8,R7,R8        ; Address of second name
        CMPC3   #8,(R7),(R8)    ; Compare names
        BLEQ    NEXT            ; Branch if in order
        MOVC3   #8,(R7),TEMP    ; Move first name to TEMP
        MOVC3   #8,(R8),(R7)    ; Move 2nd name to 1st place
        MOVC3   #8,TEMP,(R8)    ; Move 1st name to 2nd place
NEXT:   ; [next instruction]
```

(In the next section we will describe another addressing mode, displacement mode, that lets us address the second name without needing the ADDL3 instruction and a second register.)

In many applications it is necessary to test a byte to see if it contains a particular character. For example, a program that monitors the characters coming in from a terminal might check each one to see if it is a carriage return. A test for one character can certainly be done with a CMPC3 instruction using a length of one, but it is better to use a CMPB instruction because the latter takes up less space in memory, requires less typing by the programmer, and can take a literal operand. The following instruction compares the byte at CHAR to the character "+" (or more precisely, the ASCII code for a plus).

```
          CMPB     CHAR,#^A/+/
```

Bit Flags

Bit flags are used for a variety of purposes, particularly to indicate the status of tasks performed by various programs and I/O devices and to indicate properties of data. It is often useful for procedures, especially those that process input, to return flags that indicate whether or not their tasks were completed successfully. When a few flags are needed, a good choice of which positions within a register or memory location to use for them can make a program a little simpler and shorter. On many computers, the ideal position for a single flag is the sign bit because there are simple sign test instructions. For example, if a flag is stored in bit 7 of the bytes STATUS, we can test and branch using the following instructions.

```
          TSTB     STATUS
          BLSS     BIT1          ; Branch if bit 7 is 1
    BIT0:                        ; Bit 7 is 0
```

The VAX has two special instructions that make bit 0 an even better position for a flag. These are BLBS (Branch if Low Bit Set, i.e., is 1) and BLBC (Branch if Low Bit Clear, i.e., is 0). These instructions do both the indicated test and the conditional branch. They do not affect or test the condition codes. Their format is

$$\text{BLB}x \quad operand, destination$$

where x = S or C. Although only bit 0 is examined, the first operand is assumed to be a longword. (This is relevant if an addressing mode such as autoincrement is used.) The branch destination must be within roughly 127 bytes from the BLB instruction. The BLB instructions have many other uses that we will see in Chapter 12.

The JMP Instruction

For the unconditional branch instructions BRB and BRW, the destination must be specified as an address expression. For most purposes, these instructions are quite adequate, but there are situations where the destination address cannot be conveniently specified in branch mode. The JMP (JuMP) instruction may be used in such cases. Its format is

$$\text{JMP} \quad destination$$

where the destination may be specified using almost any addressing mode. (Register and literal modes would be inappropriate.) To execute this instruction, the CPU computes the operand address in the usual way and then places it in the PC, so that the instruction at that address will be executed next. For example, if R9 contains `00028E47`, the instruction

```
JMP     (R9)
```

would cause `00028E47` to be put in the PC.

Many of the realistic applications of the JMP instruction involve the use of more complex addressing modes and programming techniques than we have covered so far, so we will not give programming examples at this time.

7.2 EXAMPLE: FREE-FORMAT INPUT

To use the input conversion instructions introduced in Chapter 6, we have to know the address and number of digits in the character code representation of the integer being converted. It is a convenience for the user of a program to allow free-format input, that is, not to require that the input be typed in a specific place on the input line, and certainly not to require that the user type leading zeros on small integers. Here we will consider the problem of converting input that may appear anywhere on the input line and may even be incorrectly typed. This application illustrates implementation of several **if** statements and **while** loops.

The program segment we develop can be used repeatedly to find and convert several numbers typed in one line. A sample input line might be

```
41      379   -248        +14   12345678912      -97
```

We observe that because a leading separate numeric operand must begin with a sign (possibly blank), we must allocate a byte with a blank just ahead of the input buffer in case the user begins typing a positive number in the first position, as in the sample line above. To find the next integer, we can scan the line for a sign or digit. It is simpler, however, to scan for any nonblank character, and determine later what it is. Once we locate a number, we need to count its digits. We could stop counting when we reach a blank, but since we want to detect errors, we should stop at any nondigit. Suppose that the byte in memory following the input line happens to contain character code for a digit. We must stop counting digits when we reach the end of the line. We could use a counter initialized to the line length, but the program will be simpler if we force our loop to stop by moving a nondigit (say, a byte of zeros) into the byte following the end of the line. (Remember that a byte of zeros is not the same as a character '0' whose ASCII code is 30_{16}.)

Here is an outline for the program segment.

1. Insert 0 at the end of the input line.
2. Start the byte pointer at the beginning of the input line.
3. If the current byte contains 0, go to `END_OF_LINE`.
4. While the current byte contains a blank, increment the pointer.

5. If the current byte contains a sign, then save the current address, else save the preceding address.

6. While the current byte contains a digit, count it and increment the pointer.

7. If the number of digits is 0, go to ERROR.

8. Convert the integer to two's complement (checking for overflow).

All but the first two lines of the outline can be repeated to process each remaining integer in the input. The pointer would begin wherever it was after processing the preceding integer.

We use the following storage reservation.

```
BLANK = ^A/ /
        .BYTE    BLANK                    ; Potential "sign" for 1st integer
LINE:   .BLKB    81                       ; Zero byte at end of input buffer
PKD:    .BLKB    6
```

Register use is as follows:

```
; REGISTER USE
;
;       R6       pointer to current byte
;       R7       address of sign byte
;       R8       number of digits
;       R9       two's complement result
;       R0-R3    used by the CVT instructions
```

We assume the following initialization:

```
        READLINE   LINE
        MOVAB      LINE,R6               ; Pointer
        ADDL2      R6,R0                 ; Address of byte after input
        CLRB       (R0)                  ; Put zero byte at end of line
```

In the program segment that follows, each line from our outline appears as a comment preceding the code that implements it. The statement labels are chosen to suggest what is known or what is being done at the statements they label. The code satisfies the guidelines given earlier for organizing branches; for example, all branches go forward except those at the ends of the **while** loops.

```
        ; If the current byte contains 0, go to END_OF_LINE.
NEXT:     TSTB     (R6)
          BEQL     END_OF_LINE
;
; While current byte contains blank, increment the pointer.
TESTBLANK:CMPB     (R6)+,#BLANK
          BEQL     TESTBLANK
;
```

```
                 ; If the byte contains a sign, then save current address,
                 ;                          else save preceding address.
        NONBLANK:CMPB    -(R6),#^A/+/      ; Check for sign
                 BEQL    SIGN
                 CMPB    (R6),#^A/-/
                 BEQL    SIGN
        NOSIGN:  MOVAB   -(R6),R7          ; Save addr of preceding byte
                 BRB     DIGITS
        SIGN:    MOVL    R6,R7             ; Save address of sign
        ;
        DIGITS:  INCL    R6                ; Addr of potential 1st digit
                 CLRL    R8                ; Initialize digit counter
        ;
        ; While the current byte contains a digit do begin
        ;      count digit
        ;      increment byte pointer
        ; end
        TESTDIGIT:CMPB   (R6),#^A/0/
                 BLSS    NONDIGIT
                 CMPB    (R6),#^A/9/
                 BGTR    NONDIGIT
                 INCL    R8                ; Count the digit
                 INCL    R6                ; Increment pointer
                 BRB     TESTDIGIT
        ;
        ; If the number of digits is 0, go to ERROR.
        NONDIGIT:TSTL    R8
                 BEQL    ERROR
        ;
        ; Convert the integer to two's complement (checking for overflow).
                 CVTSP   R8,(R7),#10,PKD   ; Allow for up to 10 digits
                 BVS     ERROR             ; Branch if too many digits
                 CVTPL   #10,PKD,R9
                 BVS     ERROR             ; Some 10-digit numbers are
                                           ;    too big for a longword
        ;
        ; Store or process the converted integer and branch back to
        ; NEXT, if appropriate, to process the next one.
```

There are several exercises at the end of this chapter that explore details of this example and how it behaves when various errors appear in the input.

7.3 OPERAND ADDRESSING WITH DISPLACEMENT MODE

In high-level languages we frequently use data structures containing records which consist of several fields. High-level languages provide a notation for specifying an individual field within an individual record. For example, in Pascal we use

For this example we assume that the list of jobs to be run contains a block of information organized as shown below for each job. The BLOCKS field contains the number of disk blocks required by the job, and the RESOUCE FLAGS field contains flags indicating whether or not various system resources are needed. The roles of the other fields should be clear from their names.

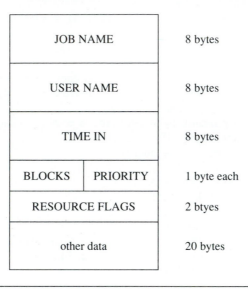

JOB NAME	8 bytes
USER NAME	8 bytes
TIME IN	8 bytes
BLOCKS / PRIORITY	1 byte each
RESOURCE FLAGS	2 btyes
other data	20 bytes

Figure 7.3   The format for a job record

recordname . fieldname

(C programmers will recognize the notation but use the terms *structure* for record and *member* for field.) In this section we introduce a new addressing mode, displacement mode, that is very convenient for specifying individual fields in assembly language. (Displacement mode is useful in many other situations also.)

   For example, suppose that a block of memory contains information on computer jobs waiting to be run. The collection of information on each job (i.e., each record) might be arranged as in Fig. 7.3. Suppose that a, the address of a record, is in R10. The addresses of the user-name and priority fields are $a + 8$ and $a + 25$, respectively. To access these fields we could use register deferred mode after using ADDL instructions to add 8 and 25 to the address in R10, but that would require more instructions, and it would require either using more registers or modifying the contents of R10, making it difficult to keep track of what is in R10 at any time (especially when there are several conditional branches).

   In displacement mode, the operand address is computed by adding a number, called a *displacement*, and the contents of a register. Thus we can refer to a field in a way that is analogous to the high-level language notation by putting the record address in a register and using the field offset for the displacement. The assembly language format is

$$dis(\text{R}n)$$

where Rn is R0, ... , R11, AP, FP, or SP. The CPU's formula for evaluating the operand specifier is

$$\text{operand address} = (\text{R}n) + dis$$

The contents of Rn will *not* be changed; the CPU computes the operand address in a scratch area.

Thus some of the fields in the example in Fig. 7.3 would be addressed as follows:

job name	0(R10) or (R10)
user name	8(R10)
priority	25(R10)

Example 7.6: Accessing Fields of a Binary Tree Node

Consider a binary tree with nodes defined by the following Pascal **type** declarations:

```
NodePtr = ↑TreeNodeType;
TreeNodeType = record
        name: array[1..8] of char;
        left, right : NodePtr
end  { TreeNodeType }
```

Each node has a field containing a name; *left* and *right* are pointer fields containing pointers to the node's left and right child, respectively, in the binary tree. Since pointers are addresses, hence longwords, each node occupies a total of 16 bytes.

Suppose that p is a pointer in R9. We want to determine if the node pointed to by p is a leaf in the binary tree. The Pascal code would be

if (p↑.left = **nil**) **and** (p↑.right = **nil**) **then** ...

The fields of the binary tree node may be addressed as follows:

p↑.name	(R9) or 0(R9)
p↑.left	8(R9)
p↑.right	12(R9)

Suppose that we have used a direct assignment statement to assign NIL = 0. The test of whether the node pointed to by p is a leaf can be coded as follows:

```
    CMPL    8(R9),#NIL
    BNEQ    CONTINUE
    CMPL    12(R9),#NIL
    BNEQ    CONTINUE
```

```
LEAF:      ; [instructions for the case where the node is a leaf]
           . . .
CONTINUE:
```

R9 has not been changed; it still contains the address of the node.

For increased readability, the programmer can use names for displacements. Direct assignment statements may be used to assign the displacement values to mnemonic symbols. For the binary tree problem, for example, we may define

```
NAME = 0
LEFT = 8
RIGHT = 12
```

We could then rewrite the leaf test in Example 7.6 as

```
        CMPL    LEFT(R9),#NIL
        BNEQ    CONTINUE
        CMPL    RIGHT(R9),#NIL
        BNEQ    CONTINUE
LEAF:
```

When the assembler translates the displacement mode operands, it looks up the symbols in the symbol table, substitutes the values for the symbols, and translates just as though the programmer had written the numeric displacements in the instructions.

Example 7.7: Comparing Character Strings Using Displacement Mode

Here we rewrite the solution for the problem in Example 7.5. R7 contains the address of an eight-character name. Another eight-character name is stored in memory immediately after the first. The problem is to program the statement

if first name > second name **then** interchange names

A solution using displacement mode is

```
        CMPC3   #8,(R7),8(R7)    ; Compare names
        BLEQ    NEXT             ; Branch if in order
        MOVC3   #8,(R7),TEMP     ; Move first name to TEMP
        MOVC3   #8,8(R7),(R7)    ; Move 2nd name to 1st place
        MOVC3   #8,TEMP,8(R7)    ; Move 1st name to 2nd place
NEXT:   ; [next instruction]
```

The displacement in a displacement mode operand may be an expression; often it is simply a decimal integer. It may be negative or positive. (It is stored in the machine code for the instruction as a two's complement integer.) There are actually three displacement modes; they differ according to how much space is used in the machine code for the displacement—a byte, a word, or a longword. The assembler normally uses as little space as possible.

The main advantages of using displacement mode are that it provides a conceptually clear way to refer to the fields in a record, it saves steps, and it decreases the likelihood of programming mistakes.

7.4 EXAMPLE: BINARY SEARCH

The Search Problem

There are many, many applications where an item must be looked up in a table. Each entry in the table may consist of several related data. For example, if we think of a dictionary as a table, each entry contains a word, its pronunciation and meaning, and perhaps its etymology and examples of its use. An entry in a telephone book contains a name, address, and telephone number. A symbol table entry contains a symbol, its value, and other information. In each case there is one datum in the entry that identifies that entry; in these examples the identifiers are the word, the name, and the symbol, respectively. The identifier for an entry in a table is often called a *key*. Usually when we must look up an item we know the key and want to find the other information associated with it, or sometimes we just want to know if a certain key is in the table at all. The general problem we are considering is called *searching*.

The most straightforward solution is to compare the key sought to the key in each entry in turn until it is found or the list is exhausted. This method is called *sequential search*. Programming a sequential search is not very difficult and is left for the exercises. The disadvantage of sequential search is that it can require a lot of work; at the worst, every entry in the list is examined, and on the average, at least half are. If the entries are sorted by key (i.e., if the keys are in numerical or alphabetical order) another method is much more efficient. It is called *binary search*.

How Binary Search Works

For the rest of this section we assume that the keys in the table to be searched are sorted in increasing order.

When describing an algorithm, it is natural to use variable names the way they are used in high-level languages—as names of data, not addresses. In the discussion of the binary search algorithm we will write variable names in italic.

Let *key* be the key sought. Suppose that we compare *key* to an entry near the middle of the list and find that it is less than the key in that entry. Then, if *key* is in the list at all, it must be in the first half because all the keys in the second half are larger than the middle one, hence larger than *key* (see Fig. 7.4 for illustration). Thus, by doing one comparison we have reduced the problem of searching for *key* in the whole table to the problem of searching only half the table. The same "trick" is used again and again until *key* is found in the table or it is determined that it is not there: *key* is always compared to the middle entry in the section of the table being searched. If *key* is larger than the key there, the second half of this section will be searched. If *key* is smaller, the first half will be searched. Of course, if the middle entry is *key*, the search terminates. The efficiency of

(We assume here that the keys are distinct, though binary search can still be used if they are not.)

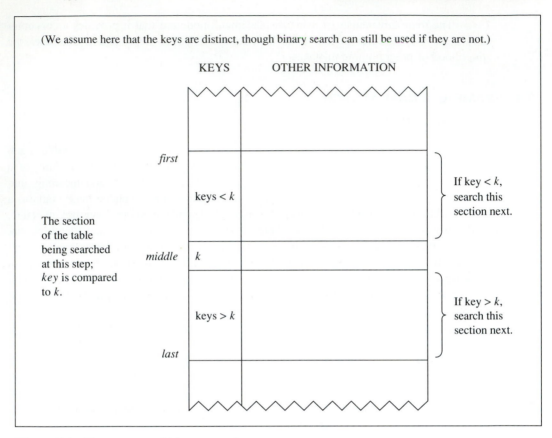

Figure 7.4   The strategy of binary search

binary search comes from the fact that when one entry in the list is examined, many other entries can be removed from consideration without ever being looked at.

As Fig. 7.4 indicates, we will use variables *first* and *last* to keep track of the beginning and end of the section of the table being searched. The index of the entry to be examined, *middle*, will be computed by averaging *first* and *last*. *Num* is the number of entries in the table.

We will assume that the desired output from the program is the index of the table entry containing *key*, or zero if *key* is not in the table. The algorithm is described in a (slightly hypothetical) high-level language below. Note the two tests in the **while** statement. The first, *index* = 0, determines that *key* has not yet been found; the second, *first* ≤ *last*, determines that the subsection to be searched is nonempty. If *first* > *last*, we can conclude that *key* is not in the table.

```
first := 1;   last := num;
index := 0;
while (index = 0) and (first ≤ last) do begin
```

```
        middle := (first + last) DIV 2;
        case
              key = table[middle]: index := middle;
              key < table[middle]: last := middle – 1;
              key > table[middle]: first := middle + 1
        endcase
    endwhile
```

Figure 7.5 shows the subsections of the table that are searched and the comparisons done in an example.

Addressing Table Entries

Most of the statements in the algorithm can be programmed easily in assembly language. One point about which there may be some questions is: How do we find the key for the entry whose index is *middle*? We will derive a formula for the address of the key, assuming it to be the first field of its table entry. Now that we are again considering address computations in assembly language, we will be using the usual convention that a name written in capital letters is a symbol. Names of other data will be written in lower-case letters. The data used in the formula are

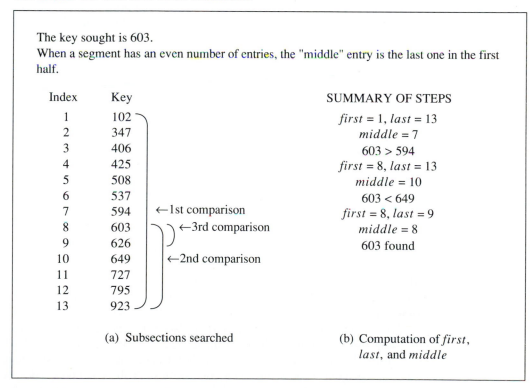

Figure 7.5   An example of binary search

TABLE	the address of the table
i	the index of the desired entry
size	the number of bytes per entry

The address of the first entry, which is also the address of its key, is TABLE; the addresses of the second and third entries (and their keys) are TABLE+*size* and TABLE+2*size*, respectively. It should be easy to see that in general, for any index *i* between 1 and *num*,

$$\text{address of } i\text{th entry} = \text{TABLE} + (i - 1) * size.$$

The only datum in the formula that varies in the binary search loop is the index *i*. The formula may be rewritten as

$$\text{address of } i\text{th entry} = \text{TABLE} - size + i * size$$

where TABLE–*size* may be computed outside the loop, leaving only two operations, * and +, to be done in the loop each time an entry address is computed.

Programming the Binary Search

The reader should observe that most of the thinking about the program has already been done. Almost all we have to do now is follow the algorithm and write the assembly language instructions to implement each statement. It is almost always an excellent idea either to write an algorithm in a high-level language or to draw a flowchart for it before writing the assembly language program. Then all the thought and planning about the problem and the algorithm for solving it can be done separately from the considerations of assembly language details. The high-level language program or flowchart can be used as a guide or outline for writing the assembly language statements. For the binary search program, we show a flowchart in Fig. 7.6 as an intermediate version between the high-level algorithm and the assembly language program. The first test in the **while** statement has been eliminated because we can branch out of the loop when *key* is found. In addition to doing the computation shown in the flowchart, the program must include the initialization and details for the computation of entry addresses, and we must make sure that the data are the correct types for the instructions in which they are used. We also give some thought to choosing between two-operand and three-operand arithmetic instructions; two-operand instructions are shorter, hence preferred, but they cannot be used where the two operands are needed later and must not be destroyed.

The program segment for the binary search appears in Fig. 7.7. Each section of instructions that corresponds to a box in the flowchart begins with a comment that indicates the correspondence. Note that well-chosen instruction labels help make the program easier to read. We have even used the "label" RESET_LAST as a comment. *First, last, middle,* and *size* are longwords because they are used in address computations. Note that in the instructions to implement the **case** statement, one conditional branch instruction immediately follows another. Conditional branch instructions do not change the condition code settings, so both are testing the condition codes that result from the comparison of keys.

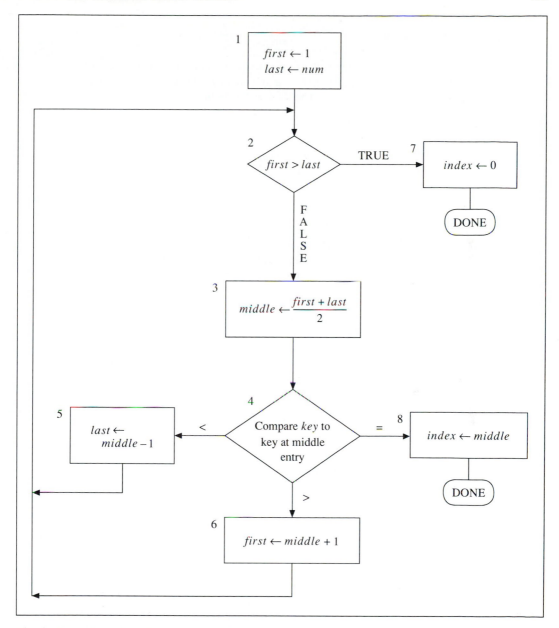

Figure 7.6 Flowchart for binary search

In writing the program for the binary search we have made a number of assumptions about various details; they are in the documentation. Some of the exercises at the end of the chapter ask the reader to consider the effects of varying these assumptions.

```
; THE PROBLEM
;
; This program segment does a binary search in a table to find
; the index of the entry for a given key. If the key is not
; in the table, it sets the index to zero.
;
; DESCRIPTION OF DATA
;
; The keys are word integers stored in increasing order. The
; entry size is an input, not a constant.
;
; GIVEN DATA
;
;       TABLE        the table to be searched (address)
;       NUM          the number of entries (word)
;       KEY          the key sought (word)
;       SIZE         the number of bytes per entry (word)
;
; OUTPUT
;       INDEX        the index of the entry containing
;                    the key sought; 0 if key is not in
;                    the table (word)
;
; VARIABLES USED IN THE PROGRAM
;
;       First, last, and middle are used as in the flowchart.
;
; REGISTER USE
;
;       R5      entry size (number of bytes)
;       R6      TABLE-size (for addressing)
;       R7      key
;       R8      first (longword)
;       R9      last (longword)
;       R10     middle (longword)
;       R11     address of entry to examine
;
; INITIALIZATION
;
        CVTWL    SIZE,R5             ; size, converted to longword
        MOVAB    TABLE,R6
        SUBL2    R5,R6              ; TABLE-size
        MOVW     KEY,R7             ; key (in register for fast access)
;
```

Figure 7.7   Binary search program (continued next page)

```
; FLOWCHART BOX 1
;
        MOVL    #1,R8            ; first := 1
        CVTWL   NUM,R9           ; last := (NUM)
;
; FLOWCHART BOX 2
;
SEARCH_LOOP:
        CMPL    R8,R9            ; Compare first and last
        BGTR    NOTFOUND         ; if first > last, key not found
;
; FLOWCHART BOX 3
;
        ADDL3   R8,R9,R10        ; first + last
        DIVL2   #2,R10           ; middle := (first+last) div 2
;
; FLOWCHART BOX 4
;
        MULL3   R10,R5,R11       ; middle*size
        ADDL2   R6,R11           ; Address of entry
        CMPW    R7,(R11)         ; Compare keys
        BEQL    FOUND            ; If keys are equal, exit loop
        BGTR    RESET_FIRST      ; If key >, search larger keys
;
; FLOWCHART BOX 5
;
; RESET_LAST:
        SUBL3   #1,R10,R9        ; last := middle-1
        BRB     SEARCH_LOOP
;
; FLOWCHART BOX 6
;
RESET_FIRST:
        ADDL3   #1,R10,R8        ; first := middle+1
        BRB     SEARCH_LOOP
;
; FLOWCHART BOXES 7 AND 8
;
NOTFOUND:
        CLRW    R10              ; index := 0
FOUND:  MOVW    R10,INDEX        ; Store index (middle or 0)
```

Figure 7.7   (continued)

7.5 LOOP CONTROL INSTRUCTIONS

The VAX has a variety of loop control instructions. Generally speaking, they increment or decrement loop indexes (counters) and may branch to a destination specified in the instruction depending on the relation between the new value of the index and the loop limit.

The VAX loop control instructions are designed to be placed at the end of the *body of the loop* (i.e., the instructions that are to be executed repeatedly). The branch destination is the first instruction of the loop body. Such a loop structure is illustrated in Fig. 7.8(a). Note, however, that since there is no test at the beginning of the loop, the instructions will always be executed at least once, even if the index is beyond the loop limit. This loop structure corresponds to the Pascal **repeat-until** statement, shown in Fig. 7.8(a), and the **do-while** in C. As we saw in Section 6.3, this can sometimes produce incorrect results; an extra test before the loop body or a different loop structure is sometimes needed. An alternative that corresponds to the Pascal and C **while** statements is shown in Fig. 7.8(b).

The loop index may be used in computation in the loop body, but usually it should not be changed.

In Section 7.1 we pointed out that conditional branching requires two steps: setting the condition codes, then testing them to determine if a branch should be taken. Usually, these steps are performed by two separate instructions. The loop instructions do both; the condition codes are set as a result of the incrementing or decrementing of the loop index. For all the loop instructions there is a limit, depending on the particular instruction, on how far away the destination may be.

The loop instructions may be divided into three groups according to their flexibility. We begin with the simplest.

SOBGTR and SOBGEQ

The names of these instructions are mnemonics for "Subtract One and Branch if GreaTeR than zero" and "Subtract One and Branch if Greater or EQual to zero." Their formats are

$$\text{SOB}xyz \quad index,destination$$

The index must be a longword, and the destination must be within roughly 127 bytes of the loop instruction. (As we mentioned earlier, that allows roughly 25–30 instructions in a loop.)

The action of the instructions may be described as follows:

SOBGTR	SOBGEQ
index ← index−1	index ← index−1
branch if index > 0	branch if index ≥ 0

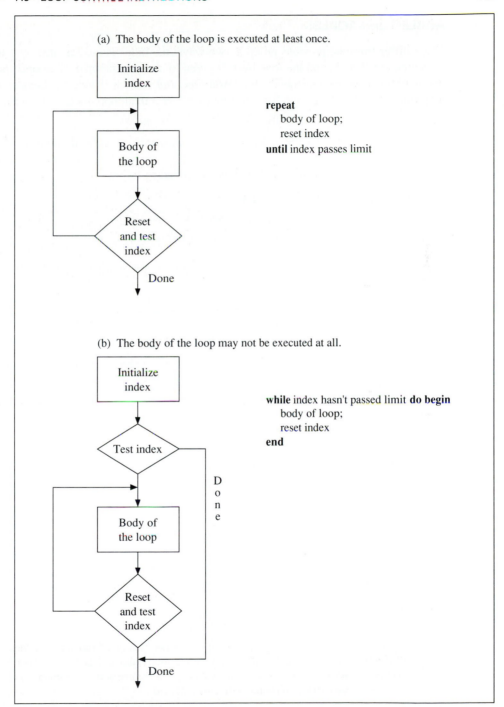

Figure 7.8 Loop structures

AOBLEQ and AOBLSS

These differ from the previous group in two ways: the index is incremented by 1 instead of decremented by 1, and the loop limit is given by the programmer as an operand. The instruction names are mnemonics for "Add One and Branch if index is Less or EQual loop limit" and "Add One and Branch if index is LeSS than loop limit." The format is

$$AOBxyz \quad limit,index,destination$$

Both the limit and the index must be longwords, and the destination must be within roughly 127 bytes.

The action of the instructions may be described as follows:

AOBLEQ	AOBLSS
index ← index+1	index ← index+1
branch if index ≤ limit	branch if index < limit

The AOBLEQ instruction is most appropriate for implementing the frequently used Pascal, C, and Fortran statements:

$$\textbf{for } index := 1 \textbf{ to } limit \textbf{ do}$$

```
for (index = 1; index <= limit; index++)
```

$$DO \; s \; INDEX = 1,LIMIT$$

We show these examples with the initial loop index value as 1 because it occurs so often, but the initial value may be anything appropriate. In general, the loops may be implemented in assembly language as follows:

```
        MOVL    initial_value,R7
        CMPL    R7,limit
        BGTR    NEXT
LOOP:
;       [body of loop]
        AOBLEQ  limit,R7,LOOP
NEXT:
```

Example 7.8: A Simple for Loop

Problem: Example 6.9 shows a program segment that stores the entry index number in each entry of a longword array LIST. The work to be done is described in the following Pascal **for** statement:

for i := 1 **to** number_of_entries **do**
    list[i] := i

SOBGTR was used to control the loop in the earlier version of this problem; here we use AOBLEQ. Note that since the initial value of the loop index is 1 and the number of entries in an array is nonnegative, we do not need an explicit comparison of the initial value and the limit; we simply check if the number of entries is zero.

Solution:

```
; PROBLEM STATEMENT
;
; This program stores in each entry of the longword array LIST
; the entry's index number. The array size is in NUM, a longword.
; If the array is empty, nothing will be stored. The indexes
; begin at 1.
;
; REGISTER USE
;
;       R6        loop index
;       R7        loop limit
;       R10       array pointer
;
; INITIALIZATION
;
        MOVL    NUM,R7          ; Loop limit
        BEQL    DONE            ; Done if (NUM) = 0
        MOVL    #1,R6           ; Initialize loop index
        MOVAL   LIST,R10        ; Initialize array pointer
;
; THE LOOP
;
STORE:  MOVL    R6,(R10)+       ; Store index, increment ptr
        AOBLEQ  R7,R6,STORE     ; Increment index, testbranch
DONE:   ; [next statement]
```

ACB*x*

In the Fortran **DO** statement and in the **for** statements in some languages (C, PL/1, and ALGOL, but not Pascal), the programmer may specify an increment for the loop index other than ±1. The increment may be positive or negative. The ACB instructions allow implementation of these more flexible loop control statements. They also allow for loop parameters that are not longwords; the loop limit, increment, and index may even be floating-point numbers.

The instruction name is mnemonic for Add, Compare, and Branch. The format is

$$\text{ACB}x \quad limit,increment,index,destination$$

where x = B, W, or L (or one of the floating-point types F, D, G, or H). The limit, increment, and index must all be type x. The destination may be up to about 32,767 bytes away. The action of the instructions is described by

index ← index + increment
if increment ≥ 0 and index ≤ limit, then branch
if increment ≤ 0 and index ≥ limit, then branch

Example 7.9: Implementing a DO Loop with ACB

The loop

        DO 10 I = J,N,INC

            [body of loop]

    10   CONTINUE

where J, N, and INC are word integers, could be implemented as follows:

```
; R9 is used for the loop index
;
        MOVW    J,R9                    ; index = (J)
;       [Test whether the loop body
;       should be executed at all.]
LOOP:
;       [body of loop]
        ACBW    N,INC,R9,LOOP           ; Loop control
```

Suppose that (J) = 5, (INC) = 3, and (N) = 28. Then the body of the loop will be executed for index values 5, 8, 11, 14, 17, 20, 23, and 26. On the last pass through the loop, when the index is 26, the ACBW instruction will increment the index to 29. Since 29 is not less than or equal to the limit (N), a branch will not be taken and the next instruction to be executed is the one that follows the ACBW.

Suppose that (J) = 5, (INC) = −3, and (N) = −13. Then the body of the loop will be executed for index values 5, 2, −1, −4, −7, −10, and −13. Since the increment is negative, on each pass through the loop the branch is taken if the new value of index is greater or equal to the limit.

7.6 EXAMPLE: CONVERTING CHARACTER CODE INPUT— HORNER'S METHOD

The Problem

In this section we will consider how to convert integers from leading separate numeric format (or character code) to two's complement format without using the powerful VAX instructions CVTSP and CVTPL. We study this problem for a number of reasons. First, it is interesting to know how the VAX instructions might actually do the conversions. Second, many computers, particularly microprocessors, do not have such powerful instructions, and hence the assembly language programmer using those machines needs to know how to convert input data. Finally, the method we will use, Horner's method for evaluating polynomials, is a useful tool that has other applications.

Suppose that we have a decimal integer represented in character code. We know that the value of the number is given by the expression

$$\overline{d}_n \times 10^n + \overline{d}_{n-1} \times 10^{n-1} + \cdots + \overline{d}_2 \times 10^2 + \overline{d}_1 \times 10^1 + \overline{d}_0$$

where $\overline{d_i}$ is the value of the digit d_i, for $0 \le i \le n$. This expression is just a special case of a polynomial whose general form is

$$p(x) = c_n x^n + c_{n-1} x^{n-1} + \cdots + c_2 x^2 + c_1 x + c_0$$

where for $0 \le i \le n$, the c_i are the coefficients. In the representation of an integer, the coefficients are the values of the digits and x is the radix; in the present problem, $x = 10$. Thus we can solve the problem of converting character code to two's complement if we can convert the individual digits and efficiently evaluate a polynomial.

Evaluating a Polynomial

There are several algorithms for evaluating a polynomial; they vary quite a bit in efficiency. The following algorithm should seem very reasonable and natural. It computes and adds each term starting with the lower powers, and to avoid unnecessary multiplication, it obtains the required power of x for each term from the previous one. The coefficients are assumed to be in the array c.

```
xpower := 1;
value := c[0];
for i := 1 to n do begin
    xpower := xpower*x;
    value := value + c[i]*xpower
end
```

To compare the efficiency of this algorithm with that of others, we need some measure of how much work is done. We could program each algorithm in assembly language and count how many instructions would be executed, but that requires programming several algorithms that we will not use. We can make very useful comparisons of algorithms by counting the number of arithmetic operations done on the data. It is easy to see that the algorithm above does $2n$ multiplications and n additions (for a polynomial of degree n).

Horner's Method for Evaluating a Polynomial

Horner's method does significantly fewer multiplications than the algorithm presented above (and the same number of additions). The key to its efficiency is a particular factorization of a polynomial. The benefit of factoring an expression to be evaluated is illustrated even with a very simple example:

$$x * y + x * z = x * (y + z)$$

The first form of the expression implies that two multiplications and one addition would be used to evaluate it, but the second form shows that only one multiplication and one addition are sufficient.

Consider the polynomial

$$7x^4 + 3x^3 - 12x^2 + 6x - 9$$

Using our first method, evaluating this polynomial would require eight multiplications. However, x divides all the terms except the constant, so we can factor as follows:

$$(7x^3 + 3x^2 - 12x + 6) * x - 9$$

The polynomial within the parentheses can be evaluated by the first method using six multiplications; thus a total of seven would be done, and we have eliminated one multiplication. But we need not stop here; we can factor the polynomial within the parentheses. Repeated factoring eventually gives

$$((((7) * x + 3) * x - 12) * x + 6) * x - 9$$

Thus we see that the polynomial can be evaluated with only four multiplications.

The general form of the factorization for Horner's method is

$$(\cdots (c_n) * x + c_{n-1}) * x + c_{n-2}) * x + \cdots + c_2) * x + c_1) * x + c_0$$

Clearly, only n multiplications and n additions are done to evaluate a polynomial of degree n. The number of multiplications has been cut in half, but the algorithm is no more complicated than the first one. In fact, it is shorter and can be programmed with a very simple loop. Beginning with the innermost parentheses, each pass through the loop computes the value of the subexpression in the next set of parentheses.

```
value := c[n];
for i := n–1 downto 0 do
    value := value*x + c[i]
```

Implementing Horner's Method to Convert Character Code

We now have an efficient polynomial evaluation algorithm. To convert a leading separate numeric integer we must convert the individual digits d_i from ASCII code to two's complement. This is very simple; the ASCII codes for digits are 48_{10} for "0" through 57_{10} for "9". Thus subtracting 48 from the ASCII code leaves the value of the digit. (The digit codes look more natural in hex; they are 30_{16}–39_{16}. The rightmost four bits are the binary representation of the digit's value.) In fact, we need not know the actual character codes for the digits; we can simply subtract the code for '0' from each digit (and let the assembler "look up" the code for '0').

The following program segment does the conversion. Note that the algorithm used in the program has been modified slightly to simplify the initialization of *value*. The modification causes the program to do an extra multiplication and addition, so it is a matter of taste whether or not it is an improvement; we opted for simplicity.

```
MINUS = ^A/-/
ZEROCODE = ^A/0/
;
; PROBLEM STATEMENT
;
; This program segment converts an integer from character code
; to a two's complement longword using Horner's polynomial
; evaluation method instead of the VAX conversion instructions.
```

```
;
; The evaluation algorithm is:
;
;          value := 0
;          for  i := n downto 0  do
;                    value := value*10 + d(i)
;
; where there are  n+1 digits, d(n)d(n-1)...d(1)d(0).
;
; We assume that the address of the character code string is in
; R9 (and the first byte is the sign), and that the number of
; digits in the integer is in R8. The result is to be stored
; in the longword at NUMBER.
;
; REGISTER USE
;
;          R6        address of digit
;          R7        two's complement value
;          R8        number of digits (loop cntr)
;          R9        address of char code
;          R10       conversion of digit
;
           CLRL    R7                    ; Value := 0
           CLRL    R10                   ; Clear for digit
           MOVAB   1(R9),R6              ; Address of first digit
;
NEXT:      MULL2   #10,R7                ; Value*10
           SUBB3   #ZEROCODE,(R6)+,R10 ; Binary value of digit
           ADDL2   R10,R7                ; Value*10 + digit
           SOBGTR  R8,NEXT
;
           CMPB    (R9),#MINUS           ; Test for minus sign
           BNEQ    STORE                 ; If no -, done
           MNEGL   R7,R7                 ; Negate value
STORE:     MOVL    R7,NUMBER             ; Store value
```

Our algorithm accomplishes what is done by the two VAX instructions CVTSP and CVTPL. Consider the part of the tasks done by each of those instructions. CVTSP does a fairly mechanical operation: It extracts the rightmost nibble of each byte, the part that represents the digit in binary, and packs them two to a byte. No numerical computation is done. The CVTPL instruction starts with the packed decimal datum, essentially a string of digits in four-bit representation, and converts it to two's complement. Thus the work done by CVTPL is most closely comparable to the polynomial evaluation we have done with Horner's method.

TABLE 7.2 LOOP CONTROL INSTRUCTIONS

Instruction		Action	Data type of loop parameters	Branch displacement[1]
SOBGTR	*index,destination*	Subtract 1; branch if >0	L	B
SOBGEQ	*index,destination*	Subtract 1; branch if ≥0		
AOBLEQ	*limit,index,dest*	Add 1; branch if ≤ *limit*	L	B
AOBLSS	*limit,index,dest*	Add 1; branch if < *limit*		
ACB*x*	*limit,incr,index,dest*	Increment *index*; branch if not beyond *limit*	*x* = B, W, L, F, D, G, or H. The increment may be negative.	W

[1] The branch displacement is the distance in bytes to the branch destination. For instructions that encode the displacement in a byte, the distance must be between −128 and 127.

7.7 SUMMARY

The condition codes are four one-bit flags in the PSW that are set by most instructions to indicate properties of one or more of their operands. The codes are N (negative or less than), Z (zero or equal), V (overflow), and C (carry or unsigned less than). Conditional branch instructions examine the condition codes to determine if the condition described in the branch instruction holds. If so, the PC is loaded with the branch destination address; otherwise, no branch is taken.

The branch destination in the conditional branch instructions must be within approximately 127 bytes from the instruction.

There are two unconditional branch instructions: BRB and BRW. The only difference between them is that the destination for the latter may be up to 32,767 bytes away.

The VAX has two instructions that test bit 0 of a longword and branch depending on whether the bit is 0 or 1.

The branch instructions are listed in Table 7.1 (in Section 7.1).

Test and compare instructions can be used to explicitly set the condition codes. Some of these instructions are TST*x* and CMP*x* (where *x* = B, W, or L) and CMPC3, for character strings. (CMPC3 uses registers R0 through R3.)

Care should be taken when using branches to organize the instructions to use as few branches as possible and to keep the flow of control (the sequence in which instructions are executed) going in one direction, down the page, except for loops.

The JMP instruction, like BRB and BRW, changes the sequential flow of control by loading the PC with the destination address, but almost any addressing mode can be used for the destination operand with JMP.

The VAX loop control instructions are summarized in Table 7.2. The instructions allow for varying amounts of flexibility, and some can be used very naturally to implement the common loop statements in high-level languages.

For the addressing mode called displacement mode, the operand address is computed by adding the displacement and the contents of a register. The contents of the register are not changed. Displacement mode is particularly useful for addressing fields within a record.

7.8 EXERCISES

1. Suppose that R6 contains 001A8EF2 and R10 contains FFFE90F2. Show the condition code values after each of the following instructions.

   (a) CMPL   R6,R10   (d) TSTB   R10
   (b) CMPB   R6,R10   (e) TSTW   R6
   (c) CMPW   R10,R6

2. Suppose that R7 contains 50FA0049 and R8 contains FF0601F3 before *each* of the following instructions. Show the condition code values after each instruction.

   (a) ADDL3   R7,R8,R9   (d) MOVW   R7,ALPHA
   (b) SUBL2   R8,R7   (e) CVTWL   R8,BETA
   (c) SUBL2   R7,R8

3. Suppose that R6 contains FFEA609C and R7 contains FFFF4079 before the following instructions are executed. Where is the instruction that is executed next, at HERE or THERE?

   ```
           CMPL    R6,R7
           BGEQ    THERE
   HERE:
   ```

4. Write instructions to branch to NOTYET if the longword at TIME is less than or equal to the longword in R8.

5. Write instructions to determine if the byte at CHAR contains the ASCII code for an uppercase letter. If not, there should be a branch to NOTUPPER.

6. Write instructions to replace the word integer in R10 by its absolute value.

7. Even though there is no P condition code to indicate that a datum is positive, we can determine if a datum is positive from the values of the N and Z codes. Could all three of the properties "negative," "zero," and "positive" be determined if there were P and Z codes instead of N and Z? What if there were P and N instead of N and Z?

8. Write assembly language statements to implement the following **if-then-else** statement, where alpha is an integer. For the assembly language solution, you may assume that ALPHA is a label on a longword in memory where the integer is stored.

   if alpha < 0 **then** print "Alpha is negative."
               else print "Alpha is not negative."

9. Suppose that there is a byte array TAGS and a character string array NAMES in which each entry has 24 characters. Each entry in the TAGS array is associated with the name in the corresponding position in the NAMES array. COUNT, a longword,

contains the number of entries in each array. Write instructions to print out all the names that have nonzero tags.

10. Rewrite the following segment of code more clearly and simply (using fewer instructions and fewer branches) without changing the effects.

```
        CMPL    (R8),(R5)
        BEQL    A
INC:    ADDL2   #4,R8
        BRB     B
A:      MOVL    R8,(R9)+
        BRB     INC
B:
```

11. Write instructions to branch to SPECIAL if the byte in R8 is 7, 11, or 13. Otherwise, the next instruction should be executed.

12. Do Exercise 49 of Chapter 6 without the assumption that the number of array entries is even. If there is an odd number of entries, the middle entry should be printed at the end of the first column.

13. Write instructions to branch to THERE if the word at WORD is between −100 and 100, and the byte at BYTE is 3 or 4.

14. Write an instruction (or instructions) to branch to ODD if the integer in the word COUNT is odd. (The integer is not necessarily positive.)

15. Suppose that ALPHA and BETA are the addresses of two quadword integers. Write instructions to branch to ABC if the quadword at ALPHA is larger than the one at BETA.

16. Using the information in Table 7.1, find a pair of conditional branch instructions (other than the one mentioned in the note at the bottom of the table) that branch on exactly the same conditions.

17. Suppose that the VAX did not have a CMPC3 instruction to compare character strings. There are two character strings in memory; their addresses are in R7 and R8. R10 contains the number of characters in each string. (The two strings have the same length.) Without using CMPC3, write instructions to compare the strings and branch to FIRST if the string whose address is in R7 comes first alphabetically, branch to SECOND if the string whose address is in R7 comes second alphabetically, and just go on to the next instruction if the strings are equal.

18. Write a program segment to find the largest entry in the word array DATA and store it in the word LARGEST. NUM, a longword, contains the number of entries in the array.

19. Write assembly language instructions that have the same effect as the following Pascal program segment. Assume that n is in the longword labeled N. Store the final value of k in the longword labeled LOG_N. (You may assume that space has already been reserved for them.)

```
        x := n;
        k := 0;
        while x > 1 do begin
            x := x DIV 2;
            k := k+1
        end
```

20. Suppose that DATA is a longword array containing integers that range in size from very small to very large. BYTES, WORDS, and LONGS are three presently empty arrays, each of the type indicated by its name. Write instructions to distribute the integers in DATA into the other three arrays so that each integer uses the smallest memory unit it fits in. You may assume that the longword NUM contains the number of entries in DATA. You should store in the longwords NUM_BYTES, NUM_WORDS, and NUM_LONGS the number of integers put into each of those arrays.

21. Consider the following program segment. It does not do exactly what it claims. Find and correct the error.

```
; This program segment searches a character string for
; the first blank.
;
; DATA
;
;       CHARS       the character string
;       LENGTH      the length of the string (longword)
;       LOCBLANK    the address of the first blank
;
; If there are no blanks in the string, 0 is stored in
; LOCBLANK.
;
; REGISTER USE
;
;       R6          pointer to current character
;       R7          loop counter
;
        MOVL    LENGTH,R7       ; Initialize loop counter
        BEQL    NOTFND          ; Branch if length = 0
        MOVAB   CHARS,R6        ; Initialize pointer
;
TEST:   CMPB    (R6)+,#^A/ /    ; Test for blank, increment ptr
        BEQL    FOUND           ; Branch if blank
        SOBGTR  R7,TEST         ; Loop control
NOTFND: CLRL    R6              ; No blank found
FOUND:  MOVL    R6,LOCBLANK     ; Store address of blank
```

22. Suppose that a two's complement integer with at most five digits is in R8.
    (a) Write instructions to convert the integer to character code. The result should go in memory beginning at the byte labeled LINE. (There are six bytes allocated beginning at LINE.) Blank out the sign character if the integer is positive.
    (b) Using the same assumptions as in part (a), write instructions to convert the integer to character code and blank out all leading zeros, if any. If the integer is positive, blank out the sign. If the integer is negative, move the minus sign so that it appears just ahead of the first nonzero digit. (For example, –12 should appear as "   -12", not "-   12".

23. In the code for processing free-format input (Section 7.2):
    (a) Why is autodecrement mode used in the CMPB instruction labeled NON-BLANK? Why is it not used in the second CMPB instruction?
    (b) Why is autodecrement mode used in the MOVAB instruction labeled NOSIGN?

24. Complete the free-format input processing example in Section 7.2 by writing the instructions to cause the code to be repeated for each number on the line, and writing appropriate instructions for the label ERROR.

25. Suppose that the free-format input processing code in Section 7.2 has been completed as described in Exercise 24. For each of the following input lines, state which integers would be converted and whether or not there would be a branch to ERROR.
    (a) -10   245xyz
    (b) 1280   385-27
    (c) 15,-42,78
    (d) 0
    (e) The sample line shown in Section 7.2.

26. Run your program written for Exercise 24 using the data in Exercise 25 to see if your answers for Exercise 25 were correct.

27. Write a complete program to read a line containing five integers (typed anywhere on the line), convert them to two's complement, and store them in the longword array ARRAY. If there are fewer than five integers in the input line, an error message should be printed at the terminal.

28. Write instructions to read a sequence of lines of varying lengths from the terminal and store them in memory beginning at TEXT in the format described in Exercise 17 of Chapter 5. You may assume that a line of length zero indicates the end of the input. Store a byte zero in memory after the last byte of text.

29. Assuming the storage format described in Exercise 17 of Chapter 5 and Exercise 28 above, write instructions to print out all the lines stored in memory beginning at TEXT.

30. Consider the binary tree node example in Section 7.3. Write an instruction to put the address of the right child of the node into R9. (This more or less implements the Pascal statement $p := p\uparrow.right$.)

31. Suppose that a person's medical record is made up of the following fields stored in memory in the order listed:

Medical record number	8 bytes
Name	22 bytes
Address	50 bytes
Phone number	7 bytes
Date of birth	6 bytes
Blood type	2 bytes
Allergies	2 bytes
Other fields	96 bytes

(a) Suppose that R6 contains the address of the record. Using displacement mode, write down operand specifiers (in assembly language source form) for the first five fields.

(b) Suppose that the next person's record is in memory immediately after this one and has the same format. Write an assembly language statement to put the address of the next record in R6.

32. Suppose that for each person who answered a questionnaire we have a block of information in the following format:

first byte

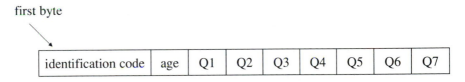

identification code	age	Q1	Q2	Q3	Q4	Q5	Q6	Q7

where the identification code is four characters, age is a byte integer, and Q1, ... , Q7 are answers to questions, each represented by an ASCII code for a number between 1 and 5. Assuming that R8 contains the address of one such block, write instructions to increment a counter in R9 if the person is in the age group 20–29 and his or her answer to the fifth question is 3 or higher. Then, whether or not the counter is incremented, change R8 to contain the address of the block of data for the next person (assuming that it immediately follows the current one in memory).

33. Does the high-level language algorithm for the binary search (Section 7.4) work properly if the table is empty (i.e., if $num = 0$)? Does the program in Fig. 7.7 work properly in this case?

34. Using data as described in the program in Fig. 7.7, except that the table may not be sorted, write a program segment that uses sequential search, instead of binary search, to find the index of the entry containing the key in KEY.

35. Show all the changes that must be made in the binary search program (Fig. 7.7) for an application where the keys are character strings of length six instead of words.

36. Show the changes that must be made in the binary search program to store the address, not the index, of the item sought. (As before, store zero if the item is not in the table.)

37. The point of this problem is to modify the binary search program for the situation where there may be more than one entry in the table with the same key. Show what changes are needed to efficiently find all occurrences of the key sought. Store the index of the first entry containing the key in INDEX, a word, and store the number of such entries in NUM_COPIES, a word. (If the key is not found, store zero in both INDEX and NUM_COPIES.)

38. Suppose that the binary search program is to be written for tables that have 32 bytes in each entry, and that the longword key occupies the last four bytes of each entry. Show the changes that should be made in the program.

39. For both sequential search and binary search (Exercise 34 and Fig. 7.7), the number of times the instructions in the search loop are executed depends on where in the table the item sought happens to be. Suppose that the table has 127 entries. Tell how many times the instructions in the search loop would be executed by each algorithm if the item sought were

(a) In the sixty-fourth place.   (d) In the ninety-sixth place.
(b) Not in the table.   (e) In the last place.
(c) In the first place.

40. What does Exercise 19 have to do with the binary search algorithm?

41. Suppose that there were no AOBLSS instruction. Write an efficient sequence of instructions that could replace

```
AOBLSS   R10,R6,LOOP
```

42. Why is the longword at NUM copied to R7 in Example 7.8, instead of just using
```
AOBLEQ    NUM,R6,STORE
```
as the loop control instruction?

43. Suppose that there were no ACBW instruction. Write an efficient sequence of instructions that could replace

```
ACBW    CNT,#7,R9,CHECK
```

44. Suppose that the instructions in a loop must be executed n times, where n is a longword in R9 and n may be zero. Write the initialization and loop control instructions to do this; use as few and as simple instructions as possible.

45. Write the instructions to test whether or not the loop body should be executed at all in Example 7.9.

46. The general form of an ALGOL **for** statement is

for index := initial_value **step** increment **until** limit **do**
   loop body

If the loop increment specified after **step** is positive, the loop body is executed for each value of the loop index, beginning at *initial_value* and incremented by *increment*, up to, but not including, the limit specified after **until**. If the increment is negative, the loop body is executed for values down to, but not including, the limit. Using appropriate VAX loop control instructions, write all the instructions needed to initialize and control loops described by the following ALGOL statements.

   (a) for I := 2*(N+4) **step** 12 **until** LEVEL2 **do**

      loop body

   (b) for CNTR := START **step** SIZE **until** LIMIT **do**

      loop body

     (SIZE may be negative or positive.)

47. ALPHA is a longword array with distinct elements, and NUM (a longword) contains the number of elements. A *run* is an increasing sequence of elements. For example, the array containing 12, 22, 2, 4, 5, 18, 10, 25, 34 has three runs: 12, 22; and 2, 4, 5, 18; and 10, 25, 34. Write instructions to count the runs in the array ALPHA, and store the number of runs in NUMRUNS, a byte.

48. BETA is a two-dimensional word array. The number of rows is stored in ROWS and the number of columns is stored in COLS (both words). Write instructions to determine if any rows in the array are *monotone*. Monotone means that as you read the row left to right, the numbers are increasing, or as you read left to right, they are decreasing. (A row is not monotone if the numbers go up and down or down and up.) You may assume that the elements in each row are distinct. For each monotone row that you find, print a message telling its row number. If you do not find any monotone rows, print a message saying that there were none.

49. Suppose that LIST is a word array, and that the longword at NUM contains the number of entries. Write instructions to rearrange the entries in LIST so that all negative entries come before all nonnegative entries. The list does not have to be sorted completely, and your solution should do less work that a sorting algorithm. (This is not difficult if you use a second array for temporary storage. Try to think of an efficient algorithm that does not require a separate array.)

50. The sorting algorithm known as the Bubble Sort puts a list in nondecreasing order as follows: Starting at the beginning of the list, compare each adjacent pair of entries (the first and the second, then the second and third, the third and fourth, and so on) and interchange the entries in a pair if they are out of order. When the entire list has been processed once in this way, it may not be completely sorted, but the largest entry will be in the last position—where it belongs. The process of comparing adjacent pairs of entries and interchanging those out of order is repeated on all but the last entry to get the next largest entry into its proper place. The process is repeated, each time ignoring the last entry from the previous pass, until there are no more pairs out of order.

    The algorithm can be improved by keeping track of the position where the last interchange occurred. If, for example, the last interchange during one pass through the list occurred at the ith position, all the entries in the $(i + 1)$st to last positions must be in their proper places and do not have to be examined again.

In the following Pascal algorithm for Bubble Sort, *last* is the index of the last entry that may be out of order, *pairs* is the number of pairs to be compared, and *num* is the number of entries in the array *list*. Note that *last* is set to zero before each pass through the list to catch the case where no interchanges are done, indicating that the list is in order.

Using the Pascal algorithm as a guide, write an assembly language program segment for Bubble Sort.

```
last := num;
while last > 0 do begin
    pairs := last – 1;
    last := 0;
    for j := 1 to pairs do
        if list[j] > list[j+1] then begin
            temp := list[j];
            list[j] := list[j+1];
            list[j+1] := temp;
            last := j
        end
    end
```

51. Suppose TEXT is a long array of characters containing a paragraph of text. The length of the text is in the longword LENGTH. There are no end-of-line marks in TEXT. Write instructions to print the paragraph at the terminal with at most 60 characters per line. You may not break a word at the end of a line, so the problem involves finding an appropriate place to end each line (i.e., finding a space between words).

8

Machine Code Formats, Translation, and Execution

8.1 AN OVERVIEW

Machine Code Formats

In this chapter we examine how instructions are encoded in machine code and how the CPU interprets and executes the code. We also consider how the assembler translates operand specifiers from assembly language statements into machine code. We will begin with some of the simpler, very commonly used addressing modes described in Chapter 4 and introduce more complex modes as we move through the chapter.

For computers in general, instructions in machine code have two major components: an opcode, i.e., a pattern of bits specifying the machine instruction to be performed, and an encoding of the operands, which includes their location, and may include the mode used to indicate the location, the data type, and other such information. Details of how instructions are encoded in machine languages vary with the different machine architectures and instruction sets. Some machines have very rigid instruction formats. For example, on IBM mainframes, an instruction to add two integers requires that one be in a register and one in memory, addressed by a mode similar to the VAX's displacement mode. A different instruction must be used to add integers if both are in registers. Thus, there, the encoding of the operands does not include any indication of the mode used, because it is implied by the opcode. Other machines allow more flexibility in a variety of

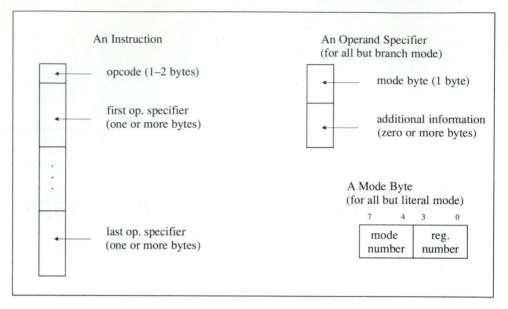

Figure 8.1   Machine code format

different directions. On some machines one instruction can be used for several data types. For example, on Motorola 68000 Family microprocessors, the same integer addition instruction is used for bytes, words, and longwords (and similarly for other integer operations). Thus, there, the encoding of the operands must include an indication of the data type. On the VAX, as we know well by now, there are different instructions for different data types, but with few restrictions, any of the addressing modes may be combined with any opcodes to form an instruction.

   Note that the term *addressing mode* usually means the way an operand is specified in machine code. In Chapter 4 we used the same term when describing how operands are specified in assembly language source statements. In general, the reader should be able to tell from the context when we are referring to source statement formats and when to machine code. Note also that we do not normally speak of "addressing" a register—memory locations, not registers, have addresses. But the term "addressing mode" is used in general for the way an operand is specified.

   Figure 8.1 illustrates the general format for VAX instructions. Instructions may begin on any byte boundary. The opcode comes first and is followed by a sequence of operand specifiers, the number of which depends on the instruction. (The maximum is six.) The order in which the operand specifiers appear in the machine code corresponds to the order in which they appear in the assembly language source statement. Opcodes for almost all instructions are one byte long. (There are two extra floating-point data types, in addition to the standard ones, whose instructions have two-byte opcodes.) Each operand specifier (with the exception of branch mode) contains a mode number and whatever additional information is needed for the particular addressing mode used.

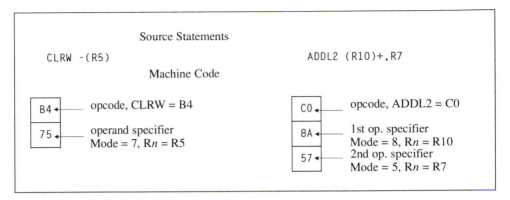

Figure 8.2 Examples of machine code

(Since branch mode *must* be used for branch destination operands, it does not require a mode number.) For most modes, the first byte of the operand specifier, the mode byte, contains the mode number in bits 7:4 and a register number in bits 3:0. (The AP, FP, SP, and PC registers are encoded as C_{16} through F_{16}.) The CPU can determine from the mode number how many additional bytes are part of the current operand. For example, if register mode is used, the operand specifier will contain the mode number, 5, and the register number. For mode 5 no additional bytes are needed.

Figure 8.2 shows the encoding of some instructions using some simple addressing modes. In these examples the operand specifiers consist only of a mode number and register number. In all examples, machine code is shown in hex.

Instruction Execution

We will describe the execution process briefly here and give examples in the next few sections. The CPU uses the program counter, PC, to keep track of its place while executing instructions. When it is ready to start a new instruction, it fetches the byte whose address is in the PC and increments the PC by 1. The CPU interprets the byte fetched as the opcode and determines from it what the instruction is and how many operands it has.[1] For each operand in turn (other than branch mode operands) the CPU first fetches[2] the byte addressed by the PC (the mode byte), incrementing the PC by 1, and determines from the mode number how many bytes of additional information are needed. It then fetches the appropriate number of additional bytes beginning at the address in the PC and increments the PC by that number. When an entire operand specifier has been examined, the CPU determines the location of the operand; that is, it determines if the operand is in

---

[1] The instructions for the G_floating and H_floating data types have two-byte opcodes. The first byte of a two-byte opcode is FD or FF; the CPU can determine from this byte if the next byte is part of the opcode. In this chapter, for simplicity, we consider only one-byte opcodes.

[2] The CPU does not actually fetch the instructions from memory byte by byte; to save time, it fetches several bytes at once and keeps them in an instruction buffer.

a register or in memory, and in the latter case, it determines the address, adjusting the contents of the register used for addressing if necessary (e.g., if the mode was autoincrement or autodecrement). Then, if this operand is to be used in the operation (as opposed to being a location for a result to be stored), the CPU fetches the actual operand. After all operand specifiers have been evaluated, the operation is carried out. The PC will contain the address of the next instruction.

The Assembler's Task

It is the assembler's main task to translate assembly language source programs into machine code. We give here a brief, somewhat simplified, description of some of the work done by the assembler so that we can understand how it translates some of the operand specifiers described in this chapter. (Some other aspects of the assembly process will be discussed in Chapter 10.)

The reader should take care to remember the distinction between assembly time and execution time. All the steps carried out by the CPU to fetch, interpret, and execute instructions occur at execution time after the assembler (and linker) have finished their tasks. Assembly—translation of the source program—is done first. In this chapter, however, we will often describe the execution process first, then consider how the assembler would have accomplished the translation. We present the discussion in this order because the machine code formats and the scheme for interpretation and execution of instructions by the CPU are fundamental to the computer (whatever computer we may be studying). The assembler is secondary; it is a program written to accomplish a particular task that is determined by the computer's architecture and instruction set.

There can be, and generally is, more than one assembler for a particular computer. Our discussion will be general enough to apply to many typical ones.

The assembler makes two passes through the module it is translating. The main purpose of the first pass is to find all the symbols used and determine their values (if possible). The assembler constructs a table, called the symbol table, containing the symbols, their values, and other information about them. Most symbols are labels on data areas and instructions. As we indicated in Chapter 4, the assembler has a location counter that it uses to keep track of the number of bytes used up so far by the data and instructions, so it can compute the address of a byte labeled by a symbol. (Since the assembler does not know where in memory the program will actually be when it is executed, it initializes the location counter to zero. Thus the values in the symbol table are computed relative to the assembler's starting point.) To compute the symbol values correctly, it is critical that the assembler be able to determine during its first pass how many bytes the encoding of each instruction will require.

During the second pass over the source program, the assembler generates the machine code. Translation of the mnemonic instruction names into opcodes is done by looking up the names in a table. Operand specifiers that do not use symbols can be encoded in a straightforward way. Wherever a symbol is used in an operand specifier, the assembler looks up the symbol value in the symbol table and encodes the operand specifier appropriately.

8.2 SOME REGISTER MODES

In this section we will discuss the implementation of the register addressing modes presented in Chapter 4 and displacement mode, introduced in Chapter 7.

The Simpler Register Modes

The first four modes may be considered in a group as their formats are very similar. They are:

		Assembly Language Format
Mode	**Mode Number**	**(Rn = R0, ... , R11, AP, FP, or SP)**
Register	5	Rn
Register deferred	6	(Rn)
Autodecrement	7	–(Rn)
Autoincrement	8	(Rn)+

For each of these modes, the operand specifier consists of only the mode byte; bits 7:4 contain the mode number and bits 3:0 the register number. (Recall that AP, FP, and SP are encoded as 12, 13, and 14, respectively.) For example,

$$\boxed{64}$$

is the operand specifier for (R4)—that is, register deferred mode using R4. The examples in Fig. 8.2 use these modes.

Since we described in Chapter 4 how these modes work, and they are fairly straightforward, we will not give execution examples here but instead will include them in other examples throughout this chapter.

Translating a source statement operand using one of these modes is very easy for the assembler to do; the mode and register number are clearly indicated by the assembly language format.

Displacement Mode

In Chapter 7 we described displacement mode as one mode, and, indeed, from the programmer's point of view there is one format for a displacement mode operand:

$$dis(Rn)$$

where Rn is R0, ... , R11, AP, FP, or SP. There are actually three displacement modes; they differ according to how much space is used for the displacement in the machine code for the operand—a byte, a word, or a longword. The operand specifier formats are shown in Fig. 8.3. The displacement may be negative or positive; it is stored in the instruction as a two's complement integer. (Recall that two's complement integers are stored in memory with the least significant byte first. Thus when written in the natural way, the first byte is at the right. This is why machine code is shown right to left on assembly program listings. In Fig. 8.3 the first byte of each operand specifier, the mode

Mode	Mode Number	Format $(n = 0, \ldots, 15_{10})$*
Byte displacement	A	dis | An
Word displacement	C	dis | Cn
Longword displacement	E	dis | En

* AP, FP, and SP are encoded as 12, 13, and 14 (C, D, and E in hex), respectively.
If $n = 15$ (for the PC), the mode is called relative mode.

Figure 8.3 Displacement modes

byte, is at the right.) When translating a displacement mode operand, the assembler will try to use as little space as possible. For example, if the displacement is between -128_{10} and 127_{10}, it will use one byte (mode A). The assembler must decide how many bytes to allow for the displacement during its first pass over the instruction so that its location counter can be incremented properly. In cases where the assembler does not have enough information to determine the displacement on its first pass, it chooses mode C, word displacement. If it later turns out that more space is needed, the linker gives an error message. The programmer may override the assembler's choice by explicitly specifying the particular mode in the following forms:

B^*dis*(R*n*)   For mode A, byte displacement
W^*dis*(R*n*)   For mode C, word displacement
L^*dis*(R*n*)   For mode E, longword displacement

If the programmer chooses a mode too small for the actual displacement, an error will result. Usually, it is best to leave the choice to the assembler.

Example 8.1: Execution of an Instruction with Displacement Mode

Suppose that PC contains 0000024E, the CPU is about to begin execution of a new instruction, and the code shown below is in memory. We will describe the steps carried out by the CPU and show where the PC is pointing at each step illustrated. The byte(s) being interpreted by the CPU at each step are boxed.

	Address	Code
PC →	0000024E	D0
	0000024F	C9
	00000250	2A
	00000251	01
	00000252	87
	00000253	D6

Fetch the byte addressed by PC; increment PC by 1.

Address	Code
0000024E	DO
PC → 0000024F	C9
00000250	2A
00000251	01
00000252	87
00000253	D6

Interpret the byte fetched, D0, as an opcode. D0 is a MOVL instruction. It requires two operands.

Fetch the byte addressed by PC; increment PC by 1.

Address	Code	Interpretation
0000024E	DO	Opcode: MOVL
0000024F	C9	
PC → 00000250	2A	
00000251	01	
00000252	87	
00000253	D6	

Interpret the byte fetched, C9, as the mode byte for the first operand. The mode number is C, so the mode is word displacement. The register used is R9. We will assume that R9 contains 00006408.

Since a word displacement is used, fetch the word (two bytes) addressed by PC and increment PC by 2.

Address	Code	Interpretation
0000024E	DO	Opcode: MOVL
0000024F	C9	Mode byte: Word displacement mode using R9
00000250	2A	
00000251	01	
PC → 00000252	87	
00000253	D6	

The displacement is 012A. Recall that the CPU's formula for evaluating a displacement mode operand specifier is

$$\text{operand address} = (Rn) + dis$$

Thus the first operand address is (R9) + displacement = 00006408 + 0000012A = 00006532. (R9 is not changed; the address computation is done in a CPU scratch area.) Fetch the operand, that is, the longword in memory at this address. (The operand is held in a CPU scratch area.)

The next byte will be interpreted as the mode byte for the second operand. Fetch it and increment PC by 1.

Address	Code	Interpretation
0000024E	D0	Opcode: MOVL
0000024F	C9	Mode byte: Word displacement mode using R9
00000250	2A	
00000251	01	Displacement: 012A
00000252	87	
PC → 00000253	D6	

The mode byte for the second operand is 87. Thus the mode is mode 8, autoincrement mode, and the register used is R7. No additional bytes are needed for autoincrement mode.

The second operand address is the address now in R7. Save it in a scratch area. Since the instruction is MOVL, the data type of the second operand is longword, so the address in R7 is incremented by 4.

Carry out the operation; that is, copy the first operand into the longword specified by the second operand address.

Now the CPU is ready to execute the next instruction. Note that the PC is pointing to the byte in memory that follows the current instruction. That byte will be interpreted as the opcode for the next instruction.

The instruction we decoded in Example 8.1 may originally have appeared in an assembly language program as

```
MOVL    298(R9),(R7)+
```

Note that the displacement is written in decimal; the assembler converts it to two's complement when it translates the instruction to machine code.

There are two details to remember about displacement mode: address computation always uses 32 bits, so the displacement is sign-extended if necessary, and the register contents will not be changed. For example, if the displacement is FF63 and the register contains 000045C2, the operand address is computed as

	(Rn)	000045C2	
+	displacement	FFFFFF63	(sign extended)
	operand address	00004525	

The contents of the register will still be 000045C2.

8.3 LITERAL MODE

Literal mode is used for encoding small nonnegative operands that are specified in the instruction itself, rather than being in a register or memory location. The assembly language format is

#*expression*

Any mode number whose leftmost two bits are zeros (i.e., modes 0 through 3) is a literal mode number; the rightmost two bits of the mode number are actually part of the literal value. Thus the form of an operand specifier for a literal is

$$\boxed{00 \quad \textit{literal}}$$

Since six bits are used for the literal value, an integer literal may be between 0 and 63. Floating-point literals will be described in Chapter 13.

Example 8.2: An Example of Literal Mode

The instruction

```
MOVW     #25,R11
```

would be encoded as

Code	Interpretation
B0	Opcode: MOVW
19	Literal. In binary: `00 | 011001`
5B	R11

When the CPU encounters a literal operand while executing an instruction, it expands the operand to the data size required by the instruction. For example, the literal in Example 8.2 would be expanded (in a CPU scratch area) to 16 bits, by adding zeros at the left, because the instruction is MOVW.

The Assembler's Task

In Chapter 4 we mentioned that although operand specifiers like #3 and #100 appear to be the same mode in assembly language, they are encoded differently in machine code; the latter is immediate mode. The assembler must decide during its first pass whether to encode an operand beginning with a # in literal mode or immediate mode. If the operand is an integer between 0 and 63 (or a floating-point number that fits in six bits), the assembler will use literal mode. If it is not in the ranges required for literals, or if the assembler cannot determine its value during the first pass over the instruction, it will encode the operand using immediate mode. We will give examples contrasting the two modes in Section 8.5, after immediate mode has been described.

The programmer can override the assembler's choice of mode and force it to use literal rather than immediate mode by writing the operand in the following format:

$$S\textasciicircum\#\textit{expression}$$

8.4 BRANCH MODE

Branch mode is used to encode the branch destination operand in all branch instructions, including loop control instructions. Because it *must* be used for the branch destination in these instructions and can be used *only* for these operands, a mode byte is not needed in the operand specifier. A branch destination is always encoded as a displacement from the contents of the PC. Thus, if the branch is to be taken, the CPU computes the destination address as follows:

$$\text{destination} = (\text{PC}) + \text{displacement}$$

and puts it in the PC.

The displacement may be positive or negative and is stored as a two's complement integer in a byte or word, depending on the particular instruction. The unconditional branch instruction BRB (BRanch, Byte displacement), all the conditional branches, and some of the loop control instructions use byte displacements. The unconditional branch instruction BRW (BRanch, Word displacement) and some loop control instructions use a word displacement.

Example 8.3: Execution of an Instruction with Branch Mode

We will go through the CPU's steps to decode and execute the instruction beginning at 00000835.

	Address	Code
PC →	00000835	F5
	00000836	58
	00000837	D2
	00000838	B6

Fetch the opcode and increment PC by 1.

	Address	Code
	00000835	F5
PC →	00000836	58
	00000837	D2
	00000838	B6

F5 is the opcode for SOBGTR. There must be two operands—the loop index and the branch destination.

Fetch the mode byte for the index and increment PC by 1.

	Address	Code	Interpretation
	00000835	F5	Opcode: SOBGTR
	00000836	58	
PC →	00000837	D2	
	00000838	B6	

The mode number is 5, register mode, and the register number is 8, so the index is in R8.

The second operand is the branch destination. Since the SOBGTR instruction always uses a byte displacement for the branch destination, fetch one byte (incrementing PC by 1).

Address	Code	Interpretation
00000835	F5	Opcode: SOBGTR
00000836	58	Mode byte: Register mode using R8
00000837	D2	
PC → 00000838	B6	

The branch displacement is D2. Now, to carry out the operation for this instruction, subtract 1 from R8 (R8 *is* changed), and determine if the branch should be taken.

If the result in R8 is not greater than zero, execution of this instruction is complete and the CPU will proceed to interpret and execute the instruction beginning at 00000838. If, on the other hand, the number in R8 is greater than zero, the branch is to be taken, so add the displacement to the PC:

current (PC)	00000838	
+ displacement	FFFFFFD2	(sign extended)
new (PC)	0000080A	

This completes execution of the instruction; the branch is effectively accomplished when the CPU begins processing the next instruction, because it uses the PC to determine where the next instruction is.

Note that because the PC is incremented when the displacement is fetched, the branch address will be the sum of the displacement and the address of the instruction that follows the branch instruction. A byte integer is in the range from -128_{10} to 127_{10}, so branch instructions with byte displacements may be used only to branch to other instructions within that range from the location of the next instruction.

Why Does Branch Mode Use a Displacement from (PC)?

In an assembly language statement, the branch destination is usually specified by a symbol that is the label on the target instruction (the one to be branched to). Why is that address encoded as a displacement from the contents of the PC rather than simply as the value of the symbol, or the address of the target instruction? Recall that the value of the symbol stored in the assembler's symbol table is the address of the instruction it labels *relative to the beginning of the module or program section* being translated. The module will be linked with others and may be loaded into memory at different places each time it is used. The true branch destination address is not known to the assembler, but when the instruction is executed, the CPU must compute the true branch address. The *distance* between the branch destination address and the contents of the PC (the address of the instruction following the branch instruction) is constant; the number of bytes used to encode the instructions between the branch instruction and the target instruction is independent of the location of the program in memory. Thus several addressing modes allow the assembler to encode address expressions as displacements from the contents of the PC. By using displacements we are assured that the program will run correctly anywhere in memory without adjustments to the operand specifiers when the program is loaded. All modern computers use some variation of this displacement scheme to translate address expressions.

The Assembler's Task

Consider the instruction in Example 8.3. It might have appeared in a program as

```
SOBGTR  R8,LOOP
```

Suppose that when the assembler encounters this statement during its first pass, . = 235_{16}. (Recall that . is the notation used for the location counter.) At this time, the assembler determines that the machine code for this statement will require three bytes: one for the opcode, one for the first operand specifier because it uses register mode, and one for the second operand specifier because SOBGTR always uses branch mode with byte displacement. The assembler can increment . to .+3 and go on to the next instruction. When the assembler encounters this instruction during its second pass, it does the translation. It encodes SOBGTR as F5 and R8 as 58, incrementing . by 1 for each byte used. When it encodes the branch destination, . = 237_{16}. To compute the displacement, the assembler looks up LOOP in the symbol table and finds, say, that LOOP = $20A_{16}$. It knows that during execution the CPU will use the formula

$$\text{destination} = (PC) + \text{displacement}$$

So the assembler solves the following equation for the displacement:

$$\text{LOOP} = \text{location of next byte} + \text{displacement}$$

$$0000020A = 00000238 + \text{displacement}$$

$$\text{displacement} = 0000020A - 00000238 = FFFFFFD2$$

Thus the third operand specifier is translated as D2. Note that in Example 8.3 we assumed that the instruction appeared in memory beginning at byte 835, not 235, and the branch destination was calculated as 0000080A, whereas here LOOP = 20A. Example 8.3 assumes that the module containing this instruction is loaded in memory beginning at byte 600. The assembler does not know that, but its computation of the displacement is correct regardless of where the program is put in memory.

If the displacement computed by the assembler is too large for one byte (i.e., is outside the range -128_{10} to 127_{10}), the assembler will issue an error message. (We do not have to convert FFFFFFD2 to decimal to check. Just observe that when truncating FFFFFFD2 to D2, we did not drop any significant bits; i.e., FFFFFFD2 = D2 with sign extension.)

8.5 SOME PROGRAM COUNTER MODES: RELATIVE MODE AND IMMEDIATE MODE

As we have seen, the PC is used by the CPU to keep track of its place in the instruction stream. But the PC is a register. What happens if it is used in an operand specifier just as R0 through R11, AP, FP, and SP may be used? For addressing modes where use of the PC would have strange and undesirable effects, it is simply prohibited. For other modes, however, the PC can be used with very useful effects, but because the effects and uses of addressing modes with the PC are very different from their effects and uses with other registers, addressing modes using the PC are given special names and must be studied carefully. Relative mode and immediate mode, introduced in Chapter 4, are special cases of displacement mode and autoincrement mode, respectively, using the PC.

Relative Mode

An operand address specified in a source statement by a symbol, or more generally, an expression, is a relative mode operand. In machine code, a relative mode operand is encoded in displacement mode using PC as the register. Thus the formula used by the CPU to determine the operand address is

$$\text{operand address} = (PC) + \text{displacement}$$

A displacement from (PC) is used for address expressions for the same reason as it is used for branch mode—to make the code independent of where the program is loaded in memory.

Any one of the three displacement modes, A, C, or E, may be used, depending on how much space is needed for the displacement. Figure 8.3 shows their formats. When used for relative mode, the rightmost nibble of the mode byte contains F, or 15, the PC's register number.

When the assembler encounters a source instruction with a relative mode operand during its first pass, it can evaluate the address expression if the symbols in the expression are already in the symbol table. It can compute the appropriate displacement using its location counter, and it will choose the mode with the smallest number of bytes needed to represent the displacement in two's complement form. If any symbol in the expression is not yet in the symbol table, the assembler will allow for the maximum possible displacement size, a longword, and either it or the linker can compute and fill in the displacement later. This is why in Chapter 4 we recommended placing storage reservation and initialization directives at the beginning of a program section. When the labels on the data areas are used as operands later in the program, they will already be in the symbol table and the assembler will be able to economize on the space used for displacements.

Example 8.4: Execution of an Instruction with Relative Mode

We will follow the steps carried out by the CPU to interpret and execute the instruction encoded below. We assume that it starts at 000013A6. Processing of the first two bytes is straightforward. The instruction is MULL3 and the first operand is the literal #3.

	Address	Code	Interpretation
	000013A6	C5	Opcode: MULL3
	000013A7	03	Literal: #3
PC →	000013A8	CF	
	000013A9	B9	
	000013AA	FE	
	000013AB	66	

Fetch the mode byte for the second operand, incrementing PC by 1.

Address	Code	Interpretation
000013A6	C5	Opcode: MULL3
000013A7	03	Literal: #3
000013A8	CF	
PC → 000013A9	B9	
000013AA	FE	
000013AB	66	

The mode byte contains CF, so the mode is C—displacement mode with word displacement. The register used is F, or 15 (i.e., the PC).

Fetch the displacement and increment PC again, but by two this time because the displacement is a word.

Address	Code	Interpretation
000013A6	C5	Opcode: MULL3
000013A7	03	Literal: #3
000013A8	CF	Mode byte: Word displacement mode using the PC
000013A9	B9	
000013AA	FE	
PC → 000013AB	66	

The displacement is FEB9. Compute the address of the second operand by adding the displacement and the current contents of the PC:

(PC)	000013AB
+displacement	FFFFFEB9
operand address	00001264

The longword beginning at 00001264 is the second operand for MULL3.

Fetch the mode byte for the third operand, incrementing PC. The mode byte is 66, so the third operand uses register deferred mode with R6. Perform the multiplication and put the result in the longword whose address is in R6.

At this point the PC contains 000013AC, the address of the next instruction. The instruction we just decoded may have originally appeared in an assembly language program as

```
MULL3   #3,SYMBOL,(R6)
```

where SYMBOL was defined earlier in the program and the instruction appears 142_{16} bytes later. Note that the assembler had to use a word for the displacement for SYMBOL because it would not fit in a byte.

Two points to remember about relative mode were illustrated by this example. At the time the operand address is computed, the PC contains the address of the next operand specifier (or the next instruction). As with displacement mode in general, the computation of the operand address is done in a CPU scratch area; the PC is unchanged.

Fortran	Assembly Language			Machine Code
	COST:	.BLKF	1	
	BASE:	.BLKF	1	
	VAR:	.BLKF	1	
	NUM:	.BLKL	1	
	.			
	.			
	.			
COST=BASE+NUM*VAR	CVTLF	NUM,R3		53DBAF4E
	MULF2	VAR,R3		53D3AF44
	ADDF3	BASE,R3,COST		C4AF53CBAF41

Figure 8.4 Example 1.1 revisited

Note that a relative mode operand requires from two to five bytes of storage, whereas all the register modes we have described, with the exception of displacement mode, use only one byte. Thus the programmer can write more compact programs by using the register modes where possible instead of address expressions.

The Assembler's Task

We have already described some of the assembler's considerations in using relative mode, so we will begin here with an example. Let us consider the first example of assembly language and machine code we presented in Section 1.1. It is reproduced in Fig. 8.4. The instructions do floating-point arithmetic, but the fact that we have not yet studied those instructions should cause no problem here, since we are interested only in the fairly mechanical task of translating into machine code.

Since we already have the machine code, we will work backward from it and figure out what the assembler did. Let us assume that when the assembler encountered the storage reservation instructions in the example, . = 2016. (We could assume that . = 0 or any other value.) When the assembler encounters the machine instructions, it will have the following entries in its symbol table:

Symbol	Value
COST	00000020
BASE	00000024
VAR	00000028
NUM	0000002C

The machine code for the first instruction (with the first byte at the right, as it appears on an assembly program listing) is

53 DB AF 4E

4E is the opcode for CVTLF, and AF is the mode byte for the first operand. Thus the assembler encoded NUM using relative mode with byte displacement. DB is the displacement. The assembler knew that when the displacement is added to the PC during execution, the PC will contain the address of the next operand specifier, following the displacement. Thus the assembler used the following equation to compute the displacement:

$$\text{NUM} = 0000002C = \text{location of next byte} + \text{displacement}$$

Since the assembler computed DB as the displacement, the location counter value for the next byte must have been 00000051 (i.e., 0000002C–FFFFFFDB). By counting back, we can determine that . = 4E at the beginning of the instruction, and we can write down the location counter value for each byte.

Location Counter	Code
0000004E	4E
0000004F	AF
00000050	DB
00000051	53

Now let us consider the second instruction:

53 D3 AF 44

44 is the opcode for MULF2, and once again the mode byte for the first operand is AF. Thus the assembler encoded the symbol VAR using relative mode with byte displacement. It used the equation

$$\text{VAR} = 00000028 = \text{location of next byte} + \text{displacement}$$

and computed D3 for the displacement. So the location of the next byte (the one containing the next operand specifier, 53) must be 00000055 (00000028–FFFFFFD3). Thus the locations of the bytes of the second instruction are

Location Counter	Code
00000052	44
00000053	AF
00000054	D3
00000055	53

The second instruction should follow immediately after the first one, and we see from our computation that it does. We leave it to the reader to decode the third instruction and see how the assembler computed the displacements for BASE and COST.

In this example we already had the machine code, so we knew that the assembler used byte displacements. We will now consider how the assembler determines the displacement and the particular relative mode to use, not knowing in advance how large the displacement is. Suppose that the operand being encoded is specified by a symbol. Because the PC will contain the address of the byte following the operand specifier

when it and the displacement are added, the equation used by the assembler to determine the displacement is

symbol value = location of byte following the operand specifier + displacement

The problem here is that there are two "unknowns" in the equation: the displacement, of course, and the location of the byte following the operand specifier. The latter is unknown because it depends on how many bytes are used for the displacement. Suppose that . = the location of the relative mode operand specifier we are working on. The assembler could first try to determine if the displacement will fit in a byte by solving for the displacement in

symbol value = .+2 + displacement

The location of the byte following the operand specifier will be .+2, because the mode byte and the displacement will each take up one byte. If the solution for the displacement is in the range -128_{10} to 127_{10}, it fits in a byte and the assembler is done. As we observed in the section on branch mode, if the displacement can be described in two hex digits, in two's complement form, it fits in a byte. For example, if we compute a negative displacement of FF7A, it cannot be stored in a byte because 7A will be interpreted as a positive number; the bits dropped are not all the same as the resulting sign bit.

If the assembler's solution for the displacement in the equation above fits in a word but not a byte, it cannot just go ahead and use that displacement. If the displacement takes up a word, the location of the byte following it will not be .+2; it will be .+3, making the solution no longer valid. It should be clear that the displacement can be corrected by decreasing it by 1. The reader can easily generalize for the case where the computed displacement requires a longword.

Immediate Mode

Immediate mode is used for assembling literal operands that are too big for the six-bit literal addressing mode. In immediate mode (as in literal mode), the operand itself (i.e., the datum to be used by the instruction) rather than the operand address is stored in the instruction. The term *immediate operand* is used with a similar meaning for most assembly languages, although the details of how the operand is stored differ for different computers.

Immediate mode is autoincrement mode, mode 8, using the PC. The mode byte contains 8F and the immediate datum is stored immediately after the mode byte. The instruction

        ADDL2   #75,R10

would be encoded as follows:

Code	Interpretation
C0	Opcode: ADDL2
8F	Mode byte: Autoincrement mode using the PC
4B	The immediate operand, first byte

00	immediate operand, second byte
00	immediate operand, third byte
00	immediate operand, fourth byte
5A	Mode byte: R10

Let us consider what happens when this instruction is executed.

Example 8.5: Execution of an Instruction with Immediate Mode

Suppose that the instruction begins at 00000472. Fetch the opcode. The instruction is ADDL2. Fetch the mode byte for the first operand. We now have

	Address	Code	Interpretation
	00000472	C0	Opcode: ADDL2
	00000473	8F	
PC →	00000474	4B	
	00000475	00	
	00000476	00	
	00000477	00	
	00000478	5A	

The mode byte is 8F; thus the mode is autoincrement and the register used is the PC. The operand address is the address now in the PC, 00000474. Since the instruction is ADDL2, fetch the operand, the longword at 00000474, and keep it in a scratch area.

As usual with autoincrement mode, increment the register by the number of bytes indicated by the data type of the operand, in this case 4 for longword. So 00000478 goes into the PC.

	Address	Code	Interpretation
	00000472	C0	Opcode: ADDL2
	00000473	8F	Mode byte: Autoincrement mode using the PC
	00000474	4B	
	00000475	00	
	00000476	00	
	00000477	00	
PC →	00000478	5A	

Note that this time the PC was incremented as a side effect of being used with autoincrement mode, not as a normal part of the instruction execution process.

Fetch the next byte and interpret it as the mode byte for the second operand. Increment PC by 1 as usual; it now points to the first byte of the next instruction. The second operand specifier is 5A, so the operand is R10.

Now, perform the operation: addition of longwords. The first operand address is 00000474, so the datum in the longword beginning at that byte, 0000004B, is added to the longword in R10. 0000004B is the longword two's complement representation of the decimal integer 75, the first operand in the source statement.

Source Statement		Machine Code							Mode of First Operand
ADDL2	#75,R10	5A	00	00	00	4B	8F	C0	immediate, longword
ADDW2	#75,R10		5A	00	4B	8F	A0		immediate, word
ADDL2	#55,R10			5A	37	C0			literal
MOVB	#^A/3/,(R8)			68	33	90			literal
MOVB	#^A/L/,(R8)		68	4C	8F	90			immediate, byte

Figure 8.5 Literal and immediate modes

The Assembler's Task

As we indicated in the discussion of literal mode, when the assembler encounters an operand beginning with a #, it must decide whether to use literal mode or immediate mode. Suppose that it has decided to use immediate mode. Then it must determine the data type of the operand and encode the datum in the proper type.

Figure 8.5 shows several source statements and the machine code for each. The bytes of machine code are shown right to left, opcode first (at the right), as they are shown on program listings. Note that #75 is encoded as a longword in the first instruction, ADDL2, but as a word in the second instruction ADDW2. Even though the third instruction operates on longword data, #55 is encoded as a literal using only one byte for the entire operand specifier. Recall that literal operands are expanded to the data type required for the instruction by the CPU at execution time.

The last two instructions in Fig. 8.5 each move a character code to a byte in memory. Note that although a byte is usually used for a character code, the assembler uses a literal for the character '3' because its code is 33_{16}, or 51_{10}, which fits in six bits. The code for the character 'L' is 4C, or 76_{10}, which does not fit in six bits, so the assembler uses immediate mode.

8.6 AN ASSEMBLY LISTING

We looked at the format of assembly language program listings in Section 5.3. There we saw, among other things, that the listing shows (reading from right to left) the assembly language source statements, the program line number, the value of the location counter at each line, the machine code and data the assembler puts in the object file, and miscellaneous other information. In this section we focus on the machine code.

Figure 8.6 shows the main part of a sample listing produced by the VAX MACRO assembler. The program is a somewhat modified and expanded version of the program segment in Example 7.3. It is worth spending some time examining the listing carefully, as it illustrates many of the addressing modes described so far in this chapter.

Let us examine one instruction in detail. Line 77 contains

Machine Code				Loc	Line	Source Statement
FF2A CF	03	00000055 8F	F9	05D0	77	CVTLP #HIGH,#3,PKD
PKD	#3	#HIGH	opcode			

Notice that the assembler listing groups the bytes in the machine code according to their roles, making the code a little easier to interpret. F9 is the opcode for CVTLP. The first operand, #HIGH, is encoded in immediate mode because HIGH = 85, which is too large for a literal. The assembler allows a longword for HIGH because the first operand of CVTLP is of longword type. The second operand, #3, is small enough for a literal, so the operand specifier is 03. The third operand is encoded in relative mode. The assembler has used a word displacement. By observing that the instruction begins at the location 05D0 and counting bytes (or by looking at the location of the next instruction), we can determine that the location of the byte following the displacement is 05DA. Thus PKD should be equal to 05DA+FF2A = 0504. Looking back to line 36 where PKD is defined, we see that this is correct.

In the program in Fig. 8.6, there were no operand specifiers that the assembler could not handle. In general, if a relative mode operand uses a symbol that is defined after the instruction that uses it, or if the symbol is not defined in the module at all, the assembler inserts EF in the mode byte and leaves a longword for the displacement. The linker will fill in the displacement. On a listing the assembler flags such operand specifiers with an apostrophe; for example:

```
56 00000000'EF D0      MOVL    SYMBOL,R6
```

8.7   MORE ADDRESSING MODES: DEFERRED AND INDEXED MODES

Deferred Addressing Modes

In all the addressing modes introduced so far for addressing operands in memory, the operand address is computed using the contents of a register (and in some cases, a displacement). There are some programming situations where the address itself is stored in memory. To perform some operation on the operand, we could first move its address from its location in memory to a register, then use register deferred mode. Two separate instructions would be needed. The "deferred addressing" modes allow us to access an operand whose address is in memory in only one step. The form of a deferred mode operand specifier is

$$@operand\_specifier$$

where the operand specifier that follows the @ may be in displacement, relative, or autoincrement mode. This operand specifier is evaluated in the usual way, producing,

```
                 0000         1  ; PROBLEM STATEMENT
                 0000         2  ;
                 0000         3  ;  The point of this program is to scan an array containing
                 0000         4  ;  names and test scores and to print the names of people
                 0000         5  ;  whose scores are between LOW and HIGH, inclusive.
                 0000         6  ;  The array is read from the DATA.DAT file.
                 0000         7  ;
                 0000         8  ; DATA
                 0000         9  ;
                 0000        10  ;   SCORES    array of names and scores.  Each entry consists
                 0000        11  ;             of a name in character code (NAME_LEN characters)
                 0000        12  ;             followed by a word integer score.
                 0000        13  ;   ENTRY_LEN the number of bytes per entry in the SCORES
                 0000        14  ;             array (NAME_LEN+2)
                 0000        15  ;   MAX       the maximum number of entries for which space
                 0000        16  ;             has been reserved
                 0000        17  ;   COUNT     the actual number of entries (longword)
                 0000        18  ;   SCORE     the displacement of the score from the
                 0000        19  ;             beginning of an entry
                 0000        20  ;
                 0000        21  ; CONSTANTS
                 0000        22  ;
             0000004B 0000    23  LOW = 75
             00000055 0000    24  HIGH = 85
             00000032 0000    25  MAX = 50
             00000016 0000    26  NAME_LEN = 22
             00000018 0000    27  ENTRY_LEN = NAME_LEN+2
             00000016 0000    28  SCORE = NAME_LEN
             0000000A 0000    29  LF = 10                        ; ASCII line feed
                 0000        30  ;
                 0000        31  ; STORAGE RESERVATION
                 0000        32  ;
             000004B0 0000    33  SCORES: .BLKB  MAX*ENTRY_LEN
             000004B4 04B0    34  COUNT:  .BLKL  1
             00000504 04B4    35  BUFFER: .BLKB  80
             00000506 0504    36  PKD:    .BLKB  2
                      0506    37  HDG:    .ASCII /People with scores between /
                      0512
                      051E

 20 68 74 69 77 20 65 6C 70 6F 6F 72 20 73 65 72 20
 65 77 74 65 62 20 73 65 20 6E 65
```

Figure 8.6 A program listing (continued next page)

```
                20 64 6E 61 20 20 20 20   0521   38   LOWSCORE: .ASCII /   and /
                00 0A 20 20 20 20         052A   39   HISCORE:  .ASCIZ /       /<LF>
                                          0530   40   ;
                                          0530   41   ;              BEGIN   SCORELIST
                                          0580   42   ;
                                          0580   43   ; This section reads the names and scores from DATA.DAT.
                                          0580   44   ; Each record contains a name and a three-digit score.
                                          0580   45   ;
                                          0580   46   ; REGISTER USE
                                          0580   47   ;
                                          0580   48   ;   R6      array pointer
                                          0580   49   ;   R8      loop counter
                                          0580   50   ;   R9      scratch
                                          0580   51   ;   R0-R5   used by MOVC3
                                          0580   52   ;
           56   FA7C CF           9E      0580   53            MOVAB   SCORES,R6              ; Initialize array pointer
                58        32      D0      0585   54            MOVL    #MAX,R8                ; Don't read more than MAX
                                          0588   55   READ:    READRCRD BUFFER               ; Get record
FF5D CF 66      FF17 CF   16      28      0598   56            MOVC3   #NAME_LEN,BUFFER,(R6)  ; Store name
        03      FF27 CF   03      09      059E   57            CVTSP   #3,BUFFER+NAME_LEN,#3,PKD
        59      FF58 CF   58      36      05A7   58            CVTPL   #3,PKD,R9
                16 A6     59      F7      05AD   59            CVTLW   R9,SCORE(R6)           ; Convert and store score
                56        18      C0      05B1   60            ADDL2   #ENTRY_LEN,R6          ; Increment array pointer
                     D1   58      F5      05B4   61            SOBGTR  R8,READ                ; Loop control
   FEF3 CF   32      58           C3      05B7   62   EOF:     SUBL3   R8,#MAX,COUNT          ; Compute number of entries
                                          05BD   63   ;
                                          05BD   64   ;
                                          05BD   65   ; This section scans the array SCORES and prints the names
                                          05BD   66   ; of people with scores between LOW and HIGH, inclusive.
                                          05BD   67   ;
                                          05BD   68   ; REGISTER USE
                                          05BD   69   ;
                                          05BD   70   ;   R6      array pointer
                                          05BD   71   ;   R8      loop counter
                                          05BD   72   ;
                                          05BD   73   ; Convert high and low scores for heading
                                          05BD   74   ;
FF3D CF 03  0000004B 8F           F9      05BD   75            CVTLP   #LOW,#3,PKD
FF51 CF 03  FF38 CF              08       05C7   76            CVTPS   #3,PKD,#3,LOWSCORE     ; Low score
```

Figure 8.6 (continued next page)

```
FF2A CF 03   00000055 8F   F9   05D0   77            CVTLP    #HIGH,#3,PKD
FF47 CF 03   FF25 CF      08   05DA   78            CVTPS    #3,PKD,#3,HISCORE   ; High score
                                 05E3   79            PRINTCHRS HDG
                                 05F3   80  :
        58   FEB9 CF      D0   05F3   81            MOVL     COUNT,R8            ; Initialize loop counter
                          27   05F8   82            BEQL     DONE               ; Branch if arrays are empty
        56   FA02 CF      9E   05FA   83            MOVAB    SCORES,R6          ; Initialize array pointer
004B 8F 16 A6              B1   05FF   84  COMPR:   CMPW     SCORE(R6),#LOW     ; Compare score to LOW
                 14        19   0605   85            BLSS     NEXT               ; If score < LOW, don't print
0055 8F 16 A6              B1   0607   86            CMPW     SCORE(R6),#HIGH    ; Compare score to HIGH
                 0C        14   060D   87            BGTR     NEXT               ; If score high, don't print
                                 060F   88            PRINTCHRS (R6),#NAME_LEN    ; Print name
        56   18           C0   061B   89  NEXT:    ADDL2    #ENTRY_LEN,R6      ; Increment array pointer
     DE 58   58           F5   061E   90            SOBGTR   R8,COMPR           ; Loop control
                                 0621   91  DONE:    EXIT
                                 0651   92            .END     SCORELIST
```

Figure 8.6 (concluded)

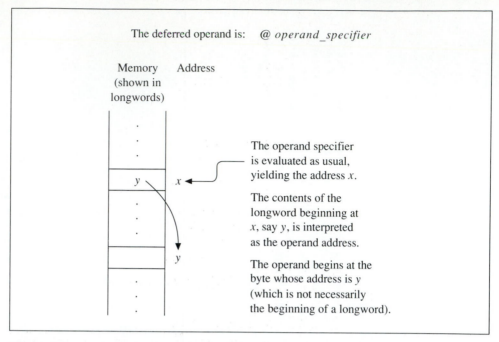

The deferred operand is: @ *operand_specifier*

Memory   Address
(shown in
longwords)

The operand specifier
is evaluated as usual,
yielding the address x.

The contents of the
longword beginning at
x, say y, is interpreted
as the operand address.

The operand begins at the
byte whose address is y
(which is not necessarily
the beginning of a longword).

Figure 8.7   Accessing a deferred operand

say, the address x. The @ indicates that x is not the address of the operand but is *the address of the address* of the operand. Suppose that the longword in memory beginning at the address x contains y. Then y will be used as the address of the operand for the instruction. Figure 8.7 illustrates deferred addressing.

Example 8.6: Displacement Deferred Mode

Consider Fig. 8.8. The effect of the MOVW instruction is to copy the word beginning at 000000F2 into R10. R10 will contain *xxxx*FF3A, where the x's indicate bits that are unchanged.

Example 8.7: Relative Deferred Mode

Suppose that LOC is a label on a longword. The operand specifier

@LOC

is an example of relative deferred mode. It indicates that the longword at LOC contains the address of the operand. After searching a table and storing the address of the item sought in LOC, we might use this operand specifier to perform some operation on the item.

Example 8.8: Autoincrement Deferred Mode

The operand specifier

@(R8)+

is an example of autoincrement deferred mode. The address in R8 is the address of the address of the operand. R8 is incremented by 4 regardless of the data type of the operand, because R8 addresses an address, which is always a longword.

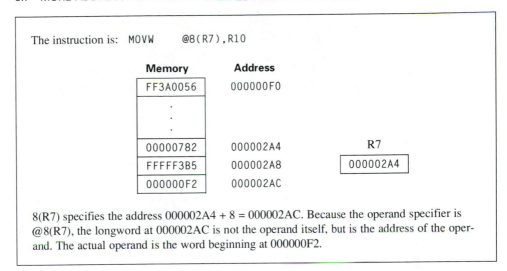

The instruction is: MOVW   @8(R7),R10

8(R7) specifies the address 000002A4 + 8 = 000002AC. Because the operand specifier is @8(R7), the longword at 000002AC is not the operand itself, but is the address of the operand. The actual operand is the word beginning at 000000F2.

Figure 8.8   An instruction that uses displacement deferred mode

Example 8.9: Using Deferred Addressing in a Program

Suppose that we have a collection of student records, each containing the name, address, grades, and other information about a student. We would like to print out a list of the students in alphabetical order. Since the records are likely to be large, it would be inefficient to move them around to rearrange them in order. Even if it were not inefficient, rearranging the records may not be allowed for other reasons; for example, it may be required that they be maintained in some other order, perhaps according to student ID number. To solve the problem, we can set up an array containing pointers to (i.e., the addresses of) the records of all the students. Initially the pointer array is in the same order as the records. The sorting algorithm will rearrange the pointers as it examines and compares student names, so that when it is done, the pointers will be in the order that corresponds to the alphabetical ordering of the student names. See Fig. 8.9 for illustration.

Suppose that R7 contains the address of an entry in the pointer array (see Fig. 8.10) and, that as part of the sorting procedure, we wish to compare the names pointed to by two adjacent pointers. The instruction to do this is

        CMPC3   #NAME_SIZE,@0(R7),@4(R7)

As we will see in the next chapter, one major application of displacement deferred mode is the accessing of procedure arguments.

Machine Code for Deferred Addressing Modes

Each of the deferred addressing modes has its own mode number. Recall that there are actually three displacement modes; they differ according to how much space is used to store the displacement (a byte, word, or longword). Also, recall that relative mode is just the special case of displacement mode where the register used is the PC. The mode

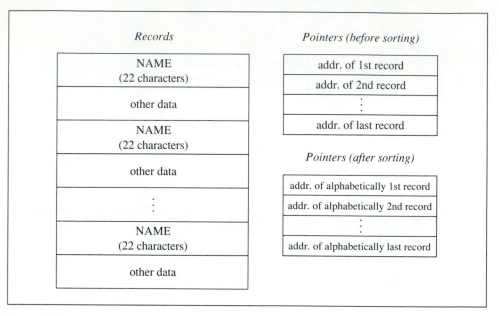

Figure 8.9   Sorting with an array of pointers

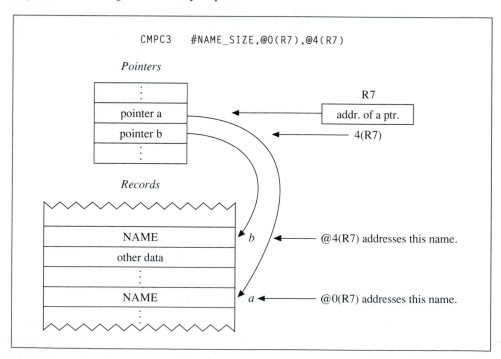

Figure 8.10   Using the pointers in Example 8.9

numbers and machine code formats are included in Table 8.1 (in the Summary, Section 8.9).

Example 8.10: Machine Code for a Relative Deferred Operand

Suppose that the value of the symbol ADDR is 00000022_{16} and the following instruction begins at byte 00000181_{16}:

```
MOVC3    #28,@ADDR,(R9)
```

The instruction is encoded as follows; the relative deferred operand occupies bytes 183–185.

Address	Code	Interpretation
00000181	28	MOVC3
00000182	1C	#28
00000183	DF	Mode byte: D = displacement deferred mode with word displacement; register = PC, hence this is relative deferred mode.
00000184	9C	Word displacement, first byte
00000185	FE	Word displacement, second byte
00000186	69	(R9)

When the instruction is executed, the displacement, FE9C, is added to 00000186 to get 00000186 + FFFFFE9C = 00000022 (i.e., ADDR). The CPU fetches the *address* for the second operand from the longword in memory beginning at 00000022. To encode the instruction, the assembler computes the displacement for ADDR in the same way as for relative mode.

Indexed Modes

Recall that our general formula for the address of the ith entry in an array is

$$\text{address of } i\text{th entry} = \text{address of array} + (i - 1)*\text{entry\_size}$$

$$= \text{address of array} - \text{entry\_size} + i*\text{entry\_size}$$

(See Fig. 6.2.) This formula uses the assumption that the array indexes start at 1. If the array indexes begin at 0, as is common in some high-level languages, the formula is

$$\text{address of entry with index } i = \text{address of array} + i*\text{entry\_size}$$

In either case, some arithmetic operations must be done just to compute the entry's address. Since array references are very common in high-level languages, the VAX provides addressing modes that compute array entry addresses. These are called *indexed modes*. The operand address is computed in two parts: a *base address* and an *index*. Any of several addressing modes already described may be used to specify the base address; the index is in a register. The general format for these operand specifiers is

$$base\_specifier[\text{R}x]$$

where Rx is R0, ... , R11, or AP, FP, or SP. The CPU determines the data type of the operand, hence the number of bytes it occupies, from the instruction's opcode. It computes the operand address as follows:

$$\text{operand address} = \text{base address} + (\text{R}x)*\text{size}$$

where *size* is the number of bytes in the operand. Thus the index register, Rx, should contain the index of the array entry to be accessed, and the base address should be the address of the first byte of the array (or the address of the array minus *size* if indexing begins at 1). The entire contents of Rx is used in the computation, so the index must be a longword.

Any addressing mode may be indexed (i.e., any mode may be used for the base address) except literal, immediate, register, branch, and index modes.

Example 8.11: Relative Index Mode

Let LIST be a word array whose entries are indexed beginning at zero. Suppose that R8 contains 00000005. In the instruction

```
TSTW    LIST[R8]
```

the operand specifier LIST[R8] addresses the array entry with index 5. The computed operand address is

$$\text{LIST} + 5 * 2$$

If the entries in LIST are indexed beginning at 1, the entry with index 5 could be addressed by LIST-2[R8].

Example 8.12: Implementing a Fortran "Computed GOTO" Statement

The Computed GOTO statement is a multiway conditional branch instruction. It has the following format:

$$\text{GOTO } (s_1, s_2, \ldots, s_k), i$$

where i is an integer variable and $s_1, \ldots, s_k$ are statement labels. If the value of the variable i is between 1 and k, the GOTO causes a branch to the statement labeled s_i. It can be implemented in assembly language by a sequence of comparisons and conditional branches that test if $i = 1$, then 2, and so on, but this could be very inefficient. The compiler can set up a table in memory containing the branch destinations and use an indexed mode to select the proper one. Suppose that the table is called GOTO_TABLE. The Computed GOTO is implemented as follows:

```
MOVL    I,R5                  ; Get i
BLEQ    BAD_INDEX             ; Branch if i <= 0
CMPL    R5,K
BGTR    BAD_INDEX             ; Branch if i > k
MOVL    GOTO_TABLE-4[R5],R6 ; Get destination address
JMP     (R6)                  ; Jump to destination
```

Machine Code for Indexed Addressing Modes

An indexed operand specifier is encoded with a mode byte for index mode (mode 4) followed by a complete operand specifier for the base address. Thus

$$base\_specifier[\text{R}x]$$

is encoded as

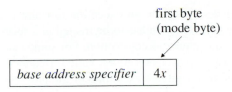

Example 8.13: Some Indexed Operand Specifiers

In these examples, the first byte of the machine code for each operand specifier is shown at the right as on program listings.

Assembly Language Format	Machine Code		
(R8)[R5]		68	45
LIST[R7]	*displ*	CF	47
@4(R7)[R10]	04	B7	4A

8.8 EXCEPTIONS, OR EXECUTION-TIME ERRORS

Exceptions

We have seen how the CPU uses the program counter to execute instructions, including branches, one after another in the proper sequence. This process may continue to run smoothly until the end of the program, or it may be interrupted by an error or an unusual condition. Whether or not the program is doing the correct computation and producing correct output is not our concern here. We are considering execution from the point of view of the CPU, which knows nothing of the programmer's intentions and simply carries out a mechanical process of decoding instructions and performing operations on data. In this section we will describe some of things that can go wrong during this process and interrupt the normal flow of execution, usually preventing completion of the program. Such situations are called *exceptions.*

What can go wrong? There are several potential problems. The byte that the CPU interprets as the opcode may not be a valid opcode or it may be privileged (not available to the ordinary user). The addressing mode used for an operand or the operand itself may be inappropriate for the instruction. There may be something wrong with the result of the operation (e.g., it may overflow).

For the beginning programmer such occurrences virtually always indicate errors in the program and should cause it to be terminated with an error message.

Our discussion up to this point is not specific to the VAX. *Exception* is a term commonly used for a problem in an instruction that causes an interruption in the normal flow of execution. The general types of exceptions that we mentioned, such as invalid opcodes or operands and improper results, can occur on other computers. As usual, there is variation in the details of exactly what events are exceptions and how the system responds to them.

On occasion a programmer does not want an exception to cause termination of a program. It may be that the exception condition has to be treated in a special way by the program, but then the program can continue to completion. For some exceptions on the VAX, it is possible to specify that a special procedure, called a condition handler, be called to handle the exception and then continue execution of the program. In this chapter we describe exceptions from the point of view of the beginning programmer, where they are most often caused by programming errors. Condition handlers will be discussed in Chapter 15.

For each type of exception described below, we give its name (assigned by DEC), its meaning, and the kind(s) of errors often made by beginning assembly language programmers that may have caused it. Note that some exceptions are called *faults* and some are called *traps*. Faults are exceptions that occur during an instruction and prevent its completion: for example, an access violation. Traps are exceptions that occur at the end of an instruction, usually because something is wrong with the result: for example, overflow. It is possible for the programmer to enable or disable some traps. If a trap is disabled, there is no interruption in execution of the program and no error message; the next instruction is executed in the usual way. If a program does quadword arithmetic, for example, the integer overflow trap should be disabled. We will indicate how traps may be enabled and disabled after describing the exceptions.

Opcode reserved to digital fault.   The opcode is invalid or privileged.

Possible cause: The program has branched into a data area or stored data in the middle of instructions.

Access control violation fault.   The program tried to reference a part of memory outside the area permitted to it.

Possible causes: The # was omitted from a literal. An address was computed improperly. A loop that processes an array continues too long.

Reserved addressing mode fault.   An inappropriate addressing mode was used. For example, a literal may have been used as a destination operand.

Possible causes: Operands written in incorrect order. Misunderstanding of the instruction by the programmer.

Reserved operand exception.   The operand accessed is not the correct data type for the instruction. We have seen that any string of bits can be interpreted as a two's complement integer, but for some data types, such as leading separate numeric, floating point, and packed decimal, some bit patterns are not valid.

Possible causes: Beginners often encounter reserved operand faults on the CVTSP instruction used to convert input data from character code. Usually, either the data themselves are improperly formatted or the address used was computed incorrectly.

Integer overflow trap.   The result of an integer arithmetic instruction requires more space than the destination operand has. (The low-order part of the result is stored in the destination operand.)

Possible causes: The programmer did not choose an appropriate data type. The wrong data were used because the operand address was computed incorrectly.

Integer divide-by-zero trap. An integer division instruction had a zero divisor.

Possible causes: Either the wrong datum was used because of an address computation error or the programmer forgot to consider the special case of a potentially zero divisor.

Floating underflow, overflow, and divide-by-zero exceptions. Floating overflow and underflow occur when the result of a floating-point arithmetic instruction has an exponent outside the range permitted for floating-point data.

Possible causes: Similar to the corresponding integer exceptions. Of course, it is possible that the data are simply outside the range that can be handled by the VAX instructions.

Decimal string overflow and divide-by-zero traps. These are for instructions that operate on data of the packed decimal type.

Enabling and Disabling Traps

The PSW contains several one-bit trap-enable flags that are accessible by the programmer. They are for the Decimal oVerflow (DV), Floating Underflow (FU), and Integer oVerflow (IV) traps. The flags are located in the PSW as follows:

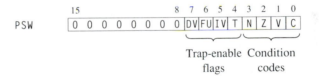

When one of the conditions described occurs, it causes an exception if and only if the corresponding trap-enable bit is set to 1. The flags are all initially zero (disabled). The IV and DV traps may be enabled or disabled at the beginning of a main program or procedure, and all three of the trap bits can be set or cleared by the machine instructions BISPSW (BIt Set in PSW) and BICPSW (BIt Clear in PSW) at any point in a program. The BEGIN macro enables the IV trap, and we will see how to control IV and DV at the beginning of procedures in the next chapter. Thus, for example, if it is expected that integer overflow might occur in a procedure but can be handled by the program itself, the programmer can disable the IV trap for that procedure and include instructions to test the overflow condition code and handle the condition appropriately without an exception occurring.

The T bit (bit 4) in the PSW is the trace trap flag; it is used by the VAX Symbolic Debugger.

Interpreting Execution-Time Error Messages

The error messages issued by the system for execution-time errors tell the programmer the kind of exception that occurred and the location of the instruction that caused it. The same information can be obtained by using the VAX Debugger, but here we are not using the debugger. The system error message describes the location of the error by giving the "rel PC" contents. The interpretation of this value depends on several factors. Usually, it is the location of the instruction that caused the exception, relative to the location of the entry point of the routine in which the error occurred. If the error is a trap, the PC would have already been incremented to contain the address of the next instruction. In such cases, the "rel PC" shown is the location of the instruction following the one that caused the exception, again relative to the entry point. If an exception occurs before the entry point, the value shown in the error message as "rel PC" is relative to the beginning of the program. (This can happen if, for example, the program accidentally branches into the data that precedes the entry point.) The location counter values shown on the program listing can be used to find the error. The interpretation of "rel PC" becomes more complicated if the program includes procedures. We will say more about it in Chapter 9.

As we have emphasized throughout this chapter, the PC is incremented as each piece of an instruction is fetched. Thus when a fault occurs, the PC may contain an address in the middle of an instruction, not its beginning. For faults (not traps) the system resets the PC to contain the address of the beginning of the instruction before printing the error message.

Example 8.14: Using an Error Message to Debug

Suppose that we ran the program shown in Fig. 8.6, but with a slight difference. Figure 8.11(a) shows the error message displayed. The error is an access violation, and it occurred at relative location 00000068. Figure 8.11(b) shows a segment of the listing. We can see that the entry point (established by the BEGIN macro) is at location 0530. Adding the relative PC gives 00000598. The instruction at location 0598 is the MOVC3 instruction on line 56. The first operand is correct; we did not forget the #. The second operand, a label, is a valid address. Thus it is likely that the third operand, (R6), is wrong (i.e., the address in R6 is improper). If we check where R6 was initialized (line 53), we see that we incorrectly used a MOVB instruction where we need MOVAB.

If we had used the debugger here, it would have told us that the error was an access violation, and it would have displayed the MOVC3 instruction in line 56 as the offending instruction. The rest of the work of determining the cause of the error (i.e., the program bug) would have been the same.

Another piece of information in execution-time error messages is often useful. The "routine name" is the entry point name. In Example 8.14, there is only one routine, but for a program with several procedures, the routine name tells the programmer which procedure has the error. (The debugger provides this information, too.)

(a) The error message.

```
%SYSTEM-F-ACCVIO, access violation, reason mask=04, virtual address=7FFED114, PC=00000BB3, PSL=0BC00024
%TRACE-F-TRACEBACK, symbolic stack dump follows
module name    routine name                    line        rel PC      abs PC

.MAIN.         SCORELIST                                   00000068    00000BB3
```

(b) Part of the listing of the incorrect program.

```
0530                        41            BEGIN   SCORELIST
0580                        42      ; This section reads the names and scores from DATA.DAT.
0580                        43      ; Each record contains a name and a three-digit score.
0580                        44      ;
0580                        45      ; REGISTER USE
0580                        46      ;
0580                        47      ;
0580                        48      ;   R6      array pointer
0580                        49      ;   R8      loop counter
0580                        50      ;   R9      scratch
0580                        51      ;   R0-R5   used by MOVC3
0580                        52      ;
0580  56 FA7C CF 90         53            MOVB    SCORES,R6             ; Initialize array pointer
0585  58 32 D0              54            MOVL    #MAX,R8               ; Don't read more than MAX
0588                        55 READ:       READRCRD BUFFER              ; Get record
0598  66 FF5D CF FF17 CF 16 28    56      MOVC3   #NAME_LEN,BUFFER,(R6) ; Store name
059E  03 FF27 CF 03 09      57            CVTSP   #3,BUFFER+NAME_LEN,#3.PKD
05A7  59 FF58 CF 03 36      58            CVTPL   #3,PKD,R9
05AD  16 A6 59 F7           59            CVTLW   R9,SCORE(R6)          ; Convert and store score
05B1  56 18 C0              60            ADDL2   #ENTRY_LEN,R6         ; Increment array pointer
05B4  D1 58 F5              61            SOBGTR  R8,READ               ; Loop control
05B7  FEF3 CF 32 58 C3      62 EOF:       SUBL3   R8,#MAX,COUNT         ; Compute number of entries
```

Figure 8-11 An execution-time error.

8.9 SUMMARY

The CPU uses the program counter, PC, as a pointer to the next byte to be processed in the instruction stream. It automatically increments the PC as it fetches each part of an instruction.

Instructions are encoded in machine code with a one- or two-byte opcode followed by an operand specifier for each operand. The ways in which operands may be specified are called addressing modes. The VAX has a large variety of addressing modes. Each operand specifier (with the exception of branch mode) starts with a mode byte that contains the addressing mode number and a register number or a literal. The CPU can determine from the mode number how many additional bytes (if any) are part of the operand specifier.

Most addressing modes use a general register in some way. For certain modes the PC may not be used. Other addressing modes, when used with the PC, are given special names and studied separately because using the PC has different effects.

In branch mode and the relative modes, the operand address is computed by adding a displacement and the contents of the PC. Thus address expressions are encoded by their position relative to the PC. This allows correct encoding of the address expression independent of where the program is loaded in memory.

Address computations are always done with 32 bits, so displacements are sign-extended if necessary.

The deferred modes allow the programmer to access an operand whose address is stored somewhere in memory without first loading the address into a register. The indexed modes are designed for addressing array entries.

Table 8.1 lists the addressing modes.

It is the assembler's job to translate assembly language source programs into machine code. Many assemblers accomplish this task by making two passes over the source program; they are called two-pass assemblers.

The main purpose of the first pass is to find all the symbols used in the module being assembled, determine their values (if possible), and build the symbol table containing the symbols and values. To determine the values of the symbols, the assembler uses a counter called a location counter, which it initializes to zero. The location counter is incremented by the number of bytes that will be used for each statement (both directives that reserve space for data and machine instructions). When the assembler encounters a symbol in the label field of an instruction, it assigns to the symbol the current value of the location counter.

During the second pass, the assembler translates the machine instructions into machine code. For some operands, several addressing modes could be used to encode them. The assembler follows a specific set of rules that control the choices it makes. Some of these are described in the text; more detail is given in the *VAX MACRO and Instruction Set Reference Manual.* There may be some address references that the assembler cannot handle; it leaves these for the linker to fill in later.

An *exception* is a problem that occurs during (or after) execution of an instruction that causes the operating system to intervene in the normal process of instruction execu-

TABLE 8.1 ADDRESSING MODES

Name	Number	Assembly format	Machine code
Register modes			
Register	5	Rn	5 n
Register deferred	6	(Rn)	6 n
Autodecrement	7	–(Rn)	7 n
Autoincrement	8	(Rn)+	8 n
Btye displacement	A	*dis*(Rn) B^*dis*(Rn)	*dis* A n
Word displacement	C	*dis*(Rn) W^*dis*(Rn)	*dis* C n
Longword displacement	E	*dis*(Rn) L^*dis*(Rn)	*dis* E n
Literal	0–3	*#expression* S^*#expression*	00 literal (6 bits)
Branch	none	*address expression*	*dis* *dis*
Program counter modes			
Immediate	8	*#expression* I^*#expression*	*datum* 8 F
Byte relative	A	*address expr.*	*dis* A F
Word relative	C	*address expr.*	*dis* C F
Longword relative	E	*address expr.*	*dis* E F
Deferred addressing modes			
Autoincrement deferred	9	@(Rn)+	9 n
Byte displacement deferred	B	@*dis*(Rn)	*dis* B n

TABLE 8.1   ADDRESSING MODES (continued)

Word displacement deferred	D	@*dis*(R*n*)		*dis*	D *n*
Longword displacement deffered	F	@*dis*(R*n*)	*dis*		F *n*
Byte relative deferred	B	@ *address expr.*		*dis*	BF
Word relative deferred	D	@ *address expr.*		*dis*	DF
Long relative deferred	F	@ *address expr.*	*dis*		EF
Index mode	4	*base_specifier*[R*x*]	. . .	*m n*	4 *x*

where *m* is the mode number and *n* is the register used for the base operand specifier, which may be any mode except register, literal, immediate, branch, and index mode.

tion. Exceptions may be caused by a bad opcode, addressing mode, address, or operand, or by some abnormal property of the result of a computation, such as overflow. Usually, especially for beginning programmers, an exception is caused by a programming error. The programmer can determine the type of error and the location of the instruction where it occurred by using the VAX Debugger or the information in the system execution-time error message.

8.10 EXERCISES

Note: In all exercises in this chapter, addresses, location counter values, symbol values, and memory and register contents are shown in hex. Although in the machine, addresses are 32 bits long, we show only four hex digits for simplicity.

1. Translate each of the following instructions into machine code.
   (a) DIVW3   R5,R11,R5   (c) DECB   (R8)
   (b) CMPC3   #6,(R7),(R8)   (d) MOVB   (R10)+,-(SP)

2. Decode the following instructions and write them as assembly language source statements. The lowest-addressed byte is at the right.
   (a) 59 63 C6   (c) 84 D5
   (b) 6A 68 0A 28

3. Each of the instructions listed below has the effect of setting all the bits of R6 to 0, but they may differ in the amount of space they require in machine code and the

amount of time it takes to execute them. For each instruction, state how many bytes it takes up in machine code. Which do you think is fastest?

(a) MOVL   #0,R6   (c) CLRL   R6

(b) SUBL2   R6,R6   (d) MULL2   #0,R6

4. Give an example of a SOBGTR instruction that uses more than three bytes in machine code.

5. Suppose a program contains the following statements:

```
FIRST:   .LONG   1
SECOND:  .LONG   2
THIRD:   .LONG   3
            .
            .
            .

         MOVAL   SECOND,R7
         MOVL    R7,(R7)+
```

(a) What will be in the longwords at FIRST, SECOND, and THIRD, and what will be in R7 after the instructions above are executed?

(b) Suppose that the last statement in part (a) is changed to

```
         MOVL    R7,-(R7)
```

What will be in the longwords at FIRST, SECOND, and THIRD, and what will be in R7 after the instructions are executed?

6. Encode the instruction

```
         BRW     NEXT
```

assuming the instruction starts at 03E5 and NEXT = 0415.

7. Show the machine code for the instruction

```
         AOBLEQ  #10,R7,LOOP
```

assuming that the instruction begins at 02D1 and LOOP = 029A.

8. In each problem below decode the instruction starting at byte 025E. (The code is shown right to left as it appears on assembly program listings.) For relative mode operands, invent a symbol and tell what address it refers to.

(a) Address: 265 264 263 262 261 260 25F 25E 25D
    Contents: AC 58 6A FF 0F CF 15 29 87

(b) Address: 262 261 260 25F 25E 25D 25C
    Contents: 57 D5 F2 59 F5 56 20

9. Suppose the assembler's location counter = 014D when the instruction

```
         SUBL3   ALPHA,R9,R10
```

is encountered. Show the encoding of the first operand specifier and the locations of the bytes it occupies for each of the following values of ALPHA.

(a) ALPHA = 00B8   (c) ALPHA = 00D0

(b) ALPHA = 003C   (d) ALPHA = 00CF

10. Suppose that for the program segment shown in Fig. 8.4, the symbol table contains the value 0038 for COST. List the values for BASE, VAR, and NUM, and determine the locations at which each of the three machine instructions begin.

11. Show the machine code for

```
ADDL2    ALPHA,ALPHA
```

assuming that ALPHA = 0042 and the instruction begins at 012A. Will the two operand specifiers be identical? Why, or why not?

12. Suppose the following two instructions appear in a program:

```
MULL2    (R4)+,BETA
MULL2    (R4)+,BETA
```

The instructions are identical. Will the translations of them into machine code be identical? Why or why not?

13. Suppose you are writing the part of an assembler that encodes relative mode operands. The value of the symbol to be encoded is in R6, and the value of the location counter is in R10. Write instructions to compute the displacement, store it in DISPL, and increment R10 so that it will contain the location of the byte following the operand specifier. Include comments to explain your computation.

14. Any symbols used in the repetition factor in a .BYTE, .WORD, or .LONG directive must be defined before the directive appears. Why?

15. Suppose BETA = 002A. Consider the instruction

```
INCB    BETA
```

(a) At what location must this instruction appear so that the displacement used in the operand specifier is 80 (i.e., -128_{10}), the largest negative byte displacement?

(b) At what location must the instruction appear so that the displacement is FF7E (or -130_{10})?

(c) Is there some location at which the instruction could appear where the displacement for BETA would be FF7F (-129_{10})? If so, what is it? If not, explain why.

16. Some computers do not have a special addressing mode for branch destinations. Branch addresses are encoded in the same way as other address expressions. Give one advantage and one disadvantage for the VAX's using branch mode instead of relative mode for branch addresses.

17. Show the machine code for each of the following instructions.

(a) SUBW2   #30,R8   (b) SUBW2   #70,R8

18. Which, if any, of the following instructions would cause an assembly-time error? (Indicate which part of the instruction is wrong.)

   (a) MNEGB   BETA,-5(R7)   where BETA = 001E and the instruction starts at 018A.

   (b) ADDL2   R7,#37

   (c) SOBGEQ   R9,LOOP   where LOOP = 00E2 and the instruction starts at 01C3.

   (d) CMPB   (R6)+,#125

19. List the main steps the assembler carries out to translate the following instruction to machine code.

    DIVW2   #MAX,R7

20. Show the machine code for each of the following instructions, assuming in each case that LOOP = 00E2 and the instruction begins at 014E.

   (a) ACBB   #50,#2,R5,LOOP   **(c)** AOBLSS #50,R8,LOOP

   (b) ACBB   #85,#2,R5,LOOP   **(d)** AOBLSS #85,R8,LOOP

21. Show the machine code for each of the following instructions.

   (a) CMPW   #^A/ /,(R5)   (There is one blank in the character constant.)

   (b) BLBS   (R6),ODD   (where ODD = 021C and this instruction starts at 0242).

   (c) MOVW   #-5,(SP)

   (d) SUBL2   #8,PLACE   (where PLACE = 1A74 and this instruction starts at 0382).

22. Using the listing in Fig. 8.6, determine how many bytes are filled by the READRCRD and PRINTCHRS macros. Is the number of bytes the same each time each macro is used?

23. Suppose that a programmer inadvertently omitted the "#" on a literal and wrote the following instruction:

    MOVL   25,R4

    What addressing mode would the assembler use when translating the first operand?

24. Give an example of a situation where the assembler will use a longword displacement to encode a relative mode operand (e.g., a label). Explain why it uses a longword instead of a byte or word for the displacement.

25. Suppose that ALPHA is a label. The following two instructions have the same effect.

    MOVAB   ALPHA,R8   and   MOVL   #ALPHA,R8

    How does the assembler encode the first operand of each instruction? Does it need assistance from the linker for either of them? If so, explain why.

26. In each problem below, decode the instruction beginning at 6E7. (The code is shown right to left as it appears on assembly program listings.) If relative mode is used for any of the operands, invent a symbol and tell what address it refers to.

(a) Address: 6EE 6ED 6EC 6EB 6EA 6E9 6E8 6E7
    Contents: 6B FD 86 CF 01   2C 8F 29

(b) Address: 6EE 6ED 6EC 6EB 6EA 6E9 6E8 6E7
    Contents: 5A 13 C5 AF AF AF AF A2

27. Decode the instruction: 5B 94 B1. (The first byte is at the right.)

28. What will be in R9 after the following instruction is executed, assuming the register and memory contents shown below?

```
MOVL    @4(R3),R9
```

	Memory	Address
R3		
00000108	0000024C	00000108
	000009A4	0000010C
	.	.
	.	.
	.	.
	00000001	0000024C
	00000002	00000250
	.	.
	.	.
	.	.
	00000003	000009A4
	00000004	000009A8

29. Beginning with the same register and memory contents as in Exercise 28, what will be in R3 and in the longword in memory beginning at 00000108 after the following instruction is executed?

```
CLRL    @(R3)+
```

If any other memory locations are changed, tell which, and tell what the new contents are.

30. The longest operand specifier we have used in any example has five bytes.

(a) Write an instruction with an operand specifier that has six bytes.

(b) Write an instruction with an operand specifier that has nine bytes.

31. List all the addressing modes used for operands in the program shown in Fig. 8.6.

32. Show the machine code for the following operand specifiers.

(a) @15(R5)

(b) @12(AP)

(c) @ALPHA
    (assuming that ALPHA = 003A and the operand specifier begins at location 00E7).

33. Consider the problem described in Example 8.9, where a collection of records is to be sorted without being physically rearranged. Using the strategy of the Bubble Sort algorithm described in Exercise 50 of Chapter 7, write a program segment to rearrange the array of pointers to reflect the ordering of the records.

34. Consider the data described in Example 8.9. Suppose that each record contains a field called UNITS that contains the number of course units the student has completed. The UNITS field is a word integer that occupies the thirty-first and thirty-second bytes of each record. Suppose that R7 contains the address of one of the pointers in the pointer array (as in Fig. 8.10, for example). Write an instruction (or instructions) to determine if the student whose record is pointed to by this pointer has completed 96 or more units. (Can a deferred addressing mode be used for this?)

35. Show the machine code for the TSTW instruction in Example 8.11 assuming that LIST = 0034 and the instruction begins at 01D5.

36. Write a program segment that uses index mode to solve the problem described in Example 6.9.

37. Suppose R6 contains 00000007 and R7 contains 00000104. Determine the address of the second operand for each instruction. If there is not enough information, say so, and tell what further information is needed.

  (a) SUBW2   #6,(R7)[R6]   **(b)** MOVB   R3,@4(R7)[R6]

38. Write a program segment that does a Bubble Sort (see Exercise 50 of Chapter 7) using index mode.

39. Consider the Binary Search program in Fig. 7.7. The instructions that compute the address of the table entry to be examined, and then compare the keys, are

```
; REGISTER USE
;
;       R5      entry size (number of bytes)
;       R6      TABLE-size (for addressing)
;       R7      key
;       R10     middle (longword)
;       R11     address of entry to examine

             .

             .

             .

        MULL3    R10,R5,R11       ; middle*size
        ADDL2    R6,R11           ; Address of entry
        CMPW     R7,(R11)         ; Compare keys
```

Would it be correct to replace the three machine instructions with the following instruction using index mode? Why, or why not?

```
        CMPW     R7,(R6)[R10]     ; Compare key to middle entry
```

40. Write three sets of instructions for the following problem, one using autoincrement mode for array addressing, one using displacement mode (with the array names as displacements), and one using index mode.

Suppose A and B are word arrays each containing 50 entries. Write instructions to add corresponding elements and put the results in the word array C. In other words, implement the following loop:

for i := 1 **to** 50 **do** C[i] := A[i] + B[i]

41. Suppose that a program does arithmetic on quadwords (using the ADDL2 and ADWC instructions). Should that program have the IV trap enabled or disabled? Why?

42. It is useful to be able to write short programs as experiments to find out exactly how certain situations are handled, study error messages, and so on. Write and assemble a program for each of the following cases. Where appropriate, examine the listing file to see the results.

   (a) Find out what happens if the destination on a conditional branch instruction is more than 128_{10} bytes away.

   (b) Use a label, rather than a constant, as a displacement in a displacement mode operand to see how the assembler handles it.

   (c) We stated (in Section 8.2) that if the programmer explicitly specifies which displacement mode to use (byte, word, or longword), the assembler will do so, but an error message will be issued if the space allotted is not sufficient. Run a test program to verify this.

   (d) Check your answer to Exercise 23.

   (e) Check your answer to Exercise 25. Run your test program using the Debugger or DUMPLONG to see that the two instructions put the same value in R8.

43. What were the values of the condition codes at the time the error occurred in the program shown in Fig. 8.11?

44. Write a short program that will terminate because of an integer overflow exception. Run the program and determine which instruction's address was in the PC when the program crashed.

45. Do you think that the first operand in

```
MOVAB    #CONST,R9
```

is legal for this instruction? Consider how the assembler might translate it and what would happen when it is executed. Consider cases where the value of CONST is small enough for literal mode and where it is not. If you decide it is illegal, explain why (i.e., what difficulties would be encountered in translation or execution). If you think it is legal, show what you think the machine code would be (say, for CONST = 5 and for CONST = 100). After forming your hypotheses, write and run a short test program to see if you are correct.

9

Procedures

9.1 ADVANTAGES OF PROCEDURES—AND IMPLEMENTATION PROBLEMS

The Advantages of Procedures

A *procedure*, or *subroutine*, is a section of code that performs a particular task and may be "called" from, or used by, other procedures or programs. A procedure acts on data given it by the routine that calls it, and when it completes its task, it returns control to the calling routine. A procedure may be assembled (or compiled, in high-level languages) independently; thus it may be developed and debugged separately from the programs that will eventually use it.

There are many reasons for using procedures. The most important is that their use makes large programs much easier to design, develop, understand, debug, and maintain. It is not that procedures have any magical properties; it is simply that they make it easy for a programmer to use a well-known technique for solving large and difficult problems: break the problem down to a set of subproblems and work on the subproblems one at a time.

It is good programming practice to code every logically separate task as a separate procedure. It is not easy to explain exactly what constitutes a "logically separate task," but examples and experience should help the beginning programmer to develop good judgment about how to break up a large program into procedures. A program that is made up of many procedures is said to be *modular*.

Since real-world programs tend to be very large (thousands of lines) and are written by several people over a long period of time, the independence of a procedure from the rest of the program is an important asset in program development. A programmer can be told what task the procedure is supposed to do, what kinds of data it will be given to work on, and what result, if any, it is to return. The programmer does not have to know anything about the rest of the program and may concentrate on one specific problem.

There are other advantages to using procedures. A procedure may be called from different places in a program, and from different procedures. The procedure is written only once and the code appears only once in memory, thus saving space and programming time.

Since procedures may be assembled or compiled separately, they may be written in different languages. The major part of a large program may be written in a high-level language, but tasks that cannot be done conveniently in that language may be done in assembly language procedures.

Again, because procedures may be written and assembled separately, procedures for common problems can be kept in a program library and used by many programmers. Procedures that perform statistical computations, input/output operations, and a variety of other tasks are often available in such libraries. They save not only programming time but also the time required to learn the technical information required to solve the problem.

We can summarize the advantages of using procedures as follows:

1. Modular programs are easier to design, debug, understand, and maintain.
2. Procedures can be called from several places in a program, saving space and programming time.
3. Procedures written in different programming languages can be combined in one program.
4. Complex and frequently used procedures can be kept in procedure libraries for use by many programmers.

The Problems

Communication between procedures and the programs that call them (including other procedures) is a complex topic. We will consider some of the problems that must be solved so that procedures can be used smoothly.

Figure 9.1 illustrates the flow of control, or the order in which sections of instructions are executed, when a program calls a procedure. The sequence of instructions that make up a procedure are stored in memory separate from the programs that may call it. After the procedure completes its task, the next instruction to be executed is the one that follows the procedure call in the calling program. Thus the first problems are to devise a method to transfer control to the procedure (by appropriately changing the PC), and to transfer back to the correct place (by resetting the PC) afterward.

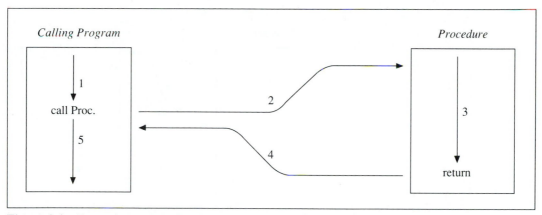

Figure 9.1   Executing a procedure

Normally, statement labels and other user-defined symbols have no meaning outside the procedure in which they are defined. They are *local* to the module where they are defined. Thus, one procedure cannot refer by name to data or instruction labels in another procedure. This is a valuable restriction, because it allows procedures to be written without worry of conflicts with symbols used elsewhere in a large program. It also forces programmers to follow the specific, narrow rules for communication between procedures, and encourages clearer, easier-to-debug programs. However, we can see that an exception to the locality of symbol definition is needed so that a program can call a procedure by name.

Many of the advantages of the modularity that is achieved by using procedures depend on the procedure's performing its task without any side effects. Consider Fig. 9.1; if the calling program puts a datum in a general register in the section of code numbered 1, that datum should still be in the register in the section of code numbered 3. But the procedure may need to use some of the registers to do its work. Thus a scheme is needed to protect the original contents of the general registers while the procedure is executing.

Another problem is that of devising convenient and flexible ways to specify to a procedure exactly what data it is to use and what to do with its results. The data operated on and the results computed by the procedure are its *arguments*. The process of giving input arguments to a procedure and telling it where to put its results is called *passing arguments*.

We can summarize the procedure communication problems as follows:

1. Transferring control to the procedure

2. Saving the contents of registers

3. Passing arguments

4. Returning to the next instruction in the calling program.

All these problems are made more difficult by the fact that procedure calls can be nested; that is, one procedure may call another which calls another, and so on. Figure 9.2

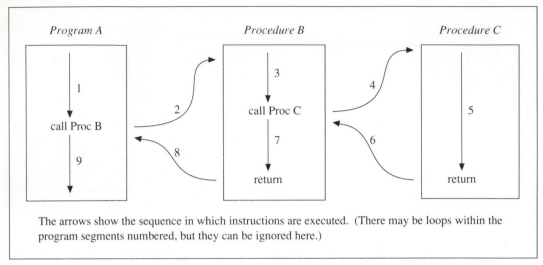

Program A   *Procedure B*   *Procedure C*

The arrows show the sequence in which instructions are executed. (There may be loops within the program segments numbered, but they can be ignored here.)

Figure 9.2   Nested procedure calls

illustrates the sequence of actions when a second procedure is called. The call to procedure C requires space to save procedure B's register contents, the return location, and information about procedure C's arguments. Meanwhile, the same items of information concerning the call to procedure B are still needed, because procedure B has not completed its work yet. It is clear that we cannot use one fixed location for passing this information between procedures.

The collection of conventions, methods, and instructions used to handle communication between procedures and calling programs is often called the *procedure linkage conventions.*[1] On the VAX it is called the VAX Procedure Calling and Condition Handling Standard.[2] (We will use the shorter title, VAX Procedure Calling Standard.) One may think of the linkage conventions as a big puzzle in which all the pieces must fit just right. There are many ways procedure linkage can be done, but if the details or methods used for one part of the whole problem are modified, the details of another part have to be changed so that the pieces still "fit together" properly. The methods used on different computers vary in sophistication and capabilities as well as in details. For example, a simpler set of conventions may be used if recursive procedures (procedures that call themselves) are not allowed. Generally, the more flexibility allowed to the programmer, the more complex are the details. The VAX has powerful and flexible linkage conventions that make complex programming techniques such as recursive and reentrant procedures easy to implement.

[1] The term *link*, as it is used here, does not mean the same thing as the LINK command (Section 5.3) that is used between assembling and running a program.

[2] Readers who wish to learn more about the VAX standard than is covered in this chapter will find it described in the manual *Introduction to VMS System Routines*.

9.2 THE STACK

What Is a Stack?

A *stack* is a list of items where all insertions and all deletions are made at one end, called the *top*. Since insertions and deletions are done at the top, the next item to be removed is always the item most recently inserted. Stacks are very useful and convenient for storing data that must be processed in this *last-in, first-out* (LIFO) order.

A stack can be set up by reserving a section of memory for it and establishing three pointers. A moving pointer is used to keep track of where the top is as items are inserted and deleted. Two fixed pointers may be used to prevent a program from removing an entry when the stack is empty and from putting into the stack more entries than there is room for. They point to the beginning, or *bottom*, of the stack, and to the other end of the reserved space, respectively.

To *push* means to insert an item into a stack, and to *pop* means to remove the top item. These terms come from the example of a stack of cafeteria trays in a spring-loaded container; when a tray is added to the stack, it pushes the others down, and when a tray is removed, the rest of the stack pops up. When a data stack is used in a computer, the entries do not actually move down and up when items are added and removed, but the terms *push* and *pop* have come to be widely used.

Figure 9.3 shows a stack as it might appear just after being set up and then again after being used for a while.

Stacks and Procedures

A stack is the natural data structure for storing much of the information that must be saved when procedures are called. This is essentially because procedures are returned from in the order opposite to that in which they were called (i.e., they are "last-in, first-out"). Consider, for example, the *return address*—the address of the next instruction in the calling program to be executed after the called procedure completes its task. When program A calls procedure B, the address of the instruction following the call is pushed on the stack. Then when procedure B calls procedure C, the address of the instruction following the call in procedure B is pushed on the stack, on top of the return address in program A. The return from procedure C is executed before the return from procedure B. Thus when procedure C completes its work, the return address it should use is the one most recently put on the stack—the one on top.

No matter how long the chain of procedure calls, the return address needed to properly return from a procedure is the one most recently pushed on the stack. The same reasoning shows that a stack is appropriate for storing register contents and other information that is saved when a procedure is called.

We have just concluded that when a procedure is called, the return address should be put on a stack. But how do we determine the return address? As we saw in so many examples in Chapter 8, when the operation specified by an instruction is carried out, the PC contains the address of the next instruction. Thus when a procedure is called, the PC contains the return address, and it can be copied onto the stack.

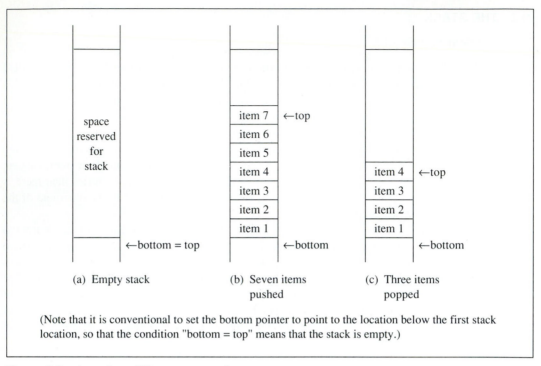

Figure 9.3   A stack at different stages of use

The User Stack on the VAX

Stacks are used on the VAX for many purposes. The operating system, for example, uses a stack for saving data needed while exceptions are being processed. The operating system also sets up a stack, called a user stack, for each program. The SP (Stack Pointer) register is intended to be used to keep track of the top of the stack; it should always contain the address of the most recently inserted item. The stack grows toward the lower-addressed end of memory; the first entry is in the highest-addressed location in the space reserved for the stack. As Fig. 9.4 illustrates, this lets us draw our diagram of the stack in a natural way, with the top of the stack toward the top of the diagram. [The operating system initializes SP to the address of the byte that follows the space reserved for the stack, where the *top* pointer is in Fig. 9-3(a).]

The user stack may be used for temporary storage for scratch work. It can be manipulated explicitly using PUSH and POP instructions and other instructions. Here we are interested primarily in its use for procedure linkage. The user stack is manipulated implicitly by the instructions that call and return from procedures. That is, the CALL and RETurn instructions push and pop data such as register contents and return addresses automatically.

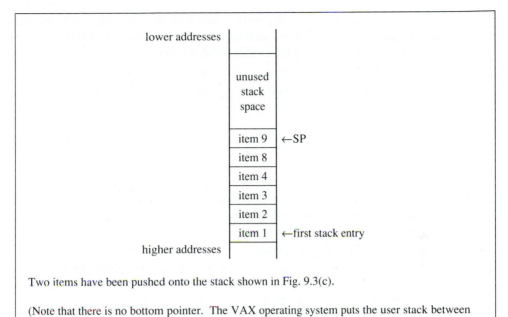

Two items have been pushed onto the stack shown in Fig. 9.3(c).

(Note that there is no bottom pointer. The VAX operating system puts the user stack between sections of memory that are inaccessible to the user's program, so pushing or popping too many items will result in a program exception.)

Figure 9.4   A user stack in the VAX

A Slight Digression—Internal Subroutines

In addition to supporting linkage conventions for procedures, the VAX (like many other large computers) provides instructions for a similar, but much simpler, situation. Since these instructions make use of one of the key ideas for solving the linkage problems of procedures—saving needed data on the stack—we will describe them here.

The simpler problem is to use, or "call," a sequence of instructions from more than one place *within one module*. DEC refers to a sequence of instructions used in this way as a *subroutine*. To emphasize the limitations of such subroutines, and to avoid confusion with the way the term *subroutine* is used in Fortran, we will call them *internal subroutines*. Internal subroutines do not have arguments in the usual sense (though they may operate on register contents that are different each time they are called). They are not assembled separately, and they may not be called from other programs. The advantage of internal subroutines is that they are much simpler to use and require very little overhead in time and space.

The only piece of information saved when an internal subroutine is called is the return address. It is saved, of course, on the stack. Thus if the contents of any registers are modified, their original contents are lost. Since there is no argument list, either the internal subroutine always works on the same data (e.g., printing out a specific array at various stages in some problem), or it uses data put in specific registers for it to work on.

The instructions that implement internal subroutines are:

BSBB	*destination*	Branch to SuBroutine
BSBW	*destination*	Branch to SuBroutine
RSB		Return from SuBroutine

In the BSB*x* instructions, the last letter indicates whether a byte or word is used to encode the branch displacement. The BSB*x* instructions push the contents of the PC—the return address for the subroutine—onto the stack and then put into PC the branch destination address. The RSB instruction simply pops the top longword from the stack and puts it in the PC, thus causing a return from the subroutine. Of course, for RSB to accomplish its intended task, if any data are added to the stack in the subroutine, they must be popped before RSB is executed.

Example 9.1: An Internal Subroutine

The following segment is part of a program that uses an internal subroutine to convert data from two's complement to character code. The subroutine is placed after the EXIT statement so that it is executed only when "called." Note that the stack is used for temporary scratch space; autodecrement and autoincrement modes perform exactly the operations needed to push and pop data on and off the stack. Since the scratch datum put on the stack is popped, RSB will find the return address at the top of the stack when it looks for it. Also note that the space for PKD is allocated after the RSB instruction, so it is outside the flow of control; that is, the CPU will not fetch the packed datum and interpret it as an instruction.

```
        . . .
        BSBW    CVTWS
        . . .
        BSBW    CVTWS
        . . .
        EXIT
;
; CVTWS
;
; This subroutine converts the word whose address is in R8
; to character code and stores the resulting string in memory
; at the address in R10. It assumes that R9 contains the
; number of digits desired in the result.
;
CVTWS:  CVTWL   (R8),-(SP)          ; Push longword on stack
        CVTLP   (SP)+,R9,PKD        ; Pop, convert to packed
        CVTPS   R9,PKD,R9,(R10)
        RSB
PKD:    .BLKB   5                   ; Allows for 9 digits
; End of subroutine CVTWS
        .END    PROGRAM
```

9.3 AN OVERVIEW OF THE VAX PROCEDURE-CALLING STANDARD

As we indicated in Section 9.1, many, many details are involved in setting up linkage conventions that will work properly. Some of the required tasks are done explicitly by the programmer; some are done by the CPU as part of the execution of certain instructions. Some of the work is done in the procedure and some in the program that calls it. All the pieces of the puzzle must fit together properly, and it may not be clear how this will happen until all the pieces have been described. To help guide the reader about what to expect, we will give a brief overview of the VAX calling standard here. The details are presented in the next three sections, along with examples. For the overview in this section we will describe the various steps, instructions, and techniques in more or less the order in which they are carried out at execution time. The registers AP (Argument Pointer), FP (Frame Pointer), and SP (Stack Pointer) all have special roles in the VAX procedure-calling standard. Recall that these are "general" registers 12, 13, and 14, respectively.

The programmer must set up an argument list for a procedure in the program that calls the procedure. The argument list may be put on the stack or in some other part of memory, and some or all of it may be set up at assembly time. When the procedure is called, the VAX puts the address of the argument list in the AP register.

Procedures are called using the CALLG or CALLS instruction. These instructions cause a lot of behind-the-scenes work to occur. They push register contents and other information onto the stack and put new data in certain registers (AP and PC, for example).

The procedure must contain an *entry mask* specified by the programmer to indicate which registers are used by the procedure. The CALL instructions use this information to determine which register contents to save on the stack.

The procedure uses AP to access its arguments. The addressing modes that are especially useful for this are displacement and displacement deferred.

The RET instruction is used in the procedure to return to the program that called it. RET pops the information that was put on the stack by the CALL instruction. It reloads the registers with the old contents that were saved on the stack.

The general organization of a procedure is shown in Fig. 9.5. The documentation for a procedure should include a list of the arguments with their roles and data types, and a description of the problem, the method used to solve it, and any special cases, details, and so on that are of interest. The .ENTRY directive is described in the next section. Figure 9.5 assumes that the procedure is in a file by itself; the .END directive should be the last statement in the file. It must not have an argument; the user transfer address should appear only on the .END directive in the file containing the main program. It is possible to include several procedures in one file (with only one .END directive, at the end of the entire file), but it is usually not a good idea. If several procedures are in one file, the labels defined in one procedure are accessible to the others. This is a possible cause of errors.

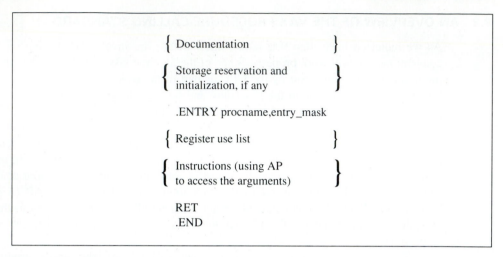

{ Documentation }

{ Storage reservation and
  initialization, if any }

.ENTRY procname,entry_mask

{ Register use list }

{ Instructions (using AP
  to access the arguments) }

RET
.END

Figure 9.5   Procedure organization

9.4 THE .ENTRY DIRECTIVE

Strategies for Saving Registers

One of the problems to be solved in procedure linkage is protection of the contents of the registers used by the calling program. We can devise many possible solutions, depending on how we answer several strategic questions. We will briefly consider some of the alternatives.

The first question is: *Where* should the old register contents be saved? For the VAX we have an obvious answer: on the stack. We should point out, though, that some machines do not have a "built-in" stack, so their standard procedure linkage conventions require that the calling program or the procedure reserve space for saving register contents.

The next question is: *Which* registers should be saved? We could save them all to be safe, but that is inefficient in its use of time and space when few registers are used. The alternatives are: the registers being used in the calling program, because these registers *may* be used and modified by the procedure, or the registers that are used in the procedure, because they *may* have contained data needed by the calling program. (Note that consistent with our emphasis on the independence of the procedure and a program that may call it, we assume that neither one actually knows which registers are used by the other.) The second alternative is the one that is generally chosen: the old contents of the registers used in the procedure are saved and put back in those registers when the procedure has completed its work. One reason for this choice is that it is more consistent with the view that the calling program be able to use a procedure easily without damaging the calling program's data. Another reason is that this choice is likely to use less space. A program may call several procedures and, using the first scheme, would have to provide information about which registers to save before each CALL. With the second

scheme, information about what registers are used in the procedure need to be represented just once in the procedure. Other reasons for saving old contents of registers used
by the procedure, rather than those used by the calling program, are related to how well
this fits with the other pieces of the linkage puzzle.

The next question is: *Who* should actually store the register contents—the calling
program or the procedure? The answer to the previous question seems to make it obvious
that the procedure should store the old register contents; the calling program would not
know which ones to save. This solution is used on some computers, but not the VAX.
The VAX CALL instructions actually store the old register contents. The CALL instruction, of course, appears in the calling program, but it might be better to think of its work
as occurring along the arrow numbered 2 in Fig. 9.1—that is, as part of the transition
from one routine to the other.

Our final question is specific to the VAX. Since the registers to be saved are those
used in the procedure, but the actual storing of the old contents is done by the CALL
instruction, how does the CALL know which ones to store? The .ENTRY directive provides the needed information.

The .ENTRY Directive

Although we can logically separate the problems involved in procedure linkage, we can
not neatly separate the solutions. The .ENTRY directive does *some* of the work that helps
solve *two* of the problems: saving registers and transferring control to the procedure. It
defines an *entry point* for the procedure and sets up an *entry mask*, or *register save mask*,
that indicates which registers are to be saved.

The form of the .ENTRY directive is

.ENTRY   *procname,regmask*

The procedure name, *procname*, is declared as an *entry point*—a point where execution
of the procedure may begin. It will be flagged to the linker as a *global* symbol—one that
is accessible from other modules. Its value will be the location of the .ENTRY directive,
so the directive should appear at the beginning of the executable portion of the procedure.

The register save mask is a 16-bit pattern whose bits are to indicate which registers
are used in the procedure and which traps are to be enabled in the procedure. Only
registers in the range R2 through R11 can be specified. For each of these registers, bit *n*
in the mask will be set to 1 if R*n* is specified. R0 and R1 are not saved because, by
convention, these registers are used to return function values from function procedures.
SP is *never* stacked, and AP, FP, and PC are *always* stacked by a CALL instruction, so
they do not have to be specified. Thus there are some bits in the mask that may be used
for other purposes. Bits 14 and 15 are used to set the IV and DV (integer and decimal
overflow) trap-enable flags in the PSW.

The programmer may specify the register save mask in the following form:

^ M<*register and trap list*>

The register and trap names in the list should be separated by commas. The assembler will construct the 16-bit mask from the registers and traps specified. The registers do not have to be listed in numerical order, but they should be. The mask will be placed at the location where the .ENTRY directive appears (the location assigned to the symbol *procname*).

Example 9.2: A Register Save Mask

$$^M<R3,R7,R8,R9,IV>$$

The assembler will construct the mask shown below in binary. Recall that the bits are numbered right to left, starting with 0.

```
0100001110001000
```

Example 9.3: An .ENTRY Directive

$$.ENTRY   OUTPUT,^M<R2,R3,R6,R7,R10>$$

The .ENTRY directive defines the symbol OUTPUT as an entry point for a procedure and indicates that the procedure uses registers R2, R3, R6, R7, and R10.

If no registers are to be saved and no trap bits set, the register mask is 0. It may be specified by 0 or ^M<>.

It is important that the programmer not tell a "lie" in the entry mask. The mask should include all registers (in the range R2 to R11) that may be changed in the procedure (including those changed as side effects of instructions like MOVC3). When the procedure is called, only the entry mask is examined to determine which registers will be saved. If a register is changed in the procedure and was not specified in the entry mask, the old contents will be lost, thus potentially causing errors after returning to the calling program.

How do the CALL instructions actually find the register mask so they can determine which registers to save? The procedure name (or more precisely, the entry point name) is an operand for the CALL instructions. Thus CALL is given the address of the register save mask and can easily examine it. Note that since the register mask takes up two bytes, the CALL will have to put the address *procname*+2 into the PC to accomplish the transfer of control to the first executable instruction of the procedure.

9.5 ARGUMENT LISTS

What Is in an Argument List?

A procedure and the program that calls it communicate via an *argument list*. That is, the data the procedure is to work with are given to it as arguments, and any results that it is to return to the calling program are returned as arguments. (Function procedures return a value in R0 and perhaps R1.) Thus the next procedure linkage problems to consider are exactly what is in the argument list, what format it has, and where it is put.

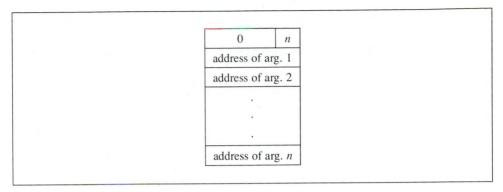

Figure 9.6   The format of an argument list

Suppose a procedure has three arguments: two input arguments that it uses in its task and one output argument that it computes and sends back to the calling program. One's first thought may be to put the two data in memory somewhere, followed by an "empty" location for the procedure's result, and to tell the procedure, by putting the address of this list in the AP, where the arguments are. This scheme will work, but not for all situations. Suppose one of the arguments is an array. It would be inefficient to copy the entire array into the argument list and later copy the possibly altered entries back to where the array belongs. Similarly, if one of the arguments is a long character string, or any datum that takes a lot of space, it may be inefficient to copy it into the argument list. Also, in both these cases, the size and structure of the argument list would depend on the size of the array or string; the procedure would need further information in order to use its argument list properly. Another way to pass an argument is to put its *address* in the list, not the datum itself. In this case, the procedure has access to the actual variable, not a copy, and may change its value. Thus this method allows implementation of the parameter-passing protocol known as *call by reference*. We will use this method as our standard argument list format, but we will also consider alternatives later.

The standard form for an argument list on the VAX (using call by reference) is shown in Fig. 9.6. Each row in the table is a longword. The number of arguments, n, is an unsigned byte integer, so $0 \le n \le 255$. The order in which the argument addresses are listed must be the same as the order in which the procedure expects them.

Where is the Argument List?

On the VAX, argument lists may be constructed on the user stack or in some other area of memory. (The CALLS instruction—"S" for stack—is used if it is on the stack, and CALLG—"G" for general memory—otherwise.) An argument list in general memory is permanent; that is, the space it occupies is reserved throughout execution of the program even if it is needed only for a short time. If the argument list is on the stack, it is popped upon return from the procedure, so the space can be reused. For recursive procedures a stack must be used for the argument lists, because each time the procedure calls itself it needs a new argument list and must not destroy the lists for the earlier calls from which it has not yet returned. Most compilers for high-level languages that allow recursion (which includes most widely used general-purpose languages) build argument lists on a stack for all procedures.

We will show how to construct argument lists both in general memory and on the stack.

Creating Argument Lists in General Memory: The .ADDRESS Directive

The .ADDRESS directive is a data initialization directive similar to the .BYTE, .WORD, and .LONG directives described in Chapter 4. Whereas the latter initialize storage to contain two's complement integers, .ADDRESS initializes storage to contain addresses. It is useful for creating argument lists at assembly time. Its format is

.ADDRESS *list_of_address_expressions*

The items in the list should be separated by commas. The assembler will put each of the addresses into memory, one after the other in the order specified, using a longword for each one. (Recall that the assembler computes the values of symbols relative to the beginning of the module or program section in which they are defined. When a procedure uses the argument list, it must have the actual addresses of the arguments. The linker makes the necessary adjustments to the values stored by the assembler.)

Example 9.4: An Argument List

Suppose a procedure has three arguments: two arrays and a longword that tells how many entries are in the arrays. If the procedure is to be called to work on the arrays NAMES and TAGS, and NUM contains the number of entries, the argument list may be set up as follows:

```
ARGLIST: .LONG    3                ; Number of arguments
         .ADDRESS NAMES,TAGS,NUM   ; Argument addresses
```

NAMES, TAGS, and NUM would of course have to be defined as usual somewhere in the program. Suppose the arrays begin at addresses 000007D4 and 00000644, respectively, and that NUM is at 00000964. The argument list set up by these directives is shown in Fig. 9.7.

Often, only part of an argument list can be created at assembly time, because some of the arguments are not known until execution time. For example, one procedure, say A, may call another and pass on to the second procedure some of the arguments pro-

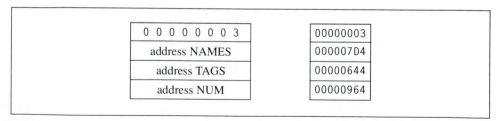

Figure 9.7   An example of an argument list (shown both symbolically and with addresses)

vided by the program that called A. Also, a procedure may be called many times, perhaps in a loop, with different arguments each time. In such cases we can reserve space for the argument list and intitialize those entries that will always be the same. Then, at execution time, we can move into the list those entries that will vary.

Example 9.5: An Argument List

Suppose a procedure has four arguments: a table, its size, an item to be looked up, and a place for some information to be returned about the item looked up. The procedure will be called many times to look up different items. The argument list might be initialized as follows:

```
ARGLIST: .LONG    4          ; Number of arguments
         .ADDRESS TABLE,SIZE  ; First two arguments
         .BLKA    1           ; Space for third argument
         .ADDRESS INFO        ; Last argument
```

Suppose that at execution time the address of the item to be looked up is in R8. It can be inserted into the argument list as follows:

```
MOVL    R8,ARGLIST+12   ; Insert 3rd arg. address
```

Creating Argument Lists on the Stack: The PUSH Instructions

The format for an argument list on the stack is the same as the format for an argument list elsewhere in memory (i.e., the format shown in Fig. 9.6). The programmer must include explicit instructions to push onto the stack the addresses of the arguments. The first longword of the argument list, the one containing the number of arguments, will be pushed by the CALLS instruction.

The VAX has several instructions that simplify pushing argument addresses onto the stack. They are

$$\text{PUSHA}x \quad operand \qquad x = \text{B, W, L, or Q}$$
$$\text{PUSHL} \quad operand$$

The PUSHA instructions push the operand address onto the top of the stack; PUSHL pushes its longword operand. Since the stack pointer contains the address of the top item on the stack, SP is decremented by 4 before the datum is moved to the stack. Thus the PUSH instructions have the same effect as

$$\text{MOVA}x \qquad operand,-(\text{SP})$$
$$\text{MOVL} \qquad operand,-(\text{SP})$$

but are shorter, and perhaps clearer. The PUSHA instructions always push a 32-bit address onto the stack. As with the MOVA instructions, the type, x, in the instruction names is relevant if the addressing mode used to address the operand is one that increments or decrements a register. For example,

```
PUSHAW  (R7)+
```

would push the address in R7 on the stack and then increment R7 by 2.

Note that argument addresses must be pushed onto the stack in the order opposite to the order in which the procedure expects them, since the one pushed first will be the bottom, or last, one in the list.

Example 9.6: Pushing an Argument List onto the Stack

To create the argument list of Example 9.5 on the stack, we could write

```
PUSHAB  INFO
PUSHL   R8
PUSHAL  SIZE
PUSHAB  TABLE
```

(Here we have arbitrarily chosen data types for the second and fourth arguments.)

Using the Arguments in a Procedure

When a procedure is called, the address of the argument list is put in AP, the Argument Pointer register. More specifically, AP will contain the address of the first byte of the list, the one containing the number of arguments. Displacement mode addressing with AP can be used to access the entries in the list. That is, 4(AP), 8(AP), and 12(AP) are the locations of the first, second, and third argument addresses, respectively. To address the arguments themselves (i.e., to get the actual data from memory) displacement deferred mode is used. Recall that in displacement deferred mode, the address specified by the operand specifier is the address of the address of the operand. One of the most frequent uses of this addressing mode is for accessing procedure arguments. 4(AP), for example, is the address of the address of the first argument. Thus to refer to the actual datum, we use @4(AP).

The contents of AP and the argument list should be treated as read-only data by the procedure. That is, the procedure should not modify AP while accessing its arguments, and it should not modify the data in the argument list or store in it results to be returned to the calling program. A procedure normally does not "know" if its argument list is on the stack or elsewhere in general memory. If it is on the stack, it is popped and discarded by the RET instruction, so all data in the list are lost. Thus, for a result to be returned by a procedure, the argument list should contain the address of a general memory location where the procedure is to store the result.

Example 9.7: An Argument List and a Search Procedure

Figure 9.8 shows a search procedure that has four arguments. Figure 9.9 shows an argument list that might be used when calling this procedure. The arrows in Fig. 9.9 show the memory locations "pointed to" by the addresses. Note that the MOVL instruction in Fig. 9.8 uses displacement mode to fetch the first argument address (the address of an array) from the argument list. The instructions that fetch the second and third arguments each use displacement deferred mode. For these, the entry in the argument list is the operand address, and a second memory reference is made to that address to get the operand. For example, using the

```
; PROCEDURE SEARCH (ARRAY,NUM,ITEM,LOC)
;
; This procedure searches for a specified item in an array
; of word integers. It uses sequential search.
;
; INPUT ARGUMENTS
;
;       ARRAY    a word array
;       NUM      the number of entries (word)
;       ITEM     the item sought
;
; OUTPUT ARGUMENT
;
;       LOC      the address of the item sought (will be 0
;                if the item is not in the list)
;
; Offsets for argument list
ARRAY = 4
NUM = 8
ITEM = 12
LOC = 16
;
; REGISTER USE
;
;       R6       ARRAY pointer
;       R7       loop counter
;       R8       item sought
;
        .ENTRY   SEARCH,^M<R6,R7,R8>
        CVTWL    @NUM(AP),R7          ; Get NUM as longword
        BLEQ     NOTFND               ; Branch if array empty
        MOVL     ARRAY(AP),R6         ; Get address of ARRAY
        MOVW     @ITEM(AP),R8         ; Get item
;
COMPR:  CMPW     R8,(R6)+             ; Compare, increment ptr
        BEQL     FOUND                ; Branch if found
        SOBGTR   R7,COMPR             ; Continue search
;
NOTFND: CLRL     @LOC(AP)             ; Store 0, item not found
        RET                           ; Return
FOUND:  MOVAW    -(R6),@LOC(AP)       ; Store address of item in LOC
        RET                           ; Return
        .END
```

Figure 9.8   A search procedure

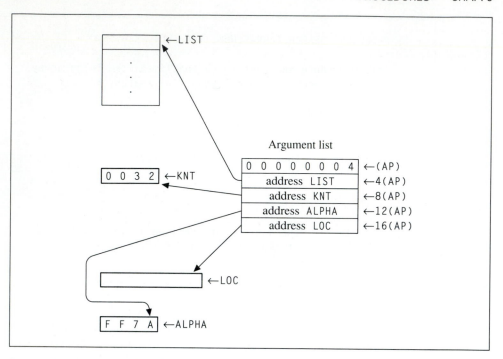

Figure 9.9   Argument list for the procedure in Fig. 9.8

argument list in Fig. 9.9, the source operand specifier @NUM(AP) in the CVTWL instruction addresses the datum 50_{10} in KNT. The operand specifier @ITEM(AP) in the MOVW instruction addresses the datum -134_{10} in ALPHA. The MOVAW instruction toward the end of the procedure uses displacement deferred mode to store its result in the memory location LOC addressed by the fourth argument, not in the argument list itself.

Note that there are no storage reservation directives within the procedure. All the data used by this procedure are reserved in the main program or other procedures. The argument list is used to tell this procedure where the data are.

The search procedure in Fig. 9.8 contains a few helpful documentation features. Since arguments are passed via the argument list, they cannot be referred to using names, or symbols, in the procedure. In the search procedure we have introduced "dummy" names for the arguments and used them for two distinct purposes. First, it is often convenient to have names for the arguments to use in the procedure documentation, both in the general description of the procedure and in the comments on the instructions. Second, we can make the references to the argument list clearer by defining symbols whose values are the displacements from the beginning of the argument list needed for each argument. Thus, for example, since we defined NUM=8, we could write

```
        CVTWL    @NUM(AP),R7
```

instead of

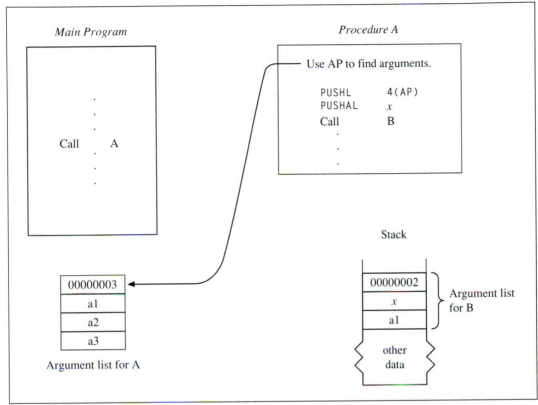

Figure 9.10   Passing an argument from one procedure to another

```
CVTWL    @8(AP),R7
```

Thus we can see exactly which argument is being referenced without having to remember or look up the format of the argument list.

Note also that the first comment line contains what looks like a high-level language procedure header statement. This line identifies the procedure and specifies to the reader the ordering of the arguments in the argument list.

Example 9.8: Passing an Argument from One Procedure to Another

Suppose that a main program calls procedure A, which has three arguments, and A calls procedure B, which has two arguments. We will consider how A can pass one of its own arguments, say the first one, to B as B's second argument. (See Fig. 9.10.) Procedure A will set up the argument list for B on the stack. It uses AP to find its own arguments. Thus it uses the instruction

```
PUSHL    4(AP)
```

to copy its own first argument (address) onto the stack as B's second argument. Next A pushes the address of B's first argument; then it calls B.

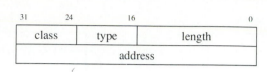

The class and type are byte integers that describe the data type of the argument. See the VAX Procedure Calling and Condition Handling Standard for details.

Figure 9.11   An argument descriptor

Variations

All the argument lists in this section pass arguments by reference (i.e., the argument list contains the addresses of the arguments). As we said earlier, this is a good general way to pass arguments, but other mechanisms are more suitable in some instances. One alternative is for the calling program to put the argument value itself in the argument list. DEC calls this the *immediate value mechanism*. A longword in the argument list is always used for each argument, whether it is passed by reference or by immediate value. This mechanism may be very convenient for constants and simple variables that are not to be changed by the procedure. It would not be used for an output argument from a procedure; the procedure never stores anything in the argument list.

Another argument passing mechanism used on the VAX is the *descriptor mechanism*. It is intended for strings (character, packed decimal, etc.) and other data types that require more than just an address to fully describe them. A character string, for example, is described by its address and length, a packed decimal datum by its address and number of digits. To pass an argument by descriptor, the calling program sets up an argument descriptor in memory and puts its address in the argument list. Figure 9.11 shows the standard descriptor format.

Instead of passing a string argument by descriptor, we could include both the address of the string and the address of its length in the argument list, using two arguments passed by reference just as machine instructions use two operands to describe such data types.

Of course, if different mechanisms are to be used to pass arguments, there must be an understanding between the calling program and the procedure about which mechanism is used for each argument. The procedure must use different addressing modes to access the argument, depending on how it is passed. For example, for the first argument, the following operand specifiers could be used:

4(AP)	If passed by immediate value
@4(AP)	If passed by reference
@4(R0)	After executing `MOVL  4(AP),R0` to get the descriptor address, if passed by descriptor

If the calling program and the procedure are being written by the same programmer, he or she may choose whatever mechanism is most convenient. If either program is in a program library or is produced by a high-level language compiler, the programmer must find out which mechanism it uses.

Protecting Data — Value Parameters

If a procedure is given the address of a variable, it can store something at that address, thus changing the value of the variable. To protect data and prevent side effects of procedures (accidental or malicious), it is often desirable to pass an argument to a procedure in such a way that the procedure cannot change the value of the actual argument, even if there is an assignment to the formal parameter in the procedure. This is the purpose of "value parameters" in Pascal, and it is the default parameter passing rule for many data types in C. We will briefly describe some ways to implement such protection. There are many relevant considerations beyond the scope of this book; this topic is discussed in more depth in programming languages courses and books.

The simplest approach to protecting a variable is to put the value of the argument, not its address, in the argument list (i.e., to use the VAX immediate value mechanism). This is straightforward for integers and floating-point numbers which occupy one longword. It is necessary, however, for the person writing the procedure (or the compiler translating a high-level language procedure) to know which entries in the argument list are values and which are addresses. For conceptual simplicity, we may insist that argument lists always contain only addresses. In that case, the calling routine can make a copy of an argument and put the address of the copy in the argument list. If the argument is an array, making the copy may take a lot of time; there is a trade-off between protection and efficiency. The best place for the copy is on the stack; it can be popped after return from the procedure. This convention—that the argument list contains addresses, but some may be addresses of copies of protected variables—combines simplicity and data protection. Another approach is to put the address of the actual argument in the argument list and trust the procedure to make a copy of the argument for its own use. This might not be a safe strategy if you are calling many procedures written in assembly language by several other programmers, but it can be relied upon if it is done systematically by a compiler for a high-level language.

In assembly language, it is up to the programmer to choose an appropriate scheme, then use it consistently in the calling and called routines. Various solutions are used by different compilers. In Section 9.10 we will see how the VAX compilers for some high-level languages handle this issue.

9.6 CALLING AND RETURNING FROM A PROCEDURE

The Call Frame

As we have indicated earlier, when a procedure is called, a lot of information is pushed onto the user stack by the CALLS or CALLG instruction. This collection of data, in a standardized format, is called the *stack frame* or *call frame*. The data in the call frame must be found and removed from the stack when the return from the procedure is executed. The procedure may put other data on the stack (including possibly a call frame for another procedure that it calls), so the stack pointer may be changed and cannot be relied on to find the call frame. The FP (Frame Pointer) register is intended for this purpose. When a procedure is called, the address of the call frame is put in FP, and FP will be used upon return to retrieve the information in the call frame.

We have already observed that the return address (the contents of the PC when a procedure is called) and the contents of the registers specified in the procedure's entry mask will be saved on the stack. We now consider some of the other data included in the call frame.

When a procedure is called, the addresses of the argument list and the call frame are put in AP and FP, respectively. If the procedure, say procedure A, calls another procedure, say procedure B, the addresses of the argument list and call frame for procedure B will be put in AP and FP. But procedure A may still need to use its argument list, and its call frame will certainly be needed later. Thus it is clear that whenever a procedure is called, the current contents of AP and FP must be saved before they are changed (i.e., the contents of AP and FP will be part of the call frame).

The contents of the registers specified in the procedure's entry mask are saved on the stack and must be popped later and put back in the registers. How will the RET instruction know which registers were saved? The call frame will contain a copy of bits 11:0 of the register save mask.

Figure 9.12 shows the format of the call frame. (Some of the data included will be described later.)

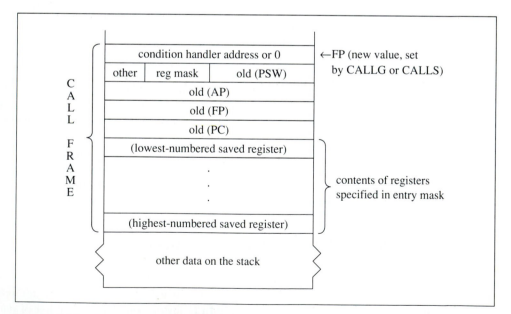

Figure 9.12   The format of the call frame

Calling a Procedure

There are two procedure call instructions: CALLG and CALLS. They construct the call frame and transfer control to the procedure. CALLS is used when the argument addresses have been pushed on the stack; CALLG is used when the argument list is set up elsewhere in memory. The formats of the two instructions are

CALLG *arglist,procname*

CALLS *numargs,procname*

The first operand of CALLG is the argument list, or more precisely, an operand specifier that indicates the address of the argument list. The first operand of CALLS is the number of arguments, usually specified by a literal. CALLS assumes that the argument addresses are on the top of the stack. The second operand of both CALL instructions is the procedure name.

Example 9.9: Calling Procedures

(a) Using CALLG

```
X:        .BLKL    1
Y:        .BLKL    1
Z:        .BLKL    1
ARGLIST:.LONG     3
          .ADDRESS X,Y,Z
             .
             .
             .
          CALLG    ARGLIST,ADD
```

(b) Using CALLS

```
X:        .BLKL    1
Y:        .BLKL    1
Z:        .BLKL    1
             .
             .
             .
          PUSHAL   Z
          PUSHAL   Y
          PUSHAL   X
          CALLS    #3,ADD
```

CALLG and CALLS are very powerful instructions. On many computers, the programmer would have to do explicitly much of the work that these instructions do automatically. Most of the work done by the two instructions is the same. We will describe the steps carried out by CALLG in detail, then describe the few differences for CALLS.

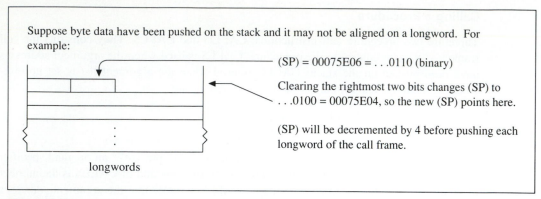

Suppose byte data have been pushed on the stack and it may not be aligned on a longword. For example:

(SP) = 00075E06 = . . .0110 (binary)

Clearing the rightmost two bits changes (SP) to . . .0100 = 00075E04, so the new (SP) points here.

(SP) will be decremented by 4 before pushing each longword of the call frame.

longwords

Figure 9.13 Aligning the stack to a longword

CALLG

1. Align the SP to a longword boundary.

   The CALL instructions push several longwords onto the stack, and for efficiency they align the SP to a longword boundary first. This is done by setting the rightmost two bits of SP to zeros. See Fig. 9.13 for an illustration. The original values of the rightmost two bits will be saved (on the stack, in step 5) so the SP can be restored to its original value by the RET instruction on return from the procedure.

2. Push contents of registers specified in the procedure's entry mask.

   The word at the address specified by *procname* is examined and interpreted as a register save mask. The registers to be saved are pushed onto the stack in decreasing order by register number (so that they appear on the stack in the natural order when read top to bottom).

3. Push contents of PC, FP, and AP.

4. Clear the condition codes in the PSW.

5. Push the PSW, register mask, and so on.

   A longword containing the following data is pushed onto the stack: the PSW (with the condition codes cleared), the part of the register mask that will be needed later (bits 11:0), a flag indicating that the procedure is being called with a CALLG instruction, and the rightmost two bits of the original address in SP. The format of this longword is shown in Fig. 9.14.

6. Push a longword of zeros onto the stack.

   The procedure may store in this longword the address of a routine (called a condition handler) to be executed if an exception occurs during execution of the procedure.

7. Copy the current contents of the SP into the FP register.

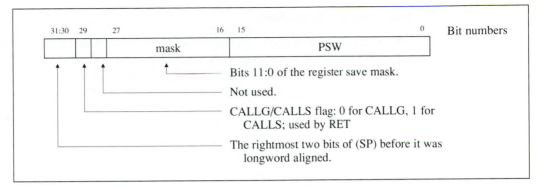

Figure 9.14 The second longword in the call frame

The SP now contains the address of the last longword pushed onto the stack. This is the beginning of the call frame for this procedure call; its address is placed in FP.

8. Put the address of the argument list in AP.

The address of the argument list is the first operand address in the CALLG instruction.

9. Set the trap bits in the PSW.

The integer overflow and decimal overflow traps are turned on or off as indicated in the register save mask.

10. Put the address *procname*+2 into the PC.

The address where execution of the procedure is to begin is *procname*+2, because the word at *procname* is the register save mask. The CALLG instruction has now completed its work, and the CPU will fetch the next instruction to be executed as usual by using the address in the PC. Thus control is transferred to the procedure.

CALLS

The argument addresses are supposed to be at the top of the stack when CALLS is used, so the first thing it does is push a longword containing the number of arguments (its first operand) onto the stack to complete the argument list. The updated address in the SP is saved in a temporary location for use in step 8, described below.

The remaining steps carried out by the CALLS instruction are almost identical to the steps carried out by CALLG. The only differences are:

In step 5: CALLS will set the CALLG/CALLS flag to 1 to indicate that CALLS is being used.

In step 8: The address put in AP will be the address saved in a temporary location just after the number of arguments was pushed onto the stack.

Returning from a Procedure

The RET (RETurn) instruction is used to return from a procedure. (It has no operands.) The RET instruction must undo the work done by the CALLG or CALLS instruction; that is, it removes the call frame from the stack and restores the orginal contents of the registers that were saved. If the procedure was called with the CALLS instruction, RET also pops the argument list from the stack.

At the time RET is executed, the SP may or may not be pointing to the beginning of the call frame. If data were added to the stack in the procedure and were not removed, the SP may be pointing to a higher position (lower-addressed position) on the stack. The FP, however, should always be pointing to the call frame. It is critical that the programmer not change the FP. RET will carry out the following steps:

1. Put (FP)+4 into SP.

   This pops anything that may have been added to the stack in the procedure, and it pops the first longword of the call frame, the one that may have contained a condition handler address.

2. Pop the next longword and save it in a temporary location.

   This longword contains the PSW, part of the register save mask, the CALLG/CALLS flag, and the rightmost two bits of the address that was in the SP before the procedure was called.

3. Pop the next three longwords and copy them into the AP, FP, and PC registers, respectively.

4. Pop and restore the contents of the saved registers.

   Bits 27:16 of the temporary location filled at step 2 are examined to determine which registers were saved on the stack. The appropriate number of longwords are popped and the registers are reloaded in increasing order.

5. Reset SP.

   At this point, the call frame has been popped from the stack and the SP points to the next longword on the stack. Bits 31:30 of the temporary location are added to the SP to reset it to its original value before the procedure was called. This undoes the operation described in Fig. 9.13.

6. Load the PSW with bits 15:0 of the temporary location.

7. If CALLS was used to call the procedure, pop the argument list.

   Bit 29 of the temporary is examined to determine which CALL instruction was used to call the procedure. If the bit is 1, CALLS was used and the argument list is at the top of the stack. The byte pointed to by SP contains the number of arguments, say n. SP is incremented by $4*(n+1)$, thus effectively popping the longword with the number of arguments and all the argument addresses.

When the RET instruction completes the steps described above, the CPU will fetch and execute the next instruction as usual. Since the PC has been reloaded with the address it contained when the CALLG or CALLS was executed, the next instruction is the one that immediately follows the CALLG or CALLS in memory.

Returning Values and Flags from Procedures

The VAX convention for returning a function value from a procedure is that the procedure leaves the value in R0; if it is a quadword or double-precision floating point number, it is left in R0 and R1. Whether or not a procedure is a function, we may want it to return one or more flags. The flags might indicate whether or not the procedure completed its task successfully, whether or not certain special conditions occurred, and so on. In particular, it may be very useful for a procedure that does input (or processes input) to return flags, because there are many things that can go wrong in such a procedure. Our READRCRD macro, for example, calls a procedure that returns a flag to indicate if the end of the DATA.DAT file has been reached.

There are two convenient places for returning flags: R0 and the condition codes. (In a function procedure, R1 might be used for flags.) On the VAX it is especially easy to use R0 because the BLBS and BLBC (Branch if Low Bit is Set, or Clear) instructions can be used to test the flag upon return from the procedure. If we did not have these instructions (and many other computers do not have similar ones), an explicit test on R0 would be needed. In that case it would be preferable to use a condition code because one conditional branch instruction could be used to test it. The VAX CALL instructions always clear the condition codes in the copy of the old PSW saved on the stack, so the programmer need only set one of the bits in the saved PSW if the condition to be indicated by the flag holds. Some of the procedures in the example in Section 9.8 return a flag by setting one of the condition codes.

9.7 RUNNING AND DEBUGGING PROGRAMS WITH PROCEDURES

In this section we review the VAX/VMS system commands to run a program with procedures, explain how to interpret run-time error messages, and show some debugger features useful with procedures.

Assemble, Link, and Run

Suppose that a program consists of a main program and four procedures, each in a separate file: main.mar, proc1.mar, proc2.mar, proc3.mar, and proc4.mar. Each file is assembled separately with the MACRO command. As usual, if a listing is desired, the /LIST option is used. If the I/O macros defined in this book are used anywhere in the program, the main program must use the BEGIN and EXIT macros (rather than .ENTRY and $EXIT_S), and it must be assembled with the I/O macro library:

MACRO/LIST MAIN+[*directory*]IOMAC/LIB

where *directory* is the directory containing the I/O macro library. Each procedure that uses any of the I/O macros is assembled similarly, with the procedure file name in place of MAIN (but the procedures use .ENTRY, not BEGIN). The I/O macro library may be omitted from the MACRO command for a procedure that does not use any of the I/O macros. For example:

MACRO/LIST PROC3

(It would not be an error to include the macro library, but it is not neeeded.) After all the files are successfully assembled, the object files produced by the assembler must be linked. The main program should be listed first in the LINK command; the order of the others is not important. If the I/O macros are used anywhere in the program, the file IOMOD.OBJ must be linked with the program. The format of the command is

LINK MAIN,PROC1,PROC2,PROC3,PROC4,[directory]IOMOD

Finally, the program is run with

RUN MAIN

When errors occur, only those files that are modified need to be reassembled. Then all the files must be linked again before rerunning the program.

Error Messages

In Chapter 8, we explained that in run-time error messages, the "rel PC" value included in the message is the location of the error relative to the entry point of the program. A program with procedures contains several entry points. For such programs, the "rel PC" is relative to the closest entry point that precedes the location of the error, usually the entry point of the procedure in which the error occurs. The message includes the entry point name, so using the listing file for the appropriate procedure, the programmer can find the error.

There is one peculiarity that can occur resulting in confusing information in the error message. Suppose that the linker has loaded the object files so that the entry point locations (all shown in hex) are

        MAIN   600
        PROC1 700
        PROC2 750
        PROC3 7B0
        PROC4 810

Now, suppose, for example, that in PROC3 there is a branch instruction that incorrectly causes a branch into the data area that precedes the entry point. A reserved opcode error may occur at, say, location 7A4. The nearest preceding entry point is PROC2 at 750. The error message will say that the error occurred in PROC2 at relative location 54.

Using the Debugger with Procedures

If we plan to use the debugger, the DEBUG option should be specified on the MACRO commands for each procedure and the main program, and on the LINK command.

When an error occurs or when the debugger suspends execution at, say, a watchpoint, we want to know not only what procedure it is in, but from where that procedure was called. The SHOW CALLS command tells us.

```
DBG> show calls
    module name      routine name                    line      rel PC      abs PC
  *.MAIN.           GETNUM                            48       0000000A    000006E1
  *.MAIN.           SETUP                             26       00000029    000007B9
  *.MAIN.           SETMAIN                            4       0000005A    00000679
```

This table is a stack of the active procedures. It indicates that execution is paused at line 48 in the routine GETNUM, which was called from line 26 in SETUP, which was called from line 4 in SETMAIN, the main program.

The STEP command, by default, treats the execution of an entire procedure as one step. That is, if the next instruction to be executed is a CALL instruction, and the STEP command is given, the debugger "steps over" the procedure. It executes the entire procedure before pausing; when it pauses, the instruction on the line following the CALL is the next instruction to be executed. If we are confident that the procedure does its work correctly, treating the entire procedure as one step is a convenience. Sometimes, though, we want to monitor the instructions within a procedure. When the debugger is paused on a CALL instruction, we can force it to step into the procedure by specifying the INTO qualifier on the STEP command. If we decide that we do not want to examine every instruction in the procedure, but would like to continue stepping through the routine that called it, we can step to the end of the procedure by using the RETURN qualifier. Here is an example.

```
DBG> step
stepped to .MAIN.\SETUP\%LINE 26
    26:         CALLG   ARGS,GETNUM            ; Get next number from input
DBG> step/into
%DEBUG-I-DYNMODSET, setting module .MAIN.
stepped to routine .MAIN.\GETNUM
    46:         MOVL    4(AP),R6              ; first byte of string
DBG> step
stepped to .MAIN.\GETNUM\%LINE 47
    47:         MOVL    8(AP),R9              ; loop limit
DBG> step/return
stepped on return from .MAIN.\GETNUM\%LINE 47 to .MAIN.\GETNUM\%LINE 73
    73:         RET                           ; return
DBG> step
stepped to .MAIN.\SETUP\%LINE 27
    27:         BLBC    R0,DONE              ; Branch if set is complete
```

We remind the reader that the STEP command should not be overused. It is better to select specific watchpoints that will help identify a problem.

9.8 EXAMPLE: LINKED LIST MANIPULATION

In this section we present an example of a program that uses twelve procedures. Many of them call others and must pass some of their own arguments to the procedures they call. Thus the program illustrates a moderately complex program organization with procedure calls sometimes going four levels deep. The example illustrates some other points about program design, too. Many of the procedures do fairly general operations and are written so that they could be used for applications with different data formats. All of the operations that depend on the specific data format are performed in a few, very short, procedures. Thus all the data-dependent operations are isolated and easy to change. To make reading the procedures easier (and to make it easy to change them without errors), symbolic names are used for constants that depend on the data format and for the displacement from the argument list address for each procedure argument. The documentation for many of the procedures includes an algorithm written in a high-level language.

The program uses a linked list. We will briefly review this basic and very useful data structure.

Linked Lists

In many of our examples and exercises we have had data stored in an array or table. The entries appear in consecutive locations in memory. Sometimes it is not convenient or efficient to maintain a list of items this way. If, for example, we want to keep the entries in numerical or alphabetical order, but we will often be adding or deleting items, it is inefficient to rearrange the entries repeatedly. Linked lists provide a way to separate the logical ordering of the entries from their physical arrangement in memory. In a linked list each entry has a pointer field that contains the address of the entry that is logically next, though it may be physically anywhere in memory. The term *node* is often used to refer to the group of bytes that constitute one entry in a linked list, including the pointer and all the data fields.

Since even the logically first node in a linked list may be located anywhere, we must keep track of its address. If we know where the first entry is, we can find the others by following the pointers. Thus with any linked list we have a pointer variable called, say *first*, pointing to the first node. The pointer field of the logically last node contains a special value called *null* or *nil* (often represented by zero) to indicate that there is no next node. Figure 9.15 shows a diagram of a linked list; it assumes that the pointer field is the first field in each node.

To describe algorithms that operate on linked lists, we need some notation to refer to the various fields of the nodes. Each node in one list will have the same format, and we can give names to the fields. To refer to a particular field in a particular node, we will use the notation

$$ptr\uparrow field\_name$$

where *ptr* is a pointer to the desired node. Thus if "link" is the name of the pointer field in each node,

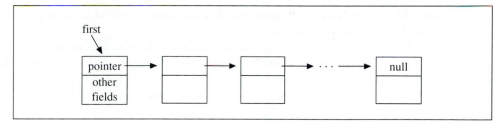

Figure 9.15   A linked list

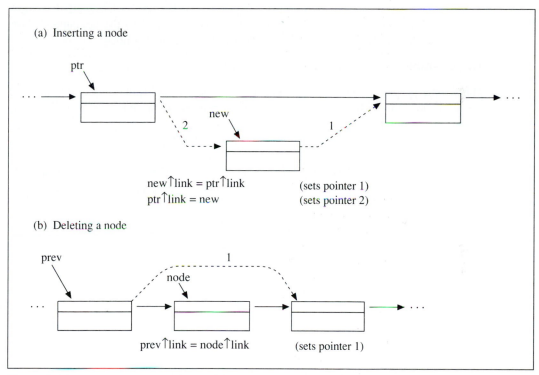

Figure 9.16   Inserting and deleting nodes

$$first \uparrow link$$

is the link field of the node pointed to by *first*. The value of *first↑link* is the contents of that field: the address of the next node.

Two operations often performed on a list are insertion of new items and deletion of existing items. In an array, these operations can require moving a lot of data. In a linked list, they require changing only one or two pointer values, as illustrated in Fig. 9.16. To standardize the steps used to insert or delete a node, it is helpful to have a fixed node at the beginning of the list that does not contain an actual entry and is never deleted (unless the entire list is no longer needed). Such a node is called a *header node*. Its use eliminates the special cases of changing *first* if a new entry is added at the beginning of the list or if the first entry is deleted.

In order to add a new item to a linked list, we must be able to find some space in memory that is not in use. Usually, a large area of memory is reserved for linked list nodes (possibly for several different lists). This space can be divided up into units of the size needed for a node, and these units, or empty nodes, can be linked up in a linked list of available nodes. When a program wants to construct a new node, it gets an empty one from the list of available nodes. When an item is deleted from a linked list, the space it occupied is "recycled"; that is, the node is returned to the available node list so that it may be used again later if more items are inserted. Since the ordering of the empty nodes is irrelevant, nodes will be removed from and returned to the beginning of the available node list. The available node list does not need a header node.

The Example

The sample program contains procedures to insert, delete, and find items, and to print all the items, in a linked list that is kept (logically) in numeric or alphabetical order. These procedures assume that the pointer field is the first field in the node, but they make no assumptions about the number, type, or size of the other fields. Thus they could be used for many different applications. They appear in Fig. 9.17.

The three data-dependent procedures are shown in Fig. 9.18. They compare, fill, and print the node key, or identifier, field. In this program the nodes contain only a pointer and a key, which is a 12-byte character string. The field names are *link* and *key*.

```
The BISB2 instruction used in these procedures has not been described yet in the text.
It sets a bit (to 1).

; AVAILABLE NODE LIST UTILITIES
;
; These procedures manage the available node pool.  They are
; in one file to share the variable AVAIL.
;
;        INIT_AVAIL (NODES, BYTES, NODE_SIZE)
;            links up all the nodes in the node pool
;
;     GET_NODE (PTR)
;         removes a node from the available node list
;         and returns a pointer to it
;
;     RET_NODE (PTR)
;         adds a given node to the available node list
;
```

Figure 9.17   Data-independent linked list routines (continued next page)

```
        ; AVAIL contains a pointer to the first node in the linked
        ; available node list.  It is initialized by INIT_AVAIL and
        ; is used by GET_NODE and RET_NODE.
        ;
        AVAIL:  .BLKL   1                       ; Ptr to first available node
        ;
        ; PROCEDURE INIT_AVAIL (NODES, BYTES, NODE_SIZE)
        ;
        ; Input arguments
        ;       NODES       the node pool
        ;       BYTES       the number of bytes in the pool (longword)
        ;       NODE_SIZE   the number of bytes per node (longword)
        ;
        ; Offsets for argument list
        NODES = 4
        BYTES = 8
        NODE_SIZE = 12
        ;
        ; REGISTER USE
        ;
        ;       R6      pointer to current node
        ;       R8      node size
        ;       R9      address of next to last node
        ;
                .ENTRY  INIT_AVAIL,^M<R6,R8,R9>
        ;
        ; Use node size to determine address of next to last node.
                MOVL    NODES(AP),R6            ; Address of first node
                MOVL    @NODE_SIZE(AP),R8       ; Node size
                ADDL3   R6,@BYTES(AP),R9        ; Address+number of bytes
                SUBL2   R8,R9                   ; Address of last node
                SUBL2   R8,R9                   ; Addr of next to last node
        ;
        ; Set pointer to first available node.
                MOVL    R6,AVAIL                ; First node is first available
        ;
        ; Link up nodes.  (Store pointer to next node in all but the
        ; last node; store null pointer in last node.)
        LINK:   ADDL3   R6,R8,(R6)              ; Store ptr to next node
                ACBL    R9,R8,R6,LINK
                CLRL    (R6)                    ; Store null ptr in last node
                RET
        ;
        ;
```

Figure 9.17   (continued next page)

```
; PROCEDURE GET_NODE (PTR)
;
; Output argument
;       PTR             pointer to an available node
;                       (will be null if none available)
;
        .ENTRY  GET_NODE,0
        MOVL    AVAIL,@4(AP)            ; Return ptr to a node
        BEQL    DONE                   ; Done if null
        MOVL    @AVAIL,AVAIL           ; Remove node from pool
DONE:   RET
;
;
; PROCEDURE RET_NODE (PTR)
;
; Input argument
;       PTR             pointer to node to be returned to list
;
        .ENTRY  RET_NODE,0
        MOVL    AVAIL,@4(AP)           ; ptr^link = avail
        MOVL    4(AP),AVAIL            ; avail = ptr
        RET
        .END
```

```
; PROCEDURE INSERT (KEY, FIRST)
;
; This procedure inserts a new item into the linked list
; whose header node is pointed to by FIRST.
; The list is assumed to be sorted.  A flag is returned
; in the Z condition code in the saved PSW to indicate
; whether or not there was room to add the new node.
;
; The algorithm is:
;
;       call getnode (new);
;       if new <> null then begin
;           call fillkey (key, new);
;           call findplace (key, first, ptr);
;           new^link = ptr^link;
;           ptr^link = new;
;           set Z to indicate success
;       end
;
```

Figure 9.17   (continued next page)

```
        ; Offsets for argument list
        KEY = 4
        FIRST = 8
        ;
        NEW:    .BLKL   1               ; For ptr to new node
        PTR:    .BLKL   1               ; For ptr returned by findplace
        ;
                .ENTRY  INSERT,0
        ;
        ; Construct node for new item.
                PUSHAL  NEW
                CALLS   #1,GET_NODE     ; Get node from pool
                TSTL    NEW             ; If new = null, return
                BEQL    RET
                PUSHL   NEW             ; Address of new node
                PUSHL   KEY(AP)         ; Address of KEY
                CALLS   #2,FILL_KEY     ; Fill key field
        ;
        ; Find position in list where new item belongs.
                PUSHAL  PTR
                PUSHL   FIRST(AP)       ; Address of FIRST
                PUSHL   KEY(AP)         ; Address of KEY
                CALLS   #3,FIND_PLACE
        ;
        ; Link in new node.
                MOVL    @PTR,@NEW       ; new^link = ptr^link
                MOVL    NEW,@PTR        ; ptr^link = new
                BISB2   #^X04,4(FP)     ; Set Z to indicate insertion
        ;
        RET:    RET
                .END
```

```
; PROCEDURE DELETE (KEY, FIRST)
;
; This procedure deletes the node with key KEY from the sorted
; linked list with header node pointed to by FIRST.  It sets
; the Z bit in the saved PSW if KEY was found in the list and
; deleted.  The deleted node is returned to the node pool.
;
; The algorithm is:
;
```

Figure 9.17   (continued next page)

```
;         call find_place (KEY,FIRST,PTR);
;         node = ptr^link;
;         if node <> null then if node^key = KEY then begin
;             ptr^link = node^link;
;             call ret_node(node);
;             set Z
;         end
;
; Offsets for argument list
KEY = 4
FIRST = 8
;
PTR:    .BLKL   1                       ; For ptr returned by findplace
;
; REGISTER USE
;
;       R6        node pointer
;
        .ENTRY  DELETE,^M<R6>
;
; Find position in list where KEY may be.
        PUSHAL  PTR
        PUSHL   FIRST(AP)               ; Address of header ptr
        PUSHL   KEY(AP)                 ; Address of key
        CALLS   #3,FIND_PLACE
        MOVL    @PTR,R6                 ; node = ptr^link
        BEQL    RET                     ; Return if node = null
;
; Determine if KEY is really there.
        PUSHL   R6                      ; Address of node
        PUSHL   KEY(AP)                 ; Address of key
        CALLS   #2,COMPARE              ; See if key is in list
        BNEQ    RET                     ; Return if key not there
;
; Delete the node.
        MOVL    (R6),@PTR               ; ptr^link = node^link
;
; Return node to available list.
        PUSHL   R6                      ; Address of node
        CALLS   #1,RET_NODE
;
; Set flag.
        BISB2   #^X04,4(FP)             ; Set Z for deletion
RET:    RET
        .END
```

Figure 9.17   (continued next page)

```
; PROCEDURE FIND (KEY,FIRST,PTR)
;
; This procedure returns a pointer (in PTR) to the node
; containing the key KEY.  FIRST is a pointer to the list
; header node.  If KEY is not in the list, the returned
; pointer will be null.
;
; The algorithm is:
;
;       call find_place (KEY,FIRST,PREV);
;       ptr = prev^link;
;       if ptr = null then return null;
;       if ptr^key <> KEY then return null
;                         else return ptr
;
; Offsets for argument list
KEY = 4
FIRST = 8
PTR = 12
;
PREV:   .BLKL   1                       ; For ptr returned by findplace
;
; REGISTER USE
;
;       R6      tentative pointer to KEY
;
        .ENTRY  FIND,^M<R6>
;
; Find position where KEY may be.
        PUSHAL  PREV                    ; For ptr returned by findplace
        PUSHL   FIRST(AP)               ; Address of header node
        PUSHL   KEY(AP)                 ; Address of KEY
        CALLS   #3,FIND_PLACE
;
; Determine if KEY is really there.
        MOVL    @PREV,R6                ; ptr = prev^link
        BEQL    STORE                   ; Return ptr if null
        PUSHL   R6                      ; Address of node
        PUSHL   KEY(AP)                 ; Address of KEY
        CALLS   #2,COMPARE              ; Compare keys
        BEQL    STORE
        CLRL    R6                      ; Null
```

Figure 9.17 (continued next page)

```
;
; Return ptr.
STORE:  MOVL    R6,@PTR(AP)             ; Return ptr or null
        RET
        .END
```

```
; PROCEDURE FIND_PLACE (KEY, FIRST, PTR)
;
; This procedure finds the place where a node with key
; KEY belongs in the sorted linked list pointed to by
; FIRST.  It returns in PTR a pointer to the node that
; would precede the one containing KEY.
;
; The algorithm is:
;
;       ptr = first;
;       next = ptr^link;
;       while next <> null do begin
;               if key <= next^key then exitloop;
;               ptr = next;
;               next = ptr^link
;       end;
;       return ptr
;
; Offsets for argument list
KEY = 4
FIRST = 8
PTR = 12
;
; REGISTER USE
;
;       R6      ptr
;       R7      next
;
        .ENTRY  FIND_PLACE,^M<R6,R7>
        MOVL    @FIRST(AP),R6           ; ptr = first
NEXT:   MOVL    (R6),R7                 ; next = ptr^link
        BEQL    FOUND                   ; If next = null, done
        PUSHL   R7                      ; Address of node
        PUSHL   KEY(AP)                 ; Address of key
        CALLS   #2,COMPARE              ; Compare keys
        BLEQ    FOUND                   ; key <= node's key
        MOVL    R7,R6                   ; ptr = next
        BRB     NEXT
```

Figure 9.17   (continued next page)

```
;
FOUND:  MOVL     R6,@PTR(AP)              ; Return ptr
        RET
        .END
```

```
; PROCEDURE PRINTLIST (TITLE, FIRST)
;
; This procedure prints out the entries in the linked list
; pointed to by FIRST.  The list is assumed to have a header
; node.  TITLE is a character string printed as a heading
; for the list.
;
; Offsets for argument list
TITLE = 4
FIRST = 8
;
; REGISTER USE
;
;       R6        pointer to current node
;
        .ENTRY   PRINTLIST,^M<R6>
        PRINTCHRS @TITLE(AP)              ; Print heading
        MOVL     @FIRST(AP),R6            ; Get ptr to header node
NEXT:   MOVL     (R6),R6                  ; Get next ptr.
        BEQL     DONE
        PUSHL    R6                       ; Push pointer
        CALLS    #1,PRINTKEY
        BRB      NEXT
DONE:   RET
        .END
```

Figure 9.17 (concluded)

The BISB2 instruction used in these procedures has not been described yet in the text. It sets a bit (to 1).

```
; PROCEDURE FILL_KEY (KEY, NODE)
;
; This procedure fills the key field of NODE with the
; key KEY.
;
; The number of bytes in the key, KEY_SIZE, and the
; offset of the key field from the beginning of the node,
; KEY_FIELD, are constants defined in this procedure.
```

Figure 9.18 Data-dependent procedures (continued next page)

```
;
KEY_SIZE = 12                          ; Number of bytes in key
KEY_FIELD = 4                          ; Offset for key field
;
; Offsets for argument list
KEY = 4
NODE = 8
;
; REGISTER USE
;
;       R6        address of node
;       R0-R5     used by MOVC3
;
        .ENTRY    FILL_KEY,^M<R2,R3,R4,R5,R6>
        MOVL      NODE(AP),R6                ; Get address of node
        MOVC3     #KEY_SIZE,@KEY(AP),KEY_FIELD(R6)  ; Store KEY
        RET
        .END
```

```
; PROCEDURE COMPARE (KEY, NODE)
;
; This procedure compares KEY with the key in NODE
; and sets the condition codes in the stacked PSW
; to indicate the relation between the two keys.
;
; The number of bytes in the key, KEY_SIZE, and the
; offset of the key field from the beginning of the node,
; KEY_FIELD, are constants defined in this procedure.
;
KEY_SIZE = 12                          ; Number of bytes per key
KEY_FIELD = 4                          ; Offset for key field
;
; Offsets for argument list
KEY = 4
NODE = 8
;
; REGISTER USE
;
;       R6        ptr
;       R0-R3     used by CMPC3
;
```

Figure 9.18   (continued next page)

```
            .ENTRY   COMPARE,^M<R2,R3,R6>
            MOVL     NODE(AP),R6              ; Address of node
            CMPC3    #KEY_SIZE,@KEY(AP),KEY_FIELD(R6)
            BGTR     RET
            BLSS     SET_N
SET_Z:      BISB2    #^X04,4(FP)             ; Set Z for equal keys
            BRB      RET
SET_N:      BISB2    #^X08,4(FP)             ; Set N if KEY < node's key
RET:        RET
            .END
```

```
; PROCEDURE PRINTKEY (NODE)
;
; This procedure prints the key in the given node.
;
; The number of bytes in the key, KEY_SIZE, and the
; offset of the key field from the beginning of a node,
; KEY_FIELD, are constants defined in this procedure.
;
KEY_SIZE = 12                           ; Number of bytes per key
KEY_FIELD = 4                           ; Offset for key field
;
; Offset for argument list
NODE = 4
;
TAB = 9
LINE:   .BYTE   TAB,0[KEY_SIZE]
;
; REGISTER USE
;
;       R6      ptr
;       R0-R5   used by MOVC3
;
        .ENTRY   PRINTKEY,^M<R2,R3,R4,R5,R6>
        MOVL     NODE(AP),R6                ; Get addr of node
        MOVC3    #KEY_SIZE,KEY_FIELD(R6),LINE+1
        PRINTCHRS LINE,#KEY_SIZE+1          ; Print key
        RET
        .END
```

Figure 9.18   (concluded)

Note that even though the data-dependent procedures are very short, it is good programming style to use them; they clearly isolate the parts of the program that would have to be changed for an application with a different node format.

For simplicity, the procedures do not do extensive testing to make sure that the argument values are valid.

Figure 9.19 shows the main program and the procedure that processes input data to test the linked list procedures. Figure 9.20 shows the data file used for the tests and the output from the program.

```
; MAIN PROGRAM
;
; This program tests the linked list procedures.  It calls
; INIT_AVAIL to link up all of the nodes, then calls TESTER
; to read and process the test data, and finally, calls
; PRINTLIST to print all the keys in the list.
;
POOL = 350                          ; Number of bytes in node pool
NODE_SIZE = 16                      ; Number of bytes per node
NODES:  .BLKB    POOL
BYTES:  .LONG    POOL
NODE_SZ:.LONG    NODE_SIZE
;
FIRST:  .BLKL    1                  ; Pointer to header node
ARGS1:  .LONG    3                  ; Argument list for INIT_AVAIL
        .ADDRESS NODES,BYTES,NODE_SZ
;
TAB = 9                             ; Tab
LF = 10                             ; Line feed
CR = 13                             ; Carriage return
TITLE1: .ASCIZ   /List is empty to start/
TITLE2: .ASCII   <LF><LF>/OUTPUT FROM PRINTLIST/
        .ASCIZ   <CR><LF><LF><TAB>/GOODIES/<LF>
;
        BEGIN    LINKED
;
        CALLG    ARGS1,INIT_AVAIL   ; Link all nodes
        PUSHAL   FIRST
        CALLS    #1,GET_NODE        ; Get a header node
        CLRL     @FIRST             ; Set ptr in header to null
;
        PUSHAL   FIRST              ; Pointer to header node
        PUSHAB   TITLE1             ; Heading for empty list
        CALLS    #2,PRINTLIST       ; Print empty list (to be sure
;                                   ; PRINTLIST works properly)
```

Figure 9.19   The main program and TESTER procedure (continued next page)

```
;
            PUSHAL   FIRST
            CALLS    #1,TESTER          ; Process test data
;
            PUSHAL   FIRST
            PUSHAB   TITLE2
            CALLS    #2,PRINTLIST       ; Print list
;
            EXIT
            .END     LINKED
```

```
; PROCEDURE TESTER (FIRST)
;
; This procedure processes input data to test the linked list
; procedures.  It reads records from DATA.DAT of the form
;
;         CODE KEY
;
; where CODE is a one-letter code telling what to do with the
; item and KEY is the item's key.  (The number of bytes in
; the keys can be varied without changing TESTER.)
; TESTER prints out all of the records processed along with
; a brief message indicating the result of the action taken.
;
FIRST = 4                                ; Offset for argument list
;
; Codes
INS = ^A/I/                             ; Insert
DEL = ^A/D/                             ; Delete
FND = ^A/F/                             ; Find
;
BUFFER: .BLKB    80
BLANKS: .BYTE    ^X20[80]
PTR:    .BLKL    1                       ; For pointer returned by FIND
;
LF = 10
TAB = 9
HDG:    .ASCIZ   <LF><LF>/TEST DATA/<LF>
INSMSG: .ASCIZ   <TAB>/inserted/
NOROOM: .ASCIZ   <TAB>/no nodes available/
DELMSG: .ASCIZ   <TAB>/deleted/
NOTIN:  .ASCIZ   <TAB>/not in the list/
ERRMSG: .ASCIZ   <TAB>/Bad code!!/
;
```

Figure 9.19   (continued next page)

```
                .ENTRY  TESTER,^M<R2,R3,R4,R5>
                PRINTCHRS HDG
;
; Read and print test record.
;
READ:   MOVC3      #80,BLANKS,BUFFER
        READRCRD   BUFFER
        PRINTCHRS BUFFER,R0
;
; Determine operation to be performed and call appropriate
; procedure.
;
        CMPB       BUFFER,#INS
        BNEQ       TRY_DEL
        PUSHL      FIRST(AP)              ; Call INSERT
        PUSHAB     BUFFER+2
        CALLS      #2,INSERT
        BEQL       IN
        PRINTCHRS NOROOM
        BRW        DONE
IN:     PRINTCHRS INSMSG
        BRW        DONE
;
TRY_DEL:CMPB       BUFFER,#DEL
        BNEQ       TRY_FND
        PUSHL      FIRST(AP)              ; Call DELETE
        PUSHAB     BUFFER+2
        CALLS      #2,DELETE
        BEQL       DELETED
        PRINTCHRS NOTIN
        BRW        DONE
DELETED:PRINTCHRS DELMSG
        BRW        DONE
;
TRY_FND:CMPB       BUFFER,#FND
        BNEQ       ERROR
        PUSHAL     PTR                    ; Call FIND
        PUSHL      FIRST(AP)
        PUSHAB     BUFFER+2
        CALLS      #3,FIND
        TSTL       PTR
        BEQL       NOTFND
        PUSHL      PTR
        CALLS      #1,PRINTKEY
        BRW        DONE
```

Figure 9.19   (continued next page)

```
NOTFND: PRINTCHRS NOTIN
        BRW      DONE
;
ERROR:  PRINTCHRS ERRMSG
DONE:   BRW      READ
;
EOF:    RET
        .END
```

Figure 9.19   (concluded)

(a) The data file.
```
I APPLES
I SPINACH
I CHOCOLATE
D PIZZA
I BROWNIES
I ICE CREAM
J COOKIES
D SPINACH
F SPINACH
I SPINACH
F SPINACH
F ICE CREAM
D APPLES
I EGGS
I MOO SHU PORK
D ALMONDS
I BANANAS
I CHEESECAKE
F COOKIES
F BROWNIES
I ALMONDS
D ZUCCHINI
I MILK
I COFFEE
I TURKEY
I YAMS
I SHRIMP
I BACON
I CHEESE
I PIZZA
I ABALONE
```

Figure 9.20   The data file and program output (continued next page)

```
I  SALMON
F  ALMONDS
F  YAMS
I  CROISSANTS
I  CANTELOPE
D  COFFEE
I  CANTELOPE
I  CASHEWS
```

(b) Output from the program.

```
List is empty to start

TEST DATA

I  APPLES
          inserted
I  SPINACH
          inserted
I  CHOCOLATE
          inserted
D  PIZZA
          not in the list
I  BROWNIES
          inserted
I  ICE CREAM
          inserted
J  COOKIES
          Bad code!!
D  SPINACH
          deleted
F  SPINACH
          not in the list
I  SPINACH
          inserted
F  SPINACH
          SPINACH
F  ICE CREAM
          ICE CREAM
D  APPLES
          deleted
I  EGGS
          inserted
I  MOO SHU PORK
          inserted
```

Figure 9.20   (continued next page)

```
D ALMONDS
        not in the list
I BANANAS
        inserted
I CHEESECAKE
        inserted
F COOKIES
        not in the list
F BROWNIES
        BROWNIES
I ALMONDS
        inserted
D ZUCCHINI
        not in the list
I MILK
        inserted
I COFFEE
        inserted
I TURKEY
        inserted
I YAMS
        inserted
I SHRIMP
        inserted
I BACON
        inserted
I CHEESE
        inserted
I PIZZA
        inserted
I ABALONE
        inserted
I SALMON
        inserted
F ALMONDS
        ALMONDS
F YAMS
        YAMS
I CROISSANTS
        inserted
I CANTELOPE
        no nodes available
D COFFEE
        deleted
```

Figure 9.20   (continued next page)

```
I CANTELOPE
        inserted
I CASHEWS
        no nodes available


OUTPUT FROM PRINTLIST

        GOODIES

        ABALONE
        ALMONDS
        BACON
        BANANAS
        BROWNIES
        CANTELOPE
        CHEESE
        CHEESECAKE
        CHOCOLATE
        CROISSANTS
        EGGS
        ICE CREAM
        MILK
        MOO SHU PORK
        PIZZA
        SALMON
        SHRIMP
        SPINACH
        TURKEY
        YAMS
```

Figure 9.20   (concluded)

9.9 LOCAL VARIABLES, RECURSION, AND REENTRANT ROUTINES

Local Variables

Procedures may contain storage reservation and initialization directives. The search procedure in Fig. 9.8 did not need any, but several procedures in the linked list example in
Section 9.8 did. The labels on the space reserved are (normally) local labels; that is, they
are not accessible from other routines in the same program. Thus storage reserved in
procedures corresponds in some ways to local variables declared in Pascal, C, and Fortran procedures, functions, and subroutines. The space allocated by a storage reservation
directive is permanent; it is reserved throughout the execution of the whole program.
This differs from local variables in Pascal; it is similar to internal static variables in C. In

Pascal, a local variable exists only while the procedure in which it is defined is executing. The space for the variable is deallocated upon return from the procedure; thus the value of the variable is lost.

The permanence of a variable defined in an assembly language routine is sometimes an asset; sometimes it is not an appropriate way to implement local variables. It has consequences and uses that may be unfamiliar to a Pascal programmer. Consider the longword labeled AVAIL in the linked list example in Section 9.8 (Fig. 9.17). The .BLKL directive initializes the longword to zero. The initialization is done once, at assembly time; it is not repeated each time the procedure is called. This is critical to the proper use of AVAIL in this program. It is supposed to contain the address of the next available node. We certainly do not want that information to disappear, as it would in Pascal, while other procedures are performing operations on the linked list. The current value of the pointer is always in the longword at AVAIL, inaccessible from other procedures, but available for use and modification by the GET_NODE and RET_NODE routines.

Another feature of a local variable reserved with a storage reservation directive is that there is just one instance of the variable (i.e., one location, of whatever type, is reserved in general memory). This may sound like a pointless observation: How many are needed? The reader familiar with recursion or reentrant code may know that the answer is: Perhaps quite a few!

Recursion

Let us review a little about recursion. First consider two nonrecursive procedures, procedure A and procedure B (which you may think of as being written in a high-level language or assembly language). Suppose that each has a local variable called X. Although they have the same name, the two variables are distinct. They occupy different places in memory. If in procedure A, X currently has the value 5, A calls B, and in B, X is assigned the value 10, then upon return to A, X still has the value 5. Now consider a recursive procedure, say P. A recursive procedure calls itself. To understand recursion, it helps to think of there being a new copy of the procedure generated each time it is called. When P calls itself, it is as if there were two copies, "P1" and "P2." If P has a local variable X whose value is 5 when "P1" calls "P2," then the value of X should be 5 after returning from "P2" to "P1." But in reality, there is only one copy of the procedure P. If, in assembly language, X is declared with a storage reservation directive, there is only one memory location for X. If while in "P2," a new value is stored in X, the original value is obliterated. Thus for recursion to work properly, each time a recursive routine is called a new instance of each local variable must be created. It can be discarded upon return. A natural place for local variables is the stack. Note that since a recursive routine may call itself many times, with different arguments each time, the argument lists should be constructed on the stack too, and CALLS should be used to call the procedure.

Example 9.10: Using Local Variables on the Stack

Suppose that a (perhaps recursive) procedure has two local integer variables. We will call them x and y. They can be allocated and used as follows. (Note that the symbols X and Y in the procedure are not labels.)

```
X = 0                                  ; Offsets from top of stack
Y = 4
        .ENTRY  PROC,^M< ... >
        SUBL2   #8,SP                  ; Reserve space for x and y
        ...
        MOVL    #5,X(SP)               ; x := 5
        ...
        ADDL2   Y(SP),X(SP)            ; x := x + y
        ...
        ADDL2   #8,SP                  ; Pop x and y from the stack
        RET
        .END
```

The ADDL2 instruction that resets the stack pointer is not actually necessary, because the RET instruction will pop everything above the call frame.

If PROC is recursive, two new longwords will be allocated on top of the call frame each time PROC is called. The currently executing instance of PROC will use the topmost instances of *x* and *y*. The RET instruction pops the call frame and argument list, and resets the stack pointer to where it was before the latest call. At that point the *x* and *y* for the previous instance of PROC will be at the top of the stack. See Fig. 9.21 for a picture of the stack.

Since local variables in Pascal and automatic variables in C are supposed to exist only while a procedure or function is executing, compilers normally allocate all local variables on the stack, not in general memory, for nonrecursive as well as recursive routines.

Another possible place for local variables is in registers. By now we are well used to using registers for variables such as loop indexes without allocating any memory space for them. This practice works fine in recursive procedures. Registers are always saved when a procedure is called, so when a recursive procedure calls itself, the data in registers during execution of one instance of the procedure, say "P1," are saved on the stack while the next instance, "P2," does its work. Upon return from "P2," the previous contents of the registers are reloaded, and "P1" can resume with the data it had.

If by now we have made the wall between each instance of a recursive routine seem so solid that they cannot communicate at all, remember that, like all procedures and functions, the various levels of the recursive routine communicate via their argument lists and, for functions, via R0 and R1, which are never saved on the stack or reloaded by RET.

Reentrant Code

When 30 people are working on a timesharing system like the VAX, all at the same time, all using the same editor, how many copies of the editor program exist? It should be clear that having 30 copies would be an inefficient use of space. A lot of software must be written so that one copy can be executed by many users at the same time. Such software is called *reentrant*. Examples of programs that should be reentrant are editors, assemblers, compilers, linkers, system utilities, and some operating system routines. The

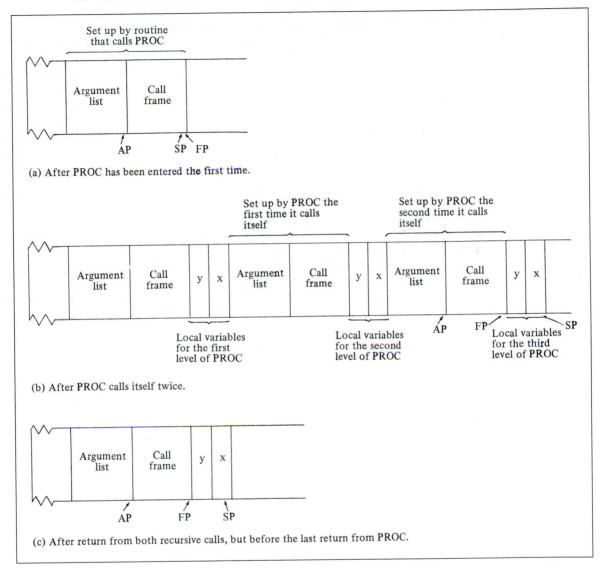

(a) After PROC has been entered the first time.

(b) After PROC calls itself twice.

(c) After return from both recursive calls, but before the last return from PROC.

Figure 9.21 Local variables on the stack

purpose of this section is to consider where space for local variables should be allocated in reentrant routines. To understand the context, we need some background about timesharing; the discussion here is very much simplified, but should be sufficient for our purpose.

The CPU does only one thing at a time, so we need to understand what is actually happening when many users are working at the same time. Computers are so fast that they can "hop around" from user to user, performing a large number of instructions on each program in such a short time that the users may not be aware that they do not have the full use of the CPU. For this to work without getting everyone's data garbled, there is some overhead. Each user program has its own area of memory; memory is large, so that is not a problem. There is only one set of general registers, and one PSL. When the CPU switches from one user to another, the program and data in memory may be left just as they are, but the contents of the registers and PSL must be saved so that the interrupted program can later be resumed at the correct position (the address in the PC) and with the correct data in the registers. Thus switching from one program to another is a little like calling and returning from a procedure. (There is more overhead in program-switching because the system has to keep track of the programs and decide whose turn it is.)

Now suppose that you are at a terminal using an editor. Think of yourself at the terminal as a main program and the editor as a library procedure that you call. Your area of memory contains a copy of the file you are editing and your user stack. There is only one copy of the editor in memory, not in your private area, but in an area accessible to all users. One example of a variable used by the editor is the current cursor position. Suppose the editor program contains a storage reservation directive reserving space labeled CURSOR where it stores the current cursor position. Your cursor is at a particular position; the location is stored at CURSOR. Now the CPU interrupts your program to work on someone else's. Suppose that person is also using the editor and that he or she moves the cursor. The location stored in CURSOR will be changed. When your program resumes, the cursor will have mysteriously jumped to a new position on the screen. This, of course, is not acceptable.

The problem comes from the fact that there is only one memory location for CURSOR. In a reentrant routine, any "variable" that is user-dependent must have a separate instance for each user. Each user has a separate user stack in the user's memory area. Space for the cursor position should be allocated on the user stack. When the editor is running for one user, the register contents are valid for that user. In particular, the SP register contains the address of the top of that user's stack. When the CPU switches to another user, the registers are reloaded with the new user's register contents, so the SP will have the address of the new user's stack. While both users are executing the same code, the code operates on different data. The general rule that we can derive from this discussion is that the programmer writing a reentrant procedure should allocate space for all user-dependent data on the user stack, not within the procedure itself.

Data used by a procedure include its arguments, of course, not just local variables. The arguments do not present a problem for a reentrant procedure. Each user's argument list is in the user's memory space. The procedure locates it via the AP as usual. Since all register contents are saved for each user, the procedure will always act on the current user's arguments.

In practice, most routines that are actually written in assembly language are operating system routines, and many must be reentrant. Thus it is good to develop the habit of allocating space for variables on the stack. Since we are not assuming any background in operating systems, we give an example that simply reads an array.

Example 9.11: A Reentrant Procedure

This procedure reads a file of character strings and stores them in an array. The buffer space for the line read from the user's file is allocated on the stack. Data that is not user-dependent, like the line of blanks, may be allocated in general memory.

```
; PROCEDURE GETSTRINGS(STRINGS: array of strings, MAX: longword,
;                                   LENGTH: byte, NUM: longword)
;
;     Reads lines from the file DATA.DAT and stores them in the
; character array STRINGS.
;     LENGTH is the (expected) length of each string. MAX is the
; maximum number of strings that fit in the array. The procedure
; will compute NUM, the number of strings actually read.
;     If a line from the file is too long, only the first LENGTH
; characters are stored in the array. If a line is too short,
; the string is padded with blanks.
;
;     This procedure expects arguments to be passed by reference.
; It is reentrant. User data (the string read) is put on the
; user stack.
;
STRINGS = 4                                  ; Offsets for argument list
MAX = 8
LENGTH = 12
NUM = 16
;
BLANK = ^A/ /
BLANKS: .BYTE    BLANK[80]
;
; REGISTER USE
;
;        R6       address for next string
;        R7       loop index
;        R8       input string length
;        R9       expected string length
;        R0-R5    used by MOVC3
;
         .ENTRY   GETSTRINGS,^M<R2,R3,R4,R5,R6,R7,R8,R9>
         MOVL     STRINGS(AP),R6       ; Array pointer
         MOVL     @MAX(AP),R7          ; Max number of strings
         CVTBL    @LENGTH(AP),R9       ; Expected string length
         SUBL2    #80,SP               ; Reserve buffer space on stack
READ:    READRCRD (SP)                 ; Read string onto stack
         MOVL     R0,R8                ; Input string length
         MOVC3    R9,BLANKS,(R6)       ; Blanks for short strings
         CMPL     R8,R9                ; Check length
```

```
              BLEQ    COPY                    ; Input length ok
              MOVL    R9,R8                   ; String too long; truncate
      COPY:   MOVC3   R8,(SP),(R6)            ; Copy string to array
              ADDL2   R9,R6                   ; Increment array pointer
              SOBGTR  R7,READ
      EOF:    SUBL3   R7,@MAX(AP),@NUM(AP)    ; Number of strings read
              ADDL2   #80,SP                  ; Pop buffer space
              RET
              .END
```

9.10 LINKING WITH HIGH-LEVEL LANGUAGES AND LIBRARY ROUTINES

We mentioned in Section 9.1 as advantages of using procedures that a program may be made up of procedures written in different languages and that a program may use library procedures. So far, we have described the VAX linkage conventions from the point of view that both the calling program and the procedure are being written by the application programmer in assembly language. Here we will consider linking with high-level languages (Fortran, Pascal, C, and COBOL) and with procedures in the VMS Run-Time Library. Aside from providing general knowledge for future use in large programs, this section can be put to use while learning VAX assembly language. For example, to avoid conversion details in assembly language, the reader may choose to write routines in his or her favorite high-level language to do all the input and output.

The VAX procedure linkage conventions were designed with the goal of allowing linkage of programs written in different languages without a lot of extra overhead. Thus for the most part the VAX high-level language compilers translate procedures and procedure calls in a way consistent with the linkage conventions described in this chapter. A high-level language CALL statement is translated to a CALLS or CALLG instruction, so an assembly language procedure to be called by a high-level language program should establish its register mask in the usual way, use AP to find its arguments, and use RET to return control to the calling program. On the other hand, the high-level language compilers will provide register masks in the translation of high-level language procedures, translate argument references to operand specifiers using AP, and use RET to return, so such procedures can be called from assembly language programs. The only real problem to consider is which argument-passing mechanisms are used.

The high-level language compilers and the procedures in the VMS Run-Time Library use the standard argument list format described in Fig. 9.6 *except* that they do not always pass arguments or expect to receive their arguments by reference (i.e., the argument lists may not contain the addresses of the arguments). Depending on the language and the argument data type, immediate values and descriptors are sometimes used. Thus to communicate properly we must know what the particular compilers do. We will summarize the compiler standards here; for more detail and examples the reader may consult the user manuals for the various languages.

The VAX Fortran compiler normally uses call by reference for all arguments except character strings; for these it uses descriptors. Thus, for example, if the Fortran program contains the statement

```
CALL SUB1 (LIST, N, 25)
```

the compiler would set up the argument list using instructions similar to these:

```
ARGLIST:.LONG     3
        .ADDRESS LIST,N,CONST25
CONST25:.LONG     25
```

(The longword containing 25 is not part of the argument list.) To interface with an assembly language procedure that does not conform to the Fortran standard, the programmer can explicitly tell the Fortran compiler how the calling program should pass an argument. The VAX Fortran functions %VAL, %REF, and %DESCR cause the argument value, address, or descriptor address, respectively, to be put in the argument list. For example,

```
CALL SUB2 (%REF(STRING), LENGTH)
```

would have the compiler put the address of STRING, a character string, in the argument list instead of constructing a descriptor for STRING and putting *its* address in the argument list.

A Fortran subroutine expects its argument list to contain the addresses of its nonstring arguments and the address of a descriptor for a string argument.

The VAX Pascal compiler uses the reference mechanism for both value parameters and var parameters. A variable passed as a value parameter must not be changed by the procedure. The Pascal compiler includes code in the procedure to copy the parameter to a temporary location and use the copy, not the actual parameter, in the procedure. (Where do you think it puts the copy?)

If an assembly language procedure to be called from a Pascal program expects an argument to be passed by a mechanism other than by reference, an appropriate specifier must be used in the formal parameter list in the procedure declaration in the Pascal program. The specifiers are %IMMED for the immediate value mechanism, %DESCR for scalar and array descriptors, and %STDESCR for string descriptors. For example, consider the following procedure declaration:

```
procedure proc   (a: integer;
                  var result: integer;
                  %immed b: real;
                  %stdescr string: alfa); extern;
```

The argument list will contain the addresses of the first two arguments (but the first argument should not be changed by the assembly language procedure *proc*). The argument list will contain the current value of the third argument and the address of a descriptor (set up by the Pascal compiler) for the last argument. The *extern* statement is required to indicate that the procedure is external to the Pascal program.

An assembly language program that calls a Pascal procedure must put the argument addresses in the argument list as usual, except for a few data types that Pascal expects to be passed in other ways. (The exceptions are dynamic arrays and procedures and functions. The reader who wishes to use these may consult the manuals for more detail.)

The VAX C compiler passes many types of arguments by the immediate value mechanism; the value of the argument is put in the argument list. Arrays are passed by the reference mechanism; the address of the array is put in the argument list. If a C program calls a procedure (perhaps written in another language) that expects an argument other than an array to be passed by reference, the argument must be preceded by the operator "&." For example, if *fibonacci* is a function, written in say, Pascal or assembly language, that expects its integer argument to be passed by reference, a C program would use the function as follows:

    v = fibonacci(&n)

On the other hand, when writing a C procedure to be called by a routine that passes arguments by reference, the C procedure must declare its parameters to be pointers.

The VAX COBOL compilers use call by reference as the standard way to pass arguments. The programmer can override the standard by writing BY VALUE or BY DESCRIPTOR in front of an argument name in a COBOL CALL statement.

The VMS Run-Time Library is a collection of assembly language utility procedures that can be called by assembly language and high-level language programs. Included are routines that do memory allocation, I/O, mathematical functions, data type conversion, error handling, and other functions. These procedures generally expect string arguments to be passed by descriptor, and some of them expect certain arguments to be passed by immediate value. Many of these procedures return status flags in R0. For the specific descriptions of the various procedures in the library and their argument formats, the reader should consult the manual *Introduction to the VMS Run-Time Library*.

9.11 SUMMARY

A procedure is a routine that performs a particular task when it is called by another routine (procedure or main program). The use of procedures makes programs much easier to develop, debug, and modify. Procedures may be assembled independently, then linked (with a main program) to form an executable program.

Procedure linkage conventions are a set of instructions and conventions that transfer control to a procedure, pass arguments to it, protect data in registers used by the calling program, and return to the calling program. The VAX Procedure Calling Standard makes heavy use of the user stack allocated for each program by the operating system. The SP (stack pointer) register contains the address of the top item on the stack.

The *call frame* is a collection of information saved on the stack when a procedure is called. Its format is shown in Fig. 9.12.

In the VAX Procedure Calling Standard a procedure has the responsibility of specifying which registers it uses so that their original contents may be stacked when the procedure is called and retrieved when control returns to the calling program. The register mask in the .ENTRY directive in the procedure provides this information. R0 and R1 are not saved; functions use these registers to pass the function value back to the calling routine.

The standard argument list format is shown in Fig. 9.6. Argument lists may be set up on the stack or elsewhere in memory. Arguments are most often passed *by reference*; that is, the argument list contains the addresses of the arguments, as in Fig. 9.6. The alternatives are to put the value of the argument or the address of an argument descriptor in the argument list. The address of the argument list is passed to the procedure in the AP register.

Procedures are called with the CALLS and CALLG instructions. They perform a large number of operations; on most machines more than one instruction is needed to accomplish similar operations. CALLS is used if the argument list is on the stack; CALLG is used when the argument list is in general memory.

The address of the call frame is passed to the procedure in the FP register. It is used by the RET instruction to find the call frame and retrieve the stored data.

Several sophisticated programming techniques can be implemented by using the stack for temporary storage. By putting local variables on the stack, one can write recursive and reentrant routines.

The VAX Procedure Calling Standard was designed to make linking of procedures written in different languages relatively easy. VAX high-level language compilers use many of the same conventions described here for assembly language programs.

Table 9.1 summarizes the new instructions and assembler directives that were introduced in this chapter.

9.12 EXERCISES

Note: Unless otherwise stated, all arguments are passed by reference; that is, argument lists contain addresses, not values, of arguments.

1. Write a procedure to print out the entries in a character string array. The arguments should be the array and the number of entries (a longword). Assume the strings are each 12 characters long.

2. Rewrite the binary search in Fig. 7.7 as a procedure. TABLE, NUM, KEY, SIZE, and INDEX, described in Fig. 7.7, should be the arguments.

3. Suppose that a main program calls procedure A, A calls B in two places, and B calls C. Suppose that the labels on the return locations are RETMN, RETA1, RETA2, and RETB. (See Fig. 9.22 for an illustration.) Suppose that C is now being executed, and

TABLE 9.1   INSTRUCTIONS AND DIRECTIVES USED WITH PROCEDURES

For transferring control		
.ENTRY	*procname,regmask*	Establish *procname* as a global symbol and as an entry point for the procedure; create the register save mask.
CALLG	*arglist,procname*	Call the procedure *procname*; the argument list is not on the stack.
CALLS	*numargs,procname*	Call the procedure *procname*; the argument list is on the stack.
RET		Return from a procedure.
For setting up argument lists		
.ADDRESS	*expressions*	Initialize longwords in memory to contain the values of the expressions.
PUSHA*x*	*operand*	Push the operand address onto the stack. (x = B, W, L, or Q)
PUSHL	*operand*	Push the operand onto the stack.
For internal subroutines		
BSBB	*destination*	Branch to subroutine (B for byte displacement,
BSBW	*destination*	W for word displacement).
RSB		Return from subroutine.

it was called by B, which was called by the *second* call in A. Draw a diagram of the stack showing which return addresses are on it and in what order. (You may use the labels to denote the return addresses, and you may ignore any other data that would also be on the stack.)

4. Write instructions to set up an argument list for the binary search procedure described in Exercise 2. Include storage reservation and/or initialization directives for the arguments. Use any reasonable data.

5. Suppose that a procedure named USEFUL must be called from several places within another procedure. The arguments are in memory in ALPHA, BETA, and the byte whose address is in R3. Write an internal subroutine that creates the argument list on the stack and calls USEFUL.

6. What addressing mode will the assembler use to encode the operand PKD in the CVTLP instruction in Example 9.1? (What size displacement will it use?)

7. Write an operand specifier that could be used to fetch

   (a) The address of the fourth argument.
   (b) The datum that is the third argument.

8. Consider the following argument list and memory contents.

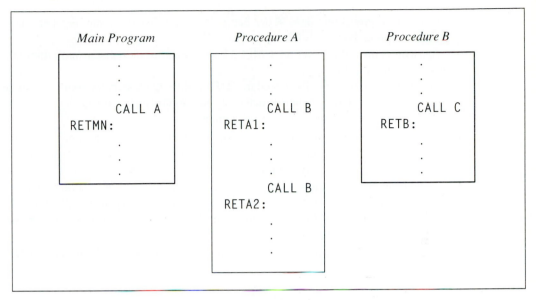

Figure 9.22 Procedures for Exercise 3

	Memory	Address
00000003 ←AP		
00001042	FFFFFF6A	0000103C
0000103C	001003C2	00001040
00001068	FF3A0047	00001044
	.	.
	.	.
	.	.
	03104200	00001068

What will be in R8 after each of the following instructions? (Assume that R8 is cleared before each instruction.)

(a) MOVW   @8(AP),R8   (b) MOVL   12(AP),R8

9. For each situation described below, state which of the following statements is true.

1. This is not an error.
2. This is an error that would cause an error message at assembly time.
3. This is an error that would cause an error message at link time.
4. This is an error that could cause an error message (program crash) at run time, or could cause incorrect output to be produced.

(a) A procedure uses R10, but R10 is not listed in the register mask in the procedure's .ENTRY directive.

(b) A procedure uses the CMPC3 instruction, but its register mask does not include R2 and R3.

(c) Procedure P calls procedure Q. Procedure Q expects its arguments to be passed by reference. When P makes up the argument list for Q, it puts the argument values, not addresses, in the argument list.

10. The selection of registers to save on the stack when calling a procedure may seem inefficient: all registers used by the procedure are saved even though some of them may not be in by the routine that is calling the procedure. Consider the strategy of saving only those registers that are used by *both* the calling routine and the procedure. For example, if the calling routine has data in R3, R8, and R9, and the procedure uses R8 and R10, then only R8 is saved. There is a very serious flaw in this strategy. What is it?

11. Suppose that there is (already written) a procedure called PRINT_ITEM with the following header:

   ; procedure PRINT_ITEM (item: word integer)

   This procedure converts the (two's complement) word integer to character code and prints it. You have an array called LIST that contains word integers. The longword NUM contains the number of entries in the array. Write instructions to print all the entries in the array, using PRINT_ITEM.

12. The procedure PRINT_ITEM in Exercise 11 expects its argument list in the standard format (i.e., containing the address of the word integer PRINT_ITEM is to print). Redo Exercise 11 so as to protect the entries in the array LIST from being changed by PRINT_ITEM.

13. Write a complete procedure to copy one character string to the end of another. The procedure should have the following header:

   ; procedure CONCATENATE (string1: character string,
   ;   length1: longword, string2: character string, length2: longword)

   The first string should be moved to the memory locations immediately following the second string. (You may assume that enough space has been reserved in memory.)

14. This exercise considers possible alternative formats for the call frame. For each alternative, assume that the CALL instructions are modified to push the data in the order that would be required. The point is to determine if any information would be lost or if the RET instruction would have difficulties retrieving the stacked data later.

(a) Could the three longwords containing the old contents of the AP, FP, and PC be arranged in a different order?

(b) Could the old contents of AP, FP, and PC be pushed before the contents of the registers specified in the register save mask?

(c) Could the longword containing the register save mask and the PSW be pushed before the contents of the registers to be saved?

15. Why does the CALLS instruction save the address of the argument list in a temporary location instead of putting it into the AP register immediately?

16. Suppose that a main program calls procedure A, and procedure A calls procedure B. Write instructions to go in procedure B that would
    (a) Put into R6 the address of procedure B's argument list.
    (b) Put into R7 the address of procedure A's argument list.
    (c) Put into R8 the address of the next instruction to be executed upon return from procedure B.

17. Suppose that a main program calls procedure A, procedure A calls procedure B, procedure B calls procedure C, and procedure C calls procedure D. Write instructions to go in procedure D that would
    (a) Put into R9 the address of procedure B's argument list.
    (b) Put into R10 the address of procedure A's condition handler.
    (c) Put into R11 the address of the next instruction to be executed upon return from procedure A.

18. Suppose that you are writing an operating systems routine to process program exceptions. Write instructions to find the most recently stacked call frame that contains a nonzero condition handler address and put the handler address in R10. (You may assume that there is a nonzero condition handler in one of the frames currently on the stack.)

19. The procedure MESSAGE has four arguments, passed by reference, described as follows (and in the order listed):

    TAG   a byte integer
    STRING1   a character string
    STRING2   another character string
    MSGLOC   a longword for the result determined by MESSAGE

    If the byte tag is negative, MESSAGE puts the address of STRING1 into MSGLOC. If the tag is nonnegative, it puts the address of STRING2 into MSGLOC. Write the procedure.

20. Write a function procedure to find the first blank character in a character string and return its address. If there are no blanks in the string, the function should return the address of the byte following the end of the string. The argument list contains the addresses of the first and last bytes of the string. (Recall that a function procedure returns its result in R0.)

21. Write the instructions needed to call the procedure PROC, which has no arguments. Use CALLS, then CALLG. Which is preferable? Why?

22. Write a solution for Exercise 47 in Chapter 7 that is a procedure with ALPHA, NUM, and NUMRUNS as arguments.

23. Write a procedure for the Bubble Sort algorithm described in Exercise 50 of Chapter 7.

24. Suppose that a true/false test with 20 questions has been given to 50 people. Each person's answers are encoded in the rightmost 20 bits of a longword, and all these longwords are in an array ANSWERS. The longword KEY contains the correct answers. There is a procedure SCORE that grades a test. Its arguments (in order) are: a person's answers, the key, and a byte in which SCORE returns the number of answers the person had correct. Assume that space is reserved for a byte array GRADES. We want to put in each entry of GRADES the number of correct answers given by the person whose answers are in the corresponding position in ANSWERS. Write instructions to set up the argument list and call the procedure SCORE as many times as necessary to grade all the tests.

25. Write a procedure GETNUM with the following arguments:

   Input arguments:

START	the first byte of a character string
END	the byte that follows the string

   Output arguments:

NUMBER	the two's complement representation of the first leading separate numeric number found in the string (a longword)
NEWSTART	the address of the byte following the first leading separate numeric number found in the string

   (The argument list, as usual, contains the addresses of the arguments described.) GETNUM should return a 1 in R0 if a leading separate numeric number is found in the character string and properly converted; it should return 0 in R0 otherwise (e.g., if no number is found or if the number found overflows a longword). In the latter cases, NUMBER and NEWSTART need not be stored.

26. Write instructions to set up an argument list using the same arguments in Example 9.5 except that the second and third arguments are to be passed by immediate value.

27. Consider the following function:

```
; FUNCTION RECURSIVE(N: LONGWORD INTEGER)
        .ENTRY   RECURSIVE,^M<R6>
        MOVL     4(AP),R6
        MOVL     #1,R0
        CMPL     R6,#1
        BLEQ     DONE
```

```
              SUBL3    #1,R6,-(SP)
              CALLS    #1,RECURSIVE
              MULL2    R6,R0
    DONE:     RET
              .END
```

Suppose that RECURSIVE is called with the following instructions:

```
              PUSHL    #3
              CALLS    #1,RECURSIVE
    NEXT:
```

(a) Which argument passing mechanism is used by this function?

(b) Consider the point during execution of this function when there are three call frames on the stack. Show clearly what is in the space below the first call frame and between the call frames. (You do not have to show the details of the call frames.)

(c) What will be in R0 when control returns to the statement labeled NEXT?

28. Using the data structure and general conventions of the example in Section 9.8, write a procedure FIND_ITH that has three arguments, FIRST, I, and PTR, where FIRST is a pointer to the header node of a linked list, I is an integer, and FIND_ITH returns in PTR a pointer to the ith node in the list (or a null pointer if there are fewer than i nodes).

29. (a) Suppose that we have an array with n entries arranged in order. How many entries must be moved, in the worst case, to insert a new entry in the proper position? (Recall that with a linked list only two pointers need be changed and no entries are moved.)

(b) Suppose that we are given a number i and we wish to find the ith entry in a list. Compare the amount of work that must be done if the list is kept in an array with the amount of work that must be done if the list is a linked list.

30. Suppose that the keys in the sample program in Section 9.8 were two's complement integers instead of character strings. Indicate which procedures would need changes and what the changes would be.

31. The INSERT procedure in Section 9.8 does not check whether the key to be inserted is already in the list. Modify INSERT to check for this condition and return a flag to the calling program to indicate if the item was not inserted because it was already in the list. Note that now INSERT must return a three-way flag: successful insertion, no insertion because no nodes are available, and no insertion because the item is a duplicate.

32. Rewrite the main program and the TESTER procedure for the example in Section 9.8 to work with two linked lists instead of one. The main program should initialize header nodes and pointers, LIST1 and LIST2, for the two lists. The data read by TESTER should have a list number, 1 or 2, in addition to the code for the operation and the key. TESTER should perform the operation on the specified list.

33. Consider the INIT_AVAIL procedure in the example in Section 9.8. Suppose that the number of bytes available for nodes (the BYTES argument) is not a multiple of the node size (the NODE_SIZE argument). Will INIT_AVAIL work correctly? (That is, will it put the pointers in the correct locations, and put the null pointer in the last complete node?)

34. Would the procedure RET_NODE in the example in Section 9.8 work correctly if its argument is the null pointer?

35. Which of the data-dependent procedures in the linked list example in Section 9.8 (Fig. 9.18) are not reentrant? Rewrite them so that they are.

10

Some Assembler Features

10.1 PROGRAM SECTIONS

PSECTS and Their Attributes

An assembly language program may be divided into several program sections that can be named by the programmer and assigned various attributes. Two of the advantages of using program sections are that they allow for the protection of instructions and read-only data from accidental overwriting, and they can be used to permit different modules to access the same data.

The .PSECT (Program SECTion) directive tells the assembler to begin a new program section (or to continue an existing one). All the data and instructions that follow the directive and precede the next .PSECT directive (or the .END directive if there are no more .PSECTs) will be part of that program section. The format of the directive is

.PSECT   *psect_name,attributes*

The psect name may be any name satisfying the rules for a symbol. We will describe a few, though not all, of the attributes that may be specified.

The WRT (WRiTe) and NOWRT (NO WRiTe) attributes indicate whether or not the contents of the program section may be modified at execution time. NOWRT may be specified for program sections containing read-only data or instructions. The default is WRT.

The EXE (EXEcute) and NOEXE (NO EXEcute) attributes indicate whether or not the program section contains executable instructions. The default is EXE. The linker checks that the program transfer address is in a program section with the EXE attribute.

The CON (CONcatenate) and OVR (OVeRlay) attributes indicate whether or not multiple .PSECT directives with the same name are to be considered as extensions to the program section or as overlays. The OVR attribute allows different modules to access the same data; we will consider examples later. The default is CON.

A word, longword, or quadword may start at any byte in memory, but efficiency of instruction execution is improved if data are aligned on appropriate boundaries—that is, if words begin at addresses divisible by 2, longwords by 4, and quadwords by 8 (i.e., aligned as if all of memory were neatly divided up into units of the same size). The alignment attribute of a program section specifies the maximum alignment that may be forced in the program section using the .ALIGN directive (described below). The program section itself is aligned to begin on a boundary indicated by its alignment attribute. The alignment may be specified by a keyword BYTE, WORD, LONG, QUAD, or PAGE. (A page boundary is an address divisible by 512_{10}.) The default is BYTE. Normally, when the assembler encounters a storage reservation or initialization directive, it reserves space or stores data beginning at the next available byte, the one whose location is given by the current value of the location counter. The .ALIGN directive tells the assembler to increase the location counter if necessary so that it will be on the next boundary of the requested type. The directive may be used as follows:

.ALIGN   *keyword*

where the keyword may be any of the keywords mentioned above for specifying the program section alignment. No .ALIGN directive may specify an alignment that exceeds the maximum for the program section.

Figure 10.1 illustrates a possible program organization for a program that contains some read-only data, some data to be used and modified by the program, and instructions. Note that one of the program section names is the same as the entry point name; this is permitted, but not required. If, during execution, an attempt is made to write in a program section with the NOWRT attribute, an error message will be displayed. Thus data can be protected.

Example 10.1: Aligning Data

When blocks of storage are being reserved for several variables and arrays, care can be taken to arrange the reservation and initialization directives to force and maintain alignment. In the first sequence of directives below, RANKS and SCORES would not be on word and longword boundaries, respectively, without the last two .ALIGN directives, but by rearranging the statements as in the second sequence, the .ALIGNs can be eliminated. Note that the statements in the second sequence are sorted in nonincreasing order by the size of the memory units being reserved.

```
        .PSECT  DATA,NOEXE,LONG
        ...
        .ALIGN  LONG
SCALE:  .BLKF   2
```

```
              .PSECT   READ_ONLY_DATA,NOWRT,NOEXE,LONG

     ; [ Data initialization directives for read-only data ]

        ;
        ;
              .PSECT   DATA,NOEXE,LONG

     ; [ Storage reservation and initialization directives ]

              .ALIGN   LONG                    ; Force alignment
     ARRAY:   .BLKL    50
        ;
        ;
              .PSECT   PROGRAM,NOWRT
              BEGIN    PROGRAM

     ; [ Instructions ]

              EXIT
              .END     PROGRAM
```

Figure 10.1 Program organization using program sections

```
     FLAGS:   .BYTE    7,0,1
              .ALIGN   WORD
     RANKS:   .BLKW    5
              .ALIGN   LONG
     SCORES:  .BLKL    10

              .PSECT   DATA,NOEXE,LONG
                 ...
              .ALIGN   LONG
     SCALE:   .BLKF    2
     SCORES:  .BLKL    10
     RANKS:   .BLKW    5
     FLAGS:   .BYTE    7,0,1
```

Processing PSECTs

We will give a brief description here of how program sections are treated by the assembler and the linker. First, taking the assembler's point of view, we consider the processing of one source module independent of the program sections that may be in other modules.

The assembler keeps a table that contains the name, attributes, current size, and a number that it assigns for each program section in the module being assembled. It creates a default program section called . BLANK . for programs that do not contain a .PSECT directive. (The periods and blanks are part of this psect name.) This psect has attributes WRT and EXE, so it may contain data and instructions. Its alignment is BYTE. Since we did not use .PSECT directives in our examples prior to this chapter, all our earlier sample programs would consist of the psect . BLANK ..

The assembler sets the location counter to zero at the beginning of each program section. The symbol table entry for each symbol contains the number of the psect in which the symbol is defined (or the psect in which it is first referenced, if it is not defined in the module). Symbol values stored in the symbol table are locations relative to the beginning of the psect. The physical arrangement of the program sections in memory is determined by the linker, so the assembler cannot completely assemble operand specifiers in an instruction in one psect that use symbols defined in another psect. It assembles a mode byte containing EF for relative mode with longword displacement, and it reserves a longword for the displacement. The linker will fill in the correct displacement value. The program listing in Fig. 10.2 illustrates the resetting of the location counter to zero at the beginning of the second psect and the way the assembler handles relative mode operands. Program listings include a "Psect synopsis" table listing the name, size, and attributes of each psect (not shown in Fig. 10.2).

Since the assembler saves the last value of the location counter for each program section (the size of the psect is the last location counter value), it can add more data or instructions to a psect later, after an intervening one. If it encounters a .PSECT directive for a psect name already in its table with the CON attribute, it will assemble the following statements (up to the next .PSECT or .END directive) as if they physically followed the last statement in the previous piece of the same psect. The linker will arrange the pieces of a program section so that they do appear consecutively in memory. (The attributes of any continuation of a psect must be the same as the attributes specified the first time; they do not have to be listed again.)

When the linker links the various modules of a program, it collects all the pieces of each program section together so that one program section will form a contiguous segment in memory. There may be parts of one program section in several modules; the linker will concatenate them one after another (unless they have the OVR attribute) and make any necessary corrections to address references. The VAX/VMS LINK command has an option /MAP that causes the linker to produce a *map file* containing a Program Section Synopsis indicating the address, size, and attributes of each program section. The map file also contains a symbol table listing the values of all the global symbols. (If the first file specified in the LINK command is, say, MAIN, the map file will have the name MAIN.MAP.)

In Chapter 9 we studied how to use procedures and how to pass arguments back and forth between them. The use of procedures and procedure arguments is, for many purposes, the best way to allow different modules to work on the same data, because this mechanism allows very tight control over what data are available to, and may be changed by, each procedure. Sometimes, though, the amount of data to be shared by a group of procedures is very large. A lot of time may be saved if long argument lists do not have to be constructed, and the programs may be clearer if they can refer to the data by name instead of indirectly via the AP register. We can set up program sections that

```
                    0000    1 ; This program adds the five entries in the word array
                    0000    2 ; ARRAY and stores the result in the word SUM.
                    0000    3 ;
                    0000    4 ; REGISTER USE
                    0000    5 ;
                    0000    6 ;     R6        array pointer
                    0000    7 ;     R7        loop index
                    0000    8 ;     R8        sum
                    0000    9 ;
                00000000    10      .PSECT  DATA,NOEXE
FFD6 0007 005D FFDE 000A 0000   11 ARRAY:  .WORD  10,-34,93,7,-42
              0000000C 000A   12 SUM:   .BLKW  1
                       000C   13 ;
                       000C   14 ;
                00000000    15      .PSECT  PROG,NOWRT
                    0000   16      BEGIN   PROG
56  00000000'EF 3E   0050   17      MOVAW  ARRAY,R6      ; Initialize pointer
    57  05 D0       0057   18      MOVL   #5,R7         ; Loop index
    58  B4          005A   19      CLRW   R8            ; Clear for sum
    58  86 A0       005C   20 ADD:  ADDW2  (R6)+R8       ; Add entry
    FA  57 F5       005F   21      SOBGTR  R7,ADD        ; Loop control
0000000A'EF 58 B0   0062   22      MOVW   R8,SUM        ; Store sum
                    0069   23      EXIT
                    0099   24      .END   PROG
```

Figure 10.2 Multiple psects

are similar to the COMMON blocks in Fortran. Each module that has access to the data would contain a copy of the program section named, say, COMMON_DATA, that contains all the storage reservation directives for the shared data. The psect would have the OVR attribute, indicating to the linker that the storage reservation directives are to overlay the same space in memory rather than reserving additional space for each module. Figure 10.3 shows a simple illustration of the use of such a program section.

```
;   The main program stores data in A and B and calls the
;   procedure PROC to add them and store the result in C.
;
          .PSECT   COMMON_DATA,OVR,NOEXE,LONG
A:        .BLKL    1
B:        .BLKL    1
C:        .BLKL    1
;
;
          .PSECT   PROG,NOWRT
          BEGIN    PROG
          MOVL     #1,A
          MOVL     #-25,B
          CALLS    #0,PROC
          DUMPLONG A,B,C
          EXIT
          .END     PROG

;   The procedure adds the first two longwords in the
;   COMMON_DATA psect and stores the result in the third.
;
          .PSECT   COMMON_DATA,OVR,NOEXE,LONG
X:        .BLKL    1
Y:        .BLKL    1
Z:        .BLKL    1
;
;
          .PSECT   PROC,NOWRT
          .ENTRY   PROC,0
          ADDL3    X,Y,Z
          RET
          .END
Output
   ** DUMPLONG OUTPUT **
   A          00000001
   B          FFFFFFE7
   C          FFFFFFE8
   **   END   DUMPLONG   **
```

Figure 10.3 A program section with the OVR attribute

10.2 TERMS AND EXPRESSIONS

We have seen that operands on machine instructions and arguments for assembler directives may be specified using expressions. For example, we have used simple expressions such as

PAGE+8   LIST–4   NUM∗SIZE

In fact, since an expression may consist of a single term; a symbol or number alone is an expression. Thus operand specifiers are, in general, described by one or more expressions along with special characters that denote the addressing mode being used (e.g., # for literals and parentheses for register deferred mode). In this section we will consider some of the general rules for forming expressions and how the assembler treats them.

Expressions are evaluated by the assembler, with help from the linker for those where not enough information is available to the assembler. They are not used like expressions in high-level languages; they do not involve computations on execution-time data. Most often, expressions are used to describe addresses and constants in forms convenient for the programmer.

Terms

Expressions are made up by combining terms. The three examples shown above use symbols and numbers, the most commonly used kinds of terms. The VAX MACRO assembler allows four different categories of terms: numbers, symbols, the location counter, and certain kinds of text strings.

A number may be specified in any of several radixes. The assembler assumes that the radix is decimal unless the number is preceded by a radix operator (or is part of an expression preceded by a radix operator). The radix operators are

Operator	Radix
$^\wedge$B	2 (binary)
$^\wedge$D	10 (decimal)
$^\wedge$X	16 (hexadecimal)
$^\wedge$O	8 (octal)

Writing $^\wedge$XF011, for example, will have the same effect as writing 61457; the assembler converts both to the bit string

0000000000000001111000000010001

A term preceded by a unary operator (e.g., a minus sign or a radix operator) is also a term. Thus –25 and $^\wedge$X20 are examples of terms.

Any symbol is a term, whether it be defined by the system (e.g., the register names) or by the user, whether a user-defined symbol be defined as a label or in a direct assignment statement. The value of a symbol defined as a label is, as always, an address, not the contents of the address; the latter is not accessible to the assembler. (The value of a symbol defined in a direct assignment statement may or may not be an address, depending on how it is defined.) We will consider the treatment of expressions containing symbols in more detail in the next section.

There are two types of textual terms: ASCII and register mask. Each is preceded by a unary operator, ^A or ^M, respectively, to indicate the type.

The format for an ASCII term is

$$^A/text/$$

The text may be from one to eight characters long, but no longer than is appropriate for the context where it is used. Often ASCII terms are used in literal or immediate operands. For example:

```
MOVL    #^A/NAME/,LINE
CMPB    (R8),#^A/-/
```

In the MOVL instruction the ASCII term could not contain more than four characters because the data type of the operand is longword. Similarly, the ASCII term in the CMPB instruction must have only one character. We have used the slash here as the delimiter for the ASCII string; as in .ASCII directives, another character may be used as a delimiter if a slash is part of the string.

We have already seen, in Chapter 9, how the ^M operator is used to set up a register save mask for a procedure in its .ENTRY directive. The format for a register mask term is

$$^M<register\_list>$$

Depending on where the term is used, there are some restrictions on what may be included in the register list. For example, we saw that a procedure's register save mask may not include R0, R1, AP, FP, SP, or PC. Our main interest here, however, is how the assembler evaluates the term. It evaluates it as a 16-bit string where a bit is on (set to 1) if the register (or trap enable designation) it corresponds to is included in the list. Thus, to the assembler, the value of the term

```
^M<R8,R5,R3,R9>
```

is equal to the value of the terms

```
^B0000001100101000
```

and

```
^X0328
```

The programmer should use whatever form is most convenient and clear.

The location counter, denoted by a period, may be used as a term in an expression. Consider the following statements:

```
TABLE:  .WORD   2,-17,45,29,-48,33,38,-21
TABLE_SIZE = .-TABLE
```

The value of . when the second statement is encountered is the location of the byte following the end of the table, so the value assigned to the symbol TABLE_SIZE will be the number of bytes in the table. (Note that defining TABLE_SIZE in this way helps to minimize work and possible errors if we later make additions or deletions in the table; only the .WORD directive setting up the table need be changed.)

The value of **.** when used in an operand specifier is the location of the first byte of that operand specifier. Consider the instruction

```
BRB       .+4
```

The value of **.** is the location of the byte containing the branch displacement. The next three bytes are at **.+1**, **.+2**, and **.+3**. Thus branching to **.+4** means skipping over the three bytes that follow the instruction. Of course, for clarity and to minimize the likelihood of making errors, we would normally put a label on the instruction at the branch destination and use that label as the operand on the BRB instruction. The situations where the location counter is used in operand specifiers are somewhat esoteric.

Expressions

Terms are combined to form expressions by using binary operators. The arithmetic operators, particularly + and −, are used most often. In addition, the VAX MACRO assembler has several operators that do logical operations on the binary representation of the values of the terms. We will not describe those here.

Terms in an expression may be grouped to form subexpressions. Since parentheses have another role in operand specifiers—they are used to denote certain addressing modes (e.g., register deferred, autoincrement)—subexpressions must be enclosed in angle brackets (< and >). Some examples are

```
SIZE*<NUM1+NUM2>
^X<3F-2B>
LIST+<3*INC>
<80-LENGTH>/2
```

As the second example illustrates, a radix operator may be applied to an entire expression, not just a single term.

Some kinds of terms, such as register names, may not be combined with others in expressions. An expression such as R5+8 simply does not make sense because the value of the term R5 is *not* the contents of R5. The assembler will issue an error message if an improper expression is used.

When the assembler evaluates an expression, it does *not* use the usual operator priorities we expect in high-level languages and ordinary mathematical expressions. All binary operators have the same priority; operations are performed left to right. The only way to override this evaluation order is to use bracketed subexpressions, as these are evaluated first. Thus if the brackets were omitted from the third example above, the resulting value would be different.

It is not always necessary that a symbol be defined (i.e., already be entered in the symbol table and have a value assigned to it) before it is used in an expression. Expressions that contain undefined symbols will be evaluated by the linker.

In general, the assembler evaluates terms and expressions as 32-bit values. (There are a few exceptions.) The result will be truncated if the context in which the expression is used requires a smaller number of bits.

10.3 SYMBOL AND EXPRESSION TYPES

Relocatable, Absolute, and External Expressions

Every expression (hence also every term) in a module is one of three types: relocatable, absolute, or external.

We have emphasized that the value assigned by the assembler to a symbol used as a label is the location of the byte it labels *relative* to the beginning of the module or program section it is in. The assembler can do no better; it does not know where in memory the program will be when it is executed. Such symbols are called relocatable. In general, an expression is *relocatable* if its value is fixed relative to the beginning of the program section in which it appears, but the actual location represented by the expression depends on where the program section is placed by the linker. Labels on data areas and labels on instructions are relocatable symbols. The location counter (for all the kinds of program sections we have considered) is a relocatable term.

An expression is *absolute* if its value is a constant, independent of where the program section containing it is placed in memory. All numbers and textual terms are absolute terms. The value of an ASCII term, for example, is the character code for the text: it is constant.

A symbol defined in a direct assignment statement may be absolute or relocatable, depending on the type of the expression that specifies the symbol value. All the symbols defined in the following statements are absolute.

```
MAX = 40
SIZE = 32
STAR = ^A/*/
TOTAL_SPACE = MAX*SIZE
```

Suppose that ARRAY is a label on an array containing 200 bytes. The symbol LAST defined by

```
LAST = ARRAY+199
```

is relocatable because its value is the location of the last byte of the array. The fact that the expression defining LAST includes the relocatable symbol ARRAY is not sufficient to determine that LAST is relocatable, however. Consider the following statements:

```
TABLE:  .WORD   2,-17,45,29,-48,33,38,-21
TABLE_SIZE = .-TABLE
```

TABLE and . are relocatable terms. Even though they are used in the expression that defines TABLE_SIZE, TABLE_SIZE is an absolute symbol. The number of bytes in the table—that is, the difference, or distance, between TABLE and the value of . in the second statement—is independent of where the program section is placed in memory. Similarly, an expression that is the difference between two relocatable symbols is an absolute expression.

Bearing in mind that the value of a relocatable symbol is an address, it should be clear that a sum (or product or quotient) of two relocatable symbols is not likely to be a useful expression. Many assemblers simply consider such expressions to be errors, but the VAX MACRO assembler accepts them. The programmer who is forming complex expressions using relocatable symbols should take extra care to be sure that the expressions are meaningful.

A symbol is *external* if it is not defined in the module being assembled. An expression is *external* if it contains any external symbols. One common example of an external symbol is a procedure entry-point name used in a CALLS or CALLG instruction. The entry-point name is defined in the .ENTRY directive in the procedure module and is a relocatable symbol there. More examples are provided by the BEGIN macro presented in Chapter 5; it contains instructions that reference external symbols that are labels on data blocks used by the I/O macros. (If you look at the symbol table on the listing from any program that uses BEGIN, you will find many external symbols along with those defined in your program.)

The assembler, of course, cannot complete the encoding of an operand specifier described by an external expression because it does not know the value of the expression. It stores a mode byte for relative mode, EF, and leaves room for a longword displacement. The linker will compute and fill in the correct displacement.

The VAX assembler assumes that any symbol not defined in the module is defined in some other module that will be linked with the present one before the program is run. Thus it classifies any undefined symbol as external. Many assemblers will not make this assumption; they expect an explicit declaration listing external symbols used in a module. If an undefined symbol is used and is not declared as external, many assemblers will issue an error message. This is helpful for catching errors such as misspellings and missing statements. Using the default assumption on the VAX, such errors are not detected until the program is linked (and possibly not even then if an undefined symbol happens to have the same name as, say, a procedure used by another module). Thus, requiring that all external symbols be declared is very helpful to the programmer, although it involves more work. The VAX programmer can use the directive

.DISABLE GLOBAL

to direct the assembler to treat any undefined symbols not declared external as errors. The directive

.EXTERNAL   list_of_symbols

tells the assembler that the symbols listed are to be considered external.

Many assemblers put restrictions on the ways in which external symbols may be combined with other terms. VAX MACRO does not, so the programmer has the responsibility of making sure that such expressions make sense.

The assembler records in the symbol table the type of each symbol it encounters. On program listings the type is indicated by an R (relocatable), X (external), or an equals sign preceding the symbol value (absolute).

Global Symbols

A symbol is *global* if it may be referenced from a module other than the one in which it is defined. Unless a symbol is made global by one of the means described below, it is local to the module where it is defined and may be accessed only in that module. This allows the same symbol name to be used in different modules without interference (like local variables in high-level languages). When the linker is attempting to fill in an address reference to an external symbol, it considers only global symbols from other modules.

A symbol may be made global in one of several ways. A procedure or main program entry point, defined in an .ENTRY directive, is always global. A symbol used as a label is global if it is followed by a double colon (::). (The labels on the data blocks used by the I/O macros are made global in this way.) A symbol defined in a direct assignment statement is global if it is followed by two equals signs instead of one. Alternatively, the programmer may define symbols in the usual ways, and include a .GLOBAL directive listing those symbols that are to be global. Many assemblers require declaring global symbols in such a directive.

Treatment of Relocatable Expressions

The distinctions between relocatable, absolute, and external expressions are important, both because the different types of expressions are treated differently by the assembler and the linker and because assemblers for many computers put restrictions on the way relocatable and global terms may be combined.

A major concern for an assembler and linker in any computer system is the translation to machine code of operand specifiers that contain relocatable expressions. When the program is executed, the machine code must specify the actual location of the data to be operated on. We have seen that on the VAX the use of relative mode addressing solves the problem in most cases. The operand specifier is encoded as a displacement from the contents of the PC. The displacement is often absolute and can be computed by the assembler, so the linker has no work to do. On computers that do not use this kind of displacement addressing, an assembler would encode the operand specifier by inserting in the instruction the value of the symbol or expression relative to the beginning of the program section (i.e., the value the assembler can compute using entries in its symbol table). The assembler would then tag the operand specifier in some way to indicate to the linker that a correction is needed. After the linker determines where each program section will be placed, it will add to each tagged operand the base address of its program section.

The use of displacement addressing has eliminated some of the work that linkers had to do, but displacements are used in machine instruction operands, not in assembler directives. Thus there are still places where the linker must correct expression values computed by the assembler by adding the program section base address. Consider the following directives to set up a procedure argument list:

```
ARGS:    .LONG    3
         .ADDRESS LIST,COUNT,ITEM
```

The argument list will be used by a procedure at execution time. The procedure expects it to contain the actual 32-bit addresses of the arguments, not their locations relative to the beginning of the program section they are in. Thus when the assembler encounters an .ADDRESS directive, it computes the values of the expressions using symbol table entries and it tags these values for the linker to correct by adding the program section base address. The assembler can correctly assemble the .LONG directive without assistance from the linker because its argument, 3, is absolute.

10.4 RESTRICTIONS ON EXPRESSIONS

Any expressions may be used in most machine instructions and assembler directives, but for some directives there are restrictions. The most common restrictions are that all symbols used in an expression must already be defined (in the same module) and that the expression must be absolute. In this section we will consider a few of the directives to which these restrictions apply, and we will see that they are necessitated by the way an assembler works and/or are reasonable in the context where the directive is used.

Recall from our discussion of assemblers in Chapter 8 that the main task performed in the first pass over the module being assembled is the construction of the symbol table. The assembler must be able to determine the values of the symbols defined in the module (relative to the beginning of the program section, of course). Thus it must be able to determine how many bytes will be allocated for each statement at the time the statement is first encountered.

Consider the following directives:

.BLK*x*   *number_of_units*

.BYTE   *arg_list*

.WORD   *arg_list*

.LONG   *arg_list*

.ADDRESS *list_of_expressions*

where the *arg_list* on .BYTE, .WORD, and .LONG are lists of items of the form

value[*repetition_ factor*]

The number of memory units to reserve, the values to be stored, the repetition factors, and the addresses to be stored by .ADDRESS are all specified by expressions. Those that affect the amount of memory used, and hence the amount by which the location counter will be incremented, must be absolute and contain no undefined symbols. Specifically, *number_of_units* and *repetition_ factor* must satisfy these restrictions. The expressions describing the values to be stored need not satisfy the restrictions because the linker can fill in the values later. The expressions listed in .ADDRESS need not satisfy the restrictions because the assembler always reserves a longword for each address.

In a direct assignment statement, the expression that describes the value to be assigned to the symbol must not contain any undefined symbols. If it did, the assembler could not determine the value of the symbol being defined during its first pass. (As we have seen in the preceding section, the expression does not have to be absolute.)

The expression that describes the register save mask in an .ENTRY directive must be absolute and not contain any undefined symbols. Since the $^\wedge$M operator is generally used for register masks, and the symbols denoting the names of the registers and the arithmetic traps are always defined, these restrictions are no inconvenience.

10.5 SUMMARY

A program may be divided into several program sections that may be given different attributes. Some of the attributes are described in Table 10.1. Breaking up a program into sections may improve the modularity of the program, allows for the protection of instructions and read-only data, and allows for several modules to access the same data directly.

Machine instruction operands and assembler directive arguments are specified using expressions that are evaluated by the assembler (or the linker). The terms that may be used to make up expressions are: numbers, symbols, the location counter, ASCII strings, and register masks. Numbers are assumed to be decimal unless they are preceded by a radix operator $^\wedge$B (binary), $^\wedge$X (hexadecimal), or $^\wedge$O (octal).

The assembler evaluates expressions containing symbols using the values in its symbol table. Expressions describe addresses or constants. They cannot be used to do computation on data that will be in memory or registers at execution time.

Expressions are evaluated left to right; there are no operator priorities. Evaluation of subexpressions can be forced by enclosing the subexpressions in angle brackets.

TABLE 10.1 SOME PROGRAM SECTION ATTRIBUTES

Default	Opposite	Meaning
WRT	NOWRT	Contents of the program section may (may not) be modified.
EXE	NOEXE	The program section contains (does not contain) executable instructions.
CON	OVR	Additional pieces of the same program section are to be concatenated (overlaid).
BYTE	WORD, LONG, QUAD, PAGE (and other values)	The keyword indicates the alignment of the program section and the maximum alignment that may be specified in an .ALIGN directive.

Expressions are normally evaluated as 32-bit quantities and truncated to the size needed.

An expression is *relocatable* if its value is fixed relative to the beginning of the program section in which it appears, but the location represented by the expression depends on where the linker places the program section. An expression is *absolute* if its value is independent of where the program section is placed. An expression is *external* if it contains any symbols that are not defined in the current module. Numbers, ASCII strings, and register masks are absolute. Symbols may be relocatable, absolute, or external.

A symbol is *global* if it may be referenced from a module other than the one in which it is defined. Procedure entry-point names are an example of global symbols.

The VAX solves the problem of encoding relocatable machine instruction operands by using the relative addressing modes. The operands are encoded as displacements from the contents of the PC; the displacements are usually constants independent of where the linker places the program. (If the assembler cannot evaluate an expression, the linker will do it later and compute the necessary displacement.) Many other computers use a similar scheme for handling relocatable operands. Others require that the linker add the program section base address to all such operands at the time the program is linked.

Restrictions are placed on the kinds of expressions that may be used in some assembler directives because the assembler must be able to determine how many bytes of memory each statement will require. For example, the expression in the .BLK*x* directives that indicates how many memory units to reserve must be absolute and contain no undefined symbols.

10.6 EXERCISES

1. Suppose that . = 0056_{16} when the assembler encounters the following statements. List the values of all the symbols defined and give the final value of the location counter.

```
        .ALIGN WORD
DELTA:  .WORD  24,-18,3
IND:    .BLKB  2
LABEL:  .ASCII /VAX/
TAG:    .BYTE  1
        .ALIGN LONG
VOLUME: .BLKL  3
```

2. Reorganize the statements in Exercise 1 to minimize the number of wasted bytes.

3. Assemble the program in Fig. 10.2, then link it using the /MAP option. Examine the map file and make a list of all the program sections. For each psect, include its starting address. (There will be some psects other than DATA and PROG, which appear explicitly in Fig. 10.2.)

4. Which of the following are valid terms?

(a) –256

(b) ^X312

(c) ^B1001110111

(d) ^X1001110111

(e) –^X2A

(f) ^A/ABCDE/

(g) ^A*25/2*

(h) ^M<R5,R10,IV,R11>

5. For which expression below is the value different from all the others?

65   ^A/A/   5*13   ^B01100101   ^X41

6. Which of the following are valid expressions? For those that are valid, state if they are relocatable or absolute.

(a) ALPHA+3   (ALPHA is relocatable.)

(b) 4*BETA   (BETA is absolute.)

(c) R7+1

(d) ^X24+15*^B111

(e) LINE+MARGIN   (Both symbols are absolute.)

(f) LINE+MARGIN   (LINE is relocatable; MARGIN is absolute.)

(g) LINE+MARGIN   (LINE is absolute; MARGIN is relocatable.)

(h) LINE+MARGIN   (Both symbols are relocatable.)

7. What is the value of each of the following expressions? (Indicate whether you are showing the value in hex or decimal.)

(a) ^X55

(b) ^A/7/

(c) RECORD+14 where RECORD = 012A and the byte at 012A contains 52.

(d) 11*^B11

(e) 5+4*2

8. Suppose that a program contains the following statements:

```
SIZE = 25
FLAG = 2
TAG:    .LONG     FLAG
CHAR:   .ASCII    /*/
ARRAY:  .BLKW     SIZE
LOC:    .ADDRESS  ARRAY
```

For each of the following expressions, state if it is absolute, relocatable, or external. Give the value for each expression, or state if there is not enough information to determine its value.

(a) LOC–TAG

(b) ARRAY+2*SIZE–FLAG

(c) FLAG*SIZE

(d) CHAR

9. (a) For each of the statements below, indicate whether the assembler can completely assemble the statement or whether the linker must do part of it.

```
MAX = 50
LIST:   .BLKB     MAX
ARGS:   .LONG     1
        .ADDRESS  LIST
```

.
.
.

```
        CALLG    ARGS,PROCEDURE
```

(b) Indicate for each of the four symbols used (MAX, LIST, ARGS, and PROCE-DURE) whether it is absolute, relocatable, or external.

10. For each situation described below, state which of the following statements is true.

    1. This is not an error.

    2. This is an error that would cause an error message at assembly time.

    3. This is an error that would cause an error message at link time.

    4. This is an error that could cause an error message (program crash) at run time, or could cause incorrect output to be produced.

  (a) There are two global symbols with the same name in different files that are part of one program.

  (b) The directive `.ADDRESS XYZ` appears in a program before XYZ is defined. (XYZ appears as a label later in the same file.)

  (c) The directive `.BLKL MAX` appears in a program before MAX is defined. (MAX is defined in a direct assignment statement later in the same file.)

  (d) A programmer misspelled the procedure name in a CALLS instruction.

  (e) The symbol LOOP is used as a label in two procedures that are linked in the same program.

  (f) The directive `.BYTE NUM` appears in a program before NUM is defined. (NUM is defined in a direct assignment statement later in the same file.)

  (g) The symbols HERE and THERE in the following direct assignment statement are relocatable symbols: `THING = THERE - HERE + 4`

  (h) The symbol XYZ is given an absolute value in a direct assignment statement and it is also used as a label in the same procedure.

11
Macros

11.1 INTRODUCTION

In Chapter 4 we listed the four types of statements that can appear in an assembly language program: machine instructions, assembler directives, direct assignment statements, and macro instructions. *Macro instructions* are pseudoinstructions that are replaced by the assembler with a sequence of assembly language statements specified in a macro definition. Thus the use of macros allows us to give a name to a sequence of instructions used often and to use that name to refer to the entire sequence.

A macro facility, or macro processor, is the part of an assembler that processes macro definitions and macro instructions.[1] Macro facilities are available with most assemblers. The discussion in this section concerns general properties of macros and would be applicable to many other assembly languages. All the specific directives and features described in later sections are for the standard VAX assembler, VAX MACRO.

A macro definition may be supplied by the programmer in the program that uses the macro, or it may be in a macro library available to one or more users. The I/O macros introduced in Chapter 5 and used in some of our programming examples are macros whose definitions are in a library.

---

[1] A macro processor can also be a separate program, not part of the assembler, that is run before the assembler to expand macros.

The process of replacing the macro instruction by the appropriate statements is called *macro expansion*, and the sequence of instructions substituted by the assembler for the macro instruction is called the *expanded macro*, or the *expansion of the macro*.

The instructions in a macro expansion need not be exactly the same each time the macro is used, or invoked. The most common way in which variations in instructions are generated is by using arguments in the macro instruction. When the macro is expanded, the assembler substitutes the actual arguments for formal arguments that appear in the macro definition. There are several other ways, some fairly simple and some quite complex, to vary the instructions in a macro expansion. We will discuss many of these later in this chapter. This ability to vary the instructions themselves provides much of the power and flexibility of macros.

Macros are defined, used, and treated by the assembler quite differently from procedures. (We cannot, for example, vary the instructions in a procedure each time it is called.) Nevertheless, the advantages of using macros are very similar to the advantages of using procedures. Specifically, macros

1. Make a program clearer by "hiding" a lot of perhaps obscure detail behind a macro name that describes the operation being done.

2. Help avoid errors by eliminating the need to write similar sequences of instructions many times.

3. Save the programmer's time (both programming time and, in some cases, time to learn how to do the task performed by a macro).

The I/O macros introduced in Chapter 5 illustrate these advantages. The reader may look at the I/O macro definitions and the procedures they call (in Appendix D) to see that the particular instructions used to, say, print a line, are rather obscure if one does not know more about the VAX/VMS I/O services. Certainly, the instruction PRINTCHRS indicates much more clearly what is being done than the statements that will be in the expanded macro.

Macro facilities vary a lot in the amount of power and flexibility they provide. For example, some (including the VAX) allow recursive macros (macros that invoke themselves), and some do not. We will not cover all the features available in the VAX macro facility or all the techniques that may be used in macros, but we will describe and illustrate many features and techniques that are common to macro facilities. Additional details about macros on the VAX may be found in the *VAX MACRO and Instruction Set Reference Manual*.

Differences Between Macros and Procedures

A macro instruction is replaced in the source program, at assembly time, by its expansion. All evidence that a macro was used is gone when the object file is constructed. The machine instructions and assembler directives in the expanded macro are assembled just as if the programmer had written them in the source program without using the macro. Macros are not a feature of the VAX (or of any computer) itself, but of an assembler for the computer. A procedure, on the other hand, is a separate module, translated by the assembler into an object module and executed when entered as the result of a CALL instruction. CALLS, CALLG, and RET are VAX machine instructions; hence they and the work they do in manipulating the procedure call frame are part of the VAX architecture.

To emphasize the differences between macros and procedures, we compare the source program, object file, and execution of a program using a macro with one using a procedure. Figure 11.1(a) shows the general appearance of the source programs. Figure 11.1(b) shows the general format of the object files. Note that the macro definition does not appear at this stage. After the assembler has used it to expand the macros during the assembly phase, the macro definition is no longer needed. The expanded macro appears in the program at each point where the macro instruction was used. The procedure appears only once. When the program that used macros is executed [Fig. 11.1(c)], the expanded macro is executed in place. Each macro expansion is executed just once (unless the macro instruction is in a loop). In the program with the procedure, each CALL statement causes a branch to the procedure's entry point, and the RET causes a branch back to the calling program. There is only one copy of the procedure; the same code is executed more than once.

11.2 MACRO DEFINITIONS AND SOME EXAMPLES

The general format of a macro definition is

.MACRO   *macro_name*   *arguments*

[*body of macro definition*]

.ENDM *macro_name*

The .MACRO directive marks the beginning of a macro definition and specifies the macro name and the formal argument names. Arguments are optional; most macros will have some, but the EXIT macro, for example, does not. The macro name and formal argument names may be any valid symbols.

The body of the macro definition may contain machine instructions, storage reservation and initialization directives, direct assignment statements, and other macro instructions; they are inserted into the source program at the point where the macro instruction appears. In all the examples in this and the next few sections, there will be nothing else, but we shall see in Sections 11.6 and 11.7 that a macro body can be somewhat more complex.

The formal argument names may be used throughout the body of the macro. During macro expansion, the assembler will treat the actual arguments as character strings with no particular interpretation of them and will substitute them wherever the corresponding formal arguments appear. Then it will translate the constructed statement.

The .ENDM directive marks the end of the macro definition.

If a macro definition is not in a macro library, it must be in any module that uses the macro, because the assembler must have access to the definition to expand the macro

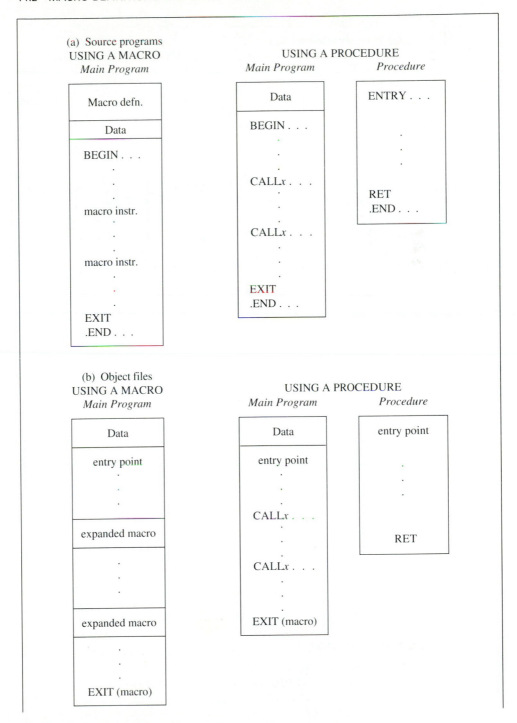

Figure 11.1 Differences between macros and procedures (continued next page)

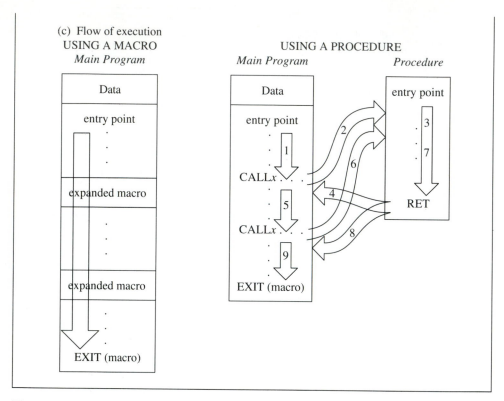

Figure 11.1   (concluded)

while assembling that module. The macro definition should be placed at the beginning of a module (just after the .PSECT directive, if .PSECT is used).

When the assembler encounters a macro definition, it simply records the name of the macro in a table and saves the body of the macro for later reference. The macro definition is used only if and when the macro instruction appears in the program. When the assembler encounters the macro instruction, it looks up the macro definition to determine what statements to substitute for it in the program.

Example 11.1: CVTSL Macro

As we saw in Chapter 6, converting a number from character code (leading separate numeric format) to two's complement requires two steps; the character code is converted to packed decimal format as an intermediate step. The following macro allows us to do the conversion using only one instruction:

```
.MACRO   CVTSL    NUM_DIGITS,LSN,LONG
CVTSP    NUM_DIGITS,LSN,NUM_DIGITS,PKD
CVTPL    NUM_DIGITS,PKD,LONG
.ENDM    CVTSL
```

Note that we used the VAX conventions for naming our macro and for the order in which the arguments are specified. NUM_DIGITS, LSN, and LONG are formal arguments; they are not symbols defined in the program.[2] When the macro is invoked, the actual macro arguments specified in the macro instruction will be substituted. Specifically, if the macro instruction

```
        CVTSL    #5,RECORD+6,R8
```

appears in the program, the assembler will insert and assemble the following instructions:

```
        CVTSP    #5,RECORD+6,#5,PKD
        CVTPL    #5,PKD,R8
```

Note that PKD was not replaced because it is not a formal argument. If this macro is to be used properly, PKD must be defined somewhere in the program.

Example 11.2: A Program Using CVTSL

This program uses the macro CVTSL defined in Example 11.1 and illustrates the placement of the macro definition.

```
; PROBLEM STATEMENT
;
; This program reads and stores two lines of data from a
; terminal. The number on the first line tells how many
; numbers are on the second line.
;
; The number on the first line is stored as a longword
; integer in NUM; the data on the second line are stored in
; the longword array DATA.
;
; The data are assumed to be in fixed format as follows:
;        First line:    sdd
;        Second line:   sdddbbsdddbb...sddd
; where d = digit, s = sign, and b = blank.
; The program will read at most 12 numbers on the second line.
;
; MACRO DEFINITION
;
        .MACRO   CVTSL    NUM_DIGITS,LSN,LONG
        CVTSP    NUM_DIGITS,LSN,NUM_DIGITS,PKD
        CVTPL    NUM_DIGITS,PKD,LONG
        .ENDM    CVTSL
;
; STORAGE RESERVATION
;
NUM:    .BLKL    1
DATA:   .BLKL    12
PKD:    .BLKB    2
BUFFER: .BLKB    80
```

---

[2] Formal argument names may be the same as symbols used elsewhere in the program; the assembler will not confuse them.

```
        ;
        ; REGISTER USE
        ;
        ;       R6        array pointer
        ;       R7        loop counter
        ;       R8        buffer pointer
        ;       R0-R3     used by CVTSL
        ;
                BEGIN   TESTCVT
                READLINE BUFFER                 ; Read number of entries
                CVTSL   #2,BUFFER,R7            ; Convert number of entries
                CMPL    R7,#12                  ; See if too many
                BLEQ    STORE
                MOVL    #12,R7                  ; Read no more than 12
        STORE:  MOVL    R7,NUM                  ; Store number of entries
        ;
                MOVAL   DATA,R6                 ; Initialize array ptr
                MOVAB   BUFFER,R8               ; Initialize buffer ptr
                READLINE BUFFER                 ; Read data line
        CVT:    CVTSL   #3,(R8),(R6)+           ; Convert to 2's complement
                ADDL2   #6,R8                   ; Increment buffer ptr
                SOBGTR  R7,CVT                  ; Loop control
        ;       [ other processing ]
                EXIT
                .END    TESTCVT
```

Example 11.3: SUM Macro

The macro SUM adds three longwords.

```
        .MACRO  SUM      A,B,C,TOTAL
        ADDL3   A,B,TOTAL
        ADDL2   C,TOTAL
        .ENDM   SUM
```

Consider the following uses of this macro.

```
SUM      4(R7),(R9)+,BETA,(R6)              SUM      #36,R5,BETA,(R9)+
```

The expansions are

```
ADDL3    4(R7),(R9)+,(R6)                   ADDL3    #36,R5,(R9)+
ADDL2    BETA,(R6)                          ADDL2    BETA,(R9)+
```

The SUM macro is used correctly in the first instance but not in the second. The instructions generated are properly formed; that is, they would not cause assembly-time errors, but the use of autoincrement mode for the argument TOTAL will have an unintended effect: R9 will be incremented by the first ADD instruction, so the destination addresses in the two ADD instructions will be different.

As Example 11.3 illustrates, several different addressing modes may be used for the actual arguments in a macro, but there are some restrictions. There are no fixed rules about which modes are permitted as macro arguments. The assembler simply substitutes the actual arguments for the formal arguments; whether or not a particular addressing mode is acceptable for a particular argument depends on how it is used in the body of the macro definition.

Example 11.4: CALL Macro

The purpose of this macro is to call a procedure. It assumes that the procedure has three arguments and sets up the procedure argument list on the stack.

```
.MACRO   CALL      PROC ARG1,ARG2,ARG3
PUSHAL   ARG3
PUSHAL   ARG2
PUSHAL   ARG1
CALLS    #3,PROC
.ENDM    CALL
```

Note that a space, not a comma, is used as a separator between the first two formal macro arguments, PROC and ARG1. Spaces and commas are both acceptable separators. Note also that the PUSHAL instruction is used to push each argument address on the stack even though the arguments may not be longwords. Will that cause any errors?

In Section 11.6 we will write a more flexible CALL macro that allows for a variable number of arguments. A general CALL macro is especially useful to have on a computer with a more primitive instruction set than the VAX has. If the programmer has to write out instructions to accomplish some of the tasks done automatically by the VAX CALLS and CALLG instructions, a macro could save a lot of bother.

Concatenation

Suppose that we want to use a macro like the SUM macro in Example 11.3, but we sometimes want to add data of a type other than longword. Instead of writing different macro definitions for each type that may be used, we can include the type as an argument and write the definition of SUM so that the actual argument specified for the type will be substituted into the middle of the instruction names in the statements generated. To do this we use an operation called *concatenation* of character strings. Concatenation means simply putting two character strings together to form a new string. In macros, arguments may be concatenated with other characters to form instruction names, operands, or any other strings that are useful. An apostrophe (') is used to indicate where concatenation is to be done.

Example 11.5: SUM Macro Using Concatenation

```
.MACRO   SUM       A,B,C,TOTAL,TYPE
ADD'TYPE'3         A,B,TOTAL
ADD'TYPE'2         C,TOTAL
.ENDM    SUM
```

The expansion of the macro instruction

```
        SUM       #36,R5,BETA,(R9),W
```

is

```
        ADDW3     #36,R5,(R9)
        ADDW2     BETA,(R9)
```

The apostrophes in the macro definition in Example 11.5 are necessary to separate the formal argument name from the surrounding characters. In general, the assembler replaces the formal argument with the actual argument only if it finds the formal argument name set off from surrounding characters by a separator (comma, space, or tab) or some other special character, such as the concatenation operator. If the first instruction in the macro definition had been written like this:

```
        ADDTYPE3      A,B,TOTAL
```

the assembler would have considered ADDTYPE3 to be one symbol and would have left it in the instruction without substituting anything for the letters TYPE (just as it did not substitute #36 for the A in ADDL3 in Example 11.3). The assembler would have generated the statement

```
        ADDTYPE3      #36,R5,(R9)
```

and then would have issued an error message because there is no instruction called ADDTYPE3.

Example 11.6: A Storage Reservation and Initialization Macro

To emphasize that the statements in the body of a macro definition need not be machine instructions, we include an example of a macro that reserves space for an array and for a variable that contains the number of elements reserved.

```
              .MACRO    RESERVE ARRAY,NUM,TYPE
ARRAY:        .BLK'TYPE NUM
ARRAY'SIZE:   .LONG     NUM
              .ENDM     RESERVE
```

This macro could be used in the storage reservation and initialization portion of a program as follows:

```
        RESERVE TAGS,50,B
```

The expansion would be

```
TAGS:        .BLKB 50
TAGSSIZE:    .LONG      50
```

Note that in the expansion of RESERVE, the assembler directives and their arguments are not lined up as they are in the macro definition. This illustrates the simple substitution of actual parameters for formal parameters in macro expansion. In the macro definition, there is only one space between `.BLK'TYPE` and `NUM`, so there is only one space in the expanded macro between `.BLKB` and `50`. For ease of reading, we may sometimes show statements in expanded macros neatly lined up even if the assembler would not produce them that way.

Macro Expansions in Program Listings

Figure 11.2 is part of a program listing. VAX assembly language program listings normally show the source program as written by the programmer. Macro definitions, if they are in the source module rather than a macro library, will appear in the program listing. Macro instructions appear in the listing but their expansions do not. The .SHOW and .NOSHOW directives may be used to override the usual listing conventions. The directive

```
.SHOW   MEB
```

will cause subsequent macro expansions (specifically, all lines that are assembled into the object file) to show in the listing. (MEB is one of several possible arguments for the .SHOW directive. It stands for Macro Expansion, Binary.) If the assembler encounters a

```
.NOSHOW MEB
```

directive, it will not show the expansions of macros that follow. The use of these directives is illustrated in Fig. 11.2.

11.3 MORE ON MACRO ARGUMENTS

Positional and Keyword Arguments

As we have seen, the assembler replaces all occurrences of formal arguments in a macro definition with the actual arguments specified when the macro is invoked. We did not explain how the assembler determines which actual argument is to replace which formal argument because the rule is natural and straightforward: the first actual argument is substituted for the first formal argument, the second actual argument is substituted for the second formal argument, and so on. That is, the role of each actual argument is determined by its position. This positional scheme is, of course, similar to the way the roles of operands for machine instructions and arguments for procedures are determined. Some macros, however, may have a very large number of arguments, and it may be inconvenient to have to remember the exact order in which they must appear. We may write the actual arguments in any order if we include a keyword for each to tell the assembler which argument is being specified. The keyword is the formal argument name. The format for specifying a keyword argument in a macro instruction is

$$formal\_arg\_name = actual\_arg$$

```
0000          1  ; PROBLEM STATEMENT
0000          2  ;
0000          3  ; This program reads and stores two lines of data from a
0000          4  ; terminal.  The number on the first line tells how many
0000          5  ; numbers are on the second line.
0000          6  ;
0000          7  ; The number on the first line is stored as a longword
0000          8  ; integer in NUM; the data on the second line are stored in
0000          9  ; the longword array DATA.
0000         10  ;
0000         11  ; The data are assumed to be in fixed format as follows:
0000         12  ;      First line:    sdd
0000         13  ;      Second line:   sdddbbbsdddbb...sddd
0000         14  ; where d = digit, s = sign, and b = blank.
0000         15  ; The program will read at most 12 numbers on the second line.
0000         16  ;
0000         17  ; MACRO DEFINITION
0000         18  ;
0000         19       .MACRO   CVTSL   NUM_DIGITS,LSN,LONG
0000         20       CVTSP    NUM_DIGITS,LSN,NUM_DIGITS,PKD
0000         21       CVTPL    NUM_DIGITS,PKD,LONG
0000         22       .ENDM    CVTSL
0000         23  ;
0000         24  ; STORAGE RESERVATION
0000         25  ;
00000004     26  NUM:    .BLKL   1                     array pointer
00000034     27  DATA:   .BLKL   12
00000036     28  PKD:    .BLKB   2
00000086     29  BUFFER: .BLKB   80
0086         30  ;
0086         31  ; REGISTER USE
0086         32  ;
0086         33  ;       R6                            array pointer
0086         34  ;       R7                            loop counter
0086         35  ;       R8                            buffer pointer
```

Figure 11.2 A listing showing macro expansions (continued next page)

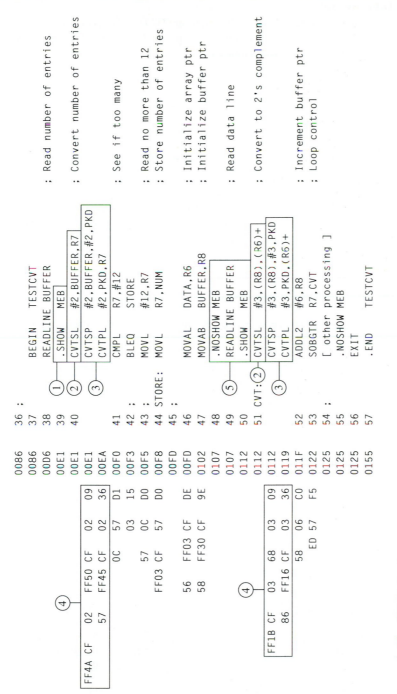

```
Addr    Object code            Line                                 Comment

        0086                    36   ;
        0086                    37        BEGIN    TESTCVT
        00D6                    38        READLINE BUFFER            ; Read number of entries
        00E1                    39  ①     .SHOW    MEB
        00E1                    40  ②     CVTSL    #2,BUFFER,R7       ; Convert number of entries
        00E1  FF50 CF 02 09     ③        CVTSP    #2,BUFFER,#2,PKD
        00EA  FF45 CF 02 36     ③        CVTPL    #2,PKD,R7
              FF4A CF 02 57  ④
        00F0  0C 57 D1          41        CMPL     R7,#12             ; See if too many
        00F3  03 15             42  ;     BLEQ     STORE
        00F5  57 0C D0          43  ;     MOVL     #12,R7             ; Read no more than 12
        00F8  FF03 CF 57 D0     44 STORE: MOVL     R7,NUM             ; Store number of entries
        00FD                    45  ;
        00FD  56 FF03 CF DE     46        MOVAL    DATA,R6            ; Initialize array ptr
        0102  58 FF30 CF 9E     47        MOVAB    BUFFER,R8          ; Initialize buffer ptr
        0107                    48  ⑤     .NOSHOW  MEB
        0107                    49        READLINE BUFFER            ; Read data line
        0112                    50        .SHOW    MEB
        0112                    51 CVT: ② CVTSL    #3,(R8),(R6)+      ; Convert to 2's complement
        0112  FF1B CF 03 68 03 09  ③     CVTSP    #3,(R8),#3,PKD
        0119  FF16 CF 03 36     ③     ④  CVTPL    #3,PKD,(R6)+
        011F  58 06 C0          52        ADDL2    #6,R8              ; Increment buffer ptr
        0122  ED 57 F5          53        SOBGTR   R7,CVT             ; Loop control
        0125                    54  ;     [ other processing ]
        0125                    55        .NOSHOW  MEB
        0125                    56        EXIT
        0155                    57        .END     TESTCVT
```

1. The .SHOW directive.
2. The macro instruction appears.
3. The expansion of the macro. Note that there are no source program line numbers on the lines generated by the assembler.
4. The object code for the expanded macro.
5. The .NOSHOW directive suppresses listing of the macro expansions until another .SHOW directive is encountered. The expansion of the READLINE macro is not shown.

Figure 11.2 (concluded)

293

Example 11.7: Using Keywords

A macro RANGE is to determine if a given integer, DATUM, is between two specified values, LOW and HIGH, and to cause a branch to a specified location, BAD, if not. RANGE is defined with the following .MACRO directive:

```
.MACRO  RANGE   LOW,HIGH,DATUM,TYPE,BAD
```

RANGE may be invoked using positional arguments in the usual way as follows:

```
RANGE   #0,#100,(R9),W,BADDATA
```

Alternatively, it may be invoked with keyword arguments like this:

```
RANGE   DATUM=(R9),LOW=#0,HIGH=#100,BAD=BADDATA,TYPE=W
```

Although the use of keyword arguments eliminates the problem of remembering the order in which the formal arguments are listed in the macro definition, it does require that the formal argument names be known to the user of the macro.

If keywords are used at all in a macro instruction, they should be used for each argument that is specified.

Default Values and Omitted Arguments

For some macros there may be one or more formal arguments for which a particular value (i.e., a particular actual argument) is used most of the time. In the macro definition we may specify this value as the default value for that argument. Then, if the argument is omitted when the macro is invoked, the assembler will use the default value. If some other value for the argument is specified when the macro is invoked, the default is ignored and the assembler uses the specified value.

A default value is specified in the .MACRO directive of a macro definition by writing

$$formal\_arg\_name = default\_value$$

instead of just writing the formal argument name.

Example 11.8: SUM Macro with a Default

Suppose that the SUM macro defined in Example 11.5 is likely to be used most often to add longwords. We can specify that the default value of the formal argument TYPE is L as follows:

```
.MACRO  SUM     A,B,C,TOTAL,TYPE=L
```

Some macro expansions are

```
SUM     R5,R6,R7,XYZ                    SUM     R5,R6,R7,XYZ,B
ADDL3   R5,R6,XYZ                       ADDB3   R5,R6,XYZ
ADDL2   R7,XYZ                          ADDB2   R7,XYZ
```

Example 11.9: A Default for PRINTCHRS

The PRINTCHRS macro has a default length of 85. Its .MACRO directive looks like this:

```
.MACRO  PRINTCHRS STRING,LENGTH=#85
```

Note that the default value includes the #, not just the number 85. The default value must appear exactly as it will be needed when substituted into instructions in the body of the macro. In the PRINTCHRS macro definition, LENGTH appears as an instruction operand, so the default has the proper form for a literal.

An argument may be omitted from a macro instruction even if no default value is specified in the macro definition. In such cases, the assembler substitutes a null string for the associated formal argument when the macro is expanded. Thus we may think of a null string as being a default value for all arguments for which the macro definition does not specify some other default value. (We will see examples in Section 11.6 where it is useful to have null arguments.)

When positional arguments are being used in a macro instruction and any argument other than the last is omitted, the comma that would ordinarily follow the argument must be included as a place holder for that argument. If the comma is omitted, the assembler will substitute the next actual argument for the formal argument that the user wishes to be null. (If one particular argument is likely to be omitted, it should be placed last in the .MACRO directive, as in Example 11.8; then the last comma may be omitted also.)

If keyword arguments are being used in a macro instruction, and some arguments are omitted, they are simply left out; commas are not needed as space holders because the order in which the arguments are specified is irrelevant. Thus keyword arguments are especially convenient for macros with a large number of arguments where many have default values that are used often. Many system I/O macros are in this category.

Keyword arguments and default values for arguments are very standard macro features. The details of how they are specified and used differ slightly in different systems.

Special Cases

If an actual argument for a macro contains a character that the assembler normally interprets as a separator (a comma, space, or tab), or a semicolon which normally indicates the beginning of a comment, the entire argument must be enclosed in delimiters to indicate that it is one argument. Angle brackets (< and >) are the standard delimiters. For example, suppose that we have a macro called PRINTMSG that displays its argument, a character string, at the terminal. We might use it like this:

```
PRINTMSG <TABLE OF TRANSACTIONS>
```

If the character string "TABLE OF TRANSACTIONS" were not delimited, the assembler would treat the spaces as separators and conclude that there were three actual arguments. If the macro definition has fewer than three formal arguments, the assembler would issue an error message.

The delimiters are not considered part of the actual argument; the assembler removes them before substituting the actual argument into the statements in the body of the macro definition.

If an angle bracket is one of the characters in an actual argument, some other character should be used as a delimiter. Any character will do, but the first delimiter must be preceded by a circumflex ($^$). For example, in

```
PRINTMSG ^/ITEMS WITH COST > $100.00/
```

the delimiter is a slash. Since the circumflex plays a special role, an actual argument that contains one must be enclosed in delimiters. For example, <^XFF00> is the proper way to specify ^XFF00 as an actual argument.

11.4 LOCAL LABELS

The Need for Local Labels

Suppose that we wish to write a macro that computes the absolute value of an integer. We could try to do it as in the following example.

Example 11.10: A Macro that Uses a Label (Unwisely, as We Shall See)

```
        .MACRO  ABS     SOURCE,DEST,TYPE=L
        MOV'TYPE        SOURCE,DEST
        BGEQ            LABEL
        MNEG'TYPE       DEST,DEST
LABEL:  .ENDM   ABS
```

Is it legal to have a label on the .ENDM statement? If so, how is the label treated by the assembler? The label is legal and is treated in the usual way. As the assembler inserts each instruction from the macro definition into the program, it assembles it (i.e., translates it) incrementing its location counter. Since there is not a machine instruction or a storage reservation or initialization directive on the line with the label, the location counter will not be incremented. Thus the next statement in the program following the macro instruction will be assembled in the location addressed by LABEL.

Although the use of the label in the definition of ABS is technically correct, it will cause an error if the macro is used more than once in one program module. Since LABEL is not an argument for the macro, the assembler leaves it in the instructions just as it appears in the macro definition. Thus if ABS is used more than once, LABEL will appear on more than one instruction and cause a "multiple definition of label" error.

Example 11.11: Expansion of ABS

Consider the program segment in Fig. 11.3(a); it invokes ABS twice. The expansions, with error messages, are shown in Fig. 11.3(b). The instructions inserted by the assembler are the ones without line numbers. Notice that the branch displacements in the machine code for both BGEQ instructions are incorrect because of the confusion between the two instances of LABEL.

The (incorrect) macro definition used here is the one shown in Example 11.10.

(a) Statements in the program

```
      ABS      R5,R5
      ADDL2    R1,R5
:  :
      ABS      (R4),ALPHA,W
      CMPW     ALPHA,BETA
```

(b) Expansions with error messages

```
                    0058   16          .SHOW    MEB
                    0058   17          ABS      R5,R5
          55        0058   D0          MOVL     R5,R5
          11        005B   18          BGEQ         LABEL
          55        005D   CE          MNEGL    R5,R5
                    0060          LABEL:

%MACRO-E-SYMOUTPHAS, Symbol out of phase

                    0060
          55        0060   C0   18     ADDL2    R1,R5
          51
                    0063   19          ;
                    0063   20          ;
                    0063   21          ABS      (R4),ALPHA,W
       99 AF        0063   B0          MOVW     (R4),ALPHA
          64
          F7        0067   18          BGEQ         LABEL
       94 AF        0069   AE          MNEGW    ALPHA,ALPHA
       92 AF
                    006E          LABEL:

%MACRO-E-MULDEFLBL, Multiple definition of label !

                    006E
       91 AF        006E   22          CMPW     ALPHA,BETA
       8F AF        B1
```

Figure 11.3 Incorrect use of a label in a macro

The ABS macro illustrates a problem that occurs in any macro facility: We often want to use labels in a macro definition, but ordinary labels cannot be used if the macro might be invoked more than once in a module. Macro facilities include a mechanism for generating labels that will differ each time a macro is invoked. In the VAX assembler, the labels generated are called *created local labels*.

Local Labels

The format of a local label is

$$n\$$$

where n is a decimal integer in the range $1 \leq n \leq 65,535$. Local labels may be used outside macros, although there are several restrictions on their use. We will discuss the use of local labels in macros only.

The assembler creates local labels beginning at 30000$. It keeps count of how many it has created so far, and whenever it creates a new one, it uses the next higher number. The programmer specifies that a local label is to be created for a macro by listing a formal argument name preceded by a question mark (e.g., ?LABEL) in the list of formal arguments on the .MACRO directive. Each time the macro is invoked, the assembler will create a new local label and substitute it for the formal name wherever it appears in the macro definition.

Example 11.12: ABS Macro Using a Local Label

A correct macro definition for ABS is

```
        .MACRO  ABS     SOURCE,DEST,TYPE=L,?LABEL
        MOV'TYPE        SOURCE,DEST
        BGEQ            LABEL
        MNEG'TYPE       DEST,DEST
LABEL:  .ENDM   ABS
```

Note that the question mark is not included in the formal label name when it appears in the body of the macro definition.

Assuming that the macro instructions in Fig. 11.3(a) are the first that are expanded in the program, the expansions would be as shown in Fig. 11.4. (Note that the branch displacements in the machine code are now correct.)

It is possible to use more than one local label in a macro. A different formal name must be specified for each.

Example 11.13: PRINTMSG Macro

The macro PRINTMSG prints a character string. It is similar to PRINTCHRS but simpler to use because the user does not have to put the string in memory. PRINTMSG could be used as follows:

```
        PRINTMSG <ACTIVE PORTS>
```

(Recall that the angle brackets are used to delimit the character string so that the assembler will not interpret "ACTIVE" and "PORTS" as two arguments.)

```
                              0058    16             .SHOW    MEB
                              0058    17             ABS      R5,R5
            55    55    D0    0058                   MOVL        R5,R5
                  03    18    005B                   BGEQ              30000$
            55    55    CE    005D                   MNEGL       R5,R5
                              0060          30000$:
            55    51    C0    0060    18             ADDL2    R1,R5
                              0063    19  ;
                              0063    20  ;
                              0063    21             ABS      (R4),ALPHA,W
         99 AF    64    B0    0063                   MOVW        (R4),ALPHA
                  05    18    0067                   BGEQ              30001$
         92 AF 94 AF    AE    0069                   MNEGW       ALPHA,ALPHA
                              006E          30001$:
         91 AF 8F AF    B1    006E    22             CMPW     ALPHA,BETA
```

Figure 11.4 Expansions of ABS using local labels

The macro definition for PRINTMSG is

```
        .MACRO     PRINTMSG MSG,?LBL,?LINE
        BRB        LBL
LINE:   .ASCIZ     /MSG/
LBL:    PRINTCHRS LINE
        .ENDM      PRINTMSG
```

We indicated in Section 11.1 that the body of a macro definition may contain a macro instruction (for another macro). Here, the PRINTMSG macro uses the PRINTCHRS macro.

Note that a branch instruction is needed to branch over the character string that will be stored in memory between machine instructions. Omitting the branch would be an error, for without it the CPU would try to execute the character code as if it were instructions.

Whenever the assembler encounters a macro instruction, it sets up an argument substitution table to use while expanding the macro. Suppose that the assembler has already created three local labels in the current module when it expands the macro instruction

```
        PRINTMSG <ACTIVE PORTS>
```

Its substitution table for this expansion would be

Formal Argument	Actual Value
MSG	ACTIVE PORTS
LBL	30003$
LINE	30004$

The actual values are substituted just as they appear in the table, as character strings, for the formal argument names in the macro. Suppose that PRINTMSG is used again to print another message immediately after the first, say as follows:

```
        PRINTMSG <User    Port    Time on>
```

The substitution table for the expansion of this instruction would be

Formal Argument	Actual Value
MSG	User Port Time on
LBL	30005$
LINE	30006$

Example 11.14: Expansions of PRINTMSG

(a)

```
        PRINTMSG <ACTIVE PORTS>


        BRB       30003$
30004$: .ASCIZ    /ACTIVE PORTS/
30003$: PRINTCHRS 30004$
```

(b)

```
        PRINTMSG <User    Port    Time on>


        BRB       30005$
30006$: .ASCIZ    /User    Port    Time on/
30005$: PRINTCHRS 30006$
```

For clarity in the example, we have not shown the expansion of PRINTCHRS.

It might occur to the reader that it would be nice to have a macro like PRINTMSG that prints the character string centered in a line. Some of the tools of Section 11.7 will be helpful for doing this.

11.5 USER-FRIENDLY MACROS

A macro is convenient to use if the user does not have to remember a lot of details, peculiarities, restrictions, and special requirements. A macro is safe to use if it is convenient (since convenience means there is less likelihood of its being used incorrectly), if it does not have unexpected side effects (e.g., destroying data in registers), and if when used incorrectly, the error is detected immediately rather than after destroying data or instructions or generating incorrect results that will be detected later when the cause is more difficult to track down. Macro definitions can be written so that they are very convenient and safe for the user, or so that they are less so. In this section we will consider some guidelines for writing user-friendly (i.e., convenient and safe) macros. These concerns are especially relevant when writing system macros, library macros that are to be used by many programmers, and even macros to be used by one programmer over a long period of time.

Some Guidelines for User-Friendly Macros

We have already seen several features of macros that suggest the following guidelines:

> Specify useful argument default values whenever possible.

> Choose natural, easy-to-remember, formal argument names, so keyword arguments are convenient to use.

> If labels are needed, use local labels.

The CVTSL macro defined in Example 11.1 is convenient to use because the macro definition adheres to the guideline:

> Use standard conventions of the assembly language whenever appropriate—for example, for naming instructions and operands, and for ordering the operands.

The required form of an actual argument depends on how it is used in the macro. Sometimes, because of the role of the argument, it is natural to have fairly stringent restrictions on its form. For example, the actual argument that replaces ARRAY in the RESERVE macro in Example 11.6 must be a symbol because it is used as a label. Sometimes, though, it is possible and desirable to allow for a variety of forms. The first three arguments of the SUM macro (Examples 11.3 and 11.5) may be specified using any operand addressing modes. Thus another guideline is:

> Write a macro definition so that a reasonable variety of forms for the actual arguments will be valid.

We saw that autoincrement mode could not be used correctly for the fourth argument in the SUM macro. In Sections 11.6 and 11.7 we will learn techniques that can be used to modify the definition of SUM so that this mode is acceptable, too.

Using Registers and Scratch Space in Macros

It is often necessary for a macro to use some registers or some scratch space in memory to accomplish its task. For example, consider the CVTSL macro (from Example 11.1).

```
.MACRO   CVTSL    NUM_DIGITS,LSN,LONG
CVTSP    NUM_DIGITS,LSN,NUM_DIGITS,PKD
CVTPL    NUM_DIGITS,PKD,LONG
.ENDM    CVTSL
```

PKD is scratch space needed for the packed decimal representation of the integer being converted from leading separate numeric to two's complement. This macro definition assumes that the user has defined PKD elsewhere in the program and has reserved enough space for it. If the user forgets to define PKD, the linker will issue an "Undefined symbol" error message, so the error will be detected quickly. However, if the user defines PKD but does not reserve enough space, the CVTSP instruction will overwrite whatever data appear in memory immediately after the space reserved for PKD; this error may be

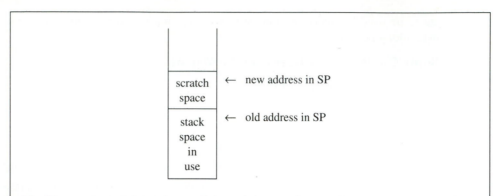

The SP must always point to the top of the stack because the operating system may, at any time, use the space above (SP). (SP) may be used to address the new scratch space reserved.

Figure 11.5   Using the stack for scratch space

much harder to detect. Thus the CVTSL macro would be both more convenient and safer to use if it reserved the scratch space needed for the packed integer. But where can the macro reserve scratch space? The answer is the user stack. To reserve temporary scratch space on the stack, we simply decrement the stack pointer by the number of bytes desired. (See Fig. 11.5.)

How many bytes should we reserve for the packed integer? Since the integer is to be stored in a longword, it should have at most ten digits. A ten-digit packed integer fits in six bytes. However, the leading separate numeric string being converted may have been incorrectly typed, or NUM_DIGITS may be specified incorrectly. In such cases, the string may have more than ten digits, and if only six bytes are reserved on the stack, other data on the stack would be overwritten, with perhaps very confusing effects. Since our aim here is to protect the user from bad side effects of errors, we should reserve more space. But how much? What is a reasonable limit? The CVTSP instruction itself will cause a reserved operand fault if the number of digits specified for either the leading separate numeric or packed operand is outside the permitted range of these data types: 0 to 31. Thus a safe macro would allow for up to 31 digits. (If the integer being converted is too large for a longword, the overflow condition code will be set by CVTPL; we may leave to the user the responsibility for checking for that error.) The improved definition of CVTSL is:

Example 11.15: A Macro That Uses the Stack for Scratch Space

```
.MACRO  CVTSL    NUM_DIGITS,LSN,LONG
SUBL2   #16,SP
CVTSP   NUM_DIGITS,LSN,NUM_DIGITS,(SP)
CVTPL   NUM_DIGITS,(SP),LONG
ADDL2   #16,SP
.ENDM   CVTSL
```

Note that the stack pointer must be reset by the macro, effectively popping the scratch data.

If a macro uses registers, it should save the original contents and reload them after finishing its work. Once again, the appropriate place for temporary storage is the user stack. There are two instructions that make it very easy to push and pop the contents of several registers. They are

$$\text{PUSHR} \qquad register\_mask$$

$$\text{POPR} \qquad register\_mask$$

The register mask is similar (but not identical) to the register mask used in an .ENTRY directive to specify the registers to be saved when a procedure is called. It is a word in which bit *n* corresponds to R*n*. Any register (except the PC) may be specified in a mask for a PUSHR or POPR instruction. Any addressing mode may be used for the mask, but a literal using the ^M operator is most common. Regardless of the order in which the registers are listed in the instruction, PUSHR will push the contents of the specified registers onto the stack so that they appear in order by register number (i.e., with higher-numbered registers stored at higher addresses). POPR copies the first longword from the stack into the lowest-numbered register listed in its mask, the second into the second-lowest register, and so on. Of course, for clarity, it is nice to list the registers in numerical order. Both PUSHR and POPR adjust the stack pointer as appropriate. They do not affect the condition codes.

Usually, the same list of registers appears in the PUSHR and corresponding POPR instructions, but the two instructions are executed independently; whatever registers are specified will be used.

Example 11.16: How PUSHR and POPR Work

```
PUSHR   #^M<R10,R5,R7,R0>
```

will cause the contents of the registers to be stacked as shown in Fig. 11.6(a).

```
POPR    #^M<R0,R8,R9,R5>
```

will cause the top four longwords on the stack to be popped and put in the registers as shown in Fig. 11.6(b).

Example 11.17: Saving Register Contents in a Macro

Recall that MOVC3 destroys the contents of R0–R5. A macro that copies a character string as part of its task should protect the data in those registers. For example:

```
PUSHR   #^M<R0,R1,R2,R3,R4,R5>
MOVC3   LEN,STR1,STR2
POPR    #^M<R0,R1,R2,R3,R4,R5>
```

The PUSHR and POPR instructions may, of course, be used outside macros. One possible use of PUSHR is to push procedure arguments onto the stack.

(a) Assume register contents as follows:

$$
\begin{array}{ll}
\text{R0:} & \text{00000000} \\
\text{R5:} & \text{00000005} \\
\text{R7:} & \text{FFFFF3A2} \\
\text{R10:} & \text{0000000A}
\end{array}
$$

The instruction

       PUSHR #^M<R10,R5,R7,R0>

will stack the register contents as follows:

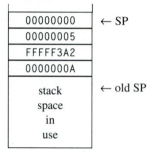

(b) The instruction

       POPR #^M<R0,R8,R9,R5>

will pop four longwords from the top of the stack, adjust the stack pointer, and put the data into the registers as follows:

$$
\begin{array}{ll}
\text{R0:} & \text{00000000} \\
\text{R5:} & \text{00000005} \\
\text{R8:} & \text{FFFFF3A2} \\
\text{R9:} & \text{0000000A}
\end{array}
$$

Figure 11.6 The effects of the PUSHR and POPR instructions

The CVTSL macro uses registers R0–R3, but they were not saved because the VAX instructions that convert between leading separate numeric, packed, and two's complement formats all use these registers. It is reasonable for the macro to adhere to the same conventions as similar VAX instructions.

Some system macros follow the convention that R0 and R1 may be used to return status flags just as procedures may do. Thus such macros generally would not save the old contents of these registers. As we indicated in Chapter 5, our I/O macros may change the contents of R0 and R1.

The examples we have just discussed illustrate several more guidelines for user-friendly macros:

A macro should not rely on the user to reserve space for scratch work done by the macro.

If scratch space is needed in a macro, the stack should be used whenever possible. It is important that the stack pointer be properly set and reset to reserve and release the space.

When scratch space is used, the maximum amount of space that may be needed should be reserved (if practical) so that other data on the stack (or elsewhere) are not overwritten by mistake.

If registers are used in a macro, the original contents should be saved (on the stack) and reloaded when the macro finishes its task. R0 and R1 may, by convention, not be saved.

11.6 CONDITIONAL ASSEMBLY

What Is Conditional Assembly?

One of the features of macro facilities that give them so much power is conditional assembly. A macro definition may specify different statements to be assembled depending on conditions that can be tested by the assembler. That is, the assembler may be told to do specified computations, test for certain conditions, and assemble certain statements depending on the results. We may think of the conditional assembly directives and some other directives used in macro definitions as making up a programming language that we use to give commands to the assembler.

Thus, in addition to machine instructions, ordinary assembler directives, direct assignments, and other macro instructions, the body of a macro definition may contain directives that control or affect the expansion of the macro. When the assembler encounters machine instructions or ordinary assembler directives (e.g., storage reservation and initialization directives), it inserts these in the program. When it encounters a macro instruction, it looks up the definition for that macro and expands it. When it encounters a directive related to conditional assembly or macro expansion, it carries out whatever steps are indicated by the particular directive.

To understand and use conditional assembly properly, we must remember that the assembler can test only conditions that exist at assembly time; it can compute only with data available at assembly time. For example, the assembler can test and do computation with the values of symbols but not the contents of memory locations or registers used in the program, because the latter simply do not exist at assembly time.

Many of the tests and computations done by the assembler are done on character strings—character strings that appear in the program itself, such as actual arguments for macros, not character strings in memory. Conditional assembly may be used, for example, to examine an actual argument for a macro to determine if it is of the proper form. We observed that the SUM macro (Examples 11.3 and 11.5) would not work correctly if the fourth argument were specified using autoincrement mode. With conditional assembly (and the tools of Section 11.7) we can modify the macro definition to test the actual argument and direct the assembler to assemble instructions that will work properly for this case. (See Exercise 28.) On the other hand, in the CVTSL macro (Example 11.15), it might be useful to know how many digits are in the leading separate numeric operand so that we do not reserve more scratch space than is needed. The number of digits *cannot* be tested at assembly time, because the leading separate numeric string is not read in and available until the program is executing.

If we are to "program" the assembler, we need some of the basic components of a programming language. We cannot use the VAX instructions, because when the assembler encounters them in a macro definition it inserts them into the source program; it does not execute them. The three major components of the "programming language" for directing the assembler that we will describe and use are variables, a conditional directive (.IF), and loop directives (.IRP, .IRPC, and .REPEAT). We will also describe several other directives that are useful in macro definitions and are typical of macro facilities in general, but we will not cover all the details of their use or all the VAX macro processor directives.

Variables

To the assembler, user-defined symbols are variables. Their values are stored in the symbol table and may be looked up, tested, and used by the assembler as needed. The values of symbols used as labels may not be changed in the course of a program module, but values of symbols defined in direct assignment statements may be changed in subsequent direct assignment statements. When such a symbol is redefined (i.e., when its value is changed) the assembler simply changes the entry in the symbol table.

To avoid conflict with symbols used in a program, symbols in a macro definition should be names not likely to be used by a programmer. Symbols for most purposes other than labels (e.g., symbols defined in direct assignment statements) can be generated during macro expansion by concatenating a created local label onto other characters. (There will be examples later.)

.IF—The Conditional Assembly Block Directive

The .IF directive is something like an **if** statement in a high-level language. If the condition specified on the .IF directive is satisfied, the statements that follow are processed by the assembler; if the condition is not satisfied, they are skipped. The format for a conditional assembly block is

.IF   *condition   argument(s)*

[*range*   ]

.ENDC

The conditions that may be specified are listed in Table 11.1. The arguments for .IF directives are the data to be tested for the specified condition; some of them may be macro arguments. If an argument for a .IF condition is an expression, it must be absolute and contain no undefined symbols.

TABLE 11.1 CONDITIONS FOR THE .IF DIRECTIVE

Condition			
Long form	Short form	Meaning	Arguments
BLANK	B	String is null	Macro argument
NOT_BLANK	NB	String is not null	Macro argument

[Note that the names of the two conditions above are misleading; the assembler tests whether or not the argument is a null string (i.e., contains no characters) not whether it is the blank, or space, character.]

IDENTICAL	IDN	Arguments are identical	Macro args., strings
DIFFERENT	DIF	Arguments are different	Macro args., strings
EQUAL	EQ	Argument = 0	Expression
NOT_EQUAL	NE	Argument ≠ 0	Expression
GREATER	GT	Argument > 0	Expression
LESS_EQUAL	LE	Argument ≤ 0	Expression
LESS_THAN	LT	Argument < 0	Expression
GREATER_EQUAL	GE	Argument ≥ 0	Expression
DEFINED	DF	Symbol is defined	Symbol
NOT_DEFINED	NDF	Symbol is not defined	Symbol

The range of a conditional block may contain any statements that could appear in a macro definition, including nested conditional blocks, looping directives, and other directives that control the expansion of the macro.

The .ENDC directive is needed to mark the end of the conditional block.

Example 11.18: CVTSL Macro with Overflow Test

Suppose that we want to add an option to the CVTSL macro that allows the user to specify if an overflow test should be performed on the two's complement result of the conversion. If this option is selected, instructions will be assembled to test for overflow and clear the longword result if overflow occurred. The user would select this option by including a fourth argument; if the fourth argument is omitted, the macro will be expanded as before. The new macro definition is

```
        .MACRO  CVTSL    NUM_DIGITS,LSN,LONG,TESTOVFL,?LBL
        SUBL2   #16,SP
        CVTSP   NUM_DIGITS,LSN,NUM_DIGITS,(SP)
        CVTPL   NUM_DIGITS,(SP),LONG
        .IF     NOT_BLANK  TESTOVFL
        BVC     LBL
        CLRL    LONG
        .ENDC
LBL:    ADDL2   #16,SP
        .ENDM   CVTSL
```

Note that the actual argument specified for TESTOVFL is irrelevant; all that matters is whether or not it is null. Two expansions are shown below.

```
        CVTSL    #3,(R8),R6                    CVTSL    #3,(R8),R6,OVFL

        SUBL2    #16,SP                        SUBL2    #16,SP
        CVTSP    #3,(R8),#3,(SP)               CVTSP    #3,(R8),#3,(SP)
        CVTPL    #3,(SP),R6                    CVTPL    #3,(SP),R6
30003$: ADDL2    #16,SP                        BVC      30003$
                                               CLRL     R6
                                      30003$:  ADDL2    #16,SP
```

Note that the label 30003$ appears in the first expansion even though the condition tested was false and the BVC instruction is not included. This is because the statement containing the label is outside the range of the .IF block. (For these examples we have arbitrarily assumed that the next local label to be created was 30003$.)

Notice the difference between the two conditional tests, .IF and BVC, in Example 11.18. One is done at assembly time, and one *may* be done at execution time. The fourth actual argument is tested by the assembler, at assembly time, to determine whether or not it is null. The assembler does not test for overflow. If the fourth argument is not null, the assembler merely inserts the BVC and CLRL instructions in the program, and the CPU will perform the overflow test when the program is executed.

If the range of an .IF directive contains only one statement, a shorter form can be used. It is called the immediate conditional assembly directive and the format is

.IIF *condition   arguments(s),statement*

The .ENDC directive is not used with .IIF, since it is not needed to mark the end of the conditional block. Example 11.19 illustrates the use of .IIF and the IDENTICAL and DIFFERENT conditions.

Example 11.19: CVT2S Macro

This macro converts an integer from two's complement to leading separate numeric. The two's complement operand may be a byte, word, or longword. Temporary scratch space on the stack is used for both the packed decimal and longword forms of the integer. Note the use of displacement mode addressing to refer to the packed decimal datum on the stack.

```
        .MACRO  CVT2S    DATUM,NUM_DIGITS,LSN,TYPE=L
        SUBL2   #20,SP
        .IIF    IDN   TYPE,L,    MOVL        DATUM,(SP)
        .IIF    DIF   TYPE,L,    CVT'TYPE'L  DATUM,(SP)
        CVTLP   (SP),NUM_DIGITS,4(SP)
        CVTPS   NUM_DIGITS,4(SP),NUM_DIGITS,LSN
        ADDL2   #20,SP
        .ENDM   CVT2S
```

As Example 11.19 illustrates, often we want one sequence of statements assembled if a condition holds and another sequence if the opposite condition holds. The VAX assembler allows us to specify both alternatives by using the .IF_FALSE directive in a conditional block structured as follows:

.IF   *condition   argument(s)*

[*statements to be assembled if condition is true*]

.IF_FALSE

[*statements to be assembled if condition is false*]

.ENDC

The action of a conditional block using .IF_FALSE is similar to an if-then-else statement in a high-level language.

.IRP—The Indefinite Repeat Block Directive

The indefinite repeat block is the most useful of the conditional assembly looping directives. It causes the assembler to generate the same sequence of statements several times, with a parameter that varies each time the statements are generated. The format of an indefinite repeat block is

.IRP   *formal_repeat_arg,<actual_arguments>*

[*range*   ]

.ENDR

The formal repeat argument may be any symbol, though it should not be one of the formal arguments of the macro. It may be used throughout the range. The actual arguments for the .IRP block are often formal arguments of the macro, though they may be other strings. The assembler will take each actual argument in turn and substitute it for the formal repeat argument throughout the range of the block. If the actual arguments for the .IRP are formal arguments of the macro, the assembler will be substituting the actual macro arguments for them, so the effect is to cause the range to be assembled for each of several actual macro arguments.

An indefinite repeat block is used below in Example 11.20, but before we examine the example, we will describe one of the new directives it uses, and extend our earlier explanation of the listing directives.

.NARG—The Number-of-Arguments Directive

In some macros, it is useful to have access to the number of actual arguments specified when the macro is invoked. The .NARG (Number of ARGuments) directive, whose format is

.NARG   *symbol*

sets the value of the symbol to the number of actual arguments.

.SHOW and .NOSHOW—Listing Control Directives

In Section 11.2 we indicated that the .SHOW and .NOSHOW directives with the argument MEB can be used to control whether or not the program listing shows statements in the macro expansion—specifically those that cause code to be inserted in the object file. It is often helpful, especially when debugging macro definitions, to see the conditional assembly directives. If .SHOW is specified with the argument ME, then the entire macro expansion, not just the statements that generate code in the object file, will show in the listing. (For other options of .SHOW and .NOSHOW, consult the *VAX MACRO and Instruction Set Reference Manual*.)

Example 11.20: CALL Macro

This CALL macro can be used to call a procedure with up to ten arguments.

```
        .MACRO   CALL     PROC ARG1,ARG2,ARG3,ARG4,ARG5,ARG6,-
                          ARG7,ARG8,ARG9,ARG10,?LBL
        .IRP     ARG,<ARG10,ARG9,ARG8,ARG7,ARG6,ARG5,ARG4,-
                 ARG3,ARG2,ARG1>
        .IIF     NOT_BLANK  <ARG>,     PUSHAB   ARG
        .ENDR
        .NARG    N'LBL
        CALLS    #N'LBL-1,PROC
        .ENDM    CALL
```

Note that long statements may be continued to a second line by putting a hyphen at the end of the line to be continued.

The formal macro arguments used as arguments in the indefinite repeat block are listed in reverse order, so that the addresses of the (nonnull) arguments will be stacked in the proper order. Note how the indefinite repeat loop and the NOT_BLANK conditional are used together, so that a PUSHAB instruction is generated for each nonnull procedure argument. The same technique is used in the DUMPLONG macro (see Appendix D) to generate instructions to dump each argument specified by the user.

Note that we concatenated a local label onto the letter "N" to generate a symbol for use in the .NARG and CALLS statements. The symbol appears as N30000$ and N30001$ in the two expansions shown in Fig. 11.7.

The formal repeat argument ARG is enclosed in angle brackets in the .IIF statement because, without the brackets, the assembler misinterprets the statement in cases when ARG is null.

.IRPC and .REPEAT—Other Loop Directives

The .IRPC (Indefinite RePeat block with Character parameter) directive is very similar to the .IRP directive. The actual arguments that get substituted for the formal repeat block argument throughout the range of the .IRPC are the individual characters of a specified string. The format of the .IRPC directive is

.IRPC *formal_repeat_arg,<string>*

For relatively simple situations where the same sequence of instructions must be assembled a fixed number of times, the .REPEAT directive may be used. Its form is

(a) Showing conditional directives

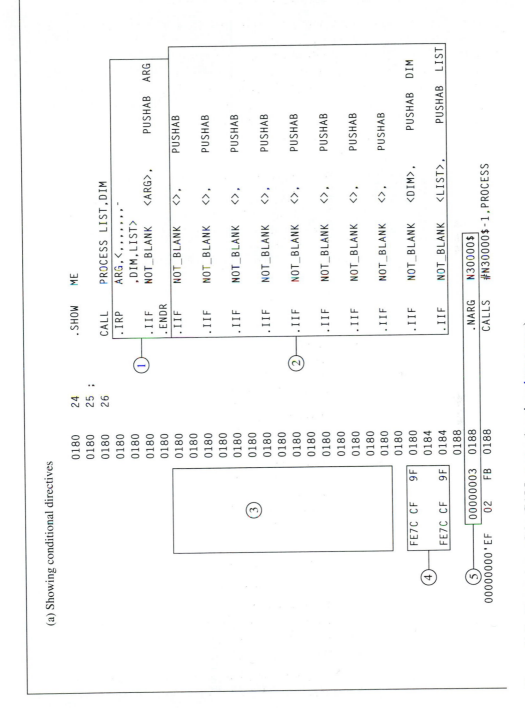

Figure 11.7 Expansions of the CALL macro (continued next page)

(b) Showing only lines that generate code

```
                   018F    28        .SHOW    MEB
                   018F    29        CALL     PROCESS LIST,DIM
        FE6D CF  9F 018F             .IIF     NOT_BLANK   <DIM>,    PUSHAB  DIM
        FE6D CF  9F 0193             .IIF     NOT_BLANK   <LIST>,   PUSHAB  LIST
00000000;EF  02  FB 0197             CALLS    #N30001$-1,PROCESS
```

6

1. The .IPR loop is shown with the arguments to be substituted for the formal repeat argument.
2. The expansion of the .IRP loop.
3. The condition is false, so no object code is generated here.
4. Object code is generated.
5. The value of N30000$ is 3.
6. A new local label was generated for the second macro expansion.

Figure 11.7 (concluded.)

.REPEAT *expression*

The expression indicates how many times the statements in the range should be processed by the assembler. It must be absolute and contain no undefined symbols.

The range for both the .IRPC and .REPEAT directives must be terminated with .ENDR.

Labels in Repeat Blocks

In Section 11.4 we considered a problem of using labels in macro definitions: the same label may not appear on more than one statement in a program module. Local labels created by the assembler solve the problem most of the time, since the assembler creates a new local label for each formal label name each time the macro is invoked. But if a label appears on a statement in the range of a repeat block, the same label may appear on many statements in the expansion. Consider the macro in Example 11.21; it attempts to compute the absolute values of up to four arguments. An expansion, with error messages, is shown in Fig. 11.8. Only the first two lines in Fig. 11.8 appeared in the program; the rest are the lines inserted by the assembler.

Example 11.21: Using Local Labels Incorrectly

```
        .MACRO   ABSVALS A1,A2,A3,A4,T=L,?LBL
        .IRP     DATUM,<A1,A2,A3,A4>
        .IF      NOT_BLANK   DATUM
        TST'T    DATUM
        BGEQ     LBL
        MNEG'T   DATUM,DATUM
LBL:    .ENDC
        .ENDR
        .ENDM    ABSVALS
```

How can we solve this problem? How can we repeatedly generate a similar sequence of instructions that contains a label, but get a different label each time? One solution, at least for the task in the macro ABSVALS, is not to use ABSVALS at all, but instead use the ABS macro of Example 11.12 repeatedly. Each time ABS is invoked, a new local label is created. Another solution, generally a better one, is to write a new macro definition containing the range of the repeat block, and to modify the repeat block in the incorrect macro so that it contains only an instruction that invokes the new macro. In the case of ABSVALS, we can use the already written ABS macro (Example 11.12) as the "new" macro, and rewrite ABSVALS to invoke ABS in the .IRP loop. The local label is now in another macro, and each time it is invoked from within the repeat block, a new label will be created. Example 11.22 incorporates this idea.

Example 11.22: ABSVALS Using ABS

```
        .MACRO   ABSVALS A1,A2,A3,A4,T=L
        .IRP     DATUM,<A1,A2,A3,A4>
        .IIF     NOT_BLANK   DATUM,    ABS    DATUM,DATUM,T
        .ENDR
        .ENDM    ABSVALS
```

Notice that the arguments for ABS are a formal repeat block argument (DATUM) and a
formal macro argument for ABSVALS (T). They will be replaced by actual arguments for
ABSVALS (or the default "L" for T). The following listing segment shows an expansion of
ABSVALS. (Only the first two lines appeared in the program; the rest are inserted by the
assembler.)

```
        .SHOW    MEB
        ABSVALS R4,R5,R6
        MOVL        R4,R4
        BGEQ            30001$
        MNEGL       R4,R4
30001$:
        MOVL        R5,R5
        BGEQ            30002$
        MNEGL       R5,R5
30002$:
        MOVL        R6,R6
        BGEQ            30003$
        MNEGL       R6,R6
30003$:
```

```
                                    0065    17          .SHOW    MEB
                                    0065    18          ABSVALS R4,R5,R6
                       54    D5     0065                TSTL    R4
                       11    18     0067                BGEQ        30000$
                 54    54    CE     0069                MNEGL   R4,R4
                                    006C        30000$:    .ENDC
%MACRO-E-SYMOUTPHAS, Symbol out of phase
                                    006C
                       55    D5     006C                TSTL    R5
                       FC    18     006E                BGEQ        30000$
                 55    55    CE     0070                MNEGL   R5,R5
                                    0073        30000$:    .ENDC
%MACRO-E-MULDEFLBL, Multiple definition of label        !
                                    0073
%MACRO-E-SYMOUTPHAS, Symbol out of phase
                                    0073
                       56    D5     0073                TSTL    R6
                       FC    18     0075                BGEQ        30000$
                 56    56    CE     0077                MNEGL   R6,R6
                                    007A        30000$:    .ENDC
%MACRO-E-MULDEFLBL, Multiple definition of label        !
                                    007A
```

Figure 11.8   Expansion of incorrect ABSVALS

.ERROR—A Directive to Display Error Messages

The .ERROR directive directs the assembler to display an error message at the terminal and include it in the program listing. It is particularly useful in macro definitions where conditional assembly directives may be used to test actual macro arguments to see that they are of the required form. A simplified format of the directive is

.ERROR   ; *message to be displayed*

Note that the error message is written as a comment. (This is a peculiarity of the VAX assembly language; it is not typical.)

.MEXIT—Macro Exit Directive

The .MEXIT directive may be used to terminate a macro expansion before reaching the .ENDM directive, or to terminate expansion of a repeat loop. If the assembler encounters .MEXIT inside a repeat loop, it will exit the loop and continue expanding the macro at the statement that follows the .ENDR. If it encounters .MEXIT outside a loop, it will exit the macro definition altogether.

Example 11.23: Using .ERROR and .MEXIT

Suppose that we want a macro definition to check that the type Q (quadword) is not specified as an actual argument in a macro that works only for B, W, and L. This could be done as follows:

```
.IF      IDENTICAL  TYPE,Q
.ERROR                          ; Q is an invalid type.
.MEXIT
.ENDC
```

If the condition is satisfied (i.e., if the type argument is Q) the error message will be displayed; the assembler will exit the macro definition and continue assembly at the statement that follows the macro instruction that was being expanded.

11.7 STRING FUNCTIONS

The VAX assembler has three string-processing functions that may be used to examine and manipulate character strings during macro expansion. Each function returns a number or a character string as its value. They may be used any place in a macro definition where the statement that results from substituting the function value would be a legal statement. Each function name begins with a percent sign to distinguish them from symbols.

The LENGTH Function

The format of the LENGTH function is

%LENGTH(*string*)

Its value is the length of (number of characters in) the string. The string may be a macro argument or a delimited string. (It may be a formal repeat block argument that is replaced by a macro argument or other string.)

The value of the length function may be assigned to a symbol and tested using conditional assembly.

Example 11.24: Using %LENGTH

Suppose that the macro WORK must process a character string argument but cannot handle strings with more than, say, eight characters. The following statements illustrate how a symbol can be set to the proper length for use in subsequent statements. (Recall that conditions like GREATER have one argument, not two; they compare the argument to zero.)

```
.MACRO  WORK     ARG,?LOCLBL
L'LOCLBL = %LENGTH(ARG)
.IIF    GREATER    L'LOCLBL-8,    L'LOCLBL = 8
```

The EXTRACT Function

The purpose of the EXTRACT function is to extract a substring from a character string. Its format is

$$\%EXTRACT(start\_position, length, string)$$

The string argument is the string from which the substring is to be extracted. It may be a macro argument or a delimited string (or a formal repeat block argument that is replaced by either of these). The start position and the length may be specified by decimal numbers or symbols. (Expressions and symbols made up using the concatenation operator with a generated local label are not permitted. These restrictions in the VAX macro processor are sometimes inconvenient, as we shall see in examples. Macro processors for some other machines allow more flexibility.) Positions in a character string are numbered left to right beginning with position 0. Thus, for example, the string "CLASS SCHEDULE" has C's in positions 0 and 7, S's in positions 3, 4, and 6, and a space in position 5.

Example 11.25: %EXTRACT

The value of %EXTRACT(0,5,<CLASS SCHEDULE>) is the character string "CLASS". The value of %EXTRACT(8,3,<CLASS SCHEDULE>) is the character string "HED".

The macro definition begun in Example 11.24 assigns to L'LOCLBL the smaller of eight and the length of the actual argument. It would seem natural to use %EXTRACT(0,L'LOCLBL,ARG) to extract the argument or its first eight characters if its length is greater than eight. Unfortunately, L'LOCLBL is not a valid argument for %EXTRACT. We could rewrite Example 11.24 using a symbol, say LENXXX, in place of L'LOCLBL, then use %EXTRACT(0,LENXXX,ARG) as needed.

The DUMPLONG macro prints only eight characters for the name of each of its arguments. It uses %EXTRACT to extract the first eight characters of the name (or the entire name if it has fewer characters). (See Appendix D for the macro definition.)

The LOCATE Function

The LOCATE function searches a string for a specified substring and returns its position if it is found. Its format is

$$\%LOCATE(target,string)$$

or

$$\%LOCATE(target,string,start\_position)$$

The target is the string to be searched for; the second argument is the string to be searched. These arguments may be macro arguments or delimited strings (or formal repeat block arguments). If the third argument, start_position, is omitted, the search begins at the beginning (position 0) of the string. If a start_position is specified, the search begins at that position in the string. Start_position may be a decimal number or a symbol. The value returned by %LOCATE is the number of the position where the target begins in the string. If the target is not found, the value returned is the length of the string searched. (Since position numbers start at 0, the length is one position past the last character in the string.)

Example 11.26: %LOCATE

The value of %LOCATE(<MA>,<GAMMA,SIGMA>) is 3.
The value of %LOCATE(<MA>,<GAMMA,SIGMA>,4) is 9.
The value of %LOCATE(<MAA>,<GAMMA,SIGMA>) is 11.

To determine whether or not a target string has been found, the following conditional block may be used.

.IF   NE   %LOCATE(target,string)–%LENGTH(string)

[*statements to assemble if target was found*]

.ENDC

Example 11.27: Using %LOCATE

Suppose that we wish to make sure that the actual argument specified for the formal argument TYPE is a B, W, or L. Example 11.23 showed how to determine if the argument was a Q, but not how to detect any other invalid character easily. The following conditional block illustrates a useful technique.

```
.IF     EQ     %LOCATE(TYPE,<BWL>)-3
.ERROR                    ; Bad type used in macro
.MEXIT
.ENDC
```

Example 11.28: Extracting Pieces of an Argument

This example illustrates how the string functions can be used together to extract individual items from a macro argument that consists of a list of items separated by commas. The macro PIECES extracts each item from the list, then invokes another macro, PROCESS, to process the item in some way.

The organization of the macro is approximately described by the following **while** loop.

while not end-of-list **do begin**
    find position of next comma;
    extract next item;
    process that item
end

The .REPEAT directive is used, along with .IF, to control the loop and limit the number of iterations to ten.

```
.MACRO  PIECES  LIST
SXXX = 0                          ; Start position for search
.REPEAT 10
.IF     GREATER_EQUAL   SXXX-%LENGTH(LIST)
.MEXIT
.ENDC
COMXXX = %LOCATE(<,>,LIST,SXXX) ; Position of next comma
LENXXX = COMXXX-SXXX             ; Length of next item
PROCESS %EXTRACT(SXXX,LENXXX,LIST)
SXXX = COMXXX+1                  ; New start position
.ENDR
.ENDM   PIECES
```

The symbols SXXX, COMXXX, and LENXXX are used instead of letters concatenated with a created local label (like N'LBL in Example 11.20) because the position and length arguments for the string functions must be a number or symbol. The concatenation operator is not permitted.

For simplicity in the sample listings, the macro PROCESS just generates an instruction to increment its argument. Its definition is

```
.MACRO  PROCESS ITEM
INCL    ITEM
.ENDM   PROCESS
```

The listing in Fig. 11.9 illustrates an expansion of the PIECES macro; it shows the conditional assembly. Notice that there are two pairs of angle brackets around the actual argument on the PIECES macro. The first is removed by the assembler when it substitutes the actual argument for the formal argument LIST. The second is needed so that the commas in the actual argument do not confuse the string functions. The listing may be a little difficult to read; the notes should help.

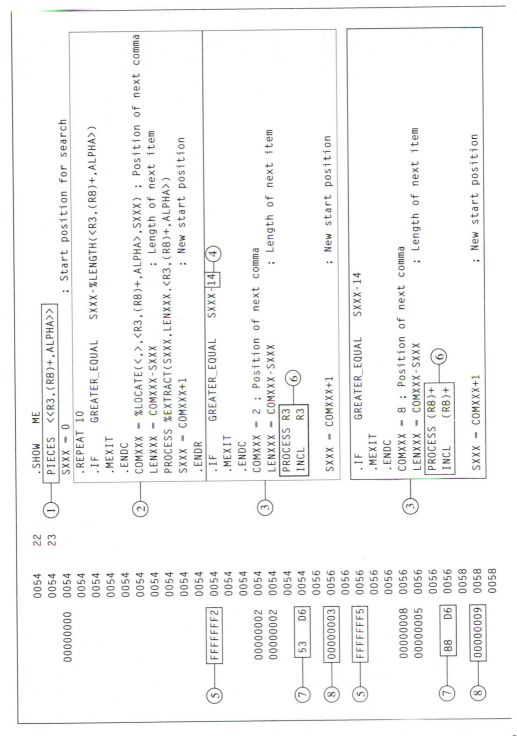

Figure 11.9 Expansion of the PIECES macro showing conditional assembly (continued next page)

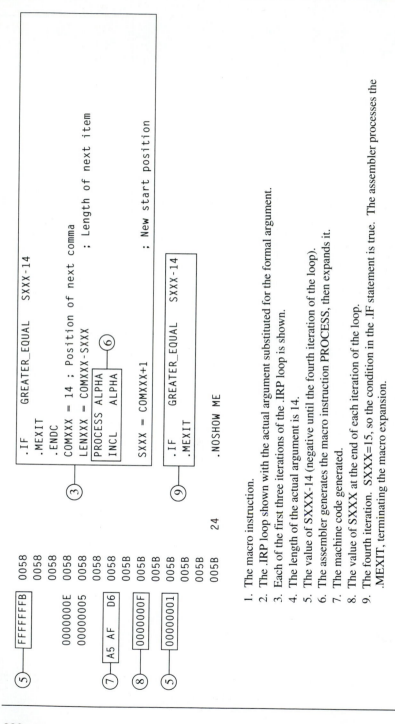

```
          ┌──────────┐
  5   0058 │FFFFFFFB  │      .IF      GREATER_EQUAL   SXXX-14
      0058 └──────────┘       .MEXIT
      0058                     .ENDC
      0058 0000000E            COMXXX = 14 ; Position of next comma
      0058 00000005            LENXXX = COMXXX-SXXX         ; Length of next item
      0058                          ┌─────────────┐
      0058 ┌────────┐          PROCESS ALPHA      │
  7   005B │A5 AF D6│          INCL   ALPHA      ⑥│
      005B └────────┘                 └────────────┘
      005B ┌────────┐
  8   005B │0000000F│          SXXX = COMXXX+1              ; New start position
      005B └────────┘
      005B ┌────────┐
  5   005B │00000001│          .IF      GREATER_EQUAL   SXXX-14
      005B └────────┘          .MEXIT
      005B
      005B
  24  005B                     .NOSHOW ME
```

1. The macro instruction.
2. The .IRP loop shown with the actual argument substituted for the formal argument.
3. Each of the first three iterations of the .IRP loop is shown.
4. The length of the actual argument is 14.
5. The value of SXXX-14 (negative until the fourth iteration of the loop).
6. The assembler generates the macro instruction PROCESS, then expands it.
7. The machine code generated.
8. The value of SXXX at the end of each iteration of the loop.
9. The fourth iteration. SXXX=15, so the condition in the .IF statement is true. The assembler processes the .MEXIT, terminating the macro expansion.

Figure 11.9 (concluded)

320

Here is the listing showing only the generated instructions.

```
             0054    22      .SHOW    MEB
             0054    23      PIECES   <<R3,(R8)+,ALPHA>>
    53   D6  0054            INCL     R3
    88   D6  0056            INCL     (R8)+
 A5 AF   D6  0058            INCL     ALPHA
             005B    24      .NOSHOW  MEB
```

11.8 SUMMARY

The macro facility of an assembly language allows a programmer to use a single statement to refer to a sequence of assembly language statements. The use of arguments and conditional assembly allows the instructions to be varied each time the macro is used. Like procedures, macros can make a program clearer, more modular, and easier to write. Unlike procedures, the actual instructions to be assembled or executed by a macro are inserted directly into the program and appear in the object file each time the macro is used.

The actual macro arguments specified in a macro instruction are directly substituted for the corresponding formal argument names used throughout the macro definition. The actual arguments may be specified positionally or with keywords (the formal argument names). Default values may be specified in the macro definition and will be used if the programmer does not specify an actual argument value when using the macro.

Instructions in macros may be varied by concatenating arguments onto other strings in the macro definition.

Ordinary labels cannot always be used in macros because the same label must not appear on more than one statement within one module. Local labels are generated by the assembler for use in macros; each time a macro using a local label is expanded, the assembler generates a distinct label.

If scratch space is needed in a macro, the user stack may be used.

Macro definitions may include conditional assembly directives. These are directives that tell the assembler to test various conditions and assemble certain statements depending on the results. The assembler may be given other directions; for example, it may be told to repeat assembly of some statements, to terminate expansion of a macro if specified conditions hold, and so on. To use conditional assembly correctly, it is crucial to remember that the assembler can test only properties that are known at assembly time. The VAX macro processor has three string functions, %LENGTH, %EXTRACT, and %LOCATE, that are particularly useful with conditional assembly.

11.9 EXERCISES

1. Write a macro that interchanges two longword data.
2. Write a macro that interchanges two data. Assume that the data are both of the same type (B, W, L, or Q) and let the type be an argument.

3. We pointed out that the last argument for the SUM macro (Example 11.3) could not be specified in autoincrement mode. Give two other addressing modes that would not be correct for that argument.

4. Write a macro definition for a macro called CVTLQ that converts its first argument from longword to quadword and puts the result in the second argument. It should leave the condition codes set to indicate the sign of the result. In other words, CVTLQ should act like the existing VAX instructions that convert between the various integer data types. Indicate what addressing modes may be used for the two macro arguments. (The list of valid modes for the second argument may be quite short.)

5. Suppose that we want to use the CALL macro from Example 11.4 to call a procedure PROC whose arguments are located as follows: The address of the first argument is in R7, the second argument is in memory at the location labeled ALPHA, and the third argument is an array named ARRAY. Write the CALL macro instruction to call the procedure.

6. What addressing modes will cause errors if used in the actual arguments for the CALL macro in Example 11.4? Explain why.

7. Write a macro definition for a macro called JOINSTRINGS with three arguments: STR1, STR2, and LENGTH. The macro is to copy the second string to the end of the first one. Both strings are in memory, and both have the same length. You may assume that the actual arguments for the strings are labels and the length is just a number.

8. Could a symbol be used as the second actual argument for the RESERVE macro (Example 11.6)? Why or why not?

9. Write a macro definition with the following header:

```
.MACRO  MOD     DIVISOR,DIVIDEND,REMAINDER
```

MOD should compute the remainder when the divisor is divided into the dividend, and store it in REMAINDER. You may assume that all arguments will be longwords.

10. One use of macros is to emulate assembly language instructions from other computers. In this exercise you are to write macros to emulate two instructions in the assembly language used on IBM mainframes. In the IBM assembly language, registers are specified by just their number, and for most instructions, the destination operand is the first operand. For example, the instruction

```
        A       5,ALPHA
```

adds the (longword) integer at ALPHA (in memory) into register 5.

(a) The IC (Insert Character) instruction copies a byte from the memory location specified by its second operand into the right end of the register specified by the first operand. The general form is

```
        IC      reg,source
```

Write a macro definition for a macro called IC that would work on the VAX and do what the IBM IC instruction does.

(b) Write a macro definition for the IBM Subtract Registers instruction which has the form

```
        SR      reg1,reg2
```

It subtracts the (longword) contents of reg2 from reg1.

11. Write a macro definition for a macro called PUSH that will push a byte, word, longword, or quadword onto the stack and correctly adjust the stack pointer (SP). Write a POP macro with similar specifications.

12. Consider the following macro definition:

```
        .MACRO  PRINTCHRS STRING,LENGTH=#85
        CVTWL   LENGTH,-(SP)
        PUSHAB  STRING
        CALLS   #2,PTCHRS
        .ENDM   PRINTCHRS
```

Show the macro expansion for

(a) PRINTCHRS LINE+8,R4   (b) PRINTCHRS RECORD

13. The PRINTCHRS macro shown in Exercise 12 calls a procedure PTCHRS to actually print the line. Assuming that PRINTCHRS has set up the arguments properly, describe the argument list expected by PTCHRS. (It is not in the standard argument list format.)

14. Why is it better for the I/O macros to call procedures to do their work rather than have the instructions in the macros themselves?

15. Referring to Exercise 20 in Chapter 6 and to the *VAX MACRO and Instruction Set Reference Manual* or the *VAX Architecture Handbook* for information on adding quadwords, write a macro definition for a macro called ADDQ2 that adds two quadwords. You may assume that the actual arguments will be specified by symbols.

16. Write a macro definition for the macro RANGE described in Example 11.7.

17. List several addressing modes that will work correctly as actual arguments for SOURCE and DEST in the ABS macro (Example 11.12). List several that would not be correct for DEST.

18. In the PRINTMSG macro defined in Example 11.13, why is the character string argument stored in memory with an .ASCIZ directive instead of on the stack?

19. What would happen if the PRINTMSG macro in Example 11.13 were used without an argument? Would it generate an assembly-time error, an execution-time error, or no error? If the latter, what would it print?

20. Write a macro definition for a macro SETREG that moves into each register Rn the longword n, for $0 \le n \le 10$. The macro definition should be short; it should not have a separate statement for each register.

21. For each situation described below, state whether or not it is an error. If the answer depends on information not given, explain in what cases it would be an error, and state whether the error would be detected by the assembler, the linker, or neither.
    (a) The number of actual macro arguments specified on a macro instruction is not the same as the number of formal arguments listed in the macro definition.
    (b) The directive .IF IDENTICAL R5,R9 is used in a macro definition to test if R5 and R9 contain the same number.
    (c) A macro uses scratch space on the stack, but does not pop the space from the stack when done.
    (d) Two procedures in separate files that will be linked as part of one program each have a (different) macro definition with the same macro name.

22. (a) Write a macro definition for a macro BZERO with two arguments, an integer and a type. The macro should generate instructions to cause a branch to the label ZERO if the integer, of the specified type, is zero. The actual argument for the integer will be specified like an instruction operand. The macro should work for types B, W, and L.
    (b) Write the macro again, but this time it should work for type Q, as well as all the types above. You may assume that if the type is Q, the datum is specified by a label. (Note that there is no TSTQ instruction.)

23. (a) Suppose that the following statements appear in a macro definition. What is the value of CNT when the assembler reaches the statement labeled NEXT (assuming that CNT does not appear in any other statements not shown)?

```
CNT = 0
        MOVL    #10,R5
LOOP:
          . . .
        CNT = CNT+1
        SOBGTR  R5,LOOP
NEXT:
```

    (b) Suppose that the following statements appear in a macro definition. What is the value of CNT when the assembler reaches the statement labeled NEXT (assuming that CNT does not appear in any other statements not shown)?

```
CNT = 0
        .REPEAT 10
          . . .
        CNT = CNT+1
        .ENDR
NEXT:
```

24. Suppose that there were no .NARG directive. Rewrite the definition of the CALL macro (Example 11.20) using direct assignments to count the procedure arguments.

25. Write a macro definition for a PUSH macro that pushes each of its arguments onto the stack. Assume that there may be any number of arguments up to ten and that all the arguments are longwords. The arguments should be pushed in the order listed.

26. Write a macro definition for a macro called ARGLIST that sets up a procedure argument list in the standard form in general memory for a procedure with at most ten arguments. Let the formal arguments for ARGLIST be LABEL, ARG1, ARG2, ... , ARG10, where LABEL is to be the label on the procedure argument list and ARG1, ... , ARG10 are the procedure arguments (all of which, you may assume, are address expressions). The number of arguments for the procedure is not an argument of ARGLIST.

27. Write a macro definition for a macro PRINTCTR that has a character string argument and prints the string centered on an 80-character line. A sample of the use of the macro instruction might be

```
        PRINTCTR <OUTPUT FROM TEST RUN>
```

(The macro definition may use PRINTCHRS.)

28. The purpose of the SUM macro below is to add the first three arguments and put the result in the fourth argument. It is a modification of the SUM macro in Example 11.5.

```
.MACRO   SUM      A,B,C,TOTAL,T=L
LXXX = %LENGTH(TOTAL)-1
.IF      IDN      +,%EXTRACT(LXXX,1,TOTAL)
ADD'T'3           A,B,%EXTRACT(0,LXXX,TOTAL)
.IF_FALSE
ADD'T'3           A,B,TOTAL
.ENDC
ADD'T'2           C,TOTAL
.ENDM    SUM
```

(a) Show the macro expansions for the following instructions. (Show only the machine instructions generated, not the conditional assembly statements.)

```
(1) SUM      #5,(R5)+,R7,ALPHA
(2) SUM      #5,R5,R7,(R10)+
(3) SUM      R4,R5,R6,BETA+8
(4) SUM      #1,X,Y,-(R7)
```

(b) Explain the purpose of the conditional assembly statements in SUM; in particular, explain how they make this version of SUM better than the one in Example 11.5.

(c) What addressing mode would cause unintended results if used for TOTAL?

29. What do you think will happen if %EXTRACT(0,N,STRING) is used in a macro definition where N is larger than the length of STRING? Will it generate an error

message? If not, what will be the value of %EXTRACT(0,N,STRING)? Write and assemble an experiment to check your hypothesis.

30. Write a macro definition for a macro ADDREGS whose first argument is a list of registers whose contents are to be added and whose second argument is the place where the sum is to be put. The registers in the first actual argument are to be separated by plus signs. For example:

```
ADDREGS R8+R2+R7,(R10)
```

The contents of the registers in the first argument should not be changed (unless one of them is specified as the second argument). You may assume that at most eight registers are added.

31. For this problem you are to write macro definitions that will replace IBM mainframe instuctions by VAX instructions that accomplish the same thing. Some of these macros will be more complicated than those in Exercise 10 (though we are simplifying the IBM instructions somewhat).

Here are the IBM instructions for which you will write macros:

IBM Format 1: Registers are specified by their number alone. A memory address may be specified by an expression or by displacement mode. [An example of displacement mode is 4(5); i.e., here too, the register, 5, is specified only by its number.]

L	reg,source	(Load. Copies the longword at source into the register.)
LA	reg,source	(Load Address. Puts the source address in the register.)
ST	reg,dest	(Store. Copies the register into the longword in memory at dest.)

IBM Format 2: For these you may assume that the branch destination is specified by an expression (as on the VAX).

B	dest	(Branch. Unconditional branch to dest.)
BE	dest	(Branch if Equal. Branch if the condition code is set for "equal.")
BCT	reg,dest	(Branch on CouNt. Subtract 1 from the register, branch to dest if result ≠ 0.)

Note that BCT does not behave quite the same as SOBGTR. BCT causes a branch if the result in the register is negative or positive (not zero); SOBGTR causes a branch only if it is positive.

IBM Format 3: In the character string instructions, the length is given as a constant in parentheses with the first operand. The string1 address will be specified by an expression. The string2 address may be specified by an expression or by displacement mode as described for Format 1.

       MVC string1(length),string2   (MoVe Characters. Copy string2 to string1.)

       CLC string1(length),string2   (Compare Characters. Compare strings, set
                                                        condition codes.)

A few examples

```
L     7,ALPHA
ST    5,2(10)
BCT   3,LOOP
MVC   THERE(100),HERE
```

Miscellaneous comments:

All the macros except B and BE will have two actual arguments. The macro processor recognizes a comma as a separator. THERE(100) would be treated by the macro processor as one argument.

Your macros should not have "side effects." IBM character instructions (e.g., MVC and CLC) do not use other registers for scratch work, but the VAX instructions MOVC3 and CMPC3 do.

Check your macro definitions. You do not have to link or run your test program; just assemble a program using a variety of IBM instructions, and look at your listing. (The sequence of instructions does not have to make any sense as a program.)

32. Most IBM mainframe instructions do not affect the condition codes. Among the instructions implemented in Exercise 31, only CLC does. Write (or revise) macro definitions for the instructions described in Exercise 31 so that the N and Z condition codes are the same after the expanded macro is executed as they were before, except of course for CLC, which must set the codes to show the result of the comparison.

12

Bit and Bit Field Operations

12.1 INTRODUCTION

For all the data types we have considered so far and the floating-point data we will consider in the next chapter, a string of eight or more bits forms a pattern that represents one datum. Instructions operate on the bit string as a unit. In this chapter we will study instructions that treat their operands as strings of independent bits or small groups of bits. Bit instructions that are commonly available on computers can shift bit strings, and test, set, clear, and complement individual bits or specified groups of bits within the operands. The bit strings may represent flags, sets, any of the usual data types, tables of small numbers packed together to save space, or anything else the programmer chooses to represent.

Many of the applications of bit instructions are in operating systems programming. Since we are not assuming that the reader is familiar with operating systems, we will mention only one or two such examples that are easy to explain and understand. The techniques illustrated in these and our other examples are useful in many applications.

We said in Chapter 1 that in some situations a programmer would use assembly language because the particular application or problem cannot be handled easily, or at all, in a high-level language. The kinds of problems for which the instructions in this chapter would be used are in that category, because many high-level languages do not allow easy manipulation of the individual bits within memory units. (The language C is an exception.) In addition to seeing how to do operations that are not done in many high-level languages, we will also see how some special data types and operations, such as the set data type in Pascal, can be implemented.

In Sections 12.2 and 12.3 we will present the VAX bit instructions that do the kinds of operations that are commonly available (though, as we have said before, the VAX instructions are more numerous and more flexible than usual). In Section 12.4 we will consider an application: the implementation of sets and set operations.

The VAX has a data type—variable-length bit fields—and instructions to operate on them, that are not available on most computers. The variable-length field instructions make some applications much easier than they would be using only the more commonly available bit operations. We will cover them in Section 12.5.

Certain terminology is used often with bit operations. A bit is *set*, or *on*, if its value is 1; a bit is *clear*, or *off*, if its value is 0. The *complement* of a bit is a bit with the opposite value. (That is, the complement of 0 is 1 and the complement of 1 is 0.) A *mask* is a pattern of bits in which the bits that are set indicate which bit positions (or data represented by them) are to be treated or operated on in some special way. For example, the bits that are set in a register mask indicate which registers are to be pushed on the stack. The masks used in this chapter indicate which bit positions in another operand are to be operated on by an instruction.

Recall that the notation for specifying a range of bit positions (in descriptions and documentation, not in machine instructions) is $l:r$, where l is the number of the leftmost bit in the range, and r is the number of the rightmost.

12.2 SIMPLE BIT OPERATIONS

In this section we will describe the VAX instructions to test, set, clear, and complement bits. For most of the instructions, one operand is a mask that specifies which bits in another operand are to be affected.

The BIT (BIt Test) instructions test specified bits in a bit string and set or clear the Z condition code to indicate whether or not all the bits tested are 0's. The instruction formats are

$$\text{BIT}x \qquad mask,bit\_string$$

where x = B, W, or L.

Example 12.1: Testing a Group of Bits

Suppose that we wish to determine if bits 13:5 in R9 are all zeros. The mask must contain 1's in positions 13:5 to indicate that those are the positions to be tested. We can construct the mask by marking these positions as shown in Fig. 12.1. The following instructions do the test and branch:

```
        BITL    #^X00003FE0,R9
        BEQL    ALL_ZERO
```

Since all the bits to be tested happen to be in the right-hand word of the register, we can use the following slightly simpler instruction for the bit test:

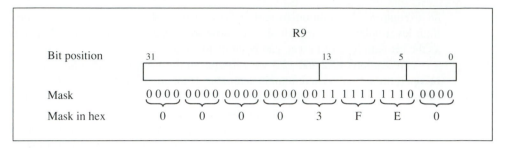

Figure 12.1   Constructing a mask for bits 13:5

```
BITW    #^X3FE0,R9
```

For this example, and in many applications, it is most convenient to specify the mask as a literal or immediate operand. Any radix may be used, but hex is usually best because it is a simple matter to convert between the bit pattern and its hex representation.

The group of bits acted on by the bit instructions do not have to be contiguous. If we wanted to determine if, say, all the odd-numbered bit positions in the longword PAIRS contain zeros, we could use the instruction

```
BITL    #^XAAAAAAAA,PAIRS
```

followed by an appropriate conditional branch.

The instructions to set, clear, and complement bits all have the same operand formats, so we consider them as a group. The instructions are

$$\left.\begin{matrix} \text{BIS} \\ \text{BIC} \\ \text{XOR} \end{matrix}\right\} x2 \quad mask,bit\_string \qquad \left.\begin{matrix} \text{BIS} \\ \text{BIC} \\ \text{XOR} \end{matrix}\right\} x3 \quad mask,source,dest$$

where x = B, W, or L. The instruction names are mnemonics for BIt Set, BIt Clear, and eXclusive OR. For all the instructions, the mask indicates which bits in the second operand are to be operated on; the other bits of the operand are unchanged. In the two-operand formats, the second operand is replaced by the result. In the three-operand formats, the result of performing the operation on the source is stored in the destination; the source is unchanged (unless it overlaps the destination). For all these instructions, the Z and N condition codes are set as they are for integer instructions. V is cleared and C is unchanged.

Example 12.2: Complementing Bits

Suppose that R7 contains 083E8AC1. After the instruction

```
XORL2   #^X0F003060,R7
```

R7 will contain 073EBAA1. The bits in positions 27:24, 13:12, and 6:5 have been complemented.

Example 12.3: Various Bit Operations

To turn off bit 15 in R4:

```
BICW2    #^X8000,R4
```

To turn off bit 15 in R4, but put the result in R8 (R4 is unchanged):

```
BICL3    #^X00008000,R4,R8
```

Note that the longword form of the instruction is needed here because BICW3 would copy only half the result to R8.

To set bits 22:18, complement bits 23 and 17, and clear the first and last byte in R10:

```
BISL2    #^X007C0000,R10     ; Set bits 22:18
XORL2    #^X00820000,R10     ; Complement bits 23 and 17
BICL2    #^XFF0000FF,R10     ; Clear end bytes
```

or, using only two instructions:

```
BISL2    #^XFF7C00FF,R10     ; Set bits 22:18 and first
                             ;   and last bytes
XORL2    #^XFF8200FF,R10     ; Complement bits 23 and 17
                             ;   and end bytes
```

Example 12.4: Converting a Digit from ASCII to Binary

In Section 7.6, when we converted integers from their character code representation to two's complement, we used a subtraction to clear the left nibble of the character code for each single digit. The result was the value of the digit in binary. The following instruction was used; R6 contained the address of the character to be processed and R10 was cleared before the conversion began.

```
SUBB3    #ZEROCODE,(R6)+,R10   ; Binary value of digit
```

We can accomplish the same thing, perhaps avoiding any confusion about why a subtraction is done and what amount to subtract, by using the following instruction instead:

```
BICB3    #^XF0,(R6)+,R10       ; Binary value of digit
```

Example 12.5: Returning a Condition Code from a Procedure

In Chapter 9 we indicated that a procedure can return flags to a calling program by setting any of the condition codes in the saved PSW that is stored in the call frame on the stack. Suppose that the procedure must set the Z bit. The saved PSW is in the first half of the second longword of the call frame, so the following instruction does the job.

```
BISB2    #^B00000100,4(FP)     ; Set saved Z bit
```

Logical Operations: AND, OR, EXCLUSIVE OR, Negation

Bits may be thought of as representing logical variables: A value of 1 represents TRUE, and a value of 0 represents FALSE. Thus the standard binary logical operations AND, denoted by $\wedge$ or $\cdot$, OR, denoted by $\vee$ or +, and EXCLUSIVE OR, denoted by $\oplus$, and the

AND	0	1
0	0	0
1	0	1

OR	0	1
0	0	1
1	1	1

$\oplus$	0	1
0	0	1
1	1	0

$\neg$	
0	1
1	0

Figure 12.2   Logical function tables

unary operation negation, or complement, denoted by $\neg$, may be performed on bits or strings of bits. The logical operations are defined by the tables of their values shown in Fig. 12.2.

Some computers provide bit instructions called AND, OR, and XOR (or some slight variation of these names) that perform the logical operations on bit strings. (The operations are defined on individual pairs of bits; when the operands are strings of bits, the operation is performed independently on bit pairs in corresponding positions in the two operands.) Although we described the VAX instructions as setting, clearing, and complementing bits, two of the instructions, BIS and XOR, do exactly the logical operations OR and EXCLUSIVE OR. BIC is very close to a logical AND. To see these connections more clearly, we will look at the bit operations again.

The following table summarizes the Bit Set operation.

BIT SET

Operand \ Mask	0 (No change)	1 (Set bit)
0	0	1
1	1	1

Now compare this table with the table in Fig. 12.2 that defines the OR operation. The two are exactly the same.

Similarly, let us look at the table for EXCLUSIVE OR in Fig. 12.2. Let the mask be the operand whose values are shown across the top of the table, and let the second operand be the one whose values are shown along the left side. Observe that in the column where the mask is 0, the results are identical to the values of the second operand;

in the column where the mask is 1, the bits of the second operand have been complemented. (Both OR and EXCLUSIVE OR are commutative operations, so it actually does not matter which operand we consider to be the mask.)

The table for the Bit Clear operation looks like this:

BIT CLEAR

	Mask	0 (No change)	1 (Clear bit)
Operand			
0		0	0
1		1	0

This is not the same as any of the logical operation tables shown in Fig. 12.2. However, the reader should easily verify that the Bit Clear operation is the same as a logical AND operation performed on the complement of the mask and the second operand.

The negation of a bit string is the same as its one's complement; the values of all the bits are reversed. The MOVe COMplemented instructions do this. The format is

$$\text{MCOM}x \qquad source,dest$$

where x = B, W, or L. The one's complement of the source is stored in the destination; the N and Z condition codes are affected in the same ways as by the other bit instructions described above. The effect of the MCOM instructions can be accomplished using XOR with a mask that consists entirely of 1's, so many computers will not have a special instruction for complementing.

Example 12.6: An AND Macro

In an application where a lot of logical operations are done, it may be convenient to have one instruction for the logical AND. We can define an AND macro as follows:

```
.MACRO  AND3    OP1,OP2,DEST,TYPE=L
MCOM'TYPE       OP1,-(SP)
BIC'TYPE'3      (SP)+,OP2,DEST
.ENDM   AND3
```

12.3 ROTATE AND SHIFT INSTRUCTIONS

Shift instructions move the bits within a register or memory location. Several kinds of shift instructions commonly are found on computers. *Logical shifts* treat all bit positions the same; none plays a special role. In *arithmetic shifts* the leftmost bit is considered as a sign bit and is treated differently than the others. In logical shifts the bits shifted out one end of the operand may be lost or they may be shifted into the other end; the latter are called *circular shifts*, or *rotations*.

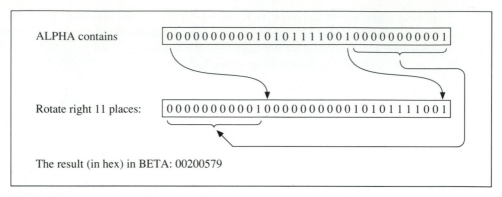

ALPHA contains   `0 0 0 0 0 0 0 0 0 0 1 0 1 0 1 1 1 1 0 0 1 0 0 0 0 0 0 0 0 0 0 1`

Rotate right 11 places: `0 0 0 0 0 0 0 0 0 0 1 0 0 0 0 0 0 0 0 0 0 1 0 1 0 1 1 1 1 0 0 1`

The result (in hex) in BETA: 00200579

Figure 12.3   An example of rotation

The VAX has a circular shift instruction, ROTL (ROTate Longword) and two arithmetic shift instructions, ASHL (Arithmetic SHift, Longword) and ASHQ (Arithmetic SHift, Quadword). The formats are

$$\left\{ \begin{array}{l} \text{ROTL} \\ \text{ASHL} \\ \text{ASHQ} \end{array} \right\} \textit{count,source,dest}$$

The first operand, *count*, is a byte that specifies the number of bit positions to shift and the direction of the shift. The number of positions is the absolute value of the count. The shift is to the left if the count is positive and to the right if it is negative.

The Rotate Instruction

ROTL works as follows, assuming for the purposes of the diagram that the shift is to the left and the number of positions to shift is *n*. A rotation to the right works similarly.

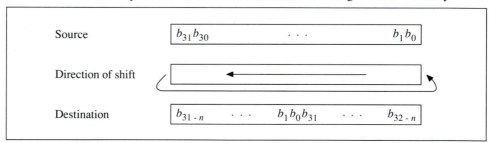

Source $b_{31}b_{30}$ $\cdots$ $b_1 b_0$

Direction of shift

Destination b_{31-n} $\cdots$ $b_1 b_0 b_{31}$ $\cdots$ b_{32-n}

ROTL sets or clears the Z and N condition codes to indicate whether the result is zero or negative. It clears V and leaves C unchanged.

Example 12.7: ROTL

Suppose that R7 contains 000013F5 and the longword at ALPHA contains 002BC801. Consider the following instruction:

```
ROTL    R7,ALPHA,BETA
```

In what direction is the rotation done? Remember that the count is a byte, so it is the rightmost byte of R7. Thus the count is F5, or -11_{10}, and the rotation is to the right. To determine the result correctly, it helps to write out the source in binary. Figure 12.3 shows the bits before and after the rotation. The Z, N, and V condition codes will be 0.

Example 12.8: Swapping Halves of a Register

To interchange the two words in R8:

```
ROTL    #16,R8,R8
```

Example 12.9: Extracting Bit Fields

Suppose that we must move bits 8:3 of R5 and bits 23:15 of R6 into the right end of R10, clearing the rest of R10. R5 and R6 should be unchanged. The result should be

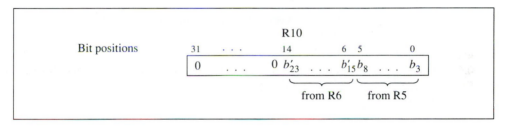

There are several ways to accomplish this task. One solution, assuming R2 is available for scratch work, is

```
BICL3    #^XFFFFFE07,R5,R10   ; Extract bits 8:3 from R5
ROTL     #-3,R10,R10          ; Move them to right end
BICL3    #^XFF007FFF,R6,R2    ; Extract 23:15 from R6
ROTL     #-9,R2,R2            ; Move to positions 14:6
BISL2    R2,R10               ; Combine the two segments
```

Example 12.10: Turning Off a Bit

See the procedure TURNOFF in Fig. 12.4. The techniques it uses are also useful for many other applications, some of which suggested in the exercises. We will see in Section 12.5 that the procedure can be made more efficient using the VAX's variable-length bit field instructions. However, since many machines do not have those instructions, the version in Fig. 12.4 is well worth studying.

Arithmetic Shifts

ASHL and ASHQ are called *arithmetic shifts* because they treat their source operands as two's complement integers, and the operations they do have the effects of multiplying and dividing by powers of 2. They affect the condition codes N, Z, and V as the integer arithmetic instructions do. Of course, these operations can be accomplished by using MUL and DIV instructions. On some computers the arithmetic shift instructions are more efficient, but a more important reason for having such instructions is that they are useful for general bit string manipulations. For this reason we include them here instead of in Chapter 6.

```
; PROCEDURE TURNOFF (BIT_STRING: longword, POSITION: byte)
;
; The procedure TURNOFF finds and turns off the rightmost bit
; that is on in its first argument. It returns the position
; number of the affected bit in its second argument.
; (If no bits are on, it returns 32.)
;
; METHOD
;
; A copy of the bit string is rotated to the right so that,
; until a 1 is found, each bit is tested when it is in the
; low bit position.
; The loop counter keeps track of the original position of the
; bit being tested and is used to construct a mask to turn the
; bit off in the original bit string.
;
; Offsets for argument list
STRING = 4
POSN = 8
;
; REGISTER USE
;
;       R6        bit string
;       R7        loop counter
;       R8        mask for turning off bit
;
        .ENTRY    TURNOFF,^M<R6,R7,R8>
;
        MOVL      @STRING(AP),R6        ; Get bit string
        BEQL      ZERO                  ; Branch if all bits off
        CLRL      R7                    ; Initialize loop counter
;
TEST:   BLBS      R6,FOUND              ; Test low bit
        ROTL      #-1,R6,R6             ; Get next bit
        AOBLEQ    #31,R7,TEST           ; Loop control
;
FOUND:  ROTL      R7,#1,R8              ; Move 1 to position
        BICL2     R8,@STRING(AP)        ; Turn off bit
        MOVB      R7,@POSN(AP)          ; Store position number
        RET                             ; Return
;
ZERO:   MOVB      #32,@POSN(AP)         ; Store position 32
        RET                             ; Return
        .END
```

Figure 12.4   The procedure TURNOFF

To see the connection between shifting and multiplication and division, consider ordinary decimal numbers. To multiply decimal integers by 10, or a power of 10, all we do is add zeros at the right end of the number. Division of a decimal integer by a power of 10 (with truncation) can be accomplished by erasing the appropriate number of digits from the right end of the number. Multiplying or dividing binary integers by powers of 2 is done similarly. Since an integer is located in a particular unit of memory or a register, we do not exactly add or erase digits at the right; we shift the number within its storage unit, dropping some bits off one end and filling the vacated bits at the other end. For multiplication, the shift is to the left and the vacated bits at the right are filled with zeros. For division, the shift is to the right and the vacated bits at the left are filled with copies of the sign bit. Thus, an ASHL instruction with a count of 3 has the effect of multiplying by 2^3, or 8; if the count is −6, the effect is to divide by 2^6, or 64.

The diagrams below illustrate the arithmetic shift operations.

Left arithmetic shift (multiplication by powers of 2):

Note that if any of the bits dropped from the left end of the operand are not equal to the original sign bit, or if the sign bit of the shifted result is not the same as the original sign, then the result, considered as a two's complement integer, has overflowed the allotted space and the V condition code will be set.

Right arithmetic shift (division by powers of 2):

Example 12.11: Arithmetic Shift

Suppose that the longword in memory at A1 contains FFFFF4A2 before the instruction

        ASHL   #-6,A1,A2

is executed. The longword at A1 will be shifted six places right. Examining the bit pattern in A1, we determine the result:

FFFFF4A2 =   11111111111111111111010010100010
Shift right, dropping
the rightmost six bits;
fill in 1's at the left: 11111111111111111111111111010010xxxxxx
Result in hex: FFFFFFD2

Thus FFFFFFD2 will be stored in the longword at A2. We can check this result by doing a division. Shifting right six places should correspond to dividing by 2^6, or 64. The longword in A1, FFFFF4A2, is -2910_{10}. Dividing by 64 give approximately -45.5_{10}. The integer division instructions truncate toward zero, so we might expect the result of the right shift to be -45_{10}. However, FFFFFFD2 is -46_{10}.

As Example 12.11 illustrates, an arithmetic right shift, interpreted as a division operation, will always truncate a negative result down, away from zero. Thus its effect is slightly different from the DIV instructions.

Sometimes masks for use in the bit instructions described in Section 12.2 must be constructed at execution time because the bit pattern needed is data-dependent. We will see an example of such an application in Section 12.4. Example 12.12 shows how a fairly general form of a mask may be constructed.

Example 12.12: Constructing Masks with ASHL

Suppose that we want to construct a mask that has n 1's beginning at bit position p; that is, bits $(p + n - 1){:}p$ should be 1's and all others 0's. The following sequence of instructions takes advantage of the fact that if the sign bit is 1, a right arithmetic shift fills the vacated bit positions with 1's. We use ASHL to generate the correct number of 1's, then use ROTL to move them into the correct positions. We assume that R6 contains n, R7 contains p, the mask is to be constructed in R8, and R3 is available for scratch work.

```
SUBB3   R6,#1,R3            ; Shift count = -(n-1)
ASHL    R3,#^X80000000,R8   ; Get n 1's
ADDB3   R6,R7,R3            ; p + n
ROTL    R3,R8,R8            ; Rotate 1's to p+n-1:p
```

After Section 12.5, this problem can be solved with only two instructions, but the method used here can be used with slight modifications on other machines that do not have variable-length bit field instructions.

12.4 EXAMPLE: SETS

Bit instructions are especially suited to doing set operations on sets represented as bit strings. We will assume that all the sets we operate on are subsets of a fixed universe set that has 32 elements. Each of the elements in the universe set is assigned an index between 0 and 31. Thus we can write

$$\text{universe} = \{x_0, x_1, x_2, \ldots, x_{29}, x_{30}, x_{31}\}$$

A set S is represented by a bit string in which each bit indicates whether or not the universe element with the same index is in S. In other words, S is represented by

$$b_{31}b_{30}b_{29} \cdots b_2b_1b_0$$

where

$$b_i = \begin{cases} 1 & \text{if } x_i \in S \\ \\ 0 & \text{if } x_i \notin S \end{cases}$$

For example, if the bit string for S is

$$00010000010111000100000010000001$$

then $S = \{x_0, x_7, x_{14}, x_{18}, x_{19}, x_{20}, x_{22}, x_{28}\}$.

The SET data type in Pascal is implemented in this way. The limit on the size of a Pascal set is usually the computer's word size or a small multiple of it. (VAX Pascal allows sets to have up to 256 elements and uses eight longwords for the representations.)

Suppose that we have reserved space for several sets, say, S, T, and V, and we have initialized S and T in some way. We will assume that the set names are the labels on the longwords that represent the sets. We would like to do the basic set operations: union, intersection, and complement, and various other useful operations.

An element is in the union of S and T if it is in either (or both) sets. Thus the union operation is a logical OR operation on the set representations and may be computed as follows:

```
        BISL3    S,T,V                ; V = S union T
```

(Either S or T could play the role of the mask, since OR is a commutative operation.)

The intersection of two sets contains all the elements that are in both sets, so it can be computed using a logical AND on the representations. The VAX does not have a logical AND instruction, but we can use the AND3 macro defined in Example 12.6 as follows:

```
        AND3     S,T,V                ; V = S intersect T
```

The complement of a set can be computed using MCOML.

There are several tests that we may want to do. For example, we may want to determine if two sets are equal, if one is a subset of the other, if a particular element is a member of a set, or if a set is empty. We may want to know how many elements are in a set.

Testing for equality of two sets may be done easily with the CMPL and BEQL (or BNEQ) instructions.

How can we determine if $S \subseteq T$? Certainly, we could write a loop that tests each bit of S in turn and checks whether each bit that is on in S is also on in T, but this would require several statements and as many as 32 passes through the loop. A much more efficient solution becomes obvious if we express the condition to be tested in another form:

$$S \subseteq T \quad \text{if and only if} \quad S \cup T = T$$

We leave it to the reader to write the instructions to test whether or not $S \cup T = T$.

Counting the elements of a set can be done using a loop similar to the one in the procedure in Fig. 12.4. It is left as an exercise, along with the other tests we mentioned above.

The task of initializing the bit string representing a set is more complicated than the set operations. The procedure in Fig. 12.5 initializes a set assuming that the universe set consists of the integers in the range 0 to 31, and the particular elements in the set being initialized are read in from the terminal in a free-format line. The procedure calls another procedure, GETNUM, to locate the input numbers within the line of characters and convert them to two's complement. GETNUM is described in Exercise 9.25.

```
; PROCEDURE SETUP (SET)
;
; This procedure initializes the longword argument SET as a
; bit string representation of the set of integers that are
; input in one line from the terminal.  The integers must
; be in the range 0 to 31.  The representation is such that
; bit i is on if and only if i is in the set.
;
; SETUP calls the procedure GETNUM to find each number in
; the input line and convert it to two's complement.  GETNUM
; returns a flag in R0 that is 1 if a number was found and
; converted, and 0 otherwise.  SETUP assumes that if GETNUM
; returns a 0 flag, all set elements have been processed.
;
; SETUP returns a success/failure flag in R0.  If the set
; is initialized without problems, R0 will contain 1.  If any
; of the numbers read are outside the range 0-31, R0 will
; contain 0 and the longword argument will not be filled.
;
LINE:    .BYTE   ^X20[81]            ; Space for input line
ARGS:    .LONG   4                   ; Argument list for GETNUM
         .BLKA   2                   ; For start and end addresses
         .ADDRESS NUMBER,RESTART
NUMBER:  .BLKL   1                   ; Set element
RESTART:.BLKA   1                    ; Where next search begins
;
; REGISTER USE
;
;        R6      the set representation
;        R7      mask
;
```

Figure 12.5 A procedure to initialize a set (continued next page)

```
                .ENTRY   SETUP,^M<R6,R7>
        ;
        ; Initialization
        ;
                CLRL     R6                 ; Set is empty to start
                READLINE LINE+1             ; Read set elements
                MOVAB    LINE,RESTART       ; Start addr. for first search
                ADDL3    #LINE+1,R0,ARGS+8  ; End address for input line
        ;
        ; Get next set element from input line.
        ;
        NEXT:   MOVL     RESTART,ARGS+4     ; Where next search begins
                CALLG    ARGS,GETNUM        ; Get next number from input
                BLBC     R0,DONE            ; Branch if set is complete
        ;
        ; Check that the number is in the correct range, 0 - 31.
        ;
                TSTL     NUMBER             ; Test sign of element number
                BLSS     BAD                ; Bad if negative
                CMPL     NUMBER,#31         ; Compare to upper limit
                BGTR     BAD                ; Bad if > 31
        ;
        ; Enter element in set.
        ;
                ASHL     NUMBER,#1,R7       ; Construct mask
                BISL2    R7,R6              ; Turn on bit in set
        ;
                BRB      NEXT               ; Go back for another
        ;
        ; Store set representation and set success/failure flag.
        ;
        DONE:   MOVL     R6,@4(AP)          ; Store the set representation
                MOVL     #1,R0              ; Set success flag
                RET                         ; Return
        ;
        BAD:    CLRL     R0                 ; Set failure flag
                RET                         ; Return
                .END
```

Figure 12.5   (concluded)

12.5 VARIABLE-LENGTH BIT FIELDS

The Data Format

A *variable-length bit field* is a string of 0 to 32 contiguous bits that does not necessarily begin on a byte boundary. Thus it may occupy zero to five contiguous bytes. Variable-length bit fields are useful for packing together several small data to save space, for working with bit tables, for manipulating (e.g., converting) data representations, and for various other kinds of applications.

The operations performed by the VAX bit field instructions can be accomplished by using appropriate combinations of other instructions presented so far (particularly some from Sections 12.2 and 12.3), but of course, the special-purpose instructions are more efficient than a sequence of several instructions. Also, the fact that these instructions can ignore byte, and even longword, boundaries is particularly handy for some applications.

Three operands are used to specify a variable-length bit field: a base address, an offset from that address, and a bit field size. The *base address* is the address of a byte in memory or is a register. The *offset*, or *position*, is the position of the first bit in the bit field relative to the first bit at the base address. That is, it is the number of bits (not bytes) separating the first bit of the bit field from the first bit of the byte at the base address. The offset is specified as a two's complement longword integer. Thus it can be positive or negative and can be quite large. The bit field *size* is the number of bits in the bit field. It is a byte operand.

Figure 12.6 illustrates how the three operands determine the bit field. Note that diagrams of bit fields show the lower-addressed bytes at the right, because VAX instructions treat memory as if the least significant bit, bit 0, is the first bit in a memory unit or register; thus bit 0 of the byte at address A (for any address A) follows immediately after the leftmost bit, bit 7, of the byte at $A-1$. The first bit of a bit field is its rightmost bit.

If a register, say Rn, is specified as the base address for a bit field and the field extends beyond bit 31 of Rn, it continues at bit 0 of R$n+1$. Thus, in diagrams, R$n+1$ is shown to the left of Rn.

In variable-length bit field machine instructions the three operands describing a bit field are always given in the following order:

$$position,size,base\_address$$

Reserved operand faults will occur for bit field instructions if the size is not in the range 0–32, or if a register is specified as the base address, the position is greater than 31, and the size is nonzero (i.e., if a nonnull field does not begin in the specified register). If $size = 0$, the bit field is empty, or null. Most of the instructions have a fairly natural interpretation for this case.

The "Find First" Instructions

The FFS (Find First Set bit) and FFC (Find First Clear bit) instructions scan a bit field (from right to left) and locate the first bit that is set or clear, depending on the instruc-

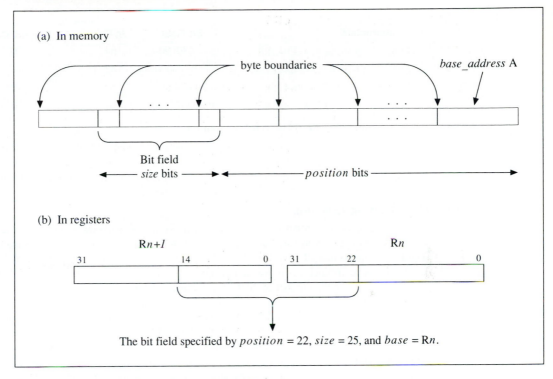

Figure 12.6 Specifying a variable-length bit field

tion. If such a bit is found, its position number is placed in the destination operand (a longword) and the Z condition code is cleared. The position is computed relative to the same base address that specifies the location of the bit field. If no bit in the desired state is found in the field, the position number of the bit following the end of (i.e., the bit to the left of) the bit field is put in the destination operand and Z is set. (As one should expect, if $size = 0$, Z is set and the destination is given the same value as the position operand.)

The instruction formats are

$$FFx \quad posn,size,base,dest$$

where $x =$ S or C.

Example 12.13: The Effects of FFS and FFC

Suppose that memory contents are as shown:

ALPHA

| F0 | 83 | 48 | 01 | 00 | 00 | 07 | FE | 24 | 44 | 00 | 89 |

Instruction		Bit Field	Results In R8	Z Cond. Code
FFS	#56,#24,ALPHA,R8	480100_{16}	64	0
FFS	#39,#3,ALPHA+2,R8	000_2	42	1
FFC	#0,#32,ALPHA,R8	24440089_{16}	1	0
FFC	#35,#10,ALPHA,R8	0011111111_2	43	0

Example 12.14: Improving the TURNOFF Procedure

In Section 12.3 we wrote a procedure TURNOFF (Fig.12.4) that finds the rightmost bit in a longword that is on, turns off the bit, and returns its position as an argument. The procedure in Fig. 12.7 uses the FFS instruction to find the bit. The search loop and some of the initialization of the earlier procedure have been eliminated.

Example 12.15: A Bit Table Disk Map

Problem: A bit table is often used by an operating system to keep track of whether or not each block on a disk is in use. Suppose that BLOCKS is the number of blocks on the disk. The blocks are numbered from 0 to BLOCKS–1. A disk map is a string of BLOCKS bits, where bit i is set if block i is in use and is clear if block i is free. The problem is to find the first clear bit, hence the number of the first disk block available for storing a file.

Discussion: The size of a variable-length bit field can be at most 32, but the disk map may contain several hundred or several thousand bits, so a loop is needed. It would seem that four operations must be done in the loop: scan for a clear bit (FFC), test to see if one was found, (if not) increment the position number by 32 to specify the next field to scan, and check that the scan does not go beyond the end of the table (in the case where no bits in the table are clear). It is desirable that operating systems programs run very quickly, so it is rather nice that the scan loop for this problem can be programmed with only two instructions. If the FFC instruction does not find a clear bit, it sets the destination operand to the position of the bit that follows the field scanned. This is the position where the next scan should start, so we use the same register for the position and destination operands. We need not test for the end of the table in the loop if we set up the table with a byte of zeros at the end to force an exit from the loop.

Solution:

```
BLOCKS = [the number of blocks on the disk]
DISK_MAP: .BLKB   BLOCKS/8+1        ; Disk map table
;              .
;              .
;              .
          CLRL   R6                 ; Initial posn = 0
SCAN:     FFC    R6,#32,DISK_MAP,R6 ; Find clear bit
          BEQL   SCAN               ; Repeat if none found
          CMPL   R6,#BLOCKS         ; See if disk is full
          BGEQ   DISK_FULL
; R6 now contains the number of an available disk block.
```

```
; PROCEDURE TURNOFF_2 (BIT_STRING: longword, POSITION: byte)
;
; This procedure finds and turns off the rightmost bit
; that is on in its first argument. It returns the position
; number of the affected bit in its second argument.
; (If no bits are on, it returns 32.)
;
; METHOD
;
; The variable-length bit field instruction FFS is used to
; find the first set bit. (Note that if no bits are set,
; FFS will return 32 as the position number.) A mask for
; turning off the bit is constructed by rotating a 1 into
; the proper position.
;
; Offsets for argument list
STRING = 4
POSITION = 8
;
; REGISTER USE
;
;       R7      position of first set bit
;       R8      mask for turning off bit
;
        .ENTRY  TURNOFF_2,^M<R7,R8>
;
        FFS     #0,#32,@STRING(AP),R7  ; Find first set bit
        BEQL    POSN                   ; Branch if all bits off
        ROTL    R7,#1,R8               ; Move 1 to position
        BICL2   R8,@STRING(AP)         ; Turn off bit
POSN:   MOVB    R7,@POSITION(AP)       ; Store position number
;
        RET                            ; Return
        .END
```

Figure 12.7   The procedure TURNOFF_2

Inserting and Extracting Bit Fields

The INS (INSert) and EXT (EXTract) instructions can be used to construct and decompose long bit strings made up of many variable-length bit fields. The instruction formats are

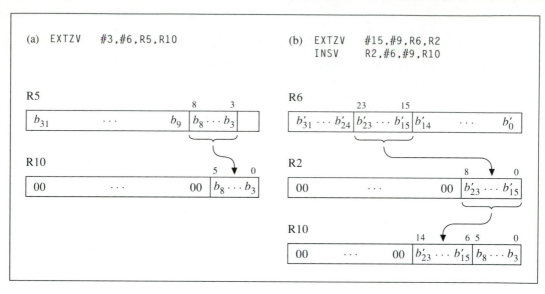

Figure 12.8   Instruction action in Example 12.16

INSV	*source,posn,size,base*
EXTV	*posn,size,base,dest*
EXTZV	*posn,size,base,dest*

INSV inserts bits (*size*−1):0 of its longword source operand into the bit field specified by the remaining operands. It does not affect the condition codes. EXTV extracts (copies) the specified bit field, extends the leftmost bit (the sign bit of the bit field), and puts the resulting longword into the destination operand; thus it treats the bit field as a two's complement integer. EXTZV (EXTract Zero-extended Variable-length bit field) performs a similar operation, but it fills the extra bits of the longword destination with zeros rather than copies of the leftmost bit of the bit field. Both EXT instructions treat a bit field of size = 0 as if it contained the integer 0. They affect the N and Z condition codes as usual, clear V, and leave C unchanged.

Example 12.16: Extracting Bit Fields

In Example 12.9 we used bit instructions to extract bit strings from two registers and pack them together in a third. By using the EXT and INS instructions, we can eliminate the ROTL's used there. The effect of each instruction below is shown in Fig. 12.8.

```
EXTZV    #3,#6,R5,R10      ; Extract bits 8:3 from R5
EXTZV    #15,#9,R6,R2      ; Extract bits 23:15 from R6
INSV     R2,#6,#9,R10      ; Insert R6 bits in R10
```

Example 12.17: Bit Matrix Graphics

For some graphics terminals the screen is represented in memory as a bit matrix. Each bit corresponds to one point, or pixel, on the screen. The bit is set if the corresponding pixel is on (lighted). To draw a picture on the screen we set the appropriate bits in the matrix.

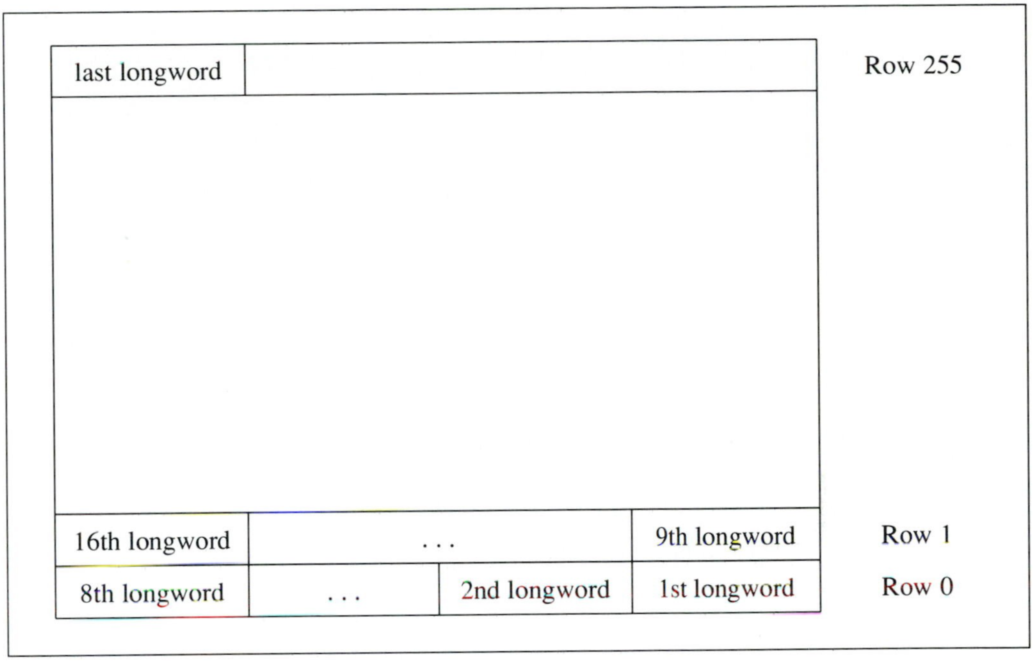

last longword		Row 255
16th longword	. . . 9th longword	Row 1
8th longword	. . . 2nd longword 1st longword	Row 0

Figure 12.9   Bit matrix for a graphics screen

We will assume that the screen dimensions are 256×256 and the matrix occupies 256×8 longwords, as shown in Fig. 12.9. Note that the lowest addressed longword is at the lower right corner. The right-to-left arrangement of the longwords should be quite familiar by now; here it ensures that adjacent bits in memory correspond to adjacent pixels on the screen. The lower addressed longwords were put at the bottom of the screen so that addresses increase in the same direction as the usual vertical axis coordinates.

Clearly, where we wish to draw lines on the screen will have nothing to do with where the longword boundaries are. One of the main advantages of the variable-length bit field instructions for this application is that we can ignore the boundaries. Another is that by specifying the exact bit field to be affected, we do not have to worry about changing parts of the screen where something else may be drawn.

For this example we will set the bits that correspond to drawing a solid rectangle on the screen, as we might wish to do as part of a bar graph. (Several other possibilities are suggested in the exercises.) We assume that we are told the location and size of the rectangle by being given its bottom row number, its height in pixels, the offset of its right side from the right edge of the screen, and its width in pixels. We assume that the width is at most 32. (See Fig. 12.10.) Since each row on the screen is represented by a string of contiguous bits, we will "draw" the rectangle one row at a time, beginning at the bottom. The first byte of the screen matrix will be the base address for the bit field instructions. The following algorithm outlines the steps to be carried out.

```
bottom_posn := bottom_row*256 + right_side_offset
for posn := bottom_posn step 256 to bottom_posn + (height–1)*256
    do Insert bit string
```

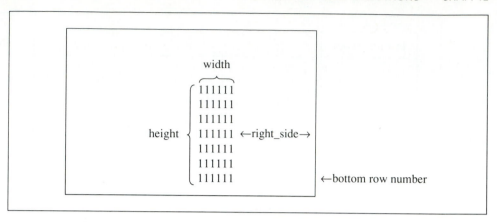

Figure 12.10   Specifications for a rectangle

The following program segment "draws" the rectangle.

```
SCREEN: .BLKL    8*256
;           .
;           .
;           .
; REGISTER USE
;
;       R6       row number of rectangle bottom
;       R7       height of rectangle (in bits)
;       R8       offset of right side (in bits,
;                from right edge of screen)
;       R9       width of rectangle (in bits)
;
; Assume that the registers above are already filled
; with the specified data.
;
;       R10      posn (loop index)
;       R11      loop limit
;
        MULL3    R6,#256,R10                ; bottom*256
        ADDL2    R8,R10                     ; bottom_posn
        SUBL3    #1,R7,R11                  ; height-1
        ASHL     #8,R11,R11                 ; (height-1)*256
        ADDL2    R10,R11                    ; Loop limit
;
DRAW:   INSV     #^XFFFFFFFF,R10,R9,SCREEN  ; Insert bit string
        ACBL     R11,#256,R10,DRAW          ; Increment posn, branch
```

Comparing Bit Fields

The bit field comparison instructions treat bit fields as integers and compare them to longword integers. (A bit field with size = 0 is treated as the integer 0.) Their main role is to affect the condition codes. They are particularly useful when many small numbers using fewer than eight bits each are packed together to save space. The instructions are

$$\text{CMPV} \qquad posn,size,base,long$$

$$\text{CMPZV} \qquad posn,size,base,long$$

CMPV (CoMPare Variable-length bit field) extracts the bit field and extends its leftmost bit to make a longword; thus it treats the bit field as a signed two's complement integer. CMPZV (CoMPare Zero-extended Variable-length bit field) extracts the field and fills in zeros at the left to make a longword; thus it treats the field as an unsigned integer. In both cases the extension is done in a CPU scratch register; the fields and the surrounding bits are not changed. The effects on the condition codes are the same as for the integer CMP instructions. N is set if and only if the first operand (i.e., the extended bit field) is less than the last operand, the longword. Z is set if and only if the operands are equal. V is cleared, and C is set if and only if the bit field operand is less than the longword when both are interpreted as unsigned integers.

Example 12.18: Comparing Bit Fields

Suppose that a questionnaire has ten questions that may be answered with numbers between 1 and 5, and each person's answers are stored in a longword with three bits for each question. The format of the longword is

```
31     29   27                            ...              5    3    2    0
   ┌───┬─────┬─────┬─────┬─────────┬─────────┬─────┬─────┬─────┐
   │   │ Q10 │ Q9  │ Q8  │         │   ...   │ Q3  │ Q2  │ Q1  │
   └───┴─────┴─────┴─────┴─────────┴─────────┴─────┴─────┴─────┘
```

Suppose that the address of the longword containing a person's answers is in R8. The following instructions determine if the person answered 4 or 5 to question 7.

```
CMPV    #18,#3,(R8),#4
BGEQ    HIGH
```

12.6 SUMMARY

Bit instructions do logical operations on bit strings; that is, for the most part, they treat each bit in an operand as if it were independent of the other bits. Bit operations include testing, setting, clearing, complementing, and shifting bits. Many of the bit instructions have one operand that is a mask—a pattern of bits that indicates which bits in another operand are to be operated on. The bit instructions presented in this chapter are listed in Table 12.1.

One application of the bit instructions is performing set operations on sets represented as bit strings. Bit instructions are also useful for working with flags, converting

TABLE 12.1   BIT INSTRUCTIONS

Instruction		Remarks	Operation
BITx	*mask,bit_string*	x = B, W, or L	Set Z condition code to indicate if all masked bits are 0's.
BISx2 BISx3	*mask,bit_string* *mask,source,dest*	x = B, W, or L x = B, W, or L	Set indicated bits (logical OR of mask and second operand).
BICx2 BICx3	*mask,bit_string* *mask,source,dest*	x = B, W, or L x = B, W, or L	Clear indicated bits (logical AND of complemented mask and second operand).
XORx2 XORx3	*mask,bit_string* *mask,source,dest*	x = B, W, or L x = B, W, or L	Complement indicated bits (logical EXCLUSIVE OR of mask and second operand).
MCOMx	*source,dest*	x = B, W, or L	One's complement of source → dest.
ROTL ASHL ASHQ	*count,source,dest* *count,source,dest* *count,source,dest*	Count is a byte; $n =$ | *count* |. Shift left if *count* > 0, right if count < 0.	Rotate *source* n places. Arithmetically shift n places. Arithmetically shift n places.

data representations, packing small data together, manipulating bit tables, and other applications.

The VAX has a data type called *variable-length bit fields*. A variable-length bit field is a string of 0 to 32 contiguous bits that does not have to begin or end on a byte or longword boundary. It is specified by a base address, the bit position number of the first bit in the field, and its size (in bits). Instructions that operate on such fields are not available on most computers; the operations performed by VAX bit field instructions can be implemented using some of the other bit instructions described in this chapter. The bit field instructions are listed in Table 12.2.

TABLE 12.2   VARIABLE-LENGTH BIT FIELD INSTRUCTIONS

Instruction		Operation
FFx x = S or C	*posn,size,base,dest*	Find first set (S) bit or first clear (C) bit. Z = 0 if found, 1 if not.
INSV EXTV EXTZV	*source,posn,size,base* *posn,size,base,dest* *posn,size,base,dest*	Copy bits (*size*−1):0 of *source* to field. Copy field to *dest*, extend sign. Copy field to *dest*; extend with 0's.
CMPV CMPZV	*posn,size,base,long* *posn,size,base,long*	Compare sign-extended field to *long*. Compare zero-extended field to *long*.

12.7 EXERCISES

1. **(a)** Write an instruction that will set bit 0 in R4 and leave the other bits unchanged.
    (b) Write an instruction that will set bit 0 in R4 and clear all the other bits.

2. Write instructions to set bits 6, 11, and 21 in R9 and clear all the other bits.

3. Write instructions to complement all the bits in the second byte (from the right) of R10 and put the result in R11.

4. Write instructions to clear the bits in even-numbered positions in R4, complement bits 1, 9, and 31, clear bit 15, and leave the others unchanged.

5. Write instructions to copy the lower-order byte of R5 into each of the other bytes in R5.

6. In Example 12.4 we saw two ways of converting a digit from character code to binary. Suppose that the character string being converted has leading blanks instead of leading zeros. Will either method work properly? Explain why or why not for each.

7. The BIT, BIS, BIC, and XOR instructions test, set, clear, or complement the bits in their second operand specified by the mask (the first operand). The MCOM instructions do the same operation as *XOR*, but to *all* the bits in the source operand; no mask is needed. For each of the other types of bit instructions, BIT, BIS, and BIC, write instructions whose effect is to accomplish the same operation, but on all the bits, without a mask.

8. Write instructions to do the following: If the rightmost bit in R7 is 0, turn on all the bits in the rightmost string of contiguous 0's; if the rightmost bit is 1, leave the string unchanged. For example, the string

    00001010111010100001111011000000

    would be changed to

    00001010111010100001111011111111

    (This can be done with only two instructions.)

9. Write instructions that clear the rightmost bit that is on in R8 by using only two instructions, no loop, and no variable-length bit field instructions. (The procedure in Fig. 12.4 does much more work to solve this problem because it must determine the position number of the affected bit.)

10. Write a macro definition for a macro ABSQ that computes the absolute value of its quadword argument SOURCE and stores the result in the argument DEST. You may assume that the actual arguments will be symbols.

11. Write instructions that, if they appear within a procedure, will cause a branch to YES if the procedure was called with a CALLS instruction.

12. Suppose that R5 contains FFFFFF07 and the longword at ALPHA contains 014A7D25. What will be in the longword at ALPHA after the following instruction is executed?

    ```
    ROTL    R5,ALPHA,ALPHA
    ```

13. What is the effect of the ROTL instruction with a count of 0? What is the effect of the ASHL instruction with a count of 0?

14. Write instructions to interchange the contents of the rightmost two bytes in R10. What happens to the other two bytes is irrelevant.

15. Show the machine code for the following instructions.

    (a) `ROTL     #-1,R9,R3`   **(c)** `ASHL     R3,#^X80000000,R8`

    (b) `ROTL     #1,R9,R3`   **(d)** `ASHQ     #63,R7,R3`

16. Consider the following program segment.

```
          MOVL    #32,R6              ; Initialize loop counter
TEST:     ROTL    #1,R5,R5            ; Test bit
          BLSS    BIT_SET
          . . .
BIT_SET:
          . . .
          SOBGTR  R6,TEST
```

Assuming that before the loop begins R5 contains

$$b_{31}b_{30}b_{29} \cdots b_2b_1b_0$$

which bit is tested first? Which bit is tested last? If the ROTL instruction were changed to

```
          ROTL    #-1,R5,R5
```

which bit would be tested first, and which last?

17. On many computers it is convenient to use the sign bit of a byte for a boolean flag; it can be tested using test and branch instructions for integers. What bit is even more convenient to use for a boolean flag on the VAX?

18. Write a macro definition for a macro called ROTATE that rotates its byte argument (which may be in memory or in a register) one bit position to the left.

19. Write a macro definition for a macro called ROTATE that has two arguments, a datum and a type (B, W, or L), and rotates the datum (which may be in memory or in a register) one place to the left. (This macro will use conditional assembly.)

20. Read the two preceding exercises. For this exercise, you are to write a definition for a three-argument macro

ROTATE   datum,count,type

The *count* argument is the number of positions by which the datum is to be rotated. You may assume that $1 \le count \le 8$. The type may be B, W, or L.

21. In the procedure TURNOFF in Fig. 12.4 a copy of the bit string argument is rotated. Rewrite the procedure using a BIT instruction and a mask so that the mask is shifted and the bit string is not. Which procedure is better?

22. If the AOBLEQ instruction in the procedure TURNOFF (Fig. 12.4) were changed to AOBLSS (and no other changes were made), for what arguments, if any, would the procedure not work properly? Does this suggest an improvement?

23. In the procedure TURNOFF in Fig. 12.4, suppose that the BEQL instruction that tests for the zero string is omitted (and the MOVB and RET at the label ZERO are omitted also). What happens if the bitstring argument is zero? Does the modified procedure work correctly?

24. Write instructions to count the bits in the longword S that are on.

25. Write a procedure to find the position of the leftmost bit in a longword that is set. The procedure should have two arguments, BIT_STRING and POSITION, as in the procedure TURNOFF (Fig. 12.4).

26. Write the procedure SCORE described in Exercise 24 of Chapter 9.

27. ASCII codes use only seven bits. The leftmost bit in a byte of character code is always zero. This allows us to use the leftmost bit position as a parity bit. (This is done to help detect errors when bytes are sent through various communications lines.) For *even parity*, the leftmost bit is turned on, or not turned on, to ensure that the total number of bits that are on (i.e., have value 1) in each byte is even.

   Assume that the byte at CHAR contains the ASCII code for a character. Write instructions to set or clear bit 7 so that the byte has even parity. (This can be done in a rather long and tedious way, or in a shorter way using an XORB instruction appropriately.)

28. Write a procedure REVERSE that reverses the ordering of the bits in its longword argument. In other words, if the argument is

$$b_{31}b_{30}b_{29} \cdots b_2b_1b_0$$

then REVERSE changes it to

$$b_0b_1b_2 \cdots b_{29}b_{30}b_{31}$$

29. Write a procedure that converts integers from character code (leading separate numeric format) to packed decimal without using the CVTSP instruction. The procedure should have three arguments:

   LSN   the leading separate numeric string
   NUM   the number of digits in the string
   PKD   the packed-decimal string produced by the procedure

   Assume the usual argument list format containing the addresses of the arguments. The procedure should return a flag in R0 to indicate if the conversion was successful; 1 indicates success, 0 failure. (Some reasons for failure would be an invalid character in the leading separate numeric string or an improper number of digits.)

30. Suppose that when the instruction

```
ASHL    BITS,R7,R7
```

   is executed, the byte at BITS contains an integer less than −32. If R7 had contained a positive longword integer, what would be in R7 afterward? Is the result consistent with the interpretation of an arithmetic shift to the right as division by a power of 2?

Answer the same questions for the case where R7 contained a negative longword integer.

31. Will the instructions in Example 12.12 achieve the intended result if $n = 0$? (Does the answer depend on whether or not the integer overflow trap is enabled?)

32. What will be in R8 after the instructions in Example 12.12 are executed if
(a) $n = 12$ and $p = 5$?   (c) $n = 20$ and $p = 25$?
(b) $n = 6$ and $p = 0$?   (d) $n = 1$ and $p = 1$?

33. Example 12.12 shows how to construct a mask consisting of a contiguous string of 1's somewhere in a register and 0's everywhere else. Suppose that we want the opposite: a contiguous string of 0's with 1's everywhere else—for example,

$$1 \ldots 100000001 \ldots 1$$

What changes, if any, should be made in Example 12.12 to construct such masks? Consider both changes in the instructions themselves and changes in how the programmer should interpret n and p, and what should be put in R6 and R7.

34. Redo Exercise 4 in Chapter 11 (writing a CVTLQ macro) using an ASH instruction. (You may assume that the actual argument for QUAD will be a symbol.) Your macro definition should be shorter than the one you wrote before.

35. The problem in this exercise is to find the longest contiguous sequence of 1's in a longword, and clear them. You are to write two procedures to do this. The first procedure is described by the following Pascal-like header:

```
;    procedure FindLongSequence(bitstring: longword; var size: byte;
;                               var position: byte)
```

This procedure determines the size and starting position of the longest sequence of 1's in its first argument. For example, the longest sequence of 1's in the following longword has size 5 and begins at position 18.

$$01110011011111011101000001100011$$

If there are two sequences of the largest length, the procedure should return the starting position of the first (rightmost) such sequence. The first argument should be passed as a value parameter; that is, the procedure should be given the address of a copy of the longword, not the address of the actual longword. If the longword contains no 1's, the Z bit in the saved PSW should be set.

The second procedure is

```
;    procedure ClearBits(var bitstring: longword; size: byte;
;                         position: byte)
```

This procedure clears (sets to 0) the sequence of *size* bits beginning at *position* in the longword *bitstring*. Both *size* and *position* should be passed as value parameters.

36. Suppose that subsets of the set of uppercase letters are to be represented in longwords, as described in Section 12.4, with b_0 representing 'A,' b_1 representing 'B,' and so on. Show the representation of the set of vowels.

37. Suppose that S and T are longwords that represent subsets of a universe set with 32 elements as described in Section 12.4. Write instructions to branch to ALL if $S \cup T$ contains all 32 elements.

38. Suppose that S and T are longwords that represent sets as described in Section 12.4. Write instructions to determine if $S \subseteq T$ and branch to SUBSET if so.

39. Suppose that S is a longword that represents a subset of the universe set containing the integers 0 through 31. Write instructions to branch to IN_SET if the integer in R8 is an element of the set.

40. Suppose that we wish to work with sets that may contain up to 256 elements. (This is the maximum size for sets in VAX Pascal.) Each set is represented by a bit string in eight consecutive longwords in memory. Write macros called UNION, INTER-SECTION, and COMPLEMENT that do the indicated set operations. You may assume that the actual macro arguments will be expressions.

41. Using the assumptions of Exercise 40, write macros called B_SUBSET, B_EQUAL, and B_EMPTY with arguments and operations described as follows:

		Branch to dest if
B_SUBSET	set1,set2,dest	set1 $\subseteq$ set2
B_EQUAL	set1,set2,dest	set1 = set2
B_EMPTY	set,dest	set = φ

42. Suppose that R6 contains F0C382D5.
    (a) What will be in R5 after each of the following instructions?

```
EXTV    #21,#3,R6,R5
EXTZV   #21,#3,R6,R5
```

    (b) Suppose that R8 contains 00000000. What will be in R8 after

```
INSV    R6,#2,#6,R8
```

43. Suppose that R5 contains FFFFFFFF. What will be in R5 after executing the following instruction?

```
EXTV    #5,#0,#^XFFFFFFFF,R5
```

44. The procedure SETUP in Fig. 12.5 uses two instructions, ASHL and BISL2 to turn on the bit whose number is stored in the longword NUMBER. Write an INSV instruction that will do the same thing.

45. The problem described in Example 12.12 of constructing a mask given its starting position and length can be solved with only two instructions. Write the instructions. (Use an instruction from Section 12.5.)

46. The procedure TURNOFF_2 (Fig. 12.7) finds the first bit that is on in a longword, turns if off, and returns its position. Write a procedure TURNOFF_3 with three arguments, BIT_STRING, START_POSN, and POSITION, where BIT_STRING and POSITION are as before, but now the search for the first set bit should begin at the bit position specified in the byte argument START_POSN. The search must "wrap around"; that is, if there is no set bit in the range 31:START_POSN, the procedure should scan bits START_POSN–1:0.

47. Using the description of the disk map problem in Example 12.15, write instructions to find an available disk block without using any of the bit field instructions.

48. In Example 12.15 we searched a disk map for a clear bit indicating an available disk block. Suppose that we need a contiguous group of n blocks, where $1 \le n \le 32$. Write instructions to find the block number of the first in a group of n available blocks or branch to NO_ROOM if no such group of blocks is available.

49. Write a sequence of instructions to determine if there is exactly one bit set in R10 and branch to ONE_BIT if so. (You might want to do this with and without instructions from Section 12.5.)

50. Consider the bit matrix graphics problem in Example 12.17. Write procedures to
   (a) Draw a horizontal line, given its row number, right endpoint (as a bit offset from the right side of the screen), and length (in bits).
   (b) Draw a vertical line, given its bottom row number, distance from the right edge of the screen (in bits), and length (in bits).
   (c) Draw the outline of a rectangle, rather than a solid rectangle, given the same specifications as in Example 12.17.
   (d) Draw a solid rectangle, given the specifications in Example 12.17, but allow for the width to be larger than 32.

51. Suppose that there were no CMPV and CMPZV instructions. For each of these, write a sequence of other instructions that does the same operation.

52. In Example 12.18 we described a representation of questionnaire answers. Write instructions to pack a person's answers into a longword as described there, assuming that the answers are in the byte array ANSWERS.

53. Write a procedure to convert a string of character code for eight hex digits to a longword hex integer. In other words, if, for example, the first argument is the character string "FFC03008", the procedure returns in its second argument the longword containing FFC03008. (This procedure was quite useful to the author for converting input for a program to test some of the examples in this chapter.)

54. Suppose that there were no CALLG and CALLS instructions, just a CALL instruction with one argument, the procedure entry point name, that causes a transfer of control to the procedure. Write instructions to do all the steps that are normally done by CALLG: that is, construct the call frame on the stack and put the appropriate new values in AP and FP. (You may assume that the entry mask does not specify any trap enables. All of the instructions you need have been covered except

MOVPSL   *dest*

which copies the PSL to *dest*.)

13

Floating Point and Packed Decimal

In this chapter we describe the floating-point and packed-decimal data types. The VAX supports both types with machine instructions that do arithmetic and miscellaneous other operations.

13.1 FLOATING-POINT DATA REPRESENTATION

Scientific Notation

"Scientific notation" is commonly used for writing very large and very small real numbers. The format is

$$\pm m \times 10^p$$

where m (called the *mantissa*) is restricted to a small range, usually $1 \le m < 10$, and p is an integer. Some examples are

$$1.48 \times 10^3 \quad -3.0083 \times 10^{28} \quad 4.87 \times 10^{-12}$$

The range of the mantissa is chosen so that any rational number can be written in this form.

The internal representation of floating-point numbers in digital computers is similar to scientific notation. The representation contains a sign, a mantissa which is a fraction (i.e., is less than 1), and a (signed) power of a radix r (generally 2, 8, or 16, rather than 10). Thus we can write floating-point numbers as

$$\pm f \times r^p \quad \text{where } 0 \le f < 1.$$

On a computer the values of f and p are restricted by the number of bits used to store them, so not all rational numbers can be represented. For those that can be, this representation is not unique (i.e., there is more than one way to write a number in this format). For example,

$$0.1101 \times 2^3 = 0.001101 \times 2^5$$

(where the fractions are shown in binary).

The Floating-Point Data Types

The VAX has two standard floating-point data types: single precision (type F_floating) and double precision (type D_floating). It also has G_floating and H_floating types; they allow for the representation of numbers with larger exponents and more significant digits.[1] For all these types a floating-point number is expressed as

$$\pm f \times 2^p \quad \text{where } 0.5 \le f < 1.$$

A single-precision floating-point number occupies a longword, a D or G floating-point number occupies a quadword, and H uses octawords. The types differ only in the number of bits used to store the exponent and fraction. The general format and the way of representing the three components (sign, fraction, and exponent) are the same.

To keep the discussion of the representations general enough to describe all the types at once, we will use t for the number of bits in the exponent and u for the number of bits in the fraction field.

A floating-point number is said to be in *normalized* form if the first digit after the radix point is nonzero. VAX floating-point numbers are always normalized; the first bit after the binary point is always 1, since $f \ge 1/2$. There are two advantages to using a normalized representation. Since the first bit is always 1, it does not have to be included in the representation; it can be assumed. The fraction bits that actually appear in the representation do not include the first bit. Thus, a floating-point representation with u fraction bits actually has $u + 1$ significant bits. The second advantage is that keeping numbers in normalized form increases the accuracy of floating-point computation. Note that the normalized representation of a nonzero number in any one of the floating data types is unique.

The single-precision (F_floating) format is

31		16	15	14		7	6		0
	f_2		S		b.exp.			f_1	

---

[1] Some floating-point types may not be available on some VAXes.

where S = the sign bit (0 is +, 1 is –, as usual)
             $f = .1f_1f_2$, and
             $b.exp. = $ "biased exponent" $= p + 128_{10}$.

Several aspects of the representation need explanation. The location of the sign bit and the arrangement of the fraction segments are certainly peculiar. It would seem more natural for the two halves of the representation to be interchanged so that the sign would be in bit 31 and the fraction would appear as a contiguous string of bits. The VAX floating-point representations were chosen for compatibility with the F and D floating-point data types on DEC's PDP-11 computers, whose basic memory unit is a 16-bit word. The representations seem a bit more natural when viewed as a sequence of words, not longwords. All four types are shown this way in Fig. 13.1.

What is a "biased exponent," and why does the F_floating representation contain $p + 128$ rather than p? The VAX uses t bits ($t = 8$ for F and D, $t = 11$ for G, and $t = 15$ for H) for the exponent, so 2^t (256, for F and D) different values can be represented. Since we want both negative and positive exponents, we could represent $-2^{t-1}, ..., 2^{t-1} - 1$ in two's complement (–128 to 127 for F and D), but this is not done. The hardware that does floating-point arithmetic can work more efficiently if the ordering of the actual exponents corresponds to the ordering of their representations interpreted as unsigned binary number. In two's complement, the sign bit makes negative integers "look" larger than positive integers. The representation used (by many computers) for the exponents simply assigns exponent values to the bit patterns in order. The assignment used by the VAX (with $t = 8$) is

Bit Pattern	Bit Pattern Value in Decimal	Exponent Represented
00000000	0	special case
00000001	1	−127
00000010	2	−126
.	.	.
.	.	.
.	.	.
01111111	127	−1
10000000	128	0
10000001	129	1
.	.	.
.	.	.
.	.	.
11111111	255	127

Thus what we call the biased exponent is simply the value of the bit pattern as an unsigned binary number. It is 2^{t-1} larger than the exponent, p, that it represents; that is, the "bias" is 2^{t-1}. A biased exponent of 0 does not represent the exponent -2^{t-1}; it is a

The number $\pm f \times 2^p$ is represented as

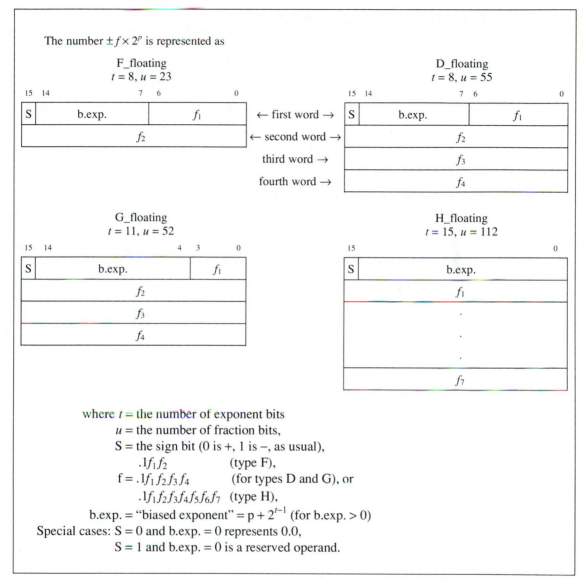

Figure 13.1 Floating-point formats

special case. A floating-point number with biased exponent 0 and sign (bit 15) 0 represents floating-point zero—that is, the number 0.0 (regardless of what is in the fraction bits). A biased exponent 0 and a sign 1 is a reserved operand—that is, an invalid number; if it is an operand in a floating-point instruction, a reserved operand fault will occur.

The ranges of values and the accuracy of numbers that can be represented in floating point on the VAX are shown in Table 13.1.

TABLE 13.1 RANGES OF FLOATING-POINT NUMBERS

Type	Exp. bits	Frac. bits	Magnitude range (approx.)	Significant digits (approx.)
F	8	23	0.29×10^{-38} to 1.7×10^{38}	7
D	8	55	0.29×10^{-38} to 1.7×10^{38}	16
G	11	52	0.56×10^{-308} to 0.9×10^{308}	15
H	15	112	0.84×10^{-4932} to 0.59×10^{4932}	33

There is nothing within a longword (or quadword or octaword) containing a floating-point number to indicate that it is, in fact, a floating-point number rather than an integer. The CPU will interpret the bit pattern as being a datum of the type appropriate for the instruction that operates on it.

In all the examples in this chapter, when we refer to floating-point numbers without specifying the type, we mean single precision, or F_floating.

Example 13.1: Interpreting a Floating-Point Number

What floating-point number is represented by 0000C150? The bit pattern is

$$\underbrace{0000000000000000}_{f_2} \; \underbrace{1}_{S} \; \underbrace{10000010}_{b.exp.} \; \underbrace{1010000}_{f_1}$$

The number is negative because $S = 1$. The biased exponent, 10000010, is 130_{10}, so the actual exponent, p, is 2. The fraction is $.1f_1f_2$, so the number is

$$-.1101 \times 2^2 = -11.01_2 = -3.25_{10}$$

(Remember that the ith position to the right of the binary point represents 2^{-i}.)

Note that the leftmost bit of the biased exponent indicates the sign of the exponent because it is the 128's place (the 2^{t-1}'s place, in general) in the binary number. The biased exponent is ≥ 128 (2^{t-1}), and $p \geq 0$, if and only if bit 14 is set.

Example 13.2: Converting to Floating-Point Representation

We convert the decimal number 5031.1875 to its floating-point representation.

$$5031.1875_{10} \quad = \quad 13A7.3_{16}$$

$$= \quad 1001110100111.0011_2$$

$$= \quad .1 \underbrace{0011101}_{f_1} \underbrace{001110011}_{f_2} \times 2^{13}$$

So $p = 13$, and the biased exponent = 141_{10}, or 10001101_2. Thus the representation is

$$001110011000000001000110100011101$$

or

$$3980469D$$

Example 13.3: Double Precision

To emphasize the arrangement of the fraction bits in a double-precision floating-point number we consider the following datum:

$$1111111111111111101000000000000000 \qquad \text{first longword}$$
$$1010101010101010000000000000000000 \qquad \text{second longword}$$

The number represented is

$$.100000001111111111111111110000000000000000001010101010101010_2$$

Initializing Storage

Floating-point constants are written in decimal. They may be written with or without a sign, with or without an exponent (a power of 10), and if the number is an integer, with or without a decimal point. If a decimal point is used, there should be at least one digit to the left of it.

Example 13.4: Floating-Point Constants

$$1.13 \quad -27.00056E15 \quad 247 \quad 0.25 \quad -5E-8$$
$$1.24E-3 = 0.124E-2 = 124E-5 = 0.00124 = 0.00000124E3$$

Storage may be initialized with the following directives:

$$.x\text{\_FLOATING} \quad \textit{list\_of\_floating\_point\_constants}$$

where $x = $ F, D, G, or H. The shorter directive names .FLOAT and .DOUBLE may be used for .F_FLOATING and .D_FLOATING, respectively. The assembler initializes the next available space in memory with the internal floating-point representations of the constants listed.

Storage for floating-point numbers may be reserved with the .BLKx directives described in Chapter 4 (where $x = $ F, D, G, or H).

Example 13.5: Reserving and Initializing Storage

```
PI:     .FLOAT  3.14159
RADIUS: .BLKF   1
AREA:   .BLKF   1
```

13.2 FLOATING-POINT OPERATIONS

The VAX instruction set includes instructions for doing floating-point arithmetic, tests and comparisons, a few other related operations, and conversion between the floating-point data types and between floating point and integer. Machine instructions that convert between floating-point and integer representations are uncommon, but not surprising for the VAX. The VAX also has a few very special powerful instructions that perform complex operations on floating-point data (the POLY*x* and EMOD*x* instructions) that we will not cover here.

Floating-point operands may be in memory, in registers, or in an instruction itself as literal or immediate operands. When a register, say R*n*, is specified for an operand of a double-precision instruction, R*n* and R*n*+1 are used; R*n* contains the first longword of the operand (with the sign, biased exponent, and most significant fraction bits), and R*n*+1 contains the additional fraction bits.

The opcodes for the G and H instructions are two bytes long.

Arithmetic and Related Instructions

The basic arithmetic instructions are

$$
\begin{Bmatrix} \text{ADD} \\ \text{SUB} \\ \text{MUL} \\ \text{DIV} \end{Bmatrix} \begin{Bmatrix} \text{F} \\ \text{D} \\ \text{G} \\ \text{H} \end{Bmatrix} \begin{Bmatrix} 2 & op1,op2 \\ 3 & op1,op2,dest \end{Bmatrix}
$$

The roles of the operands follow the same conventions as in the integer arithmetic instructions. For example, in SUBF3 the first operand is subtracted from the second and the result goes in the third. All these instructions affect the condition codes as follows:

N = 1   if and only if the result is negative (or is a reserved operand).
Z = 1   if and only if the result is zero.
V = 1   if and only if the result overflows or the divisor in a DIV instruction is 0.0.
C = 0.

Program exceptions will occur for overflow (i.e., the result's exponent is greater than 127, for F and D, or greater than $2^{10} - 1$ or $2^{14} - 1$ for G and H), reserved operands, and division by zero. The programmer can choose whether or not underflow (resulting exponent less than -127, etc.) will cause an exception by setting or clearing bit 6 of the PSW, the floating underflow trap enable bit. When underflow results from an arithmetic operation, the floating-point number 0.0 is stored in the destination operand.

Recall that 0.0 has many representations; any number with zeros in the sign and biased exponent fields is treated as zero regardless of what is in the fraction bits. However, if the result of a floating-point operation is zero, the CPU always stores the representation with zeros in all the fraction bits.

After describing the other instructions, we will examine floating-point arithmetic in more detail.

The special-purpose instructions available for floating point are

CLR*x*   *dest*

MOV*x*   *source,dest*

MOVA*x*   *source,dest*

MNEG*x*   *source,dest*

where x = F, D, G, or H. The CLRx and MOVAx instructions with x = F or D, do exactly the same operations as CLRx and MOVAx with x = L or Q, respectively. In fact, they are just alternative names for the corresponding integer instructions; the opcodes are the same. The floating-point MOV and integer MOV instructions are not identical because they do different tests to set the condition codes and determine if there is a fault. The MNEG instructions move a copy of the source operand with its sign bit complemented to the destination. (If the source = 0, the sign is not changed.) They affect the N and Z condition codes in the usual ways, and clear both V and C. There are no INC and DEC instructions for floating point.

The floating test and compare instructions are

$$\text{TST}x \qquad operand$$
$$\text{CMP}x \qquad op1,op2$$

where x = F, D, G, or H. They follow the usual conventions.

The VAX has a complete assortment of CVT instructions for conversion between any pair of the integer and floating-point data types, including two options for converting floating point to longwords: rounded or truncated conversion. The instructions are

$$\text{CVT}xy \qquad source,dest$$

where x and y may be F, D, G, H, B, W, or L, but $x \neq y$, $xy \neq$ DG, and $xy \neq$ GD, and

$$\text{CVTR}xL \qquad source,dest$$

for ConVerT Rounded, where x = F, D, G, or H. CVTxL truncates the floating-point operand to an integer rather than rounding. As usual, if the converted result cannot be represented properly in the destination, the V condition code is set.

Example 13.6: Conversions

Suppose that ALPHA is defined by

```
ALPHA:   .FLOAT  -15.9
```

The longword at ALPHA will contain 6666C27E. The table below shows the effects of several conversion instructions.

Instruction		Result in R7	
CVTFW	ALPHA,R7	xxxxFFF1	-15_{10}
CVTFL	ALPHA,R7	FFFFFFF1	-15_{10}
CVTRFL	ALPHA,R7	FFFFFFF0	-16_{10}
CVTFD	ALPHA,R7	6666C27E in R7	
		00000000 in R8	

(The x's indicate parts of R7 that are unchanged.)

Most of the CVT instructions do fairly complex operations that on other computers must be programmed with a sequence of instructions, including several bit operations. Therefore, it is worth giving some thought to how the conversions would be done if the

CVT instructions were not available. In Section 13.5 we will write a procedure to convert from floating point to longword without using CVTFL. Some of the other conversions are considered in the exercises.

Conversion from floating-point format to character code for output is an even more complex task, and not even the VAX has one or two powerful instructions to do the job. The VAX Run-Time Library contains conversion procedures that are used by the high-level language compilers and may be called directly by the assembly language programmer.

One of the groups of loop control instructions presented in Chapter 7, the ACB instructions, allows floating-point loop parameters. Recall that ACB is a mnemonic for Add, Compare, and Branch; the instruction format is

$$\text{ACB}x \qquad limit,incr,index,dest$$

where x may be F, D, G, or H (in addition to B, W, and L). These are the most flexible of the loop control instructions because they allow the programmer to specify a negative or positive loop increment, and the destination is encoded using a word, rather than byte, displacement.

Example 13.7: Floating-Point Loop Parameters

The ALGOL **for** loop

> **for** x := 2.8 **step** $-.2$ **until** 1.0 **do**
>   loop body

could be implemented as follows:

```
; REGISTER USE       R6        loop index
;
        MOVF    #2.8,R6                 ; Initialize index
LOOP:
;       [loop body]
;
        ACBF    #1.0,#-0.2,R6,LOOP    ; Loop control
```

How Arithmetic Is Done

To gain some understanding of how floating-point arithmetic is done, we will consider addition and subtraction. Some of the points discussed here can readily be applied to multiplication and division.

Suppose that we wish to add floating-point numbers $f_1 \times 2^{p_1}$ and $f_2 \times 2^{p_2}$. We cannot add the fractions as they are, unless the powers p_1 and p_2 are equal. The rules for addition may be summarized as follows:

1. Let $n = |p_1 - p_2|$.

2. Shift the fraction bits of the number with the smaller exponent to the right n places. (Now both exponents are equal to the larger of p_1 and p_2.)

3. Add the fractions.

4. Normalize the result if necessary by shifting the fraction bits and adjusting the exponent.

Before considering some additional details, we will show a simple example.

Example 13.8: Addition

Problem: Determine what will be in R8 after executing the following instruction, assuming that R6 contains 6000580C and R7 contains 90005425.

        ADDF3   R6,R7,R8

After decoding the representations, we have the following addition problem:

$$.8C6000 \times 2^{48} \quad \text{(R6)}$$
$$+.A59000 \times 2^{40} \quad \text{(R7)}$$

where the fractions have been left in hex for convenience. (The exponents are shown in decimal.) The second operand must be shifted right eight places (i.e., eight binary places, or two hex digits), yielding

$$.8C6000 \times 2^{48}$$
$$+.00A590 \times 2^{48}$$

Adding the fractions gives

$$.8D0590 \times 2^{48}$$

The sum is already in normalized form, since the first bit of 8 is 1. The result in R8 will be 0590580D.

When one of the operands is shifted right to get equal exponents for addition or subtraction, some nonzero bits may be lost. For accuracy of results, some of those bits should be used in the computation. The way the VAX does computation is equivalent to keeping two extra bits, called *guard bits*, at the right end of the fractions. Also, it allows an extra bit to the left of the binary point for a carry out of the most significant fraction position. Recall that u is the actual number of fraction bits stored in the floating-point representation; the first fraction bit is not stored. After normalization, the fraction is rounded. That is, if the first guard bit is a 1, 1 is added to the $(u + 1)$-bit fraction at the least significant place. The result is an exact result rounded to $u + 1$ bits; thus the error is at most one-half the value of the least significant bit of the fraction. (Though the error is quite small, we shall see below and in Section 13.4 that it can have a significant impact.)

Example 13.9: Addition with Rounding

Problem: Determine what will be in GAMMA after executing the following instruction, assuming that the longword at ALPHA contains 739E448D and the longword at BETA contains 947D4722.

        ADDF3   ALPHA,BETA,GAMMA

After decoding the representations we have the problem:

$$(\text{ALPHA}) \qquad 0.100011010111001110011110 \times 2^9$$
$$(\text{BETA}) \qquad +0.101000101001010001111101 \times 2^{14}$$

The first operand is shifted right five places. Three bits are dropped from the right end; two are kept as guard bits.

$$(\text{ALPHA}) \text{ shifted} \qquad 0.0000010001101011100111100\underline{11} \times 2^{14}$$
$$(\text{BETA}) \qquad +0.101000101001010001111101\underline{00} \times 2^{14}$$

Adding fractions gives

$$0.101001110000000000011001\underline{11} \times 2^{14}$$

The sum is already normalized. Since the first guard bit is 1, the result is rounded up as follows:

$$
\begin{array}{r}
0.10100111000000000001100\,1 \times 2^{14} \\
+ \qquad\qquad\qquad\qquad\qquad 1 \\
\hline
0.10100111000000000001101\,0 \ \times 2^{14}
\end{array}
$$

GAMMA will contain `001A4727`.

When is the second guard bit used? If the result of the operation requires a left shift by one place for normalization, the second guard bit is used for rounding. This is illustrated in the next example. Of course, it is possible that normalization will require a left shift by more than one place (for subtraction of positive numbers of similar magnitudes, for example). Then both guard bits and additional zeros would be shifted into the right end of the fraction.

Example 13.10: Subtraction with Normalization

Problem: Determine what will be in R7 after executing the following instruction, assuming that R7 contains `00004000` (i.e., 1/2) and R9 contains `00013F00` ($1/8 + 2^{-26}$).

```
    SUBF2    R9,R7
```

The problem is

$$
\begin{array}{c}
\text{guard bits} \\
24 \text{ bits} \quad \downarrow \\
\overbrace{} \\
0.10...00 \ \ \underline{00} \times 2^0 \\
-0.10...01 \ \ \underline{00} \times 2^{-2} \\
\hline
\end{array}
$$

First we put the operand to be subtracted in two's complement form. Note that the carry bit and the two guard bits participate in the two's complementing of the second operand.

$$
\begin{array}{r}
0.10...000\underline{0} \times 2^0 \\
+1.01...110\underline{0} \times 2^{-2} \\
\hline
\end{array}
$$

Shifting the second operand (with the carry bit treated like a sign bit and extended), and adding gives

$$
\begin{array}{r}
0.1000...0000 \times 2^0 \\
+1.1101...1\underline{1}\overline{11} \times 2^0 \\
\hline
0.0101...11\underline{11} \times 2^0
\end{array}
$$

The sum is normalized by shifting left one place:

$$0.101...111\underline{10} \times 2^{-1}$$

The first guard bit (which was the second guard bit in the sum) is added to the 24-bit fraction to round it, yielding

$$0.110...00 \times 2^{-1}$$

which is $3/8$, the correct rounded result. It will appear in R7 as `00003FC0`.

Breaking Rules

The result of the subtraction in Example 13.10 was not exact. Because only a finite number of bits are used to represent the fraction of a floating-point number, we cannot always get exact results. For the same reason, floating-point arithmetic on computers does not satisfy all the standard rules of arithmetic. Consider the following rule:

$$\text{If } a + b = b, \text{ then } a = 0.$$

Suppose that we add $1/2$ and 2^{24}, both of which can easily be put in floating-point representation. The addition is done as follows:

$$
\begin{array}{r}
0.1 \times 2^0 \\
+0.1 \times 2^{25} \\
\hline
\end{array}
$$

After shifting:

guard bits
↓

$$
\begin{array}{r}
0.0000000000000000000000000\underline{01} \times 2^{25} \\
+0.1000000000000000000000000\underline{00} \times 2^{25} \\
\hline
0.1000000000000000000000000\underline{01} \times 2^{25}
\end{array}
$$

The first guard bit is 0, so the 24-bit fraction is unchanged by rounding. The result is 2^{24}, so adding $1/2$ and 2^{24} produced 2^{24}, but $1/2 \neq 0$. Clearly, here, the difficulty arises because the numbers being added are of very different magnitudes. This is a general problem with floating-point arithmetic. To increase the accuracy of results, evaluation of long expressions should be arranged so that numbers of similar magnitudes are combined first. We will illustrate this principle with an extensive example in Section 13.4.

We leave it as an exercise for the reader to find an example to show that the associative law for addition,

$$(a + b) + c = a + (b + c)$$

does not always hold for floating-point arithmetic.

13.3 FLOATING-POINT IMMEDIATE AND LITERAL OPERANDS

Floating-point constants may be specified as literal or immediate operands in machine instructions. As with integers, the constant is preceded by a #. For example:

```
MULF3    #0.33333333,R6,AREA
MOVF     #40,R7
```

The first operand specifier in the MULF3 instruction will be assembled in immediate mode; the assembler will put the longword floating-point representation of 0.33333333 into the instruction as follows:

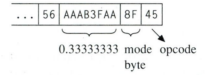

We saw that literal mode operands are used for small integer constants to save space. The leftmost two bits of the mode byte are zeros to indicate that it is a literal, and the remaining six bits contain the constant. The assembler stores certain small floating-point constants in literal mode instead of immediate mode, also to save space. The format of a floating-point literal is shown in Fig. 13.2. Three of the six available bits are used for the exponent (a true, not biased, exponent) and three for the fraction. There is no sign bit; only positive numbers can be encoded in literal mode. As with the regular floating-point representation, the most significant fraction bit is assumed to be 1 and is omitted.

Since the number 40 can be encoded as a floating-point literal, the assembler will use literal mode in the MOVF instruction above. $40_{10} = 101000_2 = .101 \times 2^6$, so the literal is 00110010. The machine code for the instruction is

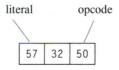

How does the CPU know, when executing an instruction, whether to interpret a literal as an integer or as a floating-point number? There is nothing in the literal byte itself to distinguish between the two types. The CPU interprets the literal as being of the type appropriate to the instruction.

Example 13.11: Interpreting Literal Mode Operands

Consider the machine code

The first instruction is SUBL2; the second is SUBF2. The first operand for both instructions is the literal mode byte 03. For the SUBL2 instruction the CPU interprets the literal as the integer 3; for the SUBF2 instruction it interprets the literal as follows:

$$00 \underbrace{000}_{p} \underbrace{011}_{f_r} = .1 \underbrace{011}_{f_r} \times 2^0 = \frac{1}{2} + \frac{1}{8} + \frac{1}{16} = 0.6875_{10}$$

For the first instruction the CPU does an integer subtraction, subtracting 3 from the contents of R9, which will be interpreted as a two's complement integer. For the second instruction the CPU does a floating-point subtraction, subtracting 0.6875_{10} from the contents of R9, which will be interpreted as a floating-point number.

When an instruction has a floating-point literal operand, the CPU expands the literal to a full-length floating-point format (depending on the instruction type) before performing the operation. Figure 13.3 shows how the expansion is done for type F. For types D, G, and H the additional longwords would contain all zeros.

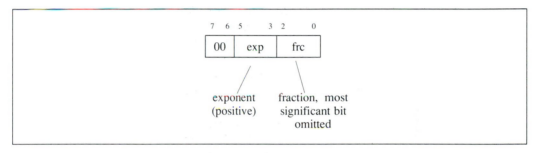

Figure 13.2 Floating-point literal format

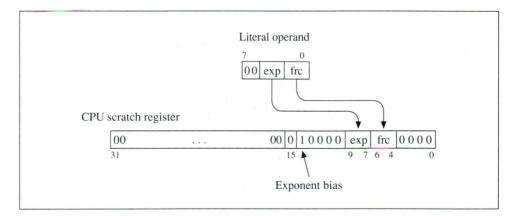

Figure 13.3 Expansion of a floating-point literal

13.4 EXAMPLE: COMPUTATIONAL ACCURACY IN COMPUTING VARIANCE

We showed in Section 13.2 that the results of floating-point arithmetic operations are not always exact, and we suggested that in long expressions, numbers of similar magnitude should be combined first. In this section we illustrate how the results may differ when the same quantity is computed using two different, but mathematically equivalent, formulas. A more thorough explanation of why the two formulas produce different results, and of how to estimate the accuracy of a computation, can be found in a numerical analysis course or textbook. Our example here is intended to alert the reader to the importance of such a course.

Suppose that we have an array of n floating-point numbers, $X(1),...,X(n)$, which we call sample points. The mean, or average, is defined as

$$\text{mean} = \frac{1}{n} \sum_{i=1}^{n} X(i)$$

The standard deviation is a measure of how far the points are from the mean. The variance is the square of the standard deviation. For this example we will compute the variance of the set of sample points. The variance is defined by

$$\text{var} = \frac{1}{n} \sum_{i=1}^{n} [X(i) - \text{mean}]^2 \tag{13.1}$$

The formula is usually simplified to

$$\text{var} = \frac{1}{n} \sum_{i=1}^{n} X(i)^2 - \text{mean}^2 \tag{13.2}$$

Procedures to compute the variance using each of these formulas are shown in Figs. 13.4 and 13.5. Formula 13.1 implies the need of two loops, one to compute the mean first, then one to do the summation shown in 13.1. Using formula 13.2, one loop can be used to compute the sum of the sample points and the sum of their squares. Thus one might expect the procedure using formula 13.2 to be slightly simpler and run slightly faster. Unfortunately, it can yield poor results. Computing and summing the differences between each sample point and the mean, as in formula 13.1, will be more accurate than computing the sums separately and taking one difference at the end.

To illustrate the difference between the formulas, both procedures were run with several sets of n sample points, where $n = 100$. For the first group of tests we generated points in normal distributions with an expected mean of 0.1234567 and expected standard deviations of 0.1, 0.01, 0.001, and 0.0001. For the second group of tests, half of the points are mean*(1 + epsilon) and half are mean*(1 − epsilon), where epsilon = 0.1, 0.01, 0.001, and 0.0001. From formula 13.1 it is clear that the correct value of the variance for this group is (mean*epsilon)^2. The third group of tests uses uniform distributions with gaps of 4*epsilon/n between points, for the same values of epsilon as above. For the second and third groups the mean is 0.1234567. Figure 13.6 shows the results of the tests. (The expected mean and variance are only estimates in the case of

```
;  PROCEDURE VARNC1 (SAMPLE, N, MEAN, VAR)
;
;  This procedure computes the mean and variance of the numbers
;  in the floating point array SAMPLE.  It uses the following
;  formula for the variance:
;
;                 1/n * SUM [(SAMPLE(i) - MEAN)^2]
;
;  INPUT ARGUMENTS
;
;        SAMPLE       sample values (floating point array)
;        N            the number of sample points (longword)
;
;  OUTPUT ARGUMENTS
;
;        MEAN         the mean (average) of the sample points
;                     (floating point)
;        VAR          variance (floating point)
;
;  OFFSETS FOR ARGUMENT LIST
;
SAMPLE = 4
N = 8
MEAN = 12
VAR = 16
;
;  REGISTER USE
;
;        R5          array pointer
;        R6          n, number of points
;        R7          loop limit (addr of last sample pt)
;        R8          scratch
;        R9          sum of sample points and mean
;        R10         variance
;
        .ENTRY  VARNC1,^M<R5,R6,R7,R8,R9,R10>
;
        MOVL    SAMPLE(AP),R5        ; Address of array
        MOVL    @N(AP),R6           ; n
        SUBL3   #1,R6,R8            ; n-1
        MULL2   #4,R8               ; 4*(n-1)
        ADDL3   R5,R8,R7            ; Loop limit
;
        CVTLF   R6,R6                ; n in floating point
;
```

Figure 13.4   Computing variance with formula 13.1 (continues next page)

```
        CLRF    R9                  ; Clear for sum of sample pts
ADD:    ADDF2   (R5),R9             ; Add sample value
        ACBL    R7,#4,R5,ADD        ; Loop control
;
        DIVF2   R6,R9               ; Compute mean
        MOVF    R9,@MEAN(AP)        ; Store mean
;
        CLRF    R10                 ; Clear for summation
        MOVL    SAMPLE(AP),R5       ; Initialize array ptr
;
TERM:   SUBF3   R9,(R5),R8          ; SAMPLE(i) - mean
        MULF2   R8,R8               ; (SAMPLE(i) - mean)^2
        ADDF2   R8,R10              ; Add square
        ACBL    R7,#4,R5,TERM       ; Loop control
;
        DIVF3   R6,R10,@VAR(AP)     ; Variance
        RET
        .END
```

Figure 13.4   (concluded)

```
; PROCEDURE VARNC2 (SAMPLE, N, MEAN, VAR)
;
; This procedure computes the mean and variance of the numbers
; in the floating point array SAMPLE.  It uses the following
; formula for the variance:
;
;               1/n * SUM [SAMPLE(i)^2]  -  MEAN^2
;
; INPUT ARGUMENTS
;
;       SAMPLE      sample values (floating point array)
;       N           the number of sample points (longword)
;
; OUTPUT ARGUMENTS
;
;       MEAN        the mean (average) of the sample points
;                   (floating point)
;       VAR         variance (floating point)
;
; OFFSETS FOR ARGUMENT LIST
;
```

Figure 13.5   Computing variance with formula 13.2 (continues next page)

```
        SAMPLE = 4
        N = 8
        MEAN = 12
        VAR = 16
        ;
        ; REGISTER USE
        ;
        ;       R5        array pointer
        ;       R6        n, number of points
        ;       R7        loop limit (addr of last sample pt)
        ;       R8        scratch
        ;       R9        sum of sample points
        ;       R10       sum of squares of sample pts
        ;
                .ENTRY    VARNC2,^M<R5,R6,R7,R8,R9,R10>
        ;
                MOVL      SAMPLE(AP),R5        ; Addr. of array
                MOVL      @N(AP),R6            ; n
                SUBL3     #1,R6,R8             ; n-1
                MULL2     #4,R8                ; 4*(n-1)
                ADDL3     R5,R8,R7             ; Loop limit
        ;
                CLRF      R9                   ; Clear for sum
                CLRF      R10                  ; Clear for sum of squares
        ;
        ADD:    ADDF2     (R5),R9              ; Add sample value
                MULF3     (R5),(R5),R8         ; (Sample point)^2
                ADDF2     R8,R10               ; Add square
                ACBL      R7,#4,R5,ADD         ; Loop control
        ;
                CVTLF     R6,R6                ; n in floating point
                DIVF2     R6,R9                ; Compute mean
                MOVF      R9,@MEAN(AP)         ; Store mean
        ;
                DIVF2     R6,R10               ; 1/n * sum of squares
                MULF2     R9,R9                ; Mean^2
                SUBF3     R9,R10,@VAR(AP)      ; Variance
        ;
                RET
                .END
```

Figure 13.5   (concluded)

NORMAL DISTRIBUTION

STD DEV	MEAN	VARIANCE 1	VARIANCE 2	EXPECTED VARIANCE
0.1000000E+00	0.1329546E+00	0.8948188E-02	0.8948196E-02	0.1000000E-01
0.1000000E-01	0.1244065E+00	0.8948187E-04	0.8948334E-04	0.1000000E-03
0.1000000E-02	0.1235517E+00	0.8948180E-06	0.8912757E-06	0.1000000E-05
0.1000000E-03	0.1234662E+00	0.8948234E-08	0.9313226E-09	0.9999999E-08

TWO POINTS

STD DEV	MEAN	VARIANCE 1	VARIANCE 2	EXPECTED VARIANCE
0.1000000E+00	0.1234565E+00	0.1524156E-03	0.1524547E-03	0.1524156E-03
0.1000000E-01	0.1234566E+00	0.1524159E-05	0.1532957E-05	0.1524156E-05
0.1000000E-02	0.1234566E+00	0.1524234E-07	0.4656613E-07	0.1524156E-07
0.1000000E-03	0.1234568E+00	0.1524199E-09	-0.1210719E-07	0.1524156E-09

UNIFORM DISTRIBUTION

STD DEV	MEAN	VARIANCE 1	VARIANCE 2	EXPECTED VARIANCE
0.1000000E+00	0.1234566E+00	0.1293599E-01	0.1293598E-01	0.1293600E-01
0.1000000E-01	0.1234568E+00	0.1293617E-03	0.1293560E-03	0.1293600E-03
0.1000000E-02	0.1234567E+00	0.1293722E-05	0.1295470E-05	0.1293600E-05
0.1000000E-03	0.1234567E+00	0.1294222E-07	0.1583248E-07	0.1293600E-07

Figure 13.6 Output from variance calculations

the normal distributions.) We can see that the results from the two formulas are similar for the first three tests in each group, but when epsilon = 0.0001, formula 13.1 still gives accurate results, while formula 13.2 is worthless.

The output shown in Fig. 13.6 was produced by a main program written in Fortran. Since the VAX Fortran compiler uses the standard procedure linkage conventions described in Chapter 9, a Fortran main program can call assembly language procedures without any unusual requirements. The Fortran statements used to call the procedures shown in Figs. 13.4 and 13.5 are

```
CALL VARNC1 (SAMPLE,N,XMEAN,VAR1)
CALL VARNC2 (SAMPLE,N,XMEAN,VAR2)
```

One advantage of using Fortran for the main program is that we can use standard Fortran I/O statements for the complex task of converting floating-point numbers from their internal representation to the character strings that appear in the output.

It should be clear that the points we have made here—that floating-point computation is tricky and care is needed to obtain accurate results—are not relevant only to the assembly language programmer. The computation steps done are the same whether a procedure is written in assembly language or a high-level language.

13.5   EXAMPLE: CONVERTING BETWEEN FLOATING POINT AND INTEGER

In this section we examine in detail the conversion of a number, say x, from floating-point representation (type F) to a two's complement longword integer, say n. We will write a function procedure that does the same operation as the CVTFL instruction. In addition to doing the conversion, the procedure sets the condition codes in the calling program's PSW saved in the stack frame. Thus on return from the procedure the condition codes will have the values they would have if the CVTFL instruction were used.

The steps carried out by the procedure are summarized below and illustrated in Fig. 13.7. The steps shown in the figure begin with x in R2. Recall that a function procedure returns its answer in R0.

1. Extract the biased exponent from bits 14:7 of x into a scratch register.
2. If the exponent of x is not positive, then $|x| < 1$, so $n = 0$. (The exponent is not positive if the biased exponent is ≤ 128.) If $n = 0$, set the Z bit in the calling program's PSW (saved on the stack in the call frame). Henceforth we assume that the exponent is positive.
3. Extract the fraction field, bits 31:16 and 6:0, into R0.
4. Set bit 7 of R0, thus inserting the most significant fraction bit that is omitted from the floating-point representation.
5. Interchange the two halves of R0 to get the fraction bits in a contiguous string in the proper order.
6. Determine how many positions the fraction bits must be shifted. To do this, observe that if we interpret the contents of R0 as an integer, its value is $1f_1f_2$, or $.1f_1f_2 \times 2^{24}$. The proper value for n is $.1f_1f_2 \times 2^p$, so R0 must be shifted (not rotated) $p - 24$ places. If $p - 24$ is negative, the shift will be to the right, as it should be. If the shift causes overflow, set the V bit in the calling program's PSW.
7. Test the sign, bit 15, of x; if x is negative, negate R0 and set the N bit in the calling program's PSW.

The procedure is shown in Fig. 13.8.

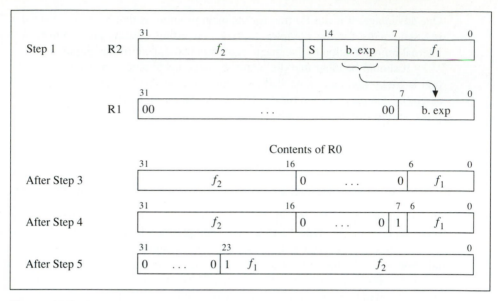

Figure 13.7 Some steps in the conversion from F_floating to integer

```
; FUNCTION CVTFL (ARG)
;
; This function converts its (single precision) floating point
; argument to a longword integer and returns the result in R0.
; The conversion truncates the fractional part of the argument.
; The appropriate condition code in the stacked calling program's
; PSW is set if the result is negative or zero or overflows.
;
; REGISTER USE
;
;       R0      longword result
;       R1      exponent
;       R2      floating point argument
;       R3      shift count
;
        .ENTRY  CVTFL,^M<R2,R3>
        MOVF    @4(AP),R2          ; Get floating pt arg
        BICL3   #^XFFFF807F,R2,R1  ; Extract biased exponent
        ROTL    #-7,R1,R1          ; Exponent in place
        CMPW    R1,#128            ; Determine if exp > 0
        BLEQ    ZERO               ; Exp <= 0, so result = 0
        BICL3   #^X0000FF80,R2,R0  ; Fraction bits in R0
```

Figure 13.8 The CVTFL procedure (continues next page)

```
               BISB2    #^X80,R0          ; Insert first fraction bit
               ROTL     #16,R0,R0         ; Fraction bits contiguous
               SUBL3    #152,R1,R3        ; Determine count for shift
               ASHL     R3,R0,R0          ; Shift fraction
               BVC      SIGN              ; Branch if no overflow
               BISB2    #^X02,4(FP)       ; Set V in stacked PSW
     SIGN:     TSTF     R2                ; Test sign
               BGEQ     DONE              ; If non-neg, then done
               MNEGL    R0,R0             ; Negate
               BISB2    #^X08,4(FP)       ; Set N in stacked PSW
     DONE:     RET
     ;
     ZERO:     CLRL     R0                ; Result = 0 if |arg| < 1
               BISB2    #^X04,4(FP)       ; Set Z in stacked PSW
               RET
               .END
```

Figure 13.8   (concluded)

We leave conversion from longword to floating point (without using CVTLF) as an exercise.

13.6   PACKED-DECIMAL DATA

We have already worked with data in packed-decimal format as an intermediate step in conversion between the two's complement integer representation and character code (Section 6.5). In this data type, an integer is represented as a string of from 0 to 31 decimal digits, packed two to a byte, and a sign, occupying the low-order nibble of the last byte in the string. (See Fig. 13.9.) The first (lowest-addressed) byte contains the most significant digit, and the remaining digits follow in natural order. [Alas, now that we have become used to reading memory "backward" (i.e., showing the lowest-addressed byte at the right in diagrams), the natural left-to-right format of packed decimal may at first be confusing.] The digits are represented in binary, and the sign is represented by the binary patterns 1010–1111—that is, A through F in hex. A, C, E, and F represent +, and B and D represent –. Signs in decimal strings generated by the CPU as the result of an operation are represented by C (+) or D (–). There are a few examples in Section 6.5.

The VAX, and many other computers, have machine instructions that do arithmetic on packed-decimal strings. Since we have a very compact and efficient representation for integers—two's complement—and a compact representation for very large numbers—floating point—it is reasonable to wonder why computer manufacturers would take the trouble to provide another data type and set of instructions for numeric computations. There are two reasons. One is that for some applications, particularly business applications involving amounts of money (e.g., budgeting, accounting), operands may be very large numbers and results must be exact to the penny; neither the integer representation

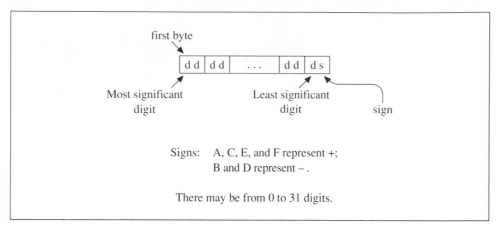

Figure 13.9   Packed-decimal string format

nor the floating-point representation may be satisfactory. Amounts in the tens or hundreds of millions of dollars cannot be represented in a longword. (We are assuming that the numbers include two decimal places for cents. The decimal point is assumed by the programmer; packed-decimal instructions treat the operands as integers.) Floating-point representation and operations are not satisfactory for such computations because of the accuracy problems described in Section 13.2.

Another reason for the use of packed decimal is that conversions between character code and two's complement (or floating point) for input and output are fairly slow operations. For integer input, for example, the character code is converted first to packed decimal by extracting the low-order nibbles from the character codes, then to two's complement by a Horner's-method computation, much as we described in Section 7.6. Although two's complement arithmetic is faster than packed-decimal arithmetic, in applications where very little arithmetic but a lot of I/O is done, it may be more efficient to leave the data in packed-decimal format. Again, an application area where this phenomenon commonly occurs is business applications. Thus, many COBOL compilers use packed decimal as the internal representation for data. The packed-decimal data type and instructions are not likely to be used by assembly language programmers.

13.7   PACKED-DECIMAL INSTRUCTIONS

Overview

Packed-decimal operands acted on by machine instructions must be in memory; they may not be in registers, and they may not be specified as immediate operands. A packed-decimal string is specified by the number of digits (not the number of bytes) in the string and the address of its first (lowest-numbered) byte. Since each string requires two instruction operands, some of the packed-decimal arithmetic instructions have four-operand and six-operand varieties, depending on whether the result replaces one of the strings or has a distinct destination.

Although many of the usual conventions are followed by the packed-decimal instructions, there are several special cases and potential problems to consider. If the number of digits is even, there will be an extra zero digit in the most significant place. If the number of digits is zero, the string occupies one byte containing a zero digit and a plus sign. (Although it is possible to represent –0 as a decimal string, the CPU always produces +0 when the result of an operation is zero and there is no overflow.)

If the result of an operation is smaller than the destination string allotted to it, the most significant digits are filled with zeros. If the result overflows the destination, a decimal overflow fault occurs and a program exception occurs if the decimal overflow trap bit (bit 7) in the PSW is set. This trap bit (like the integer overflow trap bit) is set or cleared on entrance to each procedure, depending on whether or not DV is specified in the register save mask at the procedure's entry point. Program exceptions will occur for reserved operands (a bad nibble in an operand or a number of digits outside the range 0–31) and for division by zero.

Because they work on long strings of bytes in memory (like the MOVC, CMPC, CVTSP, and some other instructions we have seen so far), the decimal instructions use some of the registers for scratch work. They all use R0–R3, and those that have a separate destination operand also use R4 and R5. R0, R2, and R4 (if used) will contain zero after the instruction executes; R1, R3, and R5 (if used) will contain the address of the byte containing the most significant digit of the first, second, and third (if any) decimal operand, respectively. These addresses may be useful to the programmer.

Warning: Unlike most VAX instructions, the six-operand decimal instructions may not work properly if the bytes in memory specified for the destination overlap either of the other decimal string operands.

All the decimal instructions affect the N, Z, and V condition codes in the usual ways. They clear C (with the exception of MOVP, which does not affect C).

Initializing Storage

The .PACKED directive is used to initialize storage with packed-decimal constants. Its formats are

.PACKED   *decimal_string*

.PACKED   *decimal_string,symbol*

The decimal string may have a sign and 0–31 digits. If a symbol is included in the directive, the assembler assigns to it the number of digits in the string; thus the symbol may be used as a literal operand in a decimal instruction to specify the number of digits.

Example 13.12: Defining a Decimal String

When the assembler encounters

```
DEC:     .PACKED -2846,DGTS
```

it assembles the constant as 02 84 6D in the bytes beginning at the current location; the value of the location counter is assigned to DEC and the value 4 is assigned to DGTS, which is an absolute symbol.

Note that since on assembly language program listings the contents of memory are shown right to left, the bytes containing the packed datum appear backward. For example, an assembler listing shows this directive as follows:

```
6D 84 02  001A      7 DEC:     .PACKED -2846,DGTS
```

(The "7" is the line number.)

Instructions

The packed-decimal arithmetic instructions are

$$\left.\begin{matrix}\text{ADDP}\\\text{SUBP}\end{matrix}\right\}\left\{\begin{matrix}4 & num\_dgts\_1,pkd1,num\_dgts\_2,pkd2\\6 & num\_dgts\_1,pkd1,num\_dgts\_2,pkd2,num\_dgts\_dest,dest\end{matrix}\right\}$$

MULP   *num_dgts_1,pkd1,num_dgts_2,pkd2,num_dgts_prod,prod*

DIVP   *num_dgts_dvsr,dvsr,num_dgts_dvdd,dvdd,num_dgts_quo,quo*

In these and all other decimal instructions, the number of digits is specified in a word operand. The DIVP instruction produces an integer quotient; it truncates toward zero, as do the integer DIV instructions. DIVP may use 16 bytes of scratch space on the stack; it will decrement SP to reserve the space and reset SP to release it when it is finished.

Example 13.13: Adding Packed-Decimal Strings

Assume the following memory contents:

SALARIES

| 00 | 04 | 37 | 82 | 60 | 0C |

TRAVEL

| 64 | 09 | 00 | 0C |

After executing

```
ADDP6   #10,SALARIES,#7,TRAVEL,#12,EXPENDITURES
```

we have the following result beginning at EXPENDITURES, and the N, Z, V, and C condition codes are clear.

EXPENDITURES

| 00 | 00 | 05 | 01 | 91 | 60 | 0C |

The MOVP instruction format is

MOVP   *num_dgts,source,dest*

The number of digits for the source and destination is the same.

There are two CMPP instructions because the numbers of digits in the two strings compared may differ. The instructions are

$$\text{CMPP3}\quad num\_dgts,pkd1,pkd2$$

$$\text{CMPP4}\quad num\_dgts\_1,pkd1,num\_dgts\_2,pkd2$$

We described the instructions that convert between packed decimal and two's complement and leading separate numeric in Section 6.5. They are included in the table of decimal instructions in the summary section that follows.

There are no CLR, MOVA, or TST instructions for packed-decimal data.

13.8   SUMMARY

The VAX has two standard floating-point data types: single precision (type F) in a longword, and double precision (type D) in a quadword, and two additional types: G and H. Floating-point numbers on the VAX may be expressed as

$$\pm f \times 2^p$$

where $0.5 \le f < 1$ and $-127 \le p \le 127$ (for types F and D)

They are always in normalized form; that is, the first bit after the binary point is a 1; that bit does not appear in the internal representation. The exponent is stored in a biased form; that is, the exponent field contains $p + 2^{t-1}$, where t is the number of bits in the exponent field. The formats are shown in Fig. 13.1.

Because only a finite number of bits are used to store the fraction part of a floating-point number, the results of arithmetic operations are not always exact. Unless care is taken in arranging the computation, large errors can result.

Decimal data may be stored in packed-decimal string format—with each decimal digit represented in binary in four bits with a sign in the last nibble of the string. (See Fig. 13.9.) Packed-decimal data and instructions are used primarily by high-level language compilers for business applications languages because fairly large integers (up to 31 digits on the VAX) may be stored and operated on with exact accuracy.

Decimal string operands are specified by two instruction operands: the number of digits in the string and the address of its first byte. All the decimal string instructions use R0–R3; the six-operand instructions also use R4 and R5.

The floating-point and packed-decimal instructions follow the usual conventions about the roles of operands and effects on condition codes. They interpret their operands as being of the type appropriate to the instruction. Program exceptions can occur for overflow, reserved operands, division by zero, and floating-point underflow. The programmer has the option of enabling or disabling the decimal overflow and floating underflow traps.

Floating-point constants may be assembled in memory using the .x_FLOATING directives (for x = F, D, G, or H). Floating-point instruction operands may use immediate or literal mode. A floating-point literal has a three-bit true exponent and three fraction bits. (See Fig. 13.2.) Decimal constants are assembled in memory using the .PACKED directive. Decimal operands may not use register, immediate, or literal mode.

The instructions described in this chapter are listed in Tables 13.2 (floating point) and 13.3 (packed decimal).

TABLE 13.2 FLOATING-POINT INSTRUCTIONS

Instruction		Types	Operation

All the instructions affect the condition codes in the usual ways.

ADDx2	$op1,op2$	x = F, D, G, or H	$op1 + op2 \rightarrow op2$
ADDx3	$op1,op2,dest$	"	$op1 + op2 \rightarrow dest$
SUBx2	$op1,op2$	"	$op2 - op1 \rightarrow op2$
SUBx3	$op1,op2,dest$	"	$op2 - op1 \rightarrow dest$
MULx2	$op1,op2$	"	$op1 * op2 \rightarrow op2$
MULx3	$op1,op2,dest$	"	$op1 * op2 \rightarrow dest$
DIVx2	$op1,op2$	"	$op2/op1 \rightarrow op2$
DIVx3	$op1,op2,dest$	"	$op2/op1 \rightarrow dest$
CLRx	$dest$	"	$0.0 \rightarrow dest$
MOVx	$source,dest$	"	$source \rightarrow dest$
MOVAx	$source,dest$	"	$source\ address \rightarrow dest$
MNEGx	$source,dest$	"	$-source \rightarrow dest$
TSTx	op	"	just affect condition
CMPx	$op1,op2$	"	codes
CVT.xy	$source,dest$	x = B,W,L,F,D,G,H	source (type x) converted to type y
		y = B,W,L,F,D,G,H	$\rightarrow dest$
		$x \neq y,\ xy \neq$ DG or GD	
CVTRxL	$source,dest$	x = F, D, G, H	source converted to L, rounded $\rightarrow dest$
ACBx	$limit,incr,index,dest$	x = F, D, G, or H	$index + incr \rightarrow index$; branch to $dest$ if $incr > 0$ and $index \leq limit$, or $incr < 0$ and $index \geq limit$

TABLE 13.3 PACKED-DECIMAL INSTRUCTIONS

Instruction		Operation

All the instructions affect the condition codes in the usual ways.

ADDP4	$num1,pkd,num2,pkd2$	$pkd1 + pkd2 \rightarrow pkd2$
ADDP6	$num1,pkd1,num2,pkd2,num\_dest,dest$	$pkd1 + pkd2 \rightarrow dest$
SUBP4	$num1,pkd1,num2,pkd2$	$pkd2 - pkd1 \rightarrow pkd2$
SUBP6	$num1,pkd1,num2,pkd2,num\_dest,dest$	$pkd2 - pkd1 \rightarrow dest$
MULP	$num1,pkd1,num2,pkd2,num\_prod,prod$	$pkd1 * pkd2 \rightarrow prod$
DIVP	$num1,pkd1,num2,pkd2,num\_quo,quo$	$pkd2/pkd1 \rightarrow quo$
MOVP	$num,source,dest$	$source \rightarrow dest$
CMPP3	$num,pkd1,pkd2$	Compare $pkd1$ and $pkd2$;
CMPP4	$num1,pkd1,num2,pkd2$	affect condition codes.
CVTLP	$long,num,pkd$	$long$, converted from 2's comp to packed $\rightarrow pkd$
CVTPL	$num,pkd,long$	pkd, converted to 2's comp $\rightarrow long$
CVTPS	num_p,pkd,num_s,lsn	pkd, converted to leading sep. numeric $\rightarrow lsn$
CVTSP	num_s,lsn,num_p,pkd	lsn, converted to packed $\rightarrow pkd$

13.9 EXERCISES

1. What floating-point number is represented by each of the following? Show your answers in decimal.

   (a) 0000BFC0
   (b) 8000C40A
   (c) 43000041
   (d) 430047A0
   (e) 00004080
   (f) C000C3B4

2. Show the floating-point representation (type F) of each of the following:

   (a) 25
   (b) –2
   (c) 1048576 $(=2^{20})$
   (d) $-41\frac{7}{16}$
   (e) 5/8
   (f) 1
   (g) $21\frac{3}{16}$

3. What does it mean to say that a floating-point number is *normalized*? What are the advantages of a normalized representation?

4. Suppose that 10 bits were used for the exponent in floating-point numbers on the VAX. Give the formula for computing the actual exponent from the biased exponent.

5. Write instructions to compute $7x^2 + 3.8xy - 5.2y^4$, where x and y are floating-point numbers (type F) stored at X and Y, respectively.

6. Suppose that R5 contains 8A004E14 and R9 contains 06004A31. What will be in R5 and R9, and how will the Z and N condition codes be set after each of the following instructions?

   (a) ADDF2   R9,R5
   (b) ADDB2   R9,R5
   (c) SUBF2 R9,R5

7. Explain what *floating-point underflow* is and how it can be caused.

8. Show the machine code for

        MULD3   #2.5,R5,-(R8)

9. On some computers, any floating-point number with zeros in all the fraction bits is interpreted as floating-point zero. Why is this not done on the VAX?

10. We observed that some floating-point instructions are identical to the corresponding integer instructions; for example, CLRF is the same instruction as CLRL. Is TSTF the same as TSTL or TSTW? If the instructions are not the same, explain how they differ.

11. What are the differences in the operations of MOVL, MOVW, and MOVF?

12. Write a program segment to estimate the area under the graph of $y = x^2$ by summing the areas of the rectangles shown in Fig. 13.10. Assume that X1, X2, and EPSILON contain floating-point numbers (type F). Use the ACBF instruction for loop control.

13. The macros defined in Examples 11.5, 11.6, and 11.12 have an argument TYPE that specifies the data type that the instructions in the macros operate on. Would F, D, G, and H be acceptable values for the TYPE argument in any or all of the macros? Why or why not?

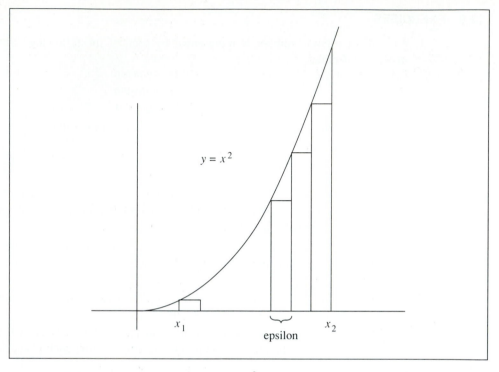

Figure 13.10   Area under the graph of $y = x^2$

14. Show (in hex) the representation for the smallest and largest positive numbers that can be represented as D_floating numbers.

15. Construct an example to show that the associative law for addition is not always satisfied by floating-point arithmetic.

16. We showed that using VAX floating-point arithmetic, $a + b = b$ does not imply that $a = 0$ by adding $1/2$ and 2^{24} and getting 2^{24} as the result. Could we have made the same point by adding $1/2$ and 2^{23}? Work out the addition in detail to show why or why not.

17. Suppose that two positive floating-point numbers are multiplied. What is the maximum number of positions the product may need to be shifted to normalize the result? Why?

18. Outline the steps that would be carried out to convert a type F floating-point number to type D without using CVTFD.

19. Write a procedure CVTFD to do the task described in Exercise 18. The procedure should set the condition codes in the calling program's PSW (in the call frame on the stack) in the same ways as the CVTFD instruction does.

20. Outline the steps that would be carried out to convert a type D floating-point number to type F without using CVTDF. (The result should be rounded.)

21. Show (in hex representation) a double-precision floating-point number that would cause overflow if used as the first operand of CVTDF.

22. Write a procedure CVTDF to do the task described in Exercise 20. The procedure should set the condition codes in the calling program's PSW (in the call frame on the stack) in the same ways as the CVTDF instruction does.

23. Outline the steps that would be carried out to convert a longword integer to floating point (type F) without using CVTLF.

24. Write a procedure CVTLF to do the task described in Exercise 23. The procedure should set the condition codes in the calling program's PSW (in the call frame on the stack) the same way the CVTLF instruction does.

25. Modify the procedure CVTFL in Fig. 13.8 so that it returns a rounded result rather than a truncated one (i.e., it should act like CVTRFL rather than CVTFL).

26. Outline the steps you would use to convert a floating point number to a character string in the following format:

$$\pm . b_1 b_2 b_3 \cdots b_{22} b_{23} b_{24} \times 2 \wedge p$$

where $b_1, \ldots, b_{24}$ are the fraction bits and p is the exponent. Write a procedure that does the conversion. (Of course, there are other formats for the output that would be more natural and more compact, but more work is required to get them. You may want to choose other output formats and write procedures for them.)

27. Show the representation of the decimal number 135,276 in each of the following data types: longword, F_floating, G_floating, leading separate numeric, and packed decimal.

28. Why is it that packed-decimal operands cannot be specified as immediate operands? (The reason has something to do with the way the operand specifier is treated at execution time.)

29. Write a macro definition for a macro TSTP that acts as a test instruction for packed-decimal data. It should have two arguments, NUM_DGTS and PKD, and should set or clear the N and Z condition codes to indicate if the specified decimal string is negative or zero. (If your macro explicitly tests the sign and digits of the decimal string, it will get quite complicated. There is a very short solution.)

30. Write a complete program to read in two numbers from the terminal, convert them to packed decimal, multiply them, and print out the result.

14

Character Strings

14.1 OVERVIEW

The VAX has a powerful collection of character string instructions that are useful for, among other things, processing input data and preparing data for output. Some of the instructions are especially helpful for text editing and similar applications where the data operated on are long segments of text. In addition to the MOVC3 and CMPC3 instructions that we have already seen, there are more complex move and compare instructions and instructions to search a string for particular characters or substrings, translate characters, and edit numeric data for output. All these operations could be programmed using other instructions; but having one instruction that performs a complex task simplifies the programmer's job, reduces the likelihood of errors, and makes programs run faster.

Most computers do not have instructions like those in this chapter. If one's purpose in reading this book is to learn basic concepts and features common to many machines and assembly languages, this chapter may be skipped.

A character string is a contiguous string of characters; for example,

/CHAPTER 14/

is a character string enclosed between delimiters (the slashes). In the context of character string operations, however, we would define a character string to be a string of character codes (ASCII codes on the VAX) occupying contiguous bytes of memory. (This might

388

more properly be called a *representation* of a character string, but for simplicity of language we will not do so.) For example:

STRING

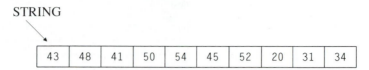

For the purposes of the character string instructions, this definition is more restrictive than need be. The instructions act on any string of bytes in memory; the bytes may contain any eight-bit patterns, even ones that are not used as ASCII codes. However, the instructions are used most often on bytes that contain character codes.

A character string is specified in an instruction by its length, or number of bytes, and the address of its first byte. (The string cannot be in a register or specified as an immediate operand.) In all the character string instructions, the length is a word operand.

As with other string data types on the VAX (e.g., packed decimal and leading separate numeric), what we would naturally consider the first, or leftmost, byte occupies the lowest-addressed byte of the string in memory, and the rest of the characters follow in natural order. Hence, in our diagrams of character strings in memory, we usually show the lowest-addressed byte at the left.

Because the operations carried out by the character string instructions require processing many bytes of operands of varying lengths, the CPU uses some registers for scratch work (for pointers and counters) just as the programmer would if he or she were writing loops to carry out the operations. In many cases the data left in the registers when execution of the instruction is completed are very useful to the programmer. For example, for the instruction, LOCC, that searches a character string for the first instance of a specified character, the CPU uses R1 as a pointer to the byte currently being examined. When the instruction terminates, R1 will contain the address of the byte containing the character sought (if it appears in the string at all). The particular registers used and the data left in them vary with the different instructions, so we provide the details when we present each instruction.

14.2   THE MOVC AND CMPC INSTRUCTIONS

We have already seen and used the MOVC3 and CMPC3 instructions:

MOVC3   *len,source,dest*

CMPC3   *len,string1,string2*

MOVC3 copies the string beginning at *source* to the bytes beginning at *dest*; CMPC3 compares the strings beginning at *string1* and *string2*. There is only one length operand because the strings are assumed to be the same length. Both instructions have a variation that allows for strings of different lengths. They are

MOVC5   *srclen,source,fill,dstlen,dest*

CMPC5   *len1,string1,fill,len2,string2*

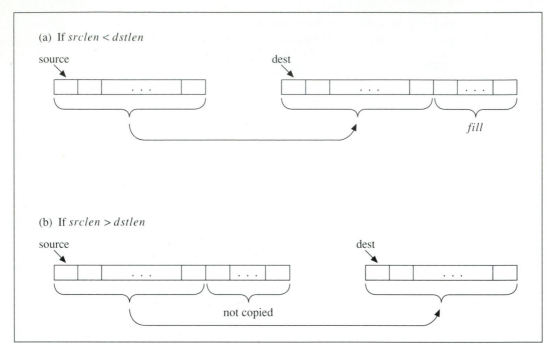

Figure 14.1   What MOVC5 does

The third operand is a fill character that is used to pad out the shorter string when necessary. All the length operands are word integers, as they are for MOVC3 and CMPC3.

MOVC5—Copy a Character String

For the MOVC5 instruction, if the source length is less than the destination length, the remaining bytes at the end of the destination string are filled with the fill character; if the source length is larger than the destination length, the extra characters at the end of the source string are not copied. Figure 14.1 illustrates these cases. Of course, if the lengths are equal, the source is copied to the destination as it would be by MOVC3.

Example 14.1: Copying Character Strings

Suppose that BUFFER is an area of memory where we are constructing a line to be printed as part of a table with several columns, each 20 spaces wide. R8 contains the address of the character string that is to appear on the current line in the third column of the table, and R9 contains its length. The item on the previous line may have been longer than the current one, so if we simply moved the new string into the buffer, extraneous characters could appear in the output. The following instruction moves the current string into the buffer and blanks out the extra spaces in the column. Here and in many other examples in this chapter, we assume that BLANK has been assigned the value ^A/ /.

```
MOVC5    R9,(R8),#BLANK,#20,BUFFER+40
```

Example 14.2: Filling a Line with a Character

If the source length in a MOVC5 instruction is zero, the destination string is filled with copies of the fill character. The following instruction creates a line of asterisks in memory beginning at LINE.

```
        MOVC5    #0,0,#^A/*/,#80,LINE
```

Note that since the source string has length zero and is not accessed by the CPU, its address can be somewhat arbitrary; we used 0 for simplicity.

The MOVC5 instruction sets the condition codes to indicate the relation between the source length and destination length. Thus, for example, a MOVC5 instruction can be followed by

```
        BGTR     TRUNC
```

to take any special action that might be needed if the destination received a truncated copy of the source string. MOVC5, like MOVC3, uses R0–R5. It leaves the following data in these registers:

R0:   the number of bytes in the source string that were not copied to the destination

R1:   the address of the byte following the last source byte copied

R2:   0

R3:   the address of the byte following the destination string

R4,R5:   0

MOVC5 will work properly even if the source and destination overlap.

Example 14.3: Formatting Output

Suppose that, as in Example 14.1, we move character strings into a buffer to be printed as part of a table, but if a string is too long for its column, we wish to print the rest of it on the next line. If no entries on a line are too long, the line of the table will be followed by a blank line. We assume that no entry needs more than 40 spaces and that BUF2 is available to set up the extra line.

```
        MOVC5    #0,0,#BLANK,#80,BUF2            ; Blank out BUF2
COL_1:     .

           .
COL_2:     .

           .
COL_3:  MOVC5    R9,(R8),#BLANK,#20,BUFFER+40  ; Copy string to colm
        BLEQ     COL_4                          ; Branch if item fits
        MOVC5    R0,(R1),#BLANK,#20,BUF2+40    ; Copy extra bytes
COL_4:     .

           .

           .
        PRINTCHRS BUFFER,#80                     ; Print table line
        PRINTCHRS BUF2,#80                       ; Print extra line
```

Note that if the BLEQ instruction had been omitted, the instruction sequence would still have worked properly; if the item copied by the first MOVC5 instruction were no longer than 20 bytes, R0 would contain 0, so the second MOVC5 instruction would move 20 blanks to BUF2+40.

CMPC5—Compare Character Strings

If the lengths of the strings compared by the CMPC5 instruction are different, the CPU treats the strings as if the shorter one had been padded at the end with copies of the fill character to make it the same length as the longer one. (No changes are actually made to the strings in memory.) CMPC5, like CMPC3, compares the strings byte by byte and stops when the bytes compared are not equal or when the ends of the strings are reached. The condition codes indicate the relation between the last bytes compared; that is, N = 1 if and only if the *string1* byte is less than the *string2* byte (as two's complement integers), Z = 1 if and only if they are equal (i.e., the ends of the strings were reached without encountering bytes that differed), and C = 1 if and only if the *string1* byte is less than the *string2* byte as unsigned integers. V is cleared.

CMPC3 and CMPC5 use R0–R3. After either instruction is executed, the contents of these registers will be as follows:

R0:   the number of bytes remaining in *string1* (counting the one that terminated the comparison if the strings were unequal, but not counting fill bytes, if any)

R1:   the address of the byte in *string1* where the comparison stopped, that is, the address of the first byte in *string1* that did not match the corresponding byte of *string2*, if there is such a byte; otherwise, the address of the byte following the end of *string1*

R2:   same as R0, but for *string2*

R3:   same as R1, but for *string2*

Example 14.4: CMPC5

Suppose that R5 contains xxxx0012 and R7 contains xxxx0007 (where the x's indicate data in the registers that are not used), and the bytes of memory beginning at STRING1 and STRING2 are as follows:

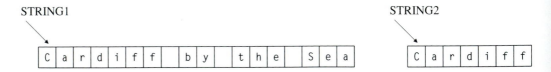

STRING1

STRING2

When the instruction

```
CMPC5    R5,STRING1,#BLANK,R7,STRING2
```

is executed, STRING2 will be padded (conceptually) with 11 blanks. The comparison will terminate at the ninth byte, where 62_{16}, the ASCII code for "b" in STRING1, will be compared to 20_{16}, the second padded blank added to STRING2. All four condition codes will be cleared because $62 > 20$, and the contents of R0–R3 will be as follows:

R0: 0000000A   (the number of bytes remaining in STRING1)
R1: STRING1+8 (the address of the "b")
R2: 00000000   (No bytes remain in STRING2.)
R3: STRING2+7 (not STRING2+8)

14.3 CHARACTER-SEARCH INSTRUCTIONS

The VAX has five character-search instructions. There are instructions that search for, or skip over, a specified character or any characters in a specified set, and an instruction that searches for a specified substring.

LOCC and SKPC—Find or Skip a Specified Character

The LOCC (LOCate Character) instruction scans a character string for the first instance of a specified character; SKPC (SKiP Character) scans a character string for the first instance of a character *other than* the one specified. The instruction formats are

$$\text{LOCC} \quad char,len,string$$

$$\text{SKPC} \quad char,len,string$$

The "result" we would want from these operations is the address of the byte at which the search terminates, but there is no destination operand for this result. LOCC and SKPC use R0 and R1 for a counter and pointer, respectively, while searching the string. The values they leave in these registers and the condition codes when they finish executing are:

R0: the number of bytes remaining in the string, including the character that was sought, if it was found

R1: the address of the byte sought, or, if none was found, the address of the byte following the end of the string

Z: cleared if a byte of the desired kind is found, set otherwise

The other condition codes are cleared.

Thus instructions that follow LOCC or SKPC can use R1 as a pointer to the byte sought (after testing Z to make sure one was found). R0 and R1 can be used particularly easily to restart the search in applications where each instance of the character sought, or each segment separated by two of them, must be processed in some way. The next example illustrates this. To focus on the use of R0 and R1, the example does a very simple task of processing the segments: counting them.

Example 14.5: Searching for a Character

Suppose that a string of text consisting of several substrings separated by slashes is in memory beginning at TEXT, and suppose that LEN is a word containing the length of the string. For example, the text might be

```
/October 3/7:30 P.M./AGENDA/
```

The following instructions count the substrings.

```
; REGISTER USE
;
;        R0       length of remaining string
;        R1       address of remaining string
;        R5       counter
;
         CLRL     R5                 ; Counter is 0
         MOVAB    TEXT,R1
         MOVW     LEN,R0             ; Length of string
;
SEARCH:  DECL     R0                 ; Skip the slash
         LOCC     #^A'/',R0,1(R1)    ; Scan for next slash
         BEQL     DONE               ; Branch if no slash
         INCL     R5                 ; Count substring
         BRB      SEARCH
DONE:
```

Care must be taken to get the lengths and address right to begin each search at the byte after the slash just found, so that the same one will not be found again.

If the processing of each character or segment found using LOCC involves printing or copying the strings, or any other operations that change the contents of R0 and R1 as side effects, the contents of R0 and R1 must be saved in other registers so that the address and length of the remaining segment of the source are not lost. (The same problem occurs with the other character instructions.)

The SKPC instruction is especially useful for skipping over blanks and finding meaningful, nonblank data in a character string. LOCC and SKPC can be used together very effectively to process free-format numerical input. The next example shows how.

Example 14.6: Processing Free-Format Input

The procedure CVTCL in Fig. 14.2 finds the first leading separate numeric string in a character string and converts it to two's complement. It assumes that the character string contains zero or more leading separate numeric strings separated by at least one blank. SKPC is used to skip over blanks and find the beginning of the first string; then LOCC finds a blank at the end of it. CVTCL returns the address of the byte that follows the leading separate numeric string and the length of the remaining part of the character string so that it can be called repeatedly to process each number in the string.

SCANC and SPANC—Searching for Sets of Characters

SCANC (SCAN Characters) searches a string for any one of a set of characters. SPANC (SPAN Characters) searches for any character not in the set specified. (Clearly, SPANC could be considered superfluous because one could specify the complementary set of characters and use SCANC. Having SPANC just makes things a bit simpler for the

```
; PROCEDURE CVTCL (STRING, LENGTH, NUMBER, NEXT, NEWLEN)
;
; This procedure searches a character string for the first
; instance of a leading separate numeric datum, converts it to
; a two's complement longword, and returns the address of the
; next byte of the string and the remaining length.  The
; procedure assumes that the leading separate numeric data in
; the string are separated by blanks.
;
; INPUT ARGUMENTS
;
;       STRING  the character string
;       LENGTH  the number of bytes in the string (word)
;
; OUTPUT ARGUMENTS
;
;       NUMBER  the two's complement representation of the
;               first number found in the string (longword)
;       NEXT    the address of the byte in the string following
;               the leading separate numeric string that was
;               found and converted.  (The argument list contains
;               the address of a longword where this address is
;               to be stored.)
;       NEWLEN  the number of bytes remaining in the string
;               (word)
;
; A flag is returned in R0 indicating whether or not a number was
; found in the string.  1 = success; 0 = failure.
; In the case of failure, no values are stored for the three
; output arguments.
;
; No error checking is done for bad characters or too many digits.
;
; METHOD
;
;    A leading separate numeric string consists of a byte
; containing a sign (which may be blank) followed by bytes
; containing digits (all in character code).  The conversion
; instruction requires the address of the string (i.e., its
; sign byte) and the number of digits.
;    SKPC is used to skip over all leading blanks.  It stops at
; the first non-blank which may be a sign or the first digit in
; the case where the sign is a blank.  In the latter case, the
; pointer is decremented by 1.  Then LOCC is used to find the
```

Figure 14.2 The procedure CVTCL (continues next page)

```
    ; blank that follows the leading separate numeric string.  Whether
    ; a blank is found or the end of the entire character string is
    ; reached, R1 will contain the address of the byte following the
    ; lsn string.
    ;
    BLANK = ^A/ /
    ZEROCODE = ^A/0/
    PKD:      .BLKB    16
    ;
    ; OFFSETS FOR ARGUMENT LIST
    ;
    STRING = 4
    LENGTH = 8
    NUMBER = 12
    NEXT = 16
    NEWLEN = 20
    ;
    ; REGISTER USE
    ;
    ;        R2-R3       used by CVTSP and CVTPL
    ;        R5          length of string
    ;        R6          address of lsn
    ;        R7          number of digits in lsn
    ;
             .ENTRY   CVTCL,^M<R2,R3,R5,R6,R7>
    ;
    ; Find beginning of lsn
    ;
             MOVW     @LENGTH(AP),R5          ; Get length of string
             BLEQ     NONE                    ; No lsn if len <= 0
             SKPC     #BLANK,R5,@STRING(AP)   ; Scan for non-blank
             BEQL     NONE                    ; No lsn if all blank
             MOVL     R1,R6                   ; Addr of first non-blank
             CMPB     (R6),#ZEROCODE          ; See if digit
             BLSS     LSN                     ; Branch if non-digit
             DECL     R6                      ; Back up to sign (blank)
    ;
    ; Find end of lsn
    ;
    LSN:     LOCC     #BLANK,R0,(R1)          ; Scan for blank
             MOVL     R1,@NEXT(AP)            ; Store addr of next byte
             MOVW     R0,@NEWLEN(AP)          ; Store remaining length
             SUBL3    R6,R1,R7                ; Number of bytes in lsn
             DECL     R7                      ; Number of digits
```

Figure 14.2   (continues next page)

```
;
; Convert
;
          CVTSP    R7,(R6),R7,PKD
          CVTPL    R7,PKD,@NUMBER(AP)          ; Store 2's comp
;
; Set flag and return
;
          MOVL     #1,R0                       ; Success
          RET
;
NONE:     CLRL     R0                          ; Failure
          RET
          .END
```

Figure 14.2 (concluded)

programmer.) There are several applications where we want to find any one of a special group of characters. A compiler, for example, may search a program statement for any operator or delimiter. We may want to count the vowels used in a long piece of text. When processing input containing numeric data, SPANC could be used to scan for bad characters—say, anything other than digits, blanks, and signs.

The instructions formats are

$$\text{SCANC} \quad \textit{len,string,table,mask}$$

$$\text{SPANC} \quad \textit{len,string,table,mask}$$

The table and mask are used to determine which characters are sought. The table is usually 256 bytes long. The contents of a byte, when treated as an unsigned integer, is between 0 and 255. SCANC and SPANC use the contents of each byte in the string as an index into the table; that is, if the byte in the string contains the number n, then the byte at the table address $+ n$ is examined to determine if the string byte is in the set desired. A simple way of distinguishing characters not wanted from those that are sought would be to put zero and nonzero entries in the appropriate places in the table. Some computers have an instruction similar to SCANC that simply scans the string until it reaches a byte whose table entry is nonzero. The VAX instructions are more flexible. A logical AND operation is performed on the table byte and the mask operand specified in the instruction. If the result is nonzero for SCANC, or zero for SPANC, the instruction stops at the current byte. (See Fig. 14.3 for an illustration.) The use of the mask means that one table can be set up to be used with several SCANC and SPANC instructions to search for different sets of characters at different times.

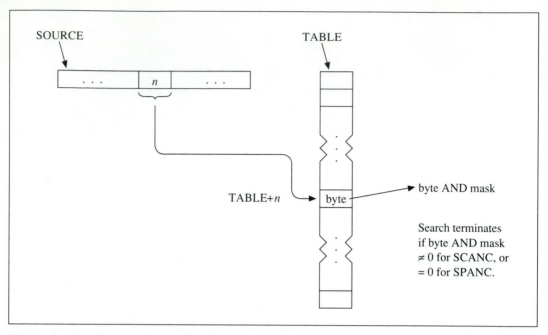

Figure 14.3   Accessing the table in SCANC and SPANC

Example 14.7: A Table for SCANC and SPANC

One of the tasks performed by a compiler, *lexical analysis*, includes finding and extracting the separate items, called *tokens*, that make up a statement. Some examples of tokens are variable names, operators, and constants. Some of the kinds of entries that we might want to have in a table to be used to extract tokens are:

Character group	Table entry (in binary)
Arithmetic operator	00000001
Relational operator	00000010
Statement terminator	00000100
(e.g., blank or ';')	
Letters (except 'E')	00010000
'E'	00110000
Digits	01100000

We are not trying to be complete here, and we are ignoring many of the special cases a compiler must handle. The main point is to illustrate how the table entries and the mask can be chosen for flexibility in specifying different sets of characters. Consider the following examples.

If we wish to search for the first arithmetic operator, we could use SCANC with the mask ^X01. We would find the first character of a variable name by scanning for a letter with the mask ^X10. We could find the end of it using SPANC with the mask ^X70 to skip over letters and digits.

Why are two bits set in the entry for digits, and why did we make the entry for 'E' a special case? 'E' could appear as a letter, hence bit 4 is on, but it can also appear in a floating-point constant to indicate an exponent. Thus we might want to include 'E' with digits sometimes by using the mask ^X20. The mask ^X40 will distinguish digits from 'E'.

The table could be set up at assembly time as shown below. For simplicity we will fill all bytes in the table not mentioned above with zeros. See the table of ASCII codes in Appendix C to check that the entries are in the correct places.

```
TABLE:  .BYTE    0[32]                      ; ASCII special chars
        .BYTE    4,0[9]                     ; Blank and special chars
        .BYTE    1,1,0,1,0,1                ; * + ' - . /
        .BYTE    ^X60[10]                   ; Digits
        .BYTE    0,4,2,2,2,0,0             ; : ; < = > ? @
        .BYTE    ^X10[4],^X30,^X10[21]     ; Letters
        .BYTE    0[6]                       ; Miscellaneous
        .BYTE    ^X10[26]                   ; Lowercase letters
        .BYTE    0[133]                     ; Misc. and non-ASCII
```

Note that if we were certain that all bytes in the source string contain valid ASCII codes, we could make the table only 128 bytes long, because TABLE+128 through TABLE+255 would not be accessed.

When the SCANC or SPANC instruction finds a byte of the type sought or reaches the end of the string, the following data are left in R0–R3 and the condition codes:

R0: the number of bytes remaining in the string, including the one that terminated the search if the search terminated because of a table entry

R1: the address of the byte in the string whose table entry terminated the search, if any; otherwise, the address of the byte following the string

R2: 0

R3: the address of the table

Z: cleared if the search was terminated by a table entry; set otherwise

The other condition codes are cleared.

R0 and R1 may be used as after LOCC and SKPC to process the character found, the segment that precedes it, and the remainder of the string as desired.

MATCHC—Match a Character String

The MATCHC instruction searches for the first instance of a specified substring, rather than a single character, in a character string. The operation it does is sometimes called pattern matching, and the substring sought is called the *pattern* or *object string*. This is an especially powerful instruction that is very useful in text-editing applications. The instruction format is

MATCHC *patrn_len,pattern,str_len,string*

MATCHC uses R0–R3 and provides information about the results of its search to the program in these registers and the Z condition code as follows:

R0:   0 if a match was found; otherwise, the length of the pattern

R1:   the address of the byte following the pattern if a match was found; otherwise, the address of the pattern

R2:   the number of bytes in the string that follow the first instance of the pattern, if any; otherwise, 0

R3:   the address of the byte following the end of the first instance of the pattern in the string, if any; otherwise, the address of the byte following the string

Z: set if a match was found; otherwise, clear

The other condition codes are cleared.

R2 and R3 (and Z) contain the information that is most useful. Subtracting the pattern length from the address in R3 gives the address of the byte where the pattern begins in the string. Note that for the other four instructions described in this section Z is cleared if the search is successful, but for MATCHC, Z is set if the search is successful.

Example 14.8: The Effects of MATCHC

Suppose that R6 contains xxxx0023, R7 contains xxxx0005, and we have the following strings in memory:

LINE

PATRN

The instruction

              MATCHC   R7,PATRN,R6,LINE

will leave the following data in Z and R0–R3:

Z: 1   (There was a match.)
R0: 00000000   (There was a match.)
R1: PATRN+5   (the address of the byte after the pattern)
R2: 0000000C   (the number of bytes in the string following the match)
R3: LINE+23   (the address of the blank after "which")

Example 14.9: Deleting a Substring

The procedure DELETE in Fig. 14.4 finds a specified substring in a string and deletes it by moving up all characters that follow the matched substring. Note that the data left in R2 and R3 by the MATCHC instruction are used as operands in the MOVC3 instruction. Also note that although the length operands are words, the pattern length was converted to a longword because it is used in the computation of an address (that of the copy of the pattern in the string).

In Chapter 7 we considered the problem of searching for a particular item in a table. We discussed two algorithms for solving the search problem: sequential search and binary search (which requires that the table be sorted). The operation of the MATCHC instruction is comparable to a sequential search. It (like the other character-string instructions) can be used even if some bytes in the operands do not contain ASCII codes. The

```
; PROCEDURE DELETE (STRING, STR_LEN, PATTERN, PAT_LEN)
;
; This procedure finds the first instance of a pattern in a
; character string and deletes it. The Z condition code in
; the stacked PSW is set if the pattern was found in the
; string and deleted.
;
; INPUT ARGUMENTS
;
;       STRING        a character string
;       STR_LEN       the length of the string (word)
;       PATTERN       a character string to be deleted from STRING
;       PAT_LEN       the length of PATTERN (word)
;
; OUTPUT ARGUMENTS
;
;       STR_LEN       is changed to the new string length after
;                     deleting the pattern.
;
; OFFSETS FOR ARGUMENT LIST
;
STRING = 4
STR_LEN = 8
PATTERN = 12
PAT_LEN = 16
;
```

Figure 14.4   The procedure DELETE (continues next page)

```
; REGISTER USE
;
;       R2       length of string segment that
;                follows pattern
;       R3       addr of byte after pattern in string
;       R4-R5    used by MOVC3
;       R6       length of string (word)
;       R7       length of pattern (longword,
;                used in address computation)
;       R8       address where pattern starts in string
;
        .ENTRY  DELETE,^M<R2,R3,R4,R5,R6,R7,R8>
        MOVW    @STR_LEN(AP),R6             ; String length
        CVTWL   @PAT_LEN(AP),R7            ; Pattern length
        MATCHC  R7,@PATTERN(AP),R6,@STRING(AP) ; Find pattern in string
        BNEQ    RETURN                     ; Return if no match
        SUBL3   R7,R3,R8                   ; Start of pattern in string
        MOVC3   R2,(R3),(R8)               ; Move up end segment
        SUBW3   R7,R6,@STR_LEN(AP)         ; New string length
        BISB2   #^X04,4(FP)                ; Success flag in Z bit
RETURN: RET
        .END
```

Figure 14.4 (concluded)

next example illustrates the use of MATCHC to find an integer datum, and it illustrates a potential hazard of using MATCHC for this purpose.

Example 14.10: Using MATCHC with Noncharacter Data

Suppose that a table beginning at TABLE contains 100 entries with 20 bytes each. Each entry begins with a key that is a word integer. We want to find the address of the entry whose key matches the one in KEY. The following instructions could be used:

```
        MATCHC  #2,KEY,#2000,TABLE   ; Search for key
        BNEQ    NOT_FOUND            ; Branch if no match
        SUBL2   #2,R3               ; Address of entry
```

But will this always work? The problem is that the bytes of the key might happen to match two bytes in some other part of one of the records. Suppose, for example, that each table entry consists of the key, a longword integer, and a 14-byte character string, and that we are searching for the entry whose key is 2074_{16}. The segment of the table below shows some of the places where 2074 could be detected—incorrectly in all but the last case. (Because the table contains integer data, the lowest-addressed byte of each entry is shown at the right. The key, or pattern, sought contains 74 in the first byte and 20 in the second byte.)

Characters	Long	Key
xxxxxxxxxxxxxxxxxxxxxxxxxxxx	xxxxxx20	74xx, ← first byte
74xxxxxxxxxxxxxxxxxxxxxxxxxx	xx2074xx	xxxx
xxxxxxxxxxxxxxxxxxxxxxxxxx20	74xxxxxx	xx20
xxxxxxxx2074xxxxxxxxxxxxxxxx	xxxxxxxx	xxxx
xxxxxxxxxxxxxxxxxxxxxxxxxxxx	xxxxxxxx	2074

To correctly find an entry whose key is 2074, we could test the address in R3 after the last instruction shown above to see if its distance from TABLE is a multiple of the entry size. The MATCHC instruction and the test would be in a loop, so that another scan could begin at the byte following the end of each incorrect instance of the key found. We leave the details to the reader.

14.4 TRANSLATING CHARACTER STRINGS: THE MOVTC AND MOVTUC INSTRUCTIONS

MOVTC–Translating a Character String

The MOVTC (MOVe Translated Characters) instruction translates a string of bytes under the control of a translation table specified as one of the operands of the instruction. It can be used to convert a character string from some other character code (e.g., EBCDIC, another widely used character code) to ASCII, or vice versa, to change all the lowercase letters to upper case, to change certain special characters, to extract and patch together fields of a record, and to scramble letters in messages to create cryptograms.

The format of the instruction is

MOVTC   srclen,source,fill,table,dstlen,dest

The translation table is usually 256 bytes long and is accessed in the same manner as the table used by a SCANC or SPANC instruction. That is, the contents of each byte in the string is treated as an unsigned binary integer (between 0 and 255) and is used as an index into the table to find the value that is to be substituted for that byte. In other words, a byte containing the number n is translated to the number in the byte whose address is the table address + n. (See Fig. 14.5 for an illustration.)

As with MOVC5, the fill character is used to pad out the end of the destination if the source length is less than the destination length. If the source is longer than the destination, the extra bytes of the source are simply not translated. The source and destination may overlap (and in many applications where the string being translated is very long, they would occupy the same space). The destination must not overlap the translation table. The condition codes are set to indicate the relation between the source length and destination length. MOVTC uses R0–R5 and leaves the following data in them:

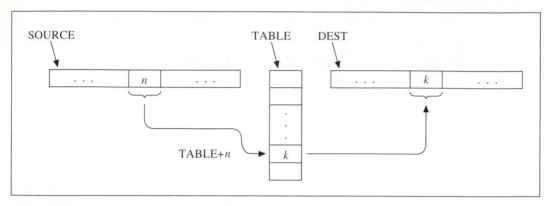

Figure 14.5   Translating a character string

R0:   the number of untranslated bytes remaining in the source string
R1:   the address of the byte following the last translated byte of the source string
R2, R4: 0
R3:   the address of the translation table
R5:   the address of the byte following the end of the destination string

Example 14.11: Translating Lower Case to Upper Case

Suppose that we wish to translate all lowercase letters in a long segment of text to upper case. Most characters will not be changed. For all entries in the translation table, say TABLE, other than those that correspond to lowercase letters, the contents of TABLE+n will be n. The ASCII codes for the lowercase letters are 97–122$_{10}$, so TABLE+97 through TABLE+122 are initialized to contain the ASCII codes for the uppercase letters.

```
TABLE: .BYTE   0,1,2,3,4,5,6,7,8,9,10,11,12,13,14,15,16,17,18,19,20
       .BYTE   21,22,23,24,25,26,27,28,29,30,31,32,33,34,35,36,37,38,39,40
       .BYTE   41,42,43,44,45,46,47,48,49,50,51,52,53,54,55,56,57,58,59,60
       .BYTE   61,62,63,64,65,66,67,68,69,70,71,72,73,74,75,76,77,78,79,80
       .BYTE   81,82,83,84,85,86,87,88,89,90,91,92,93,94,95,96
       .ASCII  /ABCDEFGHIJKLMNOPQRSTUVWXYZ/
       .BYTE   123,124,125,126,127
```

Note that we assumed that all bytes in the text contain valid ASCII codes, so we made the table only 128 bytes long.

Suppose that the string of text to be translated begins at TEXT and that its length is in R8. The following instruction does an "in-place" translation.

```
MOVTC   R8,TEXT,#0,TABLE,R8,TEXT
```

(The fill character would not be used.)

The entries in the translation table in Example 14.11 are in such a simple order that it seems unnecessarily tedious to type out all the numbers as we did in the .BYTE directives. It would be very easy to set up the table in a few simple loops at execution time, but it is inefficient to do work at execution time that can be done at assembly time. The .REPEAT directive described in Chapter 11 can be used outside macros; it is used in the next example.

A translation table would be constructed at execution time if it depended on execution-time data or computations. A program to generate cryptograms using different permutations of the letters, for example, might generate the permutations with a random number generator and fill the table at execution time.

Example 14.12: Setting Up a Table with .REPEAT

The following statements set up the same table as in Example 14.11.

```
TABLE:  .BYTE   0                ; First table byte
        CODE = 1
        .REPEAT 96               ; For CODE = 1 to 96
        .BYTE   CODE             ;   put CODE in TABLE+CODE
        CODE = CODE+1
        .ENDR
        .ASCII   /ABCDEFGHIJKLMNOPQRSTUVWXYZ/
        CODE = 123
        .REPEAT 5                ; For CODE = 123 to 127
        .BYTE   CODE             ;   put CODE in TABLE+CODE
        CODE = CODE+1
        .ENDR
```

The MOVTC instruction can be used for purposes other than translation. The next example illustrates one such use.

Example 14.13: Extracting Pieces from Records

Suppose that we have a collection of records, each say 200 bytes long and each containing a large number of fields. For each record we want to extract the data from several fields and form one string from the pieces extracted. We can do this with the MOVTC instruction with each record playing the role of the translation table. The "string" to be translated is a template containing the position numbers of the bytes to be extracted from the record. The following instructions show how to extract the nineteenth, fourth, and thirty-first five-byte segments, in that order, assuming that the address of each record to be processed will be put in R9.

```
TEMPLATE: .BYTE   90,91,92,93,94,15,16,17,18,19,150,151,152,153,154
EXCERPT:  .BLKB   15
          .
          .
          .
          MOVTC   #15,TEMPLATE,#0,(R9),#15,EXCERPT
```

MOVTUC–Translating with an "Escape"

The MOVTUC (MOVe Translated characters Until escape Character found) instruction translates a string of characters using a translation table, as does MOVTC, but it also acts as a character-search instruction. One of its operands is called the "escape" character; MOVTUC will stop translating the source string if it reaches a character in the source that would be translated to the escape character. The format of the MOVTUC instruction is

$$\text{MOVTUC} \quad srclen,source,escape,table,dstlen,dest$$

The translation proceeds as illustrated in Fig. 14.5 until the translation of a byte encountered in the source is the escape character, or the end of either the source or destination is reached. If the translation completes without an escape and the destination is longer than the source, the extra bytes in the destination are unchanged because there is no fill character operand. The program can determine whether there was an escape and, if so, where it occurred by using the information left in R0–R5 and the values of the condition codes. The registers and condition codes will contain:

R0:   the number of bytes remaining in the source string, including the one that caused the escape if one occurred

R1:   the address of the byte in the source that caused termination of the instruction, either by translating it to the escape character or by being beyond the length of the destination string, if termination occurs before the entire source string is translated; otherwise, the address of the byte that follows the source string

R2:   0

R3:   the address of the table

R4:   the number of bytes remaining in the destination string, including the one that would have received the escape character, if any

R5:   the address of the first byte of the destination string that did not receive a translated source byte, if any, either because escape occurred or because the source is shorter that the destination; otherwise, the address of the byte that follows the destination string

V: set if the search was terminated by an escape; otherwise, cleared

N, Z, C: indicate the relation between the source and destination lengths

Warning: The effects of MOVTUC are unpredictable if the destination string overlaps the source string or the translation table.

Example 14.14: Translating and Separating Lines

Suppose that BLOCK is the address of a large block of data in EBCDIC consisting of many lines, each terminated by a carriage return character (code 13_{10} in EBCDIC as well as ASCII). We want to translate the characters to ASCII and process the lines one at a time. In a realistic application the processing of the lines would probably include writing them out to a new file, but for simplicity in this example the processing will consist of just printing the line. (Only the first 85 characters will be printed if the line is longer.) We assume that the length of the entire block of data is in the word BLK_SZ, and the maximum line size in the input block is 150.

The table is constructed so that the entry in TABLE+n is the ASCII code for the character whose EBCDIC code is n. For example, the EBCDIC codes for the digits are $240-249_{10}$, so the bytes at TABLE+240 through TABLE+249 contain 48_{10} through 57_{10}, the ASCII digit codes. (Some EBCDIC codes have no ASCII translation, and some are not used; the table entries for these are zero.) The escape character is the carriage return.

```
CR = 13                                 ; Carriage return
MAX_SZ = 150                            ; Max input line size
TABLE:  .BYTE   0,1,2,3,0,9,0,0,0,0,0,11,12,13,14,15,16,17,18,0,0
        .BYTE   0,8,0,24,25,0,0,0,29,0,31,0,0,28,0,0,10,23,27,0
        .BYTE   0,0,0,0,5,6,7,0,0,22,0,0,30,0,0,0,0,0,0,20
        .BYTE   21,0,26,32,0[9],0,46,60,40,43,0,38,0[9]
        .BYTE   33,36,42,41,59,0,45,47,0[9],44,37,95,62,63,0[9],96
        .BYTE   58,35,64,39,61,34,0,97,98,99,100,101,102,103,104,105
        .BYTE   0[7],106,107,108,109,110,111,112,113,114,0[7]
        .BYTE   126,115,116,117,118,119,120,121,122,0[22],123
        .BYTE   65,66,67,68,69,70,71,72,73,0[6],125
        .BYTE   74,75,76,77,78,79,80,81,82,0[6],92,0
        .BYTE   83,84,85,86,87,88,89,90,0[6]
        .BYTE   48,49,50,51,52,53,54,55,56,57,124,0[5]
LINE:   .BLKB   MAX_SZ
                .
                .
                .

; REGISTER USE
;
;       R0,R10  length of remaining source
;       R1      address of carriage return in source
;       R4      number of unused bytes in dest
;       R6      length of line to be printed
;       R11     address of remaining source
;
        MOVAB   BLOCK,R11               ; Addr of source string
        MOVW    BLK_SZ,R10              ; Length of source
;
NEXT:   MOVTUC  R10,(R11),#CR,TABLE,#MAX_SZ,LINE ; Translate a line
        BVC     END_OR_ERROR            ; No CR found
        SUBW3   R4,#MAX_SZ,R6           ; Compute line size
        SUBL3   #1,R0,R10               ; Remaining source length
        ADDL3   #1,R1,R11               ; Addr of remaining source
        PRINTCHRS LINE,R6               ; Print line
        BRB     NEXT                    ; Get another line
END_OR_ERROR:
        TSTW    R10                     ; Any chars remaining?
        BNEQ    ERROR
END:    [processing completed]
```

Note that R10 and R11 would not be needed and the instructions could be simplified somewhat if PRINTCHRS did not use R0 and R1.

14.5   THE EDIT INSTRUCTION

In Chapter 6 we showed how to convert two's complement data to character code for
output using the CVTLP and CVTPS instructions. The result of the conversion is a
leading separate numeric string—that is, a sign followed by a certain number of digits
(in character code). If the number converted has fewer significant digits than the number
of digits specified in the CVTPS instruction, the first few digits of the result will be
zeros. For example, if, say, R7 contains FFFFFE6B, the instructions

```
CVTLP    R7,#5,PKD
CVTPS    #5,PKD,#5,LSN
```

produce

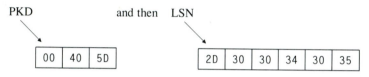

where, in this and all other diagrams of memory contents in this section, the first, or
lowest-addressed, byte is shown at the left. When LSN is printed, it appears as

-00405

For most applications, we would prefer that the output appear as

-405

Using instructions we have covered so far, we can test the string at LSN for zeros,
replace them by blanks, and move the sign. This, and any other formatting we might
wish to do, would be somewhat tedious and might require a lot of instructions.

Some computers have an EDIT instruction whose purpose is to format numeric
data for output. These instructions convert a packed-decimal datum to a character string
under the control of a pattern that specifies the format. They may be used by compilers
to accomplish the formatting done with a Fortran FORMAT statement or a picture specification in PL/1 or COBOL, and so on. Although the details vary with different
machines, the tasks that may be accomplished by an EDIT instruction (or made easier
for the programmer by it) usually include blank fill for leading zeros, insertion of a sign
immediately in front of the first significant digit, and insertion of decimal points, cur-
rency symbols, and other special characters.

The VAX EDIT instruction is

EDITPC   *num_dgts,pkd,pattern,dest*

The first two operands describe the packed-decimal datum to be edited. The pattern is a string of bytes in memory that contain "edit pattern operators"—a sequence of editing commands. Many of the operators cause one or more bytes (containing digits, a fill character, a sign, or a special character) to be stored in the next available byte or bytes of the destination. There is no length operand for the pattern in EDITPC; the end of the pattern is marked by a "pattern end" operator—a byte of zeros. There is no length operand specified for the destination because the pattern completely determines the length of the edited character string.

> ***Warning:*** *EDITPC uses R0–R5 for scratch work, destroying the original contents of those registers.*

There are 16 different pattern operators, and some of them take operands. Before we describe the details for the operators, we will consider some examples. The point of these examples is to provide motivation for the kinds of operators and features an EDIT instruction should have. We will use symbolic names for the operators. All the names begin with EO$ for Edit Operator. The names are actually system macros that initialize the bytes of the pattern, but for now we need consider them only as abstract names for the pattern operators.

Example 14.15: A Simple Editing Pattern for Positive Integers

Suppose that PKD contains the packed-decimal representation of an integer that we know is positive and has at most five digits. We want to convert the integer to character code with leading zeros replaced by blanks. EDITPC processes source digits left to right. If the next digit in the packed datum is zero and no nonzero digits have been encountered so far, we want the fill character (usually, a blank) to be stored in the next byte of the destination. If the next digit is not zero (or is zero but some nonzero digits have already been encountered), the digit must be expanded to its ASCII character code and stored in the next byte of the destination. The EO$MOVE operator acts in this way. It requires an operand, called a repeat count, that tells how many digits it is to operate on. EO$END is the pattern end operator. Thus the pattern commands are

```
EO$MOVE 5
EO$END
```

If PKD contains, say,

$$00\ 70\ 2C$$

and the pattern is properly encoded in memory at PATRN, the instruction

```
EDITPC   #5,PKD,PATRN,STRING
```

would produce

$$20\ 20\ 37\ 30\ 32$$

beginning at STRING. The first two bytes contain the ASCII code for a blank.

This pattern is not a good one to use if the integer being edited may be zero. (Why?)

Example 14.16: An Edit Pattern for Signed Integers

Again we assume that the integer to be edited has five digits, but now we make no assumptions about its sign; it may be negative, positive, or zero. The edit pattern described below blanks out leading zeros and puts the sign in front of the first significant digit. For the first four digits we use the EO$FLOAT operator. Like EO$MOVE, it replaces leading zeros with blanks, but it also "floats" the sign across these blanks. When it encounters a nonzero digit in the packed datum, it inserts the sign and the digit (expanded from four bits to the appropriate ASCII character codes) in the next two bytes of the destination. Any subsequent digits encountered by the EO$FLOAT operator will be expanded to character code and stored in the destination. The fifth digit should not be replaced by a blank even if it is zero; if the integer being edited is zero, we want one zero digit to appear in the output. The EO$END_FLOAT operator sets a flag to indicate that subsequent digits should be treated as significant digits and not replaced by the fill character. It also stores the sign character in the destination if it was not already stored. The EO$MOVE operator stores the ASCII code for the last digit in the destination. Thus the edit pattern consists of the following commands:

```
EO$FLOAT 4
EO$END_FLOAT
EO$MOVE   1
EO$END
```

Note that six bytes must be reserved for the edited result: five for digits or fill and one for the sign, which is inserted by either EO$FLOAT or EO$END_FLOAT.

Figure 14.6 shows the steps that are carried out by the instruction

```
EDITPC   #5,PKD,PATRN,STRING
```

assuming that the edit pattern has been properly encoded in memory beginning at PATRN. The significance flag and the fill and sign characters referred to in the figure are described in more detail below.

The Significance Flag

Examples 14.15 and 14.16 suggest the need for a feature common to editing instructions: a significance flag. When the EO$MOVE and EO$FLOAT operators process a zero digit, they must be able to determine whether to store it in the destination or replace it with a fill character. When EO$FLOAT encounters a nonzero digit, it must be able to determine whether to store just the digit or to also store the sign. In each case, the first option should be chosen if any significant (i.e., nonzero) digits have been encountered so far. The VAX EDITPC instruction uses the C condition code bit as the significance flag. It is cleared when EDITPC begins execution and is automatically set by the EO$MOVE and EO$FLOAT operators when they encounter a nonzero digit. It is set, cleared, and used by several other operators.

The Fill and Sign Characters

As indicated in Examples 14.15 and 14.16, the default value for the fill character—the character that replaces leading zeros—is a blank. Similarly, the default values for the sign character are a blank for positive numbers and a minus sign for negative numbers

(a) Editing the packed datum 00 30 8D

Fill = ^X20   Sign = ^X2D

Operator	Packed Source	Destination
EO$FLOAT	00 30 8D ^	20
EO$FLOAT	00 30 8D ^	20 20
EO$FLOAT	00 30 8D ^	20 20 2D 33
		Sign and digit inserted. Significance flag set.
EO$FLOAT	00 30 8D ^	20 20 2D 33 30
EO$END_FLOAT		No action since signif. flag already set.
EO$MOVE	00 30 8D ^	20 20 2D 33 30 38
EO$END		

(b) Editing the packed datum 00 00 4C

Fill = ^X20   Sign = ^X20

Operator	Packed Source	Destination
EO$FLOAT	00 00 4C ^	20
EO$FLOAT	00 00 4C ^	20 20
EO$FLOAT	00 00 4C ^	20 20 20
EO$FLOAT	00 00 4C ^	20 20 20 20
EO$END_FLOAT		20 20 20 20 20 Sign (blank) inserted. Significance flag set.
EO$MOVE	00 00 4C ^	20 20 20 20 20 34
EO$END		

Figure 14.6   Editing steps for Example 14.16

(determined by the last nibble of the packed source datum). These defaults can be changed by pattern operators. EDITPC initializes a fill register and a sign register (actually, both are parts of R2) to contain the default values. Several operators allow the programmer to load other characters into these registers at any point during the editing. There will be examples below.

Encoding the Pattern Operators

The edit pattern is a string of bytes containing the edit pattern operators and, for some operators, their operands. There are three kinds of operands: repeat counts (used with EO$FLOAT and EO$MOVE in Examples 14.15 and 14.16), characters (alternative fill or sign characters or special characters to be inserted in the output), and lengths. For operators that take a repeat count—a number indicating how many times the operator is to be applied—the operator and the repeat count share a byte. The operator is in bits 7:4 and the repeat count in bits 3:0; thus repeat counts are in the range 1–15. Operators that take no operand, or whose operand is a character or length, occupy one byte; the operand, if any, is in the next byte.

Table 14.1 lists (alphabetically) all the pattern operators and their encodings and describes the operations they perform. Each operator name is also the name of a system macro that generates the one- or two-byte encoding for the operator and its operand, if any. Although a pattern could be initialized in one line using the .BYTE directive and the encodings described in the table, the use of the names makes the pattern definitions more readable and will minimize errors.

The action and uses of many of the operators will be illustrated below in examples.

Example 14.17: The Pattern Used in Example 14.16

Using Table 14.1, we can see that the pattern used by the EDITPC instruction in Example 14.16 should be

PATRN

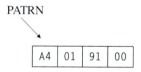

The pattern can be initialized in a program as follows:

```
PATRN:    EO$FLOAT  4
          EO$END_FLOAT
          EO$MOVE   1
          EO$END
```

Examples

As a guide for setting up patterns in the examples below, we will write out format diagrams of the result we want. The diagrams show how many digits there are, where

TABLE 14.1 EDIT PATTERN OPERATORS

Operator	Code (hex)	Operand	Operation
EO$ADJUST_INPUT	47	length	Specifies number of source digits to use, overriding the *num_digits* operand. Extra leading zeros in source are ignored or created, as needed.
EO$BLANK_ZERO	45	length	If source = 0, put fill in the last *length* bytes of the destination.
EO$CLEAR_SIGNIF	02		Clear significance flag.
EO$END	00		End of pattern.
EO$END_FLOAT	01		If significance flag is clear, set it and store sign in destination.
EO$FILL	80+r	repeat count	Store *r* copies of the fill in the destination.
EO$FLOAT	A0+r	repeat count	If signif. is set, store next digit. Else, if digit = 0, store fill. Else store sign and digit and set signif. Repeat for *r* bytes of source.
EO$INSERT	44	character	If signif. is set, store char., else store fill.
EO$LOAD_FILL	40	character	Put character in fill register.
EO$LOAD_MINUS	43	character	Put character in sign register if source < 0.
EO$LOAD_PLUS	42	character	Put character in sign register if source > 0.
EO$LOAD_SIGN	41	character	Put character in sign register.
EO$MOVE	90+r	repeat count	If signif. is set, store next digit. Else, if digit = 0, store fill. Else store digit and set signif. Repeat for *r* bytes of source.
EO$REPLACE_SIGN	46	length	If source = −0, replace sign with fill.
EO$SET_SIGNIF	03		Set significance flag.
EO$STORE_SIGN	04		Store sign in destination.

special characters should go, whether or not a sign is included, where the significance flag must be turned on, and so on. One of the advantages of using such a diagram is that it helps determine how many characters there will be in the edited result (i.e., how many bytes must be reserved for the destination operand of EDITPC). We will use the letter d to mean a digit or fill character, and the letter s to indicate a sign. The s will be shown in the first position where the sign may appear; in most of our examples the sign will float over leading fill characters and appear in front of the first significant digit. A caret will indicate the position where the significance flag must be set if it was not set earlier.

The format diagram for the simple pattern used in Example 14.15 is

$$d \quad d \quad d \quad d \quad d$$

The diagram for the pattern in Example 14.16 is

$$s \quad d \quad d \quad d \quad d \quad d$$
$$\char`^$$

Example 14.18: Inserting Special Characters

We want to define a pattern to edit a seven-digit integer with commas following the millions and thousands places. The format diagram is

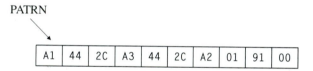

Clearly, we would not want a comma to appear if there is no significant digit to the left of it. The EO$INSERT operator stores the fill character rather than the character specified as its operand if the significance flag is not set. Note that the destination needs ten bytes. The pattern can be set up as follows:

```
PATRN:   EO$FLOAT      1
         EO$INSERT    <,>
         EO$FLOAT      3
         EO$INSERT    <,>
         EO$FLOAT      2
         EO$END_FLOAT
         EO$MOVE       1
         EO$END
```

Note that a comma must be enclosed in angle brackets; if it is not, the assembler interprets it as a separator and generates an error.

The encoding of the pattern is

PATRN

| A1 | 44 | 2C | A3 | 44 | 2C | A2 | 01 | 91 | 00 |

Example 14.19: An Alternative Fill Character

For this example we have a positive five-digit integer to be printed with three asterisks before and after the number and with asterisks in place of leading zeros. The format is

where we have shown the alternative fill character over the d's because it is not the usual blank. The pattern is initialized by

```
PATRN:   EO$LOAD_FILL *
         EO$FILL       3
         EO$MOVE       4
         EO$SET_SIGNIF
         EO$MOVE       1
         EO$FILL       3
         EO$END
```

Example 14.20: A Floating Currency Symbol in Place of a Sign

Suppose that we are editing a seven-digit number that represents an amount of money. The rightmost two digits are to be preceded by a decimal point, and a dollar sign is to appear in front of the first nonzero digit. The dollar sign will be loaded into the sign register and inserted in the appropriate place by the EO$FLOAT or EO$END_FLOAT operator. There are some problem cases to watch for: If the amount is less than a dollar, the decimal point will not appear because no significant digit precedes it. Thus we must set the significance flag before the decimal point. We will set it so that at least one digit, perhaps a zero, appears before the decimal point. Thus the format is

$$\$ \; d \; d \; , \; d \; d \; d \; . \; d \; d$$
$$\wedge$$

The pattern is initialized by

```
PATRN:   EO$LOAD_SIGN  $
         EO$FLOAT      2
         EO$INSERT     <,>
         EO$FLOAT      2
         EO$END_FLOAT
         EO$MOVE       1
         EO$INSERT     .
         EO$MOVE       2
         EO$END
```

Thus, for example, if PKD contains

$$00 \;\; 00 \;\; 00 \;\; 9C$$

the instruction

```
EDITPC   #7,PKD,PATRN,AMOUNT
```

will store the following data, beginning at AMOUNT:

$$20 \;\; 20 \;\; 20 \;\; 20 \;\; 20 \;\; 24 \;\; 30 \;\; 2E \;\; 30 \;\; 39$$

which, when printed, appears as

$$\$0.09$$

(with five blanks in front of the dollar sign).

Example 14.21: Adjusting Source Length

Suppose that we want to produce a four-digit number. A packed decimal number always has an odd number of digits. The EO$ADJUST_INPUT operator overrides the source length. If, for example, the packed datum has five digits, EO$ADJUST_INPUT with an operand of 4 will cause the EDITPC source pointer to advance one nibble, skipping the first digit. The pattern described below produces an unsigned four-digit integer with leading zeros included, not replaced by fill. The format is

$$d \; d \; d \; d$$
$$\wedge$$

The pattern is initialized by

```
PATRN:   EO$ADJUST_INPUT 4
         EO$SET_SIGNIF
         EO$MOVE          4
         EO$END
```

Condition Codes and Caveats

The EDITPC instruction affects all the condition codes. As we have seen, the C code is used as the significance flag. The N and Z bits have their usual meanings. N is set if the packed source operand has a negative sign; however, it will be cleared if all digits in the source are zeros (i.e., if the packed operand is –0). The Z bit is set if all digits are zeros. The V bit is set to indicate overflow if the EO$ADJUST_INPUT operator causes any nonzero digits to be discarded. This is the only situation in which overflow can occur. If enough room has not been reserved for the destination, EDITPC will overwrite other data.

Certainly, an instruction that does as much as EDITPC has ample opportunity to run into problems. Most of the events that cause faults are reasonable (i.e., they are situations where something is clearly wrong). A reserved operand fault will occur, as always, if the number of digits specified for the packed source datum is outside the range 0–31. The length specified for an EO$ADJUST_INPUT operator must also be in this range. (If the packed datum has a bad nibble, the results will be incorrect but a fault may not occur.) A reserved operand fault occurs if the pattern does not process all the digits in the source or if it attempts to process more digits than there are. A reserved operand fault occurs if the pattern contains an invalid operator code.

Warning: The results of EDITPC are unpredictable if the destination overlaps the packed source operand or the pattern.

14.6 SUMMARY

The VAX has a variety of character string manipulation instructions that are very useful for processing input and output data, for text editing, and for various other applications.

Character strings are specified in machine instructions by their length and the address of their first byte.

All the character string instructions use some of the general registers for scratch work—and for providing information to the program about the results of the operation performed by the instruction.

The EDITPC is the most complex of the character manipulation instructions. It edits a packed-decimal datum according to a pattern specified as one of the instruction operands. It can be used to insert special characters, blank out leading zeros, and place a sign (or other character) just in front of the first significant digit. The edit pattern commands are described in Table 14.1.

The instructions described in this chapter are listed in Table 14.2.

TABLE 14.2 CHARACTER STRING INSTRUCTIONS

Instruction		Operation	Registers used
MOVC3	*len,source,dest*	Copy string	R0–R5
MOVC5	*srclen,source,fill,dstlen,dest*	Copy string	R0–R5
CMPC3	*len,string1,string2*	Compare strings	R0–R3
CMPC5	*len1,string1,fill,len2,string2*	Compare strings	R0–R3
LOCC	*char,len,string*	Find first byte containing *char*	R0–R1
SKPC	*char,len,string*	Find first byte not containing *char*	R0–R1
SCANC	*len,string,table,mask*	Find first byte with	R0–R3
SPANC	*len,string,table,mask*	*table entry* AND *mask* $\neq 0$ (SCANC) or $= 0$ (SPANC)	
MATCHC	*patrn_len,pattern,str_len,string*	Find *pattern* in *string*	R0–R3
MOVTC	*srclen,source,fill,table,dstlen,dest*	Translate source	R0–R5
MOVTUC	*srclen,source,escape,table,dstlen,dest*	Translate with escape	R0–R5
EDITPC	*num_dgts,pkd,pattern,dest*	Edit packed datum	R0–R5

14.7 EXERCISES

1. Consider Examples 14.1 and 14.3. Suppose that if the entry for the third column is too large for a column, it is to be printed entirely on the next line beginning where column 3 begins. You may assume that it has at most 40 characters. Write the instructions to copy the string into the proper place and blank out any bytes that need it.

2. What will be in R0, R1, and R3 after the MOVC5 instruction in Example 14.2 is executed? What values will the condition codes have?

3. Consider the string and the program segment in Example 14.5. How many times is the LOCC instruction executed? What will be in R0 after the LOCC instruction is executed each time?

4. What would happen if the program segment in Example 14.5 is executed on a string where the last slash is missing?

5. Will the program segment in Example 14.5 work correctly if one of the substrings is null (i.e., if one slash appears immediately after another)? (A null string should be counted as a string.)

6. Rewrite the instructions in the loop in the program segment in Example 14.5 using fewer instructions. (Make any necessary changes in the initialization so that the segment will still work correctly.)

7. Write a procedure to do the operation done by the SKPC instruction without using any of the character string instructions introduced in this chapter. Assume that CHAR, LEN, and STRING are the arguments, taking the roles of the *char, len,* and

string operands, respectively. Your procedure should return in R0, R1, and Z the same data that would be left there by SKPC.

8. Modify the CVTCL procedure in Fig. 14.2 so that it will work properly even if the input string may have a signed leading separate numeric string immediately following another lsn string without a blank as a separator.

9. Write a procedure to count the occurrences of each of the vowels (separate counts for each) in a section of text. The procedure arguments are TEXT, LENGTH (the number of bytes in the text), and a word array VOWELS where the counts should be stored. (You should not have to test explicitly to determine which vowel has been found. Try to find an "automatic" way of incrementing the appropriate counter.)

10. Write a procedure REPLACE that finds and replaces the first instance of a specified substring in a string by another substring. REPLACE should have six arguments:

STRING	the string to be modified
STR_LEN	its length
SUB_STR_1	the substring to be replaced
STR_1_LEN	its length
SUB_STR_2	the replacement string
STR_2_LEN	its length

   STR_LEN should be changed to the new length of the modified string. You may assume that there is sufficient space after the end of the string to extend it to a total length of 150. If the replacement would cause the length to exceed 150, it should not be done. REPLACE should set a flag in R0 to distinguish among the three cases: successful replacement, pattern not found in string, and replacement would exceed length limit. Your documentation should indicate what values in R0 indicate which cases.

11. Write a program segment that finds the first entry in the table with the format described in Example 14.10 that has a key that matches the one in the word KEY.

12. Devise an algorithm to do the operation of the MATCHC instruction (i.e., to determine if one string appears anywhere in another) given the addresses and lengths of the two strings. Your algorithm should return the address where the pattern appears in the second string, or 0 if it does not appear.

13. Write a procedure to do the operation of MOVTC without using any of the character string instructions introduced in this chapter. Assume that the arguments SRC_LEN, SOURCE, FILL, TABLE, DEST_LEN, and DEST play the roles of the MOVTC operands. Your procedure should leave in R0–R5 the data that are left in them by MOVTC.

14. Write assembler directives to set up a translation table that could be used to replace all left and right square brackets ([ ]) with left and right curly brackets ({ }), respectively, and leave all other characters unchanged.

15. Is the second operand specifier in the instruction

```
MOVB    #^A/ /,TABLE+^A/0/
```

valid? Why or why not? What does the instruction do?

16. The translation table set up in Example 14.11 has only 128 bytes. What errors could occur if the string being translated had a byte containing a number larger than 127?

17. Write instructions to do the operation done in Example 14.13, but without using MOVTC.

18. Write a program that reads in lines of text from the terminal, one at a time, translates them using a table that permutes the letters but leaves punctuation unchanged, and prints out the resulting cryptogram. The program should include a procedure that constructs the permutation in a random way.

19. Show the encoding of the edit pattern used in Example 14.15.

20. If PKD contains 00 00 0C and if the EDITPC instruction and pattern in Example 14.15 are used, what will be in the bytes beginning at STRING when the instruction completes executing?

21. Would the following pattern have the same effects as the one in Example 14.16? If so, explain why. If not, give an example of a source string on which they behave differently.

```
EO$FLOAT 4
EO$SET_SIGNIF
EO$MOVE  1
EO$END
```

22. Show the encoding of the pattern in Example 14.20. How many bytes must be reserved for the edited result?

23. Show what would be in the bytes beginning at AMOUNT if the EDITPC instruction and pattern in Example 14.20 were used and PKD contained 04 89 00 1C.

24. Write a sequence of pattern commands for a pattern for a signed six-digit integer.

25. Write a procedure that converts the entries of a longword array to character code (using EDITPC) and prints them with eight numbers on a line. Assume that the array entries have at most six significant digits. The output is to be lined up in columns with a field of ten spaces per entry. The procedure arguments are the array and a longword that contains the number of entries in the array.

26. Write a sequence of pattern commands for output in the format used in Example 14.20, but with the letters CR appearing after the last digit if the number is negative.

27. Write a sequence of pattern commands for output in the format used in Example 14.21, except that an asterisk should be used for the fill character.

28. Write a sequence of pattern commands to edit a three-digit number where, if the number is negative, the minus sign is to appear after the last digit.

29. Write a sequence of pattern commands to edit a five-digit signed integer using blank fill, but where the sign is to appear in the first byte of the output.

30. Write a procedure, not using EDITPC, that takes a five-digit packed-decimal string and converts it to a character string of length six with leading zeros replaced by blanks and the sign appearing just before the first significant digit.

15

Interrupts and Exceptions

15.1 INTRODUCTION

This chapter is an introduction to interrupts. The goal is not for the reader to become proficient in interrupt programming on the VAX, but rather to understand what interrupts are and to understand the basic techniques for servicing them. The topic of interrupts is quite complex in general, and the interrupt structure and service routines on the VAX are more complex than the usual. The presentation here will be substantially simplified. The subject is studied further in courses on computer architecture and operating systems.

15.2 THE ORIGINS OF INTERRUPTS

Interrupts were invented to solve problems related to performing input and output operations. We will present a (simplified) history of these problems and various techniques for handling them.

Early computers executed one program at a time from start to finish. The program and data were prepared on punched cards or typed on a device such as a teletype. The output appeared on a line printer, punched cards, or a teletype. These systems were not interactive; the programmer submitted the program and data, and then waited, perhaps hours, for the output. Several programs in the form of punched card decks might be stacked up on a card reader waiting their turn.

While working on one program, the CPU executed instructions systematically, more or less as described in Chapter 8, although the instruction formats were generally far simpler than they are on the VAX. Input and output, however, could not be handled in the same way for two reasons: I/O involves communicating with separate devices outside the computer, and these devices are substantially slower than a CPU. Suppose that a program contains an instruction to read a character of input. The CPU can execute an instruction that sends a signal to the input device indicating that the next character should be sent. The CPU has then completed its input instruction, but it cannot go on to execute the next instruction in the program. The next instruction may perform some operation on the character that the previous instruction read, but the character may not have arrived yet in the computer's memory. The CPU must wait until the character has arrived, or, in other words, until the input operation is completed. This poses the following problem for the CPU:

> **Problem:** *How can the CPU determine when an I/O operation is complete?*

Wait-Loop Programming

One approach to the problem of communication between the CPU and an I/O device is to have specific places in memory where the two can leave messages for each other. For example, suppose that $$IOCODE is the address of a byte in memory where the I/O device stores a nonzero code to indicate the status of the operation. Such a byte is often called a *status byte*. There could be codes for "operation completed successfully" (e.g., the character has been read and stored in memory), "device not connected," "card reader is empty," and various other error conditions. The CPU "waits" for the signal from the device by executing a sequence of instructions as in the example below. Even though this is not how the problem is handled on the VAX, we use VAX-like instructions for clarity. (We assume that $$IOCODE is initially zero.)

```
WAITING:TSTB    $$IOCODE
        BEQL    WAITING
```

These instructions would be followed by instructions to examine the code in $$IOCODE and take appropriate action. If the code indicates successful completion, the program could copy the input from wherever the device put it to the desired destination in the program, then continue with whatever instructions should follow the input operation. Appropriate routines could be called to handle error conditions.

This type of programming was common on early computer systems. It is clear that the CPU wasted some time waiting for the signal from the I/O device. How significant a waste was it? The CPU on such a computer may have been able to execute roughly 100,000 instructions per second. A card reader would have taken roughly 1/100 of a second to transfer a character. In the time the CPU was waiting for the input, it could have executed 1000 instructions! The CPU is an expensive resource, so techniques were developed to make efficient use of it while I/O operations were being performed.

Multiprogramming

The program that requests an input operation cannot proceed until the operation is complete, but the CPU could use the time to work on another program. This is the idea behind multiprogramming. In a multiprogramming environment, several programs are kept in the computer's memory and are "active" at one time. When one requests input, the CPU can execute the input instruction, then put that program aside and work on another.

Of course such a scheme has overhead for the operating system and the hardware. More memory is needed to accommodate several programs at one time. With several programs in memory at the same time, there must be a mechanism for protecting one program and its data from intentional or inadvertent overwriting by another program. Putting a program aside involves saving sufficient information about the current status of the program so that execution can resume later at the correct point, with the correct data. The program itself and the data in memory may be left where they are. The new program that runs while the first is waiting for input will use the general registers, program counter, and program status register. The contents of these registers must be saved in memory with the interrupted program before the new program takes over. After the input operation is complete, the CPU can reload the registers and resume execution of the first program. Suppose that all the overhead of determining what program to run while one is waiting and the overhead of saving and reloading registers takes roughly 50–100 instructions. Clearly, multiprogramming is worthwhile; the CPU still has plenty of time to do productive work on another program.

So multiprogramming solves the problem of inefficient use of the CPU. But how does the CPU know when to resume execution of the original program? We must return to the original problem: How can the CPU determine when an I/O operation is complete?

Inventing the Interrupt

One technique that can be used is called *polling*. The CPU polls the I/O devices (examines their status bytes in memory) at regular intervals to see if they need attention. This is better than wait-loop programming because the CPU does not spend *all* its time checking the status bytes, but it is still inefficient.

Consider the following analogy. Suppose that you want to go out for pizza with a friend who lives across the street. You call her on the telephone, and she says that she can go as soon as she finishes the homework she is working on. What do you do? You could stand at your window and watch her window until you see her desklight go off. That is about as good a use of your time as wait-loop programming is for the CPU. You could do some reading, but go over to check the window every 10 minutes. That is analogous to polling. But you have probably already thought of the best solution: Tell your friend "call me when you are ready." Then you can concentrate completely on your book, or on listening to music, or washing the dishes. When the phone rings, you put aside whatever you were doing. If you thought of this solution, you reinvented the interrupt.

The essential idea of interrupts is that it is not the CPU's responsibility at all to determine when an I/O device has completed its operation; it is the responsibility of the device to send a signal to the CPU to interrupt the normal instruction execution sequence.

15.3   INTERRUPTS AND INTERRUPT PROCESSING

What Are Interrupts?

An *interrupt* is an event, or a hardware signal, that automatically interrupts the CPU, saving the current CPU status and causing a transfer of control to an operating system routine that determines the cause of the interrupt and takes appropriate action.

Although interrupts were developed to handle the I/O problem described in the preceding section, they are now used for a long list of events. In timesharing systems, the CPU switches among different users, giving a certain amount of time to each. When the timer runs out for a user, a timer interrupt occurs. There are many kinds of I/O interrupts. Program exceptions (e.g., overflow, divide by zero) cause interrupts. A power failure causes an interrupt. (Computers are so fast that when a power failure is detected, there may still be time for the CPU to execute instructions to save the current status of the machine before it stops functioning.)

Normally, the CPU responds to interrupt requests between execution of two machine instructions, rather than while an instruction is being executed. In other words, if an event causes an interrupt signal to be sent to the CPU while the CPU is in the middle of executing an instruction, the interrupt hardware mechanism lets the CPU complete the instruction before the interrupt takes over. (On computers like the VAX that have some extremely complex machine instructions that take a long time to execute, interrupts may occur at specific points in the middle of execution of such an instruction.)

We distinguish between two kinds of events that can cause interrupts. Events that are related to the program that is currently running are called *exceptions*. These are usually errors like those described in Chapter 8: overflow, divide by zero, memory access violation, reserved operand, and so forth. Not all exceptions are errors. If a debugger is being used (and the T bit in the PSW is set), a trace exception occurs between instructions so that the debugger can do its work. Events that are related to other programs, or to the system as a whole, are called *interrupts*. This group includes I/O devices, timers, power failure, and machine (hardware) errors. (Unfortunately, the word *interrupt* is used to describe this second kind of event as well as the mechanism that is used for both kinds of events. Other terminology is sometimes used; the two kinds of interrupts may be called internal interrupts and external interrupts, respectively.)

Priorities

An interrupt request can occur while another interrupt is being serviced. For example, a timer interrupt request can occur while the CPU is responding to an interrupt from an I/O device, or vice versa. It should be clear that to respond sensibly, the system must have priorities. For example, we would not want servicing of a power failure interrupt to be interrupted by the timer. Each interrupt is assigned a priority level. I/O and timer interrupts have lower priority than machine errors and power failure. In a simple system, all I/O interrupts may have the same priority; in more complex systems, there may be distinctions between different kinds of devices and/or different kinds of I/O events.

An interrupt will take effect only if its priority is higher than the priority of the currently running program, which may be an interrupt servicing routine for another interrupt. A telephone analogy may be helpful again. Think of the CPU as having a fancy telephone system with a separate line for each priority level. If a call (an interrupt) comes in on a line with a higher priority than the one the CPU is currently using, the phone rings; the CPU puts the other call on hold and answers the ringing line. If the CPU is currently occupied with a higher-priority line, the lower line does not ring. The new call (interrupt) is not lost, however. The phone system monitors the CPU activity; eventually, the CPU finishes its current task and returns to whatever it was doing before. If the CPU is now working on a lower-priority task than the new interrupt, the phone rings. If the CPU returns to another task that also has higher priority than the new interrupt, the phone system continues to keep the new call waiting. In fact, there could be several calls (interrupts) waiting at the same time. Always, the one with the highest priority will ring when the CPU returns to a low-priority task.

How does the hardware know the priority of the task the CPU is currently working on? On the VAX the field consisting of bits 20:16 of the Processor Status Longword (PSL) is called the Interrupt Priority Level field (IPL). It contains the priority level of the program currently running. The VAX has 31 interrupt priority levels. (Microprocessors generally have fewer; for example, the M68000 Family has seven.) For ordinary processing, including running user programs, the IPL field contains zero. The interrupt hardware examines the IPL field to determine whether to interrupt the CPU immediately or to wait.

Suppose that a program exception is to be serviced. What value should be put in the IPL field of the PSL? Suppose that the program that caused the exception is a user program. The exception service routine should have just as low a priority as the user program; it should be interruptable by a timer or I/O interrupt, for example. On the other hand, what if an exception occurs while servicing a high-priority interrupt? Since processing cannot proceed until the exception is handled, and the servicing of a high-priority interrupt should not be interrupted for one of lower priority, the exception service routine should have just as high a priority as the routine that caused the exception. Thus when an exception occurs, the IPL value in the PSL should not be changed. Exceptions do not have an independent priority; their priority is that of the program that caused the exception.

Processing Interrupts and Exceptions

Interrupt servicing is done partly by hardware and partly by software. There is an array, in a fixed place in memory, containing the addresses of the various interrupt service routines (software). This array is sometimes called the array of interrupt vectors, or the interrupt service table. On the VAX it is called the System Control Block. We may think of the interrupts as being numbered to correspond to the index of their associated interrupt service vector. (See Fig. 15.1.)

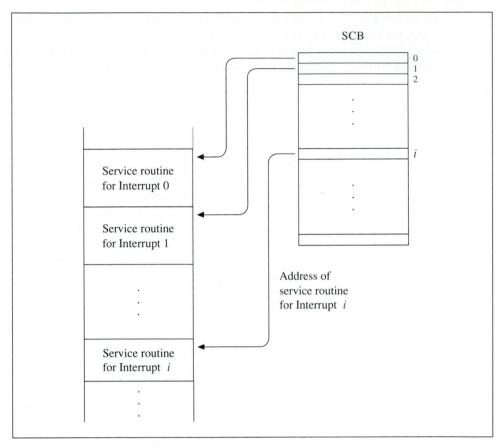

Figure 15.1   The System Control Block

The hardware carries out the following operations.

if an interrupt is requested and its priority > IPL (interrupt priority level) in the
   PSL **then**
        Stack the PSL and PC (other data may be stacked, too);
        Load the PSL with the appropriate IPL value;
        (Other fields of the PSL may be affected, too);
        Load the PC with the interrupt vector for this interrupt.

The PC has been modified, so the next instruction executed will be from the interrupt
service routine.
        The general registers are not saved by the hardware. They may be saved by the
interrupt service routine if necessary.
        One service vector may be invoked by many different causes. For example, one
I/O device may be assigned to one position in the array of interrupt vectors, but an

interrupt may result from a variety of events (e.g., successful completion of an operation or various error conditions). In some systems several I/O devices may use the same entry in the array. In such cases, the interrupt service routine may have to poll the devices to determine which one caused the interrupt. All arithmetic exceptions may be grouped as one interrupt. (They are on the VAX.)

If the interrupted program is to continue execution after the interrupt is serviced, the interrupt service routine uses the REI (Return from Exception or Interrupt) machine instruction. When REI is executed, the top two longwords on the user stack contain the saved PC and PSL of the interrupted program. REI pops them and puts them back in the PC and PSL registers. (It does some checks to make sure the new PSL is legal.) After the REI instruction is executed, the original program resumes because the address of its next instruction is in the PC.

The System Control Block on the VAX may contain roughly 128–384 interrupt service vectors (depending on the installation). We mentioned earlier that the VAX has 31 priority levels; in general, there may be many service vectors with the same priority. Microprocessors generally have fewer vectors, just as they have fewer priority levels than the VAX. There is a trade-off between space and speed. At one extreme, if we have a distinct service routine for each distinct event that can cause an interrupt, the service routine can be very quick; it knows what it has to do. On the other hand, if several devices are handled by one routine, that routine must poll the devices or check some arguments to determine which device is responsible for the interrupt. Similarly, if several events are serviced by the same routine, it must determine which event occurred.

It is very important that interrupt service routines be very efficient. Interrupts occur quite frequently. On a system like the VAX with a large number of terminals, several disks, a variety of printers, and perhaps plotters and tape drives, there may be several hundred to a few thousand interrupts per second. If interrupt servicing takes a lot of time, user programs will have little time to do their work. An even more important problem can occur if interrupt service routines are too slow: information can be lost. For example, if data is coming in from a telephone line or terminal, and the system is busy servicing higher- or equal-priority interrupts for too long a time, the data can be overwritten by subsequent input before it is accepted and processed by the system. There are ways to protect against such problems. Many systems use separate processors to perform some I/O tasks, so the main CPU is interrupted less often. "Intelligent" terminals, buffering schemes, and sophisticated communications protocols also help, but problems can still occur if the interrupt service techniques are poorly designed.

Privilege Modes

There are many situations where an operating system needs access to data and instructions that, for security reasons, an ordinary user may not use. For example, in a multiprogramming system, the operating system decides how much time each program will have control of the CPU before another program gets a turn. The operating system controls access to the I/O devices so that users do not interfere with each other. Computer systems generally have two (or more) privilege modes: *user mode* and a mode for the operating system, sometimes called *supervisor mode*. Certain instructions may not be executed in user mode, and some areas of memory may not be accessed in user mode.

Clearly, some interrupt service routines must perform operations that should not be available to ordinary users. When such an interrupt is serviced, the mode is changed to supervisor mode. When control returns to an interrupted program, the mode must be reset to the mode of that program.

Complex operating systems like that of the VAX may have more than two modes. The activities of the operating system are divided up so that even some system routines are restricted from performing more powerful operations than they need. (This is a protection against bugs in such a complex system, as well as protection against intentional misuse.) On the VAX, there are four separate modes: user mode and three levels of operating system modes. The mode in which the computer is currently executing is recorded in the Current Mode field of the PSL. This field occupies bits 25:24. When an interrupt is serviced on the VAX, the Current Mode field is changed to whichever system mode is appropriate for that interrupt. When the REI instruction is executed after the interrupt is serviced, it reloads the saved PSL from the interrupted program, thus resetting the Current Mode field.

An I/O Interrupt Service Routine

We will give a brief and somewhat simplified outline of the steps carried out to service an interrupt from a disk drive that has just completed an input operation. Some of the steps involve tasks that the operating system must carry out to manage the programs in the system, so we begin with a brief description of a few operating system tasks and data structures.

Remember that I/O operations are very slow compared to machine instruction execution. Thus while one program is waiting for an I/O operation to complete, the program that gets control of the CPU may also try to initiate an I/O operation using the same device (say, a disk) before the first I/O operation is completed. An operating system maintains a queue for each device which contains an entry for each request for the device.

In general, there will be several programs in the system that are ready to continue execution, but are simply waiting their turn. These programs are stored on a queue we may call the "ready" queue.

Now, suppose that an interrupt from the disk has occurred. The following steps are carried out. This work is not all done directly by the interrupt service routine. Standard operating system routines for some of these tasks would be called by the interrupt service routine.

- Determine which device caused the interrupt (if this information is not implicit in the interrupt routine invoked).
- Determine the cause of the interrupt (e.g., successful completion or some type of error).
- Remove the front entry from the queue for the disk that caused the interrupt.

- Copy the input data (or an error code) from the disk buffer area to the program space, as indicated in the queue entry, if the input operation itself did not automatically put the data directly into the program space.

- Clear the interrupt. (In other words, signal the disk that the interrupt has been serviced. In our informal description of interrupts as a sophisticated telephone system, this corresponds to letting the disk know that its call has been answered, so it will stop ringing.)

- Put the program that had requested this input operation on the ready queue.

- If the disk queue is not empty, initiate the I/O operation for the program that is now at the front of the queue.

- REI (Return to the interrupted program, not the one whose I/O operation just completed.)

An Exception Service Routine

We will discuss exception service routines in more detail and give an example. This discussion uses VAX terminology and includes the main ideas and operations performed by the VAX, but it is greatly simplified from what the VAX actually does. (We will mention some of the simplifications later.)

The exception service routine takes care of some overhead (bookkeeping) involved in managing the interrupt servicing; it does not do the actual processing of the exception; that is the job of routines called condition handlers. (Recall that the first longword of the call frame for a procedure is intended for a condition handler address.)

The exception service routine carries out the following operations.

1. Set up an argument list on the user stack for the condition handler. Figure 15.2 shows the (simplified) format of the argument list. The type code will be explained later.

2. Determine if the program that caused the exception has a condition handler specified. (Recall Exercise 18 in Chapter 9.) This is done by searching the user stack, using the frame pointer, FP, to find a call frame on the stack whose first longword is not zero. If no condition handler was specified by the user, a default, system condition handler is used.

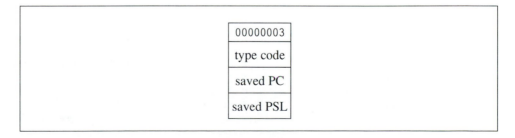

Figure 15.2 Argument list for a condition handler

3. Call the condition handler (using CALLG).

4. After return from the condition handler, determine whether the program is to be terminated or continued, and do so.

The CALLS and CALLG instructions simply fill the first longword of the procedure call frame with zero. A user may write his or her own condition-handling routine for a procedure. An instruction within the procedure itself puts the condition handler address in the first longword of the call frame. Here is an illustration.

```
.ENTRY  PROCEDURE,^M<...>
MOVAB   HANDLER,(FP)
        .
        .
        .
RET
.ENTRY  HANDLER,^M<...>
        .
        .
        .
.END
```

Alternatively, the handler procedure could be external to PROC; the same handler could be used by several procedures. The instruction

```
MOVAB   HANDLER,(FP)
```

would appear at the beginning of each procedure that uses it. (If HANDLER is defined in an .ENTRY directive, it is automatically a global symbol.)

The condition handler is called by the exception service routine like an ordinary procedure. The programmer who writes the handler must know the argument list format used by the service routine.

The argument list for the condition handler contains a type code to tell the handler what type of exception occurred. There is a system-defined code number for each kind of arithmetic exception. These are the VAX codes:

Traps		Faults	
Integer overflow	1	Floating overflow	8
Integer divide by 0	2	Floating div by 0	9
Floating overflow	3	Floating underflow	10
Floating or decimal div by 0	4		
Floating underflow	5		
Decimal overflow	6		
Subscript range	7		

Recall that after a trap (an exception that occurs after an instruction has completed execution), the PC contains the address of the next instruction. For a fault (an error that prevents completion of the instruction), the PC has been reset back to the beginning of the instruction that caused the fault.

Most systems have system-defined (global) symbols whose values are preset to the type codes. Programmers use the symbolic names rather than the actual numbers. For example, on the VAX, SS$_INTOVF = 1, and SS$_FLTUND = 5. Using the symbolic names increases the clarity of a program. (Also, the source program would not have to be modified if a new version of the system used different numbers.)

Figure 15.3 shows a condition handler for arithmetic exceptions. It determines the type of exception, prints an appropriate error message, and prints the PC and PSL from the interrupted program. (Thus it behaves a little like the system's standard condition handler that produces the error messages you have seen when your programs crash.) Note that the argument list is not in the standard form; it contains the actual arguments, not their addresses. For clarity, the handler uses a macro called PRINTHEX; we do not actually have such a macro (but you could write one).

To focus on the main steps, or ideas, we have simplified the discussion of exception servicing; this condition handler will not work on the VAX exactly as is. Some of the more complicated things actually done by the VAX are:

- Much more information is stored on the user stack, and some information is put on a system stack.
- The work we described as being done by the exception service routine is actually divided among two routines: an exception service routine and an exception dispatcher.
- The argument list for the condition handler is more complex than described here.
- The type code provided to the condition handler is not in the range 1–10; the handler must decode a more complicated number.
- R0 and R1 are saved and reloaded in case the original program resumes.

Continuing Execution of the Interrupted Program

Suppose that the exception was a trap (e.g., floating-point underflow) and the user wants a warning message printed, but wants the program to resume execution. The condition handler in Figure 15.3 ends with $EXIT, the system macro that terminates the program. The programmer should modify the handler to distinguish the case where the type code is SS$_FLTUND and, in that case, end the handler with the following instructions:

```
MOVL      #SS$_CONTINUE,RO
RET
```

SS$_CONTINUE is a system-defined symbol whose value is a code indicating that the interrupted program should be resumed. When RET is executed in the condition handler,

```
; PROCEDURE Arithmetic Exception Handler (type code, PC, PSL)
;
;    This routine determines the type of arithmetic exception
; that occurred, prints an appropriate error message, and prints
; the PC and PSL from the interrupted program.
;   To simplify selection of the appropriate error message, the
; handler uses an array of message addresses, indexed by the type
; code for each type of exception.
;
; Message headers
EXC_MSG: .ASCIZ   /An arithmetic exception occurred /
PC_MSG:  .ASCIZ   /Program counter value was /
PSL_MSG: .ASCIZ   /Processor status longword was /
;
; Array of addresses of error messages
MSGADDRS:.ADDRESS   UNKNOWN,INTOVF,INTDIV,FLTOVF,FLTDIV,FLTUND
         .ADDRESS   DECOVF,SUBRNG,FLTOVF_F,FLTDIV_F,FLTUND_F
;
; Error messages
UNKNOWN: .ASCIZ   /Unknown arithmetic exception/
INTOVF:  .ASCIZ   /Integer overflow trap/
INTDIV:  .ASCIZ   /Integer divide by 0 trap/

               .
               .
               .

FLTUND_F:.ASCIZ   /Floating-point underflow fault/
;
         .ENTRY   HANDLER,^M<R2>
         MOVL     4(AP),R2          ; Exception type code
         CMPL     R2,#1             ; Test if code in range 1-10.
         BLSS     CODE0             ; If not, assign the value 0.
         CMPL     R2,#10
         BLEQ     MSG
CODE0:   CLRL     R2
MSG:     ASHL     #2,R2,R2          ; 4*code
         PRINTCHRS   EXC_MSG        ; Print heading
         PRINTCHRS   @MSGADDRS(R2)  ; Print message
         PRINTCHRS   PC_MSG         ; Heading for PC
         PRINTHEX    8(AP)          ; Print saved PC
         PRINTCHRS   PSL_MSG        ; Heading for PSL
         PRINTHEX    12(AP)         ; Print saved PSL
         $EXIT                      ; Terminate the program
         .END
```

Figure 15.3   An example of a condition handler

control returns to the routine that called the handler, the routine we are calling the exception service routine (actually, the exception dispatcher on the VAX).

The exception dispatcher contains code like the following:

```
        CALLG   ...,...                 ; Call the handler
        CMPL    R0,#SS$_CONTINUE
        BNEQ    X
        pop all extra data from the user stack (above the
                handler argument list);
        pop the first two longwords of the handler argument list;
        REI
X:
```

When REI is executed, the top two longwords on the user stack contain the saved PC and PSL of the interrupted program (the last two longwords of the handler argument list). Recall that REI pops them and puts them back in the PC and PSL registers, thus resuming execution of the interrupted program.

15.4 INITIATING AN I/O OPERATION

We began this chapter with a discussion of the use of interrupts with I/O. We observed that when a program begins an I/O operation, it should relinquish the CPU. The program may continue executing after the CPU is interrupted by the I/O device when the operation is complete. The step in this process that has not yet been explained is how the program requests the I/O operation and relinquishes control in the first place. This may not sound like a job for an interrupt; we think of interrupts as coming from outside the current program, or as being caused by an error in the program. However, the interrupt mechanism is useful here, too.

Most computers have an instruction (or a few instructions) that may be executed by a user program to request a service from the operating system that cannot be performed in user mode (such as the actual initiation of an I/O operation). Such instructions are often called *supervisor calls*. On the VAX there are four instructions, CHMx, called CHange Mode instructions, where x indicates the desired mode. The operands of such instructions indicate the service requested by the program. Execution of any of these instructions causes an exception interrupt, and the operating system takes over to service it.

Again omitting many details in order to focus on the main ideas, here is an outline of the steps carried out when an I/O request exception occurs:

- Determine what device and what operation are requested by the program.

- Put an entry on the device queue for this program. (If the queue was empty, the operation may be initiated now.)

- Save the contents of all the general registers and the PSL in a designated place in memory.

- Remove a program from the front of the ready queue. Reload the general registers and PSL from the designated place in memory for that program.

At this point, the current-mode field in the PSL has the appropriate value for the new program (usually, user mode), and the PC has the address of the next instruction to be executed in that program. Execution continues in the usual way. The last step is a little trickier than may be obvious. For system security, care must be taken when loading anything into the PSL. The REI instruction does extensive validity checking, so it is useful here, even though we are not returning to the same program that was just interrupted. The interrupt service routine can reload the general registers for the new program and copy its saved PC and PSL to that program's user stack, then execute REI.

15.5 EXERCISES

1. Suppose that a program you wrote is currently running. After which instructions is it possible for an interrupt to occur?

2. Suppose that an interrupt request occurs while a higher-priority interrupt is being serviced. When will the new interrupt be serviced?

3. Describe some differences between exceptions and (external) interrupts.

4. Look at the error message in Fig. 8.11(a). By examining the PC shown in the error message, decide if an access violation is a trap or a fault.

5. By examining the Current Mode field of the PSL in the error message in Fig. 8.11(a), determine the VAX mode number for user mode.

6. Give two examples of interrupts where the interrupted program would *not* be resumed right after the interrupt is serviced.

7. The VAX has a BISPSW instruction available to the ordinary user. Why does it not have a BISPSL?

8. What does the REI instruction do?

9. Write a simple main program with an instruction that causes overflow. Include a condition handler that prints a message indicating that it was called. Run your program to see that your handler did indeed get executed instead of the standard system condition handler. (A condition handler for a main program is established in the same way as for a procedure. There is a call frame on the stack for your main program. Use the FP register to store the address of your condition handler in the first longword of the call frame.)

10. Suppose that you are writing a program on a machine that does not have autodecrement mode and you wish to put the longword in R8 onto the stack. Here are two ways to do it (using VAX-like instructions). Which one may cause unpredictable bugs, and why?

```
        SUBL2   #4,SP            MOVL    R8,-4(SP)
        MOVL    R8,(SP)          SUBL2   #4,SP
```

11. Rewrite the condition handler in Fig. 15.3 as described in the text so that if the exception that occurred was a floating underflow trap, execution of the program will resume after the error message is printed.

12. Suppose that a user program is interrupted by an interrupt of priority 10, after which the user program should continue. While the interrupt is being serviced, an interrupt of priority 8 is requested. We indicated in Section 15.3 that servicing of the second interrupt will occur after control returns to the user program. How many instructions in the user program will be executed between the servicing of the first and second interrupts? Explain how to interpret the phrase "control returns to the user program."

13. The text explains how to cause execution of a program to continue after a trap. Explain why the same approach will not work after a fault.

14. Suppose that there were no REI instruction, and an interrupt service routine tried to accomplish the same effect with other machine instructions.
    (a) Here is an attempt to replace the REI instruction. It has many flaws. List some of them.

```
BISPSW   4(SP)
JMP      @(SP)
```

   (b) Try to improve on the instructions in part (a). Remember that the main tasks of the REI instruction are to reload the saved PSL and PC, and to pop the saved data from the stack so that the user's stack pointer is where it was when the interrupt occurred. (Don't worry about checking that the new PSL is valid.) You will not be able to get a sequence of instructions that works. The point of this exercise is to try, that is, to write down at least one reasonable attempt, and then to analyze it and list the ways in which it fails to do the job correctly.

15. Consider a multiprogramming system where there is a timer that causes an interrupt at regular intervals to indicate that the current program must relinquish the CPU to allow another program to execute. Outline the main steps to service a timer interrupt. (Use the level of detail in the text's descriptions of a disk I/O interrupt and an I/O initiation exception, in Sections 15.3 and 15.4.)

── 16 ──

Input and Output Using RMS

16.1 INPUT AND OUTPUT

Input and output operations are among the most complex operations in a program. I/O is complex for a number of reasons. The CPU and the main memory of a computer are housed in the computer cabinet (perhaps on the same board) and communicate with each other at very high speed. As long as no I/O operations are done, the CPU can continue humming along, manipulating and moving around data in memory, oblivious to the world outside the cabinet unless someone pulls the plug. I/O operations require that the CPU communicate with physical devices of varying speeds and characteristics in the outside world. As we observed in Chapter 15, some factors that make I/O programming complex are that:

1. The physical I/O devices perform their operations at much slower speeds than the CPU.

2. To avoid wasting CPU time while I/O is being done, the CPU executes part of another program while the program requesting I/O is waiting for the operation to complete. CPU and I/O operations are asynchronous; that is, they are not naturally coordinated in time. Thus when the slow I/O operation completes, the CPU is interrupted and must respond appropriately to the event that occurred, then resume executing some program.

436

3. I/O programs must consider physical problems such as an I/O device being disconnected, a printer out of paper, or a tape drive not turned on.

In a large system shared by many users, the applications program does not directly control the I/O devices—for two reasons. One is that it is much easier for the programmer not to have to learn the many details needed. The system has a collection of programs called device drivers that communicate with specific devices such as printers, plotters, disks, terminals, and so on. These programs are tailored to the specific characteristics of the devices they "drive." The second, and more important reason is that the resources of the system can be used much more efficiently (and without conflict between users) if the operating system manages them. Thus instructions in (high-level or assembly language) programs to read or write data are actually requests to the operating system to perform the operation. To learn more about how I/O is actually done, the reader should consult a text on operating systems or the operating system manuals for a particular computer (e.g., the *VMS I/O User's Reference Manual*).

The programmer may think (and program) in terms of *logical files* and *logical I/O operations*, as opposed to physical operations. The operating system will keep track of how and where the actual data are stored and translate the logical operation requested (e.g., input a record) to the physical steps that must be carried out to find and transfer the desired data.

In this chapter we will consider I/O from a high, or logical level. Our intent here is to give the reader unfamiliar with I/O an introduction to the subject and some familiarity with the kinds of file processing and I/O services available from an operating system. In Section 16.2 we will describe how the programmer may use the VAX/VMS Record Management Services (RMS) to describe and manipulate files. The discussion is far from complete. We will cover enough detail to do straightforward I/O with disk files and at the terminal using RMS directly instead of indirectly via the macros introduced in Chapter 5.

16.2 AN INTRODUCTION TO VAX RECORD MANAGEMENT SERVICES

The VAX Record Management Services (RMS) is a collection of macros and procedures that allow the user to process records and files and, in particular, to do input and output, by describing the logical, rather than physical, organization of the records and files and by using relatively high-level operations. RMS has extensive capabilities for processing disk and tape files. It is also used for terminal I/O. We will be describing only a very small portion of RMS here. For more features and more detail about the features we present, the reader may consult the *VMS Record Management Services Manual*.

A *file* is an organized collection of related data, called *records*. In a text file (e.g., a program source file or a data file such as the DATA.DAT file used by the READRCRD macro) each line is a record.

Files are usually stored on a disk or tape, although a program may construct input and output files for a terminal. We will describe those facilities of RMS used for processing relatively simple disk files and I/O files for the terminal. We will examine the I/O macros and routines in IOMAC and IOMOD as illustrations of the use of RMS.

Files may be organized in several ways. The simplest, and the one we use for DATA.DAT and terminal I/O, is *sequential*. That is, records are arranged in a particular sequence and are processed in order. The other forms of file organization are *indexed* and *relative*. In indexed files each record has an identifier, or key, and the particular record desired is specified by its key. In relative files records may be assigned to particular positions in the file and are referred to by position number.

Communicating with RMS

In order to process a file, a program must communicate with RMS. There are two aspects to the necessary communication:

1. The program must contain blocks of data, called control blocks, that describe the files and records being processed. These control blocks are used for two-way communication; that is, the program fills some fields in the blocks with information for RMS to use, and RMS fills some fields to return information to the program.

2. The program must issue specific requests to cause action (e.g., read in a record) whenever it wants such action to occur.

The control blocks eliminate the need for very lengthy argument lists for the system procedures that carry out the I/O operations. The control blocks have a large number of fields (more than two dozen for a file control block). The data in many of the fields are examined by the I/O procedures, although all the procedures do not use the same fields. Thus if argument lists were used for all the information required by all the procedures, the lists would be long, and it would not be easy to remember just what is needed by each procedure. Instead, the control blocks are established and initialized, and they are available throughout execution of the program whenever needed by an I/O processing procedure.

RMS provides macro instructions to make reservation and initialization of the control blocks relatively easy for the programmer. It also provides macro instructions for the various processing actions; the macros set up the necessary system procedure calls. We will discuss the control blocks first, but they will be easier to understand if we know some of the terminology for the actions that may be performed on files and records. The following list briefly describes those most commonly used.

Open a file	Check that the file exists. Make it available for processing.
Create a file	Initialize a directory entry. Open the file.
Get a record	Input a record from a file.
Put a record	Output a record to a file.
Close a file	Terminate processing of the file.

We will describe two kinds of control blocks: file access blocks and record access blocks. Two other kinds of blocks may be used for providing additional information, but they are not needed for the fairly straightforward I/O that we will do.

Recall that in Chapter 10 we described how to protect data by setting up a read-only program section, that is, by using a .PSECT directive with the NOWRT (NO WRiTe) attribute. Although the I/O control blocks are normally placed in the data area of a program, some of the RMS processing macros store data into some of the fields, so the control blocks must not be put in a read-only program section.

File Access Blocks (FABs)

A *file access block* (FAB for short) is a block of 80 bytes of information describing a particular file. One file access block is needed for each file accessed in a program. A FAB has roughly 30 fields, each containing a particular item of information.

The $FAB macro may be used to reserve space for a FAB and initialize some of the fields. Some fields are filled by RMS when the file is opened or created. $FAB has 23 arguments, most of which correspond exactly to a field in the FAB. (There are fewer arguments than fields because some fields cannot be initialized by the user, and some arguments initialize more than one.) Since RMS fills some of the fields and since many of the arguments have very useful default values, very few of the arguments actually have to be specified unless the file has unusual characteristics.

Note that since the $FAB macro initializes a data area, it should be placed in the storage reservation and initialization portion of a program, not among executable instructions.

The format of the $FAB macro is

label: $FAB   arguments

Because there are so many arguments and most are usually omitted, it is convenient to specify the arguments using keywords. The list below contains the keywords and roles of some of the arguments.

Some $FAB arguments

FNM = File NaMe.   The file specification for the file described by this FAB is enclosed in angle brackets.

ORG = file ORGanization.   The options are SEQ for sequential, INDX for indexed, or REL for relative. The default is SEQ. This field is initialized by the programmer for a file to be created; for an existing file, RMS will fill the field with the actual file organization when the file is opened.

ALQ = ALlocation Quantity.   This is the number of disk blocks to be allocated when this file is created. If the file already exists, RMS will put its actual size in this field when the file is opened.

DEQ = Default file Extension Quantity.   This is the number of blocks by which the file is to be extended when space runs out. (ALQ and DEQ have useful defaults and may often be omitted.)

FAC = File ACcess options.   The particular kinds of processing that will be done on the file must be specified in advance in the FAC field. Examples of processing action are GET, PUT, DEL (delete), and UPD (update). If more than one is specified, they are enclosed in angle brackets—for example:

```
FAC = <GET,UPD>
```

The FAC field contains one bit for each option. By default, when an existing file is opened, the GET bit in the FAB is set, and when a new file is created, the PUT bit is set, so FAC may be omitted for simple I/O.

RFM = Record ForMat.   Two of the possibilities are FIX, for fixed size, and VAR, for variable size. The default is VAR.

MRS = Maximum Record Size.   This field should be filled by the programmer for a file being created. When an existing file is opened, RMS puts the actual maximum record size in the field.

One important field in the FAB that cannot be initialized by the programmer is the completion STatuS code field (STS). RMS fills this field with a success or failure code after attempting to perform an operation on the file. For example, after attempting to open a file, RMS may return the code for "file not found." If an attempt was made to access a file in a way not specified in the FAC field, RMS will return an appropriate error code.

Example 16.1: The FABs for Terminal I/O and DATA.DAT

The file access blocks for the terminal input and output files used by the READLINE, PRINTCHRS, and DUMPLONG macros and the FAB for the DATA.DAT file read by the READRCRD macro are defined by

```
INFAB:   $FAB    FNM=<SYS$INPUT>
OUTFAB:  $FAB    FNM=<SYS$OUTPUT>,MRS=85
DISKFAB: $FAB    FNM=<DATA.DAT>
```

We can rely on the default argument values and the data filled in by RMS at execution time to initialize the other fields. The file names SYS$INPUT and SYS$OUTPUT are logical names that are assigned by default to the user's terminal, but their meaning may be changed when a program is run, so that, for example, the output can be directed to a disk file instead of the terminal. (Note that in the IOMOD module shown in Appendix D, the labels DISK-FAB, INFAB, and OUTFAB are followed by two colons to declare them global symbols so they can be accessed by the I/O macros in the user's program.)

Record Access Blocks (RABs)

A record access block is a block of 68 bytes of data describing the records in a file. Each record access block is associated with a particular file access block. The $RAB macro reserves space for the RAB and does some of the initialization. Some fields may be filled by the program at execution time, and some are filled by RMS after it performs an operation. As with $FAB, $RAB has useful default values for many of its arguments. The format for $RAB is

label: $RAB   *arguments*

Some $RAB arguments

FAB = File Access Block address.   This field must contain the address of the FAB for the file containing the records described by this RAB. It is specified by writing the label used on the $FAB macro. For example, the $RAB macro initializing the RAB to be used with our terminal output file contains the argument

```
FAB=OUTFAB
```

RAC = Record ACcess mode.   The record access mode is the way records in the file are accessed or stored. Two of the options are SEQ, for sequential, and KEY. The default is SEQ.

ROP = Record processing OPtions.   There are many options that may be selected. For example, some of the options that may be used with a terminal input file and their meanings are:

PMT   A prompt message will be displayed at the terminal when an input line is requested.

CVT   All letters read from the terminal are to be converted to upper case.

TMO   There will be a time limit on how long RMS waits for input from the terminal.

If several options are specified, they are enclosed in angle brackets. For example:

```
ROP = <PMT,TMO>
```

PBF = Prompt BuFfer.   The address of a prompt message to be displayed for terminal input is specified. The user must store the prompt message in memory.

PSZ = Prompt message SiZe.   The number of bytes in the prompt message is specified. Note that if PBF and PSZ are used, PMT must be included as an option in the ROP field.

TMO = TiMe Out.   This is the maximum number of seconds allowed for completion of an RMS operation. TMO may be at most 255. Note that to use TMO, the TMO option must be included in the ROP field.

UBF = User BuFfer.   This is the buffer address for input—the address of the location in memory where the user wants RMS to put a record read in from a file. This field may be initialized in the $RAB macro if a standard location is used, or the programmer may fill this field before each *get* operation with the location for that particular record.

USZ = User buffer SiZe.   This is the length of the user buffer.

RBF = Record BuFfer.   This is the buffer address for output—the address in memory from which RMS is to take the record to be written out to the file. As with USZ, this field may be initialized in $RAB or filled by the program at execution time.

RSZ = Record SiZe.   For input, RMS fills this field with the actual number of bytes in the record read in. For output, this field must contain the size of the record to be written out to the file.

Like the FABs, the RABs have a completion STatuS code field (STS) that is filled by RMS to report a success or failure completion code after each operation.

Example 16.2: The RABs for Terminal I/O and DATA.DAT

The IOMOD module contains the following RABs and related directives:

```
LF = 10                                     ; Line feed
CR = 13                                     ; Carriage return
INRAB:  $RAB     FAB=INFAB,USZ=80,-         ; For terminal input
                 ROP=PMT,PBF=PROMPT,PSZ=5
OUTRAB: $RAB     FAB=OUTFAB                  ; For terminal output
DISKRAB:$RAB     FAB=DISKFAB,USZ=80          ; For DATA.DAT
PROMPT: .ASCII   <LF><CR>/?? /               ; Terminal prompt
```

The buffer fields (UBF for input and RBF for output) will be filled by the I/O macros READRCRD, READLINE, and PRINTCHRS. The input buffer size field USZ is initialized to 80, so no more than 80 bytes will be read in. The RAB for the terminal input file specifies that a prompt of length 5 will be displayed whenever input is requested from the terminal.

Recall that a long statement may be continued to a second line by putting a hyphen (the same character as the minus sign) at the end of the line to be continued. A comment may follow the hyphen.

We have pointed out that some fields in a RAB may be set by the program at execution time. To do so, the programmer must know something about the format of a RAB. To avoid the need to know all the details of the format (and to make it easier to modify if necessary without requiring changes in programs already written), the system provides system-defined symbolic names for the offsets for the fields. The symbolic names use a standardized pattern:

$$RAB\$type\_fieldname$$

For example, RAB$L_UBF is the offset from the beginning of a RAB for the longword field containing the address of the user buffer, and RAB$B_PSZ is the offset for the byte field containing the size of the prompt message. We use some of these symbols in the I/O procedures in IOMOD, described in examples below. There are similar system-defined symbolic names for the field offsets for FAB fields.

Processing Macros

The I/O processing macros cause action at execution time. They are placed at the point in the program where the action is to occur.

There are two kinds of processing macros: those that operate on files and those that operate on records. All the processing macros have three arguments:

FAB   address of the FAB for the file being processed, *or*

RAB   address of the RAB for the record being processed;

ERR   entry point of a routine to handle errors,

SUC   entry point of a routine to execute if the operation completes successfully.

The ERR and SUC arguments are optional; if they are omitted, the next instruction executed is the one that follows the macro in the program.

File Processing Macros

The macros for the file operations used most often are

$OPEN   makes an existing file available for processing

$CREATE   creates a new file and opens it

$CLOSE   terminates access to a file

A file must be opened before any processing may be done on it. Files should be closed when the program is finished processing them.

Some other operations available in RMS are

$ERASE   deletes the file and erases its directory entry

               (The file must be closed before it is erased.)

$EXTEND   increases the space allocated to the file

               (The file must be open before it is extended.)

Record Processing Macros

The record processing macros perform operations relating to individual records or to record access blocks. The main input and output operations are *get* and *put*. Two operations that need some explanation are *connect* and *disconnect*. Before records are read or written, the record access block to be used must be explicitly "connected" to a file access block. Recall that each RAB has a field, its FAB field, that contains the address of the associated FAB. It is possible for several RABs to specify the same FAB, so a specific RAB is chosen at execution time. (For sequential files, only one RAB may be connected to a particular FAB at one time.)

Some of the record processing macros are

$CONNECT   connects the specified RAB to its FAB, allocates buffers for
                       I/O, sets a pointer to the first record in the file.

$DISCONNECT	disconnects the RAB from its FAB.
$GET	inputs a record. RMS places the record in the area specified in the UBF field and puts its length in the RSZ field of the RAB. It sets the STS field to indicate if there were any errors or unusual conditions (e.g., end-of-file).
$PUT	outputs a record.
$REWIND	resets the file pointer to the first record in the file.

The reader can get some idea of the complexity of I/O operations from the fact that there are approximately 80 different status codes that can be returned by the $GET macro in the STS field of a RAB. Some codes indicate problems in the RAB itself (e.g., invalid data), and some indicate problems with the device, file, or operation (e.g., trying to read past the end of the file).

Example 16.3: The BEGIN and EXIT Macros

The BEGIN and EXIT macros do some of the initialization and termination work needed when using RMS. The macro definitions are

```
.MACRO  BEGIN     NAME
        .ENTRY    NAME,^M<IV>     ; Define entry point
                                  ; Set integer overflow trap
        $OPEN     FAB=INFAB       ; Open terminal input file
        $CONNECT  RAB=INRAB
        $CREATE   FAB=OUTFAB      ; Create terminal output file
        $CONNECT  RAB=OUTRAB
        $OPEN     FAB=DISKFAB     ; Open disk input file
        $CONNECT  RAB=DISKRAB
.ENDM   BEGIN
.MACRO  EXIT
        $CLOSE    FAB=INFAB       ; Close I/O files
        $CLOSE    FAB=OUTFAB      ;        "
        $CLOSE    FAB=DISKFAB     ;        "
        $EXIT_S                   ; System exit macro
.ENDM   EXIT
```

The I/O processing macros simply set up calls to system procedures to do the actual work. The system procedure names are formed by attaching "SYS" at the beginning of the corresponding macro name. For example, the expansion of

```
        $OPEN     FAB=DISKFAB
```

is

```
        PUSHAL  DISKFAB
        CALLS   #1,G^SYS$OPEN
```

The G^ indicates that the linker, not the assembler, will determine the proper addressing mode to use for the symbol SYS$OPEN.

It is within these system I/O procedures that the mode switch, from user mode to an operating system mode, described in Chapter 15, occurs. These procedures perform the type of work described for initiation of an I/O operation in Section 15.4.

To further illustrate the use of RMS, we examine our own READLINE and READRCRD macros. READLINE, READRCRD, and PRINTCHRS each calls a procedure that does the work. (These are not system procedures; they were written by the author for this book. The purpose of this extra layer, that is, of having the macros call procedures rather than doing the work themselves, is to keep the macros fairly short, so that they may be used in loops that have byte displacements for the branch destinations.)

Example 16.4: READLINE

The simplest of the I/O operations in IOMAC and IOMOD is READLINE. The READLINE macro definition is

```
.MACRO   READLINE WHERETO
         PUSHAB   WHERETO        ; Stack user buffer addr.
         CALLS    #1,RDLINE
.ENDM    READLINE
```

The RDLINE procedure is

```
; PROCEDURE RDLINE (WHERETO)
;
; This procedure gets an input line from the terminal.
; It uses the RAB labeled INRAB, which causes a prompt to be
; displayed at the terminal. The input record is stored
; in memory at WHERETO, RDLINE's argument. RDLINE returns
; the length of the record in R0.
;
         .ENTRY   RDLINE,0
         MOVL     4(AP),INRAB+RAB$L_UBF   ; Fill UBF field in RAB
         $GET     RAB=INRAB               ; Get record
         CVTWL    INRAB+RAB$W_RSZ,R0      ; Record size to R0
         RET
```

Example 16.5: READRCRD

The READRCRD macro definition is

```
.MACRO   READRCRD WHERETO,?LBL
         PUSHAB   WHERETO        ; Stack user buffer addr.
         CALLS    #1,RDRCRD      ; Returns length in R0
         BNEQ     LBL            ; Got a record
         BRW      EOF            ; End-of-file
LBL:     .ENDM    READRCRD
```

The RDRCRD procedure is

```
; PROCEDURE RDRCRD (WHERETO)
;
; This procedure reads the next record from the DATA.DAT file.
; If there was a record, it is stored in WHERETO and its
; length is put in R0. If there were no more records, the Z bit
; in the stacked PSW is set to indicate end-of-file.
; RDRCRD uses the RAB labeled DISKRAB.
;
          .ENTRY  RDRCRD,0
          MOVL    4(AP),DISKRAB+RAB$L_UBF      ; Fill UBF field in RAB
          $GET    RAB=DISKRAB                  ; Get record
          CMPL    DISKRAB+RAB$L_STS,#RMS$_EOF  ; Check STS field for EOF
          BEQL    EOF
          CVTWL   DISKRAB+RAB$W_RSZ,R0         ; Record size to R0
          RET
EOF:      BISB2   #^X04,4(FP)                  ; Set EOF flag
          RET
```

RMS$_EOF is a system-defined symbol whose value is the status code for end-of-file.

For more examples the reader may examine the PRINTCHRS macro and PTCHRS procedure that appear in Appendix D.

16.3 EXERCISES

1. The BEGIN macro (Example 16.3) opens the file DATA.DAT. What do you think will happen if the file DATA.DAT does not exist? Why?

2. Based on the example of an expansion of the $OPEN macro in Section 16.2, show how you think the following macro would be expanded.

```
       $GET      RAB=INRAB
```

3. Suppose that a file access block, record access block, and other areas are defined as follows for input from a terminal:

```
LF = 10                                    ; Line feed
CR = 13                                    ; Carriage return
INFAB:  $FAB      FNM=<SYS$INPUT>
INRAB:  $RAB      FAB=INFAB,UBF=INBUF,USZ=80,-
                  ROP=PMT,PBF=MSG,PSZ=8
INBUF:  .BLKB     80
MSG:    .ASCII    <LF><CR>/INPUT:/
LINE:   .BLKB     80
```

(a) Assuming that the file is already open, write the instruction(s) to read in a line from the terminal and store it in LINE. (Do not use the macros in IOMAC for this exercise.)

(b) What prompt will appear on the screen to tell the user that input is expected?

4. Suppose that a file access block, record access block, and other areas are defined as follows for output to a terminal:

```
LF = 10                                 ; Line feed
CR = 13                                 ; Carriage return
BLANK = ^A/ /                           ; Space
OUTFAB: $FAB     FNM=<SYS$OUTPUT>,MRS=85
OUTRAB: $RAB     FAB=OUTFAB,RBF=OUTBUF,RSZ=85
OUTBUF: .ASCII   <LF><CR>
        .BYTE    BLANK[85]
```

(a) Assuming that the file is already open, write the instruction(s) needed to print a ten-character message stored in memory at MESSAGE. (Do not use the macros in IOMAC for this exercise.)

(b) Suppose that later in the program a second message is to be printed. It is located at TITLE and has eight characters. Write the instruction(s) needed to print it. (Do not use the macros in IOMAC for this exercise.)

5. Write a program for the following problem. There are two data files on the disk, DATA1.DAT and DATA2.DAT, both containing 80-byte records that start with an eight-character key. Both files are sorted alphabetically by key. The program is to construct one new file, RECS.DAT, that contains all the records in order (i.e., the program is to merge the two files). The program should delete the two input files after merging them. (The program should be modular—that is, use procedures as appropriate.) Do not use the macros in IOMAC for this exercise.

6. After which statements in your programs does an interrupt always occur?

A

Index of Instructions

In the table below, operands are shown in the format *name.type*. (The type for string operands is given as *b*.) (Adapted with permission from the *VAX-11 Programming Card* published by Digital Equipment Corporation.)

Name	Operands	Operation	Opcode		Page
ACB*x*	*limit.x,incr.x,index.x,dest.*w *x* = B, W, L, F, D, G, or H	Add, compare, and branch	ACBB	9D	145, 366
			ACBW	3D	
			ACBL	F1	
			ACBF	4F	
			ACBD	6F	
			ACBG	4FFD	
			ACBH	6FFD	
ADD*x*2	*opl.x,op2.x* *x* = B, W, L, F, D, G, or H	Add	ADDB2	80	86, 364
			ADDW2	A0	
			ADDL2	C0	
			ADDF2	40	
			ADDD2	60	
			ADDG2	40FD	
			ADDH2	60FD	

Name	Operands	Operation	Opcode		Page
ADDx3	*op1.x,op2.x,sum x* x = B, W, L, F, D, G, or H	Add	ADDB3 ADDW3 ADDL3 ADDF3 ADDD3 ADDG3 ADDH3	81 A1 C1 41 61 41FD 61FD	86, 364
ADDP4[2]	*dgts1.w,pkd1.b,dgts2.w,pkd2.b*	Add packed	20		382
ADDP6[3]	*dgts1.w,pkd1.b,dgts2.w,pkd2.b,dgts3.w,pkd.b*		21		382
		Add packed			
ADWC	*op1.l,op2.l*	Add with carry	D8		113
AOBLEQ	*limit.l,index.l,dest.b*	Add 1; branch if ≤ 0	F3		144
AOBLSS	*limit.l,index.l,dest.b*	Add 1; branch if < 0	F2		144
ASHx	*count.b,src.x,dest.x* x = L or Q	Arithmetic shift	ASHL ASHQ	78 79	334
ASHP[2]	*count.b,srcdgts.w,src.b,round.b,dstdgts.w,dest.b*	F8 Arithmetic shift and round packed			
BBC	*posn.l,base.b,dest.b*	Branch if bit clear	E1		
BBCC	*posn.l,base.b,dest.b*	Branch if bit clear, and clear it	E5		
BBCS	*posn.l,base.b,dest.b*	Branch if bit clear, and set it	E3		
BBS	*posn.l,base.b,dest.b*	Branch if bit set	E0		
BBSC	*posn.l,base.b,dest.b*	Branch if bit set, and clear it	E4		
BBSS	*posn.l,base.b,dest.b*	Branch if bit set, and set it	E2		
BCC	*dest.b*	Branch if carry clear	1E		121
BCS	*dest.b*	Branch if carry set	1F		121
BEQL	*dest.b*	Branch if equal	13		121
BEQLU	*dest.b*	Branch if equal, unsigned	13		121
BGEQ	*dest.b*	Branch if greater or equal	18		121
BGEQU	*dest.b*	Branch if greater or equal, unsigned	1E		121
BGTR	*dest.b*	Branch if greater	14		121
BGTRU	*dest.b*	Branch if greater, unsigned	1A		121
BICx2	*mask.x,dest.x* x = B, W, or L	Bit clear	BICB2 BICW2 BICL2	8A AA CA	330

Name	Operands	Operation	Opcode		Page
BIC*x*3	*mask.x,src.x,dest.x* *x* = B, W, or L	Bit clear	BICB3 BICW3 BICL3	8B AB CB	330
BICPSW	*mask.w*	Bit clear in PSW	B9		189
BIS*x*2	*mask.x,dest.x* *x* = B, W, or L	Bit set	BISB2 BISW2 BISL2	88 A8 C8	330
BIS*x*3	*mask.x,src.x,dest.x* *x* = B, W, or L	Bit set	BISB3 BISW3 BISL3	89 A9 C9	330
BISPSW	*mask.w*	Bit set in PSW	B8		189
BIT*x*	*mask.w,src.x* *x* = B, W, or L	Bit test	BITB BITW BITL	93 B3 D3	329
BLBC	*scr.l,dest.b*	Branch if low bit clear	E9		121, 128
BLBS	*scr.l,dest.b*	Branch if low bit set	E8		121, 128
BLEQ	*dest.b*	Branch if less or equal	15		121
BLEQU	*dest.b*	Branch if less or equal, unsigned	1B		121
BLSS	*dest.b*	Branch if less	19		121
BLSSU	*dest.b*	Branch if less, unsigned	1F		121
BNEQ	*dest.b*	Branch if not equal	12		121
BNEQU	*dest.b*	Branch if not equal, unsigned	12		121
BRB	*dest.b*	Branch, byte displ.	11		121
BRW	*dest.w*	Branch, word displ.	31		121
BSBB	*dest.b*	Branch to sub-routine, byte displ.	10		208
BSBW	*dest.w*	Branch to sub-routine, word displ.	30		208
BVC	*dest.b*	Branch if overflow clear	1C		121
BVS	*dest.b*	Branch if overflow set	1D		121
CALLG	*arglst.l,proc.b*	Call procedure (general argument list)	FA		223
CALLS	*numargs.l,proc.b*	Call procedure (argument list on stack)	FB		223
CASE*x*	*selector.x,base.x,limit.x,dstlist.w* *x* = B, W, or L	Case	CASEB CASEW CASEL	8F AF CF	

Name	Operands	Operation	Opcode		Page
CLR*x*	*dest.x* *x* = B, W, L, Q, O, F, D, G, or H	Clear	CLRB	94	91, 364
			CLRW	B4	
		CLRL =	CLRF	D4	
		CLRQ = CLRD =	CLRG	7C	
		CLRO =	CLRH	7CFD	
CMP*x*	*op1.x,op2.x* *x* = B, W, L, F, D, G, or H	Compare	CMPB	91	122, 365
			CMPW	B1	
			CMPL	D1	
			CMPF	51	
			CMPD	71	
			CMPG	51FD	
			CMPH	71FD	
CMPC3[2]	*len.*w,*str1.*b,*str2.*b	Compare characters	29		126, 389
CMPC5[2]	*len.*w,*str1.*b,*fill.*b,*len2.*w,*str2.*b	Compare characters	2D		389
CMPP3[2]	*dgts.*w,*pkd1.*b,*pkd2.*b	Compare packed	35		383
CMPP4[2]	*dgts1.*w,*pkd1.*b,*dgts2.*w,*pkd2.*b	Compare packed	37		383
CMPV	*posn.*l,*size.*b,*base.*b,*long.*l	Compare bit field	EC		349
CMPZV	*posn.*l,*size.*b,*base.*b,*long.*l	Compare zero- extended bit field	ED		349
CVT*xy*	*src.x,dest.y* *xy* may be any of the 40 combinations in the CVT instructions listed below	Convert			97, 365

CVTBW 99	CVTWB 33	CVTLB F6			
CVTBL 98	CVTWL 32	CVTLW F7			
CVTBF 4C	CVTWF 4D	CVTLF 4E			
CVTBD 6C	CVTWD 6D	CVTLD 6E			
CVTBG 4CFD	CVTWG 4DFD	CVTLG 4EFD			
CVTBH 6CFD	CVTWH 6DFD	CVTLH 6EFD			
CVTFB 48	CVTDB 68	CVTGB 48FD	CVTHB 68FD		
CVTFW 49	CVTDW 69	CVTGW 49FD	CVTHW 69FD		
CVTFL 4A	CVTDL 6A	CVTGL 4AFD	CVTHL 6AFD		
CVTFD 56	CVTDF 76	CVTGF 33FD	CVTHF F6FD		
CVTFG 99FD			CVTHD F7FD		
CVTFH 98FD	CVTDH 32FD	CVTGH 56FD	CVTHG 76FD		

Name	Operands	Operation	Opcode	Page
CVTLP[2]	*scr.*l,*dgts.*w,*pkd.*b	Convert long to packed	F9	104
CVTPL[2]	*dgts.*w,*pkd.*b,*dest.*l	Convert packed to long	36	102
CVTPS[2]	*dgts1.*w,*pkd.*b,*dgts2.*w,*lsn.*b	Convert packed to leading separate numeric	08	104
CVTPT[2]	*dgts1.*w,*pkd.*b,*tbl.*b,*dgts2.*w,*trl.*b	Convert packed to trailing	24	
CVTR*x*L	src.*x*,dest.l *x* = F, D, G, or H	Convert rounded to long	CVTRFL 4B CVTRDL 6B CVTRGL 4BFD CVTRHL 6BFD	365

Name	Operands	Operation	Opcode		Page
CVTSP [2]	dgts1.w,lsn.b,dgts2.w,pkd.b	Convert lsn to packed	09		101
CVTTP [2]	dgts1.w,trl.b,tbl.b,dgts2.w,pkd.b	Convert trailing to packed	26		
DECx	op.x	Decrement	DECB	97	91
	x = B, W, or L		DECW	B7	
			DECL	D7	
DIVx2	dvsr.x,op2.x	Divide	DIVB2	86	87, 364
	x = B, W, L, F, D, G, or H		DIVW2	A6	
			DIVL2	C6	
			DIVF2	46	
			DIVD2	66	
			DIVG2	46FD	
			DIVH2	66FD	
DIVx3	dvsr.x,dvdd.x,quo.x	Divide	DIVB3	87	87, 364
	x = B, W, L, F, D, G, or H		DIVW3	A7	
			DIVL3	C7	
			DIVF3	47	
			DIVD3	67	
			DIVG3	47FD	
			DIVH3	67FD	
DIVP [3,4]	dgts1.w,dvsr.b,dgts2.w,dvdd.b,dgts3.w,quo.b	Divide packed	27		382
EDITPC [3]	dgts.w,pkd.b,patrn.b,dest.b	Edit packed	38		408
EDIV	dvsr.l,dvdd.q,quo.l,rem.l	Extended divide	7B		
EMODx	mulr.x,mulrex.b,muld.x,int.l,frac.x		EMODF	54	364
	x = F or D	Extra precision multiply	EMODD	74	
EMODx	mulr.x,mulrex.w,muld.x,int.l,frac.x		EMODG	54FD	364
	x = G or H		EMODH	74FD	
EMUL	mulr.l,muld.l,add.l,prod.q	Extended multiply	7A		
EXTV	posn.l,size.b,base.b,dest.l	Extract bit field	EE		346
EXTZV	posn.l,size.b,base.b,dest.l	Extract zero-extended bit field	EF		346
FFC	posn.l,size.b,base.b,dest.l	Find first clear bit	EB		343
FFS	posn.l,size.b,base.b,dest.l	Find first set bit	EA		343
INCx	op.x	Increment	INCB	96	91
	x = B, W, or L		INCW	B6	
			INCL	D6	
INDEX	subsc.l,low.l,high.l,size.l,base.l,offset.l	Array index computation	0A		
INSQUE	entry.b,addr.l	Insert into queue	0E		
INSV	src.l,posn.l,size.b,base.b	Insert bit field	F0		346
JMP	dest.b	Jump	17		128
JSB	dest.b	Jump to subroutine	16		
LOCC [1]	char.b,len.w,str.b	Locate character	3A		393

Name	Operands	Operation	Opcode		Page
MATCHC[2]	*len1*.w,*str1*.b,*len2*.w,*str2*.b	Match characters	39		399
MCOM*x*	*src.x,dest.x*	Move comple-	MCOMB	92	333
	x = B, W, or L	mented	MCOMW	B2	
			MCOML	D2	
MNEG*x*	*src.x,dest.x*	Move negated	MNEGB	8E	91, 364
	x = B, W, L, F, D, G, or H		MNEGW	AE	
			MNEGL	CE	
			MNEGF	52	
			MNEGD	72	
			MNEGG	52FD	
			MNEGH	72FD	
MOVA*x*	*src.x,dest*.l	Move address	MOVAB	9E	67, 364
	x = B, W, L, Q, O, F, D, G, or H		MOVAW	3E	
		MOVAL =	MOVAF	DE	
		MOVAQ = MOVAD =	MOVAG	7E	
		MOVAO =	MOVAH	7EFD	
MOV*x*	*srx.x,dest.x*	Move	MOVB	90	66, 364
	x = B, W, L, Q, O, F, D, G, or H		MOVW	B0	
			MOVL	D0	
			MOVQ	7D	
			MOVO	7DFD	
			MOVF	50	
			MOVD	70	
			MOVG	50FD	
			MOVH	70FD	
MOVC3[3]	*len*.w,*str1*.b,*str2*.b	Move characters	28		66, 389
MOVC5[3]	*len1*.w,*str1*.b,*fill*.b,*len2*.w,*str2*.b	Move characters	2C		389
MOVP[2]	*dgts*.w,*pkd1*.b,*pkd2*.b	Move packed	34		382
MOVPSL	*dest*.l	Move PSL	DC		357
MOVTC	*srclen*.w,*src*.b,*fill*.b,*tbl*.b,*dstlen*.w,*dest*.b		2E		403
		Move translated characters			
MOVTUC	*srclen*.w,*src*.b,*escape*.b,*tbl*.b,*dstlen*.w,*dest*.b		2F		406
		Move translated characters until escape			
MOVZ*xy*	*src.x,dest.y*	Move, zero-	MOVZBW	9B	115
	xy = BW, BL, or WL	extended	MOVZBL	9A	
			MOVZWL	3C	
MUL*x*2	*op1.x,op2.x*	Multiply	MULB2	84	86, 364
	x = B, W, L, F, D, G, or H		MULW2	A4	
			MULL2	C4	
			MULF2	44	
			MULD2	64	
			MULG2	44FD	
			MULH2	64FD	
MUL*x*3	*mulr.x,muld.x,prod.x*	Multiply	MULB3	85	86, 364
	x = B, W, L, F, D, G, or H		MULW3	A5	

Name	Operands	Operation	Opcode		Page
			MULL3	C5	
			MULF3	45	
			MULD3	65	
			MULG3	45FD	
			MULH3	65FD	
MULP[3]	*mulrlen*.w,*mulr*.b,*muldlen*.w,*muld*.b,*prodlen*.w,*prod*.b		25		382
		Multiply packed			
NOP		No operation	01		
POLYF[2]	*arg*.f,*degree*.w,*coefs*.b	Evaluate polynomial	55		364
POLY*x*[3]	*arg*.x,*degree*.w,*coefs*.b	Evaluate polynomial	POLYD	75	364
	x = D, G, or H		POLYG	55FD	
			POLYH	75FD	
POPR	*mask*.w	Pop to registers	BA		303
PUSHA*x*	*op*.x	Push address	PUSHAB	9F	215
	x = B, W, L, Q, O, F, D, G, or H		PUSHAW	3F	
		PUSHAL = PUSHAF	DF		
		PUSHAQ = PUSHAD = PUSHAG	7F		
		PUSHAO = PUSHAH	7FFD		
PUSHL	*long*.l	Push longword	DD		215
PUSHR	*mask*.w	Push registers	BB		303
REMQUE	*entry*.b,*addr*.l	Remove from queue	0F		
RET		Return from procedure	04		226
ROTL	*count*.b,*src*.l,*dest*.l	Rotate	9C		334
RSB		Return from subroutine	05		208
SBWC	*op1*.l,*op2*.l	Subtract with carry	D9		
SCANC[2]	*len*.w,*str*.b,*tbl*.b,*mask*.b	Scan for character	2A		397
SKPC[1]	*char*.b,*len*.w,*str*.b	Skip character	3B		393
SOBGEQ	*index*.l,*dest*.b	Subtract 1; branch if ≥ 0	F4		142
SOBGTR	*index*.l,*dest*.b	Subtract 1; branch if > 0	F5		91, 142
SPANC	*len*.w,*str*.b,*tbl*.b,*mask*.b	Span characters	2B		397
SUB*x*2	*op1*.x,*op2*.x	Subtract	SUBB2	82	87, 364
	x = B, W, L, F, D, G, or H		SUBW2	A2	
			SUBL2	C2	
			SUBF2	42	
			SUBD2	62	
			SUBG2	42FD	
			SUBH2	62FD	
SUB*x*3	*op1*.x,*op2*.x,*dif*.x	Subtract	SUBB3	83	87, 364
	x = B, W, L, F, D, G, or H		SUBW3	A3	
			SUBL3	C3	
			SUBF3	43	
			SUBD3	63	
			SUBG3	43FD	
			SUBH3	63FD	

Name	Operands	Operation	Opcode		Page
SUBP4[2]	*len1*.w,*pkd1*.b,*len2*.w,*pkd2*.b	Subtract packed	22		382
SUBP6[3]	*len1*.w,*pkd1*.b,*len2*.w,*pkd2*.b,*len3*.w,*pkd3*.b		23		382
		Subtract packed			
TST*x*	*op.x*	Test	TSTB	95	122, 365
	x = B, W, L, F, D, G, or H		TSTW	B5	
			TSTL	D5	
			TSTF	53	
			TSTD	73	
			TSTG	53FD	
			TSTH	73FD	
XFC	user defined	Extended function	FC		
XOR*x*2	*mask.x,dest.x*	Exclusive or	XORB2	8C	330
	x = B, W, or L		XORW2	AC	
			XORL2	CC	
XOR*x*3	*mask.x,src.x,dest.x*	Exclusive or	XORB3	8D	330
	x = B, W, or L		XORW3	AD	
			XORL3	CD	

Instructions used only or primarily by operating systems programs

Name	Operands	Operation	Opcode		Page
ADAWI	*op1*.w,*op2*.w	Add aligned word, interlocked	58		
BBCCI	*posn*.l,*base*.b,*dest*.b	Branch if bit clear and clear, interlocked	E7		
BBSSI	*posn*.l,*base*.b,*dest*.b	Branch if bit set and set, interlocked	E6		
BPT		Break point fault			
CHM*z*	*parameter*.w	Change mode to *z*	CHME	BD	433
	z = E (executive), K (kernel),		CHMK	BC	
	S (supervisor), or U (user)		CHMS	BE	
			CHMU	BF	
CRC	*tbl*.b,*initial*.l,*len*.w,*stream*.b,*dest*.l		0B		
		Calculate cyclic redundancy check			
HALT[5]		Halt	00		
INSQHI	*entry*.b,*header*.q	Insert at head of queue, interlocked	5C		
INSQTI	*entry*.b,*header*.q	Insert at tail of queue, interlocked	5D		
LDPCTX[5]		Load process context	06		
MFPR[5]	*procreg*.l,*dest*.l	Move from process register	DB		
MTPR[5]	*src*.l,*procreg*.l	Move to process register	DA		
PROBER	*mode*.b,*len*.w,*base*.b	Probe read access	0C		
PROBEW	*mode*.b,*len*.w,*base*.b	Probe write access	0D		

Name	Operands	Operation	Opcode	Page
REI		Return from exception or interrupt	02	427
REMQHI	*header*.q,*addr*.l	Remove entry from head of queue	5E	
REMQTI	*header*.q,*addr*.l	Remove entry from tail of queue	5F	
SVPCTX[5]		Save process context	07	

[1] Uses R0–R1

[2] Uses R0–R3

[3] Uses R0–R5

[4] Uses scratch space on the user stack

[5] May be executed in kernel mode only

B

Hex Conversion Table and Powers of 2

HEX CONVERSION TABLE

Position / Digit	Hex Digit Positional Value							
	16^7	16^6	16^5	16^4	16^3	16^2	16^1	16^0
0	0	0	0	0	0	0	0	0
1	268,435,456	16,777,216	1,048,576	65,536	4,096	256	16	1
2	536.870.912	33,554,432	2,097,152	131,072	8,192	512	32	2
3	805,306,368	50,331,648	3,145,728	196,608	12,288	768	48	3
4	1,073,741,824	67,108,864	4,194,304	262,144	16,384	1024	64	4
5	1,342,177,280	83,886,080	5,242,880	327,680	20,480	1280	80	5
6	1,610,612,736	100,663,296	6,291,456	393,216	24,576	1536	96	6
7	1,879,048,192	117,440,512	7,340,032	458,752	28,672	1792	112	7
8	2,147,483,648	134,217,728	8,388,608	524,288	32,768	2048	128	8
9	2,415,919,104	150,994,944	9,437,184	589,824	36,864	2304	144	9
A	2,684,354,560	167,772,160	10,485,760	655,360	40,960	2560	160	10
B	2,952,790,016	184,549,376	11,534,336	720,896	45,056	2816	176	11
C	3,221,225,472	201,326,592	12,582,912	786,432	49,152	3072	192	12
D	3,489,660,928	218,103,808	13,631,488	851,968	53,248	3328	208	13
E	3,758,096,384	234,881,024	14,680,064	917,504	57,344	3584	224	14
F	4,026,531,840	251,658,240	15,728,640	983,040	61,440	3840	240	15

POWERS OF 2

p	2^p	p	2^p	p	2^p	p	2^p
0	1	8	256	16	65,536	24	16,777,216
1	2	9	512	17	131,072	25	33,554,432
2	4	10	1,024	18	262,144	26	67,108,864
3	8	11	2,048	19	524,288	27	134,217,728
4	16	12	4,096	20	1,048,576	28	268,435,456
5	32	13	8,192	21	2,097,152	29	536,870,912
6	64	14	16,384	22	4,194,304	30	1,073,741,824
7	128	15	32,768	23	8,388,608	31	2,147,483,648
						32	4,294,967,296

C

ASCII Codes

Hex	Dec.	ASCII	Hex	Dec.	ASCII	Hex	Dec.	ASCII	Hex	Dec.	ASCII
00	0	NUL	20	32	SP	40	64	@	60	96	
01	1	SOH	21	33	!	41	65	A	61	97	a
02	2	STX	22	34	"	42	66	B	62	98	b
03	3	ETX	23	35	#	43	67	C	63	99	c
04	4	EOT	24	36	$	44	68	D	64	100	d
05	5	ENQ	25	37	%	45	69	E	65	101	e
06	6	ACK	26	38	&	46	70	F	66	102	f
07	7	BEL	27	39	'	47	71	G	67	103	g
08	8	BS	28	40	(	48	72	H	68	104	h
09	9	HT	29	41	)	49	73	I	69	105	i
0A	10	LF	2A	42	*	4A	74	J	6A	106	j
0B	11	VT	2B	43	+	4B	75	K	6B	107	k
0C	12	FF	2C	44	,	4C	76	L	6C	108	l
0D	13	CR	2D	45	–	4D	77	M	6D	109	m
0E	14	SO	2E	46	.	4E	78	N	6E	110	n
0F	15	SI	2F	47	/	4F	79	O	6F	111	o
10	16	DLE	30	48	0	50	80	P	70	112	p
11	17	DC1	31	49	1	51	81	Q	71	113	q
12	18	DC2	32	50	2	52	82	R	72	114	r
13	19	DC3	33	51	3	53	83	S	73	115	s
14	20	DC4	34	52	4	54	84	T	74	116	t
15	21	NAK	35	53	5	55	85	U	75	117	u
16	22	SYN	36	54	6	56	86	V	76	118	v
17	23	ETB	37	55	7	57	87	W	77	119	w
18	24	CAN	38	56	8	58	88	X	78	120	x
19	25	EM	39	57	9	59	89	Y	79	121	y
1A	26	SUB	3A	58	:	5A	90	Z	7A	122	z
1B	27	ESC	3B	59	;	5B	91	[	7B	123	{
1C	28	FS	3C	60	<	5C	92	\	7C	124		
1D	29	GS	3D	61	=	5D	93	]	7D	125	}
1E	30	RS	3E	62	>	5E	94	^	7E	126	~
1F	31	US	3F	63	?	5F	95	_	7F	127	DEL

D

I/O Macro Definitions and Procedures

THE IOMAC FILE

To create the IOMAC macro library, the macro definitions shown below should be put in a file called IOMAC.MAR. The command

LIBRARY/CREATE/MACRO IOMAC.MLB IOMAC.MAR

will create the library file IOMAC.MLB.

```
        .MACRO  BEGIN     NAME
                .ENTRY    NAME,^M<IV>     ; Define entry point
;                                         ; Set integer overflow trap
                $OPEN     FAB=INFAB       ; Open terminal input file
                $CONNECT  RAB=INRAB
                $CREATE   FAB=OUTFAB      ; Create terminal output file
                $CONNECT  RAB=OUTRAB
                $OPEN     FAB=DISKFAB     ; Open disk input file
                $CONNECT  RAB=DISKRAB
        .ENDM   BEGIN
;
        .MACRO  READLINE  WHERETO
                PUSHAB    WHERETO         ; Stack user buffer addr.
                CALLS     #1,RDLINE
        .ENDM   READLINE
;
```

```
        .MACRO   READRCRD WHERETO,?LBL
                 PUSHAB   WHERETO           ; Stack user buffer addr.
                 CALLS    #1,RDRCRD         ; Returns length in R0
                 BNEQ     LBL               ; Got a record
                 BRW      EOF               ; End-of-file
LBL:    .ENDM    READRCRD
;
        .MACRO   PRINTCHRS STRING,LENGTH=#85
                 CVTWL    LENGTH,-(SP)  ; Stack string length
                 PUSHAB   STRING        ; Stack string address
                 CALLS    #2,PTCHRS
        .ENDM    PRINTCHRS
;
        .MACRO   DUMPLONG ARG1,ARG2,ARG3,ARG4,ARG5,ARG6-
                 ARG7,ARG8,ARG9,ARG10,ARG11,ARG12
                 CALLS    #0,STARTDUMP  ; Print header
        .IRP     ARG,<ARG1,ARG2,ARG3,ARG4,ARG5,ARG6,-
                 ARG7,ARG8,ARG9,ARG10,ARG11,ARG12>
        .IF      NOT_BLANK ARG
                 MOVQ     #^A/%EXTRACT(0,8,ARG)/,-(SP)   ; Stack name
                 PUSHL    SP            ; Stack addr of name
                 PUSHL    ARG           ; Stack longword to dump
                 CALLS    #2,CVTPRT
                 ADDL2    #8,SP         ; Pop name
        .ENDC
        .ENDR
                 CALLS    #0,ENDDUMP    ; Print trailer
        .ENDM    DUMPLONG
;
        .MACRO   EXIT
                 $CLOSE   FAB=INFAB     ; Close I/O files
                 $CLOSE   FAB=OUTFAB    ;        "
                 $CLOSE   FAB=DISKFAB   ;        "
                 $EXIT_S                ; System exit macro
        .ENDM    EXIT
```

THE IOMOD MODULE

The IOMOD.OBJ module contains the FABs and RABs used by the I/O macros and the
procedures that they call to perform the I/O operations. To construct the file, the following IOMOD.MAR file should be created and then assembled with the command

MACRO IOMOD+IOMAC/LIB

```
        .PSECT   IO_DATA,LONG,WRT,NOEXE
;
LF = 10                                    ; ASCII Line feed
CR = 13                                    ; ASCII carriage return
```

```
        BLANK = ^A/ /                            ; ASCII space
        ;
        INFAB::   $FAB   FNM=<SYS$INPUT>          ; Terminal input
        OUTFAB::  $FAB   FNM=<SYS$OUTPUT>,MRS=85  ; Terminal output
        DISKFAB:: $FAB   FNM=<DATA.DAT>           ; For DATA.DAT file
        INRAB::   $RAB   FAB=INFAB,USZ=80,-
                         ROP=PMT,PBF=PROMPT,PSZ=5
        OUTRAB::  $RAB   FAB=OUTFAB
        DISKRAB:: $RAB   FAB=DISKFAB,USZ=80
        PROMPT:   .ASCII <LF><CR>/?? /
        ;
        ;

                .PSECT  IO_PROCS,NOWRT
        ;
        ; PROCEDURE RDLINE (WHERETO)
        ;
        ; This procedure gets an input line from the terminal.
        ; It uses the RAB labeled INRAB which causes a prompt to be
        ; displayed at the terminal. The input record is stored
        ; in memory at WHERETO, RDLINE's argument. RDLINE returns
        ; the length of the record in R0.
        ;
                .ENTRY  RDLINE,0
                MOVL    4(AP),INRAB+RAB$L_UBF    ; Fill UBF field in RAB
                $GET    RAB=INRAB                ; Get record
                CVTWL   INRAB+RAB$W_RSZ,R0       ; Record size to R0
                RET
        ;
        ;

        ; PROCEDURE RDRCRD (WHERETO)
        ;
        ; This procedure reads the next record from the DATA.DAT file.
        ; If there was a record, it is stored in WHERETO and its
        ; length is put in R0. If there were no more records, the Z bit
        ; in the stacked PSW is set to indicate end-of-file.
        ; RDRCRD uses the RAB labeled DISKRAB.
        ;
                .ENTRY  RDRCRD,0
                MOVL    4(AP),DISKRAB+RAB$L_UBF  ; Fill UBF field in RAB
                $GET    RAB=DISKRAB              ; Get record
                CMPL    DISKRAB+RAB$L_STS,#RMS$_EOF ; Check STS field for EOF
                BEQL    EOF
                CVTWL   DISKRAB+RAB$W_RSZ,R0     ; Record size to R0
                RET
        EOF:    BISB2   #^X04,4(FP)              ; EOF flag
                RET
        ;
        ;
```

```
;   PROCEDURE PTCHRS (STRING, MAX_LEN)
;
;  This procedure displays a character string at the terminal.
;  It sends a carriage return and line feed before the string.
;
;  Input arguments
;
;          STRING        the string to be displayed
;          MAX_LEN       the maximum string length (passed by
;                        immediate value).
;                At most MAX_LEN characters will be displayed,
;                but a byte of 0's is interpreted  as a string
;                terminator.
;
CR_LF:  .BYTE    13,10                      ; Carriage return & line feed
;
        .ENTRY   PTCHRS,0
        MOVAW    CR_LF,OUTRAB+RAB$L_RBF     ; Set RBF and RSZ fields
        MOVW     #2,OUTRAB+RAB$W_RSZ        ;    for CR and LF
        $PUT     RAB=OUTRAB                 ; Output CR and LF
        MOVL     4(AP),OUTRAB+RAB$L_RBF     ; Put STRING addr in RBF field
        LOCC     #0,8(AP),@4(AP)            ; Find 00 byte
        SUBL2    4(AP),R1                   ; Length of string
        MOVW     R1,OUTRAB+RAB$W_RSZ        ; Put length in RSZ field
        $PUT     RAB=OUTRAB                 ; Output string
        RET
;
;
;  PROCEDURE DUMP_MSGS
;
;  Prints header and trailer lines for DUMPLONG output.
;
HDR:    .ASCIZ   /** DUMPLONG OUTPUT **/
STARS:  .ASCIZ   /**   END   DUMPLONG   **/
        .ENTRY   STARTDUMP,0
        PRINTCHRS HDR
        RET
        .ENTRY   ENDDUMP,0
        PRINTCHRS STARS
        RET
;
;
;  PROCEDURE CVTPRT (LONG,NAME)
;
;  CVTPRT converts a longword to a hex character string
;  and prints it along with its name. The argument list
;  contains the longword, passed by immediate value, and
;  the address of a character string (of length at most 8)
```

```
; that is the name of the longword.
; CVTPRT uses a procedure, OTS$CVT_L_TZ, from the VAX
; Run-time Library to do the conversion.
;
        .PSECT  IO_DATA
LONG:   .BLKL   1
DUMP:   .BLKB   18                              ; For DUMPLONG's output
;
        .PSECT   IO_PROCS
DESC:   .LONG    ^X010E0008                     ; The library proc. requires
        .ADDRESS DUMP+10                        ;    a string descriptor
ARGS:   .LONG    3                              ; Arglist for library proc.
        .ADDRESS LONG,DESC
        .LONG    8
;
        .ENTRY  CVTPRT,^M<R2,R3,R4,R5>
;
        MOVC5   #0,0,#BLANK,#10,DUMP    ; Blank out DUMP buffer
        LOCC    #0,#8,@8(AP)            ; Find end of name string
        SUBL3   R0,#8,R2               ; Length of name string
        MOVC3   R2,@8(AP),DUMP         ; Move name to DUMP buffer
        MOVL    4(AP),LONG             ; Addr of longword to arglist
        CALLG   ARGS,G^OTS$CVT_L_TZ    ; Library conversion routine
        PRINTCHRS DUMP,#18             ; Output
        RET
;
        .END
```

E

Answers to Selected Exercises

This appendix contains solutions for most of the odd-numbered exercises in the text. For multipart exercises, solutions are included for only some of the parts. For some exercises that would be good programming assignments for a class, solutions are not provided.

CHAPTER 2

1. There are 8 bits in a byte, 16 bits in a word, and 32 bits in a longword.
3. The data type is determined from the context in which it is used. In other words, the computer must know what the data type is before actually looking at the data.
5. In the CPU.

CHAPTER 3

1. (a) 0010 0100 0000 1001
   (c) 1100 1010 1011
3. (a) 1116
   (c) 208
5. (a) 922

7. **(a)** 13012

9. **(a)** F290

11. Sign-magnitude: 80B6
One's complement: FF49
Two's complement: FF4A

13. −200. This is a word.

15. **(a)** FD88
(c) 0080

17. Byte: 127, −128
Word: 32767, −32768
Longword: 2147483647, −2147483648

19. The representation of 37,412 is 00009224; the representation of −548 is FFFFFDDC. The sum is 00009000.

21. If the signs of the operands are the same and the sign of the sum is different from them, overflow has occurred. Overflow does not occur in any other cases.

    One way to test for overflow is to perform an exclusive-or of the carry into the most significant digit and out of the most significant digit of the sum. If the result is 1, there is an overflow.

CHAPTER 4

1. BUFFER_SIZE = 80

3. LENGTH = 00000C74, WIDTH = 00000C76.   (Remember: The size of a word is 2.)

5. **(a)** Takes three operands, all of which are double-precision floating-point numbers. The first operand is subtracted from the second and the result goes in the third operand.

    (b) This instruction compares strings. It takes three operands. The first operand is the length, in number of bytes, of the two strings to follow. The second and third operands are the strings being compared.

    (c) Takes three operands, all of which are word integers. The first operand is divided into the second and the result goes in the third operand.

    (d) This is a conditional branch instruction. It is a "Branch if LeSS" instruction used after a comparison.

    (e) Moves (copies) an octaword.

    (f) Converts a byte integer to a longword integer.

    (g) Clear a byte.

    (h) Decrement a longword integer. ("Decrement" means subtract one.)

    (i) Adds packed decimal data.

7. The first directive creates space for one longword and initializes it to 2. The second directive creates space for two longwords and initializes them to 0.

9. (R6) + 2 * 4 = (R6) + 8

11. R5: 00183494; R8: 001A38E4

13.
```
        MOVQ    #1000000,R8
```
Using commas inside the number would have been an error.

15. MPG = ACCOUNTS+3640_{16} = $0B34+0E38_{16}$ = 0000196C

17. One way:

```
LINE:   .BLKB    80
COL1 = LINE+8
COL2 = LINE+16
COL3 = LINE+40
```

Another way:

```
LINE:   .BLKB    8
COL2:   .BLKB    8
COL2:   .BLKB    24
COL3:   .BLKB    40
```

(The first method is better.)

19. All numbers are shown in decimal.

Symbol	Values	Bytes Reserved
LF	10	0
MAX	12	0
LIST	0	48
PQR	48	16
XYZ	64	2
LINE	66	18

21. (a) `PI:     .ASCII  'Pi is approximately 22/7'`
A slash appears in the string, so we must use something else as the delimiter.
(b) `SYM_TAB: .ASCII  /**** SYMBOL TABLE ****/`

23.
```
; Program to place twice the longword at NUMBERS in the next
; longword, and to place twice that value in the following longword.
; NUMBERS can be initialized to contain any value.
;
NUMBERS:.LONG   23
        .BLKL   2
;
        .ENTRY  EX23,^M<IV>
        MULL3   #2,NUMBERS,NUMBERS+4    ; NUMBERS+4 is the address of
        MULL3   #2,NUMBERS+4,NUMBERS+8  ;   the second longword;
                                        ;   NUMBERS+8, the third.
        $EXIT_S
        .END    EX23
```

CHAPTER 5

1.
```
; This program prints out a name.
;
NAME:    .ASCIZ   /John Locke/
;
         BEGIN    PRINTNAME
         PRINTCHRS   NAME
         EXIT
         .END     PRINTNAME
```

3.
```
; This program prompts for today's date, then prints it.
;
BUFF_SIZE = 80                          ; Size of input buffer
MSG:     .ASCIZ   /What is today's date?/
BUFFER:  .BLKB    BUFF_SIZE
;
         BEGIN    DATE
         PRINTCHRS  MESSG         ; Print prompt
         READLINE   BUFFER        ; Get response
         PRINTCHRS  BUFFER,R0     ; Print it back out
         EXIT
         .END     DATE
```

5.
```
; There are several ways to do this problem. This is one way.
FIRST:   .ASCIZ   /FIRST/
SECOND:  .ASCIZ   /      SECOND/
THIRD:   .ASCIZ   /             THIRD/
;
         BEGIN   ONE23
         PRINTCHRS    FIRST
         PRINTCHRS    SECOND
         PRINTCHRS    THIRD
         EXIT
         .END    ONE23
```

7. If the buffer is used more than once, the tail end of the previous contents may be where you think a 0 ought to be.

9. Suitable for a programming assignment.

11.
```
; This program uses DUMPLONG to display the contents of
; registers R2,....,R11.
         BEGIN   DUMPREGS
         DUMPLONG R2,R3,R4,R5,R6,R7,R8,R9,R10,R11
         EXIT
         .END    DUMPREGS
```

13. **(a)** R3: 00502A3C, R4: 00502A3C
      (c) R3: 00502A3C, R4: FFDE753C

15.
```
         MOVAB   STRING+11,R10
```

17.

```
        ADDL2   #1,R10          ; Address for string
        READLINE (R10)          ; Read string
        MOVB    R0,-(R10)       ; Store length
        ADDL2   R0,R10          ; Add string length
        INCL    R10             ; Add 1 for length byte
```

Chapter 7 describes another addressing mode that makes this a little easier.

19.

```
; This program does the following:
;   Prompts the user for his or her last name, and reads it.
;   Prompts the user for his or her first name, and reads it.
;   Prints out "Hello," followed by the first and last names
;   with one space between names.
;
BUF_SZ = 80
SPACE = ^A/ /
;
FIRSTNM:.ASCIZ  /First name?/
LASTNM: .ASCIZ  /Last name?/
BUFFER  .BLKB   BUF_SIZ
MSG:    .ASCII  /Hello, /
OUTLINE:.BLKB   2*BUF_SZ+1      ; Maximum possible length
;
; REGISTER USE
;       R0       input string length
;       R6       last name length
;       R7       pointer to buffer
;
        BEGIN   HELLO
        PRINTCHRS   LASTNM      ; Print last name prompt
        READLINE    BUFFER      ; Get last name
        MOVL    R0,R6           ; Save length
        PRINTCHRS   FIRSTNM     ; Print first name prompt
        READLINE    OUTLINE     ; Get it to out buffer
        MOVAB   OUTLINE,R7      ; Establish pointer
        ADDL2   R0,R7
        MOVB    #SPACE,(R7)+     ; Insert space
        MOVC3   R6,BUFFER,(R7)   ; Copy last name
        ADDL2   R6,R7
        MOVB    #0,(R7)         ; String terminator
        PRINTCHRS   MSG         ; Print message
        EXIT
        .END    HELLO
```

21.

```
; Multiply longwords at ALPHA, BETA, and GAMMA.
;
ALPHA:  .LONG   25
BETA:   .LONG   -13
GAMMA:  .LONG   58
;
```

```
        BEGIN    MULTIPLY
        MULL3    ALPHA,BETA,R4
        MULL2    GAMMA,R4
        EXIT
        .END     MULTIPLY
```

Here is a transcript showing the use of the debugger to check the result in R4 after each instruction. Note that after the EXIT macro is executed, R4 is cleared. Note also that when R4 contains a negative integer, the debugger displays a leading zero. Ignore it.

```
$ run ex521

        VAX DEBUG Version V5.2-015

%DEBUG-I-INITIAL, language is MACRO, module set to .MAIN.

DBG> set watch R4
%DEBUG-I-WPTTRACE, non-static watchpoint, tracing every instruction
DBG> go
watch of .MAIN.\MULTIPLY\%R4 at .MAIN.\MULTIPLY\%LINE 8
     8:          MULL3    ALPHA,BETA,R4
   old value: 00000000
   new value: 0FFFFFEBB
break at .MAIN.\MULTIPLY\%LINE 9
     9:          MULL2    GAMMA,R4
DBG> examine/dec R4
.MAIN.\MULTIPLY\%R4:       -325
DBG> go
watch of .MAIN.\MULTIPLY\%R4 at .MAIN.\MULTIPLY\%LINE 9
     9:          MULL2    GAMMA,R4
   old value: 0FFFFFEBB
   new value: 0FFFFB65E
break at .MAIN.\MULTIPLY\%LINE 10
    10:          EXIT
DBG> examine/dec R4
.MAIN.\MULTIPLY\%R4:       -18850
DBG> go
%DEBUG-I-EXITSTATUS, is '%SYSTEM-S-NORMAL, normal successful completion'
DBG> examine/dec R4
0\%R4:  0
```

CHAPTER 6

```
1.      MULW3    #8,GALLONS,PINTS
3.      MULL3    #3,X,R0            ; 3x
        ADDL2    #12,R0            ; 3x+12
```

```
MULL2    X,R0                ;(3x+12)*x
SUBL3    #17,R0,Y            ; 3x^2+12x-17 in Y
```

5. Subtracting in binary: 0A − B7 = 53 (with a borrow).

Negating and adding: The two's complement of B7 is 49. 0A+49 = 53 (no carry).

7. The method works for negative integers.

9.
```
         SUBL2    R5,R5
         CLRL     R5
         MOVL     #0,R5
         MULL2    #0,R5
```

11.
```
FXD_CST: .WORD   528
DIN_CST: .WORD   19
TKT_CST: .WORD   30
TKT8_CST:.WORD   225
IND_TKTS:.WORD   76
GRP_TKTS:.WORD   3
PROFITS: .BLKW   1
;           .
;           .
;           .
         MULW3    IND_TKTS,TKT_CST,R6
         MULW3    GRP_TKTS,TKT8_CST,R7
         ADDW2    R7,R6               ; Total ticket income
         SUBW2    FXD_CST,R6          ; Income minus fixed costs
         MULW3    #8,GRP_TKTS,R7
         ADDW2    IND_TKTS,R7         ; Total number of dinners
         MULW2    DIN_CST,R7          ; Total cost of dinners
         SUBW3    R7,R6,PROFITS       ; Subtract cost of dinners
```

13. (a) R9: 00C27DEC; the longword at 00013B64: 00000829

(b) R9: 00C27DFA (Remember here that E8 is −24, not 232.)

(c) The byte at 00C27DE8: 03

(e) Overflow

(g) R4: 00013B66; the word at 00013B64: FE74

15.
```
         MOVAW    SCORES,R6
         ADDW3    (R6)+,(R6)+,R7
         ADDW2    (R6)+,R7
         ADDW2    (R6)+,R7
         ADDW2    (R6),R7
         DIVW3    #5,R7,AVERAGE
```

17.
```
         DIVL3    #2,BETA,R6
         ADDL2    ALPHA,R6
         DIVL3    BETA,R6,GAMMA
```

This method will not always work with negative data. Suppose that (ALPHA) = 11 and (BETA) = −5. The result will be −1.

19. (a) `ADDW2    #1,R3`

    (c) `SUBL3    (R5)+,#0,(R10)`   or   `MULL3    #-1,(R5)+,(R10)`

21. (a)
```
        CLRW    R6              ; Make positive word integer
        MOVB    ALPHA,R6        ;    from (ALPHA)
        CLRW    R7              ; Make positive word integer
        MOVB    BETA,R7         ;    from (BETA)
        MULW3   R6,R7,GAMMA
```
    (b)
```
        CVTBW   ALPHA,R6        ; Sign-extend (ALPHA)
        CVTBW   BATA,R7         ; Sign-extend (BETA)
        MULW3   R6,R7,GAMMA
```

23.
```
        MOVL    COUNT,R6        ; Loop counter
        MOVAL   LIST,R7         ; Array pointer
        CLRL    R8              ; For sum
LOOP:   ADDL2   (R7)+,R8
        SOBGTR  R6,LOOP
        MOVL    R8,SUM
```

25.
```
        MULL3   #2,NUM,R6
        MOVC3   R6,A1,A2
```

27. 5

29. −1 (or `FFFFFFFF`)

31. Assume that we are using row-major ordering. In the formula we use parentheses to denote contents and square brackets for grouping terms. MATRIX[I,J] is at location MATRIX+(COLS)*[(I)−1]+(J)−1. If indexes begin at 0, the formula is MATRIX+(COLS)*(I)+(J).

33. Suitable for a programming assignment.

35. No. The problem stated that the sum would be too large for a byte. At some point in the loop overflow would occur.

37.
```
        MOVL    POINTS,R8
        MOVAL   VALUES,R6
        MOVAB   DELTA,R7
LOOP:   CVTBL   (R7)+,R9
        SUBL2   R9,(R6)+
        SOBGTR  R8,LOOP
```

39. (a) 2D 34 39 32 37

41. `FFFFFB4C`

43. TEMP: 01 1C

    AGE: 20 31 31

    `My car is 11 years old.`

45.
```
    ; PROBLEM STATEMENT
    ;
    ; This program reads I, J, and LL from the terminal,
    ; computes SQR(7*I+J/LL), and prints the result.
```

```
; The numbers must be input one at a time in 6-digit
; LSN form.
;
IMSG:    .ASCIZ   /Type I/
JMSG:    .ASCIZ   /Type J/
LLMSG:   .ASCIZ   /Type LL/
RESULT:  .ASCII   /The result is /
LSN:     .BLKB    8
         .BYTE    0                        ; End of output string
PACKED:  .BLKB    4
I:       .BLKL    1
J:       .BLKL    1
LL:      .BLKL    1
;
; REGISTER USE
;
;        R6       result
;        R7       scratch
;
         BEGIN    COMPUTE
         PRINTCHRS IMSG
         READLINE LSN                      ; Read and convert I
         CVTSP    #6,LSN,#6,PACKED
         CVTPL    #6,PACKED,I
         PRINTCHRS JMSG
         READLINE LSN                      ; Read and convert J
         CVTSP    #6,LSN,#6,PACKED
         CVTPL    #6,PACKED,J
         PRINTCHRS LLMSG
         READLINE LSN                      ; Read and convert LL
         CVTSP    #6,LSN,#6,PACKED
         CVTPL    #6,PACKED,LL
         DIVL3    LL,J,R6                   ; Computation
         MULL3    #7,I,R7
         ADDL2    R7,R6
         MULL2    R6,R6
         CVTLP    R6,#7,PACKED              ; Convert and print result
         CVTPS    #7,PACKED,#7,LSN
         PRINTCHRS RESULT
         EXIT
         .END     COMPUTE
```

47. ; This program segment reads a two-dimensional longword array.
     ; The first line of input contains the number of rows, n, and
     ; columns, m. Each of the following n lines contains m integers.
     ; The format for n and m is
     ;   sddbsdd

```
        ; and the format for the numbers in the array is
        ;      bsddddd
        ; where b=blank, s=sign, d=digit.
        ;
        ; There is no error recovery for bad data.
        ;
        MAXROWS = 10
        MAXCOLS = 10
        ARRAY:  .BLKL    MAXROWS*MAXCOLS
        ROWS:   .BLKL    1
        COLS:   .BLKL    1
        LINE:   .BLKB    80              ; Input buffer
        PKD:    .BLKB    3               ; For conversions
        ;
        ; REGISTER USE
        ;
        ;       R6       array pointer
        ;       R7       m, number of columns
        ;       R8       row counter (outer loop)
        ;       R9       column counter (inner loop)
        ;       R10      buffer pointer
        ;       R0-R3    used by CVT's

                BEGIN    READARRAY
                READRCRD LINE           ; Get dimensions
                CVTSP    #2,LINE,#2,PKD  ; Convert to packed
                CVTPL    #2,PKD,R8       ; n, number of rows
                MOVL     R8,ROWS
                CVTSP    #2,LINE+4,#2,PKD ; Convert to packed
                CVTPL    #2,PKD,R7       ; m, number of columns
                MOVL     R7,COLS
                MOVAL    ARRAY,R6        ; Array address
        ;
        READ:   READRCRD LINE           ; Get row
                MOVAB    LINE+1,R10      ; Buffer pointer
                MOVL     R7,R9           ; Number of entries per line
        ;
        CNVERT: CVTSP    #5,(R10),#5,PKD
                CVTPL    #5,PKD,(R6)+    ; Convert and store entry
                ADDL2    #7,R10          ; Increment buffer pointer
                SOBGTR   R9,CNVERT       ; End of loop for each line
                SOBGTR   R8,READ         ; End outer loop
        ;
        EOF:    EXIT
                .END     READARRAY
```

49. Suitable for a programming assignment.

CHAPTER 7

1. In the order: N Z V C.
   (a) 0 0 0 1
   (c) 0 0 0 0
   (e) 1 0 0 0

3. HERE

5.
```
        CMPB    CHAR,#^A/A/
        BLSS    NOTUPPER
        CMPB    CHAR,#^A/Z/
        BGTR    NOTUPPER
```

7. Yes to both questions.

9.
```
   NLEN = 24
           MOVL     COUNT,R10
           MOVAB    TAGS,R9
           MOVAB    NAMES,R8
   LOOP:   TSTB     (R9)+
           BEQL     INCPTR
           PRINTCHRS (R8),#NLEN
   INCPTR: ADDL2    #NLEN,R8
           SOBGTR   R10,LOOP
```

11.
```
        CMPB    R8,#7
        BEQL    SPECIAL
        CMPB    R8,#11
        BEQL    SPECIAL
        CMPB    R8,#13
        BEQL    SPECIAL
```

13.
```
        CMPW    WORD,#-100
        BLSS    NEXT
        CMPW    WORD,#100
        BGTR    NEXT
        CMPB    BYTE,#3
        BEQL    THERE
        CMPB    BYTE,#4
        BEQL    THERE
   NEXT:
```

15.
```
        CMPL    ALPHA+4,BETA+4   ; Compare most significant parts
        BGTR    ABC
        BLSS    NEXT
        CMPL    ALPHA,BETA
        BGTRU   ABC
   NEXT:
```

17.
```
   LOOP:    CMPB    (R7)+,(R8)+
            BLSS    FIRST
```

```
                    BGTR      SECOND
                    SOBGTR    R10,LOOP
```

19.
```
         ; REGISTER USE
         ;
         ;          R6        x
         ;          R7        k
         ;
                    MOVL      N,R6          ; x := n
                    CLRL      R7            ; k := 0
         LOOP:      CMPL      R6,#1
                    BLEQ      DONE          ; if x <= 1, then done
                    DIVL2     #2,R6         ; x := x DIV 2
                    INCL      R7            ; k := k+1
                    BRB       LOOP          ; end of loop
         DONE:      MOVL      R7,LOG_N
```

21. The pointer to the byte being examined is incremented after each comparison by the autoincrement in the CMPB instruction, so the address in R6 at the instruction labeled FOUND is the address of the byte following the one that contains the blank. One way to correct the program segment is to replace the last two lines with

```
NOTFND:  MOVL      #1,R6
FOUND:   SUBL3     #1,R6,LOCBLANK
```

23. (a) The autoincrement at TESTBLANK will cause the pointer R6 to overshoot the first character. The autodecrement at NONBLANK, which is done before using the address in R6, will fix this. The second CMPB instruction must look at the same character, so R6 is not changed.

(b) In this case, R6 contained the address of the first digit. It must be "backed up" to the sign, which in this case is blank.

25. (a) Converts −10, 245, then branches to ERROR.
   (c) Converts 15, then branches to ERROR.
   (e) Converts 41, 379, −248, 14, then branches to ERROR.

27. Suitable for a programming assignment.

29.
```
                    MOVAB     TEXT,R10
         LOOP:      CVTBL     (R10),R7        ; Need length as longword
                                              ;   (for address calculation)
                    BEQL      DONE
                    PRINTCHRS 1(R10),R7
                    ADDL2     R7,R10
                    INCL      R10
                    BRB       LOOP
         DONE:
```

31. **(a)**

Medical record number:	0(R6)
Name:	8(R6)
Address:	30(R6)
Phone number:	80(R6)
Date of birth:	87(R6)

(b) `ADDL2    #193,R6`

33. Yes, the algorithm works in both cases. If *num* = 0, *first* will be greater than *last* and the loop is never executed. 0 is returned.

35. Remove the instruction `MOVW   KEY,R7` and replace the instruction `CMPW   R7,(R11)` with `CMPC3 #6,KEY,(R11)`

37. Replace the last few lines of the program, beginning at NOTFOUND, with the following.

```
NOTFOUND:
        CLRW    NUM_COPIES
        CLRW    INDEX
        BRB     DONE
FOUND:
;    Scan backwards, then forward from the instance of the key
; that was found, using sequential search. (If a large number
; of duplicates were expected, binary search could be used
; here too, but the code would be longer.)
;    Note that the search loops must check for the ends of the
; array, in case all entries are equal to the key and a copy
; of the key happens to be in memory before or after the array.
;
; REGISTER USE
;
;       R4      number of entries in the array
;       R5      size of entry (already initialized)
;       R6      key (already initialized)
;       R7      save address of instance of the key found
;       R8      index of first instance of the key
;       R9      index of last instance of the key
;       R10     index of instance of key already found
;               (already initialized)
;       R11     address of entry being examined (already
;               initialized)
;
        MOVL    R11,R7          ; Save current address
        SUBL3   #1,R10,R8       ; Max entries in backward scan
        BEQL    FND1            ; In case key found in first slot
```

```
          CHK1:   SUBL2    R5,R11           ; Move pointer to previous entry
                  CMPW     R6,(R11)         ; Compare keys
                  BNEQ     FND1
                  SOBGTR   R8,CHK1
          FND1:   ADDW3    #1,R8,INDEX      ; Index of first instance of key
                  CVTWL    NUM,R4           ; For forward loop limit
                  ADDL3    #1,R10,R9        ; Index of next entry
                  CMPL     R9,R4
                  BGTR     FND2             ; In case key found in last slot
                  ADDL3    R5,R7,R11        ; Address of next item
          CHK2:   CMPW     R6,(R11)
                  BNEQ     FND2
                  ADDL2    R5,R11           ; Increment address
                  AOBLEQ   R4,R9,CHK2
          FND2:   SUBW3    R8,R9,NUM_COPIES
                  DECL     R9               ; Index of last instance of key
```

39. In the order: sequential search, binary search.

    (a) 64,   1

    (c) 1,   7

    (e) 127, 7

41.
```
                  INCL     R6
                  CMPL     R6,R10
                  BLSS     LOOP
```

43.
```
                  ADDW2    #7,R9            ; Increment index
                  CMPW     R9,CNT           ; Compare to loop limit
                  BGTR     LOOPDONE
                  BRW      CHECK
          LOOPDONE:
```

Recall that the conditional branch instructions have only a byte branch displacement, but ACB has a word displacement.

45.
```
                  SUBL3    R9,N,R0          ; n-j
                  MULL2    INC,R0
                  BLSS     DONE             ; Branch past the loop
```

47. Suitable for a programming assignment.

49. Suitable for a programming assignment.

CHAPTER 8

Note: All machine code is shown with the first (lowest addressed) byte at the right.

  1. **(a)** 55 5B 55 A7

     (c) 68 97

  3. **(a)** 3 bytes

     (b) 3 bytes

(c) 2 bytes

(d) 3 bytes

(c) is fastest.

5. **(a)** FIRST contains 1; SECOND contains its own address; THIRD contains 3; R7 contains the address of THIRD.

 (b) FIRST contains the address of SECOND; SECOND contains 2; THIRD contains 3; R7 contains the address of FIRST.

7. `C5 57 0A F3`

9. In each case the operand specifier begins at byte 0000014E.

 (a) `FF 67 CF`

 (c) `80 AF`

11. `FF 11 CF FF 14 CF C0`

 The operand specifiers are not identical because when the operand addresses are calculated by the CPU, the PC will contain different addresses.

13.
```
        ADDL2   #2,R10          ; Address following op. specifier
                                ;  if byte displacement is used
        SUBL3   R10,R6,R8       ; Displacement (correct if byte)
        CMPL    R8,#127         ; Test if displ. fits in byte
        BGTR    NOTBYTE
        CMPL    R8,#-128
        BGEQ    STORE           ; Branch if byte ok
NOTBYTE:DECL    R8              ; Correct for word displacement
        INCL    R10
        CMPL    R8,#32767       ; Test if displ. fits in word
        BGTR    NOTWORD
        CMPL    R8,#-32768
        BGEQ    STORE           ; Branch if word ok
NOTWORD:SUBL2   #2,R8           ; Correct for longword displacement
        ADDL2   #2,R10
STORE:  MOVL    R8,DISPL
```

15. **(a)** 000000A7   **(b)** 000000A8

 (c) Not unless the programmer explicitly specified "W^" on the operand. In this case, the displacement would be FF7F if the instruction began at 000000A7.

17. **(a)** `58 1E A2`   **(b)** `58 00 46 8F A2`

19. **1)** Look up the opcode of the instruction, noting that it needs two operands. Increment the location counter.

 2) Look up the value of MAX in the symbol table. If $0 \le MAX \le 63$ then code it as a literal, else as immediate mode. If the latter, note that the data type is W, so the immediate value is represented in two bytes. Increment the location counter (by 1 or 3, depending on the mode used).

 3) Code the second operand as `57`. Increment the location counter.

21. **(a)** `65 20 B1`   **(c)** `6E FF FB 8F B0`

23. Relative mode (displacement from the PC). The assembler treats 25 as the operand address.

25. In the first instruction ALPHA is encoded in relative mode. In the second instruction #ALPHA is encoded as a longword immediate operand. The linker has to fill in the value; the assembler does not know the actual run-time location of ALPHA.

27. `CMPW    @(R4)+,R11`

29. R3 will contain 0000010C. The contents at memory location 00000108 will not change. The longword at 0000024C will be cleared.

31. Relative (with word displacement), register, literal, register deferred, displacement (byte), branch, immediate.

33.
```
        ; PROBLEM STATEMENT
        ; This program segment sorts an array, LIST, of pointers which
        ; are pointing to records as described in Example 8.9.
        ; It uses the bubble sort algorithm from Exercise 50 in
        ; Chapter 7. The variables last, pairs, and j are used
        ; as in that algorithm. Assume the longword NUM contains
        ; the number of records.
        ;
        KEYSIZE = 22
        ;
        ; REGISTER USE
        ;
        ;       R0      temp
        ;       R5      last
        ;       R6      pairs
        ;       R7      j
        ;       R8      address of current position in LIST
        ;
                MOVL    NUM,R5
WHILE:  TSTL    R5                      ; while last > 0 do begin
                BLEQ    DONE
                SUBL3   #1,R5,R6        ; pairs := last - 1
                BEQL    DONE            ; Done if pairs = 0
                CLRL    R5              ; last := 0
                MOVL    #1,R7           ; j := 1
                MOVAL   LIST,R8
PAIRS:  CMPC3   #KEYSIZE,@0(R8),@4(R8)  ; Compare names in records
                BLEQ    NXTPAIR
                MOVL    (R8),R0         ; Swap pointers
                MOVL    4(R8),(R8)
                MOVL    R0,4(R8)
                MOVL    R7,R5           ; last := j
NXTPAIR:ADDL2   #4,R8
                AOBLEQ  R6,R7,PAIRS     ; loop control for for-loop
                BRB     WHILE
DONE:
```

35. FE 5A CF 48 B5

37. **(a)** 00000112

   (b) Insufficient information; the address in the longword in memory at 00000108 is needed. The operand address will be that address plus 7.

39. It would not be correct. Because the data type of CMPW is word, the use of index mode would cause 2*middle to be added to the base address, but we need middle*size.

41. Disabled. Adding the least significant longwords could trigger an overflow.

43. Look at PSL=0BC00024. The condition codes are the rightmost four bits. N=0, Z=1, V=0, and C=0.

45. In the case of a constant small enough to be assembled as a literal, a reasonable guess is that the assembler flags it as an error because, at run-time, there will be no operand address. If the assembler does not flag it, but assembles the literal, we would expect a run-time error.

   In the case of a constant that must be assembled in immediate mode, the operand will have a run-time address because immediate mode is assembled as autoincrement using the PC. Hence the value in the PC is the operand address, and the CPU can execute the instruction. Thus we would not expect an error message in this case.

   An experiment shows that the assembler is clever. It recognizes that the first operand of a MOVAB instruction must have an address, so it assembles the operand in immediate mode even if it is small enough for a literal.

CHAPTER 9

1.
```
        ; PROCEDURE PRINT_STRINGS(STRINGS,NUM)
        ;
        ; This procedure prints a character-string array.
        ;
        ; Input arguments:
        ;     STRINGS    the array of strings, each 12 characters long
        ;     NUM        the number of strings (longword)
        ;
        STRINGS = 4
        NUM = 8
        STR_SIZE = 12                        ; String size
        ;
        ; REGISTER USE
        ;         R6        loop counter
        ;         R7        pointer to strings
        ;
                .ENTRY  PRINT_STRINGS,^M<R6,R7>
                MOVL    @NUM(AP),R6          ; Number of strings
```

```
             BEQL    DONE                    ; Return if no strings
             MOVL    STRINGS(AP),R7          ; String pointer
     PRINT:  PRINTCHRS  (R7),#STR_SIZE
             ADDL2   #STR_SIZE,R7            ; Increment pointer
             SOBGTR  R6,PRINT
     DONE:   RET
             .END
```

3. From the top down, the return addresses on the stack are RETB, RETA2, and RETMN.

5.
```
     ; Sets up the argument list and calls procedure USEFUL
     C_USEFUL:
             PUSHL   R3
             PUSHAL  BETA
             PUSHAL  ALPHA
             CALLS   #3,USEFUL
             RSB
```

7. **(a)** 16(AP)

   (b) @12(AP)

9. **(a)** 4

   (c) 4

11.
```
             MOVAW   LIST,R6         ; Array pointer
             MOVL    NUM,R7          ; Loop counter
     LOOP:   PUSHAW  (R6)+           ; Push, then increment item address
             CALLS   #1,PRINT_ITEM
             SOBGTR  R7,LOOP
```

13.
```
     ; procedure CONCATENATE (string1: character string,
     ;      length1: longword, string2: character string, length2: longword)
     ;
     ; This procedure copies string1 to the end of string2.
     ;
     STRING1 = 4
     LENGTH1 = 8
     STRING2 = 12
     LENGTH2 = 16
     ;
     ; REGISTER USE
     ;       R0-R5   used by MOVC3
     ;       R7      destination address
     ;
             .ENTRY  CONCATENATE,^M<R2,R3,R4,R5,R7>
             ADDL3   STRING2(AP),@LENGTH2(AP),R7   ; Address following string2
             MOVC3   @LENGTH1(AP),@STRING1(AP),(R7); Copy string1
             RET
             .END
```

15. The current value in AP must be saved in the call frame before it is overwritten.

17. (a)
```
        MOVL    12(FP),R9
        MOVL    8(R9),R9
```
(c)
```
        MOVL    12(FP),R11
        MOVL    12(R11),R11
        MOVL    12(R11),R11
        MOVL    16(R11),R11
```

19.
```
; procedure MESSAGE(tag: byte integer, string1: character string,
;     string2: character string, msgloc: longword)
;
; If the tag is negative, MESSAGE puts the address of string1 into
; msgloc. Otherwise, it puts the address of string2 into msgloc.
;
TAG = 4
STRING1 = 8
STRING2 = 12
MSGLOC = 16
;
        .ENTRY  MESSAGE,^M<>
        TSTB    @TAG(AP)
        BLSS    MOVS1
        MOVL    STRING2(AP),@MSGLOC(AP)
        RET
MOVS1:  MOVL    STRING1(AP),@MSGLOC(AP)
        RET
        .END
```

21. Using CALLS:

```
        CALLS   #0,PROC
```

Using CALLG:

```
ARGS:   .LONG   0
          . . .
        CALLG   ARGS,PROC
```

CALLS is better because it does not require the programmer to reserve a longword with the number of arguments (0).

23. Suitable for a programming assignment.

25. This procedure does less error-checking than the example in Section 7.2.

```
; PROCEDURE GETNUM (START,END,NUMBER,NEWSTART)
;
;    This procedure scans the character string beginning at
; the address START for the first occurence of a leading
; separate numeric string. (The character string ends at
; the byte preceding the address END.)
;    If a leading separate numeric string is found, GETNUM
```

```
; converts it to a two's complement longword and stores it
; in NUMBER.  NEWSTART will be assigned the address of the
; next byte following the lsn string found.
;
;   A flag is returned in R0 to indicate whether or not a
; number was found in the string. The flag is 1 if a number
; was found, 0 otherwise. If the flag is 0, nothing is
; stored at NUMBER and NEWSTART.
;
; Input arguments
;        START        the character string
;        END          the byte following the end of the string
; Output arguments
;        NUMBER       the longword two's complement representation
;                       of the first leading separate numeric
;                       number found in the string.
;        NEWSTART     the address of the byte following the first
;                       leading separate numeric string found
;
; HANDLING OF ERRORS
;
; 1) GETNUM allows for a maximum of 10 digits in the number.
;      If the number is larger, it will be truncated without
;      warning.
; 2) GETNUM assumes there are no invalid characters in the
;      string.
; 3) GETNUM assumes the leading separate numeric string has a
;      sign byte (which may be blank).
;
PKD:      .BLKB    6                        ; Space for packed decimal
;
; REGISTER USE
;        R0           flag to tell if a number was found
;        R2,R3        used by CVT instructions
;        R6           string pointer
;        R7           pointer to first byte of lsn
;        R8           number of digits in lsn
;        R9           loop limit (byte following the string)
;
          .ENTRY   GETNUM,^M<R2,R3,R6,R7,R8,R9>
          MOVL     4(AP),R6                 ; String address
          MOVL     8(AP),R9                 ; Loop limit (END)
          CMPL     R6,R9                    ; Check if string is empty
          BGEQ     BAD
SCAND:    CMPB     (R6),#^X30               ; Look for digit
          BGEQ     DIGIT
          AOBLSS   R9,R6,SCAND
          BRB      BAD                      ; No digit found
```

```
;
DIGIT:   SUBL3   #1,R6,R7                ; Save addr of first lsn byte
;
SCANB:   CMPB    (R6),#^X20              ; Scan for blank
         BEQL    ENDLSN
         AOBLSS  R9,R6,SCANB
ENDLSN:  SUBL3   R7,R6,R8                ; Length of lsn
; R6 will be pointing to the next byte after the end of the lsn
; in the case where a blank was found and in the case where the
; end of the string was reached.
         MOVL    R6,@16(AP)              ; Store NEWSTART
         DECL    R8                      ; Number of digits in lsn
;
         CMPL    R8,#10                  ; Check number of digits
         BLEQ    CONVT
         MOVL    #10,R8                  ; Chop to 10 digits if longer
CONVT:   CVTSP   R8,(R7),R8,PKD          ; Convert to packed
         CVTPL   R8,PKD,@12(AP)          ; Convert to long and store
         MOVL    #1,R0                   ; Set success flag
         RET
;
BAD:     CLRL    R0                      ; Failure flag
         RET
         .END
```

27. (a) Immediate value
    (b) Below the first call frame is the argument list for the first call. It consists of a longword containing 00000001, the number of arguments, followed by a longword containing 00000003, the argument. Below the second call frame is an argument list containing 00000001 and 00000002. Below the third call frame is an argument list containing 00000001 and 00000001.
    (c) 6 (The function computes $n!$ where n is its argument.)

29. (a) All n entries might have to be moved.
    (b) With a sorted array, we can access the ith entry in constant time. With a linked list, we have to follow i pointers, so the time is linear in i.

31. Suitable for a programming assignment.

33. INIT_AVAIL will work correctly. The address in R9 will not be the address of the next-to-last node; it will be an address somewhere inside that node, but the ACBL instruction will stop the loop after the pointer is stored.

35. The procedure PRINTKEY is not reentrant because it uses space allocated within the procedure for the line to be printed. Here is the revised procedure.

```
; PROCEDURE PRINTKEY (NODE)
;
; This procedure prints the key in the given node.
```

```
;
; The number of bytes in the key, KEY_SIZE, and the
; offset of the key field from the beginning of a node,
; KEY_FIELD, are constants defined in this procedure.
;
KEY_SIZE = 12                          ; Number of bytes per key
KEY_FIELD = 4                          ; Offset for key field
;
; Offset for argument list
NODE = 4
;
TAB = 9
;
; REGISTER USE
;        R6        ptr
;        R7        address of buffer on user stack
;        R0-R5     used by MOVC3
;
         .ENTRY    PRINTKEY,^M<R2,R3,R4,R5,R6,R7>
         MOVL      NODE(AP),R6              ; Get addr of node
         SUBL2     #KEY_SIZE+1,SP           ; Reserve buffer on stack
         MOVL      SP,R7                    ; Save buffer address
         MOVB      #TAB,(R7)                ; Store tab code
         MOVC3     #KEY_SIZE,KEY_FIELD(R6),1(R7)
         PRINTCHRS (R7),#KEY_SIZE+1         ; Print key
         ADDL2     #KEY_SIZE+1,SP           ; Pop buffer space
         RET
         .END
```

CHAPTER 10

1. DELTA = 0056
   IND = 005C
   LABEL = 005E
   TAG = 0061
   VOLUME = 0064
   final . = 0070

3. The program sections are: DATA, IO_DATA, IO_PROCS, PROG, and $RMSNAM.
   DATA and PROG are defined in the program; the others are used by the I/O macros.
   The starting addresses may vary with the system; examine your own map file.

5. ^B01100101

7. (a) 55_{16} (e) 18_{10}
   (c) 0138_{16}

9. **(a)** The linker puts the address of LIST in the longword allocated by the .ADDRESS directive. The linker puts the displacement for PROCEDURE in the CALLG instruction.

  (b) MAX is absolute; LIST and ARGS are relocatable; PROCEDURE is external.

CHAPTER 11

1.
```
        .MACRO  SWAP    A,B
        PUSHL   A                      ; Use stack for scratch space
        MOVL    B,A
        MOVL    (SP)+,B
        .ENDM   SWAP
```

3. Autodecrement and literal.

5.
```
   CALL    PROC    (R7),ALPHA,ARRAY
```

7.
```
        .MACRO  JOINSTRINGS STR1,STR2,LENGTH
        PUSHR   #^M<R0,R1,R2,R3,R4,R5>  ; Save regs used by MOVC3
        PUSHAB  STR1                    ; Use stack for scratch
        ADDL2   #LENGTH,(SP)            ; Destination address
        MOVC3   #LENGTH,STR2,@0(SP)     ; Copy string
        ADDL2   #4,SP                   ; Pop scratch work
        POPR    #^M<R0,R1,R2,R3,R4,R5>  ; Reload registers
        .ENDM   JOINSTRINGS
```

9.
```
        .MACRO  MOD     DIVISOR,DIVIDEND,REMAINDER
 ; The remainder of a DIV b is a-(a DIV b)*b
        DIVL3   DIVISOR,DIVIDEND,-(SP)  ; Use stack for scratch
        MULL2   DIVISOR,(SP)
        SUBL3   (SP)+,DIVIDEND,REMAINDER
        .ENDM   MOD
```

This macro will not work correctly if the autoincrement or autodecrement addressing modes are used for the divisor and/or dividend. Try rewriting the macro to work for those modes.

11.
```
        .MACRO  PUSH    ITEM,TYPE
        MOV'TYPE        ITEM,-(SP)
        .ENDM   PUSH

   ;

        .MACRO  POP     ITEM,TYPE
        MOV'TYPE        (SP)+,ITEM
        .ENDM   POP
```

13. The first entry in the argument list is the address of the string to print; the second entry is the actual value of the length of the string, not the address of the length.

15.
```
        .MACRO  ADDQ2   Q1,Q2
        ADDL2   Q1,Q2
        ADWC    Q1+4,Q2+4
        .ENDM   ADDQ2
```

17. All modes will work correctly for SOURCE. For DEST the following will not work: literal, immediate, autoincrement, autodecrement.

19. It prints a blank line. (There is no error.)

21. (a) It is an error (detected by the assembler) if there are more actual arguments than formal arguments. If there are fewer actual arguments, it may or may not be an error depending on the macro definition. (In the CALL macro in Example 11.20, we expect that usually the number of actual arguments is smaller than the number of formal arguments.)

(c) This would cause an error if the program using the macro was using the stack and expected certain data to be at the top of the stack. This error would not be detected by the assembler or linker; it might cause a run-time crash or incorrect output.

23. (a) CNT = 1   **(b)** CNT = 10

25.
```
        .MACRO  PUSH    A1,A2,A3,A4,A5,A6,A7,A8,A9,A10
        .IRP    A,<A1,A2,A3,A4,A5,A6,A7,A8,A9,A10>
        .IF     NOT_BLANK   A
        PUSHL   A
        .ENDC
        .ENDR
        .ENDM   PUSH
```

27. Suitable for a programming assignment.

29. There is no error; the entire string will be extracted.

31. As we indicated in the text, the VAX macro processor has some rigid, and often inconvenient rules, some of which are not documented in the manual. The following macro definitions have been tested; they work. Earlier versions that seemed quite reasonable generated error messages. For example, in the macro definition for L, the assignment to DXXX originally followed the .IF_FALSE directive, but that caused an error. Strangely, similar placement of the assignment to DXXX in the MVC macro does not cause an error message. Note also that the concatenation operator (') is not used around the "R" to concatenate it with the value of the %EXTRACT function.

Format 1
```
        .MACRO  L   REG,SOURCE
        LXXX = %LENGTH(SOURCE)
        DXXX = %LOCATE(<(>,SOURCE)+1     ; Length of displacement and '('
        .IF  EQUAL  %LOCATE(<(>,SOURCE)-LXXX    ; No paren
        MOVL    SOURCE,R'REG
        .IF_FALSE
        MOVL    %EXTRACT(0,DXXX,SOURCE)R%EXTRACT(DXXX,LXXX,SOURCE),R'REG
        .ENDC
        .ENDM   L
```

Format 2

```
        .MACRO  B       DEST
        BRW     DEST
        .ENDM   B
```

Format 3

```
        .MACRO  MVC       S1LEN,STRING2
        PUSHR   #^M<R0,R1,R2,R3,R4,R5>        ; Save regs used by MOVC3
        S1XXX = %LOCATE(<(>,S1LEN)            ; Length of string1 name
        S2XXX = %LENGTH(STRING2)              ; Length of string2 name
        SLXXX = S1XXX+1                       ; Position of length operand
        LLXXX = %LENGTH(S1LEN)-SLXXX-1        ; Length of length operand
        .IF  EQUAL  %LOCATE(<(>,STRING2)-S2XXX  ; No paren
        MOVC3   #%EXTRACT(SLXXX,LLXXX,S1LEN),-
                %EXTRACT(0,S1XXX,S1LEN),STRING2
        .IF_FALSE
        DXXX = %LOCATE(<(>,STRING2)+1       ; Length of displacement and '('
        MOVC3   #%EXTRACT(SLXXX,LLXXX,S1LEN),-
                %EXTRACT(0,S1XXX,S1LEN),-
                %EXTRACT(0,DXXX,STRING2)R%EXTRACT(DXXX,S2XXX,STRING2)
        .ENDC
        POPR    #^M<R0,R1,R2,R3,R4,R5>        ; Reload registers
        .ENDM   MVC
```

CHAPTER 12

1. (a)
```
        BISB2   #1,R4
```
(b)
```
        MOVL    #1,R4
```
3.
```
        XORL3   #^XFF00,R10,R11
```
5.
```
        MOVB    R5,R6        ; Copy byte
        ROTL    #8,R5,R5     ; Move byte to second byte
        MOVB    R6,R5        ; Insert in first byte
        MOVW    R5,R6        ; Copy two copies
        ROTL    #16,R5,R5    ; Move two bytes to left half
        MOVW    R6,R5        ; Insert right half
```

7. For BIT*x*, use TST*x*. For BIS*x*, use MOVL #−1,dest. For BIC*x*, use CLR*x*.

9.
```
        MNEGL   R8,-(SP)
        BICL2   (SP)+,R8
```

Exercise: Explain why it works.

11.
```
        BITB    #^X20,7(FP)   ; Test CALLG/CALLS flag
        BNEQ    YES           ; Flag = 1 for CALLS
```

13. No change. (If the destination is not the source, the instructions have the effect of MOV instructions.)

15. **(a)** 53 59 FF 8F 9C

     (c) 58 80000000 8F 53 78

17. Bit position 0. The test and branch can be done with one instruction: BLBS or BLBC.

19.
```
        .MACRO  ROTATE  DATUM,T
        .IF  IDENTICAL  T,L
        ROTL    #1,DATUM,DATUM
        .IF_FALSE
        CVT'T'L DATUM,-(SP)     ; Extends left bit of DATUM to bit 31
        ROTL    #1,(SP),(SP)    ; Bit 31 goes into bit 0
        MOV'T   (SP),DATUM
        ADDL2   #4,SP           ; Pop scratch work
        .ENDC
        .ENDM   ROTATE
```

21.
```
        .ENTRY  TURNOFF,^M<R6,R7,R8>
        MOVL    @STRING(AP),R6      ; Get bit string
        BEQL    ZERO                ; Branch if all bits off
        CLRL    R7                  ; Initialize loop counter
        MOVL    #1,R8               ; Mask
TEST:   BITL    R8,R6               ; Test bit
        BNEQ    FOUND               ; Branch if bit not zero
        ROTL    #1,R8,R8            ; Move mask bit left
        AOBLSS  #31,R7,TEST         ; Loop control
FOUND:  BICL2   R8,@STRING(AP)      ; Turn off bit
        MOVB    R7,@POSN(AP)        ; Store position number
        RET                         ; Return
ZERO:   MOVB    #32,@POSN(AP)       ; Store position 32
        RET                         ; Return
        .END
```

This version has four instructions in the loop instead of three, so it is slower.

23. It works. R7 will contain 32 at the end of the loop; that is the correct position value if no bits were on. The instruction that clears a bit will have no effect. Thus the procedure can be shortened by removing three instructions.

25.
```
; PROCEDURE TURNOFFLEFT (BIT_STRING: longword, POSITION: byte)
;
; The procedure TURNOFFLEFT finds and turns off the leftmost bit
; that is on in its first argument. It returns the position
; number of the affected bit in its second argument.
; (If no bits are on, it returns 32.)
;
; METHOD
;
```

```
; A copy of the bit string is rotated to the left so that,
; until a 1 is found, each bit is tested when it is in the
; sign-bit position. (The ROTL instruction sets the condition
; codes.)  The loop counter keeps track of the original
; position of the bit being tested and is used to construct a
; mask to turn the bit off in the original bit string.
;
; Offsets for argument list
STRING = 4
POSN = 8
;
; REGISTER USE
;
;       R6        bit string
;       R7        loop counter
;       R8        mask for turning off bit
;
         .ENTRY   TURNOFF,^M<R6,R7,R8>
         ROTL     #-1,@STRING(AP),R6    ; Get bit string
         BEQL     ZERO                  ; Branch if all bits off
         MOVL     #31,R7                ; Initialize loop counter
TEST:    ROTL     #1,R6,R6              ; Get next bit in sign
         BLSS     FOUND                 ; Branch if sign bit is 1
         SOBGTR   R7,TEST               ; Loop control
FOUND:   ROTL     R7,#1,R8              ; Move 1 to position
         BICL2    R8,@STRING(AP)        ; Turn off bit
         MOVB     R7,@POSN(AP)          ; Store position number
         RET                            ; Return
ZERO:    MOVB     #32,@POSN(AP)         ; Store position 32
         RET                            ; Return
         .END
```

27. Suitable for a programming assignment.

29. Suitable for a programming assignment.

31. The ASHL instruction will shift left, causing overflow. If the IV trap is disabled, the expected mask (all zeros) will be generated.

33. Observe that in Example 12.12, if $p+n > 32$, the string of 1's will wrap around the register, filling bit positions 0 through $n+p-33$. Suppose we now want to have a string of n 0's beginning at position p. Let $p' = p+n$; that is the position where the 1's begin. Let $n' = 32-n$; that is the number of 1's we want. Put n' and p' in R6 and R7, respectively; the instructions in Example 12.12 will give the desired result.

35. Suitable for a programming assignment.

37.
```
         BISL3    S,T,R3               ; Union
         CMPL     R3,#-1               ; -1 = ^XFFFFFFFF
         BEQL     ALL
```

```
39.          ROTL    R8,#1,R7          ; Make mask
             BITL    R7,S
             BNEQ    IN_SET

41.          .MACRO  B_EQUAL  SET1,SET2,DEST,?SYM
       ; Branch to DEST if the sets are equal.
             D'SYM = 0
             .REPEAT 8
             CMPL    SET1+D'SYM,SET2+D'SYM
             BNEQ    N'SYM
             D'SYM = D'SYM+4
             .ENDR
             BRB     DEST
N'SYM:       .ENDM   B_EQUAL
```

The B_SUBSET macro definition uses the UNION macro described in Exercise 40.

```
             .MACRO  B_SUBSET  SET1,SET2,DEST,?SYM
       ; Branch to DEST if the first set is a subset of the second set.
             BRW     L'SYM
S'SYM:       .BLKB   256
L'SYM:       UNION   SET1,SET2,S'SYM
             B_EQUAL SET2,S'SYM,DEST
             .ENDM   B_SUBSET
```

43. 00000000

45. This solution assumes that, as in Example 12.12, n is in R6, p is in R7, and the mask is to be constructed in R8.

```
             CLRL    R8
             INSV    #^XFFFFFFFF,R7,R6,R8
```

This solution will not cause the sequence of 1's to wrap around to the low end of R8 if $p+n > 32$ (as the instructions in Example 12.12 will do). The following instructions achieve the wrap-around, but they are not an improvement on Example 12.12.

```
             CLRL    R8
             CLRL    R9
             INSV    #^XFFFFFFFF,R7,R6,R8    ; Extends to R9 if p+n>32
             BISL2   R9,R8
```

47. ; METHOD
```
    ;     Load and search one quadword of the disk map at a time.
    ; The last quadword may not be entirely contained within the
    ; disk map, so when a clear bit is found, the position is
    ; checked to make sure it is valid.
    ;     The position number of the available disk block is left
```

```
      ; in R6.
      ;
      ; REGISTER USE
      ;        R4      address of quadword being searched
      ;        R6      bit position offset for current quadword
      ;        R7      loop index for quadword search
      ;        R8,R9   quadword being searched
      ;        R11     outer loop index
      ;
               MOVAB   DISK_MAP,R4
               CLRL    R6
               MOVL    #BLOCKS/64+1,R11     ; Number of quadwords to search
      FETCH:   MOVQ    (R4)+,R8             ; Quadword in R8 and R9
               CLRL    R7                   ; Bit position within quadword
      TEST:    BLBC    R8,FOUND
               ASHQ    #-1,R8,R8            ; Get next bit
               AOBLEQ  #63,R7,TEST
               ADDL2   #64,R6               ; Offset for next quadword
               SOBGTR  R11,FETCH
               BRB     DISK_FULL
      FOUND:   ADDL2   R7,R6                ; Position of clear bit
               CMPL    R6,#BLOCKS           ; Check if within disk map
               BGEQ    DISK_FULL
```

49.
```
               FFS     #0,#32,R10,R9    ; Find first 1
               BEQL    NEXT             ; No 1's
               FFS     R9,#32,R10,R9    ; Find next 1
               BEQL    ONE_BIT          ; If none, branch
      NEXT:
```

51. For CMPV

```
               EXTV    posn,size,base,-(SP)
               CMPL    (SP)+,long
```

For CMPVZ, use EXTVZ.

53.
```
      ; PROCEDURE CVTCB (STRING, LONG)
      ;
      ; THE PROBLEM
      ;
      ; This procedure converts the character string STRING to
      ; a longword bit pattern and puts the result in LONG.
      ; The string is assumed to be 8 characters long and should
      ; contain ASCII codes for hex digits. Thus the string
      ; "1234ABCD" would be converted to the bit pattern
      ; ^X1234ABCD. (The digits A-F must be uppercase.)
      ;
      ; CVTCB sets the Z condition code in the saved PSW in the
      ; call frame if the conversion is done successfully.
```

```
; If any characters in the string are not valid hex digits,
; Z will not be set and nothing will be stored in LONG.
;
; THE METHOD
;
; Each character is converted to a nibble containing the
; numeric value of the digit. Then the nibble is inserted
; into the right end of the result, and the result is
; shifted left 4 places to make room for the next digit.
; After processing all eight characters, the result must
; be shifted back to the right one nibble because the last
; one inserted did not have to be shifted left.
;
        .ENTRY  CVTCB,^M<R6,R7,R8,R9>
;
; REGISTER USE
;       R6      address of next character
;       R7      loop counter
;       R8      binary value of digit
;       R9      result
;
        MOVL    4(AP),R6        ; Address of STRING
        MOVL    #8,R7           ; Loop counter
        CLRL    R9              ; Clear for result
DIGIT:  SUBB3   #^X30,(R6)+,R8  ; Get 0-9
        BLSS    RET             ; Char < ^X30
        CMPB    R8,#9
        BLEQ    OK
        SUBB2   #7,R8           ; Get 10-15
        CMPB    R8,#10
        BLSS    RET             ; ^X39 < char < ^X41
        CMPB    R8,#15
        BGTR    RET             ; Char > ^X46
OK:     BISB2   R8,R9           ; Fill nibble
        ROTL    #4,R9,R9        ; Shift left
        SOBGTR  R7,DIGIT
;
        ROTL    #-4,R9,@8(AP)   ; Shift right and store
        BISB2   #^X04,4(FP)     ; Set Z in saved PSW
RET:    RET
        .END
```

CHAPTER 13

1. (a) −3/8, or −0.375   (e) 1.0
   (c) 0.0

3. The first digit after the radix point is nonzero. Maintaining normalized numbers provides more accuracy. Also, if the radix is 2, the first fraction bit must be 1, so it may be omitted from the representation and an extra low order bit may be included for more accuracy.

5.
```
        MULF3   #7,X,R2      ; 7x in R2
        MULF3   #3.8,Y,R3    ; 3.8y in R3
        ADDF2   R2,R3        ; 7x + 3.8y in R3
        MULF2   X,R3         ; x*(7x + 3.8y) in R3
        MULF3   Y,Y,R2       ; y^2 in R2
        MULF2   R2,R2        ; y^4 in R2
        MULF2   #-5.2,R2     ; -5.2y^4 in R2
        ADDF2   R2,R3        ; x*(7x + 3.8y) -5.2y^4 in R3
```

7. Floating underflow is the condition when the result of a floating point computation has an exponent smaller than the smallest exponent that can be represented in the data type of the destination operand (-127 for types F and D). It can occur after an arithmetic operation.

9. On the VAX the first bit after the radix point is assumed to be 1 and is not represented. Thus if the fraction bits are all zero, the fraction is .1, not zero.

11. MOVW copies a word. MOVL and MOVF each copy a longword, but they test different bits to determine the sign and set the condition codes.

13. The macros in all three examples will work for floating point types because the instructions used (ADDx2, ADDx3, .BLKx, MOVx, and MNEGx) all exist for types F, D, G, and H.

15. As the example near the end of Section 13.2 shows,

$$\frac{1}{2} + 2^{24} = 2^{24} \qquad \text{so} \qquad \frac{1}{2} + \left(\frac{1}{2} + 2^{24}\right) = 2^{24}.$$

However,

$$\left(\frac{1}{2} + \frac{1}{2}\right) + 2^{24} = 1 + 2^{24}.$$

17. One position. Since the fractions in the factors are each $\geq 1/2$, the product fraction will be $\geq 1/4$.

19.
```
        ; procedure CVTFD(source: F_type, dest: D_type)
        ;
        ; Converts source to dest, setting condition codes in the
        ; stacked PSW.
        ;
                .ENTRY  CVTFD,^M<R6>
                MOVL    8(AP),R6     ; Destination address
                CLRL    4(R6)        ; Clear low-order fraction bits
                MOVF    @4(AP),(R6)  ; Copy first longword, set c.c.'s
                BGTR    RET
                BLSS    SETN
                BISB2   #^X04,4(FP)  ; Set Z in stacked PSW
```

```
              RET
      SETN:   BISB2   #^X08,4(FP)    ; Set N in stacked PSW
      RET:    RET
              .END
```

21. FFFFFFFFFFFF7FFF (with the first longword at the right).

23. Let n be the absolute value of the integer. Find the leftmost bit in n that is on; let the bit position be k. The power of the floating point representation will be $k+1$. Clear bit k. Rotate right to get bit $k-1$ into bit position 6, so that the fraction bits will be in the correct positions. Clear bits 15:7 for the sign and exponent. Insert the biased exponent, $k+129$ in bits 14:7. If the original integer was negative, turn on bit 15.

25. Replace the instruction BLEQ   ZERO with BLSS   ZERO (because only a negative exponent ensures a zero result). Replace the instruction SUBL3 #152,R1,R3 with the following

```
              SUBL3    #151,R1,R3    ; -posn of first fraction bit
              BGTR     SHIFTLFT      ; No fraction bits
              ASHL     R3,R0,R0      ; Get first fraction bit in posn 0
              BLBC     R0,SHIFTRT
              INCL     R0            ; Round by adding 1
      SHIFTRT:ROTL     #-1,R0,R0     ; Drop fraction bit
              BRB      SIGN
      SHIFTLFT:DECL    R3            ; Shift count for left shift
```

27. Longword: 0002106C. F_floating: 1B004904. G_floating: 83604120. Leading separate numeric: 20 31 33 35 32 37 36. Packed decimal: 01 35 27 6C.

29.
```
              .MACRO   TSTP    NUM_DIGITS,PKD
              MOVB     #^X0C,-(SP)                 ; Packed representation of 0
              CMPP     NUM_DIGITS,PKD,#1,(SP)+ ; Compare to 0
              .ENDP    TSTP
```

CHAPTER 14

1.
```
      COL_3:   CMPL    R9,#20
               BGTR    LINE2
               MOVC5   R9,(R8),#^A/ /,#20,BUFFER+40 ; String fits on one line
               MOVC5   #0,0,#^A/ /,#40,BUF2+40      ; Blank out second line
               BRB     COL_4
      LINE2:   MOVC5   #0,0,#^A/ /,#20,BUFFER+40    ; Blank out field
               MOVC5   R9,(R8),#^A/ /,#40,BUF2+40   ; Put string on 2nd line
```

3. LOCC is executed three times. The values in R0 after each execution of LOCC are 18, 8, and 1.

5. Yes.

7.
```
      ; procedure SKPC(CHAR: character, LEN: word, STRING: character string)
      ;
      ; This procedure implements the SKPC instruction using simpler
```

```
        ; instructions. It searches for any character other than the one
        ; given as the first argument, and leaves the address of the character
        ; in R1, as the SKPC instruction does. R0 will contain the number of
        ; bytes remaining in the string, beginning with the character found.
        ;
        ; REGISTER USE
        ;       R0       address of character being tested
        ;       R1       number of characters remaining
        ;       R2       the character to skip over
        ;
                .ENTRY  SKPC,^M<R2>
                MOVB    @4(AP),R2      ; The character
                CVTWL   @8(AP),R0      ; Length of string
                MOVL    12(AP),R1      ; String address
        CMP:    CMPB    (R1)+,R2
                BNEQ    FOUND
                SOBGTR  R0,CMP
                BISB2   #^X04,4(FP)    ; No other char found, set Z
                RET
        FOUND:  DECL    R1             ; Undo autoincrement
                RET
                .END
```

9.
```
        ; PROCEDURE CNT_VOWELS(TEXT, LENGTH, VOWELS)
        ;
        ; This procedure counts the vowels in a segment of text.
        ; It counts both uppercase and lowercase letters.
        ;
        ; Input arguments
        ;       TEXT     the text
        ;       LENGTH   the number of bytes in the text (word)
        ;
        ; Output argument
        ;       VOWELS   counters (a word array)
        ;
        ; The VOWELS array is not cleared in this procedure; it may
        ; be called several times to count all the vowels in
        ; different segments of text.
        ;
        TABLE:  .BYTE   0[65],1,0[3],2,0[3],3,0[5],4,0[5],5,0[11]
                .BYTE   1,0[3],2,0[3],3,0[5],4,0[5],5,0[10],0[128]
        ; Table entries are indexes of the appropriate counters in
        ; the VOWELS array.
        ;
        ; Offsets for the argument list
        TEXT = 4
        LENGTH = 8
        VOWELS = 12
```

```
        ;
        ; REGISTER USE
        ;       R0        length of remaining text
        ;       R1        address of vowel found
        ;       R2-R3     used by SCANC
        ;       R6        vowel found
        ;       R7        table entry (VOWEL array index)
        ;       R8        VOWEL array address
        ;
                .ENTRY    CNT_VOWELS,^M<R2,R3,R6,R7,R8>
                SUBL3     #1,TEXT(AP),R1           ; SCANC uses 1(R1)
                CVTWL     @LENGTH(AP),R0           ; Text length
                SUBL3     #2,VOWELS(AP),R8         ; VOWELS array addr -2
        SCAN:   SCANC     R0,1(R1),TABLE,#^XFF     ; Find vowel
                BEQL      DONE
                CVTBL     (R1),R6                  ; Vowel
                CVTBL     TABLE[R6],R7             ; Table entry
                INCW      (R8)[R7]                 ; Increment counter
                DECL      R0                       ; Remaining length
                BRB       SCAN
        DONE:   RET
                .END
```

11.
```
                MOVAB     TABLE,R3
                MOVL      #2000,R2                 ; Table length
        SEARCH: MATCHC    #2,KEY,R2,(R3)
                BNEQ      NOT_FOUND
                SUBL3     #TABLE+2,R3,R4           ; Offset from table
                MOD       #20,R4,R5                ; The MOD macro from Exercise 11.9
                BNEQ      SEARCH
        FOUND:  SUBL2     #2,R3                    ; Address of entry sought
```

13. Suitable for a programming assignment.

15. It is valid. The operand address is TABLE+48. The instruction moves the ASCII code for a blank into the position in the table that corresponds to the character "0."

17.
```
                MOVC3     #5,18*5(R9),EXCERPT      ; 19th field
                MOVC3     #5,3*5(R9),EXCERPT+5     ; 4th field
                MOVC3     #5,30*5(R9),EXCERPT+10   ; 31st field
```

19. 95 00

21. If the number being edited has at most one nonzero digit, the pattern in the exercise will produce only five bytes of output (four blanks and the digit), whereas the pattern in Example 14.16 produces six bytes; it always includes a sign.

23. 20 24 34 2C 38 39 30 2E 30 31

25. Suitable for a programming assignment.

27.
```
        PATRN:  EO$LOAD_FILL *
                EO$ADJUST_INPUT 4
```

```
EO$MOVE         3
EO$SET_SIGNIF
EO$MOVE         1
EO$END
```

29. PATRN:
```
EO$END_FLOAT
EO$CLEAR_SIGNIF
EO$MOVE  4
EO$SET_SIGNIF
EO$MOVE  1
EO$END
```

CHAPTER 15

1. An interrupt can occur after any instruction.

3. Exceptions are caused by the currently running program, and usually are the result of an error in the program. Most external interrupts are caused by something outside the current program, and usually do not indicate an error. Processing of an exception service routine has the same priority as the program that caused the interrupt. The programmer can provide his or her own exception handling routines for some exceptions. External interrupt service routines (on a multiuser system) are usually part of the operating system.

5. 3

7. A BISPSL instruction would allow the user to change a program's Interrupt Priority Level and Current Mode fields.

9. Suitable for a programming assignment.

11. Add the following instructions after the last PRINTHEX instruction. At this point, R2 contains the exception code multiplied by 4. The code for the floating underflow trap is 5.

```
         CMPL    R2,#20          ; Test for floating underflow trap
         BNEQ    QUIT
         MOVL    #SS$_CONTINUE,R0
         RET
QUIT:
```

13. After a fault, the PC contains the address of the instruction that caused the fault. If the program is resumed at that point, the fault will occur again.

15. Save the contents of the general registers and PSL of the interrupted program in the designated area of memory. Put the program on the ready queue. Remove the first program from the ready queue. Reload the general registers and PSL from the designated place in memory for that program.

CHAPTER 16

1. A good guess would be that there is an error message. Fortunately (because we use BEGIN for many programs where we do not use a disk file), there is no error message and no problem.

3. **(a)**
```
$GET     RAB=INRAB
MOVC3    #80,INBUF,LINE
```

   (b) `INPUT:`

5. Suitable for a programming assignment.

Index

Chapter summaries are not included in the index because they do not contain new material. Only a few exercises, which contain new material are included. The appendices are not included.

A

Absolute, 274, 276
Access violation, 42, 188
.ADDRESS, 214–5, 277–8
Address, 9, 10, 67–8
Addressing modes, 40–6, 55, 160, 193–4 (*See also* specific modes)
  in macros, 289, 305
ALGOL, 145, 156
Alignment, 266–7 (*See also* Stack alignment bits)
AND macro, 333
Argument list, 209, 212–21, 225, 226
Argument pointer (AP), 14, 17, 161, 209, 211, 216, 222, 225
Arguments (of procedures), 203 (*See also* Argument list; Macro, arguments; Value parameter)
Arithmetic shift (*See* Shifting)

B

BEGIN, 64, 65, 72, 82, 189, 227, 444
Biased exponent, 359–60, 377
Binary number system, 18–23 (*For hex conversions see* Hexadecimal number system)
  converting to and from decimal, 20–2, 23, 24

Array, 45–6, 92–7
  addressing, 137–8
  allocation, 47–8
.ASCII, 50–1, 54
ASCII, 42, 49–51, 127, 406–7, 459
.ASCIZ, 50–1, 54
Assembler, 4, 5, 6 (*See also* VAX MACRO)
Assembler directives, 39, 40, 55 (*See also* specific directives)
Assembly process, 162, 167, 170, 173–5, 177
Assembly time, 7, 162, 305–6
Associative law, 369
Autodecrement mode, 46, 55, 68, 162, 163, 193
Autoincrement deferred mode, 182, 193
Autoincrement mode, 45–6, 55, 68, 124, 162, 163, 171, 175, 193
Available node list, 232–4, 249